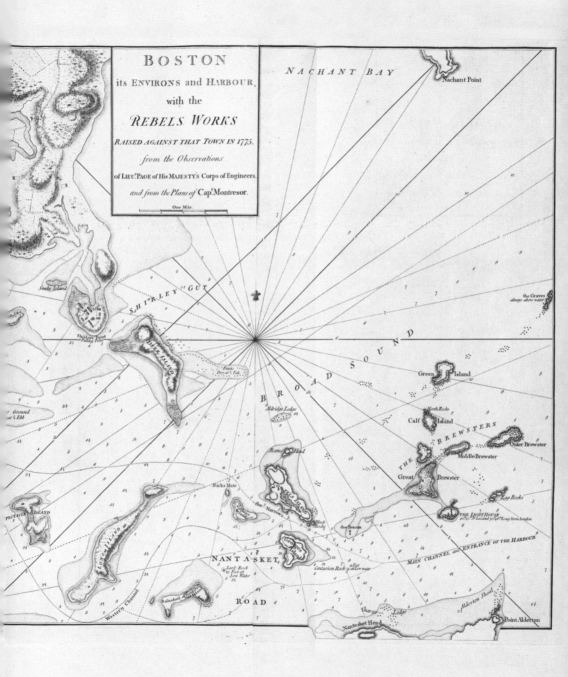

BOSTON

its ENVIRONS and HARBOUR,

with the

REBELS WORKS

RAISED AGAINST THAT TOWN IN 1775.

from the Observations

of LIEU.ᵗ PAGE of HIS MAJESTY'S Corps of Engineers,

and from the Plans of Cap.ᵗ Montresor.

One Mile

NACHANT BAY

Nachant Point

S.ᵗ HIRLEY'ˢ GUT

Snake Island

Shirleys Point

DEER ISLAND

Fauns Dry at ½ Tide

Green Island

BROAD SOUND

the Graves always above water

THE BREWSTERS

Aldridge Ledge

Rams Head

North Rocks

Calf Island

Outer Brewster

Middle Brewster

Nicks Mate

the Narrows

Great Brewster

Spectacle Island

Long Rocks

THE LIGHT HOUSE

PECTACLE ISLAND

LONG ISLAND

Spit Head

Black Rocks

the Beacon

MAIN CHANNEL and ENTRANCE OF THE HARBOUR

Georges Island

NANTASKET

Lark Rock

Centurion Rock

ROAD

Rainsford or Hospital Island

Western Channel

Nantasket Head

Quarry Ledge

Alderton Shoal

Point Alderton

Praise for *The War Before Independence*

"Though Beck only covers a short period, his excellent research brings to life the men who fought, providing readers with real, tangible heroes, not just hazy historic figures. Revolutionary War fans will rejoice in this well-written work and hope that the author has more on the way."

—*Kirkus Reviews,* Starred Review

"Popular and scholarly historians have retold parts of this tale in recent years, but none have done so in such a dramatic, cinematic, and compelling fashion. Military enthusiasts will find gripping accounts of operations, while their overall relation to the revolutionary landscape is fully manifest. I found it hard to put the volume down."

—Samuel A. Forman, author of the biography, *Dr. Joseph Warren*

Praise for *Igniting the American Revolution*

"For those who like their history rich in vivid details, Derek Beck has served up a delicious brew in this book… This one may soon become everyone's favorite."

—Thomas Fleming, author of *Liberty!*
The American Revolution

"Beck evidently relishes his subject, and he gives a fully fleshed portrait of the major patriots, both American and British…Beck's description of the 'spreading flames of rebellion' and the taking of the forts at Crown Point and Ticonderoga is as engaging as fiction. A knowledgeable, elegant account full of elaborate depictions, complete with a thorough bibliography."

—*Kirkus Reviews*

"It is in the clear, engaging telling of a complex story that *Igniting the American Revolution* by Derek W. Beck stands out... It is precise while being straightforward to read, shows the passion of the participants without taking sides, and gives equal play to the political and military affairs."

—Don N. Hagist, author of *British Soldiers, American War* and editor of *Journal of the American Revolution*

"Integrating compelling personalities with grand strategies, political maneuverings on both sides of the Atlantic, and vividly related incidents, *Igniting the American Revolution* pulls the reader into a world rending the British Empire asunder."

—Samuel A. Forman, author of the biography, *Dr. Joseph Warren*

"Recommended for history lovers, those who want a refresher on the American Revolution, and those who enjoy quality nonfiction."

—*Library Journal*, Starred Review

"Derek Beck delivers a remarkable account of the beginning of the American Revolution. The sheer depth and breadth of his research make this a must-have volume for any history buff. A magnificent resource."

—Todd Andrlik, author of *Reporting the Revolutionary War* and editor of *Journal of the American Revolution*

IGNITING THE AMERICAN REVOLUTION

THE

WAR BEFORE
Independence

1775–1776

DEREK W. BECK

To my loving parents, Katherine and Maurice.
You taught me, inspired me, and gave me the tools to write this book.
Thank you both for your love and support.

Contents

Preface

While this book can be enjoyed on its own, it is a continuation of the story left off in *Igniting the American Revolution: 1773–1775*. As described more fully in that volume's preface, I strive to paint events in this series with accuracy and objectivity. Such an unbiased approach will at times suggest the Americans are the "bad guys" and the British the "good guys". I embrace these shades of gray to present both sides of the war as authentically as possible, and my extensive research includes both Yankee and British perspectives. For the same reason, I generally avoid the word *patriot*, which means a lover of one's country, because both sides were fighting to maintain (and for the love of) their respective lands or empire. My hope is that this provides an honest look at the events of the early war. Some readers may prefer to adhere to the perspective of older history books that paint the Americans as superheroes, and thus call me an Anglophile for this unbiased attempt. But I think my continued honorable service in the modern American military refutes any such claims. Rather, I would prefer to be called a lover of truth. (Sadly, I can find no word for this: veritophile?) Truth is where real history is to be found.

Author's Note: This volume employs "logical quotations", meaning the only punctuation appearing inside quotation marks is also in that position in the original as well. So, a quotation ending with a comma inside the quotation marks, such as "quotation," indicates the comma was there in the original, while one with the comma outside the quotation marks, such as "quotation", indicates the comma is not part of the original. This style is observed for emphasis or scare quotes in the main text as well. See the bibliography for more.

ACKNOWLEDGMENTS

Because I wrote this volume simultaneously with *Igniting the American Revolution: 1773–1775*, the same gratitude I expressed in that volume should be repeated here. However, in the interest of space and avoiding repetition, I would like to give special acknowledgment to those who made the later phases of this publication possible.

First, thank you to my loving wife, Vicky, who gave up her free time with me so I could edit this book, and who ran much of our home renovation while I focused mostly on writing and working. You are a blessing.

I also wish to express my deep gratitude to my new Sourcebooks editor, Grace Menary-Winefield, who helped hone this book into something worthy of publication, and who took the lead in the final phases of the first book's publication as my champion to see it to success. And thank you to my literary agents, Doug Grad and Jacqueline Varoli Grace, as well as my first editor, Stephanie Bowen, who all took a chance on a manuscript that was really two books in one. Thanks to all of you for believing in the words on these pages and bringing them to the world.

Finally, thanks to my trusted colleague Dr. Samuel A. Forman, who kindly offered feedback and encouragement when the manuscript was still rough. And thank you to Don N. Hagist, whose insightful technical feedback helped me to understand British military units and their organization. You have both made this book stronger.

PART 1

Commitment to War
(Mid-May to October 1775)

St. Lawrence River

QUEBEC
(CANADA)

NOVA
SCOTIA

Quebec

Halifax

MASSACHUSETTS
(MAINE)

Montreal

Lake
Huron

Lake Champlain
Lake George

N.H.
GRANTS

NEW HAMPSHIRE

Lake Ontario

NEW YORK

MASSACHUSETTS

Boston

Albany

North River (Hudson)

CONN.

Lake Erie

R.I.

PENNSYLVANIA

New York

Lexington

NEW JERSEY

Concord

Philadelphia
Baltimore

Potomac R.

MD

DELAWARE

Ohio River

VIRGINIA

APPALACHIAN MTS.

Richmond

James River

Cape Fear River

NORTH CAROLINA

SOUTH CAROLINA

Santee River

Charlestown

GEORGIA

Savannah

N

NW   NE

W   E

SW   SE

S

Colonial America
1775

WEST
FLORIDA

EAST
FLORIDA

0   200   400

Scale of Miles

Gulf
of Mexico

ATLANTIC OCEAN

© 2005 Rick Britton

CHAPTER 1

MOUNTING TENSIONS

The great schism that had formed between Britons and Americans tore holes in friendships and families. One lady of Philadelphia wrote to a British officer in Boston, "I assure you that though we consider you as a public enemy, we regard you as a private friend; and while we detest the cause you are fighting for, we wish well to your own personal interest and safety."[1]

Benjamin Franklin felt this schism more directly. When he first arrived in London, he was the most noted and celebrated American, but when he left there in mid-March of 1775, he did so as a dejected outcast. This great schism was more than just a political or professional upheaval for Franklin: it also divided his own family. When he arrived in Philadelphia in early May, he cast his lot firmly with the Whigs, joining the Second Continental Congress as a Pennsylvania delegate.[2] But Franklin's forty-four-year-old son, William Franklin, who as a young man had stood by his father during his famous lightning-storm kite experiment, was now the royal governor of New Jersey and a staunch Loyalist. The political turmoil that would tear apart the colonies from their mother country would likewise tear apart this son from his father.[3]

This schism was never more apparent than in and around Boston. After the Destruction of the Tea in December 1773, Britain overreacted by closing the Port of Boston and placing large numbers of troops in the town. Tensions grew as quickly as the British garrison, and on April 19, 1775, when the British attempted to disarm the American war stores in nearby Concord, those tensions erupted into open violence, thus igniting the American Revolution. American militia forces swarmed from the countryside and chased the British back to Boston, where both sides now dug in for war—literally. While the Americans concentrated their entrenching efforts in and around nearby Cambridge to protect their new headquarters, the British fortified Boston Neck and all the hills in the peninsular town.[4]

Besides entrenching, the Americans devoted their attention to the organization of their militia forces. On May 19, 1775, Maj. Gen. Artemas Ward, the highest-ranking man in the Massachusetts Militia, was bestowed the honor of first commander in chief of the Massachusetts Army and so promoted to full general.[5] Ward received a small ceremony to mark the occasion. As John Adams described it, "Dr. [Joseph] Warren…made a harangue in the form of a charge, in the presence of the assembly, to every officer, upon the delivery of his commission; and he never failed to make the officer, as well as all the assembly, shudder upon those occasions."[6] A few days later, John Thomas, commander of the Massachusetts forces based in Roxbury (immediately across from the British via Boston Neck), was promoted to the number two position, receiving the rank of lieutenant general in the new Massachusetts Army.[7]

The Massachusetts Army was just a portion of the grander New England Army of Observation, an eclectic collection of men representing the spectrum of New England society—from out-of-work longshoremen, weatherworn farmers, and decrepit millers to youthful blacksmith apprentices, refined gentlemen lawyers, and zealous doctors. Young and old, green recruit and hardened veteran of the French and Indian War, opportunist and patriot, adventurer and reluctant soldier: together they represented every lifestyle.

Almost none wore uniforms. Instead, most wore diverse homespun clothes, a product not of the late recession resulting from the closing of Boston's port, but of the spirited Yankee refusal to accept finished goods from England. Most were Protestant Christians of one denomination or another.

Unremarkably, most were also white men, descendants of European settlers, though not all. A small number were black men who joined the Army, some perhaps as freemen, most as slaves enlisted in the stead of

PORTRAIT OF MAJ. GEN. ARTEMAS WARD (C. 1790–1795) BY CHARLES WILLSON PEALE (1741–1827). COURTESY OF THE INDEPENDENCE NATIONAL HISTORICAL PARK.

their masters.[8] Members of the "domesticated" Mahican (or Mohican) Indian tribe of western Massachusetts, living then-modern lives and locally known as Stockbridge Indians, also joined the camp, as did a few others from various tribes.[9]

The men were not the only thing conspicuously eclectic about the American Army. Rev. William Emerson, whose Old Manse stood overlooking the fight at Concord's North Bridge, wrote, "It is diverting to walk among the camps. They are as different in their form, as the owners are in their dress; and every tent is a portraiture of the temper and taste of the persons, who encamp in it. Some are made of boards, and some of sailcloth. Some partly of one and partly of the other. Again others are made of stone and turf, brick or brush. Some are thrown up in a hurry, others curiously wrought with doors and windows, done with wreaths and withes [twigs] in the manner of a basket. Some are your proper tents and marquees, looking like the regular camp of the enemy. In these are the Rhode Islanders, who are furnished with tent-equipage and every thing in the most exact English style. However, I think this great variety rather a beauty than a blemish in the army."[10] The then-small Harvard College also dedicated its few buildings to the American Army, which used them for the commissary, mess, and as officer barracks.[11]

Every day the Americans eyed their rivals across the Charles River, and sometimes the ill-disciplined Yankees fired a few potshots to harass the British in Boston. These shots had no physical effect on the British—the range was too great—but they did serve as psychological warfare against the Americans' besieged enemy. In fact, the Americans would be quite ingenious at times with psychological warfare. Lt. John Barker of the British was particularly galled when he heard the rebels had erected the British Union flag in Cambridge. As Barker explained in his diary, "they call themselves the King's Troops and us the Parliaments. Pretty Burlesque!"[12]

In Boston, Lt. Gen. Thomas Gage was well aware of much of the inner workings of the colonial leadership in Cambridge, thanks to his stifled but still functional spy network. By the end of April, Gage had received critical intelligence warning that some Yankees were discussing an attack on Boston, particularly from Dorchester Heights, which stood on a peninsula just south of Boston. Yet he had received intelligence just days earlier explicitly stating that there were no such talks of an American attack. In other words, something had changed. No doubt it was the arrival of Benedict Arnold with his scheme to collect cannon with which to bombard the town.[13]

By mid-May, Gage received further intelligence that the Americans were urging Boston's inhabitants to leave town within days if they could or suffer the consequences from an intended bombardment.[14] There was no truth to this, but Gage had to take all such warnings seriously, so he redoubled the troop guards throughout the town.[15] Still more intelligence described a rebel scheme to fortify the heights of the two nearby peninsulas—to the north at Charlestown (namely Bunker Hill) and to the south at Dorchester.[16]

As if to punctuate the accuracy of Gage's intelligence, on May 13, in broad daylight, American Brig. Gen. Israel Putnam defiantly marched at the head of some two thousand or more men across Charlestown Neck and into what had become an unspoken but understood neutral ground between the two armies. Putnam led his procession over Bunker Hill and Breed's Hill and paraded there with much pomp and circumstance, their drums and fifes blaring marching songs, all in full view of the armed British sentries in Boston, the watchful heavy cannon of the Admiral's Battery on Copp's Hill, and the many ready cannon of HMS *Somerset* on the Charles.

As the Americans marched on display, another three hundred appeared in the Cambridge Marshes across from Boston Common, parading in much the same way. At length, Putnam and his men marched to Charlestown itself and up to the very shores of the Charles, directly across from the *Somerset*, "and after giving the War-hoop opposite the *Somerset* returned as they came." As Lieutenant Barker wrote in his diary, "It was expected the Body of Charles Town woud have fired on the *Somerset*, at least it was wished for, as she had everything ready for Action, and must have destroyed great numbers of them, besides putting the Town in Ashes."[17] Doubtless, some among the Americans equally wished for battle, but it was not to be. According to Amos Farnsworth, one of the Americans there on the march, they had paraded only "to Shoe themselves to the Regulars".[18]

Old Put, as his friends called him, was not foolish for leading such a march. Rather, it built confidence among the mostly green Yankee Army. But just as important, it kept the men active. Putnam's experience had taught him that raw and undisciplined troops must be employed in some way, or they would become vicious and unmanageable. "It is better to dig a ditch every morning and fill it up at evening than to have the men idle" was a maxim he had adopted. So while Putnam kept his men busy building two redoubts he called Forts Number 1 and Number 2, both near Phipps Farm at Lechmere Point in Cambridge, the march was a much-welcomed break from the routine of entrenching.[19]

In this way, Putnam also helped boost morale, and the men who

PORTRAIT OF MAJ. GEN. ISRAEL PUTNAM (C. 1776) BY DOMINIQUE C. FABRONIUS
(1828–1894), PROBABLY AFTER A PENCIL SKETCH BY JOHN TRUMBULL
(1756–1843). COURTESY OF THE U.S. LIBRARY OF CONGRESS.

served with him grew to wholly trust his leadership. "He does not wear a large wig, nor screw his countenance into a form that belies the sentiments of his generous soul; he is no adept either at politics or religious canting and cozening: he is no shake-hand body: he therefore is totally unfit for everything but fighting."[20] Finally, the Americans were just as fearful the British might take Charlestown Heights as the British were of the Americans. So while Putnam's march taunted the British, it also allowed the Yankees to reconnoiter and familiarize themselves with that ground, should a battle for that peninsula soon come.

For this same reason, General Ward sent a warning to Lt. Gen. John Thomas in Roxbury that, should the British sally from the town and endeavor to secure Dorchester Heights, the other implicit neutral ground to the south, Thomas should be ready at a moment's notice to repulse such an enterprise. Thomas assured his commander in chief, "the Information is Simular to what I have Recvd almost Every Day this 10 Days Past. I have had For Sum Time Near Two hundred men Posted Near the Neck & Two Hundred more as a Picket that Repair there Every Night & Partt of Two Rigement more not more Then a mile & halfe Distant from the Place & am Determind to Take all Posible Care to Prevent their Taking Posesion".[21]

From the British perspective, Putnam's march combined with the latest intelligence strongly supported the likelihood of a rebel plot. Hence, Gage's new adjutant general, Lt. Col. James Abercrombie, lately arrived ahead of his 22nd Regiment that was itself bound for New York, decided to take a longboat up the Charles River to reconnoiter the American lines. According to Lieutenant Barker, Abercrombie's men were "fired upon by several of the Rebels from the Banks; several balls went thro' the boat but nobody was hurt; they made the best of their way back, and I don't hear that he has been as fond of reconnoitring since."[22] Barker later noted of the rebels, "Some of the idle Fools frequently fire small Arms at the [HMS] *Glasgow*, and at our Camp; us they never reach, but they sometimes stick a Ball in the Ship, who never returns it tho' she has it in her power to drive 'em to the D—l [Devil]."[23]

Meanwhile, all throughout May, British troops began to leave their winter barracks and again set up their white tents on and around Boston Common. While this was to be an orderly affair, in mid-May a fire swept through the barracks of the 65th Regiment, destroying much of their arms, gear, and clothing and forcing them to encamp on the Common sooner than expected.[24] There were many advantages to moving the men into summer quarters, such as a healthy respite from being cooped up with so many soldiers in close quarters and the savings that came from relinquishing rented barracks. In addition, the Common was closer to Boston Neck and the Charles River, so the troops there were in a better position to guard against rebel incursions.

The month of May also brought new troops to Boston. First, four more companies of the 65th had redeployed from Halifax and arrived on May 6. Then on May 14, the first two transports arrived of what would be the First Embarkation of fresh troops in 1775, bringing with them a portion of almost seven hundred fresh marines and officers. Within the next few days, four more transports arrived with the remaining marines.

Once they had all arrived, Marine Maj. John Pitcairn divided the marines evenly into two battalions of ten companies each, mimicking the army regiments. The veteran marines and some of the new ones were now officially named the 1st Battalion and placed under Pitcairn (who also retained overall command of the Marines), while the bulk of the new arrivals formed the 2nd Battalion under Maj. John Tupper.[25] The remainder of the First Embarkation would arrive within weeks, supplying another three full army regiments plus cavalry, an addition of nearly 1,500 fresh men and officers.[26]

Lt. Richard Williams was one of those who arrived with the First Embarkation. After assessing the toll taken on the town by the siege, he wrote in his journal that Boston was a fair town, but "as to publick buildings I can't say they shine much, the town house [Old State House] & Fanuel Hall are the only two worth notice, & are of bricks. some churches have very neat & elegant steepls of wood. no such thing as a play house, they were too puritanical a set to admit of such lewd Diversions, tho' ther's perhaps no town of its size cou'd turn out more whores than this cou'd. they have left us an ample sample of them. I walked thro' the town & was much affected at the sight of it, in a manner abandoned, almost every other shop, shut up...the trade of Boston must have been very extensive & of great consequence, the great number of store houses & warfs, which are contiguous to them shows it plainly if there were not other proofs, I can't help looking on it as a ruined Town, & I think I see the grass growing in every street."[27]

With the troops besieged on a small peninsula, their only diversion was the dreaded and ubiquitous New England rum. Once again, drunkenness became a problem among the British ranks, eroding troop discipline. Gage soon learned that the women camp followers—the many soldiers' wives and the ample prostitutes in town—were among the leading suppliers. Consequently, he issued stern orders that his officers should strictly investigate all incidents of drunkenness, and that any woman who did not observe the prohibition to sell rum and liquor to the soldiers was "to be *immediately* seized and put on board Ship."[28]

The other great burden Gage faced was that of provisions for his army. So far, the army had plenty of salt-cured meats and dry goods—there was no crisis yet. But Gage's army was in need of fresh vegetables and fruit, of which they had none, and without which the town would eventually succumb to scurvy.[29] Still, while the supply of fresh goods from the countryside had been cut off at the start of the siege, some continued to trickle in through Boston Neck thanks to a handful of industrious Yankees eager for cash.

Gage also needed fresh meat for his army, not a necessity for survival, but crucial to maintain troop morale. The disappearance of a pair of oxen at the North End gave proof of the growing desperation for fresh meat and provisions.[30] The one critical provision the army desperately lacked was hay, necessary for the horses and few livestock remaining in town. So Gage devised a plan to secure a supply from nearby Grape Island in the harbor. It was meant to be a routine foraging mission, but once again, Gage underestimated the Americans.

———— • ————

Grape Island lay just off the mainland near the town of Weymouth, in the far south of Boston Harbor, nearly ten miles by boat from Boston's Long Wharf. Gage seems to have determined on that particular hay because it was made available to him by the owner, a Tory named Lovell.[31] On May 20, a British detachment of thirty men under Lt. Thomas Innis of the 43rd embarked aboard a sloop (with its twelve guns removed) and set sail southward.[32]

The sloop dropped anchor off Grape Island, and there they remained for the night. Lieutenant Innis planned to conduct his raid the following morning, a Sabbath, expecting the local colonists to be at church. Accordingly, at perhaps eight o'clock on May 21, once the tide had sufficiently ebbed, the crew floated their few longboats and rowed to the island, grinding them to a halt on the expansive mudflats.[33] The detachment of thirty British then began hauling away the precut hay, but at seventy or eighty tons, it was more than they could take. Had they planned better, they might have taken some of the cattle there too.

In the nearby mainland town of Weymouth, the militia learned of the raid and raised the alarm, which rippled through the coastal towns all the way back to Roxbury and Cambridge. At ten o'clock, Gen. John Thomas in Roxbury received an urgent express, giving the exaggerated report that four British sloops, two armed, were landing troops at Weymouth. This was false, of course, but Thomas could take no chances, so he ordered three companies to march to Weymouth. Dr. Joseph Warren learned of the march and eagerly joined them as a volunteer.[34]

The Weymouth militia mustered at a point of land that reached closest to Grape Island. However, because it was now low tide, the few sailboats there were all beached on their sides. The Americans were thus powerless to stop the British. All they could do was glare across those mudflats and harbor waters to the hayfields of Grape Island and the bright red coats gathering hay on the island's opposite side. Though the British were well out of range, the Yankees fired a concerted volley, followed by scattered potshots, all without effect. The British sloop fired its small defensive swivel guns in return, also without effect.

As Dr. Warren anonymously reported later to the *Essex Gazette*, "Matters continued in this State for several Hours, the Soldiers pulling the Hay down to the Water-Side, our People firing at the Vessel, and they now and then swivel Guns."[35] But once the tide sufficiently flooded, sometime around two o'clock, the marooned sailboats along the Weymouth shore at last floated. The militia eagerly boarded them, hoisted sails, and began to make their way to Grape Island.

The British hurried to collect a bit more hay, then scurried toward the shoreline. Only now did Lieutenant Innis order his detachment to fire, but their volley had no effect. They then climbed aboard their longboats and rowed to their sloop, which promptly weighed anchor, just as the Americans landed on the small island's opposite shore. The Yankees rushed across the island toward the British, firing their muskets as they did so, while the sloop gave scattered swivel shot in return.[36]

Another small arms exchange came as the sloop passed around a point of land toward Boston to the north, and then the affair was over. In all, the British stole away about seven or eight tons of hay, while the

Americans burned the remaining seventy tons or so and herded away the few cattle. The King's Army could have done better, but the raid was bloodless, despite claims by both sides that they had killed a handful of the other.[37]

The British perhaps considered the Grape Island raid a success, but the Americans were now wise to the British agenda to raid the harbor islands, many of which served as pasturelands for cattle and other livestock. As a result, the Yankees would soon begin removing the herds from the other outlying islands, thereby depriving the redcoats of their greatest source of fresh meat and making another showdown with the British inevitable.

———

With both adversaries growing ever more determined to press the war, the Massachusetts Provincial Congress made a monumental decision regarding Tories, or "those persons…guilty of such atrocious and unnatural crimes against their country". On May 22, the Provincial Congress resolved "that every friend to mankind ought to forsake and detest them," and that "until they shall give evidence of a sincere repentance…no person within this colony shall take any deed, lease, or conveyance whatever, of the lands, houses, or estates of such persons."[38]

With this resolution, Loyalism was effectively made illegal; freedom of political thought taken for granted by the modern was now a crime; and all Tories were deemed outcasts unless they satisfactorily repented. Implicit within this resolution, whenever Tories *abandoned* their unsalable homes (they were not *driven* from them), the Provincial Congress was free to confiscate their private property for the Cause.

About 15 to 20 percent of white Americans are estimated to have been true Loyalists (perhaps on the lower end of that scale in New England), while the Whigs comprised no more than 45 percent of the population. Thus, the extralegal Provincial Congress, which spoke for only half of Massachusetts's population, had now stripped the rights of another sizable fraction of its people. It is one of the hypocrisies of the Revolution that those who fought for Liberty did so by stamping out the liberty of others.[39]

By mid-May, the delegates of the Provincial Congress began to devote more of their attention to the legitimacy of prosecuting the war. Though the Congress had assumed governance of the colony and now controlled an Army, its delegates were ever mindful of legality, or at least the semblance of legality, and were loath to make any attack on the British without such. Hence, they wrote a petition to the Continental Congress imploring that higher body to assume responsibility for civil government in Massachusetts and explicitly direct their Provincial Congress on how best to proceed. Their petition further expressed, "we tremble at having an army, although consisting of our own countrymen, established here, without a civil power to provide for and control it."[40]

To hand deliver this petition to Philadelphia, the colony appointed the trusted Whig—but secret British spy—Dr. Benjamin Church. Though he was the most obvious appointee, being the chairman of the Committee of Safety, the errand was much to his vexation, perhaps because he was forced to actively aid the side he was working to undermine.[41]

Indeed, the Massachusetts Congress had no legal authority over the regiments of the other colonies of Connecticut, New Hampshire, or Rhode Island, some of which were not yet arrived. Rather, these several provincial armies were bound only by the Common Cause and thus served together only by their own volition. It was therefore necessary that the Continental Congress adopt the loosely assembled New England Army as a Continental Army and assign for it a generalissimo as commander in chief. Such a generalissimo would then have legitimate authority to command all the regiments, regardless of the colony from which they hailed.

Dr. Joseph Warren decided to write privately to Samuel Adams on the matter, wishing to explain a bit more than was proper for an official petition. "I would just observe, that the application made to you respecting the taking the regulation of this army into your hands, by appointing a committee of war, or taking the command of it by appointing a generalissimo, is a matter, I think, must be managed with much delicacy. I am a little suspicious, unless great care is taken, some dissentions may arise in the army, as our soldiers, I find, will not yet be brought to obey any person of whom they do not themselves entertain a high opinion. Subordination is absolutely necessary in an army; but the strings must not be drawn too tight at first." A week later, Warren wrote a second letter, adding, "I see more and more the necessity of establishing a civil government here, and such a government as shall be sufficient to control the military forces, not only of this colony, but also such as shall be sent to us from the other colonies. The continent must strengthen and support with all its weight the civil authority here; otherwise our soldiery will lose the ideas of right and wrong, and will plunder, instead of protecting, the inhabitants."[42]

So, the groundwork was laid for a Continental Army, and for it a commander in chief.

Warren probably sent his private letter immediately by express, but the spy Dr. Church tarried for days before he departed with the Provincial Congress's petition. Knowing he would be unable to pass further intelligence to his British master for some weeks, he wrote another letter of intelligence on May 24, the day before he departed.

Sent to General Gage, Church's letter reported that the New England Army was again near twelve thousand men total between the camps at Cambridge and Roxbury, with only part of those expected from Connecticut yet arrived, and men from Rhode Island still on the march. Church also reported of the capture of Fort Ticonderoga, though Gage already knew of it. The doctor assured Gage that the Yankees would not attack Boston without the backing and support of the Continental Congress.

Finally, in an interesting insight into America's first spy, Church concluded his intelligence with a note of sorrow on the present situation, lamenting, "should hostilities be long continued & the pres^t. demands insisted upon I am fearfull of the event, may I never see the day when I shall not dare to call myself a British American... Oh for Peace & honor[?] once more." These were the words of a troubled man not wholly committed to the war, and though his treason is unforgivable, this letter gives credence to the claim that Church himself would one day provide: that he had committed his espionage only from a desire to avert war and bloodshed.[43]

Motivations aside, when this letter of intelligence resurfaced a century and a half later among Gage's papers, it proved beyond all shadow of a doubt that Church was indeed a spy against his country. For, though he did not sign this or any other of his secret letters of intelligence, he was the only man sent to the Continental Congress, and in this letter, he grumbles of his appointment.[44]

That same morning, while Church penned his perfidious letter, a thick fog blanketed Massachusetts Bay as if it were a dark omen sent by Providence herself to warn the people of Church's treachery. Yet the fog did not deter HM Sloop *Otter* as she weighed anchor, unfurled her sails, and set off southward to depart Boston Harbor before turning east-southeast to round Cape Cod. Her destination was Norfolk, Virginia, sent by Admiral Graves in reply to the repeated petitions of Virginia's Royal Governor John Murray, the 4th Earl of Dunmore, who had requested naval assistance to quell a growing rebellion there.

The fog probably burned away by midday, and by evening, the bright sun hung low in the western sky, illuminating for the *Otter* crew the rolling sea and the edge of Cape Cod ahead and starboard. Suddenly, a seaman yelled to the officer of the deck: a sail ship dead ahead! *Otter*'s captain, Matthew Squire, may have been the first to pull out his spyglass. On the horizon, he made out a full square-rigged sixth-rate 28-gun warship—with a British ensign flying at her stern. As the two ships approached one another, they each fired a series of cannon salutes.

This inbound warship was the HMS *Cerberus*, named for the three-headed dog of Greek mythology. How befitting it was that this ship, of all ships of the line, had been bestowed the honor of bringing into Boston its three dignitaries, three major generals of the British Army who held the fate of the continent in their destinies. Once *Cerberus* drew near, *Otter*'s Captain Squire, staff, and rowers all climbed into a longboat that was lowered to the water and crossed to *Cerberus*, where Capt. James Chads granted permission to come aboard.[45]

Cerberus and her crew had been sailing across the Atlantic for the past several weeks and thus remained oblivious of the Siege of Boston. So when *Otter*'s Captain Squire began telling them the news of the late battle and the turmoil that had followed, his fellow sea captain and the three major generals were eager to listen.

The most senior of these three Army generals was William Howe, forty-six. The famous Howe was highly praised and respected, even amongst the Americans, thanks in no small part to the great service of his oldest brother, Brig. Gen. George Howe, who had died heroically in the French and Indian War while leading Yankee militia at the bloody Battle of Fort Carillon (Fort Ticonderoga). The Americans were genuinely grief-stricken by the loss of George Howe, and the year after the battle, they commissioned a beautiful sculpture as a memorial, which resides to this day at Westminster Abbey. A second older brother, Richard, had risen to the rank of admiral in the Royal Navy. But William did not hide in the shadows of his two older brothers. In fact, he was an exemplary officer in his own right.

During the French and Indian War (Seven Years' War), William had been at the Second Taking of Fortress Louisbourg, had personally led a detachment of light infantry up the steep palisades to victory in the Battle on the Plains of Abraham, and later survived the deadly disease that accompanied the Battle of Havana. After that last war, thanks to his brother's heroic death, William found his surname had become a hallowed one, which helped to elevate him to the House of Commons as representative of Nottingham. He likewise rose through the Army ranks, and many considered him a leading expert in light infantry tactics and irregular warfare.[46]

A Whig in politics, during the general election of 1774, William Howe assured his constituents that if he were appointed a command in the American struggle, he would refuse, an assurance that proved necessary to gain the votes of Nottingham liberals. When Howe was indeed given a command, it was said that he asked if his appointment were a request or an order. Howe was shrewdly answered the latter, and so he submitted. The people of Nottingham were incensed, reminding Howe of his campaign promise. One constituent, Samuel Kirk, sent him a dignified but reproachful letter reminding Howe that his courage was not what was in question: "nay, your courage would be made more conspicuous by the refusal. If you should resolve, at all events, to go, I don't wish you may fall, as many do; but I cannot say I wish success to the undertaking." Howe replied, "I was ordered, and could not refuse", but noted that some opponents of the administration had lauded him for accepting the call for want of his prudence in America. He also asked Kirk to suspend his judgment and instead consider the many Loyalists in America whom he might aid.[47]

Next in seniority among the three generals aboard the *Cerberus* was Henry Clinton, who, at forty-five, was a pudgy and strange man, overly sensitive to criticism, often passive and shy of attention, yet always eager to offer his military opinions and probably the best strategist of all the generals now in America. He, like his fellow major generals, was not overjoyed to be in the American service, and would later write of the present crisis, "I was not a volunteer in that war, I was ordered by my Sovereign and I obeyed".[48] Born in America while his father was in the service, he first acquired limited experience with the militia. It was not until his return to the mother country that he quickly gained real experience in the regular service. In the last war, he had served on the European battlefields as aide-de-camp for the revered Prussian Field Marshal Ferdinand of Brunswick, a feather in his cap for which he was justly proud.[49]

The most junior among the three generals was handsome, flamboyant, haughty John Burgoyne, of fifty-two years. Burgoyne was not only an able general but also noted as a decent playwright, even by modern standards, and in late 1774, he received success as a dramatist when his first play, *The Maid of Oaks*, was produced in London. Early in his military career, Burgoyne helped to introduce an innovative form of light cavalry to the British Army. It proved very effective, and he soon climbed the ranks to command the 16th Dragoons, a light cavalry unit nicknamed "Burgoyne's Light Horse", which the King took pleasure in reviewing. Then in the last war, Burgoyne received high praise for taking strongly garrisoned Valencia de Alcántara in Spain using his dragoons alone. After the war, Burgoyne returned to his long-held seat in the Commons, serving as the representative of Midhurst, for which his outspoken, independent values drew stern criticism from the King.[50] However, Burgoyne was no supporter of the Colonial Cause, so when at last he was selected for the American Service in 1775, he declared before the Commons that America was a spoiled child. Yet Burgoyne was no warmonger either, and he further declared that he "wished to see America convinced by persuasion, rather than the sword."[51]

These were the three major generals ironically sent to Boston aboard the HMS *Cerberus*, of which one London wit wrote:[52]

Behold the Cerberus o'er the Atlantic plough,
Her precious freight Burgoyne, Clinton, Howe,
Bow! Wow! Wow!

As the three reluctant generals sat in Captain Chads's cabin drinking tea, they found themselves incredulous and dumbfounded at the news delivered by *Otter*'s Captain Squire. Upon being told Boston was surrounded by ten thousand county folk, Burgoyne reportedly asked how many regulars were now in Boston. Captain Squire overestimated the British number at nearly five thousand.[53] To this, Burgoyne cried out in astonishment, "What! Ten thousand peasants keep five thousand King's Troops shut up! Well, let *us* get in, and we'll soon find elbow-room."[54]

After their meeting, the two ships sailed their separate ways. The next morning, May 25, HMS *Cerberus* arrived in Boston Harbor, took up a pilot, and by half past ten o'clock, was navigating toward the town. Upon spotting the solid-blue admiral's flag fluttering from the fore-topmast of HMS *Preston*, the crew of *Cerberus* fired a series of maybe seventeen cannon salutes to the admiral.[55] *Cerberus* soon reached the inner harbor, and it was there that the three major generals for the first time laid eyes upon the colonial siege lines all around the beleaguered town.

As another officer described it upon his arrival days later, "the entrance in to the harbour is very beautiful, we saild by several Islands, and Castle William, which makes a noble appearance, the view of the town & ships of War, together with the different Encampments seen beyond it, enrich'd the Scene, but what a country are we come to, Discord, & civil wars began, & peace & plenty turn'd out of doors, so that all our thoughts of a Loin of Veal & Lemon sauce, vanishd with the account, of salt Pork & pease being all that was to be had."[56] Once *Cerberus* dropped her anchor, the three major generals boarded a tender and were lowered to the water. The seamen then rowed them to Long Wharf and their fate.[57]

And as fate would have it, in just a few weeks, the generals would indeed have their opportunity to find some elbow room.

When the three newly arrived major generals disembarked from *Cerberus* and came to Province House, they found His Excellency Lt. Gen. Thomas Gage busy with another urgent matter. Courtesy of his secret spy network, Gage had learned that the rebels were planning to sneak onto nearby Noddle's Island that night and destroy or carry off all the livestock thereon, "for no reason but because the owner having sold them for the Kings Use". This owner was Henry Howell Williams, and though he was a dedicated Whig whom Admiral Graves called "a notorious Rebel", he was also a merchant, and the lure of profit habitually enticed him to sell his diverse livestock and poultry to outbound British vessels.[58]

Since the Grape Island affair, Gage had been worried about access to the few remaining friendly farms on the various harbor islands and, on May 25, had successfully raided nearby Long Island for additional hay.[59] The Americans meanwhile had turned their attention to the abundant stocks on Noddle's Island and adjacent Hog Island, which they feared could feed the British for some time and thus negate their Siege of Boston.

In fact, the Americans had been pondering the removal of those livestock for a month. On May 14, the Committee of Safety had advised the selectmen of the coastal towns to consider removing the stock from those islands. When the towns did nothing even in the wake of the raid on Grape Island, the Committee of Safety resolved on May 24 to press the Provincial Congress to immediately clear those islands. It was this resolution that was transmitted to Gage through his spy network by early May 25, perhaps passed by word of mouth via Dr. Church's go-between when they delivered Church's latest intelligence.[60] In response, Gage wrote a hasty letter to Admiral Graves, urging the naval commander to order his "guard boats to be particularly Attentive, and to take such Other Measures as you may think Necessary for this night".[61]

Graves, meanwhile, was busy sorting through the dispatches just received from HMS *Cerberus*, including one explaining the almost unenforceable Restraining Act lately passed by Parliament. With it, the burden fell upon the admiral to somehow prevent New England vessels from accessing the Newfoundland fisheries and from trading to any sovereign besides Britain.[62] Also among the dispatches just received, Vice Admiral of the Blue Samuel Graves joyously discovered an official notice of his promotion, dated April 13, giving him the new rank of

Vice Admiral of the White.[63] Graves apparently decided to keep his new appointment to himself for a day, but it was with this pleasure that he received Gage's urgent appeal.

When Graves read Gage's hasty letter, his first thought was not of the livestock, but of a storehouse there of lumber, boards, and spars intended for repairs of his vessels. "The preservation of all these", he later wrote, "became of great consequence, not altogether from their intrinsic Value, but from the almost impossibility of replacing them at this Juncture."[64] It was thus with a different agenda that the admiral promptly replied to the general, affirming, "The Guard boats have orders to keep the strictest look out; and I will direct an additional One to row tonight as high up as possible between Noddles Island and the Main". Graves suggested that the best course of action, however, was to station a guard on the island.[65] Accordingly, about forty marines, perhaps drafted from those of the warships, were sent to Noddle's Island and barracked in Henry Williams's hay barn.[66]

That night, all was quiet. But the next morning, May 26, the American siege lines were startled to attention when they heard a sharp cannonade across the harbor. At eight o'clock, the HMS *Preston* crew lowered the blue admiral's flag from the ship's fore-topmast and raised in its place the flag of St. George's Cross, the famous English white flag with a red cross, while at her stern the crew replaced her blue ensign with the white equivalent, thus formally signifying Vice Admiral Graves's promotion from Blue to White. Noting the change aboard their flagship, the squadron throughout the harbor likewise exchanged their stern ensigns and then each fired thirteen cannons in salute, to which *Preston* returned thirteen.[67]

The rest of the day came and went without incident. It was not until late that evening when Massachusetts Col. John Nixon received his orders and so mustered a detachment of between two hundred and three hundred.[68] Together they marched from their camp in Cambridge through Mystick (now Medford), Malden, and Chelsea, where they waited until dawn, whose radiance began to brighten the sky at nearly four o'clock on May 27.[69]

The topography of the islands is difficult to make out today, as most of the old tidal zones and mudflats have been filled in, making both

Noddle's Island and Hog Island now part of the mainland.[70] North of the two islands ran Chelsea Creek, still extant, which separated the islands from the mainland, where the small Chelsea parish of Winnisimmet (now simply Chelsea proper) once stood. To the west and south was Boston Harbor, with Boston itself just across a narrow expanse to the west. To the east, the two islands were further separated from the mainland by narrow Belle Isle Inlet, as it is now called, which at low tide became an easily fordable, knee-high creek with wide mudflat banks. The two islands themselves were separated by an equally thin, shallow inlet, unnamed and since filled in. The mainland just east of the islands was the rolling heights known then as Chelsea Neck, now the south end of Revere before entering Winthrop. It was from there on the eastern heights that the Yankees forded Belle Isle Inlet at near ebb tide and so marched onto Hog Island.[71]

By noon, the Yankees began herding off the 6 horses, 27 horned cattle, and 411 sheep from the Hog Island farms of Whigs Oliver Wendell of Boston and Jonathan Jackson of Newburyport.[72] They did not immediately cross to Noddle's Island, presumably waiting both for a lower ebb tide and for the mission to make headway on the present island before stirring up the British encamped on the other. It was not until around one o'clock that afternoon that the Americans finally forded the unnamed creek over to Noddle's Island.[73]

Maybe just thirty Americans crossed, including Amos Farnsworth. The gentle hill centered on Noddle's Island afforded them some semblance of cover from the British marines situated on the opposite side of the island. Well aware of the marines, Farnsworth and his fellow Yankees crept along the pastures. They spotted the large herd of grazing sheep and lambs, intermingled with handfuls of horses and horned cattle, amounting to nearly a thousand livestock.[74] With such a large herd and with the marines so close, the Yankees knew they could not expect to remove many of the beasts.

Since their raid could do nothing more than harass the British, they decided to kill what animals they could and steal away still others. Yet once they fired that first shot, the marines would be on them in moments. They agreed they had but one chance to make the most of their raid. Daringly, they crept farther into the outlying pastures of the Williams farmstead until they reached a large barn "full of salt hay" (salt meadow hay or marsh grass), which stood next to an old and abandoned farmhouse. As the afternoon approached two o'clock, the Americans prepared makeshift torches, likely using their musket flints and some of the dry salt hay to do so. They then looked at one another, each with a lit torch in one hand and a musket in the other. Finally, perhaps with a nod, they threw their torches into and onto the barn and house, then quickly turned and fled. As the two wooden structures instantly took fire, billowing dark, gray smoke into the air and so drawing the attention of the marines across the field, the Americans fired their muskets at nearby horses and cattle, killing many before grabbing others to steal away.[75]

The marines may have hesitated for a moment, unsure what was happening, but the smoke and the musketry immediately made the situation clear. Their response was quick. They gathered their guns and charged toward the fleeing Americans, giving a scattered volley of musket shot as they did so. The Americans managed to slaughter some fifteen horses, two colts, and three cows, and even with the marines in hot pursuit, they now wrangled two fine English stallions, two colts, and three cows away. The remainder of the stocks would have to wait for some future raid. The Americans rushed their herd of seven beasts eastward toward adjacent Hog Island, the marines hot on their trail.[76]

With the skirmish afoot, the crew aboard HMS *Preston* in Boston Harbor took notice of both the conflagration and the billowing white smoke from the scattered musketry. Admiral Graves ordered the signal for the landing of marines, to which a sailor gathered a prearranged signal flag and promptly hoisted it up one of the masts of the flagship. As the signal flag was raised, *Preston* fired a cannon, alerting the other warships of their new orders. It only took moments, but soon all of the men-of-war were floating their longboats full of marines.

Graves next issued orders for the newly purchased and outfitted schooner *Diana*, under the command of his nephew Lt. Thomas Graves. The vessel was anchored near the path of Winnisimmet Ferry, between Winnisimmet and the north side of Noddle's Island, an ideal position to aid in the skirmish, but far enough from *Preston* that a midshipman courier must have been sent by rowboat to *Diana* to convey the orders.

Once they were received, *Diana*'s crew of thirty began to scurry across the top deck, some weighing her two bower anchors as others unfurled and trimmed her sails. Within moments of receiving her orders, the two-masted schooner was sailing swiftly along Chelsea Creek to the northeast side of the island.[77]

With the British reinforcement on its way and the marines on Noddle's Island in pursuit, the Yankee raiders soon reached the inlet separating them from Hog Island. But no sooner had they reached it, near three o'clock, than *Diana* bore down on them, unleashing a hailstorm of cannon shot from its four 4-pounders and twelve swivel guns. "But we Crost the river and about fiften of us Squated Down in a Ditch on the ma[r]sh and Stood our ground", according to Amos Farnsworth.[78] Perhaps the other fifteen Yankees led their seven stolen livestock farther onto Hog Island, leaving Farnsworth and his fellows to cover their retreat. With the schooner bearing down on them, keeping the Americans pinned in their marsh ditch, the marines from Williams Farm caught up to the fight.

The marines took up position across the narrow and shallow inlet from the Americans and their first platoon fired before falling back to reload, leaving the next platoon in the front position to then fire. While the marines continued to fire in platoons, Farnsworth and his fifteen fellow Americans popped out of their cover and gave a volley, killing or wounding a marine or two.[79] The marines continued to fire back with ferocity. As Farnsworth put it, "we had A hot fiar… But notwithstanding the Bulets flue very thitch [thick] yet thare was not A Man of us kil^d." No American died perhaps, but just as one Yankee near Farnsworth popped up to shoot, a marine took aim and fired, the lead ball smacking through one end of the Yankee's fleshy cheek and out the other, missing the bone, but instantly drawing blood that spurted down his chin and onto his collar.[80]

As these few Americans found themselves pinned down, both sides expected reinforcements. The several British longboats from HMS *Somerset*, HMS *Glasgow*, and HMS *Cerberus* had all streamed toward the island and were now disembarking a combined total of nearly a hundred additional marines. The *Glasgow* also sent her pinnace and *Somerset* sent her small sloop tender *Britannia*, each armed with swivel guns.[81] On the American side, maybe half of the more than two hundred Americans still on Hog Island began to descend toward the battle, while the remainder continued to remove the herds to Chelsea Neck.

Both adversaries' reinforcements stormed toward the small inlet that separated Hog Island from Noddle's, with the Americans on the former and the British on the latter. The odds were now about even, with nearly 150 ground forces on each side, and at last a general fusillade ensued. The British and Americans both ducked for cover in the ruts and ditches of their respective sides of the inlet, while at the same time *Diana* tried to vie for a better position, coming up to the inlet "as far as there was water" and laying anchor, even as she continued her salvo of 4-pounders and swivels. Behind her, the sloop *Britannia* hauled in and fired its swivels at the entrenched Americans, adding to the hailstorm that poured onto the marsh.[82]

The marines may have suffered an additional man or two wounded, while the Americans kept safe enough below their cover. Still, one American had a ball fly through his little finger, shearing it off. Another Yankee's gun backfired, the barrel bursting open and dusting him with burning black powder, melting his skin. But these two and maybe one more were the only Americans wounded, and none of their number was killed.[83]

In this position, with both sides entrenched and firing inherently inaccurate muskets, they found themselves at a stalemate with neither side giving up nor attempting to gain ground. With the sun falling low in the western sky, Captain Chads aboard *Cerberus* thought he would try to break the stalemate by sending ashore two of his light 3-pounder cannon with a party of seamen.[84] The seamen soon landed and mounted their guns atop a knoll on Noddle's Hill and began their cannonade, but with little effect.

By six o'clock that evening, the *Britannia* sloop had broken away from the fight. Lieutenant Graves was determined to back *Diana* away as well, partly in response to the American onslaught now mostly directed toward his schooner, and partly because of his orders from his uncle the admiral, which explicitly instructed him "not to remain in the River upon the Turn of the Tide".[85] The flooding tide up Chelsea Creek was sure to hinder *Diana*'s escape, so Lieutenant Graves complied with his orders and brought her about, hoping to move her back toward Winnisimmet.

But Lieutenant Graves found the winds calm. So he ordered *Diana's* one longboat floated, which took aboard it the kedge anchor, and by warping (dropping an anchor ahead and then pulling the boat forward, repeatedly), the crew of *Diana* fought against the slowly flooding tide and moved her away from Hog Island. Yet the incessant musketry from the Americans, coupled with the flooding tide, made the warping a struggle. At length, as many as seven longboats from the other warships, those that had been used to disembark the fresh marines, rounded Noddle's Island and joined the effort to haul off *Diana*, taking lines from the struggling schooner and attempting to tow her by rowing.

The Yankees, meanwhile, seeing the schooner in dire circumstances, turned their entire musketry in that direction, completely ignoring the marines across the inlet. *Diana* was now turned so that her stern and port side faced Hog Island, her bow aimed northwestward. The perhaps eight longboats were thus ahead of the bow, the schooner herself partially protecting them from the rebel musketry. Nevertheless, the ferocity of the American attack was daunting, and even as the seamen desperately labored to row *Diana* out from harm's way, others mounted swivels aboard each boat and fired their half-pound balls back toward shore. At the same time, the marines on Noddle's Island, seeing the colonial attack had shifted to the vulnerable *Diana*, moved into a better position, trying to draw away the rebel musketry.[86]

In spite of all the musketry and cannonading, it was mostly just noise, and few on either side were wounded, leaving *Diana* to slowly make headway westward. By sunset, just after seven o'clock, *Diana* was well out of range of the Americans on Hog Island. Colonel Nixon then ordered his men to fall back. Nearly out of ammunition, suffering from exhaustion from lack of both sleep and food, and fatigued too from their long fight that had now run nearly five hours, Amos Farnsworth and his fellow New Englanders were only happy to comply. As they left the island, they found that the other half of their force had succeeded in driving all the horses and livestock from Hog Island across to the mainland of Chelsea Neck. If only they had had the means to strip Noddle's

Island of its considerable livestock too, their mission would have been a complete success.[87]

Meanwhile, *Diana* had moved away from Hog Island, but she was not yet out of danger. As she continued to be warped and towed against the flood of Chelsea Creek, Connecticut Brig. Gen. Israel Putnam appeared on the mainland at the head of nearly three hundred men, perhaps proudly wearing a blue Connecticut militia uniform with red facings, white waistcoat, and breeches.[88] Beside him stood Dr. Joseph Warren, the able volunteer who always sought to be at the center of the action, be it political or military. Together they marched the Americans to the marshy shores and lined the riverbank somewhere east of Winnisimmet, drawing near the toiling schooner with their muskets at the ready. Just behind them was the newly formed Massachusetts artillery company under Capt. Thomas Wait Foster, maybe near forty strong. They brought with them two horse-drawn 4-pounders, which they began unlimbering atop the overlooking hills.[89]

The time was approaching eight o'clock, and dusk was quickly dissolving into a dark and moonless night. All was quiet now except for the rhythmic splashing of the oars into the water, the pulling of the hemp lines that stretched from *Diana*'s bow, and the sounds of the struggling seamen. Neither side had yet fired, but both adversaries sized up one another. Lieutenant Graves, aboard *Diana*, privately admitted that his towboats had gained him little ground. Toiling as they were against a contrary flood tide, failed as they were by the wind, and seeing too a fresh colonial force on the nearby shore, the hapless young naval officer knew his chances for escape were slim. On shore, Putnam knew it too, so he decided to offer Lieutenant Graves a way out. He stormed down to the creek's edge and sloshed into the muddy water, yelling to the schooner's crew and to the rowboats: if they would submit, they should have quarters. *Diana*'s crew looked to Lieutenant Graves for the reply. All was quiet for a moment.[90]

The fresh colonial troops waited along the north side of the riverbank in anticipation. Suddenly, two of *Diana*'s starboard cannon erupted with thunder, belching forth white smoke and flame, spitting two cannon shot that whizzed by Putnam and dispersed the Americans. Lieutenant Graves had given his reply, and the American cannon immediately fired two return shots into *Diana*. All along *Diana*'s starboard gunwales and stern, the swivels came alive once more.[91]

Putnam put his men "up to their waists in water, and covered by the bank to their necks."[92] There they immediately joined the chorus of cannon, giving a scattered bombardment across *Diana* and her tow-boats. Perhaps the 150 marines still on Noddle's Island also fired a few useless volleys from that long range across Chelsea Creek. Certainly, the two 3-pounders from *Cerberus*, still mounted on Noddle's Island, joined with their own cannonade.

Seeing the battle again renewed, General Gage in Boston sent over some of his own artillerymen with two heavy 12-pounders, along with a fresh body of one hundred to two hundred of his marines. The artillery-men soon mounted their 12s alongside the naval 3-pounders on Noddle's Island, but with twilight nearly faded to utter darkness, they could pro-vide only harassing fire. The new marines there could do nothing.[93]

Aboard the longboats, a few seamen again manned the swivels, firing at an unseen enemy obscured by the dim shoreline. The rest ducked low to avoid the whizzing balls overhead, even as they continued to row helplessly against the tide. Here it seems the British took the most casualties, with several wounded both in the schooner and the boats.[94] On the American side of the fight, Putnam encouraged his men, urging them not to fear the wayward cannon balls and musketry, all of which failed to hit their mark.

As the two sides continued with renewed ferocity, the last glimmers of light finally faded from the sky. The cannonade and musketry soon became sporadic, for all one could do was shoot in the direction of the orange, fiery blasts spewing from the opposing guns. The dark-ness forced Putnam and his men to leave their tide-pool ditches and wade deeper into the creek itself, striving to draw near enough to make out the dark vessel and her boats. So the battle continued even in the darkness, though with far less intensity. Yet under such fire, the valiant seamen persevered until, at last, nature intervened. At about half past ten o'clock on that moonless night, the flood tide having crested, the waters of Chelsea Creek slowly began to ebb once more.[95]

Now Lieutenant Graves had his opportunity, because the gently ebbing tide was advantageous to his escape. He ordered the boats to cast off, and once they had, *Diana* began to drift away from the battle westward toward Winnisimmet. No sooner had she begun to ride the current away than a contrary fresh breeze sprung up from the southwest, and with the fresh ebb tide not strong enough to counter it, *Diana* lurched sideways toward the rebels pursuing along the riverbank. Before *Diana*'s crew could regain control, "five or 6 Minutes would have secured her", she drifted into the shallow banks of the mainland near the Winnisimmet Ferry Way, running aground about 180 feet from the shore at around eleven o'clock.[96]

The sailors in the nearby longboats quickly rowed near and again took the towlines to try to free *Diana*, but the Americans concentrated all their firepower on them, enfilading the vessel and her boats. The provincial cannon meanwhile homed in on the schooner in the darkness, until it at last found its mark and began blasting holes into her starboard side. The sailors struggled hard to break *Diana* free, but soon the creek was fast ebbing away, forcing many sailors to hop from their boats and wade in the waters abeam her, braving the sporadic musket fire to push on *Diana*'s hull by hand and floundering in the mud as they tried desperately to float her.

For the British sailors, the Battle of Chelsea Creek became not one of defeating the Americans but of saving the schooner. Some aid came from the sloop *Britannia*, which again drew near, courtesy of the fresh breeze, and so provided cover fire with her complement of swivels. For hours, the sailors struggled beside *Diana* even as the Americans continued to harry them with sporadic musketry despite the darkness, all while both sides blindly cannonaded one another. Yet there was little more the British could do. With the creek continuing to ebb, the water soon fell below the seamen's knees as they floundered and pressed against the hull. At near three o'clock in the morning, *Diana* began to lurch once more, then totter, and at last fell on her beam-ends, her obstinate but valiant crew jumping or falling off her deck as she keeled over.[97]

On her side, *Diana* could no longer be manned, nor her guns fired. All the sailors could do was use the hulk as one giant shield from the American musketry while they awaited rescue. There in the shallow, ebbing, muddy water behind *Diana*, the officers and seamen took cover before wading over to the nearby *Britannia* and the longboats, at last

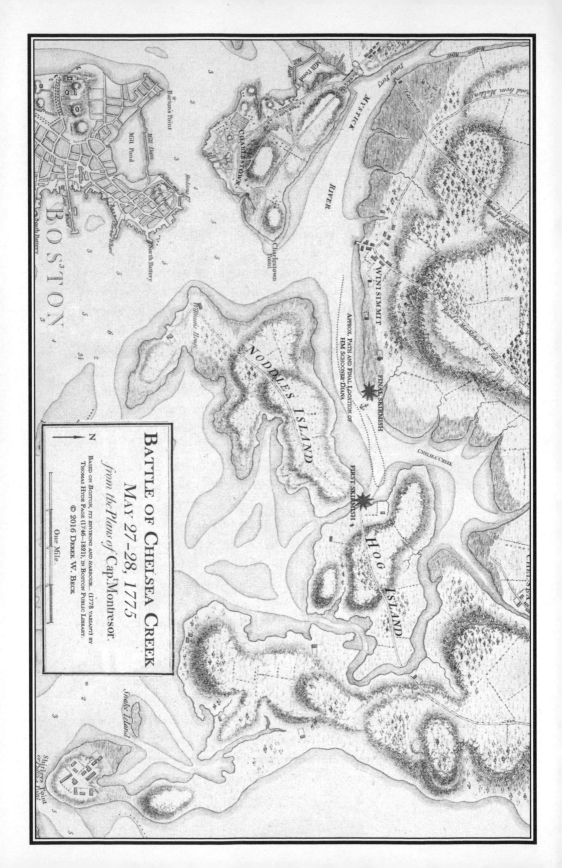

BATTLE OF CHELSEA CREEK
MAY 27–28, 1775
from the Plans of Cap.ᵗ Montresor.

BASED ON BOSTON, ITS ENVIRONS AND HARBOUR... (1775 VARIANT) BY
THOMAS HYDE PAGE (1746–1821), IN BOSTON PUBLIC LIBRARY.
© 2016 DEREK W. BECK

One Mile.

N

BOSTON.

Barton's Point

Mill Dam.

Mill Pond

North Battery

Mill Pond

Mill Pond

CHARLESTOWN

Charlestown Point

MYSTICA

RIVER

Ferry Ferry

Road from Malden

WINISIMMIT

APPROX. PATH AND FINAL LOCATION OF
HM SCHOONER DIANA

FINAL SKIRMISH

William's House

NODDLE'S ISLAND

CHELSEA CREEK

FIRST SKIRMISH

HOG ISLAND

CHELSEA FA...

Snake Island

Shirley's Point
or Pullin Point

abandoning their schooner.[98] Once they climbed aboard, the British boats rode the ebb tide away to safety, even as the water around *Diana* drained entirely away, leaving her beached on the expansive mudflats.[99]

As the British escaped, the Americans quickly swarmed onto this tidal zone and surrounded the abandoned *Diana*, just as the early light of dawn began to radiate across the sky once more. Some Yankees climbed precariously aboard the beached schooner and began to strip her of her four cannon, several swivels, and much of her rigging and sails, as well as some money found aboard.[100] The remaining Yankees began collecting hay from the mainland and stuffing it between the wet mud and the schooner's hull.

At just after four o'clock on May 28, with the sun rising above the eastern horizon, the British artillery on Noddle's Island could again target their prey. The artillery adjusted their heavy 12-pounders while the seamen adjusted their two naval 3s, and together they bore down on the American position. As the 12s opened fire, their coconut-sized iron balls thundered forth, sailed high, and splashed into the mudflats all around the American scavengers, splattering sludge everywhere.[101]

With this renewed British onslaught and the tide soon turning again to flood, Old Put grew anxious. He ordered his men to take the salvaged war stores and get back onto the mainland. Once they had, he ordered his remaining men to torch the hay stuffed beneath and throughout *Diana*, which instantly set her ablaze.[102] *Diana*'s pyre spread quickly, and soon the dancing flames filled her bowels. They reached the powder kegs still left aboard her, when, suddenly, fantastically, she exploded.[103] With this grand finale to the battle, the British conceded defeat and began to evacuate Noddle's Island by two o'clock that afternoon.[104]

The Battle of Chelsea Creek, also known as the Battle of Noddle's and Hog Island, ended with few casualties.[105] The Americans lost not a single life, with just three or four wounded, none mortally.[106] As Amos Farnsworth wrote in his diary, "thanks be unto God that so little hurt was Done us when the Bauls Sung like Bees Round our heds."[107] Though American accounts claimed otherwise, the British lost just two marines killed, plus two more wounded, along with a few seamen wounded. What had begun as a simple American raid to rob the British of livestock ended not just successfully, but amazingly so, with the destruction of His Majesty's Armed Schooner *Diana* and the acquisition of her guns.[108]

Late that same afternoon, Brigadier General Putnam returned to his quarters, the vacated Tory home of John Borland, now part of the Adams House at Harvard University.[109] The Borland House was centrally located and very near the main American encampment, and had thus become a common resort for the officers. So it was that when Putnam reached his borrowed residence, wet and covered to the waist in marsh mud, he met there Gen. Artemas Ward, who was always active when his calculus (likely bladder stones) was not flaring up. Also there was Dr. Joseph Warren, who had apparently left the battle once *Diana* was secured. Both men were eager for an update.

Without changing his clothes, Putnam gave his account of the events on Chelsea Creek. After noting that only a few Americans were wounded and none killed, he added, "I wish we could have something of this kind to do every day; it would teach our men how little danger there is from cannon balls, for tho' they have sent a great many at us, nobody has been hurt by them."[110]

Putnam was a hard-charging general, "totally unfit for everything but fighting",[111] so it was no surprise when he then told his two guests, "I would that Gage and his troops were within our reach, for we would be like hornets about their ears; as little birds follow and tease the eagle in his flight, we would every day contrive to make them uneasy."

Dr. Warren smiled but said nothing. Ward, often accused of being overly cautious, replied, "As peace and reconciliation is what we seek for, would it not be better to act only on the defensive, and give no unnecessary provocation?"

Without hesitation, Old Put turned to Warren and said, "*You know*, Dr. Warren, we shall have no peace worth anything, till we gain it by the sword."

Warren gave no reply, for while he believed Putnam was right, he shuddered at the thought of fighting the British directly. At last, Warren said only, "Your wet clothes must be uncomfortable, General, and we will take our leave that you may change them." As the doctor and General

Ward turned to leave, Warren, still contemplating Putnam's words, at last added, "I admire your spirit and respect Gen. Ward's prudence—both will be necessary for us, and one must temper the other."[112]

As Dr. Warren left the Borland House, Putnam's words continued to echo in his mind. Warren had at last accepted that war seemed now necessary and certain, yet he feared its outcome. Just days earlier, he had expressed his worries to the agent for Massachusetts in Britain, Arthur Lee, writing, "If we push this matters as far as we think we are able, to the destruction of the troops and ships of war, we shall expose Great Britain to those invasions from foreign powers which we suppose it will difficult for her to repel". Yet he admitted, "I must tell you, that those terms which would readily have been accepted before our countrymen were murdered… will not now do". Warren, however, hoped there would be no more bloodshed. "God forbid that the nation should be so infatuated as to do any thing further to irritate the colonies!"[113]

Warren was not naive. He fully expected some political struggle still ahead, particularly when it came to what he thought was a necessary overhaul of the provincial government. On the rare occasions when he found time to dwell on the grander implications of the present crisis, he began to imagine a more enlightened provincial government, which he hoped would replace the present government still officially headed by Governor Gage.

Warren wrote of his libertarian ideas to Samuel Adams in Philadelphia, explaining, "I would have such a government as should give every man the greatest liberty to do what he pleases consistent with restraining him from doing any injury to another, or such a government as would most contribute to the good of the whole, with the least inconvenience to individuals. However, it is difficult to frame a government *de novo* which will stand in need of no amendment. Experience must point out defects. And, if the people should not lose their morals, it will be easy for them to correct the errors in the first formation of government. If they *should* lose *them*, what was no good at first will be soon insupportable. My great wish therefore is, that we may restrain every thing which tends to weaken the principles of right and wrong, more especially with regard to *property*."[114]

Though it was but a minor engagement, the Battle of Chelsea Creek thus helped to solidify Warren's reluctant belief that the two belligerents would find no peace except by use of the sword. Many of his Whig colleagues had already made that determination, and there was talk of tightening the noose around Boston by fortifying the unofficially neutral heights of Charlestown to the north and Dorchester to the south. Little did they know, General Gage in Boston was well aware of those Yankee schemes and had himself privately begun to consider fortifying the same.

So while neither side knew it, as the days of May drew to a close, a race was on to secure and fortify the empty heights nearest Boston, and with it, a major military showdown became inevitable. Within a fortnight, Warren would indeed have to commit to a struggle for peace by way of the sword.

———•———

The Battle for Chelsea Creek may have been over, but the colonial scheme to remove the stock from Noddle's Island was not. Later that same day of the battle, small parties marched to the remains of *Diana* to scavenge for additional plunder.[115] On the following day, May 29, the rebels returned to Noddle's Island to drive away the nearly one thousand livestock there. Gage ordered his light infantry to muster, but before they embarked, he thought better of it and dismissed them, "and the Rebels left to do their business quietly, which by 6 oclock in the even. they effected".[116] After the Yankees successfully drove away the livestock, at about eight o'clock, they completed the day by torching most of the outbuildings of the once profitable Williams farmstead, leaving it a barren pastureland dotted with heaps of smoldering buildings. Only Williams's mansion and a few outbuildings remained intact.[117]

But on May 30, the Yankees returned once more and burned these remaining buildings too. When Admiral Graves saw this latest inferno, he was very concerned. If the rebels were willing to come all the way to the coastal mansion house, which stood underneath the guns of his warships, Graves's own rented warehouse there, with its valuable naval stores and lumber, was also at risk. He quickly issued orders, which his flagship HMS *Preston* relayed by signal flag and cannon shot. The fleet saw the new orders and immediately complied with a thunderous cannonade that effectively dispersed the Americans.

Graves then ordered ashore a large party of marines and seamen, guarded by a gunboat mounting a single heavy 12-pounder. This fatigue party spent the remainder of the day removing the warehouse stores to the warships, though they were obliged at times to pause and fire volleys at the encroaching Yankees who continued to loiter near the fiery mansion.[118] By the time the British completed their work and embarked, the mansion and outbuildings had entirely burned down, leaving only their tall, lonely brick fireplaces standing in their places, while the empty shoreline warehouse stood as the last remaining structure on Noddle's Island. Days later, it too would be razed, leaving Henry Williams with nothing.

Williams would beg recompense from the Provincial Congress for his property and livestock, declaring himself "stripped almost naked, and destitute of any place to lay his head, with a very large family of children and servants, to the amount of between forty and fifty in number, that are destitute of any business or supplies but from your memorialist." He apparently did receive some compensation, but he was never fully reimbursed. Instead, poor Henry Williams became one of the many innocent bystanders who suffered on the sidelines of the War for Independence.[119]

As for Lieutenant Thomas Graves, the hapless commander of the *Diana*, he was days later court-martialed—standard practice after the loss of a vessel, for it served as a means of inquiry into the incident. He was honorably acquitted, and the home government later concurred with the court-martial's sentence.[120]

The loss of such a plentiful supply of fresh meat from Noddle's Island would prove of great consequence in the coming weeks of the Siege of Boston, though its importance was apparently lost on British Lt. John Barker. He witlessly wrote in his diary, "it was thought hardly worth while running the risk of losing any lives by endeavouring to save a trifling property which we have no connexion with, nor indeed cou'd it be worth while[,] for it cou'd be of little consequence to us, and their burning the houses (which are only Out house and Barns I believe) can answer no other end than insulting us".[121] When fresh provisions became ever scarcer in the beleaguered town of Boston, perhaps Barker would remember with disdain the Yankee raid on Noddle's Island.

For Gage, the lesson of the Noddle's Island affair was that the Americans were willing to take the offensive. So he gave thought again to the town's defenses and decided the "Admiral's Battery" atop Copp's Hill was best controlled by the Royal Artillery and not Graves's seamen. Within days, the naval guns were removed from the battery and replaced with those of the Royal Artillery. To Graves's vexation, "insensibly it lost its original nickname" and would be called Copp's Hill Battery ever after.[122]

The brazen actions by the Americans again drew Admiral Graves's concern for his precious but vulnerable HMS *Somerset*, still moored between Charlestown and Boston. The massive 68-gun warship had been leaking since its arrival, and though extensive repairs and caulking had slowed the inflow into her bowels, new leaks were punching through her hull, forcing her crew to again almost continuously man her pumps to keep her afloat. She desperately needed a complete overhaul, but the rebel-controlled colony no longer offered a safe dock for such extensive repairs, leaving Halifax as the only nearby option. But Graves could not afford to do without *Somerset*'s superior firepower, so instead he ordered her into the harbor, though because of her mighty size, "she could be moved only by warping, and that on a flood tide". She moored just off Hancock's Wharf, while the 20-gun HMS *Lively* would days later take her place on the river to guard the Charlestown Ferry way.[123]

Meanwhile, as the last days of May passed, small parties of men from Rhode Island, part of their 1,500-man quota to the New England Army, began arriving in Roxbury. By the end of the month, their young commander also arrived: the sharp though untested thirty-three-year-old Brig. Gen. Nathanael Greene. Under Greene, the Rhode Islanders would be noted by American leadership as "the best disciplined and appointed in the whole American army."[124]

Across the Atlantic, the last days of May brought news that would utterly shock the nation, for Capt. John Derby and his private schooner *Quero* at last reached England, carrying with him the American account of the first shots of the war.

Somewhere along the southern shores of Britain, Yankee Captain Derby hid his *Quero* in some creek or cove, perhaps on the Isle of Wight, before taking a boat into nearby Southampton. He then hastily made his way to London by land, arriving in the city on May 28. He carried with him the precious American accounts of the Battle of the Nineteenth of April, but he soon learned that his intended recipient, Benjamin Franklin, had departed for Philadelphia on March 20 or 21.[125] However, Franklin's able substitute, the young American lawyer Arthur Lee, gladly stepped in to fulfill the mission. Together, Lee and Derby must have met that same day with the Whiggish Lord Mayor of London, John Wilkes, who was happy to assist in disseminating the American accounts.[126]

Though it took two days more for Dr. Warren's summary account to be printed in the London press, the rumor of the affair spread like wildfire and quickly became the talk of the town.[127] When exiled former Massachusetts Governor Thomas Hutchinson heard the rumors, he wrote in his diary, "The Opposition here rejoice that the Americans fight, after it had been generally said they would not." Hutchinson hurried to inform Colonial Secretary Lord Dartmouth of the rumors, who "was much struck with it."[128] Dartmouth tried to combat the rumors and preempt the impending publication by printing his own cautionary words the next day, but that made little difference.[129] For on May 30, Britons eagerly read the published American letter "to the Inhabitants of Great Britain", signed by Dr. Joseph Warren, a name hitherto largely unknown in England.[130]

If the mere rumor of battle could create such buzz all around London, the published version truly electrified the town. A supporter of Lord North complained, "the Bostonians are now the favourites of all the people of good hearts, and weak heads in the kingdom."[131] Lord George Germain, no friend to the colonies, wrote, "The news from America occasioned a great stir among us yesterday…the Bostonians are in the right to make the King's troops the aggressors and claim a victory."[132] Wealthy socialite and Whiggish gentleman Horace Walpole wrote, "So here is the fatal war commenced! The child that is unborn shall rue the hunting of that day!"[133] Walpole wrote in another letter, "By the waters of Babylon we sit down and weep, when we think of thee, O America! Tribulation on tribulation!"[134] The provincials had just scored a major victory in the propaganda war.

The following evening, former Governor Thomas Hutchinson joined Lt. Gen. Edward Harvey, the adjutant general, for dinner. Also joining them were two British colonels who had given service in America, and when the topic predictably turned to the American rebellion, a heated discussion ensued. When the two British officers exclaimed that Gage needed more troops, General Harvey blustered, "How often have I heard you American Colonels boast that with four battalions you would march through America; and now you think Gage with 3000 men and 40 pieces of cannon, mayn't venture out of Boston!"[135]

Those in political authority, however, waited for the official account.[136] It was not until June 9 that *Sukey* and Navy Lieutenant Nunn at last reached London, but Gage's account was too late and did little to change the public's perception.[137] One London newspaper printed, "When the news of a massacre first arrived, the...publick have suspended their judgment; they have waited the arrival of the *Sukey*; and the humane part of mankind have wished that the fatal tale related by Captain Derby might prove altogether fictitious. To the great grief of every thinking man, this is not the case."[138] Lord Dartmouth lightly chided Gage on the matter, urging that he send news of "any future Event of Importance...by one of the light Vessels of the Fleet."[139]

With the British account now received and considered, a few days later, the Lord Mayor and the aldermen of London issued a pro-American petition to King George. It read in part: "We have already expressed to your Majesty our abhorrence of the tyrannical measures pursued against our fellow-subjects in America... We desire to repeat again, that the power contended for over the Colonies, under the specious name of dignity, is to all intents and purposes, despotism... Every moment's prosecution of this fatal war may loosen irreparably the bonds of that connection on which the glory and safety of the British Empire depend... Your petitioners therefore again pray and beseech your Majesty to dismiss your present Ministers and advisers from your person and counsels for ever; to dissolve a Parliament who, by various acts of cruelty and injustice, have manifested a spirit of persecution against our brethren in America".[140]

But their petition fell on deaf ears, and news of the late Battle of the Nineteenth of April only further convinced the King and his Ministry that their policy of force and coercion was both necessary and proper. George the Third expressed his obtuse firmness succinctly when he wrote to Lord Sandwich, "when once these rebels have felt a smart blow, they will submit; and no situation can ever change my fixed resolution, either to bring the colonies to due obedience to the legislature of the mother country or to cast them off."[141] The King was too blind to realize that by his striving for obedience by the sword, he would necessarily *force* his colonies to be cast off, and thus *force* their eventual independence, not of their own desire, but by his insistence on his foolish policies.

The King and his Ministry drew comfort in knowing the bulk of their First Embarkation were due to arrive in Boston any day now, bringing an additional reinforcement of the 17th Light Dragoons and three full regiments of troops.[142] However, the Ministry did not draw comfort from Gage's abilities to wage this new war. Lord Suffolk wrote to Lord Germain, "The town is full of private letters from America which contain much more particular accounts of the skirmish than are related by the general. They don't do much credit to the discipline of our troops, but do not impeach their readiness and intrepidity." Lord Germain replied, "I must lament that General Gage, with all his good qualities, finds himself in a situation of too great importance for his talents... I doubt whether Mr. Gage will venture to take a single step beyond his instructions, or whether the troops have the opinion of him as to march with confidence of success."[143]

The Ministry also had to reconsider Gage's deputy commander, the Swiss-born Maj. Gen. Frederick Haldimand. When Gage had gone back to London on leave in 1773, Parliament was forced to pass an act to allow the foreign-born officer to hold the highest command. Now, with the war realized and the potential for Gage to be incapacitated, the situation was different. Lord Dartmouth tried to let Haldimand down gently, explaining that in the case of rebellion, the prejudices and opinions of mankind might create great difficulties should the command devolve upon any other than a natural-born subject of the King. This letter had in fact been sent weeks earlier, before London knew of the late battle, sent as a preemptive measure given the ever-more-certain conflict. It was only about now, at the end of May, that Haldimand received this disappointing news.[144]

Despite their new doubts in the abilities of General Gage, the Ministry knew the HMS *Cerberus* had already arrived at Boston, carrying aboard her the three major generals. With these generals, the King and his Ministry were confident they could properly prosecute the war.

When Lt. Gen. Thomas Gage consulted with his newly arrived major generals, they began to talk about strategies to break the siege. However, Gage could not seriously consider such operations because he knew himself to be dangerously outnumbered. His latest intelligence from Dr. Church reported the New England Army was again near 12,000, while his own force remained at about 4,000 men and officers.[145] The First Embarkation of troops was expected any day, which would add to his force nearly 1,500 men, including nearly 200 cavalry, but even with these, the British would remain outnumbered almost 2 to 1.

So in the last days of May, Gage arranged with Admiral Graves to send the sloop-of-war *Mercury* to New York with orders to reroute from there an expected Second Embarkation from Ireland. There was, after all, little reason to send troops to New York now that its inhabitants had been swayed by their local Sons of Liberty to throw in their lot with the rebellion.[146] The Second Embarkation would add to Gage's force an additional four full regiments, nearly 1,700 additional men and officers. These, plus most of the remainder of the 18th newly reassigned from New York, and replacements and recruits expected from England for the regiments already in Boston, would bring his combined force to nearly 7,800 officers and men. Unfortunately, many of these troops would take weeks yet to arrive, and Gage knew he might not have the luxury to wait that long to mount an offensive.[147]

Meanwhile, on about May 31, the colonial transport *Champion* sailed into the harbor, commandeered by a crew from the small 14-gun HM sloop *Falcon*, which arrived later on June 2. The two vessels were expected two weeks earlier, but when Commander John Linzee of the *Falcon* reported in with Graves, he gave an extraordinary tale.

Back on May 11, the 95-foot-long HM *Falcon* was cruising Buzzard's Bay on the south side of the Province of Massachusetts when it seized the transport *Champion* as she was sailing from Maryland and probably destined for Marblehead, laden with stores bound for the rebel army. The same day, *Falcon* took a second prize, a sloop "from Nantuckett for Having no Clearance."[148] From this sloop's crew, Commander Linzee learned of a third vessel then at Dartmouth, Massachusetts, owned by local Jesse Barlow, the vessel reportedly carrying within her bowels an illegally smuggled shipment from the West Indies.[149] The following morning, Linzee gave command of the captured prize sloop to a midshipman, along with a skeleton crew from the *Falcon*'s complement. Linzee then ordered the midshipman to set sail to Dartmouth to seize the smuggler's vessel.[150]

The unnamed British prize sloop reached Dartmouth probably hours later, only to discover the smuggler's vessel had already landed its cargo. Nevertheless, the small British crew seized the vessel, and together the two vessels sailed back for the *Falcon*. But Jesse Barlow and the inhabitants of Dartmouth took notice and quickly prepared the whaling sloop *Success* under the command of Captain Daniel Egery, manning it with thirty men and arming it with just two small swivel guns. Hours later, they set sail "in pursuit of these *royal* pirates."[151]

Success found the British midshipman's sloop and the commandeered smuggler's vessel anchored off Martha's Vineyard, moored about three miles apart. The *Success* tacked toward the smuggler's vessel first and quickly seized it without a shot fired. Once the Dartmouth men commandeered it, the now two American vessels sailed for the British prize sloop. The British midshipman ordered his crew to quickly hoist sail, but the two American vessels glided across the water too quickly. The British responded by firing small arms and swivels, but the Americans fired back with their equally small arms, reportedly wounding two British seamen and their midshipman commander.

Then, the two Yankee vessels crashed alongside the British prize sloop, and the American crews quickly boarded her, overwhelming the Royal Navy seamen. After a very short melee, the Yankees forced the British seamen below deck, taking command. Together, the three ships then sailed back to the coastal town of Fairhaven (northeast of Dartmouth) and there disembarked the fourteen British prisoners, some of them wounded, sending them away to the inland town of Taunton.[152]

This was the first naval skirmish of the war.

HM *Falcon* meanwhile guarded the precious *Champion* transport and in the following days took several other vessels as prizes. On about May 31, the commandeered *Champion* at last sailed into Boston Harbor, bringing with her some eight hundred barrels of flour and some corn, followed by the *Falcon* two days later.[153] And on June 4, the British transport *Charming Nancy* arrived with clothes and war stores, escorted by the 16-gun sloop *Nautilus*.[154]

June 4 was also the King's thirty-seventh birthday, and the naval ships all fired three cannon salutes in celebration. As it was a Sunday, the troops paraded on the Common at noon the following day to fire three empty volleys, followed by those of the artillery with twenty-one cannon, and then lines of troops between the Town House and Long Wharf. In the American camp in Roxbury, a few fired off rounds to taunt the British, which the British thought curious, for "they fired but 9 rounds, it's imagined some accident happen'd to their Guns as they fired no more." No accident had happened. Instead, the colonial commanders regained control of their men and chastised them for wasting their extremely limited gunpowder.[155]

On June 6, the Americans at last arranged a prisoner exchange, giving over the men taken from the late Battle of the Nineteenth of April. The ceremony was conducted with great pageantry, mostly to demonstrate that the New England Army was a bona fide military force. Dr. Warren and Brigadier General Putnam rode at the head of the parade in a phaeton pulled by two horses, together with several prisoner British officers on horseback, followed by two carts carrying the rest of the British, nine prisoners in all. Their escort was Connecticut's Wethersfield Company, commanded by Capt. John Chester, so chosen for the honor because theirs was the only complete colonial unit that had a uniform: a blue overcoat with red facings, and a white waistcoat and breeches. Putnam may have worn a similar uniform, perhaps the reason he was selected as the presiding official.[156]

The procession marched slowly across Charlestown Neck, down Bunker Hill, and into the Charlestown itself, all done in cadence to the fife and drum. They halted at Charlestown Ferry, where they were soon joined by a tender from the 20-gun HMS *Lively* anchored nearby. Maj.

Thomas Moncrieffe (or Moncrief), an old friend of Putnam's from the French and Indian War, disembarked from the tender and received the Americans. "Their Meeting was truly cordial and affectionate." [157] The British prisoners were released and boarded the tender, while Moncrieffe and his fellow British officers went with General Putnam and Dr. Warren to the nearby home of Dr. Foster in Charlestown, where they dined and entertained. At three o'clock that afternoon, the group returned to Charlestown Ferry, a signal was given, and *Lively*'s tender returned with nine colonial prisoners, who were disembarked and escorted with pageantry back to Dr. Foster's.[158] According to a perhaps biased colonial newspaper, the British prisoners all expressed their gratitude for "the genteel, kind Treatment they had received from their Captors…some of them could only do it by their Tears." The American prisoners seemed to have been treated just as humanely, though they suffered "repeated cruel Insults".[159]

Days later, on June 10, the first transports began arriving with the First Embarkation of British troops. Gage was pleased to see them disembark. Over the next several days, more transports would follow, and soon Gage would have in Boston the 17th Light Dragoons as cavalry and three new regiments of soldiers—the 35th, 49th, and 63rd—bringing his combined force to nearly 5,500 men and officers, nearly one soldier or marine for every remaining Bostonian.[160]

Meanwhile, up the coast, another naval battle was brewing.

———◆———

Admiral Graves had for some time indulged coasters (transports originating from elsewhere along the coast) to sail directly to Boston, bypassing inspection at Salem or Marblehead, provided they carried only provisions or fuel. Ever since the Battle of the Nineteenth of April, however, merchants had been loath to draw public animosity by breaking the Siege of Boston and so halted their trade with the town, leaving Graves in a conundrum.

Finding the opportunity irresistible, one intrepid Boston merchant, Ichabod Jones, proposed a scheme to supply Boston with lumber, which General Gage desired not only as firewood but also for fortification and

construction.[161] Jones's proposal was to barter with the small and isolated town of Machias, Maine, located deep within a long but narrow,
winding bay at the mouth of the Machias River. The town had been
carved from a thick and savage woodland backcountry, and thus had
plenty of lumber but little else. In exchange, Jones proposed to offer
salt provisions supplied from the Army, which he expected the few
hundred inhabitants of Machias would agree to, not because they were
Loyalist but because they were desperate. For his service, Jones presumably solicited some fee. The British accepted the scheme and so
outfitted and armed the schooner *Margaretta*, likely a purchased vessel,
which soon mounted four double-fortified 3-pounders and fourteen
swivels, along with muskets and hand grenades.[162] Graves then ordered
Midshipman James Moore, probably of the *Preston*, to take command
of *Margaretta* and escort Jones's two trading sloops *Unity* and *Polly* to
and from Machias.[163]

When the three ships arrived at Machias on June 2, Jones began
brokering the trade deal: Machias lumber for the Army's provisions
aboard *Unity* and *Polly*. At length, the town voted on the matter and,
in "considering themselves nearly as prisoners of war in the hands of
the common enemy", elected to accept Jones's offer.[164] But when Jones
began to distribute his provisions, he did so only to those who had voted
for his plan, slighting in particular two important Whigs, the young
and spirited Jeremiah O'Brien and the charismatic Benjamin Foster, a
veteran of the last war. Angered, O'Brien and Foster stormed off into
the thick backwoods to gather a few hearty, like-minded men, plotting
to return the next week to seize both Jones and Acting Lieutenant James
Moore while they were in church service.

The next week, on Sunday, June 11, Jones and Moore sat in the
meeting house for church as expected. Maybe Moore noticed the sly,
sideways glances as he listened to the sermon. Perhaps he felt uneasy and
was on guard. Suddenly, outside, he saw a party of near one hundred
men, armed with pitchforks and muskets, charging their way. Jones and
Moore sprang up. As the armed men outside swarmed to the church's
front door, Moore and a few fellow seamen climbed out a window and
dashed for the docks, though the angry mob instantly pursued. Jones
turned for the woods and apparently escaped. As the rest ran for the

docks, an alert petty officer on *Margaretta* swiftly sent a tender over. It arrived just in time for Moore and his sailors to hop in and push off, just ahead of their pursuers.

Once they were aboard *Margaretta*, the mob yelled to them from the shore, demanding they strike their colors to the Sons of Liberty. Moore may have grabbed a bullhorn when he coolly replied from the safety of his ship, inquiring what it was the mob wanted. To this, the mob bellowed for Ichabod Jones, not realizing he had escaped.[165] Rather than reveal Jones was not aboard, Moore replied "That he had express orders to protect Captain Jones; that he was determined to do his duty, whilst he had his life". But the mob soon deduced the truth, and at length, Moore demanded the mob abandon their pursuit of Jones and free his vessels, or he would burn the town.[166]

It was an idle threat, for the small *Margaretta* was hardly equipped to perform such a deed. Consequently, the townspeople ignored it and boarded Jones's sloop *Unity*, which was docked along the shore, and began to strip her of her provisions. Meanwhile, the small guns of *Margaretta* remained silent as her crew watched with disgust. As the afternoon grew late, another party of townsmen took to boats and rowed over to Jones's smaller sloop *Polly*, anchored a half mile downstream. They then boarded *Polly*, moved her up to the wharves, and anchored her just off shore. Moore meanwhile bided his time as the last dim lights of dusk faded away.

Finally, at half past eight o'clock, under a bright and nearly full moon, Moore quietly ordered his *Margaretta* crew to weigh anchor and sail near the docks, hoping to retake the sloop *Polly*. But as they did, a few townsmen still aboard *Polly* quickly slipped her cable and ran her ashore. They then fled to their boats and canoes, aligned themselves on the opposite shore, and demanded the *Margaretta* "surrender to America" while others upon the shore again demanded she strike her colors to the Sons of Liberty or suffer death if she resisted. Acting Lieutenant Moore replied, "Fire, and be damn'd!"[167]

The colonists heeded Moore's advice and fired their muskets. The twenty crew of *Margaretta* returned fire with swivels and small arms, and a "smart engagement ensued".[168] After an hour and a half of a continuous exchange of small arms, at last, the *Margaretta* slipped her cable and fell downstream half a mile until she came upon some other small sloop, where she came to and anchored nearby. There she waited for dawn, leaving the rebels to go about their business.[169]

In the middle of the night, using the near full moon to make their way, the Yankees rowed quietly toward *Margaretta*, determined to take the British schooner. *Margaretta*'s crew stood alert, and as the rebels drew near, the British opened fire. A second brisk skirmish ensued, but the British managed to beat back the Americans, suffering just one man wounded. The next morning, June 12, the British saw on the nearby shore four American boats left empty, full of holes.

Moore had had enough and decided to abandon Jones and escape, hoping to take advantage of the favorable winds and ebbing tide. He first ordered his men to lash their schooner to the sloop anchored nearby. They immediately did so, boarded her, and confiscated some boards from her storage, which they used to build barricades on their own bow and stern, hoping these would protect them against further insult from rebel small arms. The British also impressed the unlucky neighboring sloop's Captain Tobey, demanding that he serve as their pilot. Finally, they unlashed themselves and set sail eastward toward the harbor entrance.

As *Margaretta* made her escape, colonists on the shoreline gave a sort of farewell salute by firing musket shots across her bow. The shots proved harmless, but perhaps for this reason *Margaretta*'s supposedly seasoned crew, manned as they were with "twenty of the best men from the *Preston*", grew clumsy in their speedy retreat and failed to take care as they sailed running free (the wind at their backs).[170] They made a fatal turn that instantly caused an accidental jibe, slamming their sails to the opposite side and breaking their main boom and gaff. Suddenly, the *Margaretta*'s speed was crippled and she limped along with the ebb tide.

To her fortune, she soon came upon another hapless sloop inbound to Machias. *Margaretta* hailed her at gunpoint and sent her boats out to fetch her. They boarded the sloop, forced her Capt. Robert Avery to sail toward *Margaretta*, lashed the two vessels together, and then stripped the sloop of her boom, gaff, provisions, and the captain himself.

Meanwhile, with *Margaretta* nearly two miles from the wharves of Machias and out of sight, disgruntled Whig Jeremiah O'Brien decided he would pursue her. At length, he commandeered Jones's sloop *Unity*, taking with him some forty men, while another twenty commanded by the elder Benjamin Foster took to another small schooner. Together, the two vessels hoisted their canvas and began to glide across the water toward their prey.

Fortunately for the *Margaretta*, her distance ahead afforded her crew time to repair the broken boom. However, O'Brien's *Unity* was a fast ship, the faster of the two American vessels, and after taking the lead, he soon spotted the wounded *Margaretta* at a distance. O'Brien then realized that, though his men outnumbered theirs two to one, his were armed only with "guns, swords, axes, and pitchforks".[171] Noting the discrepancy in firepower and seeing too *Margaretta*'s new bow and stern deck walls, O'Brien ordered his men to build on *Unity*'s deck a breastwork of pine boards and anything else they could find.

The *Margaretta* crew hastily repaired their vessel, picking up their pace once they spotted *Unity*. Before *Unity* could draw near, *Margaretta*'s crew cut her boats from her stern to lighten her load, then weighed anchor and hoisted all the sail she could. But it was too late. *Unity* quickly came upon the escaping British schooner, just as *Margaretta* got underway and approached the entrance to the windy and narrow Machias Harbor.

Margaretta fired its stern swivels and small arms. But O'Brien, itching for a fight and hoping his pinewood barricade would hold, sailed *Unity* through the barrage and got within earshot. For a third time he demanded *Margaretta* strike her colors to the Sons of Liberty, promising to treat them well if they did, but threatening death if they refused. Moore, realizing his schooner was not swift enough to escape, ordered *Margaretta* to come about, giving O'Brien's *Unity* a broadside of swivels and small arms. (For some reason, Moore never fired *Margaretta*'s small cannon.) Both sides then erupted in small-arms fire, each "determined to conquer or die."[172]

Amid the firefight, one Yankee, manning a wall gun mounted on *Unity*'s gunwales, fired a ball into the *Margaretta*'s helmsman, killing him. As the helmsman's body fell to the deck, leaving the ship to turn freely, *Margaretta* instantly tacked to the wind just as *Unity* maneuvered closer...too close! *Unity* smashed bow-first into the British schooner, the American sloop's bowsprit running through the main shrouds of *Margaretta*, tangling and locking the two vessels in a tight V shape.[173]

The larger crew of *Unity* poured onto *Margaretta*'s deck and a violent melee erupted. *Margaretta*'s Acting Lieutenant Moore grabbed a box of hand grenades and threw two of them onto the deck of his adversary, killing or wounding several Yankees. Two Americans in turn homed in on the lieutenant-turned-grenadier and fired. Two balls smashed into Moore, one bursting into his right breast, the other into his belly, dropping the young midshipman onto the quarterdeck and into a pool of his own blood. With the fall of Moore, the British seamen lost heart, and the Americans clubbed their muskets and began beating and herding the British sailors into the hold below.

Within moments, the battle was over, with about a quarter of the men from each side either wounded or killed, including the innocent Captain Avery whose sloop had been robbed for a boom. As the Americans struck the British colors and hoisted a flag of their own, a handful of O'Brien's men lifted the dying Moore and carried him into his cabin.[174] There O'Brien asked why the colors had not been struck. Moore replied, "I preferred Death before yielding to such a set of Villains!"[175] He got his wish, and died the next day.

This was the Battle of Machias, the second naval skirmish of the war and the first American prize taken at sea. When Graves learned of the affair, he wrote, "the Event proved how totally mistaken Mr. Jones was in the temper of his Countrymen".[176] The strategic value of the victory was minimal, but the Americans gained new confidence from it, and the news spread like wildfire, encouraging many more whalers and fishermen to take to their boats and harry the Royal Navy.

In Boston, meanwhile, a far more paramount and strategic battle was looming on the horizon.

The mounting audacity of the New England Army and the declining morale of the King's forces—on top of the ever present affront at being ensnared in Boston rather than having authority over it—finally impelled Gage to act in some fashion to break the siege. The continued arrival of additional troops and the recent arrival of Major Generals Howe, Clinton, and Burgoyne stood as plain reminders of the home government's positive determination to take the offensive and squash the rebellion.

And yet, Gage was hesitant. Even with the First Embarkation of troops then arriving, the final of which would not sail in until June 15, Gage's army would swell to only 5,500 men and officers—half the size of the New England Army of Observation.[177] However, recent intelligence warned that the rebels were now earnestly discussing fortification of the commanding Charlestown Heights on the peninsula to the north and Dorchester Heights on the peninsula to the south of Boston. Gage could no longer dither and delay, nor could he wait for his Second Embarkation of troops. If he did not act soon, he would not have to. The rebels would instead force him to do battle—but on their terms, not his. So, reluctantly, Gage began to develop a plan to take the offensive.

The two commanding heights each offered a serious tactical advantage. If the Americans took either position, the British warships and ground artillery would find the heights too great for their shots to reach when fired from the harbor or low town, leaving the Americans to safely rain cannon shot onto Boston and destroy it. This of course depended on the Yankees' obtaining sufficient large cannon by which to threaten the town. So far, they lacked such firepower, having only smaller pieces that could harass the British, but nothing more. Consequently, though the Americans continued to discuss taking the two heights and thereby tightening their noose around their adversary, and Gage continued to receive intelligence of such, the Americans never made a genuine plan to attempt the enterprise.

In contrast, were the British to secure the two heights north and south of the town—and unlike the Americans, they would have to secure both—the British would then enjoy absolute security in Boston, even if the Yankees later brought in larger cannon from the two forts on Lake Champlain. Not only would such a move secure the defense of the town, but it would also secure the defense of the entire Boston Harbor, allowing British transports to continue ferrying in provisions unabated. Moreover, with fortification of those heights, the British would not be as dependent on the Royal Navy, allowing Admiral Graves to send more warships out of the harbor to secure additional provisions for the town. In fact, were the British to gain these two heights, they would practically eliminate the Yankee advantage, the siege would become little more than a nuisance, and the British would be free to maintain their occupation indefinitely.

These obvious advantages were not lost on Maj. Gen. William Howe. After assessing the disposition of the belligerents shortly after his arrival, he wrote, "The General [Gage] has not thought it prudent to Attack...nor to Extend himself upon the Heights of Dorchester, or Charles Town; which two Positions I Profess to think he should have been Master of, on the Rebels first appearance, because he could hold them both without the Least Risk." Howe concluded that Gage had not done this for fear of "a General Insurrection of the Inhabitants of The Town" of Boston "with an Intention of Massacring the Garrison, which is firmly believed to have been their intention."[178]

Despite the significant advantages of the two heights, they remained unfortified and ungarrisoned by either side. Rather, they had become an unofficial neutral ground between the two armies—each army expecting a sharp engagement from the other were they to attempt a bid for either heights. However, a more important reason also helped keep Charlestown Peninsula unfortified. While the southern Dorchester Peninsula was mostly uninhabited, Charlestown Peninsula comprised the town of Charlestown itself. The day after the Battle of the Nineteenth of April, when the British evacuated Charlestown Heights and returned to Boston, Capt. Edward Le Cras of the HMS *Somerset* sent word to the town's selectmen, warning that if they should take up arms or allow their heights to be fortified, he and the naval fleet would raze the town.[179] This was no idle threat, and the warships were more than capable of the feat. Accordingly, Charlestown's selectmen took heed and kept the New England Army from so much as encamping on Charlestown Peninsula. Neutral or not, the town was caught between two armies, so most of Charlestown's populace evacuated, leaving it a ghost town.

As Gage planned for the offensive, his first act was to ask Graves to send *Mercury* to New York to intercept the troop transports headed there and redirect them to Boston. However, this Second

Embarkation would not arrive for weeks.[180] Gage then assembled his war council.

The key members that attended the war council were His Excellency General Gage himself; his three newly arrived major generals: Howe, Clinton, and Burgoyne; probably his brigadier generals, Lord Percy, Robert Pigot, and Valentine Jones; and his Deputy Commander Maj. Gen. Frederick Haldimand; as well as staff officers and aides. At length, the council devised to commence operations to the south. The British would swarm and dominate Dorchester Peninsula, cutting it off at the thin neck where it connected to the mainland, then attack the rebel camp at Roxbury.

As Burgoyne explained, "Howe was to land the transports on the [Dorchester] point; Clinton in the centre [of Dorchester Peninsula]; and I was to cannonade from the Causeway or the [Boston] Neck; each to take advantage of circumstances."[181] Howe explained the plan was then to "proceed without loss of Time to attack the Gentry at Cambridge, & it was thought necessary before that should take place, that Boston should be left secured by a strong redoubt on the Dorchester Neck".[182] Following this, the British "would then go over with all we can muster to Charles Town Height, which is entirely commanded from Boston".[183]

Major General Haldimand was perhaps disappointed with the timing of the plan, because he had at last received his orders recalling him to England, though he arranged to sail first to New York to settle some financial affairs there. The start of the operation on Dorchester Peninsula was set for June 18.[184] Haldimand was due to depart on June 16, and so would not witness the monumental events that were about to unfold.[185]

———•———

On June 12, in preparation for the coming operation, General Gage issued a proclamation, the words of which were too magniloquent and arrogant to be his own. Once Dr. Warren and others read it, they knew by reputation that the true author was the haughty playwright Maj. Gen. John Burgoyne. It began: "Whereas, the infatuated multitudes, who have long suffered themselves to be conducted by certain well known incendiaries and traitors, in a fatal progression of crimes against the constitutional authority of the State, have at length proceeded to avowed Rebellion".

After a summary of the late skirmishes and treasons against His Majesty, the proclamation offered, "In this exigency of complicated calamities, I avail myself of the last effort within the bounds of my duty, to spare the effusion of blood; to offer, and I do hereby, in His Majesty's name, offer and promise his most gracious pardon to all persons who shall forthwith lay down their arms, and return to their duties of peaceable subjects, excepting only from the benefit of such pardon, *Samuel Adams* and *John Hancock*, whose offences are of too flagitious a nature to admit of any other consideration than that of condign punishment." The proclamation warned, however, "that no person…may plead ignorance of the consequences of refusing it", "all and every person…who have appeared in arms against the King's Government, and shall not lay down the same", or who should aid or abet the present rebellion would be henceforth deemed "Rebels and Traitors, and as such to be treated." Finally, by Governor Gage's rights and authority per the Charter of Massachusetts, the proclamation ended, "I do hereby publish, proclaim and order the use and exercise of the Law-Martial".[186]

This declaration of martial law was of little consequence, however, because the Americans no longer acknowledged Gage as their governor. The day after this "late extraordinary proclamation", Dr. Warren and four others were chosen by the Provincial Congress as a committee to draft a reply. It was drafted but never published, for urgent events far more exigent would soon supersede it.[187]

———◆———

Ever since the prisoner exchange, Brigadier General Putnam had been encouraging colonial leaders to consider fortifying the Heights of Charlestown. On one of those occasions, Dr. Warren asked Putnam something like, "If 10,000 British should march out of Boston, what number in your opinion would be competent to meet them?"

Thinking back to the late Battle of the Nineteenth of April, Putnam is said to have replied something like, "let me pick my officers, and I would not fear to meet the British with half the number—not in pitched battle to stop them at once, for no troops are better than the British—but I would fight on the retreat, and every stone wall we passed should be lined with their dead…and besides, we should only fall back on our *reserve*, while every step they advanced, the country would close on their flanks and rear."[188]

Days later, Putnam again pressed his Charlestown strategy at a meeting with Dr. Warren, General Ward, and Committee of Safety member Col. Joseph Palmer. Palmer was inclined to favor the proposal, but Ward and Warren opposed, arguing that, given the lack of gunpowder and artillery sufficient to batter the town, the endeavor was futile.

Putnam clarified himself: his aim was not to batter the town, but to draw the British from it, where the opposing forces could then meet on equal terms, and Charlestown and Dorchester were the only points where this could be done. It was a foolhardy idea, but Putnam was itching for a fight. Moreover, he rightly knew the ragtag Yankee Army needed employment to keep it together, because the men's morale was again waning from inactivity.

Warren and Ward upheld their gut convictions, objecting to the high cost in blood that such a battle might require. The Americans could succeed with guerrilla-style tactics, but they could never hope to defeat the highly disciplined British Army in a face-to-face pitched battle. Putnam did his best to change their minds, but at length he tried a different tack. He asked them to suppose the worst did happen. They would die as martyrs to the cause "and show those who seek to oppress us what men can do who are determined to live *free* or not live at all."

Considering this, Dr. Warren rose from his chair, paced around the room a moment, then returned to his chair and leaned over its back, contemplating Putnam's words. At last he replied, "Almost thou persuadest me, General Putnam—but I must still think the project a rash one. Nevertheless, if it should ever be adopted, and the strife becomes hard, you must not be surprised to find me with you in the midst of it."

"I hope not, Sir!" replied Putnam. "You are yet but a young man, and our country has much to hope from you, both in council and in war. It is only a little brush we have been contemplating—let some of us who are older and can well enough be spared *begin* the fray. There will be time enough for you hereafter, for it will not soon be ended."[189]

Nothing more came of the discussion, but on June 12 or 13, probably thanks to whispers among the British in Boston that seeped out to the Americans lines, Dr. Warren and the Provincial Congress became aware of Gage's plan to attack Dorchester Peninsula on June 18. Suddenly, the notion of a direct and open conflict with the British became very real.[190] Then on June 14, Warren received positive proof of the British plan, thanks to intelligence slipped across the lines in some unknown fashion by a Whiggish deacon still in the beleaguered town.[191]

Cambridge suddenly bustled with activity. General Ward began making all last-minute preparations he could with his army, while the Provincial Congress did the same. One of the key tasks for the Provincial Congress on June 14 was to complete the selection of its leadership for the newly formed Massachusetts Army. Ward had already been made full general and commander in chief, and John Thomas in Roxbury had been made lieutenant general. The major generals, however, had not yet been selected. For this honor, Congress nominated John Whitcomb as first major general and none other than Dr. Joseph Warren as the second.[192] Warren had initially been offered the position of surgeon general, "but, preferring a more active and hazardous employment, he accepted a major-general's commission" instead.[193]

It would take a few days for the Provincial Congress to make the new general commissions official.[194] The next day, away in Philadelphia, another general was to be nominated, for the Continental Congress would at last discuss the issue of a Continental Army and place at its head a continental commander in chief.

———•———

The Second Continental Congress had reconvened, not at the smaller Carpenter's Hall as before, but at the grand Pennsylvania State House (now Independence Hall), with its two wide, brick wings and its central white bell tower. Yet despite this grander stage, the daily sessions regarding "the State of America" proved long and fruitless.[195]

One of the chief topics for John Adams and other delegates was the petition Dr. Church had brought from Massachusetts urging the adoption of the forces outside Boston as a Continental Army and selecting a commander in chief for it. However, the discussion thus far had been uneventful, with most of the backroom politics focused on who that new commander in chief would be. Though he had essentially no military experience, John Hancock thought his extreme wealth and social standing made him well qualified for the command he so coveted. Yet the suspicious southern colonies were staunchly opposed to giving any New Englander the command, and so a push slowly emerged for the well-known Virginia planter and Militia Colonel George Washington.

Elbridge Gerry of the Massachusetts Provincial Congress wrote to their delegates in Philadelphia to give his opinion. "I should heartily rejoice to see this way the beloved Colonel Washington, and do not doubt the New-England generals would acquiesce in showing to our sister colony, Virginia, the respect she has before experienced from the continent in making him generalissimo. This is a matter in which Dr. Warren agrees with me".[196] John Adams, however, demurred to the idea of Washington at first, explaining years later, "the Delicacy of his health, and his entire Want of Experience in actual Service, though an excellent Militia Officer, were decisive Objections to him in my Mind."[197]

Adams had good reason to question Washington, for the Virginian's qualification was not obvious. Though Washington had fought in the French and Indian War with distinction, his most glaring deficiency was that he had never actually won a battle. His first real military experience was in leading a small militia and Indian force into the Ohio Valley to warn the French there of British territorial claims. In leading this mission, Washington and his small band overwhelmed a French force. Seeking revenge, a larger French and Indian force then ambushed and defeated Washington and his men on July 3, 1754, at a shoddy fort they had dubbed Necessity, located in modern southwestern Pennsylvania. This became known as the Battle of the Great Meadows, and it directly led to the start of the French and Indian War.

Washington's greatest success in that war came a year later as aide-de-camp to British Maj. Gen. Edward Braddock. On July 9, 1755, at the Battle of the Monongahela in the backcountry near modern Pittsburgh, Pennsylvania, the violently ill Lieutenant Colonel Washington left his sickbed to join the British front in time to organize the retreat and bear the mortally wounded Braddock away, a service that earned Washington fame as the Hero of the Monongahela. In gratitude for this service, he was afterward promoted to colonel and made commander in chief of the Virginia Militia. Washington would spend much of the remaining war along the western frontier, where life in the service was difficult.

By war's end, his health grew poor, so he returned to his home in Virginia. He soon after married the widow Martha Dandridge Custis and adopted her two children as his own, a union which greatly increased his social standing, wealth, and property, allowing him to settle down to a comfortable life as a gentleman farmer. But his peaceful lifestyle was disrupted when the present crisis with Britain loomed on the horizon, and he rode to Philadelphia as a delegate to the First Continental Congress, where he was noted for his prudence, judgment, moderation, and soft-spoken demeanor.

Now that he was again in Philadelphia for the Second Continental Congress, the mild-mannered Virginian's presence was far more conspicuous, for he wore each day his old Virginia Blues militia colonel uniform. Though he did so as a demonstration of solidarity for the American soldiers outside Boston, it served the dual purpose of a not-so-subtle advertisement that he was available, though perhaps not eager, to serve the Congress in a military capacity.[198]

At last, John Adams, after "apprehending daily that We should he[a]r very distressing News from Boston", met with his cousin Samuel one morning before a session of Congress to discuss the matter. Together they walked the grounds of the State House as John expounded the dangers and anxieties of the present crisis to his cousin. Samuel agreed, but said, "What shall we do?"

John answered that they should compel Congress to "declare themselves for or against something. I am determined this Morning to make a direct Motion that Congress should adopt the Army before Boston and appoint Colonel Washington Commander of it."

Samuel seemed to think seriously on the matter but said nothing.

Why did John Adams suddenly commit to supporting Washington? According to a tradition, Adams jokingly said later in life that Washington was always the logical choice because he was always the tallest man in the room. (And thus, men would always look up to him.)[199] The reality, of course, as Adams came to realize, was that only someone as respected as Washington, someone who came from a southern or middle colony instead of New England, could hope to unite the Yankee Army and the continent.

Accordingly, that same morning in Congress, John Adams arose and gave a speech, as he was fond of doing. He concluded "with a Motion in form that Congress would Adopt the Army at Cambridge and appoint a General". John Adams freely admitted that this was not the proper time to nominate a general, because the question of who was to command would be the most contentious point debated. Yet he nevertheless declared, "I had but one Gentleman in my Mind for that important command...a Gentleman whose Skill and Experience as an Officer, whose independent fortune, great Talents and excellent universal Character, would command the Approbation of all America, and unite the cordial Exertions of all the Colonies better than any other Person in the Union."

John Hancock had previously been chosen as President of the Second Congress and was thus seated in the front of the Assembly Hall, giving John Adams and the other delegates "an Opportunity to observe his Countenance". According to Adams, as he made his long introduction to his nomination, Hancock "heard me with visible pleasure, but when I came to describe Washington for the Commander, I never remarked a more sudden and sinking Change of Countenance. Mortification and resentment were expressed as forcibly as his Face could exhibit them. Mr. Samuel Adams Seconded the Motion, and that did not soften the Presidents Phisiognomy at all."[200]

The subject was postponed to a future day, but after some debate, on June 15, Congress at last unanimously voted to elect Washington as the commander in chief of the American Army, to hold the rank of full general, while the collection of provincial armies outside Boston would become the American (later Continental) Army, forerunner to the modern United States Army.[201] The next day after his appointment, the forty-three-year-old Washington gave a compelling acceptance speech, one that proved him to be a humble gentleman and a wise choice:

"Tho' I am truly sensible of the high Honour done me, in this Appointment, yet I feel great distress, from a consciousness that my abilities and military experience may not be equal to the extensive and important Trust: However, as the Congress desire it, I will enter upon the momentous duty, and exert every power I possess in their service, and for support of the glorious cause. I beg they will accept my most cordial thanks for this distinguished testimony of their approbation.

"But, lest some unlucky event should happen, unfavourable to my reputation, I beg it may be remembered, by every Gentleman in the room, that I, this day, declare with the utmost sincerity, I do not think myself equal to the Command I am honored with.

"As to pay, Sir, I beg leave to assure the Congress, that, as no pecuniary consideration could have tempted me to have accepted this arduous employment, at the expence of my domestic ease and happiness, I do not wish to make any proffit from it." Washington was committing to work without pay, an example of his selfless commitment that would be a hallmark of his command. He asked only for reimbursement of his expenses, though these would be considerable.[202]

Accordingly, Congress drafted his commission and pledged their equal support, and "that they will maintain and assist him, and adhere to him, the said George Washington, Esqr., with their lives and fortunes in the same cause."[203]

Washington's concern over his appointment was genuine. When he wrote to his wife Martha of the news, he explained, "I assure you, in the most solemn manner, that, so far from seeking this appointment I have used every endeavour in my power to avoid it, not only from my unwillingness to part with you and the Family, but from a consciousness of its being a trust too great for my Capacity… But, as it has been a kind of destiny that has thrown me upon this Service, I shall hope that my undertaking of it, is designd to answer some good purpose".[204]

John Adams was excited to give the news to his wife, Abigail, writing, "I can now inform you that the Congress have made Choice of the modest and virtuous, the amiable, generous and brave George Washington Esqr., to be the General of the American Army, and that he is to repair as soon as possible to the Camp before Boston. This Appointment will have a great Effect, in cementing and securing the Union of these Colonies."[205]

Unfortunately, Washington's able leadership would not come to Boston in time for the first major battle of the American Revolution.

CHAPTER 2

SEIZING THE OFFENSIVE

On June 15, 1775, Gage received intelligence reporting the Americans were aware of the British plan and expected "within afew Days [to] be Attacked, at Roxbury and at Charles Town." If Gage doubted whether the Americans would take action, given their newfound knowledge, the intelligence further warned that the New England rank and file were eager for a fight, or "if something is not immediately attempted [to stop the British], They will Disband [in disgust] and return to their several Homes".[1]

Indeed, the Americans had at last decided that their best course of action was to disrupt the British plan with a preemptive operation of their own, much like General Putnam had been recommending for some weeks. So on this same day, June 15, the Committee of Safety made its most monumental decision:

"Whereas, it appears of importance to the safety of this colony, that possession of the hill called Bunker's Hill in Charlestown, be securely kept and defended, and also, some one hill or hills on Dorchester Neck be likewise secured, therefore, *Resolved*, unanimously, that it be recommended to the council of war, that the above mentioned Bunker's Hill be maintained by sufficient forces being posted there, and as the particular situation of Dorchester's Neck is unknown to this committee, they advise that the council of war take and pursue such steps respecting the same, as to them shall appear to be for the security of this colony."[2]

On the question of fortifying Dorchester, Lt. Gen. John Thomas ultimately decided he lacked sufficient forces to properly take and defend those heights. As to the heights above Charlestown, the war council began laying the groundwork for the colonists' offensive operation. They would secretly put it into motion the next night, June 16, under the cover of darkness. And once the British discovered the Yankees in possession of Charlestown Heights the next morning, June 17, one day ahead of their own intended operation against Dorchester, they would be caught unprepared and forced to do battle on American terms.

———•••———

The day of June 16 was one of preparation for the Americans. Throughout the hushed Yankee encampment on and surrounding Cambridge Common, men of all ages gathered around their campfires, solemnly cleaning their muskets and clamping in new flints, others quietly filling paper cartridges, each with a musket ball and measured amount of black powder. Ranking officer Gen. Israel Putnam did the same, sitting quietly with his fifteen-year-old son at his headquarters at Borland House, servicing his two pistols and making cartridges.

Daniel, who was serving as his father's aide, could sense the earnestness in his father's demeanor but said nothing. At length, as the elder Putnam began sharpening his sword, he finally broke the silence, speaking with hesitation and in broken sentences. "You will go to Mrs. Inman's as usual tonight, and it is time you were gone. You need not return here in the morning, but stay there tomorrow; the family may want you, and if they find it is necessary to leave the house, you must go with them where they go; and try now my son, to be as serviceable to them as you can."

Daniel, though young, was wise to the fact that some military movement was planned for the next day—one that involved his father. At once, his imagination conjured images of his father helpless on some battlefield, mangled and wounded. Fighting back a wave of emotion, Daniel choked out, "*You, dear father,* may need my assistance much more than Mrs. Inman. *Pray* let me go where you are going."

"No! No, Daniel. Do as I have bid you." Old Put replied sternly, though his voice trembled and his eyes teared up. The old veteran then looked upon his son and, as if comprehending perfectly what was going through the boy's mind, replied more kindly. "You can do little, my son, where I am going, and besides, there will be enough to take care of me."

Conceding to his father's bidding, Daniel at last departed for Inman's Farm in eastern Cambridge. Its owner, devout Loyalist Ralph Inman, had fled to the safety of Boston shortly after the last battle, leaving behind his wife, Elizabeth, and her nieces, who welcomed Daniel as the new man of the house to watch over them. But on this night, the boy would hardly enjoy their chatty conversation, filled as he was with dread of some great and looming battle.[3]

In the evening twilight of June 16, on Cambridge Common amid the American encampment, nearly eight hundred men gathered around Dr. Samuel Langdon, president of Harvard College, whose institution lay just beyond.[4] Some there had perhaps assisted a day earlier in removing books and other valuables from Harvard's library to the safety of Andover, in anticipation of the impending battle.[5] But now the men were gathered for prayer before their march to battle. In that era, Harvard College was primarily concerned with educating Puritan clergy and only secondarily with educating those interested in the liberal arts. Thus, fifty-two-year-old Langdon, a minister as well as the college president, acted as chaplain for the interim New England Army and gave them a rousing prayer to encourage their hearts.[6] No doubt, these men prayed more solemnly that night, knowing it might be their last.

The men gathered there were all of Massachusetts, a little more than half of whom were detached from the regiments of Col. James Frye and Col. Ebenezer Bridge.[7] However, the majority—some three hundred men—were from the regiment of Col. William Prescott, who was to lead the entire detachment. A veteran of the Louisbourg campaigns of the French and Indian War, Prescott was now a forty-nine-year-old colonel in the militia of nearby Pepperell, though he wore no uniform to distinguish himself as such. Instead, he wore just a blue frock of home-spun cloth and kept a sword at his side.

Giving thought to the events ahead, Prescott also wore a light coat slung over his shoulder, in case the night brought chill, and he had ordered the men to bring blankets and provisions for the next day. Most of the men probably carried their blankets on their backs, rolled up and strapped over their shoulders and chest, while the few who did indeed bring provisions carried them in small bags such as the snapsack, a cylindrical leather bag that was slung over one arm.[8]

When Langdon finished his prayer, Prescott placed his broad-brimmed cocked hat on his bald head and ordered the men to form into ranks.[9] Once they had, Prescott gave the order, and the Yankees began their march eastward, with two men leading the way with "dark" lanterns (lanterns shrouded on all but the nearest side to hide their light).[10] As they made their way east, Capt. Thomas Knowlton Jr. and two hundred Connecticut men of Putnam's regiment joined them, along with at least two horse-drawn wagons of entrenching tools led by Capt. Thomas Wait Foster.[11]

At about 9:00 p.m., Massachusetts soldier Samuel Bixby in Roxbury observed, "the regulars in Boston fired an alarm, and rung the bells. We heard them drawing the carriages to the neck, & the riding of horses with great speed up to their guard and back into Boston, and there was great commotion there... The town seemed to be alive with men marching in all directions." As nothing came of it, perhaps this was intended to inure the Americans to British commotion after dark, in preparation for the intended British assault on Dorchester Heights.[12]

Meanwhile, even as the warning bells of Boston rang in the distance, Prescott's detachment continued marching onward to their destination.

———•••———

As a near full moon rose high enough to illuminate their march, the Americans crossed Charlestown Neck and soon reached the foot of Bunker Hill, passing the little earthwork redan the British had made after their retreat along the same path on April 19.[13] There, Colonel Prescott halted his column and dispatched a company of sixty men under Capt. John Nutting to keep watch from nearby abandoned Charlestown.[14] Leaving his remaining men at ease, Prescott then climbed Bunker Hill itself, where he conferred with his engineer and head of the Artillery, the highly respected sixty-five-year-old Col. Richard Gridley. Gridley's engineering skills had won him fame when he helped force the French surrender of the supposedly impregnable fortress Louisbourg during the French and Indian War.

Also joining them on Bunker Hill was General Putnam,[15] perhaps wearing a blue Connecticut militia uniform with red facings and white waistcoat and breeches.[16] Together, the three surveyed the hill and surrounding area, deciding how best to build their fortification. Prescott's orders, signed by Gen. Artemas Ward and based on the Committee of Safety's resolve the day before, were quite clear: fortify "the hill called Bunker's Hill in Charlestown".[17] Nevertheless, Gridley, Putnam, and Prescott all debated for some time about exactly *where* on the hill to build.

Charlestown was then a triangular peninsula connected at its northwestern point by a thin neck to the mainland. The broadest edge of this triangle was the south side facing Boston, demarcated by the Charles River, while the Mystic River defined the northeast side. The town itself filled just the southwest corner of this triangle and consisted of perhaps five hundred houses, a few public buildings, and a church.[18] Bunker Hill comprised the northeast portion of this triangular peninsula and, being some 110 feet high, commanded the entire peninsula, both rivers, part of the harbor, and even Boston. A fortification on its oval summit would have stood elevated above the reach of the warships' guns, while the hill's gradual slopes were easily defensible by earthworks. Furthermore, Bunker Hill guarded the only escape route across Charlestown Neck and back to the mainland, should a retreat become necessary.

As the men surveyed the grounds, Putnam was probably the advocate for taking the lower hill south of their position. That hill, known to some locals as Breed's Hill (after the owner of the farm it stood on), was certainly closer to the town of Boston and thus nearer to where the British would likely land come sunrise. However, it lacked every advantage of Bunker Hill, for it was, at 62 feet, some 50 feet lower and thus easier to overtake or encircle.[19] As engineer, Gridley no doubt petitioned for fortifying the higher Bunker Hill, but moreover, he urged a speedy decision, as it was his job to lead the construction, and the hour was getting late. At daybreak, the British would spot them, and a firefight was sure to ensue. Their only chance was to complete the defenses before the four-a.m. sunrise. So Prescott made his decision.[20]

Accordingly, Gridley descended to the lower Breed's Hill and began marking the outer boundaries of a redoubt, perhaps using a mattock to dig a line into the earth. In his haste, though Gridley was also head of the Artillery, he failed to mark cannon emplacements in his redoubt, a blunder that would cause problems later. Meanwhile, the combined Yankee force of a thousand men moved from Bunker Hill down to Breed's, bringing with them the two wagons of mattocks, picks, and spades. Soon they began to dig.

In selecting Breed's Hill, Prescott did not necessarily disobey orders. Many locals had considered the lower hill a mere extension of Bunker Hill. In fact, most period references refer to the whole area generically as Charlestown Heights. And so the redoubt was built and the battle would be fought on the slopes of Breed's Hill, though it would forever be known as the Battle of Bunker Hill.

About this time, a distant bell rang eight times in intervals of two, signifying midnight. It came from the nearby HMS *Lively*, anchored on the Charles River. Perhaps Prescott was on one of the several reconnaissance visits he made that night to Charlestown proper, in time to hear the call by *Lively*'s officer of the deck, "Eight bells and all's well."[21] If that naval officer only knew…

———— ◆ ————

Ever since Dr. Joseph Warren had left Boston on April 19, before the town was besieged and inescapable, he had lodged at the John Hunt House in Watertown. These accommodations were conveniently located near the Provincial Congress meeting place at the Edmund Fowle House, and he shared his small room with his fellow congressman and friend Elbridge Gerry.[22]

There in his room, on the eve of battle, Warren prepared to join Prescott and his men at Bunker Hill. Though the Provincial Congress had days earlier elected Warren as a major general, bureaucracy delayed his actual commissioning, and so he would instead serve as a volunteer. Gerry was probably one of those who had encouraged Warren's selection, knowing the doctor would not accept the more appropriate surgeon generalship.[23]

Gerry watched his roommate clean his fusil musket, sharpen and polish his sword, and primp his best suit, yet privately he began to lament his previous support of Warren's commission. At last, Gerry could be silent no more. He made the case that Warren, as president of the Provincial Congress and the local head of the rebellion, was too valuable to the cause of liberty to be exposed to battle. Joining the fight was brash, Gerry explained, reminding him, "We [have] not powder sufficient to maintain the desperate conflict which must ensue, and should all be cut to pieces."

"I know it," said Warren, determined to share the fate of his countrymen, "but I...should die were I to remain at home while my fellow citizens are shedding their blood for me." Indeed, the odds of a colonial success were low. Besides the limited gunpowder, they had few cannon—and none of the larger kind needed to do more than harry the British. The whole Yankee operation was at best a taunt. In contrast, the British had been embarrassed by an angry mob of mere country folk and had now been besieged in Boston for almost two months—a blemish on their honor. They were eager for retribution. When the British troops finally came, the battle would be fierce.

Gerry warned him, "As sure as you go, you will be slain."

"*Dulce et decorum est pro patria mori*," Warren replied in Latin. (It is sweet and becoming to die for one's country.)

Gerry finally realized that Warren, the hothead who would never have accepted the surgeon generalship, could not now be dissuaded from heading into battle.[24]

———◆———

On Breed's Hill, construction was well underway. Some men dug a ditch while others slowly formed the long earthen walls.[25] Their goal was to raise these walls high enough to hide behind even while standing (a breastwork). They dug as quietly as possible, but Prescott must have tensed with each loud smack into the dirt or the occasional thud of a mattock hitting rock. If their noise gave them away, and the nearby

British warships responded with a cannonade, the Americans' chances of completing the redoubt before sunrise were slim.

Ironically, the British were in fact well aware of the colonial entrenching. General Clinton, reconnoitering that night in Boston, "saw them at work". This seems unlikely at that range, even with the near full moon, but he could have *heard* them. Clinton "advised a landing in two divisions at day brake" to General Gage and General Howe in writing.[26] Howe approved, but "Gage seem[ed] to doubt their intention".[27] Gage had the final word and so, despite Clinton's misgivings ("I fear it must be deferred till…I fear to say when"), all three went to sleep.[28] British sentries in Boston also heard the entrenching but did not report it.[29] The British were not ready to believe that a handful of untrained Yankees could create a serious threat in just one night.

As far as Prescott knew, his operation remained undiscovered. Any fears he held were alleviated every half hour, literally like clockwork. For the nearby HMS *Lively*, appearing only as a dark shadow on the moonlit Charles, was a recurrent reminder that the rebels were as yet undetected, or at least ignored. Two bells, a pause, two bells, a pause, two bells more. "Six bells and all's well," were the words from *Lively*'s officer of the deck, signifying 3:00 a.m.

Though Prescott may not have heard *Lively*'s officer from Breed's Hill, he certainly heard the bells, and though he may not have been able to convert the naval time back into that of a landsman, he was still relieved every time he heard it. Nevertheless, Prescott walked down to Charlestown center several times that night, eager for a situation report from Captain Nutting and his scouts. And each time, Nutting gave the same report: all's well.

However, the fast-approaching dawn would soon illuminate that all was not well for either the British or the Americans.

———◆———

On the spar (upper) deck of the HMS *Lively*, the officer responsible for the middle watch, which ran from midnight to 4:00 a.m., was anxious to take a nap.[30] Some of the deck hands and marines may have already been napping between the guns.[31] But just as the Boston sentries had heard the

Americans at work in Charlestown, so too did the men of the *Lively*. Yet they paid it no attention. They merely considered it a curiosity.

When the sky at last started to brighten, just before the 4:06 a.m. sunrise of that fateful day, June 17, 1775, the tired officer of the *Lively*'s deck, probably a midshipman, plodded over to the half-hour glass. At four o'clock, he would flip the glass and ring out eight bells in pairs of two, signifying the end of his shift and the start of his nap.[32] His replacement would have just arrived, barely awake but ready to relieve him. Whether that first deck officer rang all eight bells is unknown, for as the two looked to the hills, they were astonished at the scene before them.

On Breed's Hill, where just last evening stood nothing but a grassy knoll, now stood a half-built redoubt, its construction still underway. The almost square fortification was about 8 square rods, or 132 feet on each side, with a bastion projecting outward toward Charlestown proper, and a sally port at the back protected by a fixed wall.[33]

One of those officers of the deck yelled: "Beat to quarters!" A drummer was always on standby, distinguished by his red coat with its white facings of the Marines, as opposed to the naval officers who wore blue.[34] The marine beat his drum, causing men to scurry onto the spar deck, ready to man one side of *Lively*'s twenty 9-pounder guns. The ship's Capt. Thomas Bishop also rushed on deck from his stern cabin. Within moments, Bishop gave the order and *Lively* lived up to her name, giving a lively bombardment that would break the morning's tranquility.[35] Copp's Hill Battery in Boston's North End soon joined in *Lively*'s cannonade chorus.[36]

When Adm. Samuel Graves heard the bombardment that morning, he was apparently at his rented home in Boston rather than aboard his flagship *Preston*, so he quickly made his way to the North End to survey the scene. One story claims that Graves first issued orders (presumably to an aide) for a cease-fire. Whether or not true, when he first laid eyes on the rebel redoubt, Graves was both stunned and furious. He immediately issued firm orders for his fleet to engage the enemy.[37]

Accordingly, seamen aboard the flagship HMS *Preston* hoisted a solid red flag nicknamed the "bloody colours", a universal signal to commence attack. *Preston* then fired a cannon or two as signal guns.[38] When the other ships' captains looked to the *Preston* and saw the new signal flag, their orders were clear: attack the redoubt at will.

Near Boston's North Battery, the 20-gun HMS *Glasgow* began to fire, even as she started to heave in her best bower anchor. Her captain intended to move her up the Charles for a better firing position. The 18-gun armed transport *Symmetry*, near the mouth of the Charles, and the 6-gun schooner *Spitfire*, near Copp's Hill, also added their facing guns to the din of the barrage.[39]

Thus began the Battle for Bunker Hill.

———•———

In Watertown, an anxious Dr. Warren darted to the stables and prepared his horse. He expected this day to be momentous, so he marked it by wearing his best suit, maybe sky blue "with covered buttons worked in silver"; worn atop a white "silk-fringed waistcoat"; a sword at his side; a dark (tricorner) cocked hat, and "his hair was curled up at the sides of his head and pinned up." He also carried with him a fusil (a light smoothbore musket).[40]

His roommate Elbridge Gerry watched from the porch of the Hunt House. Whether either man had slept that night is unknown. Warren had a splitting headache, apparently an ailment he was prone to, this one perhaps due to nervousness or lack of sleep. Whatever else Gerry may have said, hoping to still dissuade his friend, it was for nothing. If a severe headache could not keep Warren from riding to battle, Gerry's entreaties certainly could not.[41]

So Warren mounted his horse and rode off eastward into the sunrise.[42]

———•———

At the ragtag American Army headquarters in the study of the Hastings House in Cambridge, Gen. Israel Putnam debated with Gen. Artemas Ward on the military situation.[43]

Ward probably remained seated, wincing with pain, as he listened to Putnam's petition. On this of all days, Ward was again suffering a flare-up of his recurrent and debilitating calculus, and it would leave him stuck at headquarters for much of the day.[44]

If the pains in his abdomen were not enough to frustrate him, the lack of an organized command and control for the coming battle would be. Ward would find himself perpetually uninformed. When couriers did come, the vital information would often be at least an hour old—useless for a fast-moving battle.[45]

Despite these challenges, Ward's greatest difficulty in exercising his role as commander in chief was localism within the New England Army.[46] Localism—whereby, for example, a regiment from New Hampshire did not recognize authority from any but a New Hampshire officer that they themselves had elected—meant that each militia regiment (and sometimes each of its subordinate companies) was as an independent fighting unit. In many cases, even in the middle of battle, they would come and go as they pleased, taking up position where they deemed appropriate.

This autonomy had been the case ever since the start of the Siege of Boston, since whole militia companies would disappear to their farms to sow their crops.[47] That each New England province had begun enlisting a standing interim army in place of its militia helped with retention, but many regiments were enlisted out of the militia they replaced and so brought with them the same problems of localism and independency.[48] Localism was one of the many reasons why Dr. Warren and the Provincial Congress had appealed to the Continental Congress to adopt the otherwise independent provincial armies, enlist them under contracts, and unify them under an authority transcending provincial boundaries. The Congress had finally done so, just two days earlier, but it would take weeks for this to affect the troops in Boston.[49]

Putnam and his Connecticut men tried to combat localism by voluntarily submitting to Massachusetts leadership, recognizing the latter's entitlement to lead an army on their own soil. Days after the coming battle, the Connecticut legislature would make official Putnam's subordination to Ward.[50] Connecticut's recognition of the advantages of solidarity and unity of command showed advanced thinking.

Putnam's strong cooperation with Ward led many Americans to perceive Putnam as a sort of extension of Ward's authority. However, with localism and the lack of a formal unified command among the provincial armies, Putnam could not exercise true command over the battle. Even his rank of brigadier general was only meaningful in the Connecticut service. Thus, while Brigadier General Putnam was the highest-ranking officer who would serve at the battle, Colonel Prescott of Massachusetts appears to have operated independently of Putnam, commanding the redoubt by his own volition, yet for the same Common Cause of repulsing the British. Indeed, the very idea of a "Common Cause" was the only thing unifying the otherwise independent provincial armies.[51]

Ward therefore remained the actual, though impotent, commander in chief, not only of the Massachusetts men, but also of those from Connecticut. In recognition of that command, Old Put had come this morning to urge Ward to send more men to Bunker Hill. However, Ward refused to send any real reserves. Putnam implored Ward to change his decision, noting that Prescott's men had labored all night and were under the impression they were going to be relieved. In truth, Prescott himself did not expect such relief, nor would he accept it if it came, but he would gladly accept reinforcements.

Regardless, Ward was convinced that it was there, in Cambridge, that the Ministerial Troops would direct their attack, not Breed's Hill. Cambridge was where the bulk of the remaining colonial war stores and powder resided. If Ward were to send out all of his reserves to Charlestown, Gage need only cross the Charles River, as he had on April 18, and then march into Cambridge and seize control. While this was Ward's fear, it was unfounded.[52] The British had learned that crossing the river and then the Cambridge Swamp was no easy affair, and gaining an advantage against the raised militia was nearly impossible.

However, Ward was not being arbitrarily obstinate by withholding the bulk of his forces. The fact is, the British could have kept to their plan by attacking Dorchester and Roxbury and sweeping northward to Cambridge. Had Ward attempted to anticipate the British and thus sent his troops in the wrong direction, it could have meant catastrophe.

At length, Ward did concede a little. A message, perhaps delivered by Ward himself, was sent to Col. John Stark in nearby Medford requesting he send forth a detachment of his men to Charlestown straightaway. When Stark received the request, he readily obeyed, sending two hundred of his New Hampshire men under his second-in-command, Lt. Col. Isaac Wyman.[53] But Ward refused to send more until the British plan was made clear.

That plan would be clear soon enough.

Shortly after dawn, British Lieutenant General Gage gathered his key officers for a council of war at his headquarters and residence, the Province House.[54] With him were all of his major generals—Clinton, Burgoyne, Howe—and probably their respective brigadier generals: Lord Percy, Valentine Jones, and Robert Pigot, the latter described as a "little Man".[55] Also in attendance were Lt. Gov. Thomas Oliver, Gage's secretary Thomas Flucker, and the Tory civilian Timothy Ruggles, a militiaman who had formed the first Loyalist militia company, called the Associators, and so became its captain. Loyal as the Associators were, Gage never felt comfortable employing them.[56] Notably missing was Admiral Graves, due in part to his ongoing friction with Gage.[57] Aides and civil officials completed the scene.[58] The war council had but one topic to discuss: what was to be done with the rebels daring to flaunt themselves atop Breed's Hill?

Gage must have felt seriously frustrated. This day was meant to be used to prepare for the British offensive of Dorchester Heights the next morning, the first phase in their plan to create "elbow room". That plan had a reasonable chance of success, for Dorchester Peninsula was undefended, and General Thomas's American position in nearby Roxbury was weak and unfortified. At the very least, the British would have pushed the siege back far enough to give themselves a footing on the mainland beyond Boston Neck. But as Howe later wrote, "this Scheme has been entirely set aside" by the discovery of the rebel redoubt.[59] The irony of the present situation was not lost on Gage. He now had to fight to regain the very peninsula he had withdrawn from following the Battle of the Nineteenth of April just sixty days earlier. In fact, had the British built their own fort on Bunker Hill as they first planned, instead of withdrawing, the Battle of Bunker Hill probably would never have taken place.

Whether because of mere anxiety or genuine fear, most British in Boston—from General Howe to the common soldier—expected the worst this day. Howe later wrote they must "preserve the Town of Boston, which it is supposed the Rebels mean to destroy by *fire* or Sword or both".[60] In fact, the Americans had no means to destroy the town, but Gage could not know this because his intelligence was all but cut off. Thus, it would have been foolhardy for Gage to assume the new American threat was not credible.

Clinton was perhaps the most astute strategist on the war council. Though he was privately annoyed that his warning the night before had gone unheeded, he pointed out the obvious: the rebels had practically delivered themselves in a trap of their own making. All that was left to do was to close the net. Another officer wrote, "we needed only have landed in their rear and occupied the high ground above Bunker's [really Breed's] hill, by this movement we [would have] shut them up in the peninsula as in a bag".[61]

This was an overestimate of British maneuverability, however. The Mystic River behind the peninsula was too shallow for the transports to navigate, and ferrying the troops to the peninsula's back side by long-boat would have added at least an hour to the amphibious operation. Rather, it was better to land nearer to Boston and encircle the lone American redoubt by ground maneuvers, but this would only work if the British acted quickly.

Clinton knew time was of the essence, lest the rebels see the folly of their position and adjust their strategy accordingly, or lest they be reinforced. So Clinton urged Gage to act at once, offering to person-ally land with five hundred men at the "Jews burying ground", an unknown position probably just north of the town on the peninsula's western shore, well behind the American fortifications. From there, he would flank the Americans while the warships bombarded them from the Charles River. The Americans would then watch as their only escape route via Charlestown Neck was cut off, and the battle would be over almost instantly.[62]

It is easy to imagine that Lord Percy supported this plan, having gained new respect for the rebels after his retreat from Lexington two months earlier. However, as Clinton wrote, "my advice was not attended to". It seems both Howe and Gage objected. Most of the war council believed the redoubt was not yet complete, that it was only a redan, an angled earthen wall facing Boston, and thus weak and indefensible.

They thought the Americans might even be persuaded to abandon it at the mere show of force. Clinton disagreed. But the council generally underestimated Yankee ingenuity and the troops' ability to create a substantial fortification overnight.[63]

Instead, William Howe, the senior major general present, and thus the man who would lead the attack, voiced support for a landing near Boston, somewhere along Charlestown Peninsula's southern shore east of the town. There, Howe expected the troops to be well out of American musketry range, allowing the British to establish a safe beachhead for

The HON.^BLE S.^R W.^M HOWE.
Knight of the Bath, & Commander in Chief of his Majesty's Forces in America.

Mezzotint of Maj. Gen. William Howe (c. 1765 or 1777), possibly by Richard Purcell (c. 1736–c. 1766). Anne S. K. Brown Military Collection, Brown University Library.

disembarkation. Moreover, by landing on this nearest shore, the British would minimize their time in the slow-moving longboats and thus be ready for action sooner.

Regardless of these differences in strategy, all on the war council were eager for action. The rebels had issued an open challenge, and the British did not want to disappoint. "Give these Yankees a lesson they will not soon forget!" was a phrase associated with the council. While the Expedition to Concord might have taught the British what these simple country folk could do when using Indian-style warfare in closed terrain, open fighting on a field of battle was the forte of British Army tactics. "Let us take the bull by the horns" was another phrase British officers would use this day.[64]

So the plan was decided. To oversee the landing on Charlestown Peninsula's southern shore and lead the charge that would encircle by land and conquer the colonial redoubt, Lieutenant General Gage made Major General Howe the operation commander, assisted by Brigadier General Pigot (Howe's deputy). Major Generals Burgoyne and Clinton were ordered to direct the artillery from Boston (namely, Copp's Hill). Gage also gave to Clinton the special assignment of sending over Howe's reserve at the first sign of trouble, unless it was called upon sooner.[65] Lord Percy was ordered to man the lines at Boston Neck, there to occupy American General Thomas and his rebel forces across in Roxbury.[66] Finally, Howe was to meet with Graves to make the necessary arrangements with the warships, including the use of longboats for ferrying the troops across the Charles.[67]

The British plan could work, but only if they acted quickly—before American Colonel Prescott realized just how untenable his lonely redoubt was and before he received reinforcements. However, it would take time to prepare thousands of redcoats for an amphibious assault.

One necessary but minor delay came in mustering and supplying the men themselves. They were ordered to pack lightly: just their muskets with bayonets fixed, ammunition that likely had to be supplied that morning, and their blankets, because they intended to sleep that evening on the field of battle. Other bulky equipment like tents would be brought over after the battle. The men also had to wait for that day's provisions to be freshly prepared that morning, including baked bread and boiled meat.[68]

But the biggest delay came after the meeting between Admiral Graves and General Howe, which they held aboard HMS *Somerset*. Howe first inquired about bringing the larger *Somerset* and *Preston* up harbor so they could join the cannonade of the several other warships, but Graves told him there was not sufficient water depth, particularly as it was low tide. The larger ships would therefore only provide tenders for the landing as well as men and ammunition to the smaller ships to help in their bombardment. The discussion then turned to the landing itself.

While the tenders could have crossed the Charles River to dock in Charlestown at any time, Howe insisted the landing be on the beach because he was justifiably concerned about snipers in abandoned Charlestown.[69] Though if the British landed just then, with the water near low tide, the tenders would run aground in knee-deep water, forcing the troops to march into battle encumbered by wet boots, and indeed the men would fight better with dry feet. But Howe underestimated what the Americans could do with a few extra hours of preparation and decided to wait until closer to high tide that midafternoon.[70] Given that the British council of war took place sometime after dawn, perhaps as late as 6:30 a.m., about six hours had elapsed since construction on the redoubt began. With these and other British delays to come, the battle would not commence until near 4:00 p.m. The British thus gave the Americans almost twelve additional hours since being discovered at dawn in which to continue fortifying, the greatest misstep either side would make that day.[71] Unfortunately for both adversaries, each was destined to commit other great follies before the day was over.

* * *

As the long-expected cannonade commenced, Prescott and the Americans took cover in their unfinished redoubt. Though some of them were veterans of the French and Indian War, and others had tasted battle on April 19, many had no military experience. For most, their training had been limited to weekly militia drill practice in their respective towns. As a result, the intense British artillery barrage proved most effective as a psychological weapon, causing many inexperienced Yankees to cower in their redoubt. The cannonade itself offered little physical threat. Not only were the smoothbore naval guns inaccurate, but the naval gun crews also struggled to elevate their guns high enough to reach the little redoubt atop Breed's Hill. This was because, due to space limitations and practicality, naval gun truck carriages were designed with just enough vertical range to hit another ship's hull. Only on the uproll, as one's own ship crested a passing wave, was there any hope of hitting an enemy's mast.

The American redoubt was a bit too elevated, however, and the harbor too calm to give sufficient uproll, so many of the balls fired from the warships hit harmlessly on the lower slopes. Some of these nonexplosive balls instantly embedded themselves into the dirt, though others bounced dangerously up the slopes toward the redoubt. Had the Americans built on the higher Bunker Hill, they would have been entirely immune to naval guns.

Knowing this limitation, Graves had built the battery on Copp's Hill in Boston shortly after April 19, partly to harry any rebel offensive in Charlestown and partly to protect his fleet. But once Gage realized its value, the battery was turned over to the Army and renamed simply Copp's Hill Battery. Because Copp's Hill was nearly the height of Breed's, and its battery mounted five or six large 24-pounders (the largest guns fired that day), Copp's proved the greatest threat, with its balls easily reaching Breed's crown. The Yankees no doubt felt relieved when Copp's grew silent for a few hours after dawn, but the Royal Artillerymen there were simply emplacing three or four additional 24s, plus some howitzers and mortars. Soon enough, the battery's cannonade would almost literally redouble.[72]

The din was not the only frightening element of the cannonade. Due to the lack of rain, the mere act of walking about the earthen redoubt was enough to kick dirt into the air. So when British cannon balls again whistled overhead or pounded the slopes below, each ball's impact showered the Yankee working party with a cloud of dust.[73] This all conspired to terrorize many of those green Yankees, but given the range and inherent inaccuracies of smoothbore guns, killing a man was a matter of luck, not skill. Prescott knew the guns were more a source of dread than a real threat, so he ordered his cowering men to get back to work.

Noting part of their problem was range, the warship captains began vying for better positions from which their artillery could do the greatest service. *Spitfire* continued her bombardment from where she began that day, near Copp's Hill, but the nearby *Lively* repositioned downriver toward the mouth of the Charles, from which she could both fire more effectively and cover the planned landing of the British troops. Given her light draft, the armed transport *Symmetry* exerted minimal effort as she repositioned against the tide toward Charlestown Neck. As she passed Copp's Hill, two of the five gunboats there followed her, each a small barge mounting a single 12-pounder in its bow, sent forward by order of General Clinton. *Glasgow* also moved up the Charles, but in struggling against the ebb tide, she seems to have kedged to move up the shallow water. She eventually took position southwest of Charlestown center where she could rake both Charlestown Neck and the redoubt.[74]

Meanwhile, General Putnam had returned to the field after his visit to Ward's headquarters, and he probably conveyed news to Prescott of the two hundred men due to come, but soon grew impatient and rode back toward Cambridge to find out their status.[75] Also about this time, the aged engineer Colonel Gridley, who had served as foreman in the redoubt's construction, now departed the field to rest.[76]

With the redoubt almost complete, Prescott turned his attention to his next problem. It was by dawn's early light that Prescott had realized his precarious position on Breed's Hill, perhaps thinking back to the debate he had had with Putnam and Colonel Gridley the night before. Prescott could now see that by placing the redoubt on Breed's Hill, he had set up a situation in which the British could land well beyond his musketry range, fan out to follow along the Charles and Mystic Rivers, and so encircle him—which was very close to General Howe's plan.

To protect his left flank, Prescott decided to put his weary entrenching party to work on an extension to the redoubt. This breastwork would span "about twenty rods [330 feet] in length from the fort northerly". Once completed "under a very warm fire from the enemy's artillery", it would run northeastward down the slope from the northeast corner of the square redoubt, terminating at the foot of Breed's Hill, where the land became marshy and was protected by a line of trees. The two hundred New Hampshire men of Colonel Stark's regiment under Lt. Col. Isaac Wyman arrived just in time to help implement this new plan.[77]

As for Prescott's right, he hoped that abandoned Charlestown would provide some cover. Just before the bombardment at dawn, Prescott had recalled most of his scouts from there, expecting he would need them.[78] He decided that for now he would employ all his men in finishing the fortifications, but once the British began to embark, he would send a party back to Charlestown to harry the British landing.

Prescott's other problem lay with his men. They had picked up their pace in building the redoubt not only because of the cannonade, but especially because they could finally see in the morning sun what they had been doing all night and moreover, believed they were nearly finished. Imagine how their satisfaction of a job well done was shattered by orders to begin a new breastwork. The men were tired, and most had failed to heed orders to bring a day's provisions and were now hungry. Worse yet, they were under the impression that they were to be relieved that morning, yet no relief had come. The newly arrived two hundred men were not relief; they were additional laborers. The disheartened, weary men began to grumble.

One redoubt defender, Peter Brown, later wrote, "The Danger we were in made us think there was Treachery, & that we were brot there to be all slain, and I must & will venture to say that there was Treachery, Oversight or Presumption in the Conduct of our Officers... Then they [the British] began [to cannonade] pretty brisk again; and that caused some of our young Country ppl to desert, apprehending the Danger in a clearer manner than the rest, who were more diligent in digging & fortifyͬͤ ourselves against them."[79]

Noting the decreasing morale, some of the officers approached Prescott and explained the men were in no condition for action. They asked him to send a courier to General Ward requesting relief, or at least reinforcements and provisions. Prescott stated he would never consent to their being relieved. As he explained, the fortifications were the works of their hands, and they should have the honor of defending them, which they could well do without any assistance. (In truth, these fatigued laborers were now the least capable of defending them.) But Prescott did agree to send for reinforcements and refreshments, and had no doubt they would be sent promptly.[80]

Unfortunately, they would not. History does not record the name of the man Prescott sent, but since there were no horses still available, the courier was forced to walk the nearly four miles to Ward's headquarters. Once he arrived there, Dr. Joseph Warren may have greeted him. Warren of course would defer any decision on this decidedly military matter to General Ward, but he was eager for news as he spent that morning meeting with the Committee of Safety in another room of the headquarters.

The courier described the field, the need for more men, and the repositioning of the warships. Ward was eager for information from the front lines, but since Gage did not yet appear committed to an assault, neither would Ward commit more troops. The fact that Prescott sent this courier, and would send another later, suggests General Putnam never had the heart to tell him of Ward's reluctance to commit his reserves.

Meanwhile, as work began on the breastwork extending off the redoubt, the roaring but ineffective cannon shot eventually desensitized the men. Then one shot made its mark: the ball sailed over the earthen wall, probably along the breastwork construction, shearing the head off a man who may have been Asa Pollard.[81] According to Prescott, "He was so near me that my clothes were besmeared with blood and brains, which I wiped off in some degree with a handful of fresh earth. The sight was so shocking to many of the men that they left their posts and ran to view him. I ordered them back, but in vain. I then ordered him to be buried instantly."

According to Prescott, a man, "who from his appearance I judged to be a subaltern officer, came up and throwing his arm around me exclaimed, 'Dear Colonel, are you going to bury him without sending for a minister and having prayers?'"

Prescott replied, "This is the first man that has been killed, and the only one that will be buried to-day. I put him out of sight that the men may be kept in their places. God only knows who, or how many of us, will fall before it is over."

There was a solemn pause as those around the corpse realized that, by the end of the day, they too might suffer such a fate—or worse. For in that era, worse was a fatal wound that did not kill instantly, given the lack of medical procedures to deal with such injuries. Thus, this first victim of the day was buried without formality.

To encourage the men, Prescott mounted the redoubt wall, in full view and harm's way, fearlessly showing by his example that such a gruesome shot was a lucky one indeed, and the men need not worry about the cannon. Even as the balls whistled and sailed overhead, he urged the men, "To your post, my good fellow[s], and do your duty!" He continued on the parapet, rallying the work onward. In turn, the men continued their construction, finishing the redoubt and extending a breastwork northeastward down the hillside, using all the precious time the British had generously given them.[82]

Meanwhile, over on Boston's North Shore, Gage had hurried over from the Province House to survey the scene for himself. Some aides came with him, while his generals were off making the necessary preparations for the coming assault. Spectators around him had lined the riverbank or climbed on the rooftops of the nearby houses, laying out blankets to sit on. Some may have still been in their sleep attire, having rushed outside at dawn. Gage pulled out his spyglass and surveyed the little redoubt and the breastwork's construction. Seeing few Americans manning the hill, Gage felt ever more confident that victory would be his. Then something caught his eye. On top of the parapet, despite the great barrage, a man walked back and forth, urging the others. He was surely an officer.

Gage looked around and found Abijah Willard, one of his mandamus councilors. Offering him the spyglass, Gage asked, "Do you recognize this rebel?"

Willard looked. He might have been surprised for a moment to recognize Prescott, joined by one of his subordinate captains who had just climbed the wall. "I know him well. It is Colonel Prescott, my brother-in-law. I am sorry to see him there."

"Will he fight?" Gage asked.

"Yes," Willard replied, "he is an old soldier; he will fight as long as a drop of blood remains in his veins. It will be a bloody day, you may depend on it." Another version has Willard giving a different reply: "I cannot answer for his men, but he will fight you to the gates of hell."

Perhaps this shook Gage's confidence. "The works must be carried," he replied simply.[83]

———◆———

General Putnam soon rode onto the field once more, passing Prescott's courier on his way, and was happy to find the two hundred New Hampshire men had finally arrived. Old Put "walk[ed] upon the breast-work and animat[ed] the men to exert themselves."[84] Here he would repeatedly return to rally the men. Putnam next turned his attention to Bunker Hill proper, riding his horse to its crown and quickly marking out another fortification.

Meanwhile, at about 8:00 a.m., a long overdue artillery company arrived with two small cannon, perhaps both 4-pounders, commanded by Capt. Samuel Gridley. He, along with his cousin Scarborough Gridley, served in the regiment of Col. Richard Gridley, the experienced artillery officer and engineer responsible for the redoubt. Since the colonel was father to Scarborough and uncle to Samuel, the two cousins had acquired their positions due to familial connections, despite their lack of qualification, and had only received their commissions the day before. While patrimony was a tolerated practice throughout Europe, it was cause for much grumbling amongst the Americans.

Ironically, despite the elder Gridley's experience and role as artillery commander, when he had laid out the redoubt, he had forgotten to plan for embrasures for his own nephew's guns. Thus, Captain Gridley hauled two cannon up the hill by horse, only to find there was no place for them. Moreover, with the arrival of Stark's detachment of two hundred New Hampshire men, there were now more men than entrenching tools, so no tools could be had. Prescott turned to Capt. Ebenezer Bancroft and asked him to do what he could. As Captain Gridley unlimbered his cannon, Bancroft took men of his infantry company and began digging by hand into the redoubt's earthen walls, hoping to create the two embrasures necessary to accommodate the guns. Though the earthen walls were freshly piled and therefore easy to dig through, it seems odd that Prescott did not order any of his tools back from the breastwork. Growing impatient, Bancroft's men, as if to flaunt their rawness, moved the cannon into place, loaded them, and blasted away the walls, wasting precious gunpowder they could not spare and sending plumes of dirt onto their fellow soldiers. At length, they managed to place the two guns so their muzzles protruded from the front of the redoubt.[85]

As midmorning approached, the day was already becoming hot. Many of the men stripped off their coats, Prescott included.[86] They had plenty of water, as the wells of nearby Charlestown would have provided all they required. Yet the men yearned for something more thirst quenching: rum, beer, or cider. In those days, it was thought men fought better with a little alcohol in them, and in fact, the daily rations for most armies and navies included a ration of some such beverage.[87] Prescott looked more than once toward Charlestown Neck, hoping his courier was successful in getting them such provisions, as well as rein- forcements. But none came.

To add to Prescott's problems, some of the original work party had already found clever ways to desert, such as slipping out of the redoubt by feigning to help on the breastwork outside, only to disappear. Localism again played a role: even though the bulk of the men were of Massachusetts, those not of Prescott's regiment were most prone to dis- appear. But the greatest cause of desertions became the newly redoubled and accurate bombardment by Copp's Hill Battery, which incessantly pounded the redoubt's outer walls.[88]

Finally, at about nine o'clock, Prescott's officers implored him to do something. Prescott conceded and sent a second courier, this time Maj. John Brooks of his own regiment. Prescott first sent Brooks to borrow a horse of Captain Gridley's artillery, but Gridley was vehemently opposed, exclaiming that he needed his perhaps six horses to move the two cannon, should a retreat become necessary. Brooks relented. Such was the disor- ganization that no other horses were available. So, like the courier before him, Brooks walked the four miles to the Cambridge headquarters.[89]

Meanwhile, the colonial artillerymen, most having no experience and only recently selected for the duty, were confounded by the proper use of their guns. Still, they began loading and firing them as best they could. While the roar of their own cannon gave heart to the Americans, all the shots proved ineffective. A British officer in Boston observed, "from a battery in the corner of the redoubt, they fired seven or eight shot into the North end of the Town; one shot went through an old house, another through a fence, and the rest stuck in the face of Cobb's [Copp's] hill."[90] Two flew high overhead of General Burgoyne in Copp's Hill Battery, to his amusement.[91] Captain Gridley, realizing the uselessness of his men and only now fearful of wasting precious powder, "swang his Hat round three Times to the Enemy, then ceased Fire."[92] At least Captain Gridley managed to briefly rouse the spirits of his fellow Americans.

Through all of these colonial preparations, the British continued their cannonade, though it slackened somewhat due to the repositioning of the several warships. Only *Spitfire* seems to have stayed about where she had been at the start of the day. *Lively* was by now near her new position off the North Battery on the northeast side of Boston.[93] There the 14-gun armed sloop *Falcon* joined her from the harbor.

The reason *Falcon* and *Lively* took up position near North Battery was soon revealed. As the hour approached noon, several columns of redcoats became visible between the houses of Boston as they marched toward the wharf at North Battery. The Yankees watched as *Lively* floated her perhaps three tenders, which began rowing in that direction.[94] It seemed obvious the troops heading to North Battery would soon be embarking for an assault on Charlestown. Prescott and his men watched expectantly. Then, much to their confusion, *Lively*'s tenders rowed right past North Battery, continuing around the bend along Boston's coastline. The Americans quickly realized the tenders were instead heading to Boston's Long Wharf, hidden from their vantage point. Yet the sight of those several hundred redcoats gathering at North Battery had to make their senses run high. What Prescott and his men could not see: more than a thousand British regulars were now gathering at Long Wharf.

The first embarkation of the amphibious landing would soon be underway.

———◆———

At noon on that fair New England day, the hot sun was high in the clear blue sky, its rays shimmering on the Charles River, which now was flooding from the harbor toward high tide. Only the unceasing bombardment broke this otherwise serene midday.

At that great dock jutting into Boston Harbor, Long Wharf was bustling as redcoats filed in by the hundreds. There an assortment of diverse longboats, barges, yawls, and other small tenders had gathered, more than two dozen of various sizes, enlisted from all the warships throughout the harbor. The British officers effortlessly kept their disciplined men organized as they began loading into the boats.[95]

Prescott's men could only see the average foot soldiers of the main battalion lines mustering at North Battery. But collected at Long Wharf was the flower of the Army, those handpicked men divided into either of the two flank companies of each regiment. The grenadiers comprised the tallest and stoutest men, and were easily distinguished by their tall bearskin hats, worn to make them seem even taller and more ferocious than they already were. The light infantry included only the most athletic and nimble soldiers, who were employed primarily as skirmishers and flankers. Together, these two companies were the very best soldiers of their regiments, the crème de la crème. As such, they were often detached from their respective regiments and combined for special service, as had been the case for the Expedition to Concord in April. But in early June, the flank companies were formally detached and formed into their own respective corps. Now they would lead the British assault in Charlestown.

The companies mustered at Long Wharf were the grenadiers and light infantry of each of the ten eldest regiments in Boston: the 4th (King's Own), 5th, 10th, 23rd Royal Welch Fusiliers, 38th, 43rd, 47th, 52nd, 59th, and 65th, twenty flank companies in all. Of these, the 23rd Royal Welch Fusiliers was the most prestigious regiment in Boston, famous for its courageous role against French cavalry in the epic Battle of Minden of the Seven Years' War. When the 23rd had arrived in Boston, the Americans felt trepidation, believing the regiment's presence a symbol of oppression and tyranny. However, the Battle of Minden had been waged nearly sixteen years prior, and some (but not all) of the men now in the 23rd were junior recruits. Battle experience or not, the British soldiers were generally well trained, disciplined, and organized.[96]

Joining these were the 5th and the 38th regiments, eight companies each. In total, more than one thousand soldiers and one hundred officers crowded into the tenders at Long Wharf, as many as forty-five men per boat (plus the rowers and coxswain), causing each tender to settle within inches of the waterline.[97]

Of those embarking, the common rank-and-file soldier wore white or buff linen pants and waistcoats with tight-fitting, coarse, heavy, red wool coats, which for all but the light infantry had low tails that hung to the back of their knees. Each lace-decorated coat had the lapels and cuffs turned out to reveal contrasting facings colored according to their regiment. Atop these, typically, were two broad white belts, one to support a cartouche box and one for a bayonet holster and possibly a canteen, while a brass buckle adorned the point at which the two belts crossed, marking a shiny target that the Yankees could aim for. Their gear varied from one regiment to another, but generally included a buff or black haversack slung over the right shoulder that rested on the left hip. Each carried a musket with bayonet fixed, ammunition, a blanket (rolled or in knapsacks), and a day's provisions—totaling thirty pounds or so.[98]

The officers commanding them wore uniforms with added distinctions that complemented their social class. The most striking difference was their vibrant scarlet coats, colored with an expensive dye that outlasted the red dye used for the rank and file. Officers also wore as decoration bright silver gorgets that hung below their necks. Most junior officers typically carried a lighter musket called a fusil, a custom General Clinton deplored. "I reprobated the use of the fusee [fusil] for officers, argued that an officer has enough to do to keep his platoon together…[he] became[,] instead of their chief[,] the worst soldier in his platoon[,] that he would have no dependence on his men & they no confidence in him, but this had been too long an American custom". The senior officers, however, tended to carry at their side both a sword and a pistol or two. Together these distinctions made the officers, even at great distances, obvious targets for eager Yankees aiming to take them down.[99]

Perhaps General Howe was there to watch as the British finished their embarkation. The loaded boats on either side of the wharf then waited for the signal. Aboard the flagship HMS *Preston*, where Admiral Graves might now have been, seamen hoisted a blue flag up one of the masts, followed by a cannon blast or two from her bow to grab the attention of the other warships' captains. In response, the warships surrounding Charlestown redoubled their barrage while the troop tenders pushed off. With shouts from their coxswains, the perhaps six rowers per boat began to splash their oars into the softly undulating waters, lurching the tenders forward. As the two columns of boats merged from either side of Long Wharf, they formed a flotilla two boats wide by about thirteen or fourteen long.[100]

On Breed's Hill, Prescott, taking notice of the redoubled cannonade, mounted the redoubt's freshly laid wood platform to look over the six-foot-high bulwark.[101] He saw the silent, scattered puffs of smoke emanating from the warships, followed by the delayed concussion of their booms and the whistling of their cannon shots. Then he saw, coming around Boston's North End, the two perfect lines of diverse longboats, their oars rhythmically rowing them forward, each longboat filled to the gunwales with redcoats, their muskets and bayonets sparkling in the sunlight. Behind this fantastic display lay Boston—its North End, houses, and the steeple of the Old North Church—all awash with spectators.

With the British now on their way, some Yankee messenger was sent to Cambridge to sound the alarm. This may have been Putnam himself, who relayed it to his son, Capt. Israel Putnam Jr., who in turn delivered the message to General Ward at Cambridge.[102]

In the redoubt, Prescott watched for several minutes as the longboats made their way across the Charles. He soon realized they were headed to Charlestown Point, at the confluence of the Charles and Mystic Rivers, an area protected by small Moulton (Morton) Hill. By landing at Moulton Hill, the British would be well east of the redoubt, whereby they could try to encircle him.

Prescott was decisive. He turned to Capt. Thomas Knowlton, the Connecticut officer detached from Putnam's regiment, who had with him some two hundred men. Prescott's orders were simple: "go and oppose them". Prescott then sent Captain Gridley and his two useless artillery guns out of the redoubt. Gridley was to collect Capt. John Callender, who had arrived at the back of the redoubt with two more cannon, and together they were to take their four guns to support Knowlton's efforts. Prescott also ordered Lt. Col. John Robinson and Maj. Henry Woods, each with a detachment, to "flank the enemy", presumably to take up position in Charlestown along with whatever stragglers remained there from the night before. There they might safely snipe at the British landing, or so they thought.[103]

Captain Knowlton promptly gathered his Connecticut men and departed for the plain stretching from the foot of Breed's Hill's eastern slope to the Mystic River. It was now Knowlton's responsibility to form and hold this newly extended colonial left.

Knowlton marched down the back of Breed's Hill where he found a small area of trees standing by a swampy area. He studied the area beyond and noticed that several fences divided various pastures along the plain there. He saw—crossing the plain from the northeast foot of Breed's Hill, at almost a right angle to the new short breastwork and stretching to the Mystic River—a "fence half of stone and two rayles of wood. Here nature had formed something of a breast-work, or else there had been a ditch many years agone."[104]

Knowlton formulated a plan to fortify this rail fence and thus extend the colonial left flank from the redoubt's breastwork to nearly the Mystic River. Meanwhile, British General Howe, now standing at the North Battery in Boston, observed this and began formulating his own plan.

Ward's headquarters had become something of an infirmary. On the one hand, Ward himself struggled against his calculus as he tried to be useful, stopping on occasion as fits of intense pain surged through his abdomen. Throughout the day, he would be very much dependent on his aide-de-camp Maj. Samuel Osgood, his relative and secretary Joseph Ward, and his volunteer aide Henry Knox, a bookseller from Boston. Then there was Dr. Joseph Warren, who, despite a severe headache, had spent some of that morning meeting with the Committee of Safety in another room. But by late morning, Warren's headache had become intolerable, so he at last retired to a quiet room upstairs for rest.[105]

Until now, Ward had been still very much concerned about an attack on Cambridge. The simplest route to Cambridge was through Roxbury. Ward had become aware that General Thomas, manning the Roxbury lines, was under a severe bombardment from Lord Percy's British lines along Boston Neck. Thomas had gone as far as blockading the roads with abatis (felled trees, often with sharpened branches). Despite the ferocity of Percy's attack, it was but a feint to keep Thomas in check.

Col. William Heath, also serving on the American lines in Roxbury, wrote that "although several shells fell among the houses, and some [artillery] carcasses near them, and balls went through some, no other damage was sustained than the loss of one man killed by a shot driving a stone from a wall against him."[106] According to adjutant John Trumbull, son of the Connecticut governor and future art painter, that lone casualty had "no external wound, but the body over the region of the heart was black from extravasated blood."[107]

Given these diversionary bombardments, General Ward in Cambridge remained unsure of the British plan of attack. He was not yet aware of the embarkation toward Charlestown, due to the slow speed at which information then traveled. But when he suddenly heard the various bells of Cambridge peal the alarm, he knew Gage's plan was revealed at last. When couriers, including Captain Putnam Jr., arrived to confirm the news, Ward was finally determined to commit troops in that direction. Hastings House instantly bustled with activity. Ward sent couriers forth to order up all but a few reserves to what he now knew were the front lines. He then left the headquarters himself, despite his agonizing calculus, perhaps to watch firsthand as his troops departed Cambridge. Unfortunately, due to poor organization, insubordination, or fear, many of these troops would fail to reach Charlestown in time.[108]

A little later, Dr. Warren came downstairs from his rest, no doubt surprised to find the headquarters eerily empty, his only company that of Mrs. Elizabeth Cotton Hastings. As Warren drank some chamomile tea to help soothe his still throbbing head, his former medical apprentice Dr. David Townsend burst into the house and shared news of the alarm. At this, Warren declared his headache gone and immediately got ready. While Townsend stayed in Cambridge to tend to some wounded soldiers, Warren found himself a horse and galloped off to meet the British in battle.[109]

———— •◆• ————

It was now near one o'clock when the about two dozen longboats neared the shoreline at Charlestown Point. The coxswains looked back at HMS

Preston for their confirmation and saw the blue flag lowered down one of the masts and a solid red flag hoisted in its place, followed by a cannon blast from the bow as a signal for those not paying attention. This was the order to land.[110] The coxswains commanded their rowers to break column and drive forward. The boats fanned out and plowed forward with sudden speed until they ground to a halt on the sandy beach before them. The almost 1,200 redcoats and officers instantly began their disembarkation, eagerly hopping from their longboats and anxious for action that would finally break the Siege of Boston.[111]

Once formed into companies, the officers then formed the men into two lines, each two men deep, and positioned them atop Moulton Hill, even as the Royal Navy and Copp's Hill Battery continued their intense cannonade on the rebel position. The British did not march. They merely waited as their longboats along the beach pushed off and headed back, this time to North Battery and the men waiting there. The 1,200 redcoats on Moulton Hill were just the first wave. Many more were still on their way.[112]

—•—

Even now, the Americans continued to prepare for battle. Upon Bunker Hill behind the redoubt, men worked to build a new breastwork, though they did so halfheartedly, focused more on the preliminaries of the battle below. In the redoubt on Breed's Hill, Prescott looked longingly northwestward, ever hoping to see his reinforcements. Outside the redoubt, the construction of the breastwork extension was still underway. On the plain east of Breed's Hill, Knowlton and his two hundred men grounded their arms and began stripping a fence of its wooden rails, perhaps two rails per section. These they dragged back to a second rail fence, the bottom of which was a short stone wall, while the fence posts were crossing wood beams that made an X-shape, and sitting in the middle of these X posts was another wood rail or two, which formed the top half of the fence. There they wedged or suspended the additional rails onto the X-shaped posts, forming a crude barricade that stretched from the swamp and tree line at the eastern base of Breed's Hill, some 600 feet behind the redoubt and at a right angle from its outer breastwork, to almost 1,000 feet eastward, nearly to the Mystic River.[113]

It was in the gap between the redoubt's breastwork and the rail fence, behind the swamp and near the tree line, that Captains Gridley and Callender set up their cannon. Gridley, however, disgruntled with both his own inexperience and that of his men, and noting that many of his gunpowder cartridges were too large for his cannon, said "nothing could be done with them" and so ignominiously abandoned his men. But Callender's men, fresh and not yet cynical, began to fire toward the British warships, though with little effect.[114]

Meanwhile, General Putnam, coming down from Bunker Hill with some entrenching tools, made his way toward the gap near the American artillery. It seems it was under Putnam's orders that men there began constructing three V-shaped breastworks called flèches or redans, probably earthworks, though perhaps simply built from rail fence.[115]

It was also there that Putnam found Gridley's abandoned artillery. Looking to the men scattered about, Putnam furiously inquired where the officers were. The men told how the cartridges were too big and that the pieces could not be loaded. Putnam cursed and yelled, "They could be loaded!" He then took an oversized flannel cartridge out of one of the gun carriage's side boxes, broke it open, and loaded the cannon with some of its powder using a ladle. Next, he loaded a round shot and fired the gun. Old Put then supervised as the inexperienced artillerymen repeated likewise two or three times.[116]

Satisfied, Putnam left them as they continued to fire on the British. Nearby, Callender's men were already conducting their own futile cannonade. Together, Gridley and Callender's artillery soon drew the attention of the Royal Navy, which redirected its hailstorm from the redoubt to the now fully exposed colonial artillery. Since the colonial guns were at a low elevation, being at the foot of Breed's Hill, the warships had no trouble training their guns on their new targets, and so began raining cannon shot all around them. One lucky shot smashed into one of Gridley's two pieces, perhaps just shattering its carriage, but scattering its crew and likely killing some. Gridley's few remaining artillerymen had had enough. Disgusted with their ineffectiveness, they took their muskets and dissolved away into the infantry.

Captain Callender noticed that he too had many cartridges of the wrong size, but he had not observed Putnam's earlier demonstration. To make matters worse, all of his artillerymen carried muskets, and so they too began to dissolve into the infantry. Amid the constant barrage on their position, he and his artillery officers saw the odds were against them. So the inexperienced Callender decided to fall back with his two pieces. Though some would later declare he had done so to repack his oversized powder cartridges, he needed not draw off his pieces to do so. Whatever his motive, he gathered what men he still had, limbered his guns, and hastily ushered his several workhorses away with his guns toward Bunker Hill.

Meanwhile, General Putnam was riding about the field on horseback, splitting his time between the rail fence, the new Bunker Hill entrenchments, and the neck, where he expected reinforcements. When he saw Callender apparently retreating, he was furious. Putnam, described as addicted to profanity, would later confess in church for how much he swore this day.[117] Undoubtedly, then, he was swearing all the way over to Callender.

When Putnam reached Callender, he ordered the officer to stop and go back. But Callender lied, claiming he had no cartridges. (Callender's supporters would argue he meant he had no *proper-sized* cartridges.) Putnam dismounted, flung open one of the cannon's side boxes, and saw plenty of cartridges and shot. Now Putnam was beyond furious. He first made sure Callender knew how the oversized cartridges could be broken down, just as he had earlier shown Gridley's men.

Putnam then ordered Callender back, but the artillery officer remonstrated. Callender of Massachusetts was under no legal obligation to follow the orders of Putnam of Connecticut. With a few choice vulgarities and even an offer to lead the company back himself, Putnam slammed his sword onto one of the field guns, inadvertently breaking the sword and sending a shard flying toward a nearby artilleryman who fell over as he dodged it. Old Put threatened Callender with immediate death if he did not return to his post. To this, Callender conceded, turning his men back toward the swamp. Once Putnam had ridden off, the rest of Callender's men deserted him, and then he too abandoned his guns.

Thus, of the four colonial cannon on the field, one was disabled and the other three stood silent.[118]

In the redoubt, Prescott tried to keep his men encouraged, but those too patriotic to desert were still eager to depart the place of danger. Soon they had their opportunity. With construction of the redoubt nearly finished (though the breastwork outside was still underway), spades and picks began to pile up in the back of the fortification. As one story gives, Putnam rode his horse into the redoubt and told Prescott these tools should be brought up to Bunker Hill.[119] Putnam wanted to see the new fortification underway on Bunker Hill completed. But Prescott resisted, noting if he sent any of the men away with the tools, not one of them would return. "They shall every man return", supposedly replied Old Put as he sternly looked at the eager volunteers. Prescott doubted it, but a large party was sent off with the entrenching tools. Not one of those men was said to have returned, and Prescott proved to be the better judge of human nature in this instance.[120]

Meanwhile, the British longboats were again crossing the Charles, this time from nearby North Battery, ferrying over two more regiments, the 43rd and the 52nd, some five hundred men including their officers. As the first longboats fanned out and began to disembark at the same British landing site, Prescott must have noticed the few tenders still straggling at North Battery. There he saw that the remaining men were not redcoats at all, but wore dark blue coats with red facings: the Royal Artillery.[121] The sun glistened off their brass pieces as they hoisted them into the longboats. Moments later, their laden tenders began rowing across the Charles.

At Charlestown Point, this second wave of troops disembarked, formed into their respective regiments, and took position behind the two lines already atop Moulton Hill, thus forming a third line. Behind them, the artillery reached the beach and began to disembark. They had about 125 artillerymen, who worked to off-load their six brass 6-pounders and two 5½" howitzers (these eight pieces being the field artillery), as well as two heavy 12-pounder cannon. Since they had brought no horses or limbers, they then proceeded to haul on the drag ropes to pull their pieces up to the crown of Moulton Hill.[122]

With the artillery moving up the hill and taking position, one last tender ground onto the sandy beach. In it was the general's staff, along with Brigadier General Pigot and Major General Howe themselves, the two commanders that intended to lead the British to victory.

———•———

At last, Ward's colonial reinforcements were on their way. They needed only cross the flat Charlestown Neck to reach the imminent battle on the peninsula. This neck was a mere 30 feet wide, though wider than that of Boston. South of it lay a millpond, a shallow tidal area of the Charles that had long been dammed off by a break wall or milldam of stone some 300 feet offshore, a mere footpath which could not be easily used as a means to or from the peninsula.[123]

The first men to cross Charlestown Neck were probably those of Col. Samuel Gerrish of Massachusetts or Col. James Reed of New Hampshire. Reed's men were the closest to the action, stationed just on the other side of Charlestown Neck.[124] Whichever regiment was there first, perhaps their lead companies failed to notice the two floating batteries rowed up close to the milldam, just off the peninsula. Also called gondolas or gunboats, these were heavy barges with high protective bulwarks, mounting a single mast rigged with a simple lugsail, though they were also equipped with oars. Each mounted a single 12-pounder in its bow and was manned by about fifteen seamen.

Suddenly, the two floating batteries opened fire!

When those first shots buzzed across the neck, those New England companies definitely took notice. However, due to the terrain, they may not have yet seen the real threat until they proceeded still farther east. For moving into position nearer the milldam and close to the mainland was the light draft armed transport *Symmetry* with its eighteen 9-pounders. Well beyond her, but still within range, was the man-of-war HMS *Glasgow* with an additional twenty 9-pounders. The only buffer for the Americans was the millpond, which kept these deadly guns at least 300 feet offshore. Yet the guns were all still close enough to inflict serious damage.[125]

Just as the first New England companies began their crossing, *Symmetry* and *Glasgow* opened fire, magnifying the relatively feeble barrage of the two gunboats. The din of their attack was more fearful than its actual effect, but the companies broke formation and quickly turned into a helter-skelter mass running for safety across the neck—and for good reason.

It was not the round shot (the cannonball) that was to be feared, because these nonexplosive balls had to hit or bounce exactly into their target to do damage. The British gun crews knew better than to use such round shot for antipersonnel operations, especially at such range. Instead, they used the far more feared, far more deadly chain and bar shot.[126] Chain shot was two round shot tethered together by a chain. Upon leaving the muzzle, it expanded to the length of the chain, becoming a spinning projectile, each ball swinging end over end or wildly, with gruesome effect. Its sibling, the bar shot, worked with the same principle, but in place of the chain was a solid bar, making the shot look like a dumbbell. Another variety was the expanding bar shot, which had two bars that slid across each another and so expanded in flight. They were all designed to shear apart the masts of a sail ship, but here they were used to shear apart men.

As these smoothbore cannon were inaccurate, many shot missed their mark, but of those few that did make their targets, they grotesquely ripped apart their victims. One redoubt defender later declared, "One cannon cut off 3 men in two on the [Charlestown] neck".[127] The companies just then approaching the neck, upon witnessing this destruction ahead, broke formation and rushed across amid torn limbs and bodies. Though the number who died here is unknown, and though it was certainly fewer than those who successfully crossed, many of the Americans who would fall this day would do so here, at the neck.[128] Indeed, between the frightening roar of the cannon and the carnage strewn across their path, it was enough to keep many from risking crossing at all.

One of those standing back, watching the ships bombard the broken companies ahead, was Dr. Joseph Warren, who had ridden up to the edge of the neck. Warren dismounted his horse and shooed it away. The horse was a faster way to cross, to be sure, but the horse made for a much larger target as well, not to mention that it could have easily been startled by the carnage and cannon shot sailing by. However, the real reason Warren got rid of his horse was his determination to have no special advantages over the common soldier. It is easy to imagine, then, that he also chose not to run across the neck, but to walk.[129]

Arriving shortly after Warren was Col. John Stark with the remains of his New Hampshire regiment not earlier sent, about two-thirds of its total. Stark found the approach bottled up ahead as two regiments debated whether to cross, so he sent Maj. Andrew McClary ahead to tell them to cross or get out of the way. They opted for the second, and Stark ordered his men forward at a normal march. Leading his first company was Capt. Henry Dearborn, who suggested they quicken their pace. Stark would not have it. "Dearborn, one fresh man in action is worth ten fatigued ones," he said. With this, Stark's regiment continued steadily across the neck. While some of his men may have suffered a gruesome fate, they seem to have been few.[130]

Also crossing around this time was sixty-nine-year-old Seth Pomeroy, veteran of the French and Indian War and a Massachusetts Militia general, though serving this day as a volunteer. He had arrived on a borrowed horse, but as it was "too valuable to be shot", he sent it away and walked across. He would join with Stark's main body at the rail fence, amid cheers from the men. There he would wait for the battle, carrying a "gun of his own manufacture, which he had carried thirty years before at the [first] siege of Louisbourg."[131]

After crossing the neck, Dr. Warren found the Sun Tavern on the protected northwestern face of Bunker Hill, which served as a rudimentary battlefield hospital. The various physicians and less qualified (and less esteemed) surgeons there were preparing cots and supplies. Others no doubt sharpened blades for the many anticipated surgeries. Here Warren met his apprentice, Dr. William Eustis. While no record exists of their interaction, Warren's character and interest in all of his apprentices suggests he gave words of encouragement to this, his most trusted pupil.

Indeed, Warren had even secured Eustis his position in this nascent medical corps. Until that moment, Eustis was likely unaware of Warren's plan to fight in the battle. But Eustis would have quickly noticed that Warren wore a fancy suit, something entirely inappropriate for the bloody medical work expected, and noticed too that Warren carried both a sword and musket. Warren and Eustis both had their respective duties to perform this day, and after some brief exchange and farewell, the two parted ways.[132]

Warren next made his way around Bunker Hill, and for the first time he saw the battlefield, with its American lines and fortifications, and the brilliant red sea of troops now formed on Moulton Hill. Yet Warren's vantage point was sure to improve. For he was determined to have a front-row seat to the coming British assault.

What Warren and the rest of the Yankees did not realize was that the American lines had a major weakness: a secret path by which to flank them. British General Howe saw it. And he planned to seize this advantage.

———◆———

Naval cannon shot sailed overhead as Howe stepped out of his long-boat onto the beach at Charlestown Point. Eager to examine the field he expected to own by day's end, Howe and General Pigot hiked up Moulton Hill where his three troop lines and artillery awaited. There Howe took in the view. On his left was the apparently abandoned town of Charlestown, followed by the rise up to Breed's Hill and its colonial redoubt and earthen breastwork extension northeastward, which extended down the slope to a marsh protected by three flèches and a sparse line of trees, where also stood four silent American cannon. Then running east from this was a newly fortified rail fence. Beyond was Bunker Hill, with new construction underway. Howe was dismayed to see the Americans had fortified their left flank with the rail fence, because it stretched all the way across his intended path. But he was happy to see the secret way yet undiscovered by the rebels.

The plain upon which Knowlton's men had doubled up the rail fence was somewhat elevated above the Mystic River. While the rail fence stretched nearly to the eastern edge of this plain, it stopped short of a palisade, where the ground steeply dropped some eight or nine feet to a rocky beach along the river that was maybe a dozen feet wide now, at high tide. This beach lay hidden below the battlefield, so that men could march along it unseen by the Americans at either the rail fence or the redoubt. The beach continued farther northward, eventually joining the down-sloping plain well beyond the rail fence, near the foot of Bunker Hill.[133]

Could it really be this easy? Howe needed only to feint against the redoubt and rail fence while he marched another force up the beach, hidden from the battlefield, where it could easily get behind the American lines and thus encircle them, forcing either their unconditional surrender or otherwise their utter destruction. Of course, had Howe followed Clinton's proposed plan of landing troops on the peninsula's western shore, he could have encircled the American redoubt from the onset. Regardless, Howe now had his opportunity to crush the rebels. It was as if the rebels, knowing Howe had earlier refused to land behind them, determined to give him another chance to close the trap of their own making.

Unfortunately, Howe squandered this latest opportunity. As he contemplated his tactics, he watched as the first colonial reinforcements arrived on the field.

Col. Samuel Gerrish and at least a portion of his Massachusetts regiment were among the first that crossed the neck and were now atop Bunker Hill. However, upon seeing the regulars gathered at Moulton Hill, "a tremor seiz'd him [Gerrish] & he began to bellow, 'Retreat! retreat! Or you'l all be cutt off!' which so confus'd and scar'd our men, that they retreated most precipitately". Seeing this, Putnam rode up to Bunker Hill and stayed the retreat by threatening the men and slapping some with the flat side of his broken sword, certainly cursing as he did so.[134] Putnam then ordered Gerrish to collect his wits and lead his soldiers down to the battle. Yet Gerrish, exceedingly fat to the point of being unwieldy, lay prostrate on the ground, pleading exhaustion. Putnam tried to drive the men himself, treating them like badly behaved children.

Fortunately, their regimental adjutant, a Dane named Christian Febiger, was of like mind with Putnam. Febiger rallied a small number and led them down to the lines, where they would serve honorably. The rest of the men, we hope, at least worked on the incomplete breastwork atop Bunker Hill, though Putnam continued to press them forward without luck. Gerrish was later court-martialed and found guilty of conduct unbecoming an officer before being cashiered from the service.[135]

Col. James Reed's New Hampshire regiment also crossed the neck and positioned east of Knowlton's men at the sparsely defended rail fence.[136] Meanwhile, after Col. John Stark's New Hampshire men had crossed, they came up to Bunker Hill's crown, where they halted so their colonel could survey the battle lines. There he undoubtedly met Putnam, who was most grateful to have such a well-respected soldier on the field. However, the obstinate Stark of New Hampshire owed no subordination to Putnam of Connecticut, so while their meeting was cordial, Stark determined of his own accord where best to position his men.

Stark opted to march his men down toward the rail fence. His detachment sent earlier under Lieutenant Colonel Wyman soon joined them, and together they took position at the rail fence's unguarded eastern edge near the Mystic, on the American far left beyond both Knowlton and Reed's men. The double rail fence was now fully in position, but was open and transparent. So Stark put his men to work, taking heaps of cut hay lying nearby, bringing it up to the rail fence and stuffing it in, giving it the appearance of a breastwork constructed of debris and straw. Following his lead, Knowlton and Reed's men joined in.[137] Howe would say it was so sturdy it "secured those behind it from Musquettry."[138]

As other colonial reserves filed onto the field, and with the rail fence looking more secure every moment, Howe decided to call over his own reserve, which by now had gathered in Boston's North Battery. In truth, Howe had enough men to conquer the American lines, if only he had acted immediately. Instead, he sent one of his dozen aides to relay his orders.

As this aide would have to cross the Charles by boat to pass the message, Howe had time to secure his position. He sent four companies of light infantry (the 10th, 52nd, 23rd, and 4th) ahead of Moulton Hill to serve as skirmishers if the Americans dared to sally forth from their lines. These light infantry took up a forward position in a clay or marshy dell that served as a defilade (cover) against enemy fire. Howe then ordered the 38th Regiment to move left and take position behind a protective stone wall, to cover the British left flank.[139] He also ordered the 43rd to move left with orders to join with the reserve once it landed.[140]

With his flanks protected and some time to kill before his reserve would arrive, Howe allowed his troops to fall out and relax. Many would sit on Moulton Hill and eat some of their provisions from their haversacks, as if on a picnic, safely out of range of musket fire (though well within range of colonial cannon, had the Americans again attempted their use). Watching the British with envy were those fatigued Americans in the redoubt, most of whom had failed to bring food, despite orders to do so. Even when a few barrels of beer arrived, at the behest of Prescott's two messengers to Ward, it was so little that it served only to tantalize their wants.[141]

It was now half past two o'clock in the afternoon. Howe's call for his reserve would cost him another hour and a half. But the Americans were not about to remain idle while Howe strengthened his position, and so the delay would ultimately cost the British more than it gained. Many of those British soldiers were enjoying their last meals.[142]

━━◆━━

As Stark's men continued to stuff the rail fence with hay, Stark himself surveyed his left flank and soon discovered the palisade. He immediately realized it was the weakest point of the entire colonial lines. He cast his eyes down upon the beach and later said he "thought it was so plain a way that the enemy could not miss it." Stark had some of "his boys" crawl down the palisade to the beach. The narrow beach itself was firm and flat, but littered with rocks and stones, which Stark had the men collect.

There they quickly built a rock wall or cobble fence about two feet tall and stretching from the palisade to the water, which would stand as their only barricade. As the men built it, Stark walked about a hundred feet ahead, paused to gauge the distance back to his cobble fence, and then took some wood debris he found there and shoved it into sand as if it were a stake. Once this cobble fence was completed, Stark posted behind it a triple row of defenders consisting of forty to fifty men. He then crawled up the palisade and returned to the bulk of his men on the field.[143]

Howe's once-secret path was now blocked, but he thought nothing of it. As the British general saw it, the Americans had but a few men to repulse what was to be Howe's main thrust. Moreover, Howe was going to put his very best light infantry against them, led, as was tradition, by those of the commander's own regiment, which in his case was the revered 23rd Royal Welch Fusiliers.[144] Howe did not doubt victory.

In Parliament, Howe had been a supporter of Whig principles and the American Cause, but here, as a general, he had a duty to perform. Any regrets he had for the forthcoming battle were quickly put out of mind. He knew, particularly on that beach, it was going to be a slaughter.

———•—•———

As Dr. Warren descended Bunker Hill toward the rail fence, there was much excitement among the men. They knew Warren was president of the Provincial Congress and the acting head of the revolution while Samuel Adams and John Hancock were away in Philadelphia with the Second Continental Congress. And though Warren wore no uniform and had yet to receive his commission, others there already considered him a general.

At Warren's approach, Putnam dismounted his horse, showing humility both to a revered friend and to someone who was now, in his eyes, the senior-most officer on the field. Not only was Putnam the lower grade of brigadier general, but he had also willingly submitted his Connecticut forces to serve under those of Massachusetts. Yet Putnam was dismayed at Warren's arrival. Recalling their previous conversation, Old Put said, "I am sorry to see you here, General Warren. I wish you had taken my advice and left this day to us, for, from appearances, we shall have a sharp time of it. And since you are here, I am ready to submit myself to your orders."

"I came only as a volunteer," Warren assured his friend. "I know nothing of your dispositions; nor will I interfere with them. Tell me where I can be most useful."

Putnam hesitated for a moment, concerned for his friend's safety, but having known Warren long enough, he gestured to the redoubt on Breed's Hill. "You will be covered there."

Warren wanted no advantage over his fellow soldier. "Don't think I came here to seek a place of *safety*, but tell me where the onset will be most furious," he replied.

Putnam, perhaps with a smirk, referred Warren again to the redoubt. "*That* is the enemy's object," Putnam replied. "Prescott is there, and will do *his* duty, and if it *can* be defended, the day will be

WARREN TENDERING HIS SERVICES TO GENERAL PUTNAM JUST BEFORE THE BATTLE OF BUNKER HILL—ENGRAVING BY JAMES E. TAYLOR (1839–1901). COURTESY OF THE NEW YORK PUBLIC LIBRARY.

ours." Putnam knew the doctor well: Warren would only fight in the place of most danger. So Warren headed over to the redoubt. As he did, Howe's two 12-pounders opened fire from Moulton Hill, adding to the cannonade of the warships and Copp's Hill Battery, almost as if to salute Warren's arrival.[145]

Inside the redoubt, the men were now only several hundred, including the elderly, esteemed Colonel Gridley, returned after his rest. Of the original thousand, many had either gone to the rail fence or the redoubt's breastwork, been detached to Charlestown as snipers, fallen back with the entrenching tools to Bunker Hill, or simply deserted.[146] Meanwhile, reinforcements were finally filing onto the peninsula, but none came to the redoubt. The redoubt defenders were thus disheartened after seeing their numbers shrink so, even as the British still sat in safety, leisurely eating their lunches and building their strength.

So when Warren made his way into the redoubt, the disenchanted but intrepid farmers and country folk were energized at his arrival, receiving him with huzzahs. Warren urged them on, promising that some two thousand reinforcements were on their way and that he had passed by them.[147] Indeed, such reinforcements had been sent, though many would refuse to cross the neck once they saw the deadly crossfire there.

Like Putnam, Prescott too was ready to give over command to his esteemed colleague.

"I shall take no command here," replied Warren. "I have not yet received my commission. I came as a volunteer, with my musket to serve under you, and shall be happy to learn from a soldier of your experience."[148]

Prescott relented, but whether or not he ever said so, he would call upon the energizing spirit of Warren in the coming battle to help temper and encourage the men. Prescott next gave Warren the grand tour of the redoubt, bringing him to the front of the fort and onto the wooden platform, where he could see over the earthen rampart toward the British.

The longboats carrying Howe's reserve, a total force of almost 900 men and officers, rowed toward a new landing spot on the beach close to Charlestown center. This landing site was obviously picked for an easy march up to the redoubt. On the British right, the men were putting away their lunches and forming up again, this time only as two lines, since the 38th and 43rd had been repositioned left. The eight field artillery moved to the head of these two lines, ready to serve in the coming assault, leaving the heavier 12s now silent in the rear. Once the reserve landed, the total British force would be about 2,300 men led by 250 officers, plus about 125 artillerymen.[149]

As Howe made his final preparations, the warships and Copp's Hill Battery intensified their barrage of the American lines.

The ground battle was about to begin.

CHAPTER 3

BLOWS MUST DECIDE

The foreboding words King George III privately wrote to his Prime Minister Lord North late in 1774 proved to be a self-fulfilling prophecy: "I am not sorry that the line of conduct seems now chalked out...the New England Governments are in a state of rebellion, blows must decide whether they are to be subject to this country or independent."[1] The monarch and his Ministry wrongly assumed Americans were striving for independence, long before such thoughts had formed in colonial minds. This blind assumption was what had brought these two armies together now on the fields of Charlestown. Blows would indeed decide.

Thousands of spectators had gathered all around to watch the coming storm. West of Charlestown, they filled the hills of Lechmere Point in Cambridge. To the east, they watched from Chelsea across the Mystic River. To the south in Boston, they climbed on rooftops, peered from the steeple of Christ Church (the Old North Church), and lined the North End shore. It is easy to imagine spectators on the roof of a North End house helping others climb up from a second-floor dormer window, each eager to take their seats as if at a dinner theater.[2]

There is no record that Gen. Thomas Gage left Province House once the battle had begun. Perhaps he was able to witness some of the fight from the cupola of Province House. Yet, given that his career was literally on the line, it is likely that he joined the crowd at the North End at various intervals, pulling out his spyglass to see what he might.[3]

Across the Charles River, the British on Moulton Hill stood arrayed in two lines, each two deep, with six light cannon and two howitzers ahead, and the two silent 12-pounders in the rear. The front line of troops consisted of the grenadier detachment on the left and the light infantry on the right. The 5th and 52nd formed the second line and would provide support. Four of Howe's light infantry companies also remained forward in the small dell. This was the British right, and Major General William Howe would lead these men himself.

The reserve, still in their tenders and making their way over, consisted of six flank companies, the 1st Marines, and the 47th battalion companies. The two flank companies of the 35th would also land with the reserve but join Howe on the right.[4] Commanding the marines was Maj. John Pitcairn, who had served gallantly in the Expedition to Concord. He was accompanied by his recently arrived deputy Maj. John Tupper, acting commander of the 2nd Marines, and also his own son Lieutenant William Pitcairn.[5] In addition, the 38th, which remained positioned at a stone wall near Moulton Hill, and the 43rd, which had peeled off from Moulton Hill and was presently marching toward the reserve's landing zone, would both join with the reserve once it landed. Together they would comprise the entire British left, to be commanded by Howe's deputy, Brig. Gen. Robert Pigot.

Once the reserve finally landed and formed, the entire British assault force would be as two giant wings of red, the left and the right, almost evenly divided, with each having about 1,150 men plus officers.[6]

It was now about three o'clock. As they awaited the landing of the reserve, Howe and Pigot stood atop Moulton Hill with newly arrived Admiral Graves and staff, surveying their opponents. The British cannonade was now at its fiercest, causing the redoubt defenders to hide below their earthen walls and making it appear as if the redoubt was now deserted.[7]

Howe ensured that Pigot understood his plan: Howe's light infantry would peel off and march in column up the beach unseen, keeping below the battlefield's palisade, where they would bayonet the defenders at the cobble fence or send them scurrying, then pass beyond the rail fence and come up behind the rebels there, thus flanking them. Meanwhile, the grenadiers would feint a frontal assault on the rail fence to keep those colonists in check. On the left, Pigot would simply feint against the redoubt and breastwork until Howe had broken through and began encircling the redoubt from behind. Once the British surrounded the Yankees, the redcoats would swarm in toward the redoubt, trapping its colonial defenders and forcing their unconditional surrender.

At least, that was the plan.

But just as the British reserve touched shore near abandoned Charlestown and began to disembark, Prescott's colonial snipers there opened fire. With the balls whizzing by, instead of forming up properly, the British reserve tumbled out of their boats, then scurried and

PORTRAIT OF ROBERT PIGOT (C. 1765 AS A LIEUTENANT COLONEL) BY FRANCIS COTES (1726–1770). COURTESY OF CHRISTOPHER FOLEY, LANE FINE ART LIMITED.

crawled, ducking for cover. Lieutenant Waller of the 1st Marines wrote that the musketry began almost immediately as their boats hit shore. Nevertheless, he formed his men "into tolerable order with the Loss of one Man only". He then marched them forward to the knee-high grass beyond the beach, where he ordered them to lie down and take cover.[8] Nothing is said on whether the British returned fire, but those officers commanding the leftmost companies probably took the initiative, turned their men, and fired a volley or two.

At this eruption of musketry, the first small-arms fire of the battle, Pigot and Howe immediately turned their attention toward Charlestown. From Moulton Hill, all they could see were the scattered puffs of smoke emanating from the windows of the otherwise abandoned town. This was precisely the reason Howe had opted to land his main troops at Moulton Hill instead of at the Charlestown wharves. Seizing the moment, Admiral Graves turned to Howe and asked if he wanted the town burned. Howe said yes.[9]

Graves was anxious for just such an opportunity. He had ordered several of his ships—probably the *Glasgow*, *Lively*, and *Falcon*—to be ready with hot shot.[10] To prepare this type of ammunition, the seamen placed round cannon shot into a forge and then stoked its flames until it was hot enough to cause the shot to glow red. When fired, this hot shot, it was hoped, would ignite the town. The crews had to be especially careful, since their wooden warships were as much susceptible to hot shot as was their target. But in case the hot shot failed to do its job, Copp's Hill Battery was ready to lob something even more sinister at the doomed New England town.

Graves turned immediately to his naval entourage, ordering them to alert the ships and Copp's Hill Battery of their new orders. Why Graves had not arranged signal flags is unknown. Instead, messengers had to row to each warship and Copp's Hill, passing the word by mouth. While it took as long as fifteen minutes to relay the message to each location, one thing was certain: Charlestown's fate was sealed.[11]

Howe also asked Graves to redirect the five floating batteries over to the Mystic River where they could harry the rail fence from behind it, in case his plan did not go as hoped. Graves advised against this. Since the gunboats were presently at Charlestown Neck and off Copp's Hill, they would first have to row against the flood tide, and then, by the time they got around Charlestown Point and into the Mystic, they would have to again row against the tide as it ebbed back out to the harbor. They would never get around in time to be of use. Nevertheless, Howe asked for them, and a messenger was sent.[12]

Meanwhile, despite the sniping fire on the British left, the 47th and 1st Marines formed into one long line two deep, with the 43rd joining them from the right. The troops knelt or lay low, taking cover in the tall grass, waiting for their orders to march. The 38th may have also joined the left at this time, moving forward from the stone wall. The six newly landed flank companies also remained there with the reserve.[13]

It was now nearing four o'clock, and the men had grown impatient, yelling "Push on! Push on!"[14] The troops had been itching for a fight ever since the bloody retreat from Concord nearly two months prior. Howe perhaps bid his deputy good luck, then Pigot and his aides departed to command the left wing.

According to one account, Howe then exclaimed to his men, "Gentlemen, I am very happy in having the honour of commanding so fine a body of men. I do not in the least doubt but that you will behave like Englishmen, and as becometh good soldiers. If the enemy will not come from their intrenchments, we must drive them out, at all events, otherwise the town of Boston will be set on fire by them. I shall not desire one of you to go a step farther than where I go myself at your head. Remember, gentlemen, we have no recourse to any resources, if we lose Boston, but to go on board our ships, which will be very disagreeable to us all."[15] At this, and knowing the fight was about to begin, the men surely cheered and huzzahed.

As the cannonade from the warships and Copp's Hill Battery reached its climax, Howe gave the order. In response, the eight fieldpieces ahead of his two lines fired, signaling the march. With that, the sea of red that covered the southern end of the peninsula began to move forward in slow and perfect order. All along the lines, each regiment's prestigious standards flapped in the wind.[16] Behind the lines, their regimental musicians drummed and fifed to keep the lines in cadence.[17]

Howe himself, surrounded by his dozen aides, led the men forward, not from behind, but out in front; not on horse, but on foot. True to his word, he did not ask his men to march one step more than he himself would go.

As Howe's right wing moved forward, they approached the dell where the four light infantry companies had taken up forward position. These filed out of the way of their coming comrades and turned toward the Mystic River. The front right of Howe's wing, the remaining light infantry, detached and followed, the total forming a column four men abreast and eleven companies deep.[18] Where they came to the edge of the peninsula, the palisade was not yet steep, and the lights easily descended onto the Mystic beach. There they continued forward, quickly disappearing from view, hidden below the gently rising palisade.

The remainder of Howe's right wing marched calmly forward through knee-high grass, up the gentle plain toward the rail fence. Only now and then would their perfect red lines stagger slightly as they slowed to negotiate or break down the dozens of fences that crossed their path. Put up by local farmers to delineate their pastures, most were simply wooden rails on X-shaped fence posts, now hurdles for the British. As one officer wrote, "we gain'd Ground on the Enemy but slowly, as the Rails[,] Hedges & stone walls, broke at every time we got over them". Upon each fence passed, the two red lines of the British right re-formed into perfect order.[19]

Occasionally, Howe halted his right wing long enough to allow the eight fieldpieces to fire, perhaps upon passing each fence. And with British now well below Moulton Hill, the two heavier 12-pounders, still on the hill's crown, used their elevation to commence firing on the breastwork and redoubt, even as the warships and Copp's Hill Battery continued their own bombardments.

On the British left, Pigot's wing was one long line of men two deep, marching forward toward the redoubt and breastwork. Yet due to the topography, his leftmost companies had to march very near the outskirts of Charlestown and within range of the snipers there. As a result, the colonial harassing fire became almost incessant. Several times, Pigot halted his men to allow his left flank to return fire at their unseen assailants. Pigot's wing also had to surpass occasional fences under this sniping, which greatly slowed their progress, "and several Men were shot, in the Act of climbing them".[20]

As far as most Americans could see, the British had just two offensives moving forward: one on the redoubt, one on the rail fence. From Howe's perspective, it made no difference that the crossing fences and Charlestown snipers slowed his main lines. These just bought him time while his real assault force of light infantry moved unseen up the Mystic beach. Most Americans were completely unaware of this third force on which the entire British plan relied. And the only thing to stop these light infantry was a low cobble fence guarded by a handful of Stark's men.

— ❖ —

Behind the colonial lines, reinforcements continued to trickle in. One was Massachusetts Capt. John Ford's company. As he marched his men down Bunker Hill, General Putnam accosted him, asking that his company draw the three working cannon to the rail fence.

Ford protested that "they had no knowledge of the use of artillery," which was true.

Putnam was insistent, but Ford's men refused. "Captain Ford then addressed his Company in a very animated, patriotic, and brave strain, which is the characteristic of the man; the Company then seized the drag-ropes and soon drew them to the rail-fence". Putnam himself assisted in placing the guns at intervals to protrude from the rail fence.[21]

Meanwhile, the column of British lights continued their march…

— ❖ —

The 23rd Royal Welch Fusiliers marched at the van of the light infantry column making its way up the narrow, rocky beach, hidden now from the battlefield by the steep palisade on their left. The light infantry were the elite soldiers, and Stark's knee-high rock wall ahead of them was a mere speed bump on their way to taking glory from the field.

Stark's New Hampshire men—no more than fifty strong—had positioned themselves behind the wall in a tight formation, the front row kneeling, the back two offset, so that each man could fire at the same time.

The British column, however, was some 330 strong. Its commanders,

Lt. Col. George Clerk and Maj. William Butler, had ordered the men not to fire.[22] Instead, their plan was to march close in and then charge with bayonets alone, thereby overwhelming the rebels.

This was hardly an insane plan. Bayonet charges were employed in that era precisely because they worked—and worked well. Certainly, in the modern era, such a tactic would be near suicide. But unlike modern guns, muskets had an effective maximum range of only about 150 yards, though they were hardly accurate even at 50 yards. Worse yet, muskets took a long time to reload—20 to 30 seconds, depending on the soldier. (None of the participants at Bunker Hill had rifles, which were far more accurate over greater distances, but could take even longer to reload.) So while the first American volley might prove deadly for the lead ranks of the light infantry column, the British then had maybe 30 seconds to charge across the remaining distance and gut the Americans, who were defenseless against the bayonet. In fact, because few Americans had bayonets, the British expected they would flee after their first volley.

Stark's cobble-fence defenders, mere farmers and country folk in homespun clothing, could hear the chorus of the cannonade on the hidden battlefield above them. Ahead of them came only the sounds of boots rhythmically hitting the sand in perfect unison, each beat signifying the slow advance of the British column. Few, if any, of Stark's men knew this was the true British offensive before them. All they knew was that Stark had ordered them to hold their fire until the British passed the stake in the ground. And the British column was almost upon it.[23]

———•———

Up on the battlefield, the Americans waited. Without a unified command, the Yankees still seemed to operate in harmony. Prescott's command seems to have been limited to his redoubt walls, maybe the breastwork too, while Putnam seems to have been in command along much of the rail fence, though not as far as Stark's men nearer the Mystic. Others, both in the redoubt and out, considered Warren the commander, though he had opted out of such. Nevertheless, Warren's presence helped to electrify all the colonial lines.[24]

Along the rail fence, as Howe's right wing slowly approached, the Americans rested their muskets on the hay-stuffed rails to steady themselves, waiting for the order to shoot. Putnam galloped his horse along the lines, exclaiming, "every man…make sure of his mark", "pick out the officers" (those with scarlet coats), and "aim low: fire at the crossing of their belts" (referring to the shiny brass buckle in the center of the redcoats' chests). To help rally the colonial troops, at least one drummer and a fifer, possibly teenagers not old enough to fight, played the tune of "Yankee Doodle", stealing the song the British had taunted them with at Lexington and embracing it now as their own.[25]

In the redoubt, Prescott especially warned that "powder was scarce" and ordered the men to withhold their fire until he gave the word, and then to take good aim and not shoot over the redcoats' heads, but aim at their hips.[26]

The redoubt defenders, unlike the rest of the American lines, had the greatest disadvantage, despite their protective walls. Not only were they the primary British target, being in the most fortified position, but as these were the same men who had built those walls, many had been without sleep since the night before, and most had been without food for nearly as long. To add to their fatigue, the hot sun was beating down on them. Dr. Warren must have still been fighting his migraine, and the heat did not help. He was careful to hide it, however, as he was determined to be in the fight. Only adrenaline kept the redoubt defenders going as they watched Pigot and the British left wing slowly push forward, despite sniper fire from Charlestown.

Back on the British right, Howe again halted his men to allow the eight fieldpieces to fire. Following their thunderous volley, one of the artillerymen discovered, while preparing to reload his cannon, that the next round shot would not fit. The other cannon gunners were finding the same. Unaware of the problem, Howe again ordered his right wing forward. As the artillerymen began dragging their pieces, their officers checked in the side boxes and found the cannon had been supplied with mostly 12-pound shot, about an inch in diameter too large for the 6-pounder fieldpieces. Only the two howitzers were properly supplied. Howe soon halted his wing again, but when only the howitzers fired, he immediately questioned his artillery officers. They explained the problem but noted they had grapeshot. But grapeshot, unlike round shot, was useless at a distance. After chastising them, Howe ordered his artillery to peel off left and get within firing range. A tradition gives that his artillery officers balked at this, warning that the ground that way was too soft. But this was not the militia, where decisions were made by a vote. Howe did not request his artillery ahead; he ordered them, and so they complied.

So the artillerymen began dragging their pieces by hand, westward toward the swampy area ahead of the colonial flèches. Howe, meanwhile, put his right wing back in motion and soon passed beyond them. It would take some time for the artillery to reach their new position, particularly because of the fences, but once in close, they would fire their short-range grape at will. Meanwhile, the two 12-pounders back on Moulton Hill continued to play on the rebel lines, as did the guns of Copp's Hill Battery and the warships.[27]

From Boston, it looked as if two red ribbons were moving up toward the rail fence, floating forward with perfect precision, their uniformity bending and fluctuating only when they met the obstructions that crossed their path, but upon negotiating each, re-forming effortlessly.

The British slowly drew ever closer to the Americans. Suddenly, with a thunderous boom, the useless colonial cannon piercing through the rail fence came alive. Putnam is said to have dismounted his horse to fire a few shots himself, perhaps using the opportunity to teach Ford's untrained infantrymen how to use the pieces. At least one well-aimed (probably round) shot hammered through the British line, creating a gap and slaughtering some of the first British of the day. But the British did not stagger. They simply closed their ranks and coolly marched onward. The Americans were painfully slow at reloading their artillery, so while these few cannon shots gave them heart, they did little else, either now or at any other time throughout the fight.[28]

The day was dreadfully hot. As the British marched the final stretch of the field, sweat trickled down their brows. Suddenly, the warships and other British artillery halted their barrage. Now, only the rhythmic marching of boots and the swishing of legs through knee-high grass filled the air, following the beat of the regimental drums.

Neither side yet fired their muskets, except for those few snipers in

Charlestown harassing the British left—a problem that would soon be taken care of. For Graves's orders to destroy the town had just been delivered.

In Copp's Hill Battery, Burgoyne and Clinton had just received the message. One of them then turned to the blue-coated artillery officers and ordered that they prepare the carcasses, which those officers then relayed to their men. In response, the men grabbed carcass balls, each resembling a round cannon shot but with three deep holes bored into its core and situated symmetrically about the ball. Into these holes, they packed a powder mixture. They then loaded a powder charge and each carcass ball into each of their squat mortars—a heavy artillery piece designed more for lobbing than blasting.[29]

Aboard several of the warships, including *Lively*, the seamen gunners prepared their hot shot. They first put the powder charge into the cannon, then rammed in a tight wooden plug (a sabot), followed by a wad of wet rags to protect the powder from igniting prematurely. The gunners then turned to their forge, which may have been portable and close by, and carefully used a shovel-like ladle to extract the red-hot round shot, which they carefully dropped into the cannon's muzzle. Other seamen stood by with buckets of water, in case ash from the forge fell onto the ship's wooden deck. As the *Lively* was the closest to Moulton Point, she was the first to receive the order and so would be the first ready to fire on the town. *Glasgow* and *Falcon* would join *Lively* shortly thereafter.

Along the American lines, the men continued to hold their fire. The moment seemed almost tranquil, with only the swishing of grass filling the air as the British marched ever forward. Suddenly, the peace was again shattered by the familiar booms of the warships. While most of the Yankees were too distant and the sun too bright for them to realize the cannon shot was glowing as red orbs, they quickly realized the new target.

The hot shot began to crash into the buildings of Charlestown, but once the shot came to rest, most of it sat unimpressively smoldering in the debris. It took several moments before any of the wood actually caught fire. Slowly, as the warships continued their bombardment, flames began to rise.

More impressive was the carcass shot. General Clinton or (likely) Burgoyne gave the order. Seconds later, Copp's Hill Battery again thundered to life, augmenting the barrage of hot shot sailing into Charlestown. The combustion imposed on the carcasses as they discharged from their mortars immediately ignited the incendiary powder packed inside them, instantly turning these shots into balls of fire. Though the Americans could not see the glow of the hot shot from the warships, they certainly saw these fireballs from Copp's Hill with their thick, fiery smoke streaking behind. As the flaming carcasses crashed into the town, large flames quickly began to spread.[30]

This fiery hailstorm continued for several minutes, forcing the colonial snipers hiding there to scatter and retreat via a western path to stay well clear of Pigot and his left wing of British troops. Finally, to assure the town's destruction, marines landed from the nearby warships and torched the buildings nearest the water or those buildings too isolated to catch fire from their blazing neighbors. Soon, all of Charlestown was engulfed in flames and billowing black smoke.

As a southwest wind pushed this smoke across the battlefield, some Yankees believed the British aimed to use it to cover their assault. Rather, the British objective was simply to eliminate the sniper threat. In fact, the smoke seemed to have incommoded the British only, having never reached far enough northward to shroud the Americans.

And so the dying town quickly became one massive conflagration, the church steeples becoming as "great pyramids of fire above the rest".[31] British Ens. Martin Hunter of the 52nd observed, "In the steeple of a church several people were seen, while the body of the church was in one entire blaze; and as they could not get out, they were seen from Boston to fall with the steeple."[32]

Pro-Whig newspapers would later sharply criticize Howe for razing the town, but since none capitalized on the number of lives lost, few must have been killed in its destruction. By modern military standards, Howe was justified in destroying the town to protect his left flank, as there were no noncombatants there. Even so, the destruction of Charlestown horrified and emboldened the rebels. Because of this act in particular, the Americans would fight harder this day than they might have otherwise.[33]

Partly in response to the destruction of the town, some men in the redoubt fired off a few unordered shots at the coming British. Tradition holds that Prescott then mounted the parapet, kicked up their guns, and yelled to his men that if they would just obey him, not a British soldier would get into the redoubt. Another story has Prescott warning that the next man to disobey orders would be instantly shot.[34] Similarly, over at the rail fence, "a few pieces discharged before the order was given to fire. General Putnam appeared very angry, and passed along the lines quickly, with his [broken] sword drawn, and threatened to stab any man that fired without order."[35]

The destruction of Charlestown kept the battlefield's attention, but the real attack was about to commence on the unseen beach below.

Stark's triple row of defenders held their fire as the elegant column of light infantry marched up the beach toward them with their bayonets glistening. Slowly they approached that stake in the ground placed earlier by Stark. Perhaps a lead fusilier noticed it as he marched by. The British column was determined to plow through Stark's men with bayonet alone. They were nearly close enough to begin their charge. Then the dull barrels before them steadied to a level, when some New England twang gave the order.

They fired! The fifty or so cobble-fence defenders instantly disappeared in a thick plume of white smoke. Likely only half fired first; the others fired next as the first reloaded. Their musket balls formed a wall of lead that flung toward the helpless British, ripping into them and decimating their front rows, their bodies tumbling onto the beach and into the river.

The next rows of British staggered as they struggled to maneuver over the carnage that had been their brothers in arms. But the New Hampshire men kept an almost incessant fire on them, mowing them down four at a time, rank by rank. Officers and privates fell alike, their blood mingling with the small tidal pools that had collected on the beach. The officers shouted and tried to push their men on, but British discipline failed.

Without orders, some lead British blindly fired their muskets toward the white smoke that had replaced the cobble-fence defenders—a fatal mistake.[36] By awkwardly slowing to fire their muskets instead of charging ahead, the redcoats lingered within the lethal range of the American musketry, which only allowed the Yankees to slaughter still more of them, causing British bodies to pile up as hurdles of carnage for those behind.

All of this caused the column to compress on itself, the front ranks driven to a halt while the men in the back continued forward. The British officers somehow managed to drive the following companies forward in a feeble charge, but both momentum and initiative were lost. The unforgiving American musketry continued to wipe out the lead British soldiers until the column at last gave way and began to fall back.

Amazingly, the officers rallied the succeeding companies for a third attempt, but the ferocious fusillade continued to mow them down by the handfuls. The whole attack took just moments, but finally, the British officers lost control and the column began to retreat in disorder.

As legend has it, the British carried off only one wounded officer.[37] Once the smoke cleared, Stark's men erupted in huzzahs when they saw ninety-six redcoats lying dead on the beach, with many others wounded, almost a third of the entire column.[38]

Up on the battlefield, Howe heard the ferocious firefight to his right, hidden on the beach below the palisade. He next expected to hear the general noise of close-quarters combat, but instead he heard huzzahs, then silence. He knew his light infantry column had been repulsed.

Howe now thought twice about what he was doing. He had meant for his frontal attack against the fortified rail fence to be a mere feint, delaying any real assault there until his beach offensive broke through and flanked the Americans. But now he had no choice. Howe's wing would have to do what his light infantry could not: break through the thin American line and flank left toward the redoubt. If his men kept their discipline and followed their orders to drive the attack by bayonet alone, his assault had a good chance of success.

On the British left, Pigot's wing was still some distance away from the redoubt. Before Charlestown was set aflame, colonial snipers had slowed his advance. Though his left was now secure, Pigot still advanced slowly, because his offensive depended on Howe's right wing to first break the American lines.

Howe continued to lead his right wing forward, and soon they were within a few hundred feet of the rail fence. His vanguard was the line of mighty grenadiers, under the command of Lt. Col. James Abercrombie. His second line of sixteen battalion companies followed closely behind. Howe reminded them to not fire, but to drive the assault home with the bayonet alone.

The British right drew ever closer, now just two hundred feet from the Americans. But before Howe could order his bayonet charge forward, one last fence stood as a hurdle before them.

As the British approached it, the American rail-fence defenders watched and waited patiently, their muskets in the ready, steadied by resting them on the rail fence itself. Soon the British grenadiers, at the head of Howe's wing, reached that last intervening fence and began pulling off its wooden rails, just 160 feet from the Americans.

Seeing this opportunity, Captain Knowlton yelled to his Connecticut men at the western edge of the rail fence.[39] Colonel Stark did the same to his New Hampshire men at the eastern edge. And General Putnam rallied the rest as he galloped along the entire line.

Almost at once, shots erupted along the entire rail fence, shrouding it in a blanket of white smoke. Dozens of grenadiers instantly fell under the onslaught, even as they tried to tear down that last fence before them. But this was no meat grinder as it had been on the beach—the grenadiers were at the limits of musketry range, though their long line assured some shots would make their mark. Shock rippled through the grenadiers as they desperately tried to break down and climb over that last fence, made more desperate as shots kept smacking into them.

While these were the mighty grenadiers, the flower of the Army, many were inexperienced. Not yet inured to the carnage of warfare, they forgot their discipline and orders not to fire, and instinctually began to fire wildly and too high toward their assailants. The Americans, ducked behind their fortified rail fence, were difficult targets, but the grenadiers, instinctually bunching together, made for easy targets, and many of them continued to fall.

The grenadier officers yelled at their men, trying to cease their firing and charge them forward for a bayonet assault. Instead of pushing forward, the now wild grenadiers staggered, and the 5th and 52nd soon crowded up behind them, causing further chaos. All the while, the American rail-fence defenders kept up an incessant and deadly fire, each Yankee now firing at will.

Finally, seeing no hope of re-forming the lines, the officers ordered the men to fall back to just beyond musket range, a few hundred feet back. This was no retreat, and once reorganized, Howe's lines would continue their original assault. But in their wake, more than a hundred regulars lay dead or wounded on the field.[40]

Over on the British left, Pigot was still beyond musket range of the redoubt, his feint not yet committed. When he saw Howe repulsed, he halted his advance and waited.

Back on the right, as the officers and sergeants re-formed Howe's wing, Howe himself sent an aide back to Boston with orders that the British reinforcement embark at once. They had already gathered at North Battery, near five hundred additional troops plus officers. These were the eight battalion companies of the 63rd and the eight of the 2nd Marines, both regiments' flank companies already being in the fight. Howe knew this reinforcement would take time to cross (especially since the boats were still at Charlestown), but he hoped he would not need them.[41]

Back on the Mystic beach, the shattered column of light infantry had fallen back to where the palisade became low near Moulton Hill. There the light infantry officers fought to regain control, re-forming the men only with "the most passionate gestures and even to push forward ye [the] men with their swords".[42] Howe could probably see them from where he stood on the plain, but he knew it would take considerable time to reorganize the men, so he determined to continue his assault without them.

It took only a few minutes for Howe's right wing to re-form and ready to march, and it was again organized as before, with the grenadiers composing the first line, the second line being the 5th and 52nd. On the left, Pigot's wing awaited Howe's advance.[43] Then Howe gave the order, the musicians sounded the march, and the long red lines lurched forward once more.

———◆———

The British right moved in slow, perfect order, undaunted. Sweat trickled down their faces as they negotiated the same fences, though most sections were broken down from before. Howe reminded his men to assault with the bayonet alone—they needed only get close enough. The regulars soon approached their fallen comrades, some of whom were wounded, writhing in agony, and reaching out for help. Yet the troops now showed good discipline, and they marched stoically forward, stepping over the bodies of the slain as if they were logs of wood, the sanguinary knee-high grass, like tiny paintbrushes, swishing across their gaiters and speckling them with red.

As the grenadiers entered the Yankee kill zone, they expected the rebels to open fire again—yet the provincials held back. Instead, the confident colonists would wait until the British were closer still. They had to make each shot count, and the closer the regulars were, the more accurate the American shots would be. As Howe's right wing edged to within 100 feet of the rail fence, he prepared to order the charge.[44]

Over in the redoubt, Prescott knew his few defenders were anxious to get in the fight, but he also knew his powder was limited. He waited until Pigot's left wing of British drew nearer still. Finally, he thrust his sword forward as he yelled, "Now men! Now is your time! Make ready! Take aim! Fire!"[45]

Dr. Warren and the other redoubt defenders instantly fired. So too did the rail-fence defenders. All of the American lines erupted in billowing white smoke as their lead whizzed into the British troops.

At the rail fence, with Howe's troops closer than before, the onslaught was devastating. Adding to the frontal fire from the rail fence, American musketry from the breastwork and flèches raked across the British from the left, felling redcoats by the dozens. Great gaps quickly formed in their once-perfect lines as bodies fell all around, with the grenadiers in the vanguard taking the worst of it. Lieutenant Colonel Abercrombie, leading the grenadiers, fell with what appeared to be a flesh wound. He was immediately carried back, but his wound proved fatal.[46]

Despite this heavy fire, Howe gallantly led from the front, furiously trying to keep his formation, demanding his men maintain their lines and charge forward. If they could only get in close, the rebels would be defenseless against their bayonets.

But under this devastating musketry, the British were again staggered, until they succumbed to instinct and, without orders, began firing aimlessly high.[47] Capt. Henry Dearborn noticed an apple tree near him, "which had scarcely a ball in it, from the ground [to] as high as a man's head, while the trunk and branches above were literally cut to pieces." The protected American lines continued their return fire.

The white smoke soon became thick as fog around the lead British lines, causing the oncoming second line to unwittingly bunch up with the halted first, creating still more confusion and disorder.[48] Some frightened soldiers of the second line began firing too, but more than a few fired too low, killing some of their own men ahead.[49]

Under this onslaught, disorder and panic quickly swept Howe's wing. To add to this chaos, the rail-fence defenders, remembering their orders, tried to pick off the scarlet-coated officers, calling to one another when they spotted one, a tactic that proved extremely effective.[50]

As Howe continued to yell to his men to drive forward, several bullets whizzed close by. The Yankees desperately aimed for the general, but the balls continued to miss, instead picking off many of Howe's dozen or more aides. Howe's aide-de-camp, Captain Sherwin, was mortally wounded and tumbled before him, "shot thro' the Body and died the next day".[51] Another ball blasted through the ankle of nearby Lt. Thomas Page the engineer, dropping him to the ground.[52] And Lieutenant Jourdain, who had come as a volunteer to gain some military experience, was badly wounded and later died.[53] Providence had spared Howe, but he soon stood alone, surrounded only by the dead.[54] Howe later described it as "*a Moment that I never felt before.*"[55] (His emphasis.)

The entire British right was now in chaos. Some soldiers took refuge behind dead comrades, even piling up their bodies into a breastwork of carnage from which they could safely fire.[56] Amid the thick smoke, British officers yelled to keep the lines moving, ordering their men to cease fire and drive forward with bayonets alone, some officers brandishing swords, others stabbing or slapping their men to plow ahead, only to be mowed down themselves.

As some British soldiers reloaded, using the blanket of white smoke as cover, others broke formation and began to fall back. Those in the front line practically trampled those in the second line bunched up behind them. Soon the entire British right wing began swarming back in a disorderly retreat, firing scattered volleys as they did so. Left behind were hundreds of new dead or dying.[57]

On the left, General Pigot's men and Maj. John Pitcairn's marines were also taking heavy casualties. Though Pigot kept his wing in order, upon seeing the results of Howe's right wing and anticipating the loss of control of his own, he reluctantly ordered the retreat.[58]

As the entire British fell back, demoralized and afraid, the entire American lines erupted in huzzahs. Warren celebrated with his redoubt defenders, and Putnam galloped along the victorious rail-fence defenders. They had every right to be excited, for they had just repulsed a formidable army and proven to Howe that they were not to be underestimated.

However, Old Put had seen his share of fights. He knew this was far from the end of the battle. Concerning himself with the next assault, he turned his attention to Bunker Hill proper. The men on that hill, safe from the battle, had given up their construction of a second line of defense and were now standing as idle spectators. Other reinforcements were still arriving, but they too lingered there and refused to march to the front lines, mostly out of fear. With determination, Putnam kicked his horse into a gallop and rode for Bunker Hill, ready to do what he must to bring more men to the lines.

Suddenly, the American revelry was cut short. With the regulars now far enough back, the British warships began their salvo anew, causing the colonial defenders to again duck for cover. At Burgoyne's command, Copp's Hill Battery also renewed its barrage.[59]

As the battery's guns began to thunder, General Clinton, there with General Burgoyne, watched as part of Pigot's left wing fell back in disorder as far as the beach. Thinking he could be of greater service,

Clinton turned to Burgoyne and said he would cross as a volunteer to help in whatever way he could, begging Burgoyne "to save me harmless to G[eneral] G[age] for going without orders". Clinton then promptly left Copp's Hill Battery to find a boat.[60]

Elsewhere in Boston, those Whigs among the spectators, loyal to the cause yet trapped in the town, were elated at this latest development, though mindful to not openly reveal their emotions to the suspicious eyes of their Tory neighbors. Some, however, did let slip a hint of their excitement and were thus arrested. A Bostonian wrote days after, "Poor, harmless Shrimpton Hunt, standing by the door at the time of the engagement, was overheard saying he hoped our people would get the better of the others, was taken up and confined in the gaol [jail]. Sam Gore, for calling over to his sister to come and see a funeral pass, was taken up and confined some time; and a person who came out by water yesterday says Jemmy Lovell is in close gaol [jail] or in the dungeon, but nobody can tell for what."[61] Young Peter Edes, the nineteen-year-old son of the *Boston Gazette* printer Benjamin Edes who had earlier escaped from town, also exuded too much excitement when he watched the battle from Copp's Hill. Tory neighbors took note, and two days later (June 19), they tipped off a party of naval officers who arrested young Peter on a trumped-up charge of possessing illegal firearms. He would remain a prisoner until October 3.[62]

Despite the devastating British losses, the Battle of Bunker Hill was far from over.

———◆———

Inside the redoubt, the Yankee defenders took cover from the latest cannonade, while outside, between the din of the successive barrages, they could hear the wretched moaning of wounded British soldiers just dozens of feet away. In that situation Prescott's men waited, taking inventory of their remaining powder and musket balls, the results of which were not promising. Those who had premade cartridges had few, while those who charged their muskets on the fly found their deerskin pouches almost devoid of balls and their powder horns empty or nearly so. Although some on the rail fence and breastwork also ran low on ammunition, the lack of bullets and powder was far worse for the redoubt defenders, as they had fired more often to compensate for their fewer numbers. Several men literally had but a shot or two remaining. This discovery quickly dissolved any elation from having just repulsed the British.

A handful of provincials, finding themselves out of ammunition, departed the redoubt, wishing the remaining defenders good luck. This may seem a strange thing to the modern reader, but these men, whether enlisted or not, had been drawn from the militia and still felt they were mere volunteers. The *political* liberty for which they fought had led them to an extreme expectation of *personal* liberty to the point of selfishness. Patriotism and sense of duty were still new ideas for the provincial armies.[63]

Warren and Prescott tried to stymie this flow out the back of the redoubt, but without powder and balls, they could do little to impel the men to stay. Then Prescott discovered an abandoned cannon cartridge left by the artillery—nothing more than a large cylindrical flannel pouch filled with powder. He broke it open and passed it around, ordering his men "not to waste a kernel of it, but to make it certain that every shot should *tell*." For bullets, they substituted nails, scraps of iron, and rocks, or dug out balls that had been fired at them and were now embedded in the earthwork. Yet these makeshift bullets were not enough to keep some men from leaving.[64]

Though Prescott himself remained committed, he was disappointed that adequate supplies and reinforcements never arrived, at least not to the redoubt. Reinforcements had certainly come to the field, but they had all joined the rail fence or breastwork, and they were hardly the thousands expected. Prescott could see others, like Gerrish's men upon Bunker Hill, who were cowering from the battle and refusing to join the fight. More than once would Prescott glance toward Charlestown Neck, wondering whatever had happened to the remaining reinforcements promised.

Capt. John Chester led one such reinforcement company. His Connecticut men had been in Cambridge when the church bells sounded the alarm. Chester then encountered the general's son, Capt. Israel Putnam Jr., galloping into town, who verified the British embarkation. Not waiting for orders, Chester took the initiative. He quickly gathered his company of about seventy men, the other thirty of whom were already at the field, having been detached the night before to help build the redoubt.[65] His Connecticut men were perhaps the only American company that had a formal uniform, "wholly blue turned up with red", meaning they had red facings (lapels and cuffs folded open). Yet before they set off, Chester considered that their uniforms, which had been so befitting for the pageantry of the prisoner exchange just days prior, would now make them too conspicuous on the American lines, an undesirable quality in battle. For that reason, he ordered his company to cover their uniforms with their "frocks and trousers on over [their] other clothes". Only then did Chester's men march to battle, overheated as they were with two sets of clothes. The battle commenced before they could arrive, but soon they crossed Charlestown Neck, where "we were in imminent danger from the cannon-shot, which buzzed around us like hail. The musquetry began before we passed the Neck". Despite the best efforts of the gunners aboard the armed transport *Symmetry*, Chester reported no casualties and seems to have safely crossed his men.[66]

Upon reaching the peninsula, Chester's company began ascending Bunker Hill, where he then intended to descend into the battle. As they did, Chester saw "perhaps three regiments were by our side, and near us; but here they were scattered, some behind rocks and hay-cocks, and thirty men, perhaps, behind an apple-tree, and frequently twenty men round a wounded man, retreating, when not more than three or four could touch him to advantage. Others were retreating, seemingly without any excuse, and some said they had left the fort with leave of the officers, because they had been all night and day on fatigue, without sleep, victuals, or drink; and some said they had no officers to head them, which, indeed, seemed to be the case."[67]

Though annoyed, Chester at first ignored these deserters and marched his men onward. "At last I met with a considerable company, who were going off rank and file." One might guess this company was about fifty men, a typical company size. As Chester wrote later, "I called to the officer that led them, and asked why he retreated? He made me no answer. I halted my men, and told him if he went on it should be at his peril. He still seemed regardless of me. I then ordered my men to make ready [their weapons]. They immediately cocked, and declared if

I ordered they would fire. Upon that they stopped short, tried to excuse themselves; but I could not tarry to hear him, but ordered him forward, and he complied."

Chester had had enough, and his men forced this unnamed company back to the battle at gunpoint. What value this cowardly company would play in the coming assault is unknown. Chester's men, however, would fight "right of the centre, just by a poor stone fence, two or three feet high, and very thin, so that the bullets came through", that is, along the rail fence near the flèches.[68]

Other reinforcements also trickled in, but none came to the redoubt.[69] Unfortunately, a large portion that might have turned out that day never came. Many companies came as far as the neck but refused to cross, some perhaps out of ignorance or inexperience, but many out of fear or dereliction of duty. Still other companies would get "lost", as if the din of the battle were not sufficient to point them in the proper direction.

Col. James Scammans (or Scammons) first marched his men to a useless position at Lechmere Point west of Charlestown Peninsula, where he could do nothing but safely watch the battle. He later received orders "to the hill", but playing dumb, marched to nearby Cobble Hill overlooking Charlestown Neck. However, Scammans did send a messenger across the neck, asking Putnam if his men were still needed, to which Old Put vigorously replied. But by the time the messenger returned and Scammans then marched his men across, the battle was conveniently over. Later, Scammans would be court-martialed but acquitted.[70]

Maj. Scarborough Gridley of the Massachusetts Artillery, son of Col. Richard Gridley, led a large train of six or more cannon as far as Charlestown Neck. There he halted. Just then, Col. James Frye rode up on horseback, ready to rejoin his men after spending the last evening recouping from the gout. Frye asked Gridley, "why this unseasonable halt?" Gridley confessed he was daunted at crossing the neck, which was strewn with dead and wounded. Frye, recollecting aloud his victory thirty years prior at the first taking of the Fortress Louisbourg from the French, tried to rally Gridley, saying, "we shall certainly beat the enemy!" Frye then rode off. Yet Gridley still refused to drive forward and instead took post with his artillery on the safe side of the neck at Cobble Hill, maintaining later that he was covering a possible retreat.

From there he would uselessly employ his tiny guns by taking potshots at *Symmetry*.[71]

Likewise, Col. John Mansfield, who had been ordered to reinforce the troops at Charlestown, decided upon coming to the neck that he would instead keep his regiment near the artillery, to "support" Gridley's position of safety.[72] Both Mansfield and Gridley were court-martialed and cashiered from the service. Gridley's cousin Capt. Samuel Gridley was also court-martialed, but it was postponed for months. Following Scarborough's sentence, the court acquitted Samuel, to retain the favor of Colonel Gridley.[73]

One artillery officer, Capt. Samuel Trevett, bravely disobeyed his commanding officer Maj. Scarborough Gridley and took his company of 37 men ahead regardless, dragging forward his two guns by hand. They safely crossed the neck, but as they descended Bunker Hill, dragging their two pieces toward the rail fence, a British artillery shot hit its mark, shattering apart one gun's carriage and killing one man. Undaunted, Trevett's men dragged the other gun to the rail fence.[74]

Meanwhile, General Putnam had again ridden up to Bunker Hill to direct the men there to the front lines. But as he held no true command over them, in the end, despite all of his cursing and slashing of his broken sword, Putnam was unable to drive them forward. One estimate gives that at least five hundred men stood idly on Bunker Hill, doing nothing but watching the battle unfold.[75]

At the rail fence, Captain Chester's company took up position along with the wayward company they had escorted back at gunpoint. A few other newly arrived companies positioned there too, and Captain Knowlton's fatigued men there were overjoyed to see such reinforcements. Colonel Frye also arrived on the field and joined his men positioned somewhere near the redoubt's breastwork. Colonel Stark's fifty or so men on the Mystic beach must have crawled up the palisade to rejoin the fight, for they had done no service since the beach attack, and it was easy enough to slip back down there if necessary. Captain Trevett's newly arrived artillery also positioned along the rail fence. Perhaps he also donated some of his crew to help man the other cannon there, which had been otherwise manned by the inexperienced infantry of Captain Ford. Thus, the breastwork and especially the rail fence were sufficiently reinforced, but none came to the redoubt—the British main objective.

Over the course of the battle, nearly 3,500 New Englanders came onto the field, including a few black men and civilized Stockbridge Indians. However, given that desertions sometimes outweighed reinforcements, never did the Yankees have this number at one time. And too many would keep to the relative safety of Bunker Hill.[76]

In the redoubt, Colonel Prescott gave up hope for reinforcements. Worse, he fully expected the British would breach the redoubt this time, resulting in a close-quarters fight. Most of the Americans—including his—had no bayonets. And without bayonets, his redoubt defenders had no chance of repulsing such an attack, for the power of British Army tactics lay in their bayonet charge. Nevertheless, Prescott stationed his few men so armed at key points most likely to be scaled. To those without bayonets, he ordered that once the British were upon them, they were to shift to the rear of the redoubt and fire into the redcoats as they mounted the parapet.[77]

Prescott and Warren then moved among their redoubt defenders, encouraging them and raising their spirits. The men replied, "We are ready for the red coats again!" The total redoubt force now remaining was a mere 150 men or so.[78]

Finally, as the British cannonade continued, Warren stepped onto the platform to look over the parapet. There he watched as the British forces worked to re-form and reorganize, and as they did, Warren soon realized there would be nothing to stop them this time.

———— • ————

General Howe's officers surrounded him, imploring him to discontinue the battle for the sake of their men. Amid their protests, the horrified general looked at the blood-soaked field, strewn with hundreds of dead and wounded. He watched as many more wounded crawled or limped down the hill toward the boats at the beach. And all around him, still more bandaged themselves with cloth torn from their uniforms or gear, while the wealthy or high-ranking were bandaged by their attendants or indentured servants that accompanied them to the battlefield. As his broken column of light infantry rejoined him from the Mystic beach, Howe watched too as his officers tried to re-form his shattered lines. He then looked upon the sweaty, tired soldiers themselves, some hardened veterans, some young men.

Howe quickly reassessed the situation. The beach offensive had been a reasonable strategy, as had the second attempt to flank the Americans when Howe's right wing moved to attack the rail fence. However, both attacks failed, Howe realized, because he had based his strategy on two bad assumptions. First, he had expected the Americans to cower or scurry before him, rather than risk an open, pitched battle. Instead, the Yankees had steadfastly held their ground. Second, and especially disconcerting, he found British troop discipline to be unreliable. Despite their orders, the regulars had failed to charge ahead once American musketry began taking its toll, both on the beach and at the rail fence. Any new strategy would have to consider both of these elements carefully. Howe perhaps also pondered that, had he adopted General Clinton's earlier plan to land quickly behind the redoubt before the Americans could reinforce, the battle might now have been won.

Once again, Howe surveyed the opposing American lines. The Americans had proven themselves a capable fighting force, one that was well entrenched and held the high ground. He would not underestimate them again. As for his concern of troop discipline, Howe settled upon new tactics to ensure his forces would suffer fewer casualties until close enough to commit their bayonet charge. With his new strategy, Howe would at last unveil the true lethal nature of the British Army, a quality seen only when employed with careful, sound tactics and commanded by an officer who respected his adversary. The second British assault was going to be drastically different.

First, Howe's field artillery would be properly employed for the first time in the battle. Only after Howe's men had retreated from the rail fence did his field artillery arrive in their forward position near the south end of the marshy area, east of Breed's Hill and facing its breastwork extension. It was unacceptable that such trained artillery as theirs had served no use in the battle.

Next, as the forward artillery prepared their pieces, Howe passed word to all the companies, ordering them to toss off their haversacks and knapsacks. The day was still hot, and the men were growing exhausted, so they were only too happy to comply. When some of the men, drenched in sweat, decided also to toss off their red, wool coats, the officers let them be. Other soldiers, seeing the first were not chastised, followed suit, also stripping off their coats.[79]

Howe then glanced along the river, checking the progress of the gunboats. They had made it no farther than the eastern edge of Charlestown. They would be useless to him, just as Admiral Graves had warned.[80] Howe also saw his reinforcement was only now embarking at North Battery. Meanwhile, the Americans were still gaining in strength as more companies continued to trickle in. Howe made the decision not to wait for his reinforcement. Though he could not know it, General Clinton also was just embarking, but would not arrive in time for the next assault.

Finally, as Howe's officers collected around him, he explained their new plan. Whether Brigadier General Pigot came over for this council or just one of his aides, Pigot's left wing would be instrumental in this new strategy. After the short war council concluded, the officers dispersed, reassured that this time they would take the field.

The British right wing re-formed as before: the front line comprised of the grenadiers on the left and the remains of the shattered light infantry on the right, and the 5th and 52nd as the second line. But the British left wing formed into maybe five very long columns, each file within these about twelve feet apart. Within each of these files, the men packed close, one behind another. In this manner, each of the four regiments formed their own widely spaced columns, though densely packed lengthwise, while the six flank companies probably formed together as a separate, fifth column. From a distance, this would have appeared as many long queues of redcoats, each individual waiting his turn to assault the redoubt ahead.[81]

As the troops awaited the order to march, the British officers weaved among them, reminding them to drive the assault home with the bayonet alone. No one was to fire.

Meanwhile, Howe's eight fieldpieces were finally ready in their new position near the marsh, close to a brick kiln.[82] There they prepared to fire once more, this time with devastating grapeshot. Grapeshot consisted of a solid wooden disk sabot and spindle around which were stacked three tiers of three iron balls each, nine iron balls total. For the 6-pounders, each grape ball was just over an inch and a half in diameter, or roughly the size of a walnut. If the two 5½" howitzers also fired grape, their nine iron balls were each just under two and a half inches in diameter, or roughly the size of a plum. The nine balls, stacked around the spindle on the sabot, were wrapped in a canvas cover and held together with twine, making a lumpy pack that somewhat resembled a bunch of grapes.

To fire them, a black powder charge was loaded through the gun's muzzle first, followed by the grapeshot sack. A gunner then approached the breech end of the cannon, carrying a small wand, called a linstock, with a slow-burning wick-like match in its tip. With a touch to the touchhole, the match ignited the portfire, which in turn ignited the power cartridge inside, blasting the grapeshot out and sending the cannon recoiling backward. The combustion and concussion of the firing shredded the canvas bag, revealing the grape inside. The individual grapes then separated from one another in flight, forming a lethal black cloud of large iron hailstones. After flying a parabolic path over the battlefield, the balls then rained across the breastwork and flèches, shredding apart the American defenders, tearing through limbs and smashing in skulls. These antipersonnel weapons, though as inaccurate as other weapons at the battle, had nine times the chance of grotesquely slaying some number of victims with every shot fired. And they undoubtedly reaped a full harvest of carnage.[83]

As the field artillery softened up the American lines, finally, the British troops were ready. Maj. John Pitcairn and his marines on the far left, Brigadier General Pigot probably near the center of the left wing, and Major General Howe on the right wing all gave the order. And with it, the drummers beat the march, and the total British force, now no more than two-thirds of their original, lurched into motion.[84]

———•———

Inside the redoubt, the fears of Warren and Prescott were now realized. Grapeshot rained along the entire breastwork, and after each hailstorm, the redoubt defenders heard new victims writhing in agony just outside their walls. Even if the grapeshot hit just a man or two, its viciousness served wonderfully as a psychological weapon. The breastwork defenders were so ravaged by it that some of them fled into the redoubt.[85] This, combined with the earnestness of the British now marching in columns toward them with their bayonets glistening in the sun, was enough to strike fear into many of those defenders. The thought must have occurred to both Warren and Prescott, both men of intellect in their own right, that their weak position in the little redoubt was now doomed.[86]

It was now, with so few redoubt defenders and so little powder and shot remaining, that Prescott and Warren gave their strongest entreaties to make every shot count. These last defenders were the staunchest, the ones who had not used the various opportunities that day to escape this place of danger. They fully intended to hold their redoubt so long as shot remained in their pouches, and then many would hold it even still.

Prescott rallied his men, perhaps yelling that famous line that many gave that day: "Don't fire until you see the whites of their eyes!"[87]

———— • ————

On the British left, the columns marched coolly up the field, branching slightly away from one another so they might surround the redoubt. On the British right, Howe's wing marched toward the rail fence. All the while, the artillery in their forward position continued to rain grape onto the colonial lines. Despite the terror that some of those Yankees felt, they all held steadfast. This time, they would wait until the British drew even closer than before.

The warships, Copp's Hill Battery, and the two 12s on Moulton Hill again ceased fire as the British assault advanced. Once the British neared their forward field artillery, these too stopped firing.

And then the field was again silent, just the marching of boots and the swishing of grass, except for the few drummers beating the march and the Charlestown fire still blazing nearby.

The British drew near. But the Americans held their fire, waiting until the redcoats were still closer—uncomfortably closer.

Suddenly, all at once, the British left wing broke their stride and charged forward, rushing up toward the redoubt!

On the British right, the front line comprised of grenadiers and light infantry charged forward and began a feint, firing at the rail fence from a safe distance. Simultaneously, the second line of the British right wing suddenly maneuvered into a column and surged left. Led by Howe himself, they instantly charged leftward toward the redoubt's breastwork, passing the British field artillery.

In an instant, almost the entire British assault had become a swarm of columns rushing toward the weakly defended redoubt and breastwork. This surprised the redoubt defenders, but Prescott and his men held their fire. Over at the rail fence, it was obvious that position was no longer the objective, so its defenders immediately began firing.

Then, all at once, the grenadiers suddenly broke from the front line of the British right, probably wheeling by platoons themselves as they became a column. This new column of grenadiers immediately charged toward the flèches and the end of the breastwork, leaving the light infantry alone to harry the rail fence and keep the colonials in check.[88] Captain Knowlton and others there quickly realized they were being flanked and so urged their men westward to help man the flèches.

Still, the redoubt defenders held their fire as the British swarmed toward them from all sides, rushing past the heaps of their dead comrades. The beating of British boots filled the air, but for the redoubt defenders, their hearts were pounding just as loudly. On the extreme British left, Major Pitcairn urged his marines forward to the redoubt's western wall. Brigadier General Pigot, near what were now the center columns, led them to the southern face. And Major General Howe led his columns toward the eastern face and its extended breastwork.

Just as the regulars closed to within sixty feet of the redoubt, Prescott gave the order. And the Yankees fired![89]

The deadly volley staggered the British for a moment, but the regulars held their fire and continued to charge forward. Prescott's men then fired at will. "As fast as the front man was shot down, the next stepped forward into his place, but our men dropt them so fast, they were a long time coming up."[90]

White smoke began to blanket the entire colonial lines as they fired incessantly into the oncoming British, felling many, yet the redcoats kept coming. Howe's new tactic of charging in columns gave the troops momentum that was proving to be unstoppable.

On the far British left, Major Pitcairn and his column of marines charged toward the ditch below the redoubt's western wall, but a heavy volley momentarily checked their drive.[91] Fearless, Pitcairn raised his sword as he rallied his marines behind him. As he did, another ferocious volley exploded from the redoubt, as many as four shots smacking into him, felling him backward, the wounds mortal.

Myth surrounds the question of who fired the fatal shot, but the old myths are all dubious. Multiple shots by multiple men felled the major, and given the literal fog of war—from the dust in the redoubt to the smoke of the guns—those who fired the shots might not have known it.

His son, Lt. William Pitcairn, rushed up to him and promised to get him a doctor. The younger Pitcairn then pulled his father from the fight amid heavy musketry, and with the help of other marines, carried him toward the boats, there sending him off with a kiss. Though his father was soon in Boston, he expired a couple hours later. A story claims that Lieutenant Pitcairn, perhaps upon seeing his wounded father rowed away, cried out, "I have lost my father!" The marines around him then replied, "We have lost our father!"[92]

Meanwhile, west of the redoubt, the incessant American fire finally forced the column of marines to take cover behind some hedges maybe a dozen yards off. But once there, they quickly found themselves pinned down by the heavy fire.[93]

Inside the redoubt, the Yankees found a second artillery cartridge, which they quickly broke open and passed around for its powder.[94] All the while, Prescott ordered his redoubt defenders from one side to the other and back again, trying to man the weakest points, focusing their fire on the strongest British thrusts.[95] Warren also rallied the men, but neither he nor Prescott could do much. There were too many British.

From the south and southeast, Pigot's columns forced their way through heavy fire and converged on the redoubt, becoming jumbled as they did so. Once they reached the ditch outside, they fanned out and took cover from the constant musketry, hugging the outside of the redoubt's walls for what little protection they provided. The British then found themselves pinned down here, and the Americans took advantage, sporadically popping up from behind their walls to fire a quick shot before ducking again. In response, the British began an almost blind return fire. But when that proved fruitless, the bravest of the redcoats mounted the ramparts, hoping to break in, only to be quickly gunned down.

From the east, Howe's columns plowed forward, ready to put their steel blades to work. Howe himself was near the 5th and 52nd, leading their charge to break through the breastwork. One report gives that a shot hit the ground near Howe and bounced, hitting his ankle, but if true, he was not injured. Farther ahead, Howe's grenadiers assaulted the northern half of the breastwork and the three flèches. The light infantry remained before the rail fence, keeping its defenders in check.[96]

Along the breastwork, an American "marksman" was "standing upon something near three feet higher than the rest of the troops, as their hats were not visible. This man had no sooner discharged one musket, than another was handed to him, and continued firing in that manner for ten or twelve minutes". The story gives that he shot not less than twenty officers, an impossibly large number, though there is little doubt that was his aim. Yet this daring Yankee made himself a critical target, and the grenadiers of the 23rd Welch Fusiliers finally mowed him down.[97]

Private Abel Parker of Prescott's regiment was one of those defending the breastwork. As the British endeavored to breach the breastwork walls by mounting its parapet and firing in, one shot smashed into one of Parker's calves, lodging there, barely missing the two bones but instantly dropping him. Down to his last ball, he fired a return shot, but his musket jammed. So he resorted to using his otherwise worthless gun as a crutch to painfully hobble away to the relative safety of the redoubt.[98]

Elsewhere along the breastwork, Capt. George Harris of the 5th Grenadiers tried to rally his men up the parapet. Harris wrote, "We had made a breach in their fortifications," meaning some of his men had successfully climbed over the wall, "which I had twice mounted, encouraging the men to follow me, and was ascending a third time, when a ball grazed the top of my head, and I fell deprived of sense and motion. My lieutenant, Lord Rawdon, caught me in his arms, and, believing me dead, endeavored to remove me from the spot, to save my body from being trampled on. The motion, while it hurt me, restored my senses, and I articulated, 'For God's sake, let me die in peace.'" Rawdon, realizing only now that his captain was alive, ordered four soldiers to pull Harris back. They hesitated under the heavy fire, knowing they were safer in the ditch, but finally they pulled Harris off to the protection of some nearby trees, three of them receiving wounds in the process. Harris would recover from his wound and live a long life.[99]

Lt. Francis, Lord Rawdon continued to rally the 5th Grenadiers, but he was impressed with the steadfast rebel defense: "there are few instances of regular troops defending a redoubt till the enemy were in the very ditch of it, and I can assure you that I myself saw several pop their heads up and fire even after some of our men were upon the berm [between the ditch and the start of the rampart wall]."[100] Rawdon himself was nearly killed, receiving a shot through a (nonregulation) catskin cap he wore that day.[101]

Another officer nearby, Maj. Arthur Williams of the 52nd, was also shot and mortally wounded. Rawdon asked the 52nd's Ens. Martin Hunter to fetch him a surgeon, but Hunter, after seeing those who had carried off Captain Harris get shot, wrote later that "though a very young soldier, I had sense enough to know that I was much safer close under the works than I could be at a few yards from it, as the enemy could not depress their arms sufficiently to do any execution to those that were close under, and to have gone to the rear to look for a surgeon would have been almost certain death". It did not matter. Williams was soon dead.[102]

Back on the western side of the redoubt, the marines remained pinned down, using the hedges for cover. Marine Lt. John Waller wrote, "we remained about Ten Minutes or near a Quarter of an Hour in this dangerous situation, where the poor Fellows were kill'd as I was directing the Files how to level their Fire". Waller finally was "at length half mad with standing in this situation & doing nothing towards Reducing the Redoubt." He noticed that part of the 47th Regiment was now on his left, along with their commander, Lt. Col. William Nesbitt, for the marines and they had become jumbled in their charge toward the redoubt.

On his right, Waller found several companies, including the 2nd Marine Light Infantry, led by his friend Capt. Archibald Campbell. Also among those to his right was Lt. Jesse Adair, the marine who, sixty days earlier, had charged the British onto Lexington Green and so begun the first skirmish of the war. Waller asked both Nesbitt and Campbell to form as files on his flanks and together charge the redoubt with their bayonets. The officers all agreed, and together their three files stormed past the hedges, through the ditch, over the berm, and up the rampart.[103]

Inside the redoubt, Prescott quickly refocused his Yankee defenders in that direction, meeting the valiant British charge with stiff resistance. The regulars took heavy casualties, including British Captain Campbell, shot dead as his men swarmed up the redoubt. But there were too many redcoats for the rebel defenders to repulse.[104]

As the British began mounting the western parapet, Prescott's men fired into them, mowing them down. The next wave of soldiers instantly took their place, mounting the parapet and firing into the redoubt, one shot smacking through the thigh of Col. Richard Gridley.[105]

With the American musketry beginning to slacken for want of ammunition, the British poured into the redoubt. Lt. Jesse Adair of the Marines was among the first. A moment later, the British poured in from all sides.[106]

The battle at the redoubt instantly became a vicious and bloody melee. The British swarmed in, bayonets first, disemboweling the front-line Yankees. Lieutenant Waller wrote, "I cannot pretend to describe the Horror of the Scene within the Redoubt, when we enter'd it, 'twas streaming with Blood & strew'd with dead & dying Men, the Soldiers stabbing some and dashing out the Brains of other[s,] was a sight too dreadful for me to dwell any longer on".[107]

Thick dust filled the air, along with a white blanket of smoke from the musketry. Those few colonists with shots remaining used this reduced visibility to reload, firing once or twice more. Some would fire, then instantly retreat, using the smoke as cover. Others decided to dabble in the dire experiment of firing stones for want of musket shot. While sometimes this worked, often the pebbles failed to fire properly, and sometimes they shattered upon firing, coating their intended target only with sand.[108]

Of those few Americans who had bayonets, they did some service within the limits of their skill, insignificant as this was in the face of trained regulars. Most Americans resorted to smashing the incoming regulars with rocks or using their muskets as if they were clubs and, when their stocks broke, using the barrels.[109] The British, pouring in from all sides now, could not risk shooting one of their own, so continued to attack with bayonet only.

At last, Prescott and Warren called the retreat, though many, including Warren, steadfastly remained. Warren used his sword to parry the bayonet strikes, just as Prescott was doing nearby. Soon there were so many British in the redoubt that Prescott was barely able to dodge the many bayonets coming at him. Several pierced his banyan and waistcoat.[110] Though the claim is unauthenticated, Warren may have received an injury to his arm at some point, perhaps by bayonet, during this melee.[111]

The close-quarters combat continued to grow more vicious. All around, regulars skewered and disentrailed weary Americans, while Yankees beat and bashed the redcoats to a bloody death. The redoubt floor was literally drenched in blood, guts, and brains.

With the gunfire in the redoubt now ceased, the white smoke dissipated, replaced instead by a brown cloud of dust that became so thick the Americans had to feel their way out.[112] The fight continued to push deeper into the redoubt, forcing the Americans back until they bottlenecked at the sally port. Prescott and Warren kept their cool, parrying the bayonets and urging the stout defenders to retreat. Finally, the men were out. Prescott and Warren followed…as did the British.[113]

Behind the redoubt, the retreating defenders found Howe's column, which had breached the breastwork and was now attempting to cut them off. Abel Parker, using his musket as a crutch to hobble away, had only retreated to just a few yards beyond the redoubt when a British volley felled two Americans on either side of him, just as a third ball pierced his sleeve, narrowly missing his arm. Yet despite the oncoming mass of British, most of the redoubt defenders, Parker included, slipped by the redcoats and retreated beyond the rail fence. And because the rail-fence defenders still had ammunition, they kept an incessant fire on the pursuing British as they slowly fell back with regularity to cover the retreat. Or, as General Burgoyne observed from Copp's Hill Battery, "the retreat was no flight: it was even covered with bravery and military skill".[114] So too did the men atop Bunker Hill finally give some service, covering the retreat of the front lines.

With the last of the redoubt defenders falling back, Dr. Warren turned to a handful of the retreating stragglers and, with a thrust forward of his sword, called for another shot into their British pursuers. As the Americans raised their weapons, several redcoats fired first.

One British pursuer made his mark, his shot smacking into Warren's left cheek near his nose, blasting out the base of his skull in the back, blowing out his brains, instantly killing him.

Dr. Joseph Warren was dead!

His lifeless body collapsed to the ground, blood pouring out his face and down his front. Who killed Warren is unknown, but it was likely a pistol shot from close range, thus an officer or an officer's servant or aide. Shocked, nearby Americans instantly fired at Warren's killer, annihilating him.

Some then tried desperately to grab Warren's body, against the crashing tide of oncoming British. But the stout Yankees were forced to fall back as the British surged toward them and past Warren's remains.[115]

As Prescott's redoubt defenders retreated toward Bunker Hill, the Americans at the rail fence slowly fell back to provide covering fire. Their retreat then continued with great order and discipline as they took cover behind fences and walls, firing off a scattered shot here and there before dropping back to the next place of cover to fire again.[116]

Somewhere along the rail fence, the beloved old veteran and Militia General Seth Pomeroy, serving that day as a volunteer, continued to animate the men around him, even as the British broke though the American lines. Suddenly, a musket shot slammed into Pomeroy's gun, shattering it. Pomeroy needed no more persuasion, so he reluctantly joined the retreat, taking with him his shattered musket. When he later heard of Dr. Warren's fall, he lamented on the blindness of fortune: that, of the two volunteer generals in the battle, Warren the young and chivalrous soldier, the eloquent and enlightened legislator, should fall, while he escaped, old, unhurt, and useless.[117]

With the Americans streaming away from the rail fence, Artillery Captain Trevett was compelled to abandon his field cannon there.

The Battle of Bunker's Hill, June 17, 1775 (and the Death of General Warren) by John Trumbull (1756–1843). Courtesy of the Yale University Art Gallery.

But along Bunker Hill's slope, he found his second cannon, salvageable though disabled due to its shattered wooden carriage. Trevett knew the Americans had very few cannon, and each piece was crucial for their future operations. So, collecting his few artillerymen nearby and enlisting some infantrymen, Trevett and at least a dozen men dragged the gun from its splintered wreckage by its drag ropes—no small feat. Depending on its size, it weighed between one and two thousand pounds.

At the same time, the battered British light infantry, aligned in broken formation against the now abandoned rail fence, surmounted the hay-stuffed barrier and surged forward, driving back the American retreat under a flurry of musketry. The grenadiers too continued to swarm forward, over the flèches and the redoubt's extended breastwork, picking off Yankee stragglers.

Like a lion chasing the slowest gazelle in the herd, one broken British company turned to pursue Trevett and his volunteers as they labored to drag off their heavy cannon. When the British got within 90 feet, they fired, sending a wall of lead toward the Yankees, killing one and wounding another. As Trevett's men struggled to pull off their cannon, some of

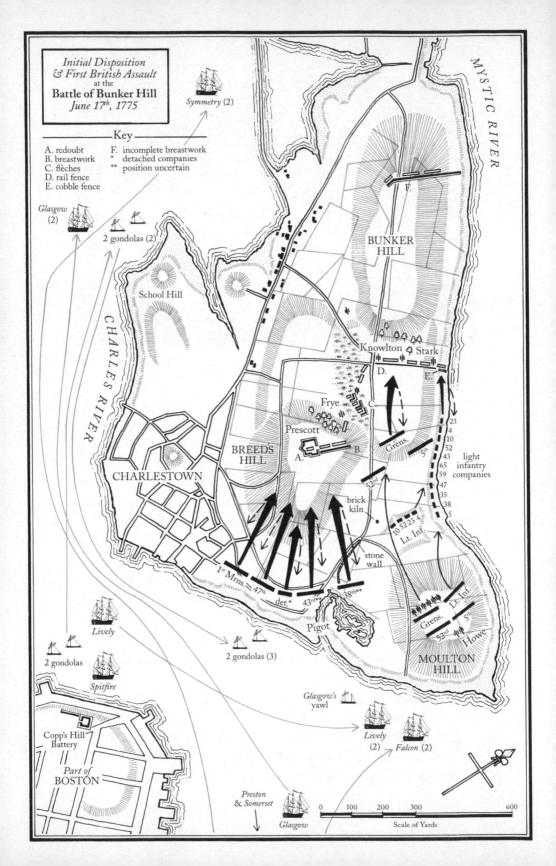

Initial Disposition
& First Assault
at the
Battle of Bunker Hill
June 17th, 1775

Symmetry (2)

MYSTIC RIVER

─── Key ───
A. redoubt
B. breastwork
C. flèches
D. rail fence
E. cobble fence

F. incomplete breastwork
*   detached companies
** position uncertain

Glasgow (2)

2 gondolas (2)

BUNKER HILL

F.

School Hill

Knowlton   Stark

D.   E.

Frye   C.

23
4
10
Prescott   52
43   light
BREEDS   B.   65   infantry
HILL   Grens.   59   companies
A.   5ᵗʰ   47
52ⁿᵈ   35
brick   38
CHARLESTOWN   kiln   5

10 52 23
Lt. Inf.

stone
wall

Lt. Inf.

1ˢᵗ Mrns. ≈ 47ᵗʰ
det.*   43ʳᵈ**   38ᵗʰ**

Pigot

Grens. Lt. Inf.
52ⁿᵈ   5ᵗʰ
Howe

MOULTON
HILL

Lively

2 gondolas   2 gondolas (3)

Spitfire

Glasgow's
yawl

Copp's Hill
Battery

Lively (2)

Falcon (2)

Part of
BOSTON

Preston
& Somerset
↓

Glasgow

0   100   200   300   600

Scale of Yards

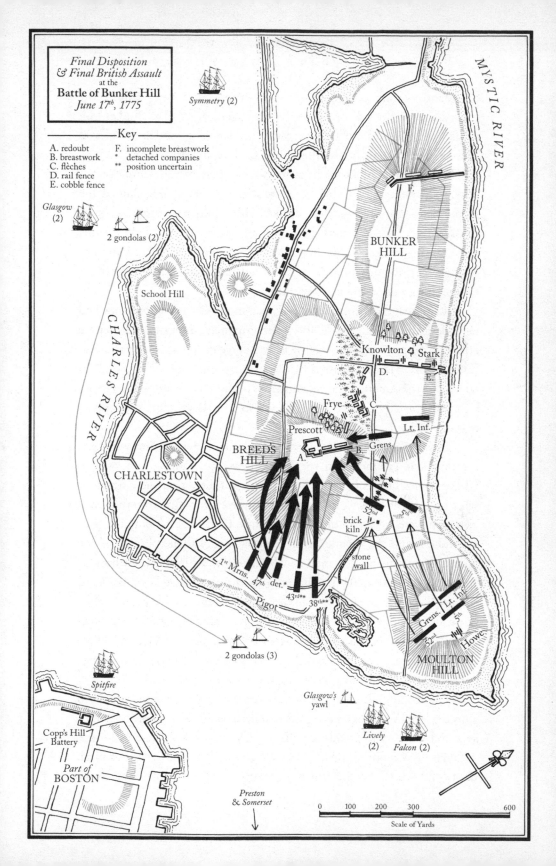

Final Disposition
& Final British Assault
at the
Battle of Bunker Hill
June 17ᵗʰ, 1775

Symmetry (2)

— Key —
A. redoubt   F. incomplete breastwork
B. breastwork   * detached companies
C. flèches   ** position uncertain
D. rail fence
E. cobble fence

Glasgow
(2)

2 gondolas (2)

MYSTIC RIVER

School Hill

CHARLES RIVER

BUNKER HILL

F.

Knowlton   Stark
D.
E.

Frye   C.
Prescott   Lt. Inf.
BREED'S   B. Grens.
HILL   A.

CHARLESTOWN

52ⁿᵈ   5ᵗʰ

brick
kiln

stone
wall

1ˢᵗ Mrns. 47ᵗʰ det.*
Pigot   43ʳᵈ** 38ᵗʰ**

Grens.   Lt. Inf.
52ⁿᵈ   5ᵗʰ
      Howe.

MOULTON
HILL

2 gondolas (3)

Spitfire

*Glasgow's
yawl*

Copp's Hill
Battery

Lively
(2)

Falcon (2)

Part of
BOSTON

*Preston
& Somerset*

0   100   200   300   600

Scale of Yards

his infantry volunteers provided covering fire. Other Americans nearby turned against the tide of the retreat and again descended Bunker Hill to give aid. A localized firefight suddenly ensued from both sides as Trevett's men fought to pull their piece back from harm's way.[118]

On Bunker Hill, Putnam cursed as he tried to rally some of the retreating men, yelling, "Make a stand here!" Perhaps he hoped the incomplete entrenchments on Bunker Hill could now serve as a new colonial line. "We can stop them yet," he exclaimed. "In God's name, form, and give them one shot more!"[119] While he managed to turn enough men for one more volley, Putnam could not stay the retreat's momentum, and soon he too withdrew.

Few British gave chase, however, for most of their companies had been devastated in the battle. In some companies, all of the officers were either killed or wounded, leaving only a sergeant or a senior private to lead them.[120] Many exhausted British gave up pursuit as they took firm control of the American entrenchments, perhaps celebrating the victory with halfhearted huzzahs. There they rested as they waited for support to come up.

That support came in the form of Maj. Gen. Henry Clinton. When his longboat ground onto the beach near the flaming wreckage of Charlestown, bullets from the few snipers still lingering there began to whiz by, or as he later wrote, they had "landed under fire from the town, two men were wounded in the boat before I left it". Assessing the situation, he found the "whole left in Confusion". "I then collected all the guards & such wounded men as would follow which to their honour were many & advanced in column with as much parade as possible to impres[?] on the enemy".[121] Clinton's column must have been sizable, but it seems doubtful that any of his troops included the 562 reinforcements, which were still just making their way across the Charles. These would land too late to "have their share of the success, though they marched with the utmost haste as soon as they were landed."[122]

Clinton soon joined Howe on the summit of Breed's Hill, hoping to gain the latter's permission to pursue the rebels to the end of the peninsula and then on to Cambridge. But Howe just stood there in horror. Though he was not injured, he looked as if he had been, with his black boots and white breeches splattered with blood from marching twice across the field of death. Howe had seen his dozen aides picked off around him, only one of whom would survive his wounds.[123] Moreover, he had watched as his lines were repeatedly slaughtered, decimated, and broken. Now he surveyed the field in shock, viewing the many bodies strewn across the bloody grass, some dead, others writhing in agony and crying out, and weaving between these, the many more wounded, crawling or limping back toward the beach and the waiting longboats there.

Howe was thankful to have Clinton by his side. According to Clinton, Howe "told me I had saved him for his left was gone".[124] Despite Clinton's pleas, Howe feared his losses were too great to warrant a pursuit into Cambridge now. Given the American skill at Indian-style warfare, the road to Cambridge would prove as deadly as it had been in the march back from Concord sixty days earlier. Had the Americans been routed, perhaps a British pursuit would still be in order. But the Americans had retreated with discipline, and Howe had learned the hard lesson that he must respect these Yankees and their ability to fight. So Howe gave Clinton permission to advance his column, but only to the neck and no farther.[125]

Meanwhile, as the Americans streamed toward the neck, they passed the makeshift field hospital where Dr. Eustis was busy doing triage. Even as he hastily attended the wounded, Eustis must have asked many walking by if they had seen his mentor, Dr. Warren. Those at the head of the retreat professed Warren was still coming, not knowing he had fallen. Those at the rear assumed Warren was somewhere ahead. Others just shook their heads as they sullenly walked by. But since Boston's most famous doctor was among the last to depart the redoubt, few had witnessed his fall. And Eustis had no idea *where* along the lines his mentor had taken position, so he could not know with whom to inquire. Poor Dr. Eustis would not learn of his mentor's demise until sometime after the battle.

Despite his trepidation, Dr. Eustis and the other physicians and surgeons went about their duty in haste, trying to prepare the wounded for the retreat. The Americans were ill prepared, having few litters and horse-drawn carriages, though a very few officers were afforded the next closest thing: a blanket stretched across two rails. The rest had to be carried off on the backs of volunteers, no doubt an agonizing experience depending on the victim's wounds. Litters or not, the Americans pulled off nearly all of their wounded. Just thirty-one men were left behind and taken as prisoners. Most of these were mortally wounded and would die within days after their capture.[126]

As the American retreat reached the neck, just feet from the mainland, the gunners aboard the armed transport *Symmetry* again trained her guns and opened fire, unleashing a final hailstorm of chain shot that raked all along the narrow pathway.[127]

Despite the sharp bombardment and flying carnage, Captain Trevett's volunteers, breaking their backs under the weight of their salvaged gun, somehow darted past the intense enfilade unscathed and pulled their cannon to safety. It would be the only artillery piece recovered that day, leaving the other five on the field to fall into British hands. Ironically, Trevett was later confused with the other derelict Artillery officers and so briefly arrested, but once the error was known, he was quickly released and commended for his gallantry.[128]

Meanwhile, General Clinton pursued the retreating Americans, leading his column from the front and marching it along a road situated west of the redoubt, quickly overtaking Pigot and his exhausted forces. As his column advanced, colonial snipers took up positions in various scattered farmhouses and began to harry them. Clinton wanted to push on, but thought a detachment should be left to overwhelm the houses and kill the snipers inside. Just then, Lord Rawdon, who had led his weary grenadiers from the breastwork, joined Clinton and insisted on having the honor of storming the houses, but Clinton refused to let the grenadiers further risk themselves.[129]

At length, Clinton advanced ahead, and though the entire road was lined with houses, many with snipers, he mostly ignored them and plowed forward, set on cutting off the American retreat. Lord Rawdon wrote that the rebels "continued a running fight from one fence, or wall, to another, till we entirely drove them off the peninsula of Charlestown."[130]

When Clinton approached the western slopes of Bunker Hill, he expected to find the rebels making a final stand at the half-demolished redoubt that the British had built (and later tore down) following their retreat from Concord. Clinton wrote, "expecting that the redoubt…was occupied, & for that I assembled all I could, but found hardly to be believed that they had left it in a state serviceable only to us". In fact, it remained just as the British had left it: only a V-shaped flèche, its point toward the neck and its open side facing Clinton as he marched up.[131]

Taking full advantage of the Yankees' mistake, Clinton poured some of his men into the flèche, where they took cover from the few remaining rebels that were darting from house to house to harry the British. Clinton then "ordered a fire to be kept up tho sparingly to prevent their men seeing us & to cover the cannon." While Clinton's men kept the rebel stragglers in check, he sent back to Howe, asking that the cannon and howitzers come up with carcasses to raze the scattered houses there. Clinton further requested the support of the remaining light infantry and grenadiers. But Howe had lost his nerve and did not approve Clinton's scheme. So Clinton returned to Howe, gave his opinions on building fortifications, and then returned to Boston, having been there only as a volunteer.[132]

Finally, by about six o'clock that evening, most American stragglers had been driven from the peninsula. With the fighting over, Lt. John Dutton of the 38th, afflicted with the gout and exhausted, wandered a few feet from his company to rest and change his stockings. As he sat down in the grass, two colonists approached with muskets in hand. Dutton's servant warned his master, but Dutton laughed, stating they were coming to surrender. Then the Yankees fired, killing both Dutton and his servant. Dutton's company, no more than fifty feet away, responded in kind, firing into the two brave but foolish Yankees, felling them.[133]

Now that the British controlled the peninsula, Howe formed several entrenching parties to help solidify their position. He also reconsidered Clinton's scheme and ordered the artillery up to the neck to post with the troops there.[134] The remaining troops were tasked with collecting the wounded and take them to the waiting boats, though the progress of this would slow drastically with the fast approaching sunset.

On the mainland, General Putnam rallied the Yankees, hoping to lead a quick attack across Charlestown Neck. But his zeal quickly ended when a British 12-pounder moved into position opposite the neck and began to fire.[135] Major McClary of Stark's regiment was also reconnoitering the neck when a stray naval artillery shot smashed through him, catapulting him "two or three feet from the ground…and [he] fell dead upon his face."[136]

Colonel Prescott too was anxious for another chance against the British. He marched all the way to the Cambridge headquarters to assure General Ward that British confidence was shaken, and that if he could have but three regiments, fifteen hundred men, well equipped with ammunition and bayonets, he could retake the hill that night. Ward doubted so many bayonets could be had and doubted too the success of such a bold measure, so he refused Prescott's plan.[137]

Meanwhile, Putnam put the men to work on new entrenchments atop Winter Hill, about a mile and a half west of Charlestown Neck.[138] The next morning, Putnam would lead more entrenching parties to the neighboring Prospect Hill, which stood still closer.[139]

The Yankee strategy was a sound one, and as Howe learned of these new entrenchments, he lamented, "The intention of these Wretches are to fortify every Post in our way; wait to be attack'd at every One, having their rear secure, destroying as many of us as they can before they set out to their next strong Situation, &, in this defensive mode, (the whole Country coming into them upon every Action) they must in the end get the better of our small Numbers."[140]

Burgoyne added, "near Boston—it is all fortification. Driven from one hill, you will see the enemy continually retrenched upon the next; and every step we move must be the slow step of a siege. Could we at last penetrate ten miles, perhaps we should not obtain a single sheep or an ounce of flour by our laborious progress, for they remove every article of provisions as they go."[141] Just as Burgoyne had predicted, the newly arrived major generals indeed made some elbow room, but in an anonymous letter surely authored by this same magniloquent general, he humbly ate his words when he wrote, "We have got a little elbow-room, but I think we have paid too dearly for it."[142]

With the battle now over, perhaps one of Howe's subordinates congratulated him on taking the field. But with so many casualties, Howe did not feel victorious. A phrase oft repeated among the troops was "Damn the rebels. They would not flinch."[143]

Ironically, neither did the Americans initially feel themselves the victors, having lost the field and their beloved Dr. Warren. Rather, a hint of sullenness now loomed over the once energized colonial siege lines. But as the Americans reflected on the battle, they came to appreciate it as a victory. Colonel Stark soon reported to the New Hampshire Provincial Congress, "we remain in good spirits as yet, being well satisfied that where we have lost one, they have lost three."[144] James Knowles of Captain Chester's company thought it "a Glorious Day to N America" and "proof of Yankey Bravery." Brig. Gen. Nathanael Greene in Roxbury wrote, "I wish [we] could Sell them another Hill at the same Price as we did Bunkers Hill."[145] Ultimately, the battle gave the Americans courage, signaled to the British that the provincials could hold their own, and helped to unite the four New England armies.

The human toll was staggering. Of the British officers alone, they suffered 19 dead and 70 wounded, two of whom would die days later, totaling more than one-third of the officers in the battle, testament to the Yankees' ability to pick off the brightest scarlet coats. About 188 British soldiers were also killed, with another 761 wounded, 23 of whom were mortally wounded and died soon after. In all, the British suffered approximately 1,038 casualties, or 41 percent of their entire assault force.[146] The Battle of Bunker Hill was a Pyrrhic victory. Clinton summarized it simply: it was "a dear bought victory, another such would have ruined us."[147]

The colonial losses paled in comparison, though there are slightly varied accounts. One colonist explained, "our loss can never be ascertained with precision, as the order, regularity, and discipline, of the troops from this province, is so deficient that no return can be made which is to be relied upon. However, the returns, for many reasons…will exceed rather than fall short of the real loss."[148] The reason they exceeded the actual loss was the "good old American custom, ante-dating the French and Indian wars, which led soldiers to exaggerate their ills… [to secure] future special remuneration from a grateful government. At all events, hundreds of petitions are still in existence from alleged veterans of Bunker Hill praying for… a pension, bonus, adjusted compensation, [etc.]."[149]

Despite these difficulties, George Washington would later estimate about 139 killed, 36 missing (including the 31 taken prisoners), with another 278 wounded (including four colonels: Jonathan Brewer, Ebenezer Bridge, Richard Gridley, and John Nixon).[150] The Americans also lost 5 of their 6 field artillery, 5 swivel guns, and many of their entrenching tools, all abandoned to the British.[151]

The battle greatly affected General Howe, who wrote to a friend, "I freely confess to you, when I look to the consequences of it, in the loss of so many brave Officers, I do it with horror—The Success is too dearly bought."[152]

General Gage in Boston was also horrified with the results. His official letter to the home government was plain and factual, but he included with it a private letter to Lord Dartmouth, giving a more inclusive assessment. "The Tryals we have had shew that the Rebels are not the despicable Rabble too many have supposed them to be, and I find it owing to a Military Spirit encouraged amongst them for a few years past, joined with an uncommon Degree of Zeal and Enthousiasm that they are otherwise. Wherever they find Cover they make a good Stand, and the Country, Naturaly Strong, affords it them, and they are taught to assisst it's Natural Strength by Art, for they entrench and raise Batterys."[153]

A day later, Gage wrote more openly to Lord Barrington, warning, "They are now Spirited up by a Rage and Enthousiasm, as great as ever People were possessed of, and you must proceed in earnest or give the Business up. A small body Acting in one Spot, will not avail. You must have large Armys, making Divertions on different sides, to divide their force. The loss we have Sustained, is greater than we can bear. Small Armys cant afford such losses, especially when the Advantage gained tends to little more than the gaining of a Post. A material one indeed, as our own Security depended on it." Then, in a moment of remarkable openness atypical of his letters and uncharacteristic of the man, Gage confided, "I wish this Cursed place was burned".[154]

General Clinton repeated Gage's thoughts, adding, "give us 25000 for the next Campgn or leave the war to the Navy".[155] General Burgoyne wrote similarly, "America is to be subdued by Arms—or to be given up—If the Confederacy be general, no intermediate Measure can be taken but what must be productive of fruitless expense, Loss of Blood, and a series of Disappointments."[156] Even junior officer Capt. Walter Laurie of the 43rd wrote such sentiments back to the home government, adding, "we have every mortal in the whole four Provinces able to bear Arms (by choice or compulsion) to conquer in the Field, or reduce to submission".[157]

With the battle over, both adversaries continued to entrench, the Americans building on the mainland, the British building on Charlestown Peninsula. And as if to punctuate their ongoing work, at about six o'clock that evening, the British artillery at Boston Neck renewed its barrage upon the Americans at Roxbury, though "with little spirit and less effect".[158] By nightfall, the cannonade was ended, leaving both adversaries a little peace by which to ponder the horrors of the day.

For the British, reminders of those horrors were strewn everywhere on the field of battle. While the work of collecting the British wounded would continue throughout the night, so too would the moaning of the wounded and the dying. And the glowing mound that was once Charlestown now resembled a burnt forest after a great fire, the many brick chimneys not unlike spindly tree trunks, each marking where a house once stood, while all around, crackling heaps of red embers and dying flames continued to throw their eerie light into the night sky.[159] "I shall never forget the night of the 17th of June," wrote British Ens. Martin Hunter. "The cries of the wounded… Charlestown on fire, and the recollection of the loss of so many friends was a very trying scene for so young a soldier."[160]

Now, an uneasy peace returned to the Boston area. And both armies rested.

CHAPTER 4

PASSING OF BATONS

Throughout the night following June 17, lanterns bobbed across the battlefield, pausing for a moment here and there before continuing forward. These were the British surgeons and their litter bearers, dutifully performing their morbid triage, zigzagging across the field as they were beckoned by the sound of the moaning wounded. Aided by the moonlight, the surgeons picked out those redcoats who were treatable and ordered them carried off to the boats waiting on the Charles riverbank. For those too far gone, the surgeons could only look at them in pity, shake their heads, then move on, leaving these unchosen behind. For every boat full of wounded that left Charlestown, another empty one arrived in its place, grinding to a halt on the sandy beach to await a fresh load.

In Boston, carts and wagons gathered at the North Battery to collect the arriving wounded as they were hoisted from the longboats. Many British officers and some soldiers had brought their families with them to Boston. Now these grief-stricken families and others crowded the wharves, raising their lanterns over the wounded, hoping not to see a husband or father among those hoisted out. Customs Commissioner Henry Hulton wrote, "In the evening the streets were filled with the wounded and the dying; the sight of which, with the lamentations of the women and children over their husbands and fathers, pierced one to the soul. We were now every moment hearing of some officer, or other of our friends and acquaintance, who had fallen in our defence, and in supporting the honor of our country."[1]

Ens. Jeremy Lister, still recovering from a shattered elbow received during the Concord affair, heard that his comrade Lt. Waldron Kelly was wounded, which he "suppos'd Mortally". When he informed Mrs. Kelly, she "for some time sat motionless with two small Children close by her. so soon as her grief gave the least vent she took her leave and went home to meet her Husband who was brought home scarcely alive". Yet Lieutenant Kelly would eventually recover. Lister had made this same wrong prognosis for Lt. William Sutherland, wounded at Concord, and so twice now had needlessly scared the wife of one of his comrades.[2]

Horse-drawn wagons overloaded with wounded and dying were sent to the few hospitals in Boston: the almshouse, a workhouse, and a recently converted old factory opposite the granary.[3] All three were quickly overtaxed with the numbers of casualties. Moreover, the hospitals were crude, even by that era's standards. The British had simply not been ready for such massive losses. With the hospital staffs woefully undermanned, some of the women camp followers were permitted to serve as nurses in exchange for army rations.[4] The hospitals also lacked sufficient space. The almshouse was the nearest thing to a genuine hospital in Boston, yet it may have had just eight beds.[5] So the wounded were taken from the wagons and laid outside the hospitals to wait, some hemorrhaging to death as they lay unattended.

For those wounded who did make it inside, the medical care was both a blessing and a curse. Sometimes the mildest of injuries would still result in death, given the premodern medical system. While a few surgeons had proper training, limited as it was then, and the care was relatively good for the era, none knew of bacteria or cleanliness. They would use the same saw or scalpel on countless soldiers—and sometimes the same bloodied bandages—thereby spreading disease. Healers did know of lead poisoning, however, and thus knew musket balls had to be removed. Those injured with chest or head wounds would suffer probing with surgical pliers until the bullet or shrapnel was found.

Those unfortunate enough to have leg or arm injuries—and there were many, for the Yankees had been ordered to deliberately aim low— generally faced amputation, considered the only reliable remedy for such injuries. All of these procedures were undergone without anesthesia. The best a wounded man could hope for before undertaking the knife was a swig or two of West Indies rum, but even the strongest rum did not dull the pain. The hospitals were filled with men crying in agony. Surgeons' mates selected for their size and strength pinned down the wounded as their limbs were sawed off or their torsos prodded for bullets. The floors, covered with sand to soak up the blood, were nevertheless slick from all the gore. Amputated limbs were stacked in piles near the work areas. The whole building reeked of death.

Dr. Alexander Grant, a British physician at one of the Boston hospitals, took a few minutes amid these horrible scenes to write a friend. "I have scarce time sufficient to eat my meals, therefore you must expect but a very few lines: I have been up two nights, assisted with four mates, dressing our men of the wounds they received in the last engagement; many of the wounded are daily dying; and many must have both legs amputated. The Provincials had either exhausted their ball, or they were determined that every wound should prove fatal; their muskets were charged with old nails and angular pieces of iron; and from most of our men being wounded in the legs, we are inclined to believe it was their design, not wishing to kill the men, but leave them as burdens on us, to exhaust our provisions and engage our attention, a[s] well as to intimidate the rest of the soldiery."[6]

The endless stream of casualties indeed intimidated and demoralized the men. Rumors even began to spread that "the rebellious rascals" had "both poisoned and chewed the musket balls, in order to make them the more fatal."[7] Henry Hulton summarized the British sentiment of the evening: "In this army are many of noble family, many very respectable, virtuous, and amiable characters, and it grieves one, that gentlemen, brave British soldiers, should fall by the hands of such despicable wretches as compose the banditti of the country; amongst whom there is not one that has the least pretension to be called a gentleman. They are a most rude, depraved, degenerate race, and it is a mortification to us that they speak English, and can trace themselves from that stock."[8]

With so much death around Boston, one anonymous British officer wrote critically, "We are all wrong at the head. My mind cannot help dwelling upon our cursed mistakes. Such ill conduct at the first out-set argues a gross ignorance of the common rules of the profession, and gives us for the future anxious forebodings. I have lost some of those I most valued. This madness or ignorance nothing can excuse. The brave men's lives were wantonly thrown away. Our conductor [Howe] as much murdered them as if he had cut their throats himself on Boston common. Had he fallen, ought we to have regretted him?"[9] While Howe should have regrouped following the failed beach attack, this anonymous officer failed to recognize that troop discipline under fire was the greatest contributor to British losses.

But many other British officers astutely realized troop discipline was the root cause. As Lt. Francis, Lord Rawdon noted, "Our confidence in our own troops is much lessened since the 17th of June. Some of them did, indeed, behave with infinite courage, but others behaved as remarkably ill. We have great want of discipline both amongst officers and men."[10] General Clinton was so horror-struck by this revelation that he could only put his thoughts down in cipher: "All was in Confusion[;] officers told me that they could not command their men and I never saw so great a want of order and [our victory was] more luck[?] than which[?] I never saw".[11] And General Burgoyne wrote, "Though my letter passes in security, I tremble while I write it; and let it not pass even in a whisper from your Lordship to more than *one* person: the zeal and intrepidity of the officers, which was without exception exemplary, was ill seconded by the private men. Discipline, not to say courage, was wanting. In the critical moment of carrying the redoubt, the officers of some corps were almost alone; and what was the worst part of the confusion of these corps—all the wounds of the officers were not received from the enemy [but by their own men]… it will require some training under such generals as Howe and Clinton before they can prudently be instructed in many exploits against such odds".[12]

As Burgoyne implied, though troop discipline was the root cause, British military leadership was ultimately responsible for its failure to provide adequate training. This was a problem inherent in the British Army as a whole, not the failure of General Gage alone. But Gage was the local commander, and once news of the battle reached Britain, and Parliament found itself under public scrutiny, Gage made for an easy scapegoat. Whether Gage guessed it or not, his tragic victory at Bunker Hill would mark the end of an otherwise honorable career.

On the American side, another leader's honorable career had been cut short. The beloved Dr. Joseph Warren's crumpled body spent the night lying amid the dead on Breed's Hill. He would not be discovered until the next day.

With the many hundreds of British wounded strewn across the battlefield, the squalid affair of removing them to Boston would take days. As for those American wounded left on the field and taken prisoner, most were soon dead.[13] It remains unknown whether their mortality rate was due to the severity of their wounds (and hence why they were abandoned) or to being given little attention by the overworked British surgeons. In Cambridge, the Americans too spent the night and following days treating their wounded, aided by such physicians as Dr. William Eustis and Dr. Isaac Foster of Charlestown, the chief surgeon.[14]

With both adversaries across Charlestown Neck entrenching throughout the night, by sunrise on June 18, it was clear that a new assault against either side would mean hundreds more casualties. The British did not have the stomach or the soldiers for such an assault. The Americans, on the other hand, had neither the gunpowder nor the motive.

Meanwhile, though General Gage had intended to send his wife back to England for safety, she had not yet departed. Upon witnessing the horrific numbers of wounded British officers in Boston, Mrs. Gage "sent all her fowls, fish, and what little fresh meat she had in the house, to the wounded officers, scarcely leaving a sufficiency for herself and the General." Her generosity on this day after the battle much endeared her to the officers.[15]

The morning of June 18 also brought new general orders for the British in Charlestown. General Howe ordered tents to be brought over so the men could build an encampment on the peninsula. He also ordered work parties to collect the dead and bury them in mass graves.[16]

Capt. Walter Sloan Laurie, who had held command at North Bridge in Concord, was placed in charge of one such burial detail. When his party came across the body of Dr. Joseph Warren atop Breed's Hill, Laurie immediately recognized it as the doctor.

Sometime following the battle's conclusion, perhaps now, some officer took the slain doctor's sword as a souvenir. The sword would eventually be handed down to a servant who would then sell it back to an American, though its present whereabouts are unknown.[17] The burial detail next examined the doctor's clothes for personal effects. "He died in his best clothes; everybody remembered his fine, silk-fringed waistcoat."[18] Unfortunately, they also found in Warren's pocket six letters, probably related to his business with the Committee of Safety, incriminating at least two Bostonians including John Lovell, who were immediately imprisoned.[19]

Finally, as Captain Laurie's burial detail dug a small grave, some say they stripped Warren of his clothes.[20] They then tossed in the grave some unnamed farmer wearing a frock, before tossing Warren's body in along with it.[21] Captain Laurie enjoyed burying Warren, for he smugly wrote later, "Doctr. Warren… I found among the slain, and stuffed the scoundrell with another Rebel into one hole, and there he & his seditious principles may remain".[22] The British soldiers then unceremoniously filled in Warren's grave.

Meanwhile, among the American lines, Dr. John Warren, youngest of Joseph's three brothers, was apprehensively inquiring into the whereabouts of his eldest sibling. John had been at his home in nearby Salem when he first heard news of the battle and later saw the smoke rising from Charlestown. Further news reported devastating losses, that the Americans had been defeated, and that his brother was thought to have been in the engagement. Though anxious, John determined to get a few hours' sleep before departing. But after a restless nap, he left Salem on horseback at two o'clock in the morning. Upon reaching Medford, John learned the distressing news that his brother was missing.

"Upon this dreadful intelligence I went immediately to Cambridge, and inquired of almost every person I saw whether they could give me any information of him. Some told me he was undoubtedly alive and well, others, that he was wounded; and others, that he fell on the field. This perplexed me almost to distraction. I went on inquiring, with a solicitude which was such a mixture of hope and fear, as none but one who has felt it can form any conception of. In this manner I passed several days, every day's information diminishing the probability of his safety."[23]

Finally, John Warren had had enough. He was determined, being in grief and not in his right mind, to go across Charlestown Neck to inquire there. He became so overzealous with a British sentinel guarding the neck that the sentinel bayoneted him. Though it is not recorded where he received this injury, it took the sharp pain of a steel blade to snap him back into a proper state of mind. He was forced to give up his search and assume the worst. His physical wound would eventually heal over with a scar, but only that intangible bandage known as closure could heal his emotional wound.

Yet such closure could not come until Charlestown was again in provincial hands. Only then might he hope to find the remains of his fallen brother. Perhaps in part as homage to his sibling, Dr. John Warren focused his grief toward good by joining the Americans as a physician. He would serve with them for the next two years of the war.[24]

News of the battle had come as quickly to Worcester as it had to Salem. Miss Mercy Scollay, residing there with Warren's four children in their rented farmhouse, was stricken with grief upon hearing the news, probably told to her by her landlord, Dr. Dix. Mercy knew her beloved fiancé Dr. Warren was certainly among those who had fought. Rumors followed for days, but Mercy showed great strength of heart. When confirmation of Warren's death came, perhaps from Dr. John Warren or even Dr. William Eustis, she accepted the dread that was in her heart and only then told the children. These poor children, who had lost their mother only two years prior, were now orphans. They had been in Mercy's care for a few months, though they had known her for a year or more. Their grandmother Mary Warren in Roxbury had been more of a mother figure. But Mercy remembered her promise to her dead fiancé and so prepared herself mentally for the struggle of raising four children alone, without her beloved Joseph. The Dix household became a house of mourning, and Mercy adorned herself in black.[25]

Mercy was not alone in her mourning. Abigail Adams wrote her husband, John, still in Philadelphia with Congress, "Not all the havoc and devastation they have made has wounded me like the death of Warren.

We want him in the Senate; we want him in his profession; we want him in the field. We mourn for the citizen, the senator, the physician, and the warrior. May we have others raised up in his room."[26]

Two days after the battle, on June 19, James Warren (no relation) was voted President of the Massachusetts Provincial Congress, "in the room of the Hon. Joseph Warren, Esq., supposed to be killed in the late battle at Bunker's Hill." The Congress also elected William Heath, lately selected for brigadier general, as major general in Warren's stead.[27]

On the same day, another doctor came to Cambridge looking for Dr. Joseph Warren. Upon learning of Dr. Warren's presumed fate, and knowing the two other prominent Sons of Liberty, Samuel Adams and John Hancock, were busy in distant Philadelphia from whence he had just traveled, the traitor Dr. Benjamin Church easily became one of the most influential members of the Provincial Congress.[28]

———————•◦•———————

In the days after the battle, both the Americans and the British continued to entrench. Though both sides exchanged an occasional cannonade or musket fire from time to time, they each bided their time.

The Americans fortified all the hills between Charlestown and Cambridge, some of which they had begun to entrench even before the recent battle. Strangely, however, the colonials had neglected making serious entrenchments to the south. It was only after the battle that they sought to remedy this situation, building strong lines opposing Boston Neck and a fort on a hill overlooking Roxbury.

Col. Richard Gridley probably played some role in these efforts, as did Col. Rufus Putnam of Massachusetts (distantly related to Old Put). But a new face was also helping to entrench there. This was the twenty-five-year-old Henry Knox, perhaps recognizable by his conspicuous attempts to veil his disfigured left hand with a handkerchief, his pinkie and ring fingers having been lost two years earlier when his gun misfired during a hunting accident. Prior to the recent crisis, Knox had passed the slow hours at his Boston shop, *The London Book-Store*, by reading about artillery and engineering. Though he had been trapped in the besieged town for a time, he had managed to sneak out with his Loyalist wife, Lucy Flucker Knox, sometime before the latest battle. He then joined the American Cause as a volunteer, at first serving General Ward as an aide. Now, at last, Knox was putting all of his book learning to use.

Among his first accomplishments, Knox helped to create a new American line east of Roxbury, designed to defend against British incursions from across Dorchester Neck. Unfortunately, the town of Roxbury itself had become little more than a ghost town, its "once busy, crowded street is now occupied only by a picket-guard. The houses are deserted, the windows taken out, and many shot-holes visible. Some have been burnt, and others pulled down to make room for the fortifications."[29]

Knox and the entrenching crews in Roxbury were not the only ones contemplating Dorchester Peninsula. Undeterred by the British losses, General Clinton was determined to continue with the original plan to conquer that unguarded peninsula to the south. In a council of war on the day after the battle, Clinton urged the possession of Dorchester Heights, "as they lay directly on our Water Communication and more seriously annoyed the Port of Boston than those of Charles Town did."[30] At a minimum, Clinton urged that they take Dorchester Neck or Foster's Hill, a small height on Dorchester, nearest to Boston, that commanded the town and Boston Neck.

The artillerymen and engineers disagreed with Clinton, stating that the Americans "never could annoy us from that side" and that "if the Enemy possessed themselves of Fosters Hill we could from our side blow them to atoms." Clinton remonstrated, "if we were ever driven from Boston it would be by the Enemy batteries at foster Hill."[31] But Gage, now indecisive after the devastating late battle, decided to delay the planned operation until the following Friday. When Friday came, it was not until the troops were actually in their boats that the assault was again put off, this time for good.[32]

Clinton grew frustrated with their inactivity and was certain some decisive victory was needed to raise the spirits of the British soldiers. "Seeing the troops so totally disperrited I saw no chance of recovering their courage more likely than some well considered move against the Enemy. I wanted to try their Countenance by a Cannonade, following it up or not as occasion should offer and making it pass as a reconnoisance if we should not judge it right to attack them. I was not attended to."[33]

Clinton continued to push for action, and Gage at least once placated his eagerness. "…the Enemy was kept constantly alert notwithstanding which the little corps I went out with did penetrate the Roxbury lines, also threw them into the greatest confusion, & if I had been permitted to have followed it up[,] which I am sure might have been done without risk against such miserable parish school gentry[,] the most important consequences might have followed, but Mr. Gage[,] who was pleased to come with me as far as the line[,] not having the confidence in me which I flatter myself he would have had had we served longer together, ordered me to call in the troops".[34]

The Battle of Bunker Hill had made both Generals Gage and Howe reluctant. Their new strategy was simply to fortify Boston and Charlestown and wait for more troops.

Charlestown remained under Howe's command, garrisoned by all of the troops who had come over in the battle, including the reinforcement of the 63rd and 2nd Marines who had come too late for action. The troops had begun fortifying Bunker Hill proper immediately following the battle, but unlike the quick construction from the Yankees, theirs was an evolutionary process that took many weeks to finish. Once completed, the multilevel fort spanned the hill's entire crown, shaped as a narrow pentagon with its farthest vertex forming a long salient projecting southeastward. A broad wall faced the neck to the northwest and was close enough that artillery and even musketry from inside could rake that only path from the mainland. The fort was ditched, palisaded, fraised with long pikes aimed outward, and armed with many cannon. The British would also strengthen the colonial works on Breed's Hill, but Fort Bunker Hill was their main defense, and it soon became impenetrable. Never again would the Americans seriously talk of assaulting that peninsula.[35]

The British also added fortifications in Boston. The original double line at Boston Neck was moved forward, ahead of the neck to the Roxbury side, where the walls could be expanded and better fortified. This new double line was flanked by tidal salt marshes, which were themselves ditched and stockaded. Farther ahead were built two V-shaped flèches, each with a picket of twenty or twenty-five men. Various flèches and batteries also sprang up across Boston Peninsula, particularly facing Back Bay and Cambridge. In addition, some of the roads were fortified with breastworks, in case the outer works were compromised. On the Dorchester side, all Gage did was build a blockhouse mounted with cannon and guarded by an earthwork in front. Thus, Gage prepared for an attack from Roxbury or Cambridge, but ignored his weakness from Dorchester to the south.[36]

With defensive preparations underway, a few promotions were given to replace fallen officers lost in the recent battle. Most notably, Maj. John Tupper assumed command of the marine battalions after the death of Maj. John Pitcairn. Additionally, both Lt. Jesse Adair, the instigator of the Skirmish at Lexington, and Lt. William Pitcairn, son of the deceased major, were promoted to captain by the end of July.[37]

Gage also began to receive, piecemeal, four more regiments from the Second Embarkation of troops to America. These had been sent to New York, but Gage had sent a ship to intercept them and redirect them to Boston. The first arrived on June 22, the rest by July 19.[38]

Gage was not the only one to have new men arriving. The Americans were about to receive their new generalissimo.

———— ·•· ————

At about two o'clock in the afternoon on July 2, 1775, a rainy and dreary day, a tall man on horseback arrived at the American encampment of Cambridge Common, soaking wet and half-sick. The disheveled colonial troops peeked out from their diverse tents to look up at this gentlemen stranger, conspicuous not only by his aura, but by his distinct blue officer's uniform with buff facings. Of the small entourage on horseback behind him, perhaps only one other had a uniform.[39] Whispers spread through the encampment as this gentlemen rode his horse through the Common, pausing only briefly in the rain to survey the camp.[40]

It was with this unceremonious arrival that Gen. George Washington, commander in chief of the new and yet unestablished Continental Army, first came before his men. Besides his entourage, he was escorted by two provincial congressmen: Moses Gill and Dr. Church the spy, both sent days earlier to nearby Springfield to serve as the general's escort through Worcester and into Cambridge.[41]

Washington's first stop was Ward's headquarters at nearby Hastings

House, where he met with James Warren and other leaders of the Provincial Congress, along with Massachusetts Gen. Artemas Ward and maybe Connecticut Brig. Gen. Israel Putnam. Both Ward and Putnam had received major generalships in the new Continental Army and may have received their formal commissions that evening.[42] Washington's entourage included his aide-de-camp, Maj. Thomas Mifflin, and his secretary, Lt. Col. and Dr. Joseph Reed.[43] The most notable character in Washington's entourage was Maj. Gen. Charles Lee, an experienced, retired British officer who had been on half-pay but was now Washington's third-in-command, behind Ward. Perhaps Lee was in a uniform similar to that of Washington.[44] Horatio Gates, a British Army veteran with experience in two wars, rounded out the newly arrived senior staff. Gates's commission came four days later, giving him the rank of brigadier general and the post of adjutant general.[45]

Washington's first act upon arriving at Hastings House was simply to remove his wet coat. He and his men then gathered by the fireplace to dry themselves. Ward entertained his new boss until a dinner banquet was served in the high fashion of upper-class gentlemen. Tradition tells that it included free-flowing wine, storytelling, and patriotic singing.[46] What was discussed that evening is not recorded, but after dining, Washington, fatigued from traveling and eager to get settled, called it a night. The next morning he would rise early to begin his new office.

Quarters had been arranged at the house of the president of Harvard College, often called the Benjamin Wadsworth House, which still stands. But after a few days, deciding the house too small to act as his headquarters, Washington asked the Provincial Congress to arrange for him to take over the abandoned Tory home known then as the Vassal House, later the Longfellow or Craigie House, which is also still standing. It was a few days more before Washington would move into the Vassal House and make it his headquarters.[47]

On the day after his arrival, July 3, 1775, Washington rose early, prepared himself, and then officially assumed command without ceremony. A tradition persists that he held a formal change-of-command ceremony underneath an elm at Cambridge Common, but that story, perpetuated almost a hundred years after, has since been debunked.[48] In truth, "near 2000…[Rhode Island] Troops musterd [in Roxbury and marched] toward Cambrid[ge] to waight on the new Generals But was Rejected By the General Who said they did not want to have time spent in waiting on them."[49] The change of command was a non-event. Washington "merely took over the orderly book of the previous Commander-in-Chief, General Artemas Ward, and started issuing orders. That was all."[50] His first general orders included an order for a true return of each regiment's manning so that he could get a sense of the size of his force and how they might be reorganized as a Continental Army.[51]

Thus, without fanfare, Washington was now commander of the forces in Cambridge. But this force was no true Army, and Washington would find it riddled with jealousies and unruliness. It was now his duty to temper and sculpt these men into a capable and disciplined fighting force, all while keeping the enemy at bay just a few hundred yards off. With a sigh perhaps, he mounted his horse, and together with Major Generals Ward and Lee, rode off to survey his ragtag force and the difficult task that lay before him.

———•———

His Excellency Gen. George Washington's first order of business was to inspect the American lines in Cambridge and hear firsthand accounts of the battle.[52] He would also observe the British-occupied battlefield, though only via a spyglass from across the river. Assisting him was his steady companion William "Billy" Lee, a black slave who today carried Washington's spyglass strapped across him in a leather case.[53]

Throughout the day, Washington heard accounts of those men who had served gallantly in the recent battle, men like Prescott, Stark, Knowlton, and Warren. General Ward also informed the new chief of those men who had performed dishonorably, men like Captain Callender of the Artillery, whose court-martial was presently underway. His Excellency also visited the wounded, likely escorted by Dr. Church himself, who was soon to be given charge of the Army hospitals. Inspecting the lines and the ragtag Army would consume the better part of Washington's first day as commander in chief.

Washington also found time to meet with the Provincial Congress in Watertown. They warmly received him and promised their utmost support, but also warned him about the want of discipline in the Army:

"We would not presume to prescribe to your Excellency, but supposing you would choose to be informed of the general Character of the Soldiers, who compose this Army[,] beg leave to represent, that the greatest part of them have not before seen Service. And altho' naturally brave and of good understanding, yet for want of Experience in military Life, have but little knowledge of divers things most essential to the preservation of Health and even of Life.

"The Youth in the Army are not possess'd of the absolute Necessity of Cleanliness in their Dress, and Lodging, continual Excercise, and strict Temperance to preserve them from Diseases frequently prevailing in Camps; especially among those who, from their Childhood, have been us'd to a laborious Life."[54]

In the humble and optimistic manner that was a hallmark of Washington's public life, he responded, "The Course of human Affairs forbids an Expectation, that Troops formd under such Circumstances, should at once posses the Order, Regularity & Discipline of Veterans— Whatever Deficiencies there may be, will I doubt not, soon be made up by the Activity & Zeal of the Officers".[55]

On the next day, July 4, 1775, exactly one year to the day before the Continental Congress would declare independence, Washington turned his attention to the reorganization of the troops and the enlistment of the diverse interim provincial armies into a new Continental Army. His general orders for the day formally announced the selection of the first major generals of this new Army. They were, in order of their seniority, Artemas Ward, Charles Lee, Philip Schuyler, and Israel Putnam.[56] Major General Schuyler, the only one not in Cambridge, was stationed outside the Tory stronghold of New York with a body of Connecticut troops to watch the movements of the powerful Royal Governor William Tryon.

This day's general orders continued with Washington's first attempt to break the age-old localism that continued to plague the Army. "The Continental Congress having now taken all the Troops of the several Colonies, which have been raised, or which may be hereafter raised, for the support and defence of the Liberties of America; into their Pay and Service: They are now the Troops of the United Provinces of North

America; and it is hoped that all Distinctions of Colonies will be laid aside; so that one and the same spirit may animate the whole, and the only Contest be, who shall render, on this great and trying occasion, the most essential service to the great and common cause in which we are all engaged."[57]

Part of Washington's challenge was that he effectively had three kinds of American forces to deal with. First was the militia, a short-term reserve force, comprised primarily of only nearby towns at this date, plus other volunteers. Second were the four provincial (or interim) armies, which the New England colonies had recently created as standing armies in response to the new war. And finally was the new Continental Army as authorized by the Continental Congress. It was Washington's job to replace the ragtag, cavalier militia and interim armies with a legitimate Continental Army that was to be disciplined and trained, its troops all bound by enlistments so they could not go back to their farms whenever they pleased or otherwise dissolve away. The reorganization of the men required the reorganization of their officers too. No longer would officers be elected from among their ranks and thus be forced to pander to their men in hopes of keeping their officership.

To this end, His Excellency instituted new, higher standards for officers, which included opportunities for both reward and punishment. Reward came in the form of commissions in the new Continental Army—more than a few provincial officers would *not* receive such. Punishment was to be meted out to those that did not exhibit good officership. As an example, a court-martial sentenced Captain Callender of the Artillery for his cowardly behavior at Bunker Hill, granting him the undesirable distinction of being the first officer to receive a disciplinary action under Washington. Accordingly, on July 7, Washington gave in his general orders of the day:

"It is with inexpressible Concern that the General upon his first Arrival in the army, should find an Officer sentenced by a General Court Martial to be cashier'd for Cowardice—A Crime of all others, the most infamous in a Soldier, the most injurious to an Army, and the last to be forgiven; inasmuch as it may, and often does happen, that the Cowardice of a single Officer may prove the Distruction of the whole Army: The General therefore (tho' with great Concern, and more especially, as the Transaction happened before he had the Command of the Troops) thinks himself obliged for the good of the service, to approve the Judgment of the Court Martial with respect to Capt. John Callender, who is hereby sentenced to be cashiered".[58]

The cashiering (ceremonial dismissal) of Callender was likely done at the head of paraded troops accompanied by beating drums, all watching as the former officer was marched away in disgrace.[59] Many more courts-martial would follow.

His Excellency, always fair and stoic in public, revealed in private his true feelings about the men to his distant cousin, Lund Washington, who managed his affairs at Mount Vernon. "The People of this Government [Massachusetts] have obtained a Character which they by no means deserved—their Officers generally speaking are the most indifferent kind of People I ever saw. I have already broke one Colo. and five Captain's for Cowardice, & for drawing more Pay & Provision's than they had Men in their Companies. there is two more Colos. now under arrest, & to be tried for the same Offences—in short they are by no means such Troops, in any respect, as you are led to believe of them from the Accts which are published, but I need not make myself Enemies among them, by this declaration, although it is consistent with truth. I daresay the Men would fight very well (if properly Officered) although they are an exceeding dirty & nasty people."[60]

One of the root causes of the indiscipline Washington found was the rhetoric of the Revolution itself. The rebellion was a concerted effort of social insubordination: the lower-class colonists were rejecting their social place amid the Empire, refusing subordination to and instead demanding equality with their better-educated and ostensibly altruistic English nobles. The crux of this argument was that all (white) men are created equal, which in turn influenced the breakdown of colonial social classes. But in opposition to this, the organization of any army, with its rigid rank system, is inherently a class system, the two macro classes being the enlisted men and the commissioned officers appointed over them, a system reinforced in that era by the fact that officers were generally drawn from the upper social classes, such as landowners.

Consequently, America's public insubordination to those considered socially superior (the Empire) enticed some in the American Army to also defy military superiors. It is somewhat ironic, then, that while Britain faced the disobedience of its American subjects and hoped to bring them back into submission, Washington faced the disobedience of his soldiers and likewise struggled to bring them under control. This was Washington's challenge—to temper that defiant enthusiasm, to ensure the spirit of rebellion did not spill over from the battlefield and into the discipline of his Continental Army.

The aristocratic colonist Benjamin Thompson thought that it was impossible to introduce a proper degree of subordination into the American Army because of "the great degree of equality as to birth, fortune and education that universally prevails among them. For men cannot bear to be commanded by others that are their superiors in nothing but in having had the good fortune to get a superior commission, for which perhaps they stood equally fair. And in addition to this, the officers and men are not only in general very nearly upon a par as to birth, fortune, etc., but in particular regiments are most commonly neighbours and acquaintances, and as such can with less patience submit to that degree of absolute submission and subordination which is necessary to form a well-disciplined corps."[61]

Years later, the Prussian Frederick von Steuben, commissioned a major general in the Continental Army to serve as inspector general, would lament to a European friend, "You say to your soldier, 'Do this,' and he doeth it; but I am obliged to say to mine, 'This is the reason why you ought to do that;' and then he does it."[62]

Throughout the war, this new, pervasive mind-set of equality would plague Washington in his efforts to establish discipline within the new Continental Army.

Washington's attempts to instill discipline during his first days in command were noted by Rev. William Emerson, a chaplain in the Army and grandfather to essayist Ralph Waldo Emerson. "There is great overturning in the camp, as to order and regularity. New lords new laws. The Generals Washington and Lee are upon the lines every day. New orders from his Excellency are read to the respective regiments every morning after prayers. The strictest government is taking place, and great distinction is made between officers and soldiers. Every one is made to know his place and keep in it, or be tied up and receive thirty or forty lashes according to his crime. Thousands are at work every day from four till eleven o'clock in the morning. It is surprising how much work has been done".[63] Washington began to exact discipline for profanity, gambling, drunkenness, and nonattendance to daily worship, and he ordered the officers to see to the neatness of their men and the camp, and to prevent their men wandering off or abusing private property.[64]

More often than not, the disciplinary orders Washington was forced to make were, to the modern soldier, obvious and should have gone without saying. On July 15, for instance, Washington's orders gave: "the General hears with astonishment, that not only Soldiers, but Officers unauthorized, are continually conversing with the Officers and Sentrys of the Enemy[.] any Officer, Non Commissioned Officer or Soldier, or any Person whatsoever, who is detected holding any Conversation, or carrying on any Correspondence with any of the Officers or Sentrys of the advanc'd posts of the enemy, will be immediately brought before a General Court Martial, and punished with the utmost severity. The General is alone to judge of the propriety of any intercourse with the enemy and no one else is to presume to interfere."[65]

Exacting this new discipline helped to add to Washington's esteem, not tarnish it. Wherever he went, he was warmly received. On July 20, Dr. James Thacher wrote, "I have been much gratified this day with a view of General Washington. His Excellency was on horseback, in company with several military gentlemen. It was not difficult to distinguish him from all others; his personal appearance is truly noble and majestic, being tall and well-proportioned. His dress is a blue coat with buff-colored facings, a rich epaulette on each shoulder, buff under dress, and an elegant small-sword; a black cockade in his hat."[66]

Abigail Adams wrote on July 16 to her husband, John, in Philadelphia, "I was struck with General Washington. You had prepaired me to entertain a favorable opinion of him, but I thought the one half was not told me. Dignity with ease, and complacency, the Gentleman and Soldier look agreably blended in him. Modesty marks every line and feture of his face". Then she added, "General Lee looks like a careless hardy Veteran".[67]

Gen. Charles Lee was so tall, thin, and oddly featured that a caricature of him has been said to be his best likeness. He was characterized as "a perfect original, a good scholar and soldier, and an odd genius; full of fire and passion, and but little good manners; a great sloven, wretchedly profane, and a great admirer of dogs", as well as critical of his superiors and egotistic. When he was serving in America as a British officer during the Seven Years' War, the Indians named him "Boiling Water" because of his restlessness. In the following peace, he served under the King of Poland. When troubles came to America, he returned, buying land in Virginia and taking up the Whig cause.

Though made third-in-command of the Continental Army, Lee secretly sought the position of commander in chief, and waited for an opportunity for Washington to fail. Lee eccentrically called his headquarters in Medford "Hobgoblin Hall", and his hospitality was said to be as careless as his dress—so much so that when Lee once asked Abigail Adams to dine with him, along with some other ladies present, she excused herself.[68]

Upon General Burgoyne's first arrival in Boston, Lee (not yet being a Continental) wrote his once fellow officer and still dear friend a long letter on the despotism of the English Government, advising Burgoyne not to be deceived by the Ministry as General Gage had been. When General Lee arrived later in Cambridge, Burgoyne wrote him a long letter in reply, arguing for the sovereignty of the government and recommending a meeting at Brown's House between the lines at Boston Neck to discuss the politics further and thereby "induce such explanation as might tend in their consequences to peace." Lee was open and transparent with these letters, and with Washington's consent, Lee petitioned the Massachusetts Congress for permission to hold the suggested meeting and asked that they appoint a witness. The Provincial Congress expressed concern, thinking it would arouse jealousy among the men, but appointed Elbridge Gerry as witness and left the decision up to Lee, "if you shall think proper to proceed in it". Lee thought better of it, knowing Burgoyne wanted to meet only to convince him that he was on the wrong side of the war. So Lee wrote again to Burgoyne, stating he would postpone the interview "until the subversion [or end] of the present tyrannical Ministry and system, which...must be in a few months, as...Great Britain cannot stand the contest." And with that, the two masters of pomp and flourish ended their lofty attempts at persuading the other.[69]

Washington also exerted much energy on supplying the Army. The need for blankets was particularly felt, because many soldiers had abandoned theirs on Bunker Hill. For those manning the trenches, a blanket was often the only protection from the rain, valued particularly for keeping one's precious gunpowder dry. Shortly after the late battle, General Ward had put in a requisition with the Provincial Congress for replacement blankets. But although the nearby towns were pressed, the stores could obtain neither clothing, nor socks, nor blankets. The effort now fell to Washington, and eventually such supplies came in from the other colonies.[70]

On July 9, Washington was relieved to receive a return that the Army had 308 barrels of gunpowder, a small but sufficient supply. Three weeks later, he learned that his subordinates had not troubled to actually count those barrels and had simply given him the number on hand in early June, much of which had been expended in the recent Battle of Bunker Hill. When Washington found he had in fact only 90 barrels, enough for only nine shots per man, he was dismayed at how critical his situation really was.[71] Gage had been wise to raid the Powder House a year prior, because the dire powder situation the Continentals now faced would prohibit them from making any real offensive.

All Washington could do was press the Continental Congress for powder from anywhere it could be had. Some trickled in from militia stores in surrounding towns, but nothing of consequence. The powder situation was so desperate that Washington was forced to prohibit the firing of guns even for shooting practice. In late July, he ordered, "Notwithstanding the strict and repeated Orders, that have been given against firing small arms, it is hourly practised, All Officers commanding Guards, posts and detachments, to be alert in apprehending all future Trangressors."[72] Other critical shortages, such as guns and cannon, would vex Washington for many months.

Before Washington's arrival, General Ward, noting that the lack of bayonets had in part led to the American defeat at Breed's Hill, asked the Provincial Congress for the next best thing: 1,500 spears, twelve feet in length with metal tips, either to be purchased or hired. By Washington's arrival, just 215 had been delivered, sent to General Thomas on the Roxbury lines. Washington responded by putting the men to work making their own spears of thirteen feet. The men were also employed in constructing various entrenching components, including fascines and gabions.[73]

Washington also sought ten thousand hunting shirts to serve as a crude uniform, not only to unify the men, but also because many had come with only the clothes on their backs, and these had since become ragged. Unfortunately, the Continental Congress did not take up this request, and though Washington would continue to press it, the Army was kept in its nondescript state. So His Excellency improvised, declaring that he, his generals, and the aides-de-camp were to be distinguished by light-blue, pink, and green ribbons, respectively, worn diagonally across the breast between the coat and waistcoat. The field officers could wear red or pink cockades in their hats, the captains yellow or buff, the subalterns green. Sergeants could wear an epaulette or strip of red cloth upon the right shoulder, the corporals one of green. It was not until 1776 that a uniform was adopted, modeled after Washington's own Virginia Blues design.[74]

Amid all of these changes, a welcome distraction came to the troops on July 18 and the days following, when there was read to the divisions of the Army "A Declaration by the Representatives of the United Colonies of North America, now met in General Congress at Philadelphia, setting forth the causes and necessity of their taking up arms." It was received with much enthusiasm and huzzahs, particularly on Prospect Hill, where General Putnam's men listened to both it and an "animated and pathetick address" by a minister, then huzzahed when a new flag standard lately sent was unfurled, bearing on one side the motto "An Appeal to Heaven" and on the other, the Latin phrase "*Qui transtulit sustinet*" (He who transplanted us sustains us). As one countryman summarized it, "And the Philistines on Bunker's Hill [the British] 'heard the shout of the Israelites [the Americans], and, being very fearful, paraded themselves in battle array.'"[75]

Meanwhile, Washington's mind was also burdened with the Army's very organization, made worse by frustrating delays in receiving the returns on the numbers of men actually at his disposal. On this he wrote, "could I have conceivd, that which ought, and in a regular Army would have been done in an hour, would employ eight days, I should have sent an Express off the 2d Morning after I arrivd with a genl acct of things. but expecting in the Morning to receive the Returns in the Evening, and in the Evening surely to find them in the Morning (& at last getting them full of Imperfections) I have been drilled on from day to day, till I am ashamed to look back at the time which has elapsed since my arrival here."[76]

Finally, on July 10, he had his return. The results were far worse than expected. While he had been told to expect some 18,000 to 20,000 troops when he arrived, he in fact had no more than 14,000 fit for duty.[77] In contrast, Washington believed Gage to have between 10,000 and 12,000 British troops in Boston.[78] In fact, once the remainder of the British Second Embarkation of troops landed on July 19, Gage would have just under 7,300 redcoats and artillerymen (outnumbering the trapped Bostonian civilians by about 1,000).[79]

On the same day, Washington wrote to John Hancock, President of the Continental Congress. "From the Number of Boys, Deserters, & Negroes which have been enlisted in the Troops of this Province [Massachusetts], I entertain some Doubts whether the Number required can be raised here; and all the General Officers agree that no Dependance can be put on the Militia for a Continuance in Camp, or Regularity and Discipline during the short Time they may stay. This unhappy & devoted Province has been so long in a State of Anarchy, & the Yoke of ministerial Oppression has been laid so heavily on it that great Allowances are to be made for Troops raised under such Circumstances. The Deficiency of Numbers, Discipline & Stores can only lead to this Conclusion, that their Spirit has exceeded their Strength. But at the same Time I would humbly submit to the Consideration of the Congress, the Propriety of making some farther Provision of Men from the other Colonies."[80] In other words, Washington urged Congress for more troops, but troops from the other colonies. He needed better-disciplined men than the "dirty & nasty people" of Massachusetts, which seemed to have none left to give.

Those forces fit for duty were also greatly reduced by another calamity: the dreaded "distemper", a severe dysentery that had started to sweep the camp by July. One observer wrote, "They have no woman in the camp to do washing for the men, and they in general not being used to doing things of this sort, and thinking it rather a disparagement to them, choose rather to let their linen, etc., rot upon their backs than to be at the trouble of cleaning 'em themselves. And to this nasty way of life, and to the change of their diet from meat, vegetables, etc., to living almost intirely upon flesh, must be attributed those putrid, malignant, and infectious disorders which broke out among them soon after their taking the field, and which have prevailed with unabating fury during the whole summer."[81]

The epidemic spread throughout eastern Massachusetts, and soon it was at Abigail Adams's doorstep in Braintree. She wrote to her husband, "The small-pox in the natural way was not more mortal than this distemper has proved in this and many neighboring towns. Eighteen have been buried since you left us, in Mr. Weld's parish. Four, three, and two funerals in a day, for many days." So too had the epidemic spread into Boston and the British encampments in Charlestown. It was not until late October that it began to decline.[82]

Amid all of these troubles, Washington also had to form the Continental Army out of the hodgepodge interim New England armies and militia units surrounding Boston, even as they maintained the Siege of Boston. Much was riding on Washington's unproven abilities as commander in chief.

To begin his arduous task of forming the Continental Army, Washington started at the top. The brigadier generalships were nominated and selected by the Continental Congress, but their appointed seniority was not well received. Petty politics in the form of age, experience, militia or provincial rank, social standing, political influence, and provincial allegiance all had to be dealt with, and Washington would spend weeks sorting it out. The Continental Congress selected Seth Pomeroy of Massachusetts as the senior-most brigadier, followed by Richard Montgomery of New York, David Wooster of Connecticut, William Heath of Massachusetts, Joseph Spencer of Connecticut, John Thomas of Massachusetts, John Sullivan of New Hampshire, and finally Nathanael Greene of Rhode Island. That William Heath was given higher seniority than his Massachusetts Army commander John Thomas made for an awkward situation, though the honorable and humble Thomas did not let it affect him or his duty. Even so, when it became clear that the elderly Pomeroy had no intention of serving, Washington, without waiting for congressional approval, gave the topmost slot to Thomas.[83]

Meanwhile, Joseph Spencer felt slighted by the fact that Israel Putnam had been given a major generalship over him, even though both he and David Wooster outranked Putnam in the Connecticut service. So without informing Washington, Spencer simply abandoned his men in Roxbury and returned to Connecticut. Spencer's officers and Connecticut Governor Jonathan Trumbull pleaded with Spencer to return, just as they pleaded with Washington to redress Spencer's grievances. But Washington replied to the governor, "in such a Cause I should hope every Post would be deemed honourable which gave a Man Opportunity to serve his Country." At length, the sensitive Spencer returned to Roxbury and accepted his appointed commission.[84]

But while Spencer at last showed humility, Connecticut Militia Maj. Gen. David Wooster would not, considering the lesser rank a slight. Instead, Wooster, serving with the Connecticut troops under Major General Schuyler outside New York, rejected his commission, politely returning it to John Hancock with the reply, "I have already a commission from the assembly of Connecticut." He decided to remain a militiaman.[85]

The reorganization of general officers meant too a reorganization of troops into three grand divisions of two brigades each, one division being posted outside Charlestown, one in Cambridge, and one in Roxbury. And with this came the commissioning of the colonels. Among the many selected, Bunker Hill veterans John Stark and William Prescott both received commissions.[86]

Other key positions remained unfilled for some time, including the commissary general and the paymaster general, the latter being critical to maintaining troop morale. Another critical position was given to Maj. Thomas Mifflin, Washington's aide-de-camp, who was made the first quartermaster general in August.[87] The artillery regiment was also a concern. Before Washington's arrival, Col. Richard Gridley had announced his desire to leave the service, though he had agreed to remain a few months more until a permanent replacement could be found.

The company and field grade officers presented a different sort of problem. The militia had always elected their own officers, and in response, the officers had to "make interest" with their men, not unlike politicians.[88] As such, officers were picked based on their popularity, not on their ability. Officially, in the creation of the interim New England armies, officers were no longer selected by the men, though most were just given the same position they had held in the militia units from which they were drawn.

In late August, Washington wrote, "As we have now nearly compleated our Lines of Defence, we have nothing more, in [my o]pinion, to fear from the Enemy provided we can keep our men to their duty and ma[ke] them watchful & vigilant; but it is among the most difficult tasks I ever undertook in my life to induce these people to believe that there is, or can be, danger till the Bayonet is pushed at their Breasts; not that it proceeds from any uncommon prowess, but rather from an unaccountable kind of stupidity in the lower class of these people, which believe me prevails but too generally among the Officers of the Massachusets part of the Army, who are ne[ar]ly of the same Kidney with the Privates; and adds not a little to my difficulties; as there is no such thing as getting Officers of this stamp to exert themselves in carrying orders into execution—to curry favour with the men (by whom they were chosen, & on whose Smiles possibly they may think they may again rely) seems to be one of the principal objects of their attention."[89]

To a newly appointed officer, uneasy about his lack of military experience, Washington gave this advice: "be strict in your discipline; that is, to require nothing unreasonable of your officers and men, but see that whatever is required be punctually complied with. Reward and punish every man according to his merit, without partiality or prejudice; hear his complaints; if well founded, redress them; if otherwise, discourage them, in order to prevent frivolous ones. Discourage vice in every shape, and impress upon the mind of every man, from the first to the lowest, the importance of the cause, and what it is they are contending for".[90]

The soldiers themselves were essentially adopted from the interim armies. That is, they were simply transferred to Washington's command, without any extension to their enlistment contracts or formal commitments to the new Continental service. This was a crucial problem because, while the exact date of their enlistment termination varied by province, Washington was at risk of watching the disciplined Army he was laboring to build dissolve around Christmastime. He could not presently dwell on this problem, however, though he knew by year's end, it would return to the forefront of his mind.[91]

In the meantime, though Washington was often distressed about the apparent lack of progress in establishing discipline and was forced to constantly repeat himself in each day's general orders, he was in fact slowly tempering the men into a legitimate army. And the best way in which he kept the men sharp was to allow them on occasion to engage the enemy.

Throughout the summer, sporadic skirmishes would be waged, though all were of little consequence. But on the night of August 26, Washington seized Plowed Hill, along the Mystic River northwest of Bunker Hill, "within point blank shot of the Enemy on Charles Town Neck". With some 1,200 men, the Americans entrenched it overnight in the style of the taking of Breed's Hill. By morning, the Americans had "an Intrenchment in such forwardness as to bid defiance to their [British] Cannon." Washington was further tightening his noose around the British. By nine o'clock that morning, the British on Bunker Hill opened up with "a heavy Cannonade which continued through the day without any injury to our work, and with the loss of four [American] Men only, two of which were killed through their own folly".[92]

This folly was the foolish Yankee sport of catching cannonballs. "Every ball, as soon as it fell, was surrounded with a great number of men, to see who would get it first, and the shells themselves had scarcely time to break before they would surround them to pick up the pieces of them".[93] This was at first encouraged with a reward, "in order to familiarize our raw soldiers to this exposure...but it produced also a very unfortunate result, for when the soldiers saw a ball roll sluggishly along, they would attempt to stop it, by which means several brave lads had their feet badly crushed, whereupon the order was withdrawn."[94]

Washington was happy with his new entrenchment on Plowed Hill, but lamented not having gunpowder enough to return the "salute" the British had given him. "The Insult of the Cannonade however we were obliged to submit to with impunity, not daring to make use of Artillery on Acct of the consumption of powder, except with one Nine pounder placed on a point, with which we silenced, & indeed sunk, one of their Floating Batteries."[95]

So Washington continued forming the Continental Army, strengthening and entrenching the American lines, establishing discipline, and urging for supplies such as gunpowder. The Continental Army did not spring up overnight in place of the loose confederation of diverse provincial armies. Rather, this laborious effort consumed Washington from his arrival until winter. Once winter arrived, new problems would present themselves, such as the lack of proper clothing, barracks, blankets, wood for fire and food, and the end of the soldiers' enlistments.

His Excellency had another problem too. The spy Dr. Benjamin Church was yet unsuspected by all, and so on July 27 was made director-general and chief physician of the newly formed Hospital Department (later the Medical Department), a position that would evolve to the modern position of surgeon general. His prescribed duties were "to furnish medicines, Bedding and all other necessaries, to pay for the same, superintend the whole, and make his report to, and receive orders from the commander in chief."[96] But under everyone's nose, he continued his espionage, passing information on Washington's progress to the British.

By August, shiploads of British soldiers unfit for duty were herded aboard vessels for transfer back to England. Mrs. Gage also finally embarked for home aboard the *Charming Nancy* transport, crowded together with hundreds of maimed and sickly soldiers. Her ship first arrived in Plymouth, England, and the description of its arrival paints the picture of what most of those ships must have been like: "one hundred and seventy sick and wounded soldiers and officers… A few of the men came on shore, when never hardly were seen such objects! some without legs, others without arms; and their cloaths hanging on them like a loose morning gown, so much were they fallen away by sickness and want of proper nourishment. There were moreover near sixty women and children on board; the widows and children of the men who were slain. Some of these too exhibited a most shocking spectacle; and even the vessel itself, though very large, was almost intolerable, from the stench".[97]

Sending away the sick and wounded helped General Gage manage the limited rations he had in Boston. However, with the siege still underway, the British remained in want of fresh provisions. They had plenty of salt pork, flour, butter, dry peas, and some dry rice, but little else.[98] Bostonian John Andrews explained, "We have now and then a carcase [carcass] offer'd for sale in the market, which formerly we would not have pick'd up in the street; but bad as it is, it readily sells… Was it not for a triffle of salt provissions that we have, 'twould be impossible for us to live. Pork and beans one day, and beans and pork another, and fish when we can catch it."[99] Ens. Martin Hunter noted an officer's horse was "stolen, killed, and sold in the market for beef."[100] Deacon Timothy Newell "was invited by two gentlemen to dine upon *rats*."[101] And scurvy was spreading due to the lack of fresh vegetables.[102] The only things the British had plenty of were powder and weapons.

The problem was not that England had failed to send Gage fresh provisions, but that the American siege was very effective. New England whaleboats had formed into a sort of loose "navy", and they were now capturing many of the transports intended for the British in Boston. While some "whaleboats" were actually whaling sloops, most were quite small, "remarkable for rowing quick, they are made light & sharp at both ends, some of them carry [only] 8 or 10 men, including the rowers… no man of War's boat can come up with them in smooth water. they drag them on shore & can carry them on their shoulders."[103]

The affairs of Grape and Noddle's Islands had proven that the Royal Navy did not possess the supremacy of the harbor that had been supposed. As one historian later noted, "Quite as [General] Gage, on land, learned that the provincial farmer was dangerous as a bush fighter and even behind breastworks, so [Admiral] Graves was to learn that the fisherman and whaler, while helpless against his great ships, could do harm to his smaller boats, his communications, and his prestige."[104]

The Americans collected whaleboats in large numbers, equipped themselves with small arms, stripped the harbor islands of hay and livestock, and in so doing, deprived the British Army. Washington hoped that these endeavors would so increase the British "Desertions,

Discouragement, and a Dissatisfaction with the Service, besides weakening their strength… and, if continued, might afford the fairest Hope of Success, without a further Effusion of human Blood."[105] Despite the best efforts of the whaleboaters, however, British provisions did continue to trickle in. On August 15, a fleet of transports returned from a secret mission, bringing from nearby islands "about two thousand sheep, one hundred and ten oxen, butter, eggs, &c., &c."[106]

As the whaleboaters gained confidence, a few naval skirmishes ensued, though most were of little importance. One involved the burning of a key navigational lighthouse near Nantasket Roads at the entrance of Boston Harbor. The British promptly sent carpenters to rebuild it, supported by a guard of thirty marines. On the night of July 30, the carpenters, who had smuggled rum with them against orders, got many of the marines drunk. At dawn the next day, American whaleboaters landed and attacked them, the marines being mostly useless and still a little drunk. The two sides exchanged shots, and a few marines died, while the remaining British were taken aboard the whaleboats as prisoners. The whaleboaters then burned everything there they could, before escaping just as British warships bore down on their position.[107]

The whaleboat "navy" soon grew to near three hundred small vessels.[108] As other such naval skirmishes ensued, the weak and timid Admiral Graves began to fear for his warships. While it is true that his battered warships were not as prepared for war as they should have been, many in need of desperate repair given the decline in naval funding during peacetime, responsibility still sat squarely on his shoulders. Yet Graves refused to take the initiative, despite his unquestioned authority to do so, claiming his only explicit orders were to support General Gage and the Army.

While Graves was more than eager to raze Charlestown during the Battle of Bunker Hill and, in fact, had desired to do so ever since the Expedition to Concord, he only preached such hostility when the responsibility of the outcome was not his to bear. Now, when the situation called for his independent decision-making, he hesitated and fumbled, allowing the American whaleboats to gain dominance in New England waters.[109] Burgoyne deservedly summarized Graves's inaction in a scathing and flamboyant letter typical of his prose:

"It may be asked in England, 'What is the Admiral doing?'

"I wish I were able to answer that question satisfactorily; but I can only say what he is *not* doing.

"That he is *not* supplying us with sheep and oxen, the dinners of the best of us bear meagre testimony; the state of our hospitals bears a more melancholy one.

"He is *not* defending his own flocks and herds, for the enemy have repeatedly plundered his own islands.

"He is *not* defending the other islands in the harbour, for the enemy in force landed from a great number of boats, and burned the lighthouse at noonday (having first killed and taken the party of marines which was posted there) almost under the guns of two or three men-of-war.

"He is *not* employing his ships to keep up communication and intelligence with the King's servants and friends at the different parts of the continent, for I do not believe General Gage has received a letter from any correspondent out of Boston these six weeks.

"He is intent upon greater objects, you will think,—supporting in the great points the dignity of the British flag,—and where a number of boats have been built for the enemy; privateers fitted out; prizes carried in; the King's armed vessels sunk; the crews made prisoners, the officers killed,—he is doubtless enforcing instant restitution and reparation by the voice of his cannon and laying the towns in ashes that refuse his terms? Alas! he is not."[110]

The lack of fresh provisions, along with the casualties from Bunker Hill and the ongoing siege, conspired to lower morale in Boston. The bleak outlook for the British campaign further exacerbated troop morale. Gage showed the same timidity as Graves, skulking away from a ripe opportunity to take the unclaimed Dorchester Peninsula south of Boston, despite his newly arrived troops. To be fair, Boston was no longer tenable, and Gage's major generals agreed. By mid-August, both Burgoyne and Clinton were giving Gage their proposals and justifications for altogether abandoning Boston by the coming winter. Their plan, which Burgoyne claimed was of unanimous consent amongst the major generals, was to move the entire campaign to the Loyalist bastion of New York, citing its obvious advantages of being an island and thus easily defended by the Royal Navy, that it was friendly territory, and

more to the point, that such a relocation would end the besiegement. Gage considered their plan, but was not yet willing to remove his army from Boston.[111]

While Gage may have been inclined to maintain the status quo, the home government had a much different opinion. Late in July, London received the news of the late and epic battle. In response, Prime Minister Lord North warned the King, "the War is now grown to such a height, that it must be treated as a foreign war, & that every expedient which would be used in the latter case should be applied in the former."[112]

In Parliament, the Whig minority would use news of the battle to decry the aggression taken by Lord North's Ministry, citing the massive British casualties suffered for little military gain. But Lord North's Tory majority would use the incident as proof that it was not Massachusetts alone, but all of New England that was in open rebellion, and that they would soon be aided by the colonies to the south. Furthermore, while the Skirmishes of Lexington and Concord could be dismissed as tensions pushed to the breaking point, instigated by Gage's march through the countryside, Bunker Hill was indisputably instigated by the provincials and undertaken—the Tory majority was convinced—in hopes of destroying Boston.

Such action proved that the colonies were not merely defending their "liberties", but had become an aggressive mob that must be pacified. The English gentleman Horace Walpole, who spent more time entertaining and relaxing than considering politics, wrote that the Americans "do not pique themselves upon modern good breeding, but level only at the officers, of whom they have slain a vast number. We are a little disappointed, indeed, at their fighting at all, which was not in our calculation."[113] Walpole's sentiment was probably indicative of most English gentry. Until Bunker Hill, England had expected that the Americans would eventually cower as the British ratcheted up the pressure. That they had not meant it was now time for more aggressive action.

King George was particularly displeased, though unwavering. "I am clear as to one point," he wrote Lord North, "that we must persist and not be dismayed by any difficulties that may arise on either Side of the Atlantick; I know I am doing my Duty and therefore can never wish to

retract". Though even now there was still the chance for reconciliation, the British government opted to dig in its heels.[114]

To this end, Lord Dartmouth inquired of the King about sending to Boston additional forces. However, as Britain was not yet officially in a state of war, there were few reserves available at home. As the King later relayed to Lord North, "I told him very fairly that I feared except Highlanders and Marines none could be prepared till Spring which agreed with his own ideas; that preparations ought to be made and if possible some 50. Gun Ships sent as a reinforcement the Admiral thinking them the best qualified for that Service."[115] Only by ramping up recruiting efforts could England have men enough to send to America by spring.

Neither Parliament nor the King's Ministry would accept that they had some blame for the current crisis. If not them, then who was to blame? In another discussion, Lord Dartmouth and King George considered Gage's conduct and the viability of retaining him in his post as commander in chief of North America. As the King explained later to Lord North, "I have desired Lord Dartmouth to acquaint Lt. G. Gage that as he thinks nothing further can be done this Campaign in the Province of Massachusets Bay that he is desired instantly to come over that he may explain the various wants for carrying on the next Campaign; I think on Second thoughts You had better not say any thing but leave the Subject of reward untouched untill his arrival. Howe to Command during the General's absence the Troops now at Boston[,] Carleton being fully employed in forming the Canadians."[116]

However, Gage's recall was not for a mere consultation. Rather, Dartmouth and the King had decided to let Gage down easy, as they no longer required his services. Lord Dartmouth went to work writing the letter that would recall Gage and leave Howe in charge, under the pretext that nothing more could be done that year. But the real reason for Gage's recall lay perhaps in the last unfinished statement of the King's letter to Lord North: "I do think the Admiral's removal as necessary if what is reported is founded as the mild General [unfinished]".[117]

Gage would not know of this decision for several weeks to come, while Graves's own recall would arrive soon after.

As for Maj. Gen. Guy Carleton in Canada, though he was next in the

line of succession before Howe, he was busy with other affairs.[118] The backcountry had been astir ever since the Taking of Fort Ticonderoga, and though Carleton did not yet know it, the war effort of the United Colonies was about to come knocking on his very doorstep.

———•———

With Benedict Arnold and Ethan Allen having taken both Fort Ticonderoga and Crown Point on May 10 and a British sloop on May 18, the joint forces of Vermont, Connecticut, and Massachusetts now controlled the entire Lake Champlain region of upper New York. With the questions of command left unfinished, Ethan Allen would stay at Fort Ticonderoga, acting as the nominal commander of its new American garrison, while Colonel Arnold would keep to his captured sloop *Enterprise*.[119]

Connecticut and Massachusetts had meant only to take the chain of forts along the Champlain and to go no farther. The legality of their actions was defensible because the forts resided in colonial lands, namely New York, but the decision was nevertheless a bold one. Yet soon the Continental Congress hesitated and even considered returning the forts to the British, though only after stripping them of their warlike stores. At this, the New England provincial governments as well as the city of Albany immediately protested. They cited the strategic value of the forts, noting if the British were indeed allowed to reclaim them and strengthen their meager walls, they could effectively cut New England off from the rest of the continent.

Such a plan was exactly what General Carleton hoped to do once reinforced. Arnold and Allen joined the chorus of protests by writing letters to the Continental Congress, marking one of the few times when these two men were in agreement. On May 31, Congress finally conceded, resolving to retain the forts.[120]

Despite the Continental Congress's hesitation and concerns, with Lake Champlain secured, Arnold turned his attention northward toward Canada. He sent messengers to Montreal to ascertain the strength and disposition of the large British garrison there under General Carleton, collected what information he could, and formed a plan for an

expedition into Canada, which he forwarded to both the Massachusetts and Continental Congresses.

All the while, the garrison at Fort Ticonderoga sent letters of complaint against Arnold to the congresses of both Connecticut and Massachusetts. The latter finally decided to send a committee to Lake Champlain to inquire about Arnold's conduct and to place him under the command of Connecticut Col. Benjamin Hinman. When Arnold received the committee, he was indignant, stating that he had served the terms of his commission honorably. However, Arnold's unbridled ego would not permit him to be "second in command to any person whomsoever". Rather than serve under Hinman, a man of the same rank, he delivered the Massachusetts committee a list of grievances along with his resignation. Out of spite, his last act was to disband the two or three hundred troops he had recruited. However, the committee instantly reenlisted them under Massachusetts Col. James Easton.[121]

To add to Arnold's torment, he received news that his wife had died on June 19. Fortunately, his sister Hannah had taken over as caregiver for Arnold's three sons, aged seven, six, and three.[122]

Unemployed and devastated, Arnold hurried back to Cambridge, arriving probably in mid-July, where he met General Washington for the first time. Arnold would spend much of the next month arguing with the Massachusetts government about his conduct. But away in Philadelphia, the Continental Congress was discussing a new military operation that would give Arnold an independent command and help raise him to the title of hero.

Before adjourning in August, the Continental Congress began to consider whether it was wise to make a preemptive attack against the British in Canada, much as Benedict Arnold and Ethan Allen had proposed since the Taking of Ticonderoga.

The American colonies feared the Canadian threat for many reasons. For one, many Canadian inhabitants were of French descent, the traditional enemy of both Britain and British America. Prior to 1763, lands east of the Mississippi River but west of the British Colonies were known as New France, which the French ceded to the British in the Treaty of Paris that ended the Seven Years' War (the French and Indian War). The northernmost part of this territory was a nebulous region called Canada, which Britain proclaimed in 1763 as the new Province of Quebec (a name that for a time became synonymous with Canada).

One of the major political reasons to fear Canada was the Quebec Act, which Parliament did not intend as a Coercive Act, though the Americans deemed it as such. The Quebec Act had four primary elements. The first more clearly defined Quebec's boundaries, extending Canada southwest deep into the Ohio Valley, contrary to the claims of Connecticut, Pennsylvania, and Virginia. The second formed a Governor's Council, but no sister assembly, which was placed under direct control of the Crown, contrary to the free assemblies of the other colonies. The third allowed for Catholic worship, a necessary provision to appease the formerly French inhabitants, but contrary to the beliefs of the intolerant Protestants in the lower British Colonies. The fourth set up English law for criminal matters, but allowed for the "custom of Paris" for all civil affairs. The result for the Canadians was a benevolent and liberal government, one providing religious tolerance and recognition of their French heritage. The Quebec Act was far in advance of its time.[123]

For the rebellious Thirteen Colonies, their greatest concern was that a colony to the north stood opposed to their political interests and beliefs. The new territorial claims on the frontier were of particular concern, not merely for the land itself, but for the resources it could provide and its access to the lucrative Indian trade that could now be denied the Lower Colonies. The Americans were also, despite all of their enlightened political thought, especially appalled at the recognition of Catholicism.

Even so, the First Continental Congress had, in late 1774, written to their northern neighbors asking for cooperation and promising religious tolerance, an appeal that was met with warmth from the Canadians. But Congress's duplicity was later discovered when it also wrote to Parliament, lambasting the Quebec Act and, in particular, the establishment on American soil of a "religion that has deluged your island in blood, and dispersed impiety, bigotry, persecution, murder, and rebellion through every part of the world." Fortunately for the Lower Colonies, this incident was quickly forgotten.[124]

More important to the Continental Congress as it debated a preemptive campaign was that Canada presented a strengthening British military threat that could be unleashed at any time. Because the Habeas Corpus Act did not apply there, nor had it any elected legislature, Canada was effectively under military rule, with Maj. Gen. Guy Carleton as its military governor. Additionally, the British had great influence over the backcountry Indians, and without careful conciliatory measures to appease the natives, the Americans might be subjected to frontier raids and butchery, as they had seen firsthand in the war of over a decade earlier. Also, Canada had been the key to victory in the last war against the French and Indians, and many believed it would again be such. Finally, because Canada was a conquered province of the French, it was widely expected that the Canadians too yearned for and would seek the liberties the Thirteen Colonies sought, and would so become allies and join in any campaign against the British in Canada.

Thus, with the growing war around Boston, the Continental Congress determined to take a preemptive strike at Canada. Their hope was either to conquer the sparse British posts in Quebec, thereby eliminating it as a threat and freeing its citizens, or to keep Carleton occupied and penned up, thereby preventing him from cutting off New England from the continent. The unknown variable was the Indians, and to that end, messengers were sent abroad to seek their neutrality, which was done even before the war had formally begun.

Back in May, Col. Jonathan Brewer of Connecticut had proposed to Congress a plan to attack Canada: by going up the Kennebec River through the wilderness of Maine and then via the St. Lawrence River to Quebec City and Montreal. That proposal had come too early for Congress to take such bold measures, and on June 1, Congress resolved to prohibit any colony from sending troops into Canada. However, with the Battle of Bunker Hill recently waged, and the war now official, the time was now ripe.[125]

On June 27, Congress detached Maj. Gen. Philip Schuyler northward from New York to put the Lake Champlain region under command of the Continental Army. They also ordered that, if he "finds it practicable, and that it will not be disagreeable to the Canadians," to immediately take the Fort St. Johns (or Saint-Jean, at modern Saint-Jean-sur-Richelieu) and also Montreal.[126]

Schuyler would indeed find it practicable. His expedition into Canada marked the first truly aggressive, warlike act the Americans undertook. Until this point, after the Skirmishes of Lexington and Concord, the Americans could have argued they were acting in self-defense. Even after fortifying Breed's Hill, they could have argued that it was a necessary defensive move, given their credible intelligence of an imminent attack by Gage. No such argument could now be made. Schuyler would clearly

PORTRAIT OF MAJ. GEN. PHILIP SCHUYLER (C. 1886) BY JACOB HART
LAZARUS (1822–1891), AFTER JOHN TRUMBULL (1756–1843). COURTESY
OF THE INDEPENDENCE NATIONAL HISTORICAL PARK.

be on the offensive, and the Americans were now to be unequivocally in an open war.

The forty-one-year-old Schuyler (pronounced *Sky-ler*), third major general behind Artemas Ward and Charles Lee, was, despite his lack of military experience, given command because of his high social standing among New York's elite. He would serve as the head of this semi-independent army later known as the Northern Department.[127]

At Schuyler's side was brilliant and aggressive Brig. Gen. Richard Montgomery, age thirty-eight. An Irishman and veteran of the French and Indian Wars, Montgomery had fought at Louisbourg, Fort

PORTRAIT OF BRIG. GEN. RICHARD MONTGOMERY (c. 1784–1786) BY
CHARLES WILLSON PEALE (1741–1827), POSSIBLY FROM AN ENGRAVING.
COURTESY OF THE INDEPENDENCE NATIONAL HISTORICAL PARK.

Ticonderoga, and Montreal. After the last war, he had languished in the British Army as a captain while lesser officers with greater social influence obtained their majority promotions over him. Disgruntled, he left the Army, vowed never to take up arms again, and immigrated to New York to become a gentleman farmer. Despite his vow, Montgomery then married into the prominent Livingston family, and the social connections such a marriage entailed swept him into the cause of his surrogate country. He served for a time in the New York Provincial Congress, and later, when the brigadier generalship was thrust upon him, he reluctantly accepted.[128]

Unpreparedness caused weeks of delay, and Schuyler did not arrive at Fort Ticonderoga until July 18. He left in his place in New York the able Connecticut Militia Maj. Gen. David Wooster, charged with both watching the movements of the formidable Royal Governor William Tryon and confirming that the newest expected troops from Britain, part of the Second Embarkation, had indeed rerouted north to Boston.

When Schuyler at last reached Fort Ticonderoga, he was appalled at the lack of defenses and vigilance. "A Centinel on being informed I was in the boat quitted his post to go and awake the guard, consisting of three men, in which he had no success. I walked up and came to another, a serjeant's Guard. Here the centinel challenged, but suffered me to come up to him, the whole guard, like the first, in the soundest sleep. With a penknife only I could have cut off both guards, and then have set fire to the blockhouse, destroyed the stores, and starved the people here." Assessing the rest of the camp, he was dismayed at the meager numbers of soldiers waiting for him there.

Schuyler also learned through intelligence that General Carleton had strengthened Fort St. Johns, was building two armed schooners there, and had perhaps four hundred regulars.[129] Finally, jealousies among the Green Mountain Boys militia had led to their ousting their commander Col. Ethan Allen and replacing him with Seth Warner, whom they elected a lieutenant colonel. While Warner would prove a better subordinate, Allen petitioned Schuyler to remain with the Army. Schuyler wrote, "I always dreaded his impatience of subordination; and it was not until after a solemn promise, made me in the presence of several officers, that he would demean himself properly, that I would permit him to attend the Army". Allen would serve only as a volunteer, often given scouting and recruiting missions to keep him far away from the action.[130]

In preparation for operations on Lake Champlain, Schuyler began an industrious effort to build ten large batteaux and two row galleys of sixty foot in length, together capable of handling some three hundred men. Unfortunately, while the galleys had capacity for five 12-pounder cannon each, Schuyler could only mount one per vessel, for while he had plenty of cannon, he had no carriages. Once completed, the galleys would be christened *Schuyler* and *Hancock*. These, combined with the two vessels Benedict Arnold had captured, the sloop *Enterprise* and the schooner *Liberty*, plus his ten old batteaux and the ten freshly built, comprised the first American Navy sanctioned by the Continental Congress.[131]

On August 17, Schuyler traveled to Albany to make peace with an Iroquois (Six Nations) Indian delegation. Schuyler was ultimately successful in having them commit to neutrality, but his treaty negotiations would take months. The Iroquois, an Indian confederacy of six tribes, had great influence, but they did not represent every tribe in the area. Some other Indians and even a few wayward ones from the Six Nations would fight with the British throughout the campaign.[132]

Meanwhile, Brigadier General Montgomery learned that the two British schooners under construction at Fort St. Johns to the north would soon be ready. And so, unafraid of responsibility and not waiting for Schuyler in Albany, Montgomery took the initiative to move north against the fort with nearly one thousand men, though he sent word to Schuyler begging him to follow. The team of Schuyler and Montgomery was a perfect one, each balancing the other, and Schuyler had implicit trust in Montgomery's ability as the latter set off.[133]

By the end of August, Schuyler was back in Ticonderoga, ordering some eight hundred additional troops and some artillery northward to meet with Montgomery's meager force gathered south of St. Johns. Then Schuyler embarked northward as well, ahead of the reinforcements. On September 4, at Isla la Motte on the north end of Lake Champlain, Schuyler took command of the force. Together with Montgomery, they advanced forward to Île aux Noix (Nut Island) at the head of the Richelieu River, twelve miles south of Fort St. Johns.

On September 6, Schuyler's navy landed his thousand men along the western bank of the Richelieu, south of the fort. Unfortunately, Schuyler, who had long suffered from rheumatism and bilious fever, was too ill and so stayed at the landing site, leaving Montgomery to lead what was to be a reconnaissance mission to probe British defenses. The Americans marched through wetlands and thick woods, but before they got far, a small hundred-man Indian unit led by British officers, waiting in ambush, spotted them.

A short firefight ensued. Several Americans were felled dead during the first onslaught. The woods were thick and the smoke was even thicker, with each side vying for a better firing position. Scattered gunshots rang through the dark, untamed forest. After a half hour, the Indians had had enough and retreated to Fort St. Johns. Each side suffered perhaps eight killed or mortally wounded, with just as many injured. Montgomery, knowing he had lost the element of surprise, and still uncertain about the enemy strength at the fort, decided to fall back and await nightfall.

That night, back at the landing zone, the Americans gained critical intelligence from a credible informant, the name of whom Schuyler kept secret because the local man was fearful of retribution. His news was bleak. Shortly after Arnold's raid in May, the fort had been strengthened, and her small garrison was now ready. The Indian ambuscade had confirmed that much. Furthermore, despite Schuyler's having just days earlier sent Ethan Allen northward to curry favor with the Canadians, the informant doubted the Canadians would offer assistance, maintaining they instead preferred to wait and see what happened. Like this informant, the Canadians feared retribution were they to choose the losing side.

Finally, the informant told Schuyler that one of the two British schooners, well protected by the fort, was nearly ready for action: "the Vessel was launched & had one Mast in and the Other ready to raise…she would be ready to sail in three or four Days and is to carry 16 Guns". (The other schooner was still finishing construction.) This, combined with the fact that the Americans had but two small cannon with them, made their prospects of taking the fort (or even preventing the completion of the vessels) dubious. So Schuyler's war council opted to regroup at Île aux Noix to the south and await the coming reinforcements and additional artillery Schuyler had earlier ordered forward.[134]

As Montgomery's men fortified the river island Île aux Noix, the British at Fort St. Johns completed their first schooner, christening her *Royal Savage*. Montgomery knew if *Royal Savage* could get into Lake Champlain to the south, it would have free rein to harass the Americans at Ticonderoga. The easiest way to control such a swift beast was to keep her caged in. So Montgomery had his men install a log boom across the Richelieu River to obstruct her escape.

But as the American reinforcements began arriving, Montgomery grew anxious to meet the *Royal Savage* on his terms and so made plans to attack Fort St. Johns once more. He was further encouraged when James Livingston, a Canadian merchant sympathetic to the cause and based in nearby Chambly north of St. Johns, informed him that "a considerable party of Canadians" would help in the next assault. While Montgomery made his preparations, General Schuyler again opted to stay behind, owing to his ailing condition.[135]

Montgomery's plan was to advance with his force of now some 1,700 men plus five light cannon and three mortars. His hodgepodge flotilla of two row galleys, a sloop, a schooner, and a dozen or more batteaux was to land his force near the fort, then lie in the Richelieu River and prevent the escape of the *Royal Savage*. On the evening of September 10, the task force was put into motion. The night was pitch-black, and upon landing, the divisions lost their way, two of them running into one another, causing alarm. A few British grapeshot increased the panic, and an entrenched British unit opened fire, completing the terror.

The green colonial troops, scared and ill experienced, fell back in retreat with hardly a fight, despite the best efforts of Montgomery to prevent them from doing so. The Americans spent the night at the same landing zone as before. On the next day, Montgomery was hopeful for a third attempt, but when word came that the *Royal Savage* was on its way, the troops demanded to retreat. In disgust, Montgomery conceded, and they retreated again to Île aux Noix. Montgomery would later push for courts-martial, but few of the soldiers would testify against one another.

At Île aux Noix, with no sign of the *Royal Savage*, the troops began to realize their cowardice and felt guilty. Montgomery encouraged their downtrodden mood. "I have endeavored to make them ashamed of themselves, and hope that this won't happen again." He thought privately that their behavior could be "palliated by saying they were young troops" and their rough edges would "wear off with a little practice". As he reported to Schuyler, the men were "unable to bear the reproach of their late unbecoming behavior."[136]

As a few more reinforcements arrived, a most fortunate affair helped raise the morale of the troops. A small British gunboat, reconnoitering the waterways, discovered the American base at Île aux Noix and opened fire. The colonial gunners responded in kind with one of their cannon shot blasting squarely into her, sinking her and, they supposed, all her crew.[137] The action was short, but it marked the first victory of the Canadian Campaign and so energized the men.

Montgomery was anxious to capitalize on the newfound enthusiasm and so made preparations for yet another assault on Fort St. Johns. But his plans were delayed several days when a thunderstorm reached Île aux Noix and turned it into a cesspool of disease. Many had been growing sick with the poor sanitary conditions there, but the change in weather exacerbated the problems.

Schuyler's own illness grew worse too. On September 16, he gave formal command of the force over to Montgomery and then set back for Fort Ticonderoga. Though not on the front lines, Schuyler would toil long hours fighting to acquire supplies and troops from a half-invested Congress to send forward to Montgomery. Schuyler's tireless work made Montgomery's expedition possible, and without Schuyler's diligence, the Canadian Expedition would have failed even before it had begun.[138]

On the same day as Schuyler's departure, September 16, the weather cleared, and Montgomery initiated his plan for yet another attempt on Fort St. Johns. This time, he was determined to be successful.

———— • ————

Once back at Fort Ticonderoga, General Schuyler pressed forward all newly arriving Continentals to Île aux Noix. Soon Montgomery's forces there swelled to nearly 2,000, including Seth Warner with some 170 Green Mountain Boys and Col. Timothy Bedel with 100 New Hampshire Rangers. However, some reinforcements found one reason or another to beg for furloughs. These, plus the disease spreading in the unsanitary camp at Île aux Noix, served to deplete the American force. So with only 1,400, Montgomery set forth on his third attempt to assail Fort St. Johns. His hodgepodge navy landed them near the fort on September 17. But the redcoats were ready this time.

British General Carleton had just two regiments in all of Canada: the 7th Royal Fusiliers, with an effective strength of 376 men, and the 26th (Cameronians) Regiment of Foot, with 263 soldiers. During the first two failed assaults against Fort St. Johns, Major Preston of the 26th had but 200 men drawn from both regiments plus about 100 Indians and some artillerymen. But Carleton capitalized on the brief respite since Montgomery's last attempt and reinforced the British post with the bulk of his remaining regulars, plus some 100 Canadian volunteers and a company of Highlanders, 70 strong, comprised of volunteers that had emigrated from Scotland. In all, Preston now had some 725 men. To guard the supply train and protect the escape route, should a retreat become necessary, Chambly, farther downriver (downriver being north here), was also posted with 83 troops from the 7th.[139] Meanwhile, Carleton attempted to recruit Canadians as militia, but found the finicky locals unwilling to pick sides in the crisis. "The Canadians are not now what they were at the Conquest," wrote Carleton, referring to the British victory in the French and Indian War, "they had been long trained to Obedience and inured to War...left to themselves for so many Years, can it be believed, they would immediately, and with Pleasure, submit to a Subordination".[140]

Ironically, it was the well-connected Maj. Charles Preston of the 26th, new commander of Fort St. Johns, who had some years earlier purchased a majority commission over then British Captain Montgomery. Now fate had brought them together again—as opposing commanders.

That night, Montgomery's Americans bivouacked near their landing zone south of St. Johns and experienced uneasy sleep under sporadic fire from the fort. The next morning, September 18, as they prepared for assault, they heard distant musketry, which caused a stir throughout the men.

Montgomery had decided he would lead this third assault personally, so he quickly selected 500 men, and together they crept through the woods to the opposite side of the fort, toward the musketry. Soon they found it. It was his own scouting party under Maj. John Brown—sent out a few days prior and now engaged in a running fight! Brown's about 134 men had ambushed a convoy of eight British supply wagons making their way to St. Johns, when some 200 British troops under Capt. John Strong had emerged from the fort to give pursuit. The Yankees hesitated, but Montgomery's leadership and charisma rallied them forward, forcing the British to give up the wagons and fall back to the safety of their fort.[141]

As Montgomery and his men pursued, all at once, Fort St. Johns came alive, bombarding their position. Montgomery drove his men to cover, and despite the onslaught, they began digging entrenchments, mounting their artillery, and placing men at various posts to guard the western approaches to the fort. To the south, his little navy guarded the Richelieu River to prevent the escape of the *Royal Savage*, which was helpless in the confined waters of the river and so kept close to the fort for protection. So began the Siege of Fort St. Johns.

As the Americans entrenched all around, the British maintained a heavy bombardment, to which the newly built American batteries feebly replied. This bombardment continued incessantly for days as the Americans continued to fortify their lines. On September 22, as Montgomery climbed an entrenchment to inspect his works, just as he turned, a cannon shot whizzed by, slicing off the end of his coat. The men were astounded and their respect for Montgomery redoubled, for they saw that "this did not seem to hurt or frighten him".[142]

The excitement of those first days of the siege soon gave way to monotony, day in and day out, with useless daily cannonades in both directions. The provincials lacked sufficient artillery to truly threaten the fort, while the British outnumbered their guns two to one. Even so, each was unable to make a dent in the other, and few casualties mounted on either side. Days turned into weeks, and the two little armies were at a stalemate. With winter fast approaching, the Americans lost valuable time.

To break the stalemate, Preston hoped for additional reinforcements, while Montgomery waited for more artillery to arrive. In the meantime, the American general sent parties out to recruit sympathetic Canadians. Col. Ethan Allen, who retained his title mostly as a courtesy, along with

Lt. Col. Seth Warner and Maj. John Brown, led three such efforts. On September 21, Warner set off with two hundred men to take the weak outposts of La Prairie and Longueuil, situated opposite Montreal, where the Americans could then guard against British reinforcements sent by land to Fort St. Johns.[143]

Colonel Allen went one step further. Overzealous as always, he led about thirty "English Americans" (probably New Englanders) and eighty recruited Canadians to the St. Lawrence riverbank opposite weakly defended Montreal, just west of the mouth of the Richelieu. Allen had received encouraging intelligence that the Montreal Canadians would rise up to support his small force should he attack, thereby allowing him to quickly take the city. He later claimed he had also expected to meet Major Brown and his small force there, though no evidence exists to show Brown ever agreed to such.[144]

On the night of September 24, Allen's men crossed the St. Lawrence to the island that is Montreal, but had so few canoes that it took three trips. By daylight, there was no sign of Brown, and the signal Allen expected from a friendly in the town never came. Instead, the weak garrison of perhaps forty British regulars swarmed from the town, augmented by both Canadian and English townspeople, plus a few Indians, near five hundred total. Indeed, the Canadians rose up as Allen expected, but against him, not for him. With so few canoes to escape Montreal's island, Allen was trapped.

Sometimes called the Battle of Longue-Pointe, a small and short-lived skirmish ensued. Though Allen fought until the end, it was a losing battle, with many of his own Canadians melting away at the first sign of trouble, leaving just two dozen men to stave off a swarm of five hundred. One Indian nearly killed Allen before it was over, with Allen and the others taken prisoner. He would remain imprisoned for nearly three years, spending most of that in England before being returned in a prisoner exchange in 1778.[145] Allen had briefly excited the Canadians, but "at a stroke he had lost his prestige, shown the weakness of American pretentions, made the Canadians again hesitate, [and] turned the Indians toward the British." Washington, Schuyler, and Montgomery would all blame him.[146]

Meanwhile, the Siege of Fort St. Johns continued. Montgomery did what he could, but what he required were more men and artillery. Some would come from Fort Ticonderoga, but the greatest support to his siege would come from another direction altogether, for General Washington had just sent forth a second expedition into Canada.

In late August, just before the first attempt on Fort St. Johns, several delegates of the Continental Congress were back in Cambridge, taking advantage of a congressional recess.[147] There they met with Washington to discuss the plan for Canada. Together they made the decision—based perhaps on the proposal of Arnold or remembered from Brewer's proposal months earlier—to send a second Canadian expedition northward. The mission was to meet with General Schuyler's force and cooperate with his expedition or otherwise serve as a diversion to allow Schuyler's success.

To lead this second expedition, Washington commissioned Benedict Arnold as colonel in the Continental Army and, on September 5, put under his command about 1,100 men, consisting of eleven New England musket companies and three newly arrived rifle companies, one from Virginia and two from Pennsylvania. Among his men were Capt. Henry Dearborn and Christian Febiger, both of whom had valiantly served at Bunker Hill. Arnold's personal aide was volunteer Capt. Aaron Burr, who would become infamous almost thirty years later in a duel with Alexander Hamilton. And leading the Virginia riflemen was Capt. Daniel Morgan, soon to be famous.[148]

Rifles were rare and hard to come by in the colonies, and while they were popular in the backwoods and wilderness areas, they were so unheard of around Boston that John Adams had to explain them, with some excitement, to his dear wife Abigail. "The Continent is really in earnest in defending the Country. They have voted Ten Companies of Rifle Men to be sent from Pensylvania, Maryland and Virginia, to join the Army before Boston. These are an excellent Species of Light Infantry. They use a peculiar Kind of Musket call'd a Rifle—it has circular or [word worn away: helical? rifled?] Grooves within the Barrell, and carries a Ball, with great Exactness to great Distances. They are the most accurate Marksmen in the World."[149]

Despite an accuracy of more than 200 yards, rifles took longer to reload because the shot had to be forcefully rammed in for a snug fit. Furthermore, these were weapons for hunting, not war, and so had no bayonet mount, leaving the owner defenseless in close combat. These deficiencies meant riflemen had to be escorted by musketmen. While riflemen would serve throughout the war in greater and greater capacities, the musket would remain the workhorse of the Continental Army.[150]

The accuracy of the rifle also gave its wielder an air of cockiness. The riflemen's egos were further intensified by their exclusion from fatigue or work details (such as entrenching), a policy thought necessary

Engraved portrait of Benedict Arnold (c. 1777) by Henry Bryan Hall (1808–1884). Anne S. K. Brown Military Collection, Brown University Library.

to curry the favor and loyalty of these otherwise independent-minded backwoodsmen. True, on the occasional skirmishes along the Boston lines, riflemen came in handy, accurately picking off handfuls of British troops from afar. But their privileged place in the Army quickly made them insolent troublemakers, wholly unsuited for the disciplined army Washington was forging.

The riflemen's belligerence came to a climax on September 10. On Prospect Hill, northeast of central Cambridge, the adjutant for Col. William Thompson's Pennsylvania Rifle Battalion confined a sergeant for neglect of duty. Twice before, riflemen of their battalion had been arrested for similar small crimes, and twice they had been broken out by their rebellious comrades. Now, again, the men began to murmur and threaten to break their sergeant out. The adjutant responded by arresting the key mutineer.

All seemed calm as the regiment's officers sat down for dinner together, but they were soon interrupted by huzzahing and whooping throughout the camp. They rushed outside to discover that the two arrested men had been broken out of their holding shack and were now surrounded by dozens of soldiers haughtily celebrating the accomplishment. Colonel Thompson and several of his officers acted decisively, seizing the original insubordinate sergeant and ordering an armed guard to escort him straightaway to the Main Guard in Cambridge. The sergeant was taken into custody without opposition from the mob, and he and his escort promptly made their way toward Cambridge, probably by wagon or horse.

The crisis seemed averted, and the officers turned to go back inside and eat their dinners. Twenty minutes later, thirty-two men of Capt. James Ross's company gathered, loaded rifles in hand, and swore they would release the arrested man or lose their lives trying. Before they could be stopped, they ran toward Cambridge in pursuit of their comrade. Colonel Thompson again acted decisively, sending an express to Washington's headquarters.

This was the Army's first mutiny, and Washington, not to bullied, was determined to teach these men the consequences of such insubordination. His Excellency ordered the Main Guard surrounded by some five hundred troops, bayonets fixed, guns loaded. He also issued orders to Col. Daniel Hitchcock's regiment and several other companies of Brig. Gen. Nathanael Greene's brigade, all near Prospect Hill, to cut off the mutineers and subdue them with force if necessary. Washington and General Lee, joining Greene, then rode out toward Prospect Hill to intercept the mutineers personally.

Seeing more than a regiment under arms and ready to stop them, the mutineers' zeal quickly waned. They took cover behind some trees and reconsidered their plan. One of the generals, probably Washington, ordered the mutineers to ground their weapons, which they did immediately. As if to restore some honor to the wayward rifle battalion, Capt. George Nagle's company of the same Pennsylvania Rifle Battalion then surrounded the mutineers. They arrested the six principal actors, binding the two ringleaders, and then marched all six off to the Main Guard to join their companion. The rest were sent back to their camp for discipline there.

So ended the first mutiny, and so ended all indulgences for the rifle battalions. The following morning, September 11, Washington's daily general orders stated: "Col. Thompson's Battalion of Rifle-men posted upon Prospect-hill, to take their share of all duty of Guard and Fatigue, with the Brigade they encamp with. A General Court Martial to sit as soon as possible to try the men of that Regiment, who are now prisoners in the main Guard, and at Prospect-hill, and accused of '*mutiny*'. The Riflemen posted at Roxbury, and towards Letchmore's point, are to do duty with the brigade they are posted with." No longer would the riflemen lounge around the camp while the rest of the Army did the hard labor and guard duty.[151]

The court-martial met the next day, September 12, and sentenced all thirty-two mutineers plus the original insubordinate sergeant to a slap on the wrist: a dock in pay of a mere twenty shillings each (to "be paid to Dr Church for the use of the General hospital"), except for one John Leamon, who was additionally sentenced to six days in prison. One embarrassed fellow rifleman called it "too small a punishment for so base a crime and mitigated no doubt on account of their having come so far to serve the cause and its being the first crime. The men are returned to their camp, seem exceedingly sorry for their misbehavior and promise amendment. This will, I hope, awaken the attention of our officers to their duty (for to their remissness I charge our whole disgrace)…this much I can say for them [the soldiers that subdued the mutineers?]: that upon every alarm it was impossible for men to behave with more readiness or attend better to their duty".[152]

Days before this incident, Washington had assigned two of Colonel Thompson's rifle companies to Benedict Arnold's expedition into Canada. It is unknown whether Captain Ross's mutinous company was intended to be among them, but if so, it was stripped of that honor. Instead, the two companies of Captains William Hendricks and Matthew Smith were given the responsibility of restoring glory to the battalion and so assigned to Arnold's great expedition. Doubtless, some in the camp were eager to see fewer riflemen around after this incident.[153]

Arnold's officers made their final preparations for the expedition, including issuing new coats and linen frocks to each man.[154] On September 14, Washington gave Colonel Arnold explicit instructions and ordered him to set forth on his expedition. Washington knew too well of Arnold's ego, so one of his instructions was: "In Case of an Union with General Schuyler, or if he should be in Canada upon your Arrival there, you are by no means to consider yourself as upon a Seperate & independant Command but are to put yourself under him & follow his Directions. Upon this Occasion & all others I recommend most earnestly to avoid all Contention about Rank—In such a Cause every Post is honourable in which a Man can serve his Country." Washington also issued a declaration of friendship in both French and English to be given to the inhabitants of Canada.[155]

With these orders and a copy of the map and diary of the route taken some fifteen years earlier by the British engineer John Montresor, Arnold departed the same day, September 14. Their mission was no secret, however, and General Gage's spies immediately notified the besieged governor of the expedition, and he in turn sent word by sea to General Carleton in Canada.[156]

Arnold marched his men the several days' journey from Cambridge to Newburyport. On September 18, the men boarded a mixed fleet of eleven sloops and schooners, and the next morning set sail northward for the Kennebec River in Maine. On September 20, the flotilla stopped at Gardiner along the Kennebec to disembark about one hundred of the men before continuing the remaining six miles upriver to Fort Western (opposite modern Augusta).

The men at Gardiner gathered one hundred new pine batteaux waiting there, built within just two weeks, and rowed them the same day up to Fort Western to rejoin their comrades. These batteaux were small boats with a capacity of just five to seven people. Since most of the expedition was upriver and against the current, the batteaux's primary purpose was as waterborne wagons for each company's provisions, tents, and camp equipage.

The expeditionary force tarried at Fort Western for several days more, preparing for the rigorous journey ahead, gathering supplies, and loading their batteaux. Finally, on September 25, the first divisions departed up the Kennebec, beginning their long toil by batteaux and on foot through an untamed wilderness.[157]

Washington's choice of Benedict Arnold as expeditionary commander would prove to be a wise choice indeed, for this was Arnold the brave, long before any thought of treachery or treason would enter his heart. Meanwhile, the first real traitor of the war, Dr. Benjamin Church Jr., was about to make a fatal mistake.

By September 1775, various regimental surgeons, complaining of not receiving necessary medical supplies at the unit level, accused Dr. Church of hoarding such supplies for the camp hospitals. Many of the accusations seem to have stemmed from politics, the regiments still not yet accustomed to the hierarchy of the Continental Army. Nevertheless, Washington felt obliged to begin a series of inquiries into the matter, the results of which, one at a time, exonerated Church from any wrongdoing.

Meanwhile, as these inquiries continued, the spy Dr. Church struggled to find ways to relay his intelligence into the hands of the British in Boston. Even in the early days of the siege, the not-so-good doctor had found ways to do so. But once Washington took command, it became almost impossible.[158]

So Church attempted ever more clandestine means at passing his intelligence. "Three attempts I have made without success," Church later wrote, never describing the first two. "In effecting the last, the man was discovered in attempting his escape; but fortunately my letter was sewed in this waistband of his breeches. He was confined a few days, during which time you may guess my feelings; but a little art and a little cash settled the matter."[159] Nervous as he was, Church used both cunning and bribery to secure the prisoner's breeches and the treacherous letter sewn inside. He also likely secured the courier's release, to ensure the man would not rat him out.

Church then learned of a circuitous method to pass intelligence into Boston. By way of the Royal Navy that still controlled Newport, Rhode Island, one could deliver a letter (or one's self) to Capt. James Wallace of the HMS *Rose*, to be sent around to Boston on the next vessel. To this end, the doctor employed a woman "he kept", a mistress perhaps, though others suggest she was a prostitute, calling her "a Girl of Pleasure".[160]

Mindful of his safety, Church wrote his latest correspondence using a substitution cipher of Greek, Latin, and entirely unique symbols. Addressed to a Major Cane in Boston, apparently one of General Gage's two aides-de-camp, it was less military-related and more a plea that the British seek an accommodation for peace, warning that the Continental Army grew stronger each day. Church much exaggerated this last point by overstating the colonial strength in both men and supplies, particularly gunpowder. He also wrote about the American plans to attack Canada, his recent trip to Philadelphia, and the mood of the Continental Congress: "they were united, determined in opposition, and appeared assured of success." He concluded the letter with an arrangement on how to send the reply and, in finishing, wrote as if he knew the future: "Make use of every precaution, or I perish." He left the letter unsigned.[161] Church then gave the sealed letter to his mistress with orders to deliver it to Captain Wallace of the *Rose*, otherwise to Royal Collector Charles Dudley or Loyalist merchant George Rome.

The woman, whose name remains uncertain, was incompetent with her charge. With the letter hidden in her stocking, she made her way to Rhode Island and met with Godfrey Wenwood (or Wainwood), a local baker and her former lover, seeking his help in gaining an introduction to Captain Wallace or one of the other Loyalists.[162] Wenwood was no friend of the Crown, but instead an astute Whig. Upon learning the letter was intended for Boston, Wenwood warned the woman she was in imminent danger if she attempted to deliver the secret dispatch to any of the men named and so convinced her to entrust the letter to him.

Once he had the letter, Wenwood kept it quiet for a time before he consulted his friend, a local schoolmaster named Adam Maxwell, and together they decided to open it. Seeing it in cipher and so unable to read it, they knew they had acted in the best interest of the cause by not forwarding it.

By late September, Church somehow became aware that the letter had not yet reached Boston. Fearful of being revealed, he pressed his mistress, who wrote Wenwood to inquire about its status. This alerted Wenwood and Maxwell that the author of the cipher letter was still in contact with Boston, so they took it to Henry Ward, secretary of the rebel government in Providence, who had them forward it to fellow Rhode Islander General Greene in Cambridge, who promptly brought it to the attention of Washington.

Washington immediately ordered the woman arrested. Though she refused to reveal any information for some time, she finally confessed that the author was Church, and in exchange, Washington kept her identity a secret. Washington must have felt both anguish and fury over such a high Son of Liberty being in correspondence with the enemy. He gave immediate orders to have Church arrested and all his papers confiscated. A theory proposes that some confidant of Church was privy to the situation and disposed of any incriminating evidence before the doctor's papers were seized. Whether true or not, in the end, Washington would have only the cipher letter as his sole proof against the doctor.[163]

Two different teams soon translated the cipher letter: Col. Elisha Porter of the Massachusetts Militia (assisted by Elbridge Gerry) and Rev. Samuel West.[164] The two translations agreed, and Church, who never denied being the author, verified the translations to be accurate.

Church argued that his plan "was to influence the Enemy to propose immediate Terms of Accommodation", hoping that by convincing the British that the Americans were stronger than they were, the British might be induced to offer peace. Furthermore, the letter was not addressed to Gage but to Major Cane, who effectively served as an intermediary. Church argued that the letter was in fact intended for his "brother" (really his brother-in-law) John Fleeming *via* Cane. He admitted his indiscretion in acting in secret, but begged for compassion, citing that his intention was in fact in support of the cause.[165]

Washington would not hear Church's pleas. On October 3, a court-martial convened to consider the matter. Church would steadfastly claim his ultimate goal was peace, and that he abhorred the struggle between the mother country and her colonies. The following day, the court unanimously agreed that he had carried on a criminal correspondence with the enemy. The newly written Articles of War had not contemplated treason, so Church was sentenced to confinement until the Continental Congress should determine his punishment.[166]

Church was also tried by the new House of Representatives of Massachusetts, which had replaced the ad hoc Provincial Congress on July 19 and so became a quasi-legitimate body, since it was authorized under the Massachusetts Charter.[167] Church astutely resigned his seat in the House, but argued his case himself, without a lawyer, explaining his cipher letter paragraph by paragraph. But sentiment was strong against him. The former Provincial Congress had long known their secrets were being compromised, with Gage learning of their resolutions almost as quickly as the resolutions were made. There were also the suspicions about Church's visit to Boston and to Gage shortly after the Expedition to Concord.

Most detrimental to Church's case was the idea that so high an officer in the Whig movement could be in collusion with the enemy, a burden too great for the public to bear. The House resolved to "utterly expel" him, denied him "any of that special Privilege and Protection which every worthy and honest Member of this Body is by the Law and Constitution entitled to," and declared that if he should be released from military custody, he would be immediately apprehended by the colony and tried and punished by the laws of the Massachusetts.[168]

Still, there were some who held sympathy for Dr. Church. At the time of his court-martial, the only positive evidence against him was the cipher letter, which was grossly inaccurate in its Continental Army dispositions and lacked detail of any critical military value. It seemed to some he was being treated as a scapegoat and given an unfair military trial without a lawyer. As General Greene wrote to his wife, "With art and ingenuity surpassing whatever you saw he veiled the villany of his conduct, and by implication transformed vice into virtue. But notwithstanding all his art and address, and his faculty of making the worse appear the better reason, he could not establish his innocence either satisfactory to the public in general or the General Court in particular." Note Greene wrote that Church could not *establish* his innocence, suggesting the sentiment of the day was indeed a witch hunt—Church was guilty until proven innocent.

John Adams may have suspended his own judgment, but he was no less appalled. As he wrote to General Lee, "At the Story of the Surgeon General, I stand astonished. A Man of Genius, of Learning, of Family, of Character, a Writer of Liberty Songs and good ones too, a Speaker of Liberty orations, a Member of the Boston Committee of Correspondence, a Member of the Massachusetts Congress, an Agent for that Congress to the Continental Congress, a Member of the House, a Director General of the Hospital and Surgeon General—Good God! What shall We say of human Nature? What shall We say of American Patriots?"[169]

Yet with so little evidence against him, historians long doubted whether Church was indeed America's first notable spy. It was not until more than a century later, upon the acquisition of Gage's papers, that his letters of intelligence were discovered, giving absolute certainty that Church was indeed in the service of the British Army.

Despite Church's defense that he only desired to bring about peace, his true primary motive was money. Paul Revere wrote years later, "I fell in company with a Gentleman who studied with Church… He said, He did not doubt that He was in the Interest of the British; and it was He who informed Gen. Gage[.] That he knew for Certain, that a Short time before the Battle of Lexington, (for He then lived with Him, and took Care of his Business and Books) He had no money by him, and was much drove for money; that all at once, He had several Hundred New British Guineas; and that He thought at the time, where they came from."[170]

Shortly after Church's trials, another traitor revealed himself. He was Benjamin Thompson, a Loyalist later known as Count Rumford. Thompson was a man of science and invention, said to be second in

North American only to Benjamin Franklin. Suspicion surrounding Thompson began in 1774 when he secretly helped two Army deserters return to Boston, deserters much coveted by local militia companies as drillmasters. Though suspicion would follow him ever more and he was subjected to formal inquiries as a result, there was never any proof of treason, leading many for generations since to believe he was ultimately turned traitor by a relentless witch hunt. But like Church, he too would be confirmed guilty once Gage's papers became public more than a century later.

Knowing his treason to be secret, Thompson feigned being a Whig for some time, perhaps so he might sell off his lucrative property unabated, for the Massachusetts government had placed a moratorium on the sale of all Loyalist property. He may have also been one of Church's go-betweens, relaying or even writing one or more of Church's early letters of intelligence to Gage. Thompson's espionage culminated in a letter, written May 6, 1775, on the surface appearing to be a short message of no consequence. The remaining space of the large parchment was filled with a second letter written in invisible ink, addressed to "Sir" (presumably Gage), and included intelligence on American troop levels, possible colonial plans of attack, the political sentiments of their leaders, the status of certain British prisoners, and finally, Thompson's reassurance that he remained loyal to the Crown.

Thompson might have continued his espionage indefinitely, but with Church's capture, he was finally inspired to seek the safety of Boston. On October 13, Thompson left Cambridge for Newport, Rhode Island and, via arrangement with Captain Wallace of the HMS *Rose*, was safely transported by the HMS *Scarborough* into Boston following the same path that had been intended for Church's cipher letter. He would later make his way to England, receive a commission in the British Army, and serve against his birth country later in the war.[171]

As for Church, after his trial, he was held in a series of jails, the first in Connecticut. When his health began to fail him, some family, presumably his father and brothers, petitioned the Continental Congress to allow him fresh air and exercise, which was granted. Accordingly, he was returned to Massachusetts, where he might have some liberty though under close guard.

James Warren, President of the Massachusetts House, was astounded at this resolution. To John Adams he wrote, "Is not your resolve relative to him somewhat Extraordinary? I fear the People will kill him if at large. The Night before last he went to Lodge at Waltham[,] was saved by the interposition of the selectmen but by Jumping out of A Chamber Window and flying. His Life is of no great Consequence, but such A Step [of setting him free] has a tendency to lessen the Confidence of the People in the doings of the Congress."[172]

Upon hearing of Church's wretched state, General Howe in 1777 arranged for a prisoner exchange, intending to send Church to England. One story gives that Church was actually aboard a vessel when a mob rose up to prevent his departure, so Church was recommitted to jail with even his supervised freedom now stripped away. All the while, Church's wife had pleaded compassion, though ultimately she too gave up, sailing with their four children for England, where she received a comfortable British pension.

With pressure mounting to punish Church, but with his health fading and his value to the war effort now irrelevant, the new Massachusetts government voted on January 12, 1778, "to remove Doct. Benj. Church on Board the Sloop *Welcome*, Cap. James Smithwick master[,] bound for the Island of Martineco [Martinique]". That vessel set sail shortly thereafter, but the ship and all her crew were lost at sea. Dr. Benjamin Church Jr. was never heard from again.[173]

Just as Church's career was about to be ended by the discovery of his cipher letter, so too was Gage's career about to end, with the arrival of a different sort of letter.

On September 26, 1775, the HMS *Scarborough* arrived from London with a packet from the home government.[174] It included the orders from Lord Dartmouth, written in the most polite language possible, recalling Gage to England: "…the King is led to conclude that you have little Expectation of effecting any thing further this Campaign, and had therefore commanded me to signify to you His Majesty's pleasure that you do, as soon as conveniently may be after you receive this Letter, return to England, in order to give His Majesty exact Information of every thing".[175] Further instructions were included for Howe to temporarily act as commander in chief upon Gage's absence and Major General Carleton to act independently as commander in chief in Canada, thus allowing Gage to retain his permanent title even while in England.[176] Despite the flowery language, however, Gage was quite aware that he would not be returning to America.

When Admiral Graves learned of his rival's recall, he must have been joyous. Unbeknownst to him, the Admiralty Secretary Sir Philip Stephens had just five days earlier penned a letter to Graves demanding his own recall. The British Admiralty next sent a letter to Molyneux Shuldham, rear admiral of the white, to take command of the 50-gun HMS *Chatham* at Portsmouth and sail with the fifth-rate HMS *Orpheus* to Boston. Shuldham would set sail in late October, and Graves would not learn of this news for almost three months. For now, ignorant of his own sealed fate, he was free to gloat as Gage prepared to depart for England.[177]

Gage was too much the gentleman to complain of his fate, but he did write a private letter to Lord Barrington, placing the fault of the American situation squarely on the shoulders of the home government.[178] As news of his recall spread, Gage received several addresses of sincere gratitude for his good governorship from Loyalists in Boston, the countryside, and his mandamus councilors. In a written response, Gage lamented the state of affairs and gave a welcomed assurance that during his absence his successors would afford them every favor and protection.[179]

Gage would spend many days preparing for his departure. He wrote to Graves, assuring his political rival, "I will not distress you by an Application for a Ship of War to carry me and have therefore Ordered a transport to be got into readiness".[180] Gage then organized and passed necessary documents to his successor, Howe, and gave him what instructions he thought wise. He also conveyed to his civilian deputy Lt. Gov. Thomas Oliver that civil authority was now passed unto him.[181] Finally, Gage packed his effects and made ready for a public change-of-command ceremony, whereby he would formally pass his command to Howe. Accordingly, on October 10, Gage received his last salute as commander in chief, and Howe received his first. The next evening, without fanfare, Gage departed Boston aboard the transport *Pallas*, along with his secretary Thomas Flucker.

Aboard ship, he wrote perhaps his last official letter to Lord Dartmouth, declaring his honest opinions on the matter of America. "I am convinced that the Promoters of this Rebellion have no real Desire of Peace, unless they have a Carte-Blanche. Their whole Conduct has been one Scene of Fallacy, Duplicity and Dissimulation, by which they have duped many well inclined People."[182] Gage was despondent about the situation in America, but as his letter shows, he still failed to understand the political revolution underway. He arrived in London on November 14 with as little ceremony as his Boston departure.

The next day, Gage met with King George III. While the King received him graciously, many of the politicians and councilors were eager for a scapegoat and ready to condemn him. Writing to General Clinton, a London-based artillery captain observed, "Gage poor wretch is scarcely thought of, he is below contempt—no party thinks of him and he breaths a private man unthought of—".[183] Former British officer and now American Maj. Gen. Charles Lee haughtily wrote, "damn him! let him alone to the hell of his own conscience and infamy which must inevitably attend him!" This was a surprising declaration by Lee, who had served beside Gage in the ill-fated Battle of Monongahela during the French and Indian War. In fact, in 1774, Lee had written to Gage, "I have had a real affection for very few men—but that these few, I have lov'd with warmth zeal ardor. You, sir, [are] amongst these few".[184]

Not all were so vituperative, however. Governor Wentworth of New Hampshire called Gage "a good and wise man...surrounded with difficulties." The minority party of pro-American Whigs in Parliament also came to his defense. Before the House of Commons, Charles James Fox ridiculed the government for prating about firmness in 1774 but sending only meager military forces to enforce their will. He severely rebuked the cabinet for trying to shift blame from their own shoulders to General Gage.[185]

Indeed, Fox was right. Gage had been an able administrator, and though he lacked the military aggression Parliament may have wanted, he was precisely what the situation had called for. It is to his credit that the Revolutionary War was delayed for as long as it was, and under the command of another type of general, America might have declared independence far earlier than 1776.

Nevertheless, the hardliners in Parliament were blinded by their rage and eager to divert the blame to someone besides themselves. Gage soon fell into obscurity, and by April 18, 1776, Lord George Germain, newly chosen Secretary of the Colonies, stripped Gage of his titular status as commander in chief, making Howe the official commander in America. Gage would never again serve in a position of importance.

Yet Gage found some solace at home in England. He wrote Clinton that he had at least one advantage over his fellow general officer: he was surrounded by his children, while Clinton was exiled from his. So too was he reunited with his wife, Margaret Kemble Gage, and the two apparently remained happily together to the end of their days.[186]

Meanwhile, Major General Howe, who had stayed in Charlestown since the Battle of Bunker Hill, removed himself to Boston, probably taking up residence in Province House. He sent Clinton to take command in Charlestown in his stead.[187]

Howe had no more expectation of accomplishing much in what was left of 1775 than Gage had had. Just after the Battle of Bunker Hill, Howe had written, "We can do no more this Campaign than endeavor to preserve the Town of Boston…tho' should anything offer in our favor, I should hope we may not let pass the Opportunity."[188] Howe would have no such opportunity, and the British would remain in a defensive posture for the rest of the year.

And so the batons were passed, first on the American side, from the de facto leader Dr. Joseph Warren to the de jure commander Gen. George Washington, and then on the British side, from the peacetime Lt. Gen. Thomas Gage to the wartime Maj. Gen. William Howe. Warren and Gage had at first sought a peaceful political resolution to those trying times. Now Washington and Howe would seek a military resolution to the question of colonial liberty.

Still, that colonial desire for liberty was not a desire for independence. However, with both sides further entrenching and preparing for battle, with two formal armies now arrayed against one another, and with Parliament becoming more staunchly in favor of rule by military force, even the moderates in the Continental Congress were slowly coming to believe that the only means to break the impasse was a declaration of independence. And so it can perhaps be argued that the last glimmer of hope for a peaceful resolution sailed away with Lt. Gen. Thomas Gage on the transport *Pallas*.

In Canada, meanwhile, the war was just beginning...

PART 2

Crucible
(October 1775 to Spring 1776)

CHAPTER 5

STRUGGLES OF AUTUMN

As the Siege of Boston stretched endlessly onward, so too did the Siege of Fort St. Johns. When a few additional forces trickled in at St. Johns, particularly Capt. John Lamb's artillery company on September 21, Brig. Gen. Richard Montgomery devised a new strategy. He was fully aware that his cannon were essentially useless in their present position across the river east of the fort, so he decided to construct a new gun battery close in on the fort's northwest side. Only from there could the Americans bombard the fort with any effect. Such a close position was of course a dangerous one, for the enemy cannon would surely assail his defenseless men as they built their new entrenchment. However, if the Americans were to ever take the fort, Montgomery thought it an acceptable risk. Others thought differently.

Maj. John Brown alerted the general that his men would desert before taking such an untenable position. Flustered, Montgomery called a war council comprising of his field officers and company commanders. They too echoed Brown's warning. The zeal of the continent's spirit to resist the Ministry's authority inspired the independent-minded soldiers to question all authority over them, leading them to rebuff even military orders they did not agree with or understand.

Montgomery privately debated resignation but thought better of it. "Were I not afraid the example would be too generally followed, and that the publick service might suffer," the veteran general pondered, "I would not stay an hour [more] at the head of troops whose operations I cannot direct." So Montgomery conceded to his officers and withdrew his plan—against his better judgment. Instead, he turned his attention southward, hoping daily for the arrival of still more troops and artillery.[1]

In early October, the Continental Congress, in reply to Major General Schuyler's pleas for more men, sent Connecticut Maj. Gen. David Wooster's provincial regiment from outside New York City to join the Canadian Campaign. They promptly headed northward, leaving behind a small detachment to watch New York. But when Wooster's regiment finally arrived in Albany, they found orders from Schuyler (at Ticonderoga) to remain there, given the lack of supplies at the fort. Then, as the weather grew colder and men became sick, and with the Siege of Fort St. Johns dragging on, Schuyler finally decided to send Wooster up to join Montgomery. When the first of his Connecticut troops arrived at Ticonderoga en route, they exhibited typical militia independence and *chose* to go no farther until Wooster himself arrived.

Appalled, Schuyler wrote to Congress, "Do not choose to move! Strange language in an Army; but the irresistible force of necessity obliges me to put up with it." When Wooster did arrive, Schuyler assured him that, though he might be a major general in the Connecticut service, he was by no means senior to Brigadier General Montgomery of the Continentals. Wooster had in fact been on the list to be commissioned a brigadier in the Continentals, with seniority less than Montgomery, but had politely rejected it and sent his commission back to John Hancock, though Congress still considered it open. In response to Schuyler, Wooster "thought hard of being superseded," but he knew his men would never serve under Montgomery without him, so he willingly submitted to Montgomery's command for the public good and soon after accepted his Continental commission as a brigadier general. Once Wooster had collected all of his 335 men at Fort Ticonderoga, they set sail northward to join Montgomery at Fort St. Johns.[2]

As for the sick, many began to stream from Montgomery's siege lines back to Fort Ticonderoga, though some merely feigned sickness. Most had known what hardships they would face when they first signed up as "rangers" or "pioneers", having experienced similar conditions during the French and Indian War. Yet the soldiers had good reason to want for home, given their lack of supplies, tents, and clothing, particularly with the coming winter. Their spirits also were gloomy as the siege stretched on into ever colder weather. Many would die of exposure, diarrhea, dysentery, and pneumonia. Few would serve with full bellies; most would be suspicious of treachery; and all would remember their warm beds at home while they shivered on the many cold, snowy nights to come. But the great majority, despite their grumblings, would persevere, giving the siege a prospect.

In the halfhearted but continuous bombardments between the two opposing forces at St. Johns, the Americans scored a victory on October 14. The small colonial flotilla had kept *Royal Savage* bottled up in the river, unmaneuverable since the beginning of the siege, forcing the British to keep her close to the fort for her protection. Finally, the American cannon did some work on her, blasting holes below her waterline. Montgomery wrote to Schuyler, "They have not been very anxious to save her, else they might easily have protracted her fate." She sank in place, settling to the shallow riverbed but resting still mostly above the waterline. Her cannon might still have been in a usable position, but it would have taken a major salvage operation for the British to get her out again, something quite impossible while the American cannon kept watch. As to the second schooner nearby, the British never quite completed her, so she posed no threat.[3]

While the stalemate continued, James Livingston, the sympathetic Canadian of nearby Chambly, finally came through by recruiting a force of three hundred Canadians. He suggested to Montgomery that they attack the small British post at Chambly, which guarded the northern river approach to Fort St. Johns, thereby cutting off the last means of resupplying St. Johns and its only defense in a retreat. (The land approaches to Fort St. Johns had already been secured when the Americans took the small frontier posts of La Prairie and Longueuil.) Fort Chambly was a small, two-story stone structure (which still stands), commanded by the weak Maj. Joseph Stopford. It was garrisoned by just eighty-three men of the 7th Royal Fusiliers.

Eager for action, Montgomery seized on the scheme, placing Maj. John Brown in charge of the task force. The three hundred Canadians, along with fifty Americans and two 9-pounders, slipped past Fort St.

Johns on the night of October 16. Once at Fort Chambly, Brown and Livingston put their two meager cannon to service. They harried the outpost for two days (it was hardly a bombardment), creating just a few holes in its walls and knocking down a chimney, but inflicting no casualties. Even so, with no real fight in him, Major Stopford abruptly negotiated his surrender on October 18, giving up the fort the next morning.

The capture of Fort Chambly, as simple an affair as it was, reinvigorated the Americans. The spoils were of particular value, including a sizable supply of arms and warlike stores, and a large quantity of food. Most notable were the 124 barrels of gunpowder. The American-Canadian force also took the 7th Regiment's flag standard. This battle trophy, the first of its kind ever taken by the Americans, quickly became a source of pride for Montgomery's troops. It was promptly sent to Schuyler and then on to the Continental Congress.[4]

When Schuyler wrote of the victory to Washington, he included Montgomery's inventory of the spoils, which ended with the line: "Royal Fusileers, 83. Accoutrements, 83." Washington's reply included one of

7TH REGIMENT OF FOOT'S COLOR STANDARD CAPTURED AT THE SIEGE OF FORT ST. JOHNS, PRESENTLY ON DISPLAY AT THE WEST POINT MUSEUM COLLECTIONS, U.S. MILITARY ACADEMY.

his few recorded laughs: "We laugh at his Idea of Classing the Royal Fuzileers with the Stores: Does he [Montgomery] consider them as Inanimates or as a Treasure?" As happy as this news made Washington, with the Siege of Fort St. Johns dragging on, he added his hope that the next letter would be dated from Montreal.[5]

With Major Stopford's surrender at Fort Chambly, Montgomery took the opportunity to press a humanitarian issue he thought important. He had received accurate intelligence that after being captured outside Montreal, Ethan Allen had been handled roughly and sent in irons aboard a ship set for England. Montgomery wrote Stopford that, should Governor Carleton persist in this severe treatment of prisoners of war, "I must appeal to your own candour whether my duty to the troops committed to my charge, does not demand retaliation." Montgomery made it clear he desired no such escalation, but told Stopford to relate the capitulation of Fort Chambly to Carleton and warn him of the dangers of such continued barbarity.[6] Carleton received Montgomery's letter, but refused to have correspondence with the rebels. He instead wrote Lord Dartmouth on the matter, declaring, "I shall treat all their threats with silent contempt".[7]

Just as the victory over Fort Chambly raised the spirits of the besieging American Army, so too did Wooster's arrival on October 26, at head of his 335 Connecticut men. The 225 men of the 4th New York Continentals arrived soon after. Montgomery's forces, including the Canadians under Livingston, now swelled to more than 2,000 effectives. With this new level of esprit de corps, Montgomery again proposed to his officers his old plan to erect an artillery emplacement close to Fort St. Johns. This time, his officers assented. Preparations were immediately put underway.[8]

Meanwhile, in nearby Montreal, Carleton was aware of the desperate situation surrounding Fort St. Johns and prepared a task force of his own. Carleton sent an express to Col. Allan Maclean in Quebec City to sally forth with all available men and converge with him at Fort St. Johns. Maclean had been busy augmenting Quebec's defense force by raising a regiment of Royal Highlander Emigrants, Army veterans who had emigrated from Scotland. By now, he had eighty or more, which he quickly embarked on ships and set sail for the Richelieu River.[9] Carleton

PORTRAIT OF MAJ. GEN. SIR GUY CARLETON (DATE UNKNOWN) BY UNKNOWN ARTIST.
COURTESY OF THE LIBRARY AND ARCHIVES CANADA.

himself embarked with a fleet of thirty-four small vessels of various sizes, loaded with some five or six hundred men, mostly Canadian militia, plus one hundred Indians and whatever few regulars he still had.

On October 30, as the British flotilla departed Montreal, they soon approached Longueuil, where three hundred of Seth Warner's Green Mountain Boys and the several-hundred-strong 2nd Regiment of New Yorkers sat in wait. As the flotilla drew near, Warner gave the word, and their cannon opened up with a thunderous boom, catching Carleton by surprise. The British ships scrambled to tack. Once the British brought their cannon to bear, they fired back without effect. Carleton then ordered his men to the boats: they would weed out the Americans by land. But as the longboats approached the shore, the Green Mountain Boys and the New Yorkers replied with a heavy onslaught of cannon and musketry.

The British soldiers and militia were sitting ducks in their longboats, and they began to take immediate losses. The coxswains called the boats to fall back, but after regrouping, they tried to land once more. The small British landing parties gave a valiant effort but were repulsed several times. After five hours of continuous bombardment, Carleton called the retreat, and the British flotilla fell back toward Montreal. They suffered twenty killed, fifty wounded, and four prisoners taken, while the Americans had not a single casualty. Meanwhile, Maclean, having heard the news of Carleton's repulse, anchored his vessels east of the Richelieu River near the town of Sorel, there to await further instructions.[10]

Back at Fort St. Johns, Montgomery's men began construction of their new battery just 250 yards northwest of the fort and on the same side of the Richelieu River. The British garrison continuously bombarded their new position, but on November 1, the battery was completed and armed with four 12-pounders and five "Royals" (brass 5½" mortars). With plenty of shells and powder from Chambly, Montgomery opened up a sustained and powerful barrage on Fort St. Johns, its booming chorus joined by his four-gun battery to the east. From their new close-in position, the Americans for the first time began to cause massive damage, though they inflicted few casualties.

Later the same day, Montgomery halted his fire and sent a letter to Major Preston via a prisoner captured from Longueuil. It informed Preston of Carleton's defeat, urged him to spare the lives of his brave garrison, and concluded, "Should you continue to…persist in a defence which cannot avail you—I…shall deem myself innocent of the melancholy consequences which may attend it."[11]

That night, one of Carleton's secret couriers was caught trying to sneak into Fort St. Johns. His message to Preston was, "Hold out and you shall be relieved." Preston never received this message, instead lamenting, "Not a Syllable of Intelligence from General Carleton arrived altho' we sent repeated Messengers to Montreal."[12]

Agonizing over what to do, Preston sent a reply to Montgomery, stating he would surrender the fort if he were not relieved in four days. Montgomery by this time knew of Benedict Arnold's expedition into Canada, meant to combine with his. Moreover, with the season growing late, he was anxious to move out. So Montgomery replied, "if you do not surrender this day, it will be unnecessary to make any future proposals; the garrison shall be prisoners of war, without the honours of war".[13]

Preston opted to stall. On November 2, he sent out several officers to parley, including Lt. John André, who as a major five years later would help Benedict Arnold commit his infamous treason. André realized the fort's situation was indeed desperate and so advised Preston to surrender. So Preston conceded and negotiated with Montgomery the terms of capitulation: the British garrison was to be permitted to march out with all honors of war, the officers could keep their side arms and the soldiers their baggage, but all the garrison were to be shipped southward to be detained by the Colonies. Accordingly, on the morning of November 3, the British marched out of the fort, grounded their arms, and boarded the small colonial flotilla bound for Connecticut.[14]

On the British side, the total losses throughout the siege were just 20 killed and 23 wounded.[15] On the American side, the numbers remain unclear but seem to have been even fewer. The greatest scourge was camp sickness, with Schuyler reporting in mid-October some 937 soldiers unfit for duty.[16]

The spoils taken from Fort St. Johns were considerable. Besides limited food, it had some thirty-nine cannons, seven mortars, and two howitzers, plus ammunition, as well as the two schooners. *Royal Savage* would be raised and repaired for service. The other, missing just its masts and rigging, would be completed and christened the *Revenge*.[17]

The siege may have been mundane, and Montgomery may have been the victor, but Preston performed admirably, his stiff resistance holding Montgomery in position for almost fifty days. Washington had even suggested to Schuyler that he ignore Fort St. Johns entirely and move on, but Schuyler rightfully feared having such a strong British post at his rear.[18] Consequently, the long delay forced Montgomery to continue his campaign into the worst of the severe Canadian winter. Worse yet, he now had only two months before many of his men's enlistments expired.

And more than a few were counting the days until they could march home to their warm beds.

To add to Montgomery's troubles, with many of the men ill equipped for the winter, some became disgruntled and near mutinous when they saw that the British garrison were permitted to keep their belongings. The undisciplined Americans were anxious for the garments as spoils of war to replace their own ragged clothes. "I wish some method could be fallen upon of engaging *gentlemen* to serve; a point of honour and more knowledge of the world, to be found in that class of men, would greatly reform discipline, and render the troops much more tractable", complained Montgomery. "I would not have sullied my own reputation, nor disgraced the Continental arms, by such a breach of capitulation, for the universe; there was no driving it into their noddles, that the clothing was really the property of the soldier".[19] To quell the grumbling men, Montgomery promised they would get all the clothing they required at their next objective: Montreal.

As the American force prepared to muster for their march north-westward, a winter storm socked them, unleashing sleet and rain, and miring the roads. Morale again declined, and many began to talk about marching home early. All Montgomery could do was coax the men forward with the promise that those who went as far as Montreal would be free to leave once they took the city. Montgomery had always trusted his fate to Fortune and expected she would smile upon him once more. With a victory at Montreal, he hoped they might seize General Carleton himself. Displeased as they were, the men accepted Montgomery's offer. And so together, the expeditionary force plodded forward, against the winter storm.

But Fortune was against Montgomery this time, and he would sorely regret his promise to release the men. For Carleton had no intention of making his stand at Montreal, and the American general would desperately need those men instead at Quebec City.

———————•—•———————

Meanwhile, by the end of September, all of Benedict Arnold's expedition had departed Fort Western and were slowly making their way up the

Kennebec River. About half the men marched, while the rest tended the batteaux that served as floating supply wagons, sometimes rowing or, more frequently, dragging them upriver and portaging them around the numerous severe rapids and steep waterfalls. In other areas, the currents were so strong, but the river's edge so entangled, that the men best spent their energy wading in the river, while pulling or pushing their boats along.[20]

As much of their journey was to be upriver, the batteaux were something of a burden at times, causing some companies to rotate out the boatmen with those marching. One of the few advantages they offered was as lean-to shelters for the many rainy nights. However, the batteaux, newly built from green timber, were unseasoned, and so unfit for the treacherous path ahead. After only the first day of the expedition, several began to open at the seams and leak. One of the expedition's two physicians, Dr. Isaac Senter, was so concerned for his medical supplies that he resorted to buying a seasoned canoe for a very hefty price at an outpost along the Kennebec. The countless rapids and associated frequent beatings against rocks and tree roots further damaged the new batteaux. Within a week into the trek, most of the boats were splintered and breaking. Some were condemned to the side of the river, while soldier-carpenters patched others as best they could with what little they had. The loss of so many batteaux would not in itself halt the expedition, since more than half the men were following the riverbank on foot. Rather, their loss would prevent bringing along the bulky supplies necessary for the camp—including provisions, tents, and camp equipage—and so could mean starvation for the expedition.

To exacerbate these problems, the casks used for the provisions were not waterproof. After just a few days in, many of the vital provisions became ruined. Soggy bread and dried peas swelled to the point of bursting their casks. Pork and beef were ruined by the washing away of their salt preservative. This was an ominous sign. Though the men would fish when they could, their long and difficult path allowed little recess for such leisurely pursuits. However, at least two oxen were ushered alongside the rear of the cavalcade to serve as self-transporting meals when the provisions at last grew scarce.

With every day that passed, the hardships continued to mount. Spoiled rations and wet weather colluded to plague the men with dysentery. As more and more batteaux began to fall apart, the few remaining seaworthy ones were overloaded with camp equipage. Exhaustion set in for all, but particularly for those manning the now-overburdened batteaux. And as the portages became more frequent, the men awkwardly struggled under the weight of their overladen boats up the ever-steeper terrain.

Hardships such as these—man against nature—made for the ideal mission for Colonel Arnold. Here in the wilderness, far removed from his superiors, he was master of all and subordinate to none, free to determine his own course and unfettered with the bureaucracy of a chain of command. At Fort Western, Arnold had waited with the rear of his caravan to see the entire detachment set off. Soon he had passed to the front of the main body and was shortly some days ahead of the main divisions.

Well ahead of even Arnold was his first division of pioneers, led by Lt. Archibald Steele, supported by Captain Morgan's Virginia riflemen. These were literal trailblazers. Probably having left days before the main divisions, they cut paths through the dense thicket and underbrush at the portages, cleared logs and obstructions from the river, and marked the path for the others to follow. For speed, they traveled with the lightest provisions, but theirs was the toughest labor. They sometimes traversed the same paths several times as they reported to Arnold, made contact with the French in Canada, and arranged to have provisions sent back to the main body.

On October 6, Steele's pioneers reached the Great Carrying Place, a long portage interspersed with low ridges and three small lakes. Crossing here afforded the men a shortcut to the Dead River, which poured into the Kennebec some miles to the north, thereby allowing them to bypass a long bend of upriver paddling and steep terrain. Also known as the Twelve-Mile Carrying Place, the portage was rigorous and slow, thickly wooded and steep, despite the paths the pioneers cut. The main divisions came upon it some three days after Steele's pioneers. Some crews, such as that of Abner Stocking, took three days to cross it. At difficult portages such as this, each company would have to cross several times to get all their supplies across. Despite the difficulty, the icy cold lakes were a welcome sight, not for the easy boating across, but for the abundance of trout they offered up to the hungry trekkers.

As the cold, rainy weather turned to light snow squalls, and noting the rising number of cases of dysentery, the Americans built near the Great Carrying Place at least one and maybe two shacks, which they imaginatively called field hospitals. Dr. Senter wrote in his journal on October 16 that one hospital was "no sooner finished than filled."[21]

After crossing the long portage, the men reached the Dead River. In that era, it was an open expanse, since dammed up to form Flagstaff Lake. It was a breathless wonder to behold, a placid wide stream surrounded by densely wooded mountains. Its name derived either from its dead-still stagnancy near the carrying place or from its deadly upriver waters near its source, so narrow there that the river became riddled with countless impassable rapids and falls.

Around October 19, the weather took a turn for the worse, becoming an intense storm that rained on the weary men for three or four days straight. The Dead River swelled into a torrent, rising some ten feet and forcing the men to portage alongside its mired banks. Countless new tributaries obstructed its much-expanded riverbanks, forcing the men to walk across slippery, muddy terrain for sometimes several miles away just to find a place narrow enough to cross. When they could not, the men were forced to wade in knee-deep, frigid water, losing all sensation in their feet and risking hypothermia. The whole of the expedition slowed to a crawl. As the storm grew to an intense gale, trees broke apart and toppled over, causing still more obstructions and great anxiety among the men, who feared camping underneath.

For days, the rain showed no sign of ending. Their only solace was the oxen, which were now sent up from the rear, slaughtered, and distributed among the men. For the first time in weeks, they tasted fresh meat, though each man was given just one pound. The men consumed the last of their other rations soon after. Then they turned to a paltry sample of flour mixed with water to make slurry, and after that was gone, some experimented with shoe leather as a meal. Two dogs, brought along as pets, would also become meals before journey's end. At least one division successfully hunted a moose, but even that did not last long among these famished souls.

As the men pressed forward, their hardships seemed to increase with each step. No sooner had the rains let up than snow began to fall. On October 25, some six inches fell overnight.

With provisions now scant, Lt. Col. Christopher Greene halted his division to wait for the rear, commanded by Lt. Col. Roger Enos. Having all the paths cleared before him, Enos's rearguard was also given the bulk of the heavy supplies. This disposition allowed the front divisions, those with the greatest labor in cutting paths for the caravan, such as Steele's pioneers, to travel lightly. Enos's rear was also charged with contending with the sick and sending them back to Fort Western.

When Enos finally came up and met with Greene, they called together a meeting of their officers to decide if they should proceed without provisions. They would have to make their own decision, as Colonel Arnold was days ahead and out of reach. Enos's officers grumbled about the hardships, despite their units having the easiest labor and still having sufficient rations that included the entire force's reserve supply. The officers took a vote. Enos, like Greene, voted to proceed, but Enos's officers voted to return. Enos then declared that, as their commander, he should go with his men. He then laid claim to the few rations they had left, but after a brief but heated discussion finally consented to give Greene a meager portion of flour before departing. And so ended the meeting. Unbeknownst to Arnold, a sizable portion of his men had just turned for home.

Enos perhaps had some technical justification to turn back. On the day before, Arnold had sent a letter back along the caravan ordering Enos to supply what men he could with fifteen days' provisions "and that the remainder [of the men], whether sick or well, should be immediately sent back".[22] But Arnold would later write to Washington, "Enos's division…I am surprised to hear, are all gone back".[23] In any event, upon Enos's return to Cambridge, he was placed under arrest and court-martialed, but acquitted. He stood in stark contrast to the men who pressed on successfully, and so public sentiment was strong against him. "Go hang thyself," he was told. Enos resigned his commission shortly thereafter.[24]

Despite no hope of further provisions, the rest of Arnold's men pressed onward. As the expedition approached the Dead River's source, batteaux became useless, first because of the obstructed floodwaters due to the storm and then the shallow and narrow rapids. Colonel Arnold, well ahead of his main divisions, even sent word back recommending they abandon the batteaux there. Only Captain Morgan, a strict disciplinarian, opted to drive his Virginia riflemen forward with their remaining seven batteaux.[25] Others kept just one per company to help ferry their remaining provisions and camp supplies. The Dead River's source was in the deepest wilderness, approaching a large ridge of mountains that are part of the northern reaches of the Appalachians.

As the men trudged up still more difficult, snow-blanketed terrain, they crossed the heights of the continental divide and so into Canada, from where the waters thereafter flowed north. And for the first time they laid eyes on their rally point: Lake Megantic, also called Chaudière Pond, which flowed into River Chaudière and then the St. Lawrence near their objective. Some of the divisions struggled through many bogs and streams approaching Lake Megantic; others received Arnold's message to cut straight north, avoiding the lake altogether and instead merging with the Chaudière along a shorter route.

The men then followed alongside the Chaudière northward, almost none of them having batteaux. A group of Morgan's riflemen, however, overzealous to complete their journey, rode one of their batteaux downstream, though the river was exceedingly rocky and rapid. Somewhere well north of Lake Megantic they found themselves caught in the river's strong rapids and pulled toward a small but turbulent waterfall. Out of control, their batteau capsized, their few supplies lost, leaving the men to frantically struggle to swim to shore. One rifleman was not so lucky. He feebly swam against the current until he plummeted to his death over the falls.

The men continued along the Chaudière, starving and freezing, disheveled and exhausted, some sick with dysentery. It was on October 30 that Arnold himself arrived at the first French Canadian houses in the backwoods post of Sartigan, probably modern Saint-Georges. From willing traders he acquired new provisions, including cattle, which he ordered driven back along the river to his famished men, who eagerly butchered several to feast upon. A few days later, all of the men arrived at Sartigan, and there they rested for several days. Of the 1,100 men that began the 240-mile journey, only 600 completed it, of whom many were sick, leaving Arnold with an effective force of only about 500.[26]

Once rested and fed, the men set off again, leaving the river and marching two or three days northeastward to Pointe-Lévy (Point Levi), modern Lévis on the St. Lawrence, where they arrived on November 8. From there, Arnold looked across the wide expanse of the St. Lawrence River to its opposite shore and the military objective they had so long marched toward: the formidable and impervious walled fortress of Quebec City, surmounting a steep promontory, supported by river wharves below it. The waters before him were filled with about fifteen transports and guarded by the 28-gun HMS *Lizard* and the 10-gun sloop-of-war *Hunter*.[27]

Perhaps somewhere in the back of Arnold's egotistical mind he knew the truth. With his battered men, ill equipped and without cannon, he really had no chance of conquering Quebec City. Yet he was determined to try.[28]

In Boston, Gen. William Howe was aware of the situation in Canada and had ordered the 2nd Battalion of Marines to be ready to embark for Quebec, "but, on Consulting with the Sea Officers, thought impracticable to get up the river."[29] Winter was now too near to send such a reinforcement, for the St. Lawrence could well be frozen before the transports rounded Nova Scotia.

Meanwhile, Admiral Graves had no idea that by mid-October his recall orders were already in the hands of his successor, who was making ready in England to set sail. It is somewhat ironic, then, that only now, for the first time since hostilities began, did Graves decide to take the offensive. He settled upon a plan to exact judgment on certain seditious coastal towns that had previously acted against his fleet.

Falmouth (modern Portland, Maine) had seized masts earmarked for the Navy and had briefly imprisoned a naval officer, Lt. Henry Mowat. Cape Ann Harbor (specifically Gloucester, aided by neighboring Ipswich) had fired on HM Sloop *Falcon*, wounding several and taking many prisoners, while Gloucester also had seized a British schooner. Machias had captured the Navy's purchased schooner *Margaretta* and two trading sloops, and with them was now threatening Nova Scotia.[30] Portsmouth had fired on one of HMS *Scarborough*'s boats. Marblehead and Salem were probably on Graves's list because they were home to the whaleboaters that harried his ships and had long been hotbeds for rebellious activity in support of Boston. And Newburyport worked with Falmouth and Saco in securing supplies for the American Army. Thus, Graves decided to exact the severest consequences on each town in turn.[31]

Before General Gage's recall, the admiral had explained his plan and requested use of some troops, which he required as landing parties since most of his marines were now on shore duty. Gage had approved, and Graves received about one hundred troops, plus free use of the Army's armed transport *Symmetry* and sloop *Spitfire*. Graves added to his task force the only Navy ships he could afford to dedicate to the venture: the armed vessel *Canceaux* and the schooner *Halifax*. Both were small, armed with just six carronades (short but more powerful and advanced cannon), plus swivels.[32] These four ships were placed under the command of Lt. Henry Mowat, who was more than eager for the opportunity to exact revenge on Falmouth for having once imprisoned him. It took about a month to outfit the ships for the expedition. Finally, in early October, Graves gave Mowat his orders: he was to "burn destroy and lay waste" the towns.[33]

As Mowat made final preparations to destroy the coastal towns to the north, the small British naval squadron to the south at Rhode Island began to terrorize the people of Bristol. This was the squadron commanded by Capt. James Wallace of the 20-gun HMS *Rose*. His fleet included the sloop-of-war *Swan*, the armed schooner *Hope*, and several smaller vessels, as well as HMS *Glasgow*, recently down from Boston. Wallace's squadron had been dominating Narragansett Bay since hostilities began, but the inhabitants of Rhode Island were growing weary of resupplying them.

So on October 7, Wallace arrayed his ships in battle formation before the town of Bristol and then sent a lieutenant ashore to issue his resupply demands. The town committee considered the demands but tarried too long. After the appointed time had expired, Wallace signaled to his ships and they began a massive bombardment of shells and carcasses into the town. In the midst of it all, a local militia colonel hailed the

Rose and was brought aboard. Wallace ordered the cease-fire and gave the town several hours more to reply to his demands of two hundred sheep and thirty fat cattle. The town replied they had already driven off most of their stock, save a few sheep and milk cows. To this reply, Wallace sent the following: "I have this one proposal to make: if you will promise to supply me with forty sheep, at or before twelve o'clock, I will assure you that another gun shall not be discharged." The Bristol committee, faced with little alternative, punctually complied with Wallace's demand, buying off the destruction of their town.[34]

In Boston, perhaps that same day, Mowat sailed northward aboard the *Canceaux*, escorted by the *Halifax* and his two borrowed ships *Symmetry* and *Spitfire*.[35] His flotilla captured an armed schooner along the journey, possibly the same schooner they spotted at sea and chased until she ran ashore at Cape Cod.[36] His first target was Gloucester, but after arriving there, Mowat deemed the houses too scattered for an effective naval bombardment, so he continued sailing to the town upon which he had long desired to exact his revenge.

Thus on October 17, Mowat's flotilla reached Falmouth and laid anchor. He promptly sent an envoy to the town selectmen with his message: "you have been guilty of the most unpardonable rebellion…having it in orders to execute a just punishment on the Town…remove without delay the human species out of the said Town, for which purpose I give you the time of two hours".[37]

Despite the many months of war, Falmouth was unprepared for retaliation for its rebellious acts. The town sent a committee to parley with Mowat, guessing he was rattling the saber and in fact merely required supplies. But once aboard *Canceaux*, they learned the magnitude of his orders: "to fall upon and destroy" the town.[38] At first the committee protested, but then, with tears in their eyes, conceded and begged for more time. Mowat offered to postpone the bombardment until the next morning at eight o'clock, provided they turned in their weapons. They agreed, but turned in fewer than a dozen muskets, stating that the five cannon Mowat once knew to be in the town had been removed to the countryside upon sighting his flotilla. These few muskets bought the town another half day.

Throughout the night, the small band of the local Sons of Liberty sent word to the neighboring towns, collecting what few militiamen they could. But the zealous colonials did not improve the situation and instead made it clear to the inhabitants "that if any compliance or submission was made, they would burn it [Falmouth] to ashes." In other words, the Sons of Liberty wanted Falmouth to fall as a martyr to the cause rather than submit. Except for the few soldiers mustering in town, the people of Falmouth seem to have squandered their last night away.[39]

The next morning, October 18, Mowat granted a slight extension. "Perceiving woman and children still in the town, I made it forty minutes after nine before the Signal was hoisted, which was done with a gun". The cannon shot drew the attention of the other vessels' captains, who saw hoisted upon *Canceaux*'s main topgallant masthead a red pennant.[40] With that, all five British vessels began their bombardment of a "horrible shower of balls, from three to nine pounds weight, bombs, carcasses, live shells, grape-shot and musket balls." Yet with fewer than two hundred dwellings in Falmouth, not built close together, the event took some time. "The firing lasted, without many minutes cessation, until about six o'clock P.M., during which time several parties came ashore and set buildings on fire by hand." The Falmouth militia fired a few musket shots in response, but despite what they thought, no one was injured on either side.[41]

Falmouth paid dearly for its rebellion: "...about three-quarters of the buildings...are consumed...many of which held two or three families apiece, besides barns, and almost every store and warehouse in town. St. Paul's Church, a large new building, with the bell; a very elegant and costly new court-house, not quite finished; a fine engine, almost new; the old town house and the publick library, were all consumed." One or two wharves survived, but most of the vessels in the harbor were destroyed. Those dwellings that did survive were riddled with cannon shot holes.[42]

This judgment upon Falmouth did more to harm the British cause than it did to help it. The town was on the edge of wilderness, with no countryside to support it, and the townspeople, perhaps some three hundred families, were scattered into the woods in despair. With the coming of winter, the destruction of Falmouth for so small a crime only served to inflame the Americans.

For General Washington, this meant that many of his troops from coastal towns were now clamoring to head home, hoping to see to the safety of their own families, and Washington granted some furloughs as a result. Furthermore, Portsmouth was known to be the next target, so he sent Brig. Gen. John Sullivan there to help defend it.[43] But Mowat would not destroy any other coastal town, deciding instead to return to Boston, as much of his ammunition had been spent in the difficult task of razing Falmouth, and his flimsy vessels, particularly *Spitfire*, were battered by their own guns' recoil.[44] In the end, this was Graves's only foray into taking the offensive, but the destruction of Falmouth left him an infamous legacy with the Americans.

***

Following the Battle of Bunker Hill, moderates in the Continental Congress, led by John Dickinson of Pennsylvania, urged a second appeal to the King for reconciliation and accommodation of their grievances. But the Massachusetts delegates were strongly opposed to this, given all that had happened in their colony. John Adams reminded his colleagues that the First Continental Congress had sent a similar petition in late 1774, which the King had received graciously but had laid before the Parliament, where it was utterly ignored. Still, some in Congress were convinced that hope for peace was not yet lost and that all of their troubles stemmed from a wicked Ministry that had deceived their King. After some debate, on July 8, they adopted a new and final appeal to the King, known afterward as the Olive Branch Petition.[45]

Congress entrusted this petition to Richard Penn, who sailed for England four days later and arrived in London on August 14. Though Penn was a grandson of Pennsylvania founder William Penn and himself a former lieutenant governor of that colony, and although he had the London-based colonial agent Arthur Lee to assist him, still he could find no minister to give him an audience. "The King and his cabinet," according to Lord Suffolk, "are determined to listen to nothing from the illegal congress, to treat with the colonies only one by one, and in no event to recognize them in any form or association." By August 21, Penn and Lee had only managed to send a copy of the petition to Lord Dartmouth, Secretary of the Colonies.[46]

The King was determined to ignore the congressional agents because, for weeks, he had been receiving news of the mounting tumults in America, including the Taking of Fort Ticonderoga and the Battle of Bunker Hill. He thought, how could these deluded people be imploring for peace on the one hand, while preparing for and making war on the other? The King was indeed encouraged to war by his ministers, but he quickly grew to wholeheartedly support it himself.

Thus, on August 23, His Majesty issued "A Proclamation for Suppressing Rebellion and Sedition". It declared: "many of Our Subjects in divers Parts of Our Colonies and Plantations in *North America*…forgetting the Allegiance which they owe to the Power that has protected and sustained them…have at length proceeded to open and avowed Rebellion, by…traitorously preparing, ordering and levying War against Us". After further proclaiming it treason to assist those in rebellion and declaring that the government would give their "utmost Endeavours to suppress such Rebellion, and to bring the Traitors to Justice", the Royal Proclamation ended as all of them do: "God Save the King." Thus marked the first public declaration of rebellion given by the King himself, not his Ministry or Parliament. With this proclamation, the King widened the gulf between the mother country and her colonies beyond any hope of peace.[47]

Despite this grave development, Penn and Lee continued to press Lord Dartmouth for an audience. It was not until September 1, "the first moment that was permitted us", that they were able to deliver in person the original petition to Dartmouth, who promised in turn to lay it before the King. Penn and Lee urged Dartmouth to get a reply, and Dartmouth did his part within a day, but they afterward learned that, since the King had refused to formally receive the petition on the throne, "no answer would be given."[48]

At the end of October, General Washington in Cambridge received a copy of "A Proclamation for Suppressing Rebellion and Sedition", perhaps sent out from the British in Boston. Washington promptly forwarded it on to the Continental Congress, but days before its arrival, Congress received a letter from Penn and Lee relaying the King's refusal to respond to the Olive Branch Petition.[49] Consequently, when the copy of the Proclamation was read before Congress days later, it effectively served as the King's response. The Proclamation would undermine congressional moderates' efforts to work toward a peaceful resolution. Instead, with their King now publicly in support of his Ministry's Coercive Acts, there was no authority left to intercede, and moderates would soon come to accept the war now thrust upon them.

Nevertheless, in their reply to the Proclamation, which they adopted weeks later, Congress made it clear: "We will not, on our part, lose the distinction between the King and his Ministers", though Congress also reaffirmed their right to oppose the "cruel and illegal attacks, which…have no foundation in the royal authority."[50]

Meanwhile, on October 26, King George III made his way from St. James's Palace to the Houses of Parliament at Westminster amid great pomp and fanfare. Once he arrived in the House of Lords, "adorned with his crown and regal ornaments, and attended by his Officers of State, (the Lords being in their robes)," the King sat on his ornate, golden throne, where he then commanded the Gentleman Usher of the Black Rod to summon the members of the House of Commons.[51] Once they too arrived, the King issued the traditional Speech from the Throne that opened the next session of Parliament and, in doing so, reaffirmed his intent to press the war:

"Those who have long too successfully laboured to inflame my people in America, by gross misrepresentations, and to infuse into their minds a system of opinions repugnant to the true constitution of the Colonies, and to their subordinate relation to Great Britain, now openly avow their revolt, hostility, and rebellion," the King told Parliament. Calling it a "desperate conspiracy", the King responded directly to the Olive Branch Petition: "They meant only to amuse, by vague expressions of attachment to the parent State, and the strongest protestations of loyalty to me, whilst they were preparing for a general revolt." Repeating the opinion of his Tory Parliament, the King avowed, "The rebellious war now levied…is manifestly carried on for the purpose of establishing an independent Empire."

He then declared his solution: "It is now become the part of wisdom, and (in its effects) of clemency, to put a speedy end to these disorders by the most decisive exertions. For this purpose I have increased my naval establishment, and greatly augmented my land forces" and "have received the most friendly offers of foreign assistance". Finally, the King offered a way out for the Americans, stating that, "When the unhappy and deluded multitude, against whom this force will be directed, shall become sensible of their error, I shall be ready to receive the misled with tenderness and mercy," promising to authorize certain persons power to grant pardons to individuals or any colony.[52]

The Tories, the political party that enjoyed a large majority in Parliament, met the King's address with strong applause and support. Yet the minority pro-American Whigs would not allow the King's speech to go unchallenged, and it would afterward spark some of the fiercest debates in Parliament.

Following the King's departure and then that of the Members of the Commons, the Lords briefly recessed to unrobe. When they reconvened moments later, the Whigs immediately mounted a valiant opposition. Referring to the Ministry, Lord Shelburne asked, "Is it their intention, by thus perpetually sounding independence in the ears of the Americans, to lead them to it…or compel them into that which must be our ruin?" The Duke of Grafton boldly asserted that Parliament must repeal every act since 1763 relative to America.[53]

It was likewise in the House of Commons, where Charles Fox censured Lord North "as a blundering pilot who had brought the nation into its present difficulties." "Alexander the Great," Fox added, "never gained more in one campaign than the noble lord [North] has lost—he has lost a whole continent!" George Johnstone exclaimed, "To see an irregular peasantry commanded by a physician [Dr. Joseph Warren], inferior in number, opposed by every circumstance of cannon and bombs that could terrify timid minds, calmly waiting the attack of the gallant Howe leading on the best troops in the world…who can reflect on such scenes, and not adore the Constitution of Government which could breed such men! Who…is there that can dismiss all doubts on the justice of the cause which can inspire such conscious rectitude?" Despite the best eloquence and vociferousness of the Whigs, the majority Tories held firm to their conviction for war. Over the coming months, Prime Minister Lord North and his Tory sycophants would in turn soundly defeat all propositions toward peace that the Whigs brought to the floor.[54]

The debate waged outside Parliament too, becoming the subject of taverns, newspapers, and pamphlets. Political philosopher Richard Price argued there was no advantage to the war: neither revenue nor trade could be had from the colonies if they were actually conquered. The Briton commoners were already witnessing the truth in Price's prediction. With all trade to Britain's primary consumer market now cut off, a massive depression rippled through the British Isles, driving many out of work. The public debate also stymied the Ministry's recruiting efforts, with many would-be soldiers expressing a general reluctance to fight their own brethren. In consequence, Parliament began to consider the hiring of German mercenaries, as suggested by the King's speech.[55]

Despite the public outcry in Britain, the well-entrenched Tory party was too blind and too committed to concede Parliamentary sovereignty. To do so would require both them and the King to admit to poor judgment in pressing their agenda of coercion. The war was by now too political for such a concession.

So at last, the King and his Ministry effectively ousted from the Empire all of the Thirteen Colonies, long before they had ousted themselves. It would take a few months more for America to come to this realization, but once it had, a formal Declaration of Independence was inevitable.

<hr/>

While the Siege of Boston was accompanied by occasional skirmishes, most were of little consequence. But on November 9, General Clinton, now in charge at Charlestown and having been itching since Bunker Hill to take the offensive, prepared for a raid on Phipps's Farm on adjacent Lechmere Point, where some cattle grazed freely. "…we had long accustomed them to look with unconcern on our padling in boats about the harbour," Clinton wrote, "& this day about 300 light Infantry were amusing themselves in a Careless manner, with orders to attempt nothing without signal. I went aboard a man-of-war near the spot to be attacked and from whence I could see part of the motion of the Enemy, I saw a favorable moment made the signal, & in two minutes the boats got into order and were rowing towards the shore, where they arrived without receiving scarcely any fire," just a few wayward shots from American cannon. The British swarmed onto the shore about 11:00

a.m., surprising the Americans, who fled in haste. As some light infantry lined up along a stone wall to guard the approach, the rest drove forty-five cattle across Charlestown Neck.[56] The Americans, meanwhile, regrouped and returned, seven hundred strong, bringing with them riflemen. They fired their guns and blasted their cannon as the British safely paddled away, and then the Yankees deluded themselves into thinking they had forced the retreat.[57]

The skirmish emboldened the Americans to fortify Cobble Hill, which guarded the approach to Charlestown Neck and was very close to the British outer works. Following the pattern that was now common to the Americans, Washington ordered an entrenchment thrown up there on the night of November 22. To the British, yet another fort suddenly appeared the next morning. The Americans at Cobble Hill could now command both Phipps's Farm and Charlestown Neck, and a few of their cannon could even reach Boston, though barely.

The Americans also leisurely began building an additional fort on Phipps's Farm itself, though it would not be completed until late January due to snow and frozen ground. This farm on Lechmere's Point protruded into the Charles River to within 1,200 yards of the northwest tip of Boston. The proximity of this new fort caused quite a stir amongst the British, and they began a new battery immediately across in Boston to counter it. Meanwhile, the British kept up a sporadic cannonade on the new American positions for several weeks. Washington's cannon, however, remained silent, because he could not afford the powder to return fire.[58]

Trifling as these events may seem, Washington's noose around the British was again cranked tighter. These new positions would play an important role in the final stroke Washington was hoping to make against the British in Boston.

———— •◦• ————

Of the many difficulties Washington faced as he continued to mold his hodgepodge provincial armies into a unified Continental Army, his greatest burden was localism—soldiers of one colony unwilling to subordinate to officers of another.

The size of the regiments of the several provincial armies varied considerably, from 590 for most of the New England regiments to 1,000 men for those of Connecticut. Washington was especially annoyed with Rhode Island's system, which had far too many officers for far too few men, thus drawing extra pay and soaking up resources but providing no extra value.[59] Because of this, Washington desired to reshape the regiments to a uniform size, irrespective of which colony the men had come from. Together with a committee from the Continental Congress, Washington determined that, in contrast to the 40 irregular provincial regiments he currently had, the Army should consist of not less than 20,372 men, 28 regiments of a uniform 728 men each, including officers, each having 8 companies.[60]

Another impetus for re-forming the regiments was to integrate the officers of different colonies and give positions to those more worthy of command, such as those of the southern colonies, which had been crowded out by the New Englanders. It was for this reason that Capt. Aaron Burr and Maj. Mathias Ogden, both of New Jersey, had volunteered to march with Colonel Arnold's expedition. With no men at their command, Washington had no other place for them.

By early November, Washington and his general staff had begun paring down the many provincial regiments to the uniform Continental ones. In the process, they planned to intermix the officers and reduce their numbers. While politicking by ambitious officers made the transition delicate and tedious work, it was the lack of nationalism that stood as the greatest obstacle. Most officers banded together, asserting that a regiment of one colony would not accept officers from another. Washington expected more from his officers. He summarized the problem: "Connecticut wants no Massachusets-man in their Corp—Massachusets thinks their is no necessity for a Rhode Islander to be Introduced amongst them—& New Hampshire Says, it's very hard that her valuable & experienc'd Officers (who are willing to serve) should be discarded, because her own Regiments, under the New Establishment cannot provide for them."[61] Washington was prepared to lose some officers, but in the end, he had to concede—all the regiments would remain homogeneous by colony, both their officers and their men.[62]

Under this new establishment, Col. Asa Whitcomb of Massachusetts was one of those left without a regiment. But unlike many of his colleagues, Whitcomb was a true leader, exhorting his men "not to abandon the Interest of their country" and declaring he would himself "continue in the service, *even* as a private Soldier," rather than be a "bad example, when the Enemy are gathering Strength". Meanwhile, Col. Jonathan Brewer of Massachusetts was one of those who did indeed receive a regiment, but he was so moved by Whitcomb's selflessness that he relinquished his command to Whitcomb. Washington was equally moved by the loyalty and patriotism of these two men, qualities he wished more of his officers exhibited. Unwilling to part with either of them, Washington upheld the transfer of Brewer's regiment to Whitcomb, but further ordered, "Col. Brewer will be appointed Barrack Master, until something better worth his Acceptance can be provided."[63]

Washington's real difficulties, however, were still ahead. Since arriving in Cambridge, he had worked tirelessly to form a reasonable semblance of a disciplined army. Now, with the end of the year fast approaching, that army was on the verge of dissolving away overnight, as most enlistments were due to expire on December 31. So on November 12, Washington ordered his officers to begin enlisting under the new establishment of twenty-eight regiments.

The term for the new enlistments was until December 31, 1776. Officers were instructed to ensure no duplicate enlistments by other officers, on pain of cashiering. Financial incentives were provided to soldiers who could provide their own blankets or arms. Pay was set at the same rate as 1775. Tories, vagabonds, black men (free or not), boys unable to bear arms, and old men unable to endure the hardships of service were all barred from service. Washington stressed, "The Officers are to be careful not to inlist any person, suspected of being unfriendly to the Liberties of America [Tories]... The Rights of mankind and the freedom of America will have Numbers sufficient to support them, without resorting to such wretched assistance".[64]

Recruiting new soldiers was always an option, but the initial focus was on reenlisting the men of the provincial armies into the Continental regiments. The Army could not risk watching their veterans walk off at the end of the year, nor could it successfully wage a war with green recruit replacements. Unfortunately, given the one-year terms (deemed necessary for recruitment), the Army would face this same enlistment problem the following year. For now, to encourage provincial veterans reenlisting, all furloughs were canceled for men under the old establishment and were to be granted only to those who enlisted under the new, at a rate of fifty per regiment, for a duration of ten days plus travel time to and from home.[65]

After the first week of the reenlistment drive, the results were bleak. Of the 11 regiments Washington received results for, their grand total was a mere 966 men.[66] Part of this was because men were reluctant to reenlist due to the lack of proper clothing as the cold New England winter set in. While some companies were now turning in their tents and transitioning to barracks, there were not yet enough barracks for all. However, more than any, the biggest issue was and would continue to be pay.[67]

Weeks earlier, Washington had written the President of the Continental Congress, John Hancock, explaining, "my Situation is inexpressibly distressing, to see the Winter, fast approaching upon a naked Army: The Time of their Service within a few Weeks of expiring, & no Provision, yet made for such important Events. Added to these, the Military Chest is totally exhausted. The Paymaster has not a single Dollar in Hand. The Commissary General assures me, he has strained his Credit for the Subsistance of the Army to the utmost. The Quarter Master General is precisely in the same Situation: And the greater Part of the Troops are in a State not far from Mutiny, upon the Deduction from their stated Allowance. I know not to whom I am to impute this Failure, but I am of Opinion, if the Evil is not immediately remedied & more punctuality observed in future, the Army must absolutely break up".[68] Now that it was mid-November, with his men still unpaid for October, Washington wrote Hancock again: "there must be Some other Stimulus besides, Love for their Country, to make men fond of the Service".[69]

Another source of potential veterans for the reenlistment effort was those of the militia, though localism again played a role here. As many of the Massachusetts Militia had seen little use enlisting even in the Massachusetts Interim Army, many would also refuse enlistment into the Continental Army. The militiamen preferred not being bound to any long commitment, though since the war was in their backyards, they could, in case of emergency, readily augment the Continental Army as reservists. But once a crisis was dealt with, the militia units would immediately dissolve away and head back to their homes, as was tradition.

With so few of the soldiers around Boston willing to reenlist, officers were dispersed to the various colonies to raise up new recruits, these to be sent to Cambridge as fast as they were recruited.[70] Meanwhile, as another incentive to reenlist, Washington ordered that any soldier wishing to be discharged would first be required to surrender his gun to the Army. Any gun that was privately owned would be assessed and paid for at fair value.[71] The general staff also got directly involved in the reenlistment effort, parading the men and giving them spirited and impassioned speeches to elicit moral and patriotic sentiment.[72] This may have helped slightly, and the numbers for the second week of the reenlistment drive were better, but they were still very discouraging.[73]

Despondent, Washington wrote on the matter to Joseph Reed, his trusted confidant and former secretary, who had been obliged to return to Philadelphia in late October to attend to his private affairs, much to Washington's chagrin. "Such a dearth of Publick Spirit, & want of Virtue; such stock jobbing, and fertility in all the low Arts to obtain advantages, of one kind or another, in this great change of Military arrangemt I never saw before, and pray God I may never be Witness to again…such a dirty, mercenary Spirit pervades the whole, that I should not be at all surprizd at any disaster that may happen—In short…our lines will be so weakend that the Minute Men and Militia must be call'd in for their defence—these being under no kind of Government themselves, will destroy the little subordination I have been labouring to establish, and run me into one evil, whilst I am endeavouring to avoid another; but the lesser must be chosen. could I have foreseen what I have, & am like to experience, no consideration upon Earth should have induced me to accept this Command."[74]

In another letter to Reed, Washington added, "I have often thought, how much happier I should have been, if, instead of accepting of a command under such Circumstances I had taken my Musket upon my Shoulder & enterd the Ranks, or, if I could have justified the Measure to Posterity, & my own Conscience, had retir'd to the back Country, & livd in a Wig-wam".[75]

Washington faced the same enlistment problems with both his hodgepodge navy and artillery, as they were part of the Army and not yet separate departments.[76] Despite these recruiting difficulties, on

November 10, the Continental Congress resolved: "That two Battalions of marines be raised…and that they be considered as part of…the continental Army", thus laying the groundwork for the modern United States Marine Corps. Meanwhile, Col. Richard Gridley, Commander of the Artillery, who had determined to retire shortly after Bunker Hill, finally did so. In respect for his service, Congress resolved to pay him the half-pay he had given up from his former British service. The next artillery officers in succession felt themselves too old to take on the burdens of command and instead wholeheartedly supported the relatively unknown Boston bookseller Henry Knox. Knox had been serving as a volunteer since Bunker Hill, and it was only on November 17 that Congress commissioned him into the Army, giving him the rank of colonel.[77]

However, since Congress was in distant Philadelphia, Knox was

PORTRAIT OF COL. HENRY KNOX (C. 1805, DEPICTED AS A MAJOR GENERAL) BY GILBERT STUART (1755–1828). PHOTOGRAPH © 2015 MUSEUM OF FINE ARTS, BOSTON.

unaware of his impending commission when Washington, on the day before, ordered him first to New York to inventory the artillery supplies and then onward to Fort Ticonderoga. For some time, Washington had been anxious to take the offensive against the British in Boston, but with so few cannon and so little gunpowder, he hardly had the means to act, even defensively. Knox's mission was to fulfill the plan laid out by Benedict Arnold so many months earlier: to collect from Fort Ticonderoga all the artillery pieces he could and transport them back to Cambridge. As Washington implored, "the want of them is so great, that no trouble or expence must be spared to obtain them."[78]

Thus, Colonel Knox set off for a brief visit to New York before proceeding on to Fort Ticonderoga to meet with General Schuyler, with the fate of Boston dependent on his success.

Since November 8, Col. Benedict Arnold and his men had been encamped at Point Levi, directly across the St. Lawrence from Quebec City. But that was as far as they could go. They had no means to cross the wide and frigid river, for along their journey the men had either lost or abandoned all of their batteaux.

Upon crossing into Canada, Arnold had hoped to receive word from General Montgomery. Arnold had also sent several messages himself. At least one he entrusted to an Indian courier, but instead of taking the letter to Montgomery, the Indian scout reported Arnold's whereabouts to the British. In response to this intelligence, the British stole all boats from the Point Levi side of the river. It was because of this treachery that Arnold now found himself stranded with no way to cross his men.

Arnold had in fact purchased a few canoes along the way from Sartigan, but they were hardly enough to ferry his expeditionary force. It took several days at Point Levi for him to scrounge or purchase what few canoes the British had failed to steal. Some came from neighboring towns, others from Indians, but finally he procured forty small canoes in all.[79]

With so few canoes, it would take three trips to ferry across his 550 men, but he could do no better.[80] And with HMS *Lizard* and HM sloop *Hunter* guarding the waters, he would have to wait until nightfall to attempt the crossing. The men's ability to maintain absolute silence was now crucial, lest they be discovered. If the first ferry was successful but the rest were caught crossing, the few men on the Quebec side would be sitting ducks and would be easily decimated by Quebec's garrison. Arnold needed every man he had if there was to be any hope of success against the city. He hoped Montgomery's force would join them there soon, and hopefully, they would bring cannon. As yet, Arnold had heard nothing from Montgomery and so knew nothing of his whereabouts or successes.

Just days earlier, British Col. Allan Maclean had taken the bulk of Quebec's defenders, including his Highland Regiment Emigrants, aboard two ships to rendezvous with General Carleton from Montreal, hoping to together relieve the Siege of Fort St. Johns. When Carleton's flotilla was repulsed from Longueuil, Maclean was anchored off Sorel to the east, at the mouth of the Richelieu River. There he lingered, awaiting further instructions. But after the Yankees took Fort St. Johns days later, American General Montgomery sent Maj. John Brown to Sorel both to block the St. Lawrence and to ensure no British forces sailed from Quebec to aid Montreal. At Sorel, on about November 8, Brown discovered Maclean's forces, and a small skirmish ensued. Maclean wisely took to his two ships, the schooner *Providence* and the snow *Fell*, and his small force departed down the St. Lawrence River back to Quebec.[81]

Meanwhile, Montgomery's forces made their way amid sleet and rain along the mired fifteen-mile road from St. Johns, encumbered by their heavy artillery but finally reaching La Prairie. There they halted to prepare to cross the St. Lawrence River and head into Montreal. On November 10, part of Brigadier General Wooster's regiment was the first to cross. However, like Arnold, Montgomery lacked sufficient boats, for his little navy could not exit the Lake Champlain region due to the several small waterfalls north of St. Johns. With few boats and poor weather, Montgomery's dangerous crossing was to be a two-day affair.

Inside Montreal, General Carleton had opted to abandon the town and instead make his stand downriver at Quebec. So as Montgomery continued to cross his men, Carleton handed over the disposition of Montreal to the civil government and then concentrated his efforts on hastily embarking what military stores they could and destroying the rest. By the time the bulk of Montgomery's lead forces crossed the river and made their way to the suburbs of Montreal, Carleton had boarded the small armed brigantine *Gaspee*, escorted by two armed vessels and eight small transports, all laden with provisions.[82] On November 11, probably late that evening, they set sail northeastward under a fair wind, just hours ahead of Montgomery's arrival.

But luck was not with the British. The weather turned into a cold, fierce gale, the river became choppy, and on the next day, one of their ships ran aground. They got it back afloat, but all they could do was anchor off Sorel and weather the storm. Despite the rough waters, Montgomery meanwhile had crossed the remainder of his forces to Montreal.

Without military support, the civil government knew any attempt to hold the town was futile, so the best they could hope for was to preserve their personal property and liberty. Accordingly, Montreal officials sent couriers to Montgomery to meet him on the road, even before he arrived outside the town, to present terms for their immediate surrender. To their surprise, Montgomery stated they had no right to terms as they had no means of defense, but he assured them his forces came not as enemies but as friends to protect them, and that they would be safe and there would be no plundering. Thus, on November 12, Montgomery issued his own terms of surrender, which were accepted, and on the next morning took possession of the town. Unaware that Carleton had fled, Montgomery's troops then immediately searched the town for the governor, only to learn he had already escaped.[83]

Downriver at Point Levi, Benedict Arnold prepared to cross to Quebec City. However, the same weather that hampered Carleton's escape also delayed Arnold. In fact, Arnold was ready to cross as early as November 11, but he was unwilling to risk his men in a nighttime crossing under such adverse conditions. Yet by tarrying too long, Arnold lost the advantage. On November 12, despite the gale, Col. Allan Maclean returned with his garrison and two vessels and retook command of the city from irresolute Lieutenant Governor Hector Cramahé, who happily secluded himself in his house for the remainder of the winter.[84] When

Arnold learned of Maclean's return, he cursed his luck and delays. "Had I been ten Days sooner, Quebec must inevitably have fallen into Our Hands, as there was not a Man there to oppose us".[85]

On the next day, the weather broke, so Arnold committed to attempting his crossing that night. As they spent the day preparing, Arnold finally received positive intelligence of Montgomery's whereabouts via a letter from perhaps Col. James Easton at Sorel. Arnold sent off a hasty dispatch back to Montgomery that night. The two prongs of the Canadian expedition were finally in contact and would soon be in concert.[86]

Starting at about nine o'clock that night of November 13, as a waning gibbous moon rose into the night sky, Arnold's force began to cross the St. Lawrence, one-third at a time.[87] Silence was critical to get past the small gunboat patrols and the perhaps four ships patrolling the river.[88] To add to their problems, though Arnold's men had built scaling ladders in hopes of breaching the walls of Quebec, they discovered the ladders too cumbersome to ferry on their small canoes and so abandoned them at Point Levi.

With muffled oars, the force silently made their way across. After two-thirds of his men had crossed, the last set off. Suddenly, one rather flimsy canoe, overladen with men, burst open, dumping all its passengers into the icy river. Despite the paralyzing cold, they managed to swim to nearby canoes and scramble aboard. But poor Lt. Archibald Steele could find no canoe with room to take him. All they could do was tow him over as he shivered and grew numb.[89]

The commotion of the bursting canoe was what probably led to their discovery by a "frigate's barge", possibly the *Hunter*'s longboat. It opened fire! Most of Arnold's men paddled as quickly as they could, but some fired muskets back at their assailants, killing three of the barge's men and obliging it to turn away. Arnold had just lost any hope of taking Quebec by surprise.[90]

By four o'clock in the morning, Arnold's entire force was crossed, landing at Wolfe's Cove, where they promptly built a secluded fire to warm up poor Lieutenant Steele. They then ascended the cliffs to the Plains of Abraham, the same plains upon which the famous British Maj. Gen. James Wolfe had defeated the French Marquis de Montcalm in the decisive victory of 1759 that spelled the end of French rule in Canada. Unlike Wolfe's forces, however, who had to ascend a steep acclivity, Arnold's scaled it easily via a slanting road cut since.[91] As dawn approached, they laid their eyes for the first time on the great western wall of the Quebec fortress, with its six massive granite bastions jutting toward the fatigued Americans as if to flaunt the city's mighty bulwarks, and all along it, gleaming cannon. The fortress that was Quebec City had never been taken by storm, and Arnold knew it.

It was now daylight, and the Scotsman Colonel Maclean acted decisively. The weather was cold and getting colder, and the Americans were ragged and tired. So Maclean sent forth a few troops, and as the Americans were crossing the expansive Plains of Abraham toward the city, Maclean's men set fire to the intervening and now abandoned suburb of St. John (Saint-Jean-Baptiste) and to other scattered houses outside the fortress walls, and managed to capture a rifleman sentry.[92] Undaunted, Arnold marched his men through billowing smoke and flame to within 800 yards of the great walled city. There they halted and huzzahed three times.

Maclean had some 1,011 British, including his now complete regiment of 200 Royal Highlander Emigrants and the marines and crew of *Hunter* and *Lizard*, their ships having been beached in anticipation of the river freezing over. This also included the remaining 63 officers and men of the 7th Royal Fusiliers. Additionally, he had some 300 Canadian militia. (All told, there were about 5,000 souls inside the walls of Quebec who might have come to the aid of either adversary.) So it was that Maclean's mix of 1,311 armed men replied to the Americans with three huzzahs of their own. The British then "saluted" the American arrival by blasting at them with grapeshot and canister shot, quickly scattering Arnold's men.[93]

Arnold next sent an officer under a flag of truce toward the city, carrying with him terms of surrender. The British must have laughed. They saw 550 men with no cannon, no ladders, standing outside the great walled city that many deemed impenetrable, the entire city armed as it was with something approaching 140 cannon.[94] Maclean had no reason to fear an assault. All he feared was how long his provisions would last with so many people inside Quebec. He noted days after Arnold's arrival that it was a "very disagreeable situation we are in...so that we can get nothing into the Town".[95]

As the New Jersey volunteer Maj. Matthias Ogden approached under a flag of truce, the British fired at him with an 18-pounder. The artillerymen must have laughed as the envoy turned and quickly ran back, narrowly escaping the cannon shot. Arnold was appalled, stating that the response was "contrary to humanity and the laws of nations". He gave the British a day before trying again. The next morning, Ogden was again sent, and again he was fired upon. The British laughed as before, thoroughly enjoying their target practice and hoping Arnold would send a third target for them. Arnold did, and the British fired on the courier a third time. Finally, Arnold gave up his attempt to parley.[96] There was to be no negotiation, and Arnold was slightly peeved that the British did not take him seriously. However, he knew he could not presently assault the town, so he waited in anticipation for Montgomery's arrival and particularly for his cannon.

Montgomery had problems of his own. Now that he had taken Montreal, he was obliged to hold true to his promise to allow those men desiring to depart early, ahead of their enlistments, to do so. Much to his chagrin, a mass exodus followed, including nearly all the New Englanders, such as Seth Warner's Green Mountain Boys and Colonel Bedel's New Hampshire Rangers. Fortunately, the valiant New Yorkers were determined to see the campaign to its conclusion, probably due to localism, because Montgomery was a New Yorker. Wooster's Connecticut regiment also remained. As for the rest, Montgomery pleaded with them to stay on, but they would not have it. He could not comprehend how so many could depart with victory so close. Nevertheless, with disappointment and despair, Montgomery watched as more than half his army left him.[97]

General Schuyler learned of the exodus as the men made their way southward via Fort Ticonderoga. Writing to Congress, he bemoaned, "It might have been expected that men influenced by a sense of liberty would not have required such a promise [as to be sent home after Montreal], and that others, to whom it was not immediately intended, would not have taken the advantage of it; but all this flows from the same unhappy source with the other disorders too prevalent in our troops—a want of subordination and discipline, an evil which may prove fatal to us."[98]

The exodus quickly deflated the morale of the meager force that remained in Montreal, though Montgomery bolstered their spirits some when he ordered the town's military spoils dispersed. The men were especially cheerful when they received their new coats, but not just any coats: British redcoats! It was a strange sight to behold: American troops donning the red coats of their adversary!

Administration aside, Montgomery was anxious to join Arnold at Quebec. But first, he had one more problem to deal with. Carleton's flotilla had anchored off Sorel. Montgomery knew this and had immediately dispatched batteaux armed with small cannon to seek the governor out. Meanwhile, on November 15, the concealed Americans in Sorel proper moved their cannon into an advantageous position and began firing. Because the St. Lawrence grows quite narrow near Sorel, other American forces began setting up cannon immediately across the river in hopes of pinning the British in a deadly crossfire. An American gunboat also revealed itself and cautiously moved in to harry the British.

The winds were still contrary for a drive to Quebec, so the British fleet could only shift its anchorage upriver (westward) and out of range of the Sorel cannon. The new American commander at Sorel, Col. James Easton, sent a rowboat under a flag of truce with the following proposal: "Sir by this you will learn that General Montgomery is in Possession of the Fortress Montreal—You are very Sensible that I am in Possession at this Place, and that from the Strength of the United Colonies on both sides your own situation is Rendered Very disagreeable…I am therefore induced to make you the following Proposal, viz—That if you will Resign your Fleet to me Immediately without destroying the Effects on Board, You and Your men shall be used with due civility together with women & Children on Board—to this I expect Your direct and Immediate answer. Should you Neglect You will Cheerfully take the Consequences which will follow—".[99]

Carleton weighed his options. He could not see from his position the number of cannon at Sorel, though he might have spotted Montgomery's armed batteaux making their way from the southwest. All he knew was that his force had but thirty guns including those on his flagship *Gaspee*, which mounted just six carronades.[100] While he could take a chance at running the blockade, the contrary wind and the resulting inability to maneuver left his naval officers unconvinced.

Biding his time, Carleton doubted the invincibility of the blockade and said so to Easton's courier, to which the American invited Carleton to send someone over to inspect their batteries. Carleton accepted the offer and sent some observer back with Easton's courier to Sorel. In truth, the Americans had only a handful of small cannon at Sorel, but by trickery and double-talk, they managed to dupe the British observer into thinking the situation more dire than it was. Had Carleton known better, he should have run the blockade. At any rate, this jockeying seems to have bought the British another day.

Finally, Carleton and his officers agreed that what was most important was getting the governor to Quebec, for the very fate of the colony depended on it. They settled upon a plan to sneak Carleton past the blockade that night, November 16.

As the night grew darkest, Carleton, dressed like a Canadian peasant, got into a birch canoe with maybe six men, perhaps two of which were officers. One of these was a French-Canadian named Jean Baptiste Bouchette, known to be a skilled and swift pilot, affectionately nicknamed *La Tourte* (The Pigeon). After being quietly lowered to the water, they softly rowed toward Sorel's batteries with muffled oars. Once in close, they cautiously paddled forward with their bare hands, holding their breath as they did so.

Aboard ship, command devolved to Carleton's deputy, Brig. Gen. Richard Prescott. The next morning, the British ships dumped their powder and cannon shot into the river, and then immediately surrendered. Easton's men were happy with the easy victory, and they quickly moved to secure the considerable provisions and stores. They also took prisoner some 144 regulars including their officers, probably the remainder of the 26th Regiment. But again, they found no governor.[101]

Governor Carleton's canoe was instead making its way safely down the St. Lawrence. The canoe was spotted the next morning by the British snow *Fell*, out on patrol. Once her precious cargo was safely aboard, the vessel came about and made for Quebec.[102]

Montgomery was embarrassed for his former British comrades, giving up their ships without a fight. "Such an instance of base poltroonery I never met with! and all because we had a half-a-dozen cannon on the bank of the river to annoy him in his retreat."[103]

At Quebec, Colonel Maclean had set to making war preparations. When he heard the news of Montreal's fall and yet knew nothing of Carleton's escape, he mourned, "I have the misfortune to be the Oldest King's Officer in Canada".[104] Maclean, now believing the defense of the province had fallen to him, prepared to attack Arnold immediately.

Arnold received intelligence on November 19 that Maclean was indeed preparing to sally forth with his garrison and make an attack. Accordingly, Arnold assessed his situation. His men inspected their gunpowder cartridges, only to discover many were wet from the sleet and snow, and so unfit for use. They also had only enough ammunition for four rounds per man. Entrenching was impossible because the ground was frozen solid. Finally, the men were greatly fatigued, some sick, and most without proper clothing. Instead of facing what he believed was an overwhelming force under such disadvantageous circumstances, Arnold opted to retreat back some nineteen miles southwest along the St. Lawrence to Pointe-aux-Trembles (modern Neuville). They departed immediately at three o'clock in the morning and marched all the next day. As they made their way, they saw the *Fell* with Carleton aboard making her way to Quebec, escorted by a small schooner, perhaps the *Providence*.[105]

Back in Montreal, Montgomery still lingered. One administrative delay after another kept him there, such as dealing with the prisoners captured from Carleton's flotilla. The Americans were especially excited with the capture of General Prescott, for it was now widely known that it was he who had treated Ethan Allen harshly before shipping him off to England, and the troops wanted retribution. Though Montgomery treated Prescott with contempt, he would not allow himself to sink to Prescott's level. At this, some of Montgomery's officers became mutinous and, as he explained to Schuyler, "presumed to remonstrate against the indulgence I had given some of the officers of the King's troops. Such an insult I could not bear, and immediately resigned. Today they qualified it by such an apology as puts it in my power to resume command."[106]

The idea of resigning his command would continually linger on Montgomery's mind. He remained particularly affected by the quitting of so many of his troops. He wrote to Schuyler, "Will not your health permit you to reside at Montreal this winter?... I am weary of power, and totally [in] want [of] that patience and temper so requisite for such a command." In the same letter, he also mused, "I think [Gen. Charles] Lee ought by all means to have the command here."[107] Montgomery was especially homesick. He had given up the life of a soldier once for that of a gentleman farmer, and he and his wife of just two years had looked forward to a quiet life. That dream was shattered when he found himself swept up in the continental struggle.[108]

Schuyler was equally affected upon seeing the exodus from Montreal as it passed by Fort Ticonderoga. Being unable to persuade them to turn back and continue through the campaign, he considered Montgomery's example. In writing to Congress of Montgomery's intention to retire, Schuyler added, "My sentiments...exactly coincide with his... I shall, however, do every thing in my power to put a finishing stroke on the campaign, and make the best arrangement in my power in order to ensure success to the next; this done, I must beg leave to retire."[109] Schuyler further explained to Washington, "Our Army requires to be put on quite a different Footing. Gentlemen in Command, find It very disagreeable to Coax, wheedle and even to Lye, to carry on the Service. Habituated to Order, I cannot without the most extreme Pain, see that Disregard of Discipline, Confusion & Inattention which reigns so General in this Quarter, & am therefore determined to retire, of this Resolution I have advised Congress."[110]

John Hancock, as president of the Continental Congress, personally wrote letters to both Schuyler and Montgomery, begging them to stay. To Montgomery he explained, "the Loss of so brave and experienced an Officer will be universally regretted as a Misfortune to all America. But they [America] still hope that upon reconsidering the Matter, the same generous and patriotic Motives, which first induced you to take so capital a Part in opposing the unprovoked Hostilities of an unnatural Enemy, will prompt you to persevere in the Cause, and to continue gathering fresh Laurels, till you find our Oppressions reduced to Reason, and America restored to her constitutional Liberties."[111]

However, it was George Washington's reply that was most poignant. He wrote to Schuyler, "I am very sorry to find…that both you and General Montgomery incline to quit the Service—Let me ask you Sir, when is the Time for brave Men to exert themselves in the Cause of Liberty and their Country, if this is not? Should any Difficulties that they may have to encounter at this important Crisis deter them? God knows there is not a Difficulty that you both (very justly) complain of that I have not in an eminent Degree experienced; that I am not every Day experiencing, but we must bear up against them, and make the best of Mankind as they are, since we cannot have them as we wish— Let me therefore conjure you and Mr Montgomery to lay aside such Thoughts—Thoughts injurious to yourselves and excessively so to your Country which calls aloud for Gentlemen of your abilities."[112]

Schuyler decided to stay on, but on December 7, hoping more comfortable surroundings might help his ailments, he would relocate his headquarters to his home in Albany.

Montgomery, being too much the soldier to quit now, also decided to serve a little longer. "I have courted fortune and found her kind. I have one more favor to solicit and then I have done."[113]

Meanwhile, as it was now the end of November, Montgomery's greatest administrative concern was that he had but a month left until many of his men's enlistments officially expired. Some, such as Col. Rudolphus Ritzma's 1st New York Regiment, renewed their enlistments for another six months, extending their term until mid-April. But most did not.[114] To help augment his depleted force, Montgomery decided to officially recognize Canadian James Livingston's help to the cause and so commissioned him a colonel with his perhaps now only two hundred volunteers formed into a Canadian regiment.[115]

Finally, after far too many delays, on November 28, Montgomery was ready to depart Montreal. He left behind a large part of his force under the command of Brigadier General Wooster. The rest boarded the captured vessel *Gaspee* and the schooner *Maria*, perhaps a meager three hundred American troops in all, along with four fieldpieces and six mortars. Colonel Livingston's Canadian force of about two hundred was to march to Quebec separately.[116]

On December 1, snow began to fall at Pointe-aux-Trembles, where Arnold's forces were waiting. Their clothes were tattered, but no wool or

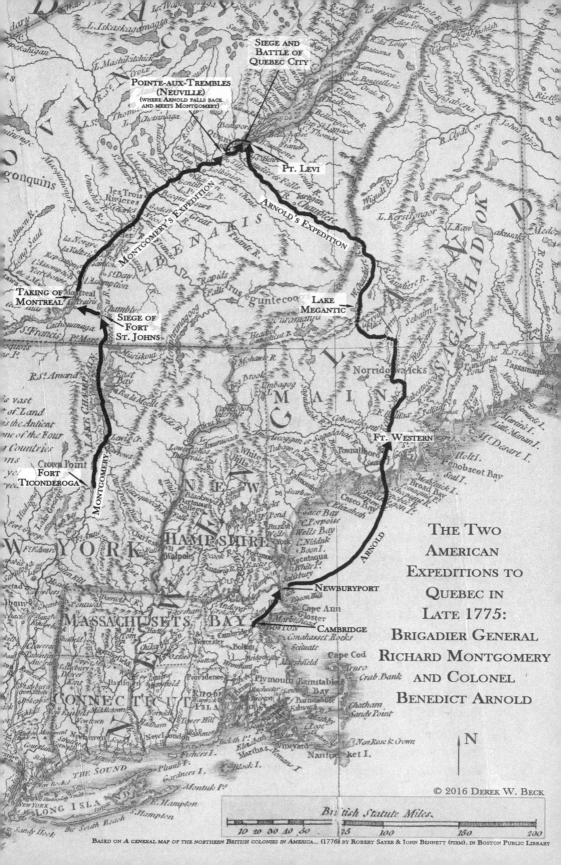

SIEGE AND
BATTLE OF
QUEBEC CITY

POINTE-AUX-TREMBLES
(NEUVILLE)
(WHERE ARNOLD FALLS BACK
AND MEETS MONTGOMERY)

PT. LEVI

ARNOLD'S EXPEDITION

MONTGOMERY'S EXPEDITION

TAKING OF
MONTREAL

SIEGE OF
FORT
ST. JOHNS

LAKE
MEGANTIC

Norridgewocks

FT. WESTERN

CROWN POINT
FORT
TICONDEROGA

MONTGOMERY

ARNOLD

NEWBURYPORT

CAMBRIDGE

THE TWO
AMERICAN
EXPEDITIONS TO
QUEBEC IN
LATE 1775:
BRIGADIER GENERAL
RICHARD MONTGOMERY
AND COLONEL
BENEDICT ARNOLD

N

© 2016 DEREK W. BECK

British Statute Miles.

10 20 30 40 50   75   100   150   200

BASED ON A GENERAL MAP OF THE NORTHERN BRITISH COLONIES IN AMERICA... (1776) BY ROBERT SAYER & JOHN BENNETT (FIRM), IN BOSTON PUBLIC LIBRARY cloth was locally available by which to make new ones. All they could do was fabricate moccasins out of sealskin leather, stuffing them with hay or leaves for warmth, as was the local custom.[117]

———•———

Then, on December 2, Montgomery's two ships arrived at Pointe-aux-Trembles amid cheers and huzzahs from Arnold's exhausted men. It was on this day that Richard Montgomery and Benedict Arnold met for the first time, and each was quite impressed with the other. Montgomery then gave a short but "energetic and elegant" speech that encouraged Arnold's men, who continued to huzzah throughout.[118] All were immediately taken with Montgomery, one noting, "He is a genteel appearing man, tall and slender of make, bald on the Top of his head, resolute [word unintelligible] and mild, of an agreeable temper, and a virtuous General".[119] Another added, "His easy and affable condescension to both officers and men, while it forbids an improper familiarity, creates love and esteem; and exhibits him the gentleman and soldier."[120] Montgomery was equally impressed with Arnold's soldiers, writing Schuyler, "There is a style of discipline among them, much superior to what I have been used to see this campaign."[121]

The two forces spent a day there for reorganization and dispersing of provisions, for which Arnold's men were especially thankful, particularly for the red coats to cover their naked backs and the food to fill their empty bellies. Finally, the combined army set off. Most marched, while provisions and cannon proceeded by boat, all moving toward Quebec. By December 4, they had arrived. And within days, the new siege of the fortress city was well underway, but unlike the previous attempt, which had been Colonel Arnold versus Colonel Maclean, it was now General Montgomery versus General Carleton.

The total American force was only about 1,100 men, many conspicuously dressed in red coats.[122] In contrast, when Carleton had reached Quebec days earlier, he had but 1,300.[123] Carleton acted decisively. The city had plenty of supplies to survive through the spring, but Carleton refused to feed those able-bodied Canadians who refused to serve as militia. Moreover, as British Maj. Henry Caldwell put it, "We could guard against open and avowed enemies, but not against those lurking about town".[124] So back on November 22, almost immediately upon his return to the city, Carleton had issued an ultimatum: all such miscreants unwilling to take up arms for the defense of the city or who were otherwise unsure of their loyalties were to quit the town within four days, leaving behind their arms, "Under pain of being treated as Rebels or Spies".[125] Certainly, a few who departed joined with the Americans, but most dispersed to the countryside. Of those who remained, even if their motive was only to protect their property, they were now compelled to take up arms. As Major Caldwell noted, with the miscreants purged, "everybody seemed zealous for the public service".[126] So with the newly augmented militia, the British Canadian force was now near 1,800 men.[127]

Given his insufficient cannon and men, Montgomery should have simply continued his siege until more Continental troops arrived to his support. However, a clock was ticking against him, and he knew that by the end of the month, with enlistments expiring, many of his men would depart. His only hope was to take the offensive. If successful, he would thereby secure all of the Province of Quebec. So he again put his faith in Fortune, as he so often did. He wrote on December 5 to Schuyler, "Fortune often baffles the sanguine expectations of poor mortals. I am not intoxicated with the favours I have received at her hands, but I do think there is a fair prospect of success."[128]

Under this time constraint, Montgomery and Arnold prepared to attack the mighty fortress that was Quebec City. But Carleton and Maclean knew the attack would come, and they were more than ready.

CHAPTER 6

DESPERATE MEASURES

The British in Massachusetts were doing very little throughout the winter. Charlestown's garrison had been reduced to a small one, instead of building new barracks there. In Boston, the regulars had by late October all moved into their winter quarters, including newly built barracks and, courtesy of enforcement of the Quartering Act, barns and unoccupied homes. (It is a myth that the Quartering Act allowed for occupied homes to be given over to the soldiers. No citizens were turned out of their homes. Inns, stables, barns, and uninhabited homes were used. The act also required the colonies to pay for supplying the Army, but given the open war, none would do so.)[1]

Since the Siege of Boston remained at a stalemate, fresh provisions continued to be in short supply, particularly as whaleboat privateers and Washington's navy gained confidence and skill in interdicting supply boats. Smallpox also began to fester in the city, and sickness and pestilence quickly spread. As one British officer noted, "Thirty bodies are frequently thrown into a trench at a time, like those of so many dogs, no bell being suffered to toll upon the occasion."[2] The Blockade of Boston even prevented fuel from being brought into the town, forcing the British to pull down empty houses, fences, and trees, all for use in heating homes and preparing meals. The British also took over the Old South Meeting House, which they stripped of its pulpit and pews, most destined for fuel. However, one beautifully carved box pew with its silk furniture was carried to an officer's house and made into a pigpen. The emptied Old South was then turned into a riding school for the 17th Light Dragoons.[3]

Despite Washington's best efforts to tighten his siege around Boston and blockade it, the British continued to get the occasional supply ship into the harbor, always, it seemed, just as the situation was becoming desperate. Salt provisions they had plenty of, but on November 19, a large ship arrived from England with every kind of provisions, "dead and alive"—hogs, sheep, fowls, ducks, eggs, mincemeat, and even gingerbread for the holiday season.[4] Despite the arrival of the few supply ships, Howe decided to expel some three hundred citizens from Boston by vessel to nearby Point Shirley in late November. Most were poor, some had the pox, and all were draining Howe's scant resources.[5]

The difficulty of this situation conspired against troop morale, and the British began to question the strategy and wisdom of their present course. One officer wrote, "If we hear a gun fired upon the Neck, we are all under arms in a moment, and tremble least the Provincials should force their way into the town and put us all to the sword for our cruelty at Lexington and setting fire to…Charlestown. Certainly our conduct at both places was alike inhuman and unjustifiable; and if heaven punishes us for it, it is no more than we deserve… But the glorious expedition we are upon is approved of by an all-wise, all-merciful Ministry; and therefore all must be right… 'Tis well for our generals that we have no where to run to; for could the men desert, I am of opinion that they would soon be left by themselves; but situated as we are, we must unavoidably live and die together."[6] Occasionally, soldiers did attempt to desert, but they seem to have been few, for the enterprise was now difficult, with the British always on guard for an attack. At least one soldier was caught deserting and was hanged before the camp, probably in Boston Common, to serve as a gruesome warning for other soldiers harboring such thoughts.[7]

Frustrations were not limited to the lowly British soldier.[8] Gen. John Burgoyne was the junior of the three major generals, and he quickly found his services of little use in Boston. To occupy himself, he turned to his hobby as a playwright. He helped produce the ambitious tragedy *Zara*, writing for it a prologue and epilogue that "exhorted the conquering Britons to mercy, and the rebellious Americans to return to their duty." *Zara* opened at Faneuil Hall to a packed crowd and would play several times throughout the late fall.[9] This was a welcomed diversion for bored soldiers and unemployed citizens alike.

But Burgoyne was restless. He had done little in way of the assault on Breed's Hill, and with the Army now languishing behind the Siege and no British plan to break free, he began writing to the home government for permission to return to England. Burgoyne's petitions were finally approved, and on December 5, he sailed for home aboard HMS *Boyne*.[10] On his departure, one newspaper commented, "We hear that General Burgoyne, giving over all hopes of obtaining that elbow room he expected, is absolutely going home."[11]

A few other British Army changes took place at this time. Lord Percy, officially a colonel with the brevet rank of brigadier in American only, was breveted to major general in America only. And Lt. Col. Francis Smith, of the Expedition to Concord fiasco, was made aide-de-camp to the King, officially promoted to full colonel, and breveted to brigadier in America only—likely causing grumblings amongst the men.[12] Finally, each regiment was to be increased from ten companies to twelve (excluding the two extras on permanent recruiting service at home), and each company was to be expanded from thirty-nine to fifty-six soldiers.[13] However, it would take some time to recruit, equip, and ship these additional men to America.

Washington's own reorganization was also still underway, including the raising of an official Navy. First, the ragtag fleet of whaleboats—self-proclaimed privateers—was legitimized by the issuing of letters of marque. Even so, the privateers were an ever-present headache for the American commander in chief. "Our Rascally privateers-men, go on at the old rate, Mutinying if they can not do as they please," he wrote his trusted former secretary Joseph Reed.[14] Next, Congress on December 11 resolved to have built a Continental squadron of frigates consisting of five 32-gun ships, an equal number with 28-guns, and three 23-gun ships—thirteen total, though they would not be ready until 1776.[15]

In the meantime, Washington commissioned his own navy. The first vessel was the schooner *Hannah*, which sailed on September 5.[16] About a month later, *Hannah*'s crew was "removd to a vessell of better fame for Sailing"—the *Lynch*—one of six additional schooners that had been acquired and fitted for naval warfare, most of which set sail by late October.[17] The largest of these six was the *Washington*, armed with ten light guns, while the others mounted maybe just four 4-pounders. With such a small armament, the value of this navy was not in its firepower but in its speed and agility to raid against unsuspecting transports, armed or otherwise. Washington's fleet posed no threat to a British man-of-war. However, the dawn of the genuine American Navy did not end Washington's problems at sea.[18]

While Washington's small fleet enjoyed some success attacking unarmed supply ships of all kinds, the legality of their seizures became a pressing issue. Upon off-loading the cargoes in New England harbors, the sailors often found that much of the supply ships' stores were privately owned, not those of the military. Under the accepted rules of war, private cargoes had immunity against a legally conducted naval raid. Congress and Washington were especially careful to conduct their agenda in a legally defensible manner. To address these issues, Washington urged the formation of an admiralty court. Congress dawdled, and instead Massachusetts led the way. However, it would be well into 1776 before the Massachusetts Admiralty Court was operational.[19]

The problems with the seamen did not end with this officially sanctioned navy. Washington wrote to Congress, "the plague trouble & vexation I have had with the Crews of all the armed vessells, is inexpressable, I do believe there is not on earth, a more disorderly Set, every time they Come into port, we hear of Nothing but mutinous Complaints…the Crews of the Washington & Harrison have Actually deserted them".[20] To be sure, the sailors had some reason to complain. General Washington's agent reported, "After repairing on board the brig [*Washington*] Saturday night, enquiring into the cause of the uneasiness [a polite way to describe their dereliction of duty] among the people and finding it principally owing to their want of clothing, and after supplying them with what they wanted, the whole crew, to a man, gave three cheers and declared their readiness to go to sea the next morning."[21] Clothing may have helped some, but what they really required was the example of a naval success. Fortunately, a shining star was about to rise as that example for all the fleet and so justify all of Washington's naval burdens.

That star was Capt. John Manly of the schooner *Lee*, fitted with four 4-pounders and ten swivels and manned by fifty sailors.[22] When Washington gained intelligence that the British were particularly worried about the *Nancy* transport's safe arrival to Boston, he naturally put his armed vessels on the lookout for her. In November, the brigantine *Nancy* was still making her way across the Atlantic. She was unarmed but protected by an armed convoy. Weather had dealt its hand, however, and *Nancy* became separated from her protectors.

Unescorted, she made her way toward Boston and even reached the mouth of the harbor before being driven back by poor weather. Finally, from the deck of his schooner *Lee*, Captain Manly spotted her on the horizon. Manly brought the *Lee* fast about, and with her fair curves and smooth lines, she made swift speed to the struggling British transport. Master Robert Hunter surrendered his defenseless *Nancy* without a fight, and the *Lee* escorted her into Gloucester on about November 29.[23] Gloucester militiamen then provided security while *Nancy*'s stores were disembarked.

And what stores they were! She had no gunpowder, but had every other war-making store that Washington desperately required. He had been begging for flints, and with one stroke, he now had one hundred thousand. Many of his volunteers had no guns, while others had relics inherited from the French and Indian War, and now Washington had two thousand new guns, complete with bayonets, rammers, and fittings. Musket balls were aplenty: more than thirty-one tons. Every kind of military equipment he could desire was there, from entrenching tools and encampment supplies, to artillery supply wagons and rounds. The most impressive find, however, was a massive 13-inch brass mortar, which they christened the Congress. In honor of this fortuitous seizure, they celebrated as only soldiers and sailors can, temporarily turning the Congress into a punchbowl.[24]

This was among the first of many naval victories to come. Congress would continue to legitimize the American Navy and, on December 22, would name Esek Hopkins the first commander in chief of the Continental Navy.[25]

Nancy's cache of military stores solved one of Washington's many critical problems, but the problem of the Army reenlistment was ever weighing on his mind. Just as it was with Montgomery's army in Quebec, Washington knew that unless something changed, his army in Massachusetts was set to dissolve in just a few weeks.

While enlistments continued to trickle in, by December 4, Washington had just 4,800 committed for the next year, less than a quarter he had hoped for.[26] He was particularly frustrated with the dismal support from the Connecticut men. They, more than any of the others, were keen on leaving under all circumstances. The immediacy of the problem was exacerbated because, unlike the rest of the colonies, Connecticut's enlistments expired on December 10.

Washington had been working with Whiggish Gov. Jonathan Trumbull of Connecticut to raise up new enlisted recruits in place of those determined to leave, but as early as December 2, the Connecticut men began an exodus—eight days early. These men left without approval or discharge. They simply packed up and moved out. Washington was astonished. He issued general orders warning that any who left without an official discharge would be treated as deserters. He also sent an express to Governor Trumbull with the names of those who had departed early, so "that they may be dealt with, in a manner suited to the Ignominy of their behaviour."[27]

As for the rest of the Connecticut soldiers, many were counting down the days, despite their officers' pleas to stay on. Simeon Lyman was one such Connecticuter that refused to be bullied into staying a single day more. As he wrote in his journal for November 29, his regiment was ordered to parade before "the genera[l's] door", probably that of Gen. Charles Lee's headquarters, Hobgoblin Hall. The general then gave the men a spirited speech soliciting them to stay on for another year. Some one hundred agreed, but the rest, maybe another three hundred, refused. A few days later, they were paraded again, and this time, both General Lee and Brig. Gen. John Sullivan begged the men to stay on, but just four days longer. Yet the men refused even this. According to Lyman, Lee then formed them up into a hollow square, and from its center he shouted, "'Men, I do not know what to call you; [you] are the worst of all creatures,' and flung and curst and swore at us, and said if [we] would not stay he would order us to go on [to British-controlled] Bunker Hill and if we would not go he would order the riflemen to fire at us, and they talked they would take our guns and take our names down, and our lieutenants begged of us to stay". One Connecticuter thought of departing immediately, and upon asking if any would join him, was seen by General Lee, who "catched his gun out of his hands and struck him on the head and ordered him to be put under guard." However, for all of Lee's threats and showmanship, he was unable to convince more to commit beyond their enlistment date. By December 2, "a paper was set up on the general's door not to let the soldiers have any victuals if they would not stay 3 weeks longer," with similar warnings supposedly given throughout the countryside for fifty miles. According to Lyman, "the paper was took down as soon as it was dark, and another put up that General Lee was a fool". The Connecticut men were paraded and harangued daily until the eve of their discharge, but Lyman, along with the greater part of his regiment, refused to be swayed. On December 10, they turned in their guns and ammunition, and promptly left the encampment.[28]

The void left by the Connecticut men was like a poison that infected the other troops and hindered the reenlistment effort. Gen. Nathanael Greene lamented that the troops of Rhode Island seemed on the verge of following the same example, biding their time until December 31. "I was in hopes...that ours would not have deserted the cause of their country... The Connecticut troops are going home in shoals this day... New-Hampshire behaves nobly; their troops engage cheerfully... But I fear the Colony of Rhode Island is upon the decline... I sent home some recruiting officers, they got scarcely a man, and report there are none to be had there".[29]

Why were these men, so zealous for the cause, now so eager to depart? While poor camp conditions, lack of supplies, and late pay were some reasons, Governor Trumbull suggested another to Washington. "The pulse of a New England man beats high for liberty—His engagement in the service he thinks purely voluntary—therefore in his estimation, when the time of inlistment is out, he thinks himself not holden, without further engagement, this was the case in the last war, I greatly fear its operation amongst the Soldiers of the other Colonies, as I am sensible this is the genius and spirit of our People."[30]

As the Connecticut troops marched away on December 10, though they were fully in their rights to do so, the various towns along the way received them with indignation. Some Connecticut men were even spurned upon reaching their hometowns. Meanwhile, to fill the now vacant ranks in the Continental Army, the Connecticut men were temporarily replaced with five thousand militia reserve, three thousand from Massachusetts and two from New Hampshire.[31]

Washington was greatly concerned with the arrival of these militia units, fearing that the discipline he had worked so hard to establish among the Continentals would again be broken. Yet when they arrived, it turned out many of these were the older men, veterans of the French and Indian War. Despite the bad conditions they were met with (there were still not yet enough barracks to receive them, and sufficient blankets and firewood were lacking), they served remarkably well, and Washington was quite pleased with their service.[32]

As 1775 drew to a close, those that had reenlisted were to remain with their old regiments until the end of the year. All the while, new recruits were trickling in and required training. Thus, the officers spent the last weeks of the year pulling double duty, tending both to their old and new regiments.

Despite all of his troubles, Washington still found time to write many detailed letters to his cousin Lund Washington, steward of the general's business affairs and caretaker of Mount Vernon. Washington also often wrote to his wife, Martha, and he was pleased that she accepted his invitation to stay the winter with him in Cambridge. She would arrive December 11.[33]

Just as Washington worked to hold together his army to maintain the Siege of Boston, Montgomery prepared to attack besieged Quebec before his own men's enlistments expired.

Outside Quebec City, Brig. Gen. Richard Montgomery and Col. Benedict Arnold contemplated their strategy. Quebec was a fortress city situated atop the eastern tip of a promontory known as Cape Diamond (Cap Diamant), formed by the confluence of a bend in the St. Lawrence to the south and east and the much smaller St. Charles River to the north, thus surrounded by water on three sides. The easternmost tip of these heights fell to near river level, upon which lay a waterfront district known as Lower Town, consisting mostly of warehouses, homes, and wharves. Overshadowing the Lower Town from the promontory's peak was the larger, main part of the city, known as Upper Town, the elevation of which varied from 200 to more than 300 feet at the southern edge, and had for its southern boundary a steep palisade that dropped to the St. Lawrence, leaving only a footpath along a narrow southern beach. Protecting the Upper Town were surrounding fortress walls of granite averaging 40 feet high and between 4 and 7 feet thick. The fortress also featured six prominent bastions facing westward toward the Heights or Plains of Abraham and what was left there of the suburb of St. John, the same suburb that Colonel Maclean had burned upon Arnold's arrival. Moreover, the walls were strong and intact, having never been battered by cannon, despite the former battle outside them in the French and Indian War. Access to the Upper Town fortress was through one of four strongly reinforced gates: St. John's Gate and the smaller St. Louis Gate to the west, Palace Gate to the north, which faced the suburb of St. Roch and guarded the only reasonable land approach to the Lower Town, and Prescott's Gate on the promontory's eastern face, through which passed the only road connecting the Lower Town to the Upper. As the Lower Town stood outside the great walls of the Upper, it was relatively unguarded, defended only by a few blockhouses and small palisades. However, in preparation for the anticipated rebel attack, the inhabitants of the Lower Town were evacuated to the Upper, and all its streets had been rigged with barricades and pickets. Furthermore, the British had something near 140 cannons throughout the Upper and Lower Towns, all mounted and ready for Quebec's defense.[34]

Before attacking this formidable fortress, Montgomery felt obliged to send a message of warning to its commander, General Carleton. Arnold alerted Montgomery that the British had fired upon his previous messengers, so Montgomery devised another means, employing an old local woman, a noncombatant, to take the message into the great walled city. She was successful in delivering the message, but Carleton was not amused at its words. It began, "the feelings of humanity induce me to have recourse of this expedient to save you from the Destruction which hangs over you." It then described that a city with such expansive walls could not be defended by such a meager and motley force as Carleton had. "I am at the head of troops, accustomed to success…it is with difficulty I restrain them till my Batteries are ready… Should you persist in an unwarrantable defense, the consequences be on your Head." Carleton however looked upon the note with contempt and, true to what he had told Lord Dartmouth, refused to respond to the rebels. Instead, with pomp and ceremony, accompanied by a drummer, the letter was handled by tongs, as if it were diseased, and promptly thrown into the fireplace.[35]

On the same day, December 6, Montgomery tried a second ploy. Appealing to the merchants and property owners, he wrote, "I find myself reduced to Measures which may overwhelm you with Distress. The City in Flames at this severe Season… We came with the professed Intention of eradicating Tyranny, and giving Liberty and Security to this oppressed Province, Private Property having ever by us been deemed sacred". (Perhaps he forgot about the private East India tea dumped during the Boston Tea Party, apparently not deemed sacred.) This message Montgomery sent with a second woman, but Carleton was aware of the plot, and so had her arrested and thrown in jail for a few days before she was drummed out of town.[36]

A few days later, Montgomery sent similar letters over the walls by bow and arrow, each "full of threats and scurrility."[37] That they yielded no results was not surprising, because they were bluffs and Montgomery knew it. All he could do was harry the British.

Arnold had previously written Montgomery to bring more mortars than cannon, as the walls would prove indestructible to any cannon available to the Americans. With mortars, they hoped to lob balls into the city and destroy the houses, but even these would have little effect, for the city was quite expansive. Regardless, few mortars were available, and Montgomery only brought a handful to complement his cannon.

The only real annoyance the rebels could offer came from their riflemen. Thomas Ainslie, a captain in Quebec's British militia, swore at their dastardly sniping. "Skulking Riflemen watching to fire on those who appear on the ramparts—We saw a man drop; we pop at all those who come within musket shot knowing their intention is to kill any single person walking on the ramparts—this is the American way of making war…they are worse than Savages, they will ever be held in contempt with men of courage. Lie in wait to shoot a sentry! a deed worthy of a Yanky men of war."[38]

The old way of thinking is now quite humorous: such audacity to shoot your enemy with a precise weapon such as a rifle! Ainslie was right in one regard—it did indeed take greater courage to dodge a wall of incoming gunshots in hopes of getting in close enough to run your enemy through with the bayonet.

Carleton felt reasonably secure in his fortress. He had enough provisions to last the winter and was due a massive reinforcement and supplies in the spring. More importantly, he knew well the lessons of history. In 1759, the arrogant French Marquis de Montcalm, anxious to answer British taunts, foolishly sallied forth from the then-French city-fortress with all his forces, meeting Gen. James Wolfe outside for the epic Battle of the Plains of Abraham. Both military leaders perished, but the English took the field, Quebec City, and ultimately all of Canada. Carleton would not make the same mistake Montcalm did. He would remain in the fortress walls and wait for Mother Nature to destroy his opponent by either sickness, cold, or starvation.

For now, the Americans took up residence in the many abandoned houses of the otherwise inhabited St. Roch suburb to the north, plus those few nearer houses that had escaped the conflagration of Maclean's earlier raid, remnants of the suburb of St. John. Montgomery and Arnold may have together shared the Holland House, which served as the American headquarters. It stood two miles southwest of the city's main St. John's Gate.[39]

The Americans' greatest problem was that winter had set in, preventing them from properly conducting the siege. Ordinarily, they would have built an ever-tightening line of entrenchments to bring their cannon and mortars ever closer to the city, but since the ground was now frozen solid and covered with snow, this was impossible. Instead, the American cannon were forced to take worthless potshots at the fortress from distant positions like St. Roch.

The best position for American artillery was on the Plains of Abraham, though there they would have no cover. Nevertheless, the Yankee artillerymen decided to experiment with an "ice battery", wicker gabions filled with snow and coated with water, which quickly froze, making an icy breastwork, intermixed with fascines. Before they tested it, Montgomery made a third attempt to parley with Carleton, sending his aide-de-camp along with Benedict Arnold and a drummer toward the city under a white flag of truce. But Carleton refused the meeting and they were turned away, though at least they were not fired upon as Colonel Maclean had done.

With that, Montgomery ordered Capt. John Lamb to commence firing from his ice battery. Outfitted with a mix of 9- and 12-pounders, five total plus a howitzer, Lamb gave the order and his ice battery came alive. Unfortunately, just like the occasional cannonades from St. Roch, this too was weak and useless. Instead, the ice battery's wimpy assault only drew the attention of the British artillerymen, who began amusing themselves by barraging it with their massive 32-pounders. The British scored multiple direct hits, dismounting several of Lamb's cannon, killing three Americans and injuring several others. The British continued to pound at the battery, huzzahing and jeering as they watched it shatter. Despite the untenable position, Lamb and his artillerymen clung to their little battery for maybe two days.

Amid the continuous bombardment, Montgomery came to the ice battery to inspect it. Turning to his artillery captain, he calmly commented, "This is a warm work, sir."

"It is indeed! And certainly no place for you, sir," Lamb told Montgomery.

"Why so, Captain?"

"Because there are enough of us here to be killed without the loss of you, which would be irreparable," Lamb replied.

By December 19, the ice battery was totally destroyed and left abandoned.[40]

Montgomery's best hope was to wait out the winter, devote his troops to foraging and gathering wood, and strengthen his position however he could. Yet he justifiably feared that the American reinforcements he expected in the spring would not arrive before those of Carleton. Were the British reinforced first, Montgomery would be severely outnumbered, and he knew he could not count on the finicky Canadians to rise up to his aid. In fact, few local Canadians were to be found, most having fled either to the safety of Quebec City or to distant villages. Montgomery could only hope they would join the American Cause once Quebec was reduced.

As he explained to Schuyler, "The enemy are expending the ammunition most liberally, and I fear the Canadians will not relish a union with the Colonies till they see the whole country in our hands, and defended by such a force as may relieve them from the apprehensions of again falling under the Ministerial lash. Were it not for these reasons, I should have been inclined to a blockade till towards the first of April, by which time the garrison would probably be much distressed for provisions and wood."[41] Yet Montgomery also knew he could not count on having much of an army past December, let alone April.

Meanwhile, occasional useless cannonades continued between both sides, with the British being unsuccessful only because the Americans learned to not venture too close. As Montgomery wrote to Brigadier General Wooster at Montreal, "I never expected any other advantage from our artillery than to amuse the enemy and blind them as to my real intention."[42]

What was his real intention? Whether to excite the men and so induce them to reenlist, or to simply use his meager forces before their enlistments expired, Montgomery determined his only course of action was to launch an attack on the city. His warning to Carleton was true enough: the city walls were indeed too extensive to man with such a small garrison as his. Carleton could not watch every corner of every wall at every hour. With Arnold's blessing, the two American commanders devised a strategy to attack the city by the end of the month. To aid in their element of surprise, they would wait until the next massive snowstorm. In the meantime, they began preparations for the eventual attack, including the building of scaling ladders.[43]

Days faded away, and still no snowstorm. By Christmas Day, Montgomery was worried, fearing he would lose perhaps half of his small force in only a week. He tried to encourage the men and gave them a spirited speech, noting that if they succeeded in taking the city, they would "rescue a province from the British yoke…and obtain for ourselves immortal honor." While some found it "sensible and concise", Abner Stocking thought it "rash and imprudent, but did not think proper to make any objections, lest I should be considered wanting in courage." Even so, Stocking observed that, for most of his brothers in arms, "the fire of patriotism kindled in our breasts, and we resolved to follow wherever he should lead."[44] As Montgomery wrote Schuyler, "I then had reason to believe the troops well inclined for a *coup-de-main*."[45]

Meanwhile, Schuyler, now at Albany, received Montgomery's latest letter with anticipation. "It has relieved me from a most distressing anxiety, occasioned by a report which prevailed here, that General Montgomery was killed, Colonel Arnold taken prisoner, and our Army totally defeated."[46] That nasty rumor had been circulating in Albany for some time, and while untrue, still served as an ill omen.

Washington in Cambridge and the Continental Congress in Philadelphia waited with anticipation, hoping to hear of Montgomery's success against Quebec. Washington wrote to Schuyler, "I flatter myself that your next Favour will give me an Account of General Montgomery's joining Colonel Arnold and that Quebec is or soon will be reduced to our possession".[47]

As cold weather and sickness took their toll, smallpox also began to plague the Americans outside Quebec. Montgomery had "not much above 800 men fit for duty exclusive of a few ragamuffin Canadians." These extra ragamuffins were some 200 Canadian locals that the Americans had managed to sway to join them.[48]

Finally, on December 27, a major snowstorm hit Quebec, giving Montgomery the ideal obscuration for his attack. His troops were put on standby, the newly built scaling ladders were made ready, those Americans dressed as redcoats affixed sprigs of hemlock to their hats to distinguish themselves, and once all was prepared, they waited for the word.[49] Montgomery wanted to commence the operation late that night, securing the greatest element of surprise.

And then…it stopped snowing!

Montgomery reluctantly called off the attack, and good thing. A

British prisoner, recently captured, had escaped back to the city, having "effected it by getting a bottle of rum, and making the sentry over him drunk." He took with him a cold and dejected American deserter, and both immediately informed the British of the American plan. As a cloudless, starry sky gave way to daylight, Montgomery could see the British had shifted their defenses to precisely the points on the Upper Town against which he had hoped to attack.[50]

Despite the setback, American spirits continued to run high. But with just four days until the end of the year, Montgomery watched the skies, praying for a raging storm.

Montgomery's original, compromised plan was to attack the Upper Town in earnest.[51] Had he done so, it would have been as waves against a cliff, smashing and breaking apart, but the walls would have still remained. Moreover, the snowy weather was sure to make any assault more difficult, and to guarantee the Upper Town's defense, British parties sallied forth almost daily to shovel away the snow from their outer walls, clearing their ditch to prevent the Americans from merely ascending snow heaps and into the city.

Captain Ainslie of the British militia was confident in the city's defenses. "Can these men pretend that there is a possibility of approaching our walls loaden with ladders, sinking to the middle every step in snow! Where shall we be then? shall we be looking on cross arm'd? It will be a fatal attempt for them, they will never scale the walls."[52] Ainslie was right: the Americans never would. So instead, they now planned to break in from the weaker Lower Town.

First, Montgomery would set off with his detachment of New Yorkers and perhaps a few Canadian locals, about 275 total, southward across the Plains of Abraham, down the steep palisade, and then eastward along the narrow St. Lawrence beach, which had now become an obstacle course of ice boulders pushed up by the repeated tides of the frozen river. Their objective was the coastal Lower Town on the east side of Cape Diamond, entering it from the south corner. Arnold meanwhile would approach from the northern suburb of St. Roch with some 480 men, including Captain Lamb's artillerymen, local Canadians, and Indians. They would enter the Lower Town from the north side. The two attacks, Montgomery's and Arnold's, would fight their way past the barricades and guards, meet in the middle, and attempt to breach into the walled Upper Town through the connecting roadway at Prescott's Gate. Meanwhile, to give the British the attack they expected, Col. James Livingston's Canadian regiment, augmented with Canadian locals, a force near 250, would attack the great Upper Town walls from the west, attempting to breach through St. John's Gate or at least serve as a diversion. Additionally, Maj. John Brown would lead a portion of these in an attack on the guard at Cape Diamond bastion at the southwesternmost corner of the Upper Town ramparts. Brown would also fire rockets as a signal to Arnold once Montgomery had begun his final approach along the St. Lawrence beach. Finally, Capt. Isaiah Wool would command a small battery of five mortars and two cannon from St. Roch and lob into the Upper Town as many shells as he could.[53] The plan was audacious, but just days prior, Montgomery had written his brother-in-law, "*Audaces fortuna juvat.*" Fortune favors the brave.[54]

Finally, as if Fortune had answered Montgomery's beckoning, on December 30, the sky grew darker and darker, and the wind began to blow. As the early sunset came and went, the wind grew to gale strength, snow began to pour, ice pellets began to hail, and the temperature dropped to frigid, with the men risking frostbite from even the shortest exposure.[55]

At two o'clock in the morning of December 31, the men began making preparations. Those wearing British redcoats were to put white paper in their cocked hats, "across their caps from the front to the acmé", to distinguish themselves from the enemy.[56] The men then gathered their scaling ladders, and the advance parties moved silently across the Plains of Abraham to take up their positions. Meanwhile, the respective artillery crews of Captain Wool and Captain Lamb prepared their guns.

At five o'clock in the morning, while the blizzard raged with still greater ferocity, the American assault on Quebec was finally set to begin.

In Cambridge, though Washington always worried about his undersupplied and undersupported Army, he waxed almost philosophical when he considered the feat undertaken thus far: "…search the vast volumes of history through, & I much question whether a case similar to ours is to be found. to wit, to maintain a Post against the flower of the British Troops for Six Months together without—and at the end of them to have one Army disbanded and another to raise within the same distance of a Reinforced Enemy—it is too much to attempt—what may be the final Issue of the last Manouvre time only can tell".[57]

Washington's reenlistment drive results continued to be gloomy. By December 15, the numbers were at a mere 5,917. But true to the American way of doing things, as the deadline approached, the rate of both recruitment and reenlistment began to increase, and by December 31, Washington reported 9,650 total enlistments for the new year.[58] This was just half of what he had hoped, or half those that had first besieged Boston after the Expedition to Concord. Some whose enlistments were up would remain into the new year, serving as volunteers until more recruits came in. And Washington would of course continue to enlist new troops, though recruitment would remain difficult throughout the entire war, despite a colonial population that could support a force sufficient to overwhelm the British.[59] Nevertheless, Washington's army, temporarily augmented as it was by some 5,000 militia reservists, gave him a combined force of almost 15,000, nearly double that of the British in Boston and Charlestown.[60]

Amid these difficulties, Washington wondered why the British failed to capitalize on their advantage. "I have been convinced by General Howe[']s conduct that he has either been very ignorant of our Situation (which I do not believe) or, that he has received positive Orders (w[hi]ch I think is natural to conclude) not to put any thing to the hazard till his reinforcements arrive—otherwise, there has [not] been a time since the first of December that we must have fought like men to have maintaind these Lines, so great in their extent".[61]

Howe had no orders prohibiting him from taking the offensive. Rather, he was still rattled by his Pyrrhic victory at Bunker Hill. His newfound timidity was embodied in his halfhearted cannonades against the encroaching rebels, who continued to build works ever closer to Boston, tightening the siege around the British one breastwork at a time. In fact, Howe had determined to remain in the town now only to winter, given the lack of transports and the massive undertaking.[62]

Once the spring thaw came, Howe hoped to be ready to remove his garrison from Boston and take up a more tenable and strategic position, one defensible by the Royal Navy, easily supplied by transport vessels, and with strong Loyalist support amongst its population. Only one location on the entire continent offered all these advantages, and both Burgoyne and Clinton had been urging since August to relocate there: the city of New York.[63]

Meanwhile, on December 30, the 50-gun HMS *Chatham* sailed into Boston Harbor. When the Boston fleet saw that she flew a rear admiral's flag from her mizzenmast, they fired a proper cannon salute to honor her arrival.[64] Sailing in with her were several transports carrying provisions and about half of the 17th and 55th Regiments of Foot, the remainder of the 17th having already arrived in early November, as had another four companies of artillery. These were part of a Third Embarkation of troops, but as it was now anticipated that the British would soon depart Boston, most were earmarked for Halifax and Quebec. Once these new troops disembarked, it would bring the total number of British in Boston to almost 8,100 men and officers, including artillerymen and marines.[65]

Aboard *Chatham*, Rear Admiral of the White Molyneux Shuldham carried orders that gave him the uncomfortable task of relieving his superior, Vice Admiral of the White Samuel Graves. Though Shuldham would not learn of it until May, he had been promoted to vice admiral of the blue since setting sail from England and was therefore just one grade lower than Graves.

"Nothing could be more unexpected or extraordinary than this Recall," Graves wrote. Shuldham was beyond reproach as he carried out his duty. On January 15, 1776, Graves transferred his flag to Shuldham in a formal change-of-command ceremony likely aboard HMS *Preston*, making the *Chatham* the new flagship. Then after other administrative tasks and waiting for fair sailing weather, on February 1, Graves finally left Boston aboard *Preston*, following the same path that his professional rival, Gen. Thomas Gage, had gone just months before.[66]

Finally, on about the last day of the year, Washington received the results of a very important vote from the Continental Congress. Back on the 22nd, Congress had resolved, "that if General Washington and his council of war should be of opinion, that a successful attack may be made on the troops in Boston, he do it in any manner he may think expedient, notwithstanding the town and the property in it may thereby be destroyed."[67] John Hancock, the richest man of Boston, with valuable real estate and property there, forwarded the results of this resolve to Washington, adding, "I most heartily wish it, tho' individually I may be the greatest sufferer."[68] Washington now had explicit permission to attack Boston—and destroy her if need be—in order to eliminate the British threat.

Even with this new permission, it would take time and resources to plan such an attack. And so 1775 ended quietly for Boston, with the siege still at a stalemate. The Siege of Quebec, however, was set to ring in the New Year with violence and bloodshed.

CHAPTER 7

BATTLE AMID THE BLIZZARD

It was just after five o'clock in the morning, December 31, 1775. The nor'easter snowstorm continued its terrible fury as the Americans commenced their assault on Quebec. While General Montgomery and his men began their descent from the Plains of Abraham down the narrow palisade road to the St. Lawrence riverbank below, Major Brown's men began their diversionary feint on Cape Diamond Bastion at the southwest corner of the Upper Town's great walls. Simultaneously, Colonel Livingston and his Canadians began their spirited demonstration against St. John's Gate on the west wall of the Upper Town. This commotion signaled Captain Wool in the northern suburb of St. Roch, who brought to life his battery of five mortars and two small cannon, each throwing rounds over the high north wall of the Upper Town.[1]

In response, the sleeping giant that was Quebec City awoke with a roar. Her bells began to furiously peal, joined quickly by drums that beat the call to muster, alerting the militia to turn out. General Carleton, whose headquarters was at the Governor's House in the Fort or Château St. Louis, was said to have been sleeping in his uniform, ready for the assault.[2] Upon hearing the attack, he rushed from his bedroom to his office where he was immediately met with aides and officers, hurrying into the headquarters with timely intelligence.

Moments later, the ramparts of the great walled city came alive with musketry, raining down on the halfhearted American attacks against the

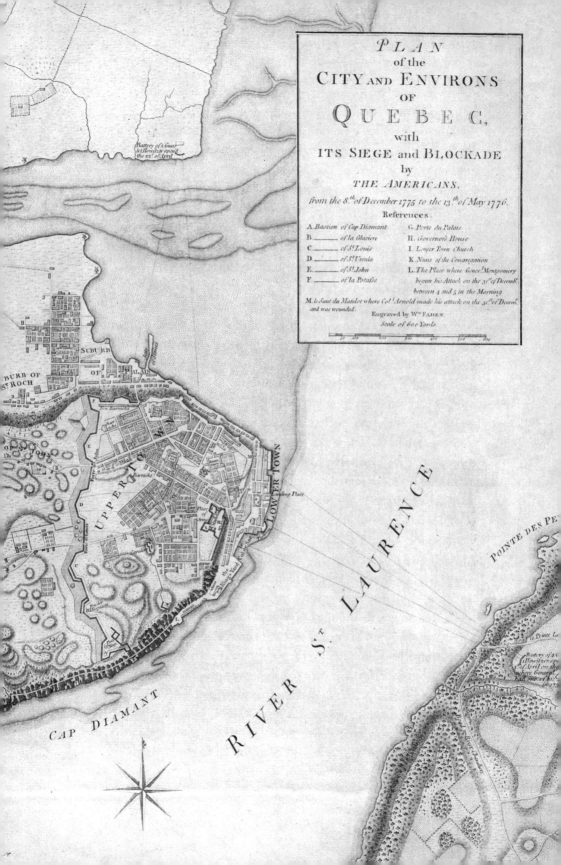

PLAN
of the
CITY AND ENVIRONS
OF
QUEBEC,
with
ITS SIEGE and BLOCKADE
by
THE AMERICANS.

from the 8.th of December 1775 to the 13.th of May 1776.

References.

A. *Bastion of Cap Diamant*
B. _____ *of la Glaciere*
C. _____ *of St Louis*
D. _____ *of St Ursula*
E. _____ *of St John*
F. _____ *of la Potasse*

G. *Porte du Palais*
H. *Governor's House*
I. *Lower Town Church*
K. *Nuns of the Congregation*
L. *The Place where Gener.l Montgomery begun his Attack on the 31.st of Decemb.r between 4 and 5 in the Morning*

M. *le Saut du Matelot where Col.l Arnold made his attack on the 31.st of Decem.r and was wounded.*

Engraved by W.m Faden.

Scale of 600 Yards.

Battery of 2 Guns & 1 Howitzer open'd the 22.d of April

SUBURB OF ST ROCH

SUBURB OF ... ALAIS

New Barracks

UPPER TOWN

LOWER TOWN

Landing Place

Place of Arms

Cavalier

Powder Magazine

Prison

CAP DIAMANT

RIVER S.t LAURENCE

POINTE DES PE...

Pointe Le...

Battery of 4 ... Howitzer open... of April on the ... where General ... had one or ... 177...

Upper Town. Carleton, however, knew the Upper Town was impregnable by such a small and ill-equipped force.[3] He suspected the two frontal assaults there were but feints, and sent Maj. Henry Caldwell to the farthest corner at Cape Diamond Bastion to ascertain whether this supposition was correct. Until he knew for sure, Carleton would not commit his sizable militia reserves.[4]

During Major Brown's diversionary attack against nearby Cape Diamond Bastion, Montgomery and his force of fewer than three hundred silently descended the steep palisade, reaching the riverfront path that passed eastward beneath the walls of the Upper Town. On cue, Brown's men fired two or three rockets into the sky, signaling the two real attacks to commence.[5]

Montgomery was the first prong in this real attack, and with the signal given, he hurried his men along the perilous, icy riverbank toward the Lower Town. The St. Lawrence was mostly frozen over, but the constant tides had heaved large, rugged chunks of ice onto their footpath. Montgomery and his men were "obliged in several places to scramble up the slant of the Rocks & then descending by pulling the Skirt of our Coats under us & sliding down 15 or 20 foot, & this repeated several times before we got to first Barrier [of the Lower Town]."[6]

Montgomery marched at the head of his troops, leading them forward. His aide-de-camp, Capt. John Macpherson, and his first company, led by Capt. Jacob Cheeseman, were close behind, as was volunteer Capt. Aaron Burr. Col. Donald Campbell, a mere quartermaster who conspicuously carried a large two-edged Scottish broadsword known as a claymore, was the second highest-ranking man on Montgomery's force and was also near the van.[7]

The narrow path and the heavy snow squall quickly made the assault force one long line of men. They struggled against a biting snow that blew almost horizontally into their face, but slowly they drove ahead.

As Montgomery's men worked their way around the south palisade of the promontory, Arnold, in the north suburb of St. Roch, prepared to get underway, having seen the rocket signal. He had all of his men mustered except Capt. Henry Dearborn's company, which, due to lack of suitable housing in St. Roch, had been forced to dwell across the small St. Charles tributary to the north. That frozen tributary now hindered

Dearborn's arrival, but Arnold could wait no longer. So Arnold gave the order to march, commencing the second prong of the American attack.[8]

Like Montgomery, Arnold led from the front of his nearly five hundred men. They made their way along the northeast shores of the St. Lawrence toward the north end of the Lower Town. Captain Lamb's artillery company was with them, struggling to drag a single brass 6-pounder cannon mounted on a sleigh.[9] The rest of the men carried long scaling ladders constructed just for this event. The snow was blinding and powerful, and the men bent their backs under the weight of the ladders as they tried to navigate the waist-high snowdrifts. Lamb's artillerymen struggled so much with their cannon, which repeatedly sank into the fresh, unpacked snow, that they finally abandoned it, marching ahead now as musketmen.

As Arnold's men approached the Lower Town, they had on their left the northerly bend in the St. Lawrence. Its bank was filled with a number of vessels, beached to protect them as the river iced over.[10] On their right was the palisade atop which stood the Upper Town's ramparts. The Americans slowly made their way near the Lower Town.

The only sound was of whipping gales.

Suddenly, the walls on the American right all erupted with immense musketry! Balls whizzed all around. Shots picked off Arnold's men one at a time, dropping men to the ground in agony and painting the snow red.

The blizzard was so blinding that it made for almost whiteout conditions. Unable to see their assailants, all Arnold's men could do was drive forward, popping off a few aimless shots at the walls as they did so. The dark night, the blinding snow, the intense musketry from the Upper Town walls, the unfamiliar and winding path as they entered the outskirts of the Lower Town—all of this led to confusion, and the rear companies were soon separated from the main force, only to wander aimlessly along other paths before realizing their error and backtracking toward the main attack.

The Lower Town was unprotected by rampart walls and thus was the weakest link for the city. But Carleton was a wise general and had littered each pathway with pickets and barricades, each armed with soldiers and cannon. Nevertheless, were the Americans to actually get into the Lower Town, and were Montgomery and Arnold to actually meet up from their opposing *entrées*, they would still have to fight their way into the walled Upper Town.

Despite the heavy musketry, Arnold's force plowed ahead, entering the narrow street Rue du Sault au Matelot. There they faced the first barricade, built on the wharf next to the river. Arnold's plan had been to blast it with Lamb's cannon as a diversion while the soldiers came at it from the sides, climbed into it through its gun ports, and then killed its defenders or otherwise sent them fleeing. But as Arnold now had no cannon, he quickly decided on a diversionary frontal assault. Simultaneously, Captain Morgan's riflemen were to venture onto the frozen St. Lawrence, encircle the barricade from the river, and fire into its defenders from their rear.

The street was narrow, just 20 feet wide, and the Americans were sitting ducks. As Arnold rushed forward, yelling to his troops to attack, one of the many whizzing musket balls hit nearby, bounced off a rock, shattered into several pieces, and a part of its shrapnel smacked into Arnold's left lower leg through the front, just missing the two bones. His leg instantly buckled and he collapsed.[11]

Captain Morgan, though not the senior officer there, straightaway took command. He first ordered Arnold back, and two soldiers helped the broken colonel up. One was the volunteer Major Ogden, who had just received a ball through his left shoulder. Even as Arnold was pulled back to safety, he continued to rally the men. Fortunately, Morgan was just as capable a leader as he was a soldier.

As Morgan and the men drove forward, the barricade's two 12-pounder cannon came alive, firing grapeshot into the onrushing Americans.[12] The thunderous cannon joined the pernicious chorus of musketry, which continued to rain into the narrow corridor from the Upper Town ramparts, some houses, and the barricade itself.

Then, relative silence. The British artillery prepared to fire their next grapeshot volley and the barricade defenders reloaded their muskets. This was their chance. Morgan's riflemen, still out front, raised their pieces and fired with deadly accuracy through the barricade's gun embrasures, dropping several British gunners. The American musketmen rushed up to the two gun ports, climbed over the cannon into the crowd of terrified defenders, and fired!

Or at least they tried to fire… A few shots went off, but to the mortification of the Americans, many of the colonial guns would not fire.

The Americans had attempted to cover their guns with their coats to protect them from the wet snow, but this proved useless. The storm was too intense, and the heat of their bodies melted any snow that collected on their coats, which in turn soiled their guns' priming powder. When they pulled the trigger, the flintlock struck the pan, but the spark could not ignite the wet powder.

The British defenders, however, had managed to keep their guns dry. Fortunately for the Americans, the thirty or so defenders were also Canadian militia, instead of the few regulars left in the city, and so they quickly opted to flee or surrender.[13] Some of the Americans then seized the guns of their British Canadian counterparts, tossing their own soiled muskets aside.

Wasting no time, Morgan pushed his men past the now-silent barricade and along Rue du Sault au Matelot. They ran down the narrow street, following its circular course of about three hundred yards, but the blizzard grew still more intense and the corridor was so dark and unfamiliar that many men lost their way. The few that followed the proper path met a second barricade near twelve feet high and more heavily defended.

New musketry instantly began to pour into them, and here the street was so narrow that hardly a ball could miss. From a platform on a knoll behind the barricade, maybe two cannon also opened fire, raining grape or canister shot. One ball the size of a walnut grazed Captain Lamb's cheek, gruesomely tearing off flesh and barely missing his skull.[14] Morgan's riflemen sniped at the artillerymen, quickly felling them and drawing the guns' silence. Faced with such deadly accuracy, no other British defender was willing to risk manning the cannon afterward.

Amid the barrage of musketry, several Americans attempted to scale the barricade. As they tried to climb over, a hailstorm of musket balls flew into them. Those who survived long enough to look over to the opposite side saw maybe one hundred or more barricade defenders with a sea of bayonets there waiting for them.[15]

City defenders began swarming in, taking up key positions in adjacent buildings and augmenting those behind the barricade. Other Canadians began to pop out from numerous places behind the Americans, firing their muskets into the American rear before dodging back into circuitous alleyways. Musket balls continued to whiz into the Americans with deadly effect.

Captain Hendricks, head of one of the rifle companies, took aim at one of the enemy, but as he did, a ball smacked into his chest. He staggered backward and dropped dead into the blood-spattered snow. Another ball smacked into rifleman Lieutenant Humphrey, felling him, blood spurting from his chest. Lieutenant Steele, the pioneer who had led the way through the Maine wilderness, took aim with his rifle, only to watch a musket ball blow off three of his fingers.[16]

Only perhaps now did Morgan realize how few men he had, maybe fewer than a hundred! Many had lost their way; others were now dead. As several more Americans dropped dead or wounded onto the red, slushy ground, Morgan finally ordered his men into the houses. They broke through the windows and quickly rushed in for cover. There they could fire with some measure of safety as their assailants continued to close in.

Morgan decided to keep his men there until dawn, just minutes away, which he hoped would allow the many straggling American companies to make their way up to his position. More importantly, he hoped Montgomery's attack would break through and soon merge with his.

On the south side of the Lower Town, Montgomery was still silently leading his force forward. They had come upon the first picketed barricade, but strangely, it had been left undefended. Montgomery personally helped cut away with a saw several of its pickets, enough that his men could pour in and move forward. He and his advance party, which had gotten somewhat ahead of his main force due to the rugged terrain and blinding snow, then reached the next picket and began to saw through it as before.[17]

As they did, the hidden British defenders watched.

———— •·• ————

A two-story blockhouse (the Pot Ash) and its adjoining road barricade, together fortified with seven small 3-pounders, guarded the Lower Town's southern approach (called Près-de-Ville) and concealed a ragtag force of around fifty anxious, waiting defenders. These included thirty

French and eight British Canadian militia; a British corporal; a transport captain named Barnsfare; and nine of his seamen who, like other ships' crews, had been impressed into defense. One militiaman was John Coffin, a Boston Loyalist who had lately moved to Quebec with his wife and twelve children in hopes of avoiding the war.

As Montgomery finished sawing a picket, he tossed it aside and rushed forward. Surely he saw the blockhouse, despite the blizzard conditions, and maybe he saw its defenders too. Barnsfare told everyone to hold their fire, declaring, "he would not fire till he was sure of doing execution."[18] The cannon were loaded with grapeshot, which for 3-pounders, consisted of nine balls, each near an inch and a half in diameter, twice the caliber of ordinary musket balls.[19]

Montgomery's advance force, still well ahead of his main body, zealously charged forward, ascending the incline and into the Lower Town. As they reached within thirty yards of the blockhouse, both Coffin and Barnsfare turned to their respective artillery and yelled "Fire!"

Smoke plumed from the blockhouse and barricade as a rain of grapeshot and musketry smashed into the oncoming Americans—three balls hitting Montgomery alone. One flew through one of his thighs, shattering the bone, another slammed into his groin, a third smashed though his chin into his skull, instantly killing him.[20]

As Montgomery's body tumbled to the snow, other shots slammed into Captain Cheeseman and Captain Macpherson, along with several others.[21] Their shattered bodies crumbled beside their fearless commander.[22] Of those few who had charged beyond this second fence, all were now dead. Many just behind the picketed barricade had also fallen, most only injured though groaning in misery.

As the smoke quickly cleared, courtesy of the gale winds, the blockhouse defenders saw the bloodied snow and the heap of dead bodies. The rest of the Americans visible just behind the barricade shrank backward.

Montgomery's main force just then came up to the second barricade, and as Col. Donald Campbell was now the senior officer present, command devolved to him. Campbell, the quartermaster, lacked the stomach of a soldier, despite what he may have looked like, carrying that ridiculous claymore at his side. Instead of rallying the men, as Captain Morgan had done in place of Arnold, the cowardly Campbell ordered retreat. So the men immediately turned and fled, following the very path they had come, not even attempting to steal away their commander's body before doing so. As the snow continued to fall, Montgomery and his fallen comrades were soon buried in frozen, white graves.[23]

British Major Caldwell wrote of Montgomery's men, "Had they acted with more spirit, they might have pushed in at first and possessed themselves of the whole of the Lower Town, and let their friends in at the other side, before our people had time to have recovered from a certain degree of panic, which seized them on the first news of the post being surprised."[24] Captain Ainslie of the British militia thought differently: "allow for a moment that they had carried the Lower Town, they wou'd have been but little advanc'd towards getting possession of the upper town, from whence we can burn the houses below us at any time. Shells wou'd soon have reduced it to a heap of rubbish."[25]

At that moment, the blockhouse received news of the attack by Arnold's force on the other side of the Lower Town. Fearing they would be overrun, the thirty or so French Canadians fled. With half the garrison run off, the rest also considered fleeing. But before they could, Loyalist John Coffin drew his bayonet and said he would put to death the next man who laid down his arms or attempted to abandon the post. Then, with the assistance of Captain Barnsfare, he turned two of their cannon inward, toward the Lower Town, in case Arnold's force was indeed successful in approaching as far south as their position.[26]

Arnold himself was of course being carried back to a makeshift colonial hospital in St. Roch, but Captain Morgan, with Arnold's remaining force, was pinned down. He desperately hoped to see Montgomery's men break through to them and provide relief against the advancing British and Canadian defenders. But poor Morgan had no idea of Montgomery's fall, or of his subordinate Campbell's cowardice.

Fortune, which Montgomery had so entrusted, had betrayed them all. The entire assault was now doomed.

━━━◆━━━

By rapid reconnoitering, General Carleton learned that the American attacks by Brown and Livingston on the Upper Town's front walls were but feints. Given this, he finally unleashed his reserves, first Captain Laws with about sixty or seventy men, then Captain McDougal with about sixty of Colonel Maclean's Royal Highlander Emigrants. Major Caldwell, who had seen the feint at Cape Diamond Bastion firsthand, also learned of Arnold's attack and hurried toward the fight, bringing with him a number of his militia and a company of the British 7th Royal Fusiliers. This total force, about two hundred in all, emerged from the Palace Gate on the north side of the Upper Town facing St. Roch. From there they turned hard right and followed the path toward the Lower Town, expecting to come on Arnold's rear and trap him.[27]

Dawn was fast approaching. With it, Captain Dearborn's company, which had struggled to join Arnold's force in time for the attack, was finally nearing the Lower Town. Just as Arnold's main body had done earlier, they passed alongside the Upper Town walls and were met with intense musketry. But Dearborn did not know the way through the crooked streets to the main fight, and soon he was lost, with his company divided. As they blindly wandered, some of the fresh British reinforcement unknowingly converged on Dearborn's position, approaching from back roads and coming so close that only a tall fence of pickets stood between them.

The Death of General Montgomery in the Attack on Quebec, December 31, 1775 by John Trumbull (1756–1843). Courtesy of the Yale University Art Gallery.

Amid the blowing snow, both enemies halted on either side of the pickets, unable to see the other. Then one of the British yelled to Dearborn, asking who he was.

"A friend", Dearborn replied.

"A friend to who?" came the reply.

"To Liberty!" Dearborn exclaimed.

"God-damn you!" replied the soldier. He raised himself partly above the pickets and fired!

Dearborn pulled his trigger, but to his mortification, it would not fire! Just as Arnold's men had discovered earlier, Dearborn's men found their priming powder soiled by melted snow.

But the British had no trouble at all and fired into them with ferocity.

Dearborn's men scattered. They broke into the lower floors of several houses, hoping to re-prime their guns. It was no use. With the remainder of the British reinforcement coming up, Dearborn saw he was greatly outnumbered. He surrendered, and they were promptly disarmed and made prisoners.[28]

With Dearborn's surrender, the last hope for Captain Morgan and his pinned troops was gone. The British reinforcement was about to hem the Americans in from the north, while the severe fire from the barricade and houses trapped them from all other sides.

As Captain Laws's two-hundred-strong reinforcement advanced, he was so anxious to see his company ahead of that of his comrade McDougal, that in his zeal, he got ahead of even his own company and so alone encountered a rear company of Americans. Unfazed, he proudly ordered them to lay down their arms, for his men would be up in a moment. The Americans laughed at him and seized him, but as they did, the British reinforcement did indeed come up, led by McDougal and his company. The British immediately moved to encircle this American rear, but those Canadians and Indians among the Americans, rather than surrender, quickly fled across the frozen St. Lawrence, despite the "danger in the meeting with air holes, deceptively covered by the bed of snow." Outnumbered, the remaining American rear released Laws and promptly surrendered.[29]

By now, the sun had risen and thus the streets became navigable, despite the still raging storm. At the second barricade, where Morgan's men were pinned down, the British Captain Anderson and a small body of troops unlatched the barricade gate and began to emerge. From inside an adjacent house, Morgan carefully aimed his rifle and shot the captain through the head, felling him. The British troops wisely fell back at once, dragging with them their dead officer, a streak of bloody packed snow marking the path. Yet this move signaled that the British were now confident, thanks to their swelling numbers.

About then, some of the straggling American companies finally came up, though they found themselves quickly pinned down, just as Morgan's were. In their desperation, they surged toward the barricade with their scaling ladders and took cover close to its walls to avoid the deadly British fire.

At the same time, British Major Caldwell arrived, coming up from inside the barricade it seems, using back roads to get around the fighting. He brought with him some fifty seamen, part of the British reinforcement, whom the barricade defenders were happy to have join them. Caldwell noted when he arrived that he "found things, though not in a good way, yet not desperate."[30]

Caldwell ordered those men with bayonets through the house windows to dislodge Morgan's American forces hiding therein. Meanwhile, the Americans swarming in front of the barricade struggled to get their ladders raised. They threw one ladder over the barricade, hoping to use it to scale back down amid the British defenders, but Caldwell's men snatched it. Giving this up, the Americans then hoisted their ladders against the nearby houses and quickly scaled to their upper levels, while the British used their snatched ladder to do the same.

Instantly, the battle shifted to a close-quarters fight within the adjacent houses—up and down stairwells and in bedrooms, a confused melee—with many wounded or killed.[31]

Caldwell next ordered some of his men under Captain Nairne to head toward the wharf, come around the barricade, and then encircle the Americans. A few moments later, Caldwell himself decided to go the same way, hoping to reconnoiter the American position. As Nairne's men came around the wharf first, they encountered some of Morgan's colonial forces taking cover in a house near the barricade. Nairne's men dislodged these Americans and repulsed them back toward the wharf.

Morgan's men then found new cover in a house on the wharf, just as Caldwell was coming upon it. With Morgan's men inside and Caldwell outside but away from the windows, they heard but could not see each other. They both halted.

Unable to see Caldwell, the Americans cautiously called out, "Who is there?"

"A friend," Caldwell replied. He was not sure if these were the Americans or his own men under Captain Nairne. "Who are you?" he asked, to be certain.

"Captain Morgan's Company," was the reply.

Caldwell, alone and now realizing his peril, thought quickly. "Have good heart for you will soon be in the town," he said before jumping behind a nearby pile of boards and escaping to the next wharf over. From there, with some other British men, he brought a 9-pound cannon to bear on the house with Morgan's men and fired, killing one and wounding another.[32]

The house-to-house melee continued until about nine o'clock that morning.[33] Some of Morgan's company considered holding out until nighttime, but the arrival of the British reinforcement assured them they were surrounded. At last, the remainder of the American troops began to surrender. Refusing to surrender to the British, Morgan saw a priest among the spectators who had now gathered. Rushing to him, he gave the priest his sword, while angrily announcing, "I give my sword to you; but not a scoundrel of those cowards shall take it out of my hands!"[34]

The Battle of Quebec was now over. The Americans were defeated.

Back at the General Hospital in St. Roch, Dr. Senter was attending Arnold and other wounded. Senter had earlier requested Arnold's permission to participate in the attack, but Arnold knew the good doctor's services would be needed at the hospital. As wounded continued to stream in, one from Montgomery's ill-fated attack told the bedridden Arnold the solemn news. Horror filled the room, but this was quickly replaced with dread when another messenger rushed in, warning that a British detachment was now on its way there. Just then, Captain Wool's incessant cannonade outside abruptly fell silent, followed by scattered musketry, then silence.

Arnold immediately sent a messenger to St. Roch's Canadian militia captains, begging that they turn out. Though they had been friendly until now, these local Canadians offered no help and instead fled to the countryside. Dr. Senter entreated Arnold to be carried back to the countryside as well, but Arnold would not have it. "He would neither be removed, nor suffer a man from the Hospital to retreat. He ordered his pistols loaded, with a sword on his bed, &c., adding that he was determined to kill as many as possible if they came into his room. We were now all soldiers, even to the wounded in their beds were ordered a gun by their side."[35]

But the attack never came. The British, satisfied with capturing Wool's annoying battery and Lamb's fieldpiece, which they found still on its sleigh, retreated with their new ordnance, their mission accomplished.[36] However, the British would continue to barrage St. Roch throughout the night and into the coming days.

Sometime that night, Colonel Arnold sent an express to Brigadier General Wooster in Montreal, alerting him of the situation. His injury quite bad, Arnold also immediately turned over his command to Colonel Campbell.[37] However, when Arnold learned of Campbell's cowardice, perhaps the next day, he would take back his command and serve as a bedridden commander until Wooster himself could come up.[38]

While the Battle of Quebec proved tragic for the Americans, it would take a few days more for them to realize just how devastating a loss it really was.

———— •‖• ————

In the aftermath of the battle, the British concluded: "our success at least was equal to a reinforcement of 500 men; the garrison was in high spirits and wished for nothing more than a second attack."[39] British morale was high in part because they had suffered few casualties: just five killed and thirteen wounded (two mortally), or eighteen total.[40] But for the Americans, spirits were especially low.

Once the fog of war had lifted, Arnold found that something like 330 able-bodied American men and officers had been taken prisoner, most confined to the Seminary building in Quebec. When British Major Caldwell inspected these prisoners, he jeered, "Of those we took, one

Major was a blacksmith, another a hatter; of their captains, there was a butcher, a —, a tanner, a shoemaker, a tavernkeeper, &c., &c. Yet they all pretended to be gentlemen."[41] The prisoners attempted a few times to break out, but each try was unsuccessful. Almost half would shamefully bargain for their freedom by joining the British forces in the fight against their own countrymen.[42] The rest would remain imprisoned for about a year, some being sent to places like New York and Halifax before being released via prisoner exchanges.

Another sixty or so Americans were killed or wounded prisoners held by the British.[43] American volunteer John Henry, a prisoner himself, wrote of the wounded, "To the great honor of General Carleton, they were all, whether friends or enemies, treated with like attention and humanity." In fact, time and again, the prisoners wrote in their journals of the humanity and benevolence of Carleton. Henry would later call him "an ornament such as would grace any nation", adding, "If such men as Washington, Carleton, and Montgomery, had had the entire direction of the adverse war, the contention, in the event, might have happily terminated to the advantage of both sections of the nation."[44]

These were not the only American losses. More wounded were in the American hospital in St. Roch, under the care of Dr. Senter. And days after the battle, with the outlook so dim and their enlistments up, "Upwards of One hundred Officers, and Soldiers, Instantly set of[f] for Montreal [and thus back to New York]," the bedridden Arnold wrote Washington, "and it was, with the greatest dificulty I could persaude the rest to make a stand. The Panick soon subsided, I aranged the Men in such Order, as effectually, to Blockade the City, and enable them to Assist each other if Attacked." Given the departures plus his losses to the British, by mid-January, Arnold had but seven hundred men, including his many sick and wounded.[45] He pressed Wooster in Montreal for more men, but Wooster's numbers were also quickly dwindling, though he sent what he could. Wooster also dispatched a message to Seth Warner and the Green Mountain Boys of modern Vermont to again request their aid.[46]

For those Americans who remained outside Quebec, esprit de corps was especially low, not only in seeing their army dwindle, but also from the loss of Montgomery. It took almost two weeks for General

Schuyler to learn of it. When he wrote the horrible news to Washington, he lamented, "I wish I had no Occasion to send My Dear General this Melancholly Account. My Amiable Friend the Gallant Montgomery is no more. The Brave Arnold is wounded & we have met with a severe Check, in an unsuccessful Attempt on Quebec; May Heaven be graciously pleased that the Misfortune may terminate here".[47]

Washington replied a few days later, "I...am heartily sorry & most sincerely condole with you upon the unhappy Fall of the brave and worthy Montgomery & those gallant officers & Men, who have experienced a like Fate. In the Death of this Gentleman, America has sustained a heavy Loss, as he had approved himself a steady Friend to her Rights and of Ability to render her the most essential Services. I am much concerned for the intrepid and enterprizing Arnold and greatly fear that Consequences of the most alarming Nature will result from this well intended but unfortunate Attempt."[48] But General Lee encouraged Washington, writing, "Poor Brave Montgomery! but it is not a time to cry but to revenge".[49]

On January 1, the morning after the battle, Montgomery's body was found where he had fallen, frozen and covered in snow, his ornamental sword, with its ivory handle and silver dog's-head pommel, lying by his side. The garrison engineer who found him assumed he was a man of importance, so several of the American prisoners were consulted for the identification.

The British looked on Montgomery's death with solemn dismay, remembering the great service he had once given to the Empire as a British officer. Captain Ainslie wrote, "those who knew him formerly in this place, sincerely lament his late infatuation, they say he was a genteel man, and an agreeable companion." A fine coffin was ordered for his body, and on January 4, he was buried in a private ceremony.[50]

The American prisoners were permitted to see his funeral procession as it passed their quarters. American prisoner John Henry wrote, "The coffin, covered with pall, surmounted by transverse swords, was borne by men. The regular troops, with reversed arms, and scarfs on the left elbow, accompanied the corpse to the grave. The funerals for the other officers, both friends and enemies, were performed this day. From many of us it drew tears of greeting and thankfulness towards

General Carleton."[51] American prisoner Maj. Return Meigs wrote of Montgomery, "He had the voluntary love, esteem, and confidence of the whole army. His death, though honourable, is lamented, not only as the death of an amiable, worthy friend, but as an experienced, brave general, whose country suffers greatly by such a loss at this time."[52]

Montgomery's remains would lie buried at Quebec until 1818, when they were at last transferred down the same water path he had followed up to the city, coming to their final resting place at St. Paul's Church in New York City.[53]

Though he did not live to learn of it, Montgomery died as a major general, with news of his promotion still on its way. Then a few days into the new year, before Congress knew of the tragedy at Quebec, they also promoted Arnold to brigadier. Hence, Arnold was promoted for his services rendered, not as some automatic promotion given Montgomery's death, though perhaps the latter is how the men perceived it.[54]

Montgomery's death was not all in vain. His fall would become a source of heroism, a recruiting tool, and a banner by which to rally the men. His name would frequently be used in conjunction with that of Dr. Joseph Warren, the two men being perhaps the two great martyrs of the entire war and certainly of 1775.[55]

But Montgomery's death also brought to the forefront of public debate the question of whether the Canadian Expedition was a sound strategy at all. Writing to Wooster in Montreal, Washington explained, "I need not mention to you the Importance of Canada in the scale of our Affairs—to whomsoever It belongs, in their favour probably, will the Ballance Turn—If it is ours, success will crown our virtuous Struggles—If our Enemies, the Contest at best, will be doubtfull, hazardous & bloody".[56] But the tragedy of the loss weighed on His Excellency's mind. In another letter to Joseph Reed, Washington tried to find the silver lining, noting that had Canada "been subdued by such a handful of Men 'tis more than probable that it would have been left to the defence of a few, & rescued from us in the Spring—Our Eyes will now, not only be open to the Importance of holding it, but the numbers which are requisite to that end."[57]

Montgomery's death was also the impetus for much discourse on the question of American enlistments.[58] Had Montgomery not been concerned with losing his men at the first of the year, he could have waited for sufficient reinforcements and artillery, or otherwise continued to blockade the city. The current policy of annual enlistments was thus to blame for Montgomery's death. Washington wrote to John Hancock, "That this cause precipitated the fate of the brave, and much to be lamented Genl Montgomerie, & brought on the defeat which followed thereupon, I have not the most distant doubt of; for had he not been apprehensive of the Troops leaving him at so important a crisis, but continued the Blockade of Quebec, a Capitulation, from the best Accts I have been able to collect, must inevitably have followed."[59]

The ensuing discussion of enlistment terms would take most of the next year. Not until September 24, 1776, would Congress finally decide upon having the colonies "engage the troops to serve during the continuance of the war", enticing soldiers with a twenty-dollar bounty and one hundred acres of land.[60] This, however, did not help Washington's present army, many of whom would be eager to depart at the end of 1776, just as many had in 1775.

Meanwhile, the Siege of Quebec would continue until the spring of 1776, with nothing of consequence occurring until then. Though Arnold would build batteries across the St. Lawrence to hit Quebec from different angles, they would have little effect. At any time, Carleton might have sallied forth from the great fortress and easily crushed the remainder of the American Army, "but he still (perhaps with propriety) adhered steadily to his resolution of running no risk as to the safety of the place. No body was more ready than he was at all time to expose his person, his timidity was only shown in respect to others, and the safety of the town."[61] Yet despite the many odds against him, Arnold remained valiant, writing, "I am in the way of my duty, and know no fear."[62]

And so 1775 came to a close, with two sieges at a stalemate, two beloved generals lost, and two American armies dwindling as enlistments expired and men marched home.

CHAPTER 8

A NEW YEAR BEGINS

The New Year of 1776 was a time of mourning for the American troops in Canada. In Boston, it was rung in by droves of men marching for home, their enlistments now expired, and all pleas for them to stay at last spent. Not all was lost for the American Cause, however. For the seed of the Revolution was at last fomenting in the other colonies. In Norfolk, Virginia, the events of New Year's Day would at last fully commit the southern colonies to the war.

Like most of the Loyalist colonial governors, Royal Governor John Murray, 4th Earl of Dunmore, was slowly losing control of Virginia. However, unlike his fellow governors, Lord Dunmore opted for an aggressive policy to stamp out the rebellion. To provide him aid and support, a small naval squadron was sent there, including the 20-gun HMS *Liverpool* and the two 16-gun sloops-of-war *Otter* and *Kingfisher*.[1]

In his attempts to quell the upheaval, Dunmore issued a monumental proclamation to emancipate all slaves and indentured servants who would take up arms against their rebellious masters.[2] However, as most of his authority had already been stripped, he possessed little means to enforce this. So it was left to the slaves themselves to manage their escape, but for the many who did, they would be afforded the governor's protection, supported by some two hundred regulars at his disposal. Hundreds of escaped slaves would eventually join with Dunmore, to be equipped and formed into Lord Dunmore's so-called

Ethiopian Regiment. Many more Black Loyalist regiments would follow as the war continued.

Hostilities in Virginia first came to a head on December 9, 1775, when a mix of Continental and militia troops built a strong entrenchment across the Great Bridge near a small British fort that guarded the southern approach to Norfolk. At the encouragement of Lord Dunmore, the Royal Navy responded by landing there a small force of two hundred regulars, plus some three hundred former black slaves and white indentured servants. These five hundred audaciously assailed against two thousand well-fortified rebels. It was another Battle of Bunker Hill but in miniature, this time with the odds greatly stacked against the British. The British losses were not substantial, and the Americans had but one man wounded, but the significance of the incident came when the British were repulsed and the Americans held their ground.[3]

On January 1, 1776, Dunmore decided to exact revenge on the people of Virginia, ordering the Royal Navy to open fire on Norfolk and lay waste and destroy it. The bombardment commenced at about three thirty in the afternoon and continued until ten o'clock that night. Landing parties augmented the barrage by torching the scattered buildings and ensuring the town's conflagration. Though the Americans fired at these British landing parties, occasionally repulsing them, they could not stop the town's destruction. The flames quickly became general and widespread. By the next day, Norfolk was a heap of embers.[4]

Dunmore's aggressive policy brought the war to the South. The unintended consequence was that he almost singlehandedly cemented the uncommitted southern colonies to the cause.[5]

Outside Boston, General Washington wrote of Dunmore, "If…that Man is not crushed before Spring, he will become the most formidable Enemy America has—his strength will Increase as a Snow ball by Rolling; and faster, if some expedient cannot be hit upon to convince the Slaves and Servants of the Impotency of His designs… I do not think that forcing his Lordship on Ship board is sufficient; nothing less than depriving him of life or liberty will secure peace to Virginia; as motives of Resentment actuates his conduct to a degree equal to the total destruction of the Colony."[6]

Meanwhile, as Norfolk burned, Gen. William Howe in Boston

spent the first days of the new year going through the various dispatches received with Adm. Molyneux Shuldham's arrival. One was a copy of the King's Speech from the Throne given at the opening of Parliament in late October. After reading it, Howe thought it proper to send a copy past the front lines to the Americans. It was the first time any in the Continental Army read it, but soon it was printed and circulated among the camp. Washington must have felt a measure of dread when he read it, for he now knew that Great Britain was going to push the war to its final outcome.[7]

Still, Washington found humor in the irony that, on the same day, January 1, prior to their receiving the King's Speech, the Americans atop Prospect Hill in Cambridge "had hoisted the Union Flag in compliment to the United Colonies, but behold! it was receivd in Boston as a token of the deep Impression the Speech had made upon Us, and as a signal of Submission". The flag raised was probably the standard British Union Flag of the old 1606 design, which closely resembles the modern British flag designed in 1801. Perhaps a second flag was raised beneath it, one of thirteen red-and-white stripes, meant to signify the union of the colonies.[8]

So the Americans remained defiant, but the British had another idea in the works to induce colonial submission. North Carolina's Royal Governor Josiah Martin, less aggressive than Virginia's Lord Dunmore, had for some time been pressing the home government for a Southern Expedition. After long delays, it was decided to send five regiments and two artillery companies directly from Britain to the Carolinas. Maj. Gen. Charles, Lord Cornwallis, requested permission that his regiment join the force, and so it was granted. Maj. Gen. Henry Clinton was to be detached from Boston and rendezvous with the task force at Cape Fear, North Carolina, to take command of the expedition. Their mission was to establish a foothold in the South and begin moving northward.

To this end, Clinton embarked aboard HMS *Mercury* and, on January 20, sailed southward along with three transports.[9] Learning of Clinton's departure and of an intended attack in the South, Washington sent Maj. Gen. Charles Lee to head up the new Southern Department.[10] Once the new British regiments finally arrived off Cape Fear, Clinton decided to launch an attack on Charlestown (now Charleston), South

Carolina. It would be the first of many battles in the southern colonies and would serve only to further solidify their support.[11]

Meanwhile, news of the latest Coercive Act was on its way to America. The Prohibitory Act, which received its royal assent on December 22, prohibited all trade whatsoever with all Thirteen Colonies, provided for the seizure of colonial ships, whether for trade or war, and allowed for the impressments of colonial sailors into the Royal Navy. While the latter provision was seen as the most grievous, the Prohibitory Act was mostly irrelevant given the war now being waged.[12]

At last, with both adversaries now fully committed to prosecuting the war, Washington began plotting a finishing stroke to the Siege of Boston.

———◆———

Washington was anxious to end the stalemate with the British in Boston. His hope was an extremely cold winter, one that would freeze over the Back Bay and allow him to send troops across the frozen Charles River and so enter Boston beyond the main British fortifications. But the winter remained mild, and the river did not freeze. So he settled for yet another minor skirmish. On the night of January 8, he sent Maj. Thomas Knowlton (of Bunker Hill fame) with two hundred troops across the narrow Charlestown milldam to burn the fourteen houses remaining there.

Meanwhile, the latest British diversion was a play titled *The Blockade of Boston*, authored by John Burgoyne before he had sailed for England. It was expected to be very amusing, as it featured hilarious caricatures of Washington and his men. The farce was set to begin in Faneuil Hall at about nine o'clock that same night, with General Howe himself attending.

As the audience gathered, Knowlton and his men tiptoed across the rocks that formed the milldam, their path illuminated by a near full moon. Once they reached Charlestown, an alert sentry there spotted them, but while Knowlton offered to take him prisoner, the sentry resisted. One of Knowlton's men then shot the sentry dead, the musket's report instantly alarming the small British garrison still left in Charlestown. The British began to swarm in confusion to their fortifications, blindly firing hundreds of shots frantically toward Knowlton's position. But the Americans exhibited sensible discipline and so did not engage. Instead they rushed toward the fourteen houses and set them aflame. They also captured a sergeant and four privates as prisoners before they hurried back across the milldam.

Across the river in Boston, a sergeant of the guard heard the shots and "immediately ran into the playhouse, got upon the stage, and cried 'Turn out! Turn out! They are hard at it, hammer and tongs.'" The whole audience thought the sergeant was acting a part in *The Blockade of Boston* and thought he performed it so well that the playhouse burst into applause, drowning him out as he tried to plea with them. Finally, he conceded, waited for the clapping to end, and then bellowed, "What the deuce are you all about? If you won't believe me, by Jasus you need only go to the door, and there you will see and hear both!" There was a pause in the audience, then, tradition claims, it was General Howe who decisively yelled for the men to man their posts. Women shrieked as the soldiers and officers immediately poured out of the hall. Knowlton was successful in harrying the British, but the British believed the rebels had intentionally timed it with the farce so as to end it abruptly.[13]

While minor victories such as this always served to raise esprit de corps, Washington was anxious for a more general and decisive action. Yet powder remained his biggest problem, despite gains as in the taking of the *Nancy* transport. Powder-making facilities were popping up throughout the colonies, but a critical ingredient, saltpeter, was in extremely short supply. Without black powder, Washington could never seriously consider engaging the enemy in a direct offensive.

Nevertheless, on January 16, Washington called together a council of war, which included John Adams, home briefly from Philadelphia. Washington laid before the council "the indispensible necessity of making a Bold attempt to Conquer the Ministerial Troops in Boston, before they can be reinforced in the Spring". The council agreed an offensive should take place. However, because sickness and weather had reduced Washington's feeble army to fewer than nine thousand effectives, they advised he seek additional troops from the local militia to aid in any such endeavor. Accordingly, Washington sent a request throughout New England to raise up additional militia reserves.[14]

Even if Washington could collect men and gunpowder, he still had little chance of success without proper artillery. The cannon he did have were too small and too few. To solve this problem, Washington had dispatched Col. Henry Knox to Fort Ticonderoga to bring to Cambridge all the ordnance he could.

Weeks earlier, on December 5, Knox had arrived at the former British fort and taken inventory of the artillery and cannon shot. Of the mortars, he selected fourteen of various sizes, most of which were average, though he must have been elated to find the three iron 13-inch mortars, short but massive, perhaps a ton each. For cannon, he could only find one large brass 24-pounder, but he was able to find thirteen 18-pounders plus ten 12s. These plus other smaller cannon gave him forty-three pieces total, some brass (really bronze), some iron. He also collected two howitzers, both of 8-inch caliber. There were also many artillery rounds available, though Knox did not collect these. Instead, most would come from different routes, some cast new, otherwise stolen from the King's store in New York.[15]

Before setting out from Fort Ticonderoga on December 6, Knox optimistically wrote to Washington, "I hope in 16 or 17 days to be able to present to your Excellency a Noble train of Artillery". In fact, the journey would take much longer. The first step of this arduous expedition was to transport the artillery by gondola a short distance on Lake Champlain, where they were then dragged by cattle over land and over a bridge to nearby Lake George.[16] There the guns were loaded onto three vessels: a scow, a large batteau, and a boat that Knox called a "Pettianger". The scow was at first overloaded and sank in the low water, but Knox's hired men managed to "bail her out and tow her to the leward shore…and by halling the cannon aft ballanc'd her, and now she stands ready for sail". The three vessels were then sailed or rowed southward to decommissioned Fort George at lake's end.[17]

Once there, many delays slowed the continued progress of the expedition. Though a storm piled on them an "exceeding fine Snow" some two feet deep, Knox soon realized the snow was too deep. He was also having trouble securing their next mode of transportation. Local Stillwater native George Palmer was supposed to supply 80 yoke of oxen and sleighs to drag the guns, but when Palmer met with Knox in Albany to negotiate a near 30 percent premium over what Knox thought an acceptable price, "The treaty broke off abruptly & Mr Palmer was dismiss'd." However, this was no immediate crisis because "By reports from all parts the snow is too deep for the Cannon to set out, even if the Sleds were ready." Without oxen or sleighs, Knox "Sent out his Waggon Master & other people to all parts of the Country to immediately send up their slays [sleighs] with horses suitable," and in the end hired "horses in the whole amounting to near 124 pairs with Slays [sleighs], which I'm afraid are not strong enough for the heavy Cannon". In fact, the horses would prove capable enough, and Knox ended up saving money over hiring oxen. Finally, after weeks of delay, Knox's hired New York crews mounted the artillery onto the sleighs, and by about December 30, the expedition was again moving south.[18]

THE NOBLE TRAIN OF ARTILLERY BY TOM LOVELL (1909–1997). REPRODUCED WITH KIND PERMISSION OF THE DIXON TICONDEROGA COMPANY. ALL RIGHTS RESERVED. THIS PAINTING IS INACCURATE BECAUSE KNOX USED PRIMARILY HORSES, NOT OXEN.

Leaving Fort George, the artillery was conducted along a difficult and exceedingly slow route following the Hudson River, with the crews forced to cross the frozen Hudson four times before reaching Albany. Instead of one long caravan, Knox's noble train of horse-drawn sleighs became a series of fragmented companies sometimes miles apart, conducting their respective sleighs with teams of two or sometimes up to eight horses, though at times augmenting these with additional beasts, including oxen when available, to surpass particularly high snowdrifts or difficult terrain.[19]

Meanwhile, awaiting his train of sleighs in Albany, Knox dined one early evening with Gen. Philip Schuyler at his home. Their dinner was suddenly interrupted when a messenger reported that one of the heavier cannon had broken through the ice at nearby Half Moon Ferry and fallen into the Hudson. Knox immediately departed from Schuyler's home to see to the crossing of the other guns himself, arriving at the ferry at dusk. Apparently, the sunken cannon there was now abandoned, and the man who had been in charge of it, one Mr. Schuyler (likely related to the general), was now at Sloss's Ferry some seven miles distant. Fearing for his other guns, Knox sent an express to Sloss's Ferry, reprimanding Mr. Schuyler for his carelessness and commanding him not to attempt the crossing until Knox's arrival, though an express soon returned, informing Knox that the guns were already successfully crossed and that the ice there was thicker. Knox then sent an express to a Mr. Swartz, in charge of another section of the artillery train and who was bound to Half Moon Ferry, "the usual place of crossing", redirecting him instead to Sloss's Ferry.[20]

Over the next few days, Knox supervised the crossing of the remaining guns into Albany, but as the end of the train reached Sloss's Ferry, Mother Nature forsook them with a "cruel thaw", delaying their effort for days (but allowing Knox to admire nearby Cohoes Falls). New snow came, and by January 6, all artillery were safely across Sloss's Ferry and into Albany. On the following day, they were to cross the river again to the shore opposite the town. At this final river crossing, Knox's teams had managed to successfully cross ten of the eleven laden sleighs, when the final sleigh fell through and "broke all the Ice for 14 feet around it." Nightfall soon came, but on the next day, with much effort and aided by the people of Albany, Knox's men pulled the "drown'd Cannon" back out. Out of gratitude, Knox christened it the Albany.[21]

The noble train next passed eastward over the Berkshires, from "which we might almost have seen all the Kingdoms of the Earth," and so into Massachusetts. This was the most difficult part of the journey, and here the horses at times proved insufficient for pulling the heavier pieces over the mountains. Knox continued to seek out oxen to augment his horses, but only occasionally did he find any to hire.[22]

The rest of the journey continued without much difficulty. The New York teamsters conducted the artillery as far as Springfield, where Massachusetts men then took up the task. Finally, the artillery began to arrive in Framingham, some twenty miles outside Boston, on about January 25—almost fifty days since the start of the expedition, far exceeding Knox's original hope for a "16 or 17 days" journey. With the exception of some of the lighter pieces, sent immediately to the lines and mounted in the American entrenchments, most of the pieces were probably then kept in Framingham until Washington called them up.[23]

With the cannon arriving and Washington's fort at Lechmere's Point finally completed after months of delays due to snow and frost, he again called together his council of war.[24] On February 16, Washington laid before them his proposal. He noted that "the severe freezing Weather formed some pretty strong Ice" in the bays, and "knowing the Ice could not last", he submitted that the time was now ripe for an assault. "I proposed it in Council; but behold! though we had been waiting all the year for this favourable Event, the enterprize was thought too dangerous! perhaps it was—perhaps the irksomeness of my Situation led me to undertake more than could be warranted by prudence—I did not think so".[25] But Washington conceded to the wisdom of his council. Instead, the war council agreed that a bombardment of the town should commence "as soon as there shall be a proper Supply of powder & not before, & that in the mean Time, preparations should be made to take possession of Dorchester Hill, with a view of drawing out the Enemy."[26]

The idea was as old as the siege itself, with Dr. Joseph Warren and Gen. Artemas Ward having discussed the merits of the idea shortly after the Expedition to Concord. British General Clinton had even been on the verge of taking Dorchester Peninsula shortly after Bunker Hill, but by then, Generals Gage and Howe had lost their nerve. The British had doubted too whether they had sufficient troops to garrison the peninsula were they to capture it. Now the unofficial neutral ground of Dorchester Heights, which offered all the advantages that Bunker and Breed's Hill offered, was to be the Yankee objective. Preparations were immediately put underway, but this would be all that was done until more gunpowder could be found.

Howe was well aware of Washington's preparations, courtesy of the occasional American deserter. So he too began making preparations. The British first built two strong batteries in Boston facing southward toward Dorchester. Then, in mid-February, a British sortie crossed the frozen water from Castle William to Dorchester Peninsula, torched the handful of houses there, and took prisoner six rebel scouts. Finally, the British barricaded and fortified the streets of Boston, in case the American attack turned toward the town.[27]

Then, a stroke a luck befell Washington. The city of New York, though a center of Loyalism, had its share of active rebels. The Royal Navy therefore blockaded the city, but out of complacency, maintained an unwritten agreement that they would allow trade ships to pass as long as the Navy's warships could still obtain fresh provisions from shore. Merchants were keen to profit from the foolish albeit unofficial policy, smuggling powder and munitions in whenever possible. On February 29, three tons of powder arrived in New York, with three tons more expected shortly thereafter. Most of this made its way to Washington's army outside Boston.[28]

Finally, Washington had everything he required to assault Boston: permission from Congress to destroy the town if need be, cannon and gunpowder by which to effect the attack, agreement from his war council now that he had the requisite powder, and preparations already underway to take Dorchester Peninsula. The fate of Boston was at last at hand.

In early March, Washington's army was now fully employed in preparations for the fortification of Dorchester Heights. His Excellency himself met with his general staff to devise the attack strategy.[29]

Dorchester was at that time an approximately rectangular peninsula, connected to the mainland at its southwest corner by a broad neck perhaps half a mile wide. Foster's Hill (or Nook's Hill, since leveled) dominated the peninsula's northwest tip, which, at a distance of about a half a mile, was the closest eminence to Boston Neck and stood well behind the main British stockade there. A small distance southeast of Foster's were the Twin Hills, the westernmost being the tallest hill on the peninsula, known as Signal Tree Hill (now Telegraph Hill), which stood some 140 feet high. The other of the Twins was Middle Hill, and together they were generically known as Dorchester Heights. Still other minor hills dotted the peninsula. The northeast tip of the peninsula was Dorchester Point, which reached to within about a half mile of Castle Island and the strong Castle William thereon. The whole of Dorchester Peninsula was surrounded by a wide tidal flat, becoming a muddy expanse at low tide, with just four to six feet in depth at high tide, and thus was impossible to approach by warship. The small town of Dorchester itself was on the mainland to the southwest. The peninsula then was largely countryside, with just a few houses there until General Howe had them burned. The peninsula is today what is known as South Boston, as landfill has since nearly melded it to Boston proper.[30]

After Washington considered the peninsula's topography, he decided upon a strategy to build his fortifications on the high eminences of Dorchester Heights. From there the forts would command the whole of the peninsula, a large part of Boston, and even part of the harbor. He further chose Foster's Hill as a secondary objective. From there he could position cannon close in and enfilade the whole of Boston Neck.

There was one problem to fortifying Dorchester, however. Though the winter weather had become mild and the temperature slowly rose above freezing, the ground there remained frozen solid, the frost about a foot and a half thick.[31] So an idea was seized upon to create a fort not of earth, but of wood. It would be a breastwork of fascines: bundles of sticks held in place by wooden frames called chandeliers. The advantage of this design was that it could be entirely prefabricated.[32] Then, once Washington gave the order, the whole of it could be hauled by wagon train across Dorchester Neck. Washington decided they would assemble it all in the course of one night, following the tried-and-proven Yankee method of nighttime fortification.

Washington befittingly delegated the preparations to the top-ranking Massachusetts officer—Maj. Gen. Artemas Ward. Fascines and gabions were built for the breastwork. Trees were felled to serve as abatis. Barrels were collected and filled with dirt, to be rolled down the hills if the enemy should attack. Hay was pressed and bundled, to act as a blind to cover the wagon train's movements across Dorchester Neck. And wagons were collected or procured in sufficient numbers necessary for the enterprise.[33]

The Americans were in good spirits and worked heartily, hoping for a culmination to a long ten-and-a-half-month siege. A rumor circulated throughout the American camps that General Howe had sworn that if the Americans broke ground on neutral Dorchester, he would sally forth and attack it. If so, the Americans thought Howe was "sure of looseing two thirds of his army. This is what we wish for, trusting (through the assistance of Heaven) this would be a means of rescueing from their hands our capital and many of our friends".[34]

Conversely, the British were very well acquainted with these preparations, and they too looked forward to a decisive action that would end the long stalemate. The British in Boston kept busy as they completed their new batteries that faced southward toward Dorchester. They also cut a trench across Boston Neck and further strengthened the lines there, and in so doing, changed Boston from a peninsula into an island.[35]

Meanwhile, as Ward managed the American preparations, Washington further refined his strategy. First, to aid in the coming action, he requested further support of local militia units from the surrounding communities to serve as an emergency reserve for three days. Also, to cover the noise associated with fortifying, he intended a general bombardment from the Roxbury lines and the new fort at Lechmere's Point, which, to inure the British so they might let down their guard, would commence several days in advance and run each night until his plan was set in motion.

With the new, large cannon from Fort Ticonderoga, combined with the commanding height and proximity offered by Dorchester Heights, the British would wake to find themselves in a very precarious position indeed. Like the situation at Breed's Hill, the naval ships would be unable to bombard the fort on Dorchester, due to its height. The British in Boston would then have to either ignore the fort altogether and risk watching the town around them be decimated, or mount an amphibious landing to attack the fort with ground forces, as they had against Breed's Hill. Such an assailment, Washington hoped, would be as devastating for the British as it had been in the Battle of Bunker Hill. To ensure such a disaster, riflemen were to be positioned on the hill where they might pick off the British officers from afar, even as they landed. But Washington had another trick up his sleeve too.

If the British did indeed sally forth from Boston to attack Dorchester, Washington would have ready on the opposite side of Boston a large landing party of four thousand troops in two divisions, one under Brig. Gen. Nathanael Greene, the other under Brig. Gen. John Sullivan, the whole to be commanded by Maj. Gen. Israel Putnam. A signal system was arranged, perhaps by fire beacon. They were to wait for the signal at Lechmere's Point, ready to row across the Charles River and enter the town of Boston if it was left weakly defended.[36]

Finally, the date of the great enterprise was set. It would be the night of March 4, so that the next day, should a battle ensue, it would be March 5—the sixth anniversary of the 1770 incident best known by its misnomer: the "Boston Massacre". On that anniversary, Washington knew he could count on his New Englanders to fight most ardently.

———— ◆ ————

With final preparations underway to fortify Dorchester Heights, on the night of March 2, the American works at Lechmere's Point and Roxbury opened fire. The Bombardment of Boston had begun, though it was only a prelude to the real planned event.

This "caused a good deal of Surprize and alarm in Town, as many of the Soldiery said they never heard or thought we had Mortars or Shells: That several of the Officers acknowledged they were well and properly directed".[37] Lechmere's Point was especially effective, enfilading Boston Neck and its lines with great effect. Never before had an American Army cannonaded with such severity or such firepower, for only now had they the massive firepower of the cannon from Fort Ticonderoga and the powder and shells by which to use them. The British immediately opened a return salvo, and the two sides bombarded each other throughout the night. As dawn approached, the Americans ceased fire and the British followed suit, but on the evening of March 3, they started anew.

Little came of these bombardments, with the British reporting just six men wounded in the whole affair and little damage to the buildings.[38] Washington reported just as few casualties, "One a Lieutenant by a Cannon Ball's taking off his thigh, the other a private by the explosion of a shell which also slightly wounded four or five more."[39] Unluckily for the Americans, five of their mortars burst, owing to being overcharged or improperly mounted. These included two of their large 13-inch mortars, one being the Congress, taken from the ordnance brig *Nancy*.[40]

Both adversaries conducted their cannonades with great ferocity, "and a nobler scene it was impossible to behold: sheets of fire seem'd to come from our [British] Batteries; some of the shells crossed one another in the air, and then bursting look'd beautiful. The inhabitants were in a horrid situation, particularly the women, who were several times drove from their houses by shot, and crying for protection."[41] Yet the exchange of cannon fire was mostly noise, and fortunately for the Bostonians, few were wounded.

Finally, on the night of March 4, after another daylong cease-fire, the two sides renewed their mutual barrages. This was the third night of bombardment, the eve of the "Boston Massacre" anniversary. The cannonade successfully kept the British attacking with so severe a counter-bombardment that it was deafening to them. Thus, they were largely unaware as the Americans put into motion their grand enterprise.

By early evening, some of the emergency local militia had arrived at the Roxbury camp. Nighttime also brought mild weather and a hazy fog that settled along the harbor, obscuring the lights of Boston from the hills of Dorchester. As soon as the last flicker of twilight faded away, leaving the night sufficiently dark, though illuminated by a bright, full moon just rising above the hills, the Americans got underway.[42]

At about seven o'clock, a covering party of some 800 men, including perhaps some of the newly arrived militia, marched across Dorchester Neck. They immediately split up, about half marching toward the farthest Dorchester Point to guard against incursions from the garrison at nearby Castle William, and about half marching to the northwest point at Foster's Hill to guard against a British incursion from Boston Neck, while a few handfuls headed toward the back side of Dorchester.[43] Immediately following across Dorchester Neck was a work party of 1,200 men, led by Brig. Gen. John Thomas. Directly behind these followed the train of some 360 ox-drawn wagons laden with fascines, gabions, and entrenching tools, plus a few pieces of artillery. The total force employed was about 3,000 men.[44] As the wagons slowly proceeded, men laid a total of 700 or 800 bundles of hay along the short neck to act as a screen for their movements. The work party meanwhile made for Dorchester Heights, reaching their crowns at about eight o'clock. (The lower Foster's Hill, though nearer to Boston, would not be fortified this night.)

Atop the two peaks of Dorchester Heights, Col. Henry Knox, assisted by volunteer and retired Col. Richard Gridley, marked with stakes the perimeters of the two fortifications.[45] The wagon crews meanwhile emptied their burdens and returned to Roxbury, there to load up again. They would make some three or four trips that night while the work party diligently built their prefabricated forts, one on each of the two peaks. In just two hours, by ten o'clock, the two forts were sufficient to repulse small arms and grapeshot.

Despite the noisy bombardment intended as a screen, the Americans were not undiscovered, given away perhaps by the full moon. British Lt. Col. John Campbell reported to Brig. Gen. Francis Smith, "the rebels were at work on Dorchester heights."[46] Amazingly, it was exactly the same situation as the eve of Bunker Hill, when credible witnesses warned of the Americans fortifying. Now, again, the British had forewarning. Yet this time it was given to Francis Smith, the same dolt who had led the British to failure in the Expedition to Concord. "The news required instant action; but action and Smith were irreconcilable terms." The British failed yet again to take the initiative, failed to turn a gun toward Dorchester, failed to man their new batteries facing southward, failed even to inform General Howe, who, it might be guessed, would not have made the same mistake twice.[47]

Construction continued "with the utmost spirit" until the American work party was relieved at about three o'clock in the morning.[48] The relief was some three thousand fresh troops, plus five companies of riflemen. They came partly to complete the works and partly to man them at the fast-approaching dawn, now just three hours away. It seems, however, that many of the original work party refused to be relieved, and so by morning, the provincials were perhaps double this number.[49]

As six o'clock approached on the fifth of March, the sky began to brighten, and the mild New England night gave way to a very windy morning. The first British sentries to see the spectacle upon Dorchester Heights must have been horrified. The troops in Boston began to scurry.

General Howe was immediately alerted to the news, and he too must have hurried to the South Battery to observe the sight firsthand. There upon Dorchester Heights stood two new forts, "that appeared more like majick than the work of human begins. They were each of them near 200 ft. long on the side next the town, and seemed to be strong cases of packed hay about 10 ft. high with an Abattis of vast thickness round both." The small valley between the two hills yet separated the fortifications, but otherwise both posts were very nearly complete, their gun embrasures already mounted with gleaming cannon taken from Fort Ticonderoga. To add to the formidability of the scene, maybe six thousand provincials now manned the lines.[50]

The British cannonade, which had until now been directed at Roxbury and Lechmere's Point, was now redirected to Dorchester Heights. As the artillery at Boston Neck turned to the south, Boston's South Battery at last came alive. Each position fired a series of volleys but quickly discovered it futile—the forts were too high and at too far a range to hit. They even "Endeavoured to Elevate their Cannon, so as to reach our works, by sinking the Hinder wheels of the Cannon into the Earth, but after an unsuccessful Fire of about two Hours, they grew weary of it, & Desisted."[51] The Royal Navy, it seems, never even attempted to fire at so distant and great a height.[52]

Though the British could not fire on the Americans, the danger was that, with the advantage of height in their favor, the Americans could easily cannonade the British. The Continentals could bombard Boston, the neck, and even the warships throughout the harbor, yet they enjoyed complete freedom from counter-bombardment. Given their advantage, the Americans surely fired a few shots across the neck, to rattle their sabers and thus reveal the position's superiority. But otherwise, the Americans essentially remained silent, waiting instead for Howe to make the next move.

According to one anecdote, Howe said that the rebels "had done more work in one night than his whole army would have done in six months."[53] Howe was indeed astounded at this Yankee feat, though he had previously seen a marvel as this on Breed's Hill. Writing later to Lord Dartmouth, Howe thought the fortification "must have been [accomplished by] the employment of at least twelve thousand men".[54]

Another claim gives that Howe "was seen to scratch his head and heard to say by those that were about him that he did not know what he should do".[55] This is hard to believe, for Howe was competent, though perhaps he paused a moment to consider his options. He then acted decisively, ordering an immediate attack. The ardor of the British troops, anxious to break free from Boston once and for all, encouraged him in this hazardous endeavor. By ten o'clock that morning, the regulars were ready to embark at Long Wharf. Brig. Gen. Valentine Jones was to command this initial force, consisting of just five regiments and maybe a company or two of artillery—a force of only 1,200 men, not counting officers and any possible artillerymen.[56]

This was quite a small force. While the initial British assault force that had deployed at the Battle of Bunker Hill was nearly the same at 1,500 men, Howe had then decided that number insufficient and thus brought over his reserve, bringing his total to some 2,300 soldiers plus officers before he finally assailed the Americans on Breed's Hill.[57] But in this present contest, the entrenched American force on Dorchester Heights was much larger than it had been at Breed's Hill. In fact, the entrenched Americans now outnumbered the British force by more than four to one. And unlike at Breed's Hill, the American lines now included thousands of fresh men and plenty of artillery. What, then, was Howe thinking in sending so few troops to Dorchester Peninsula?

First, Howe's entire force was only about eight thousand, with a significant portion sick with illness or smallpox.[58] His effective force may have been just five or six thousand. Second, he was well aware of the American troops at Lechmere's Point and so required part of his men to defend Boston, not to mention the garrison required to man the Charlestown lines.[59] In other words, Howe simply did not have the men to mount a proper attack.

Howe's only hope was to land at Dorchester Point, charge his men in column toward the eastern face of the Heights—that is, against the American right flank of the eastern fort—and without firing, drive the attack home with the bayonet alone. But upon examining the American forts, the British engineer Capt. Lt. Archibald Robertson thought them too strong for a successful attack. He tried to gain an audience with Howe to discourage the assault, but Howe felt obliged to attack for the honor of the British Army.[60]

Long Wharf "was thronged with soldiers…the provincials rejoiced at seeing it, clapped their hands and wished for the expected attack."[61] In preparation for this imminent assault, Washington sent two thousand additional colonial troops over to Dorchester Peninsula to oppose them.[62]

The British expeditiously embarked aboard five transports, and at about half past eleven o'clock that morning, they set off for Castle William.[63] Only from there, given the wide tidal flats protecting the north and south sides of Dorchester Peninsula, could the British easily cross onto Dorchester Point and then attack the Americans from the east.

Meanwhile, as in the prelude to the Battle of Bunker Hill, throngs of civilian spectators began to turn out, all throughout Boston and the neighboring communities. Soon they dotted the hills, watching with anticipation for a spectacle that was sure to become a very bloody battle.

With the wind beginning to howl, the Americans continued to strengthen their forts, beginning a long breastwork that would stretch down the one hill and up the other, thus connecting the two posts together. General Washington himself came to the American lines, and as the men continued their arduous work, he eyed the British transports as they got underway. He then turned and yelled to his army, "Remember it is the fifth of March, and avenge the death of your brethren!" Huzzahs erupted and rippled along as his words were quickly repeated down the lines.[64]

But Nature intervened.

The previous mild night gave way to a horribly windy day, with a massive storm brewing on the horizon. The British troop transports,

WASHINGTON AT DORCHESTER HEIGHTS BY EMANUEL GOTTLIEB LEUTZE (1816–1868).
COURTESY OF THE TRUSTEES OF THE BOSTON PUBLIC LIBRARY. WASHINGTON IS MISSING
HIS RANK SASH IN THIS RENDITION.

now under sail, thrashed against the chop, struggling even to get as far as Castle William. As the gusty wind began to pick up speed, two transports ran aground near the east end of Dorchester Peninsula, though they managed to get off quickly and without damage, just as the Americans dragged over a nearby fieldpiece to fire upon them.[65] However, by the time the transports all reached Castle William, they had missed high tide.[66] While the tidal flats were much narrower at Castle William and nearby Dorchester Point, the British would have been under a great disadvantage if they had continued the landing with the water receding.

And if the British were to have any chance of success, outnumbered as they were, they at least needed easy access to a beachhead from which to mount their attack. The ebbing tide also meant the warships could not draw in close to provide support.

The next flood tide was not until after midnight, so this became the plan—to attack the rebels in a dangerous night operation, guided by a waning full moon. Perhaps this was a better plan, because the American riflemen would have some difficulty aiming at their targets in the dark. British Brig. Gen. Valentine Jones was to stay aboard ship with his troops off Castle William, while General Howe and Lord Percy would meet him at nine o'clock that night with additional men. Together they would land the troops and storm the American forts.[67]

However, as the day stretched on, the storm grew to gale force, and with it, any high spirits among the British soon evaporated. It became "generally thought it would have been a second Bunker's Hill."[68] In the interim, with no attack from the British, despite the battering winds, the Americans continued to fortify their works. By two o'clock that afternoon, they completed the breastwork between the two forts of Dorchester Heights.[69]

As night approached, the British troops were kept under arms until one o'clock in the morning, still expecting to attack.[70] But the gales became so powerful, "it was such a storm as scarce any one remembered".[71] Deacon Timothy Newell called it "a Hurrycane, or terrible sudden storm which arose, in the evening prevented, or a pretence only, can't say—nothing was attempted,—Indeed the violence of the storm rendered it impossible for any boat to land—Some of the Transports were driven on Governors Island, but got off and returned."[72] Rev. William Gordon pleased himself "with the reflection that the Lord might be working deliverance for us and preventing the effusion of human blood."[73]

Howe was forced to postpone the night landing until the next day. Nothing is said of how the American troops fared that night, but they continued to strengthen their positions even as the tempest grew to a torrential downpour.

The next morning, March 6, the storm continued with such violence that it again pushed at least one of the British vessels ashore, though they were able to get it off again. Howe, fighting the stinging rain that flew into his face, made his way to a position to survey the Americans. Just as he suspected, he found their works redoubled, or as one officer put it, "the enemy were entrenched up to their necks".[74] The storm would rage on until eight o'clock that morning.[75]

Howe made his way to back to Province House, and there he met with his general staff and engineer Capt. John Montresor. Montresor was probably the man who "declared that the works had been so strengthened as to render any present attack very doubtful, and that should the enemy augment their works upon that peninsular from such a commanding height we should inevitably be drove from the town."[76] Howe already knew this, but he needed to hear it from his specialist. His staff seems to have agreed with the engineer's assessment.

Privately, Howe knew the storm's intervention had allowed him to save face, avoiding a futile attack on the Americans while still retaining the honor of King and Country. "I could promise myself little success by attacking them under all the disadvantages I had to encounter," he was forced to conclude, "wherefore I judged it most advisable to prepare for the evacuation of the town".[77]

What a momentous decision! With that admission, the Stalemate of Boston was to be broken: the British would quit the town, Washington would have the first military victory of his career, and the Revolutionary Spirit would be given fresh fuel for its fire.

———— ◆ ————

Gen. William Howe had relented to the odds stacked against him and so decided to evacuate Boston. But evacuate to where? His plan had always been to quit the town and move the war into New York with the coming spring. That Washington took Dorchester Heights simply sped up Howe's timetable. However, the British garrison had but six weeks' provisions left.[78] Furthermore, the additional troops and transports Howe required before taking the war into New York had not yet arrived, and he knew there would be rebel resistance there. So Howe was forced to rethink his plan. "I am sensible how much more conducive it would be to His Majesty's service, if the army was in a situation to proceed immediately

to New York; but the present condition of the troops, crowded in transports…and all the incumbrances with which I am clogged, effectually
disable me from the exertion of this force in any offensive operation".
Howe decided to evacuate to British-controlled Halifax, Nova Scotia.
There he could wait for his supplies and troops to come in, unhampered
by Yankee ingenuity or harassment, and there he could get reorganized.
Yet he feared giving "the rebels time to form an army in…New York,"
and hoped somehow "to check the encouragement they will receive from
the apparent activity of the King's army retired to Halifax".[79]

Portrait of Capt. John Montresor (c. 1771) by John Singleton Copley
(1738–1815). Courtesy of the Detroit Institute of Arts.

With the decision made, the British commander in chief knew he would face "A thousand difficulties" in carrying out this massive undertaking. Admiral Shuldham must have attended the war council, where he reaffirmed that the Royal Navy would provide all the assistance it could. Howe then ordered his field officers to begin preparing for the exodus.[80]

The Royal Navy had few ships in the harbor, of which Admiral Shuldham had even fewer transports, including the *Adventure* and one he quickly procured specifically for the evacuation, the *Francis*. The five Army transports that had been engaged for the aborted landing at Dorchester Peninsula were also used. These few vessels were sure to be quickly overburdened. The British had to find room for the troops, provisions, military stores, and those Loyalists wishing to stay under the protection of the King. Shuldham also employed the *Richmond* as a hospital ship to care for all the British sick and wounded, many of whom were suffering from smallpox.[81]

Passengers, probably just the officers and the Loyalist male gentry, were allowed one ton of personal belongings per person. The majority of the storage was reserved for military use, and inventory was kept as best as possible. All of Boston's extensive military stores were to be evacuated or otherwise destroyed, given the lack of space and want of time. The artillery crews were forced to spike a considerable quantity of their heavy ordnance to render it useless. Wool was also to be carried off, "the want of which is more distressing to the enemy than any other article whatever". Finally, several vessels detained at Boston were either to be refitted and manned, or otherwise scuttled, "to prevent their being of use to the Rebels, among which are two Vessels of Three hundred Tons belonging to the Notorious Rebel Hancock, which were upon the Stocks."[82]

An unscrupulous Irish opportunist named Crean Brush was given charge of yet another transport, the brigantine *Elizabeth*. Though Howe's evacuation orders prohibited looting, Brush and his gang raided houses and confiscated anything of value. Meanwhile, with the embarkation apparent, Washington sent express orders to Capt. John Manly aboard his American schooner *Lee* to harry the British once they left the harbor. Manly would successfully take *Elizabeth*, the only British ship captured, and bring Brush and his confiscated goods back to Boston.[83]

With the town preparing for exodus, it quickly became "nothing but hurry and confusion".[84] The soldiers worked night and day to bring provisions and stores to the wharves where they were then loaded onto the ships.

As to the inhabitants, "The Tories were thunder-struck, and terribly dejected."[85] The Whigs too were fearful of what might come. The Boston selectmen sought an audience with General Howe and petitioned that he not burn the town. Howe replied "if the Enemy molested him in his retreat he would certainly burn it; if not, he would leave the town standing." The selectmen thought it a fair compromise.[86]

Accordingly, on March 8, Howe sent a messenger beyond the British lines under a flag of truce to inform General Washington.[87] Washington would honor the agreement, for not only did he not wish to see the town destroyed unnecessarily, but he could not afford to spend his gunpowder wantonly, merely to fruitlessly harass the British as they departed. Washington was already sure Howe's next target would be New York, and there the use of his precious powder would be better served. Interestingly, the proud General Howe did not address this message to Washington directly, nor did he sign it. Washington decided "as It was not addressed to me or any one else, nor authenticated by the signature of Genl Howe or any other act obliging him to a performance of the promise mentioned on his part, that I shou'd give it no Answer". Instead, Washington followed Howe's precedent, sending back a generic response stating only that the letter was indeed laid before Washington and citing the reasons it was given no response.[88]

Meanwhile, to be sure he was not caught unprepared should Howe change his plan, Washington moved to strengthen his positions. First, on the night of March 9, the Americans began assembly of the previously envisioned star fort atop Foster's Hill, directly across from Boston Neck. But the British discovered the work in progress and cannonaded the hill, scattering the Americans. Construction was then postponed for several days. Washington next devised building a new bulwark on Dorchester Peninsula's eastern end to better attack the shipping, and soon the Yankees were put to work on it. But each time the Americans moved to strengthen their positions, the British responded with an insignificant barrage to discourage them. At length, with the British having embarked the bulk of their artillery or having spiked those that were to stay, they could do nothing more to prevent Washington from further tightening his noose around them. By March 17, the small fort on Foster's Hill would be complete.[89]

As the British evacuation became more and more certain, not merely a ruse, Washington considered how best to array his troops. "Notwithstanding the report…that Hallifax is the place of their destination, I have no doubt, but that they are going to the Southward of this, and I apprehend to New York…I shall hold…our Troops in readiness to march at a moments warning, and Govern my movements by the events that happen".[90]

For eight days, the British prepared for their exodus. By March 11, Howe issued the following general orders: "The Troops to have all their Baggage on board Ship by five O'Clock this Afternoon, if any is found on the Wharfs after six, it will be thrown into the Sea."[91] Once the stores were loaded aboard the ships, the troops and Loyalists began to embark. Shuldham's flagship, the 50-gun HMS *Chatham*, along with the equally armed HMS *Centurion*, were so overladen with stores and men that they drew too much water to be moved from Boston except by a favorable wind. So with the first opportunity, they moved deeper into the harbor at King's Roads. HMS *Fowey* meanwhile repositioned to Boston to guard the embarkation of the troops.[92] Howe further ordered the grenadiers and light infantry to serve as the rear guard and cover the retreat. They were to relieve the sentries at the advance British lines so that the latter could embark aboard their assigned transports.

Due to the scarcity of vessels, the conditions aboard the ships were less than ideal, "crowded with two Regts. in each ship, and nothing could be more horrid."[93] One local aristocrat lamented that he had to sleep in a cabin with thirty-six others, "men, women, and children; parents, masters, and mistresses, obliged to pig together on the floor, there being no berths."[94]

Two days more were required to await favorable winds. Finally, in the early morning hours of March 17, St. Patrick's Day, the remaining troops began to embark. Capt. Jesse Adair, the headstrong marine who had led the British onto Lexington Green but was acting this day as an engineer, was ordered to strew crow's feet (caltrops) across Boston Neck to impede any rebel advance as the remainder of the rear guard got to their ships. "Being an Irishman, he began scattering the crowfeet about from the gate towards the enemy, and, of course, had to walk over them on his return, which detained him so long that he was nearly taken prisoner."[95]

As the rear guard made its way to its ship at Long Wharf, they laid down chevaux-de-frise (spiked logs) across the wharf and fired some houses there, in case "there had appeared any Enemy in our rear, but none appeared."[96] The rear guard then got aboard ship about nine o'clock that morning, and thus the entire British Army was embarked without a shot fired, or "without the least loss, irregularity, or accident."[97]

The last of the ships then pushed off from Boston and headed into the harbor, leaving only the few remaining Whigs in town. The expelled included more than 8,000 soldiers and officers, plus ancillaries including staff, commissary department, provost, jailers, sutlers (civilian suppliers), and camp followers of all kinds. Of the uncounted camp followers, an incomplete list gives some 667 women and 553 children, these belonging just to the artillery and six of the regiments of foot. The actual numbers were more than twice that, with at least 2,400 camp followers total. Add to these some 1,100 Loyalists, not counting perhaps an equal number that had quit the town earlier in the Siege. In all, something near 11,500 souls crowded the ships. Most would never return. Nor would they have a place to return to, had they sought to do so, for the Massachusetts government was to confiscate all Loyalist property shortly after the British Evacuation.[98]

General Howe himself, along with Lord Percy, General Pigot, and his aides and staff, were among the last to leave the town, perhaps boarding the HMS *Fowey*. One can only wonder what thoughts went through Howe's mind as he gazed for the last time upon Boston. *Fowey* and the other ships then sailed southward, passing Castle William, its garrison also preparing for evacuation. Just before noon, the last of the ships came upon the waiting flotilla at King's Roads, something more than thirty vessels in all, including HMS *Chatham* and HMS *Centurion*.[99]

A tender then rowed Howe and his entourage to the flagship HMS *Chatham*. As he made his way onto the warship, she saluted him with the blast of fifteen guns. Then the whole flotilla sailed farther to Nantasket Roads at the south end of the harbor.[100]

At this, the thousands of Americans soldiers and spectators that dotted the miles of the town's surrounding entrenchments erupted in huzzahs and laughter. Washington was among the crowd as they watched the Evacuation of Boston. Perhaps he viewed the scene from Dorchester Heights, accompanied by Col. Henry Knox.[101] And just maybe, Washington allowed himself that uncharacteristic indulgence of a smile, for he stood for the first time as a victorious general on the field of battle.

The honor of triumphantly marching into Boston was given to Gen. Israel Putnam, joined as tradition has it, by Gen. Artemas Ward. Because of the town's smallpox epidemic, Putnam led some one thousand troops that had previously had the disease, marching them into the forlorn town the same day the British departed: Evacuation Day.[102]

As they approached the British lines, the Continentals observed British sentries still on guard. The Americans moved in cautiously, guns at the ready, but they "found the Centinels to be Images dressed in the Soldiers Habit with Laced Hatts and for a Gorget an Horse Shoe with Paper Ruffles their Pieces Shouldred fixed Bayonets". The sentinels were

GENERAL HOWE EVACUATING BOSTON—ART BY MICHAEL ANGELO WAGEMAN (1820–UNKNOWN), ENGRAVING BY JOHN GODFREY (C. 1817–1889). ANNE S. K. BROWN MILITARY COLLECTION, BROWN UNIVERSITY LIBRARY.

but scarecrows, some made of hay, dressed in red coats. More stood guard at the British works on Bunker Hill.[103]

Once inside, the Americans found Boston "almost impregnable every avenue fortified", with many of the streets barricaded with small guard posts. The hasty British departure had left the town a mess, but it was altogether whole, with the exception of the few houses and the many fences and trees that had been harvested for fuel. Washington later wrote, "The hurry in which they have Imbark'd is inconceivable, they have not, from a rough estimate, left less than 30,000£s worth of his Majestys Property behind them, in Provision's and Stores, Vessels, Rugs Blankets &ca." As part of this mess, massive quantities of ruined military stores and disabled ordnance were left everywhere. Some thirty pieces of "fine heavy Cannon" and a mortar or two were salvageable, their spikes later drilled out, but the majority were rendered useless. Shots and shells were found in abundance, as were artillery carts and powder wagons, some damaged, "others, after a little cutting & hacking were thrown into the harbour & now visiting every shore." Strangely, valuable sailing vessels sat abandoned with only a mast or bowsprit cut down, fully reparable, some of them even loaded with supplies.[104] (Why did the British not use these to ease their transportation burden?)

The Continentals took all of this in as Putnam marched them to the Heights of Boston, where they immediately began new fortifications intended for defense from the sea, should the British return.[105]

Meanwhile, civilians (especially those immune to smallpox) began to trickle into Boston. One was Rev. Samuel Cooper, who quickly surveyed his home. As he wrote to Benjamin Franklin, "Boston stands, to the Surprize of Many, but much plunder'd—I am a Sufferer among a Multitude of Others. My House was let to a Capt Cockran of the British Army… He had the Use of all my Furniture, but has not left a Bed, Coverlid, Sheet, or any Pewter, China, or Crockery—many other Things of great Value carried off or destroy'd—but This is a small Specimen of the Perfidy & Villainy of British Officers & Soldiers—I esteem it however an Honor in such a Cause to suffer with & for my Country." Despite all that had happened, it is clear Reverend Cooper was only just beginning to contemplate colonial independence when he added, "Shall we have a Nego[tia]tion this Summer—Must we return to the mild and gracious Governm't of Britain?"[106]

A few days later, Washington himself entered Boston. He was most impressed by the British works, all left standing, "upon examination of which, especially that at Bunkers Hill, we find amazingly strong. 20,000 Men could not have carried it against one thousd had that work been well defended."[107] Washington also inspected John Hancock's mansion for damage. He then, with "a particular pleasure", wrote the president of the Congress that his "house has receiv'd no damage worth mentioning. Your furniture is in tolerable Order and the family pictures are all left entire and untouch'd." Though Hancock was willing to see the town destroyed, his property was mostly saved. Only his two sailing vessels were damaged or destroyed.[108]

Meanwhile, at Castle William, the British garrison tarried as they prepared for the fort's destruction. Once they were nearly ready, engineer Capt. Lt. Archibald Robertson joined them to inspect the mines and ensure they were properly set for optimal effect. The garrison then spiked and broke the trunnions off their cannon. Finally, in the early morning of March 20, once all was set and the garrison evacuated, they detonated the mines. The fortress walls blasted apart in a thunderous explosion, reducing the castle to a cloud of smoke and debris that rained down along the island. For the finale, the garrison set fire to all the wooden parts of the fort and the few houses there, creating a towering blaze that was seen even by the fleet at Nantasket Roads. With their task complete, the last of the garrison then departed by boat, leaving behind Castle Island. Where once reigned a redoubtable fortress now stood a blazing trash heap.[109]

As the British fleet awaited favorable winds, Admiral Shuldham sent an express armed ship to advise the different governors on the continent of the British removal from Boston. General Howe also sent a message back to Lord Dartmouth, regretfully informing the home government of the evacuation and advising that all ships set to sail to the New World be rerouted to Halifax.

Once the news arrived in London, some pro-war members of Parliament would sharply criticize Howe's decision to evacuate. However, these critical politicians thought only in terms of abstract ideals. Had Howe indeed attacked the Americans at Dorchester Heights, the result would have been another devastating British defeat. Such a crushing loss would have destroyed the backbone of the British Army and perhaps dissuaded Britain's limited public support at home for the war, thereby ruining any hope the British had of an eventual victory in the Revolution. The decision to give up Boston and regroup in Halifax was absolutely necessary if the British intended to fully prosecute the war.

For several days, the British tarried at Nantasket Roads, taking aboard water and awaiting favorable winds. This made Washington nervous: "The whole Fleet is now in Nantasket & Kings Roads waiting for, I know not what, unless to give us a parting blow; for which I shall endeavour to be prepared." Nevertheless, His Excellency ordered his riflemen and five of his regiments to New York, though he lamented, "I cannot spare more whilst the Fleet hover in our harbour."[110]

It was not until March 27 that a fair wind blew, and so the British departed for Halifax. Only a few ships remained, including HMS *Renown*, left to ward off any British supply ships still making their way across the Atlantic.[111] Once Washington received definite intelligence of their departure, he sent six more regiments to New York. He would send the remainder in the following days, leaving but a garrison to fortify and defend Boston.[112]

Though Brig. Gen. Benedict Arnold's meager forces in Canada remained at a stalemate in their Siege of Quebec, Gen. George Washington's forces had successfully triumphed in his Siege of Boston. More importantly, Arnold and Brig. Gen. Richard Montgomery had successfully occupied the other major British force in North America long enough for Washington to get artillery from Fort Ticonderoga by which to force the Evacuation of Boston to occur. The Canadian Campaign thus made possible the success of the Boston Campaign.

As those last British ships sailed from Boston Harbor, for the first time since September 28, 1768, Boston was completely devoid of British troops.[113] As one Boston selectman observed, "Thus was this unhappy town...relieved from a set of men whose unparalleled wickedness, profanity, debauchery and cruelty is inexpressible, enduring a siege from the 19th April 1775 to the 17th March 1776."[114]

Epilogue

After the British Evacuation, Dr. John Warren was finally free to search out the body of his beloved older brother, Joseph Warren, buried somewhere on the field at Breed's Hill. It was not until April 4, 1776, when John, along with brother Eben and their friend, Paul Revere, found the unmarked grave.[1] "Gen. Warren's body had mouldered in the grave for ten months…in the same grave with a person with a frock on. Warren's body was found stripped of its covering, while the other was buried in its common habiliments… [Joseph's] two brothers…were satisfied of the identity of the body, by many circumstances…[including] that afforded by Col. Revere, who set the artificial tooth…and who recollected the wire he used in fastening it in".[2]

As an accomplished silversmith, Paul Revere had found use for the trade in dentistry as well. Revere noted his own handiwork, where "the left upper cuspidatus, or eye-tooth, had been secured in its place by a golden wire."[3] Revere's use of dentistry to identify the remains is cited as the first known use of dental forensics.

On April 8, Warren's remains were brought back to Boston, honored in a large funeral procession, and given a proper ceremony. His remains were reinterred later that day, buried with the "customary solemnities of the craft" of the Lodge of Freemasons (of which he was a Grand Master) at the Granary Burying Ground within the tomb of a friend of the family.[4] His remains would be reinterred twice more, finally to be laid to rest in the Warren family tomb in Boston's Forest Hills Cemetery on August 8, 1856, where they remain to this day.

Mercy Scollay and later John Warren would care for Joseph's four orphan children. Benedict Arnold would send handsome donations to help, until Arnold and Samuel Adams at last convinced Congress to provide direct financial support in respect of Joseph Warren's service.

For decades, Joseph Warren's fame would rival even that of Washington, a distinction that remains evident in the dozens of U.S. cities, counties, and streets that still bear his surname.[5]

———•———

The slow increase in aggression by the British would drive the Americans to suppose their only way out was independence. In 1775, this was hardly the agenda of any but the most radical minds. In fact, in March of that year, Benjamin Franklin had wrote Lord Chatham, "I never had heard in any Conversation from any Person drunk or sober, the least Expression of a Wish for a Separation, or Hint that such a Thing would be advantageous to America."[6] Even such zealots as Samuel Adams did not dare speak openly about independence in 1775.

But the British always suspected independence was the object and acted accordingly. This drove the wedge deeper between the mother country and her colonies until at last the British invoked from the colonies the very call for independence they so ardently sought to avoid. The seedling of independence was nurtured further when, in early 1776, the relatively unknown Thomas Paine published a small pro-independence pamphlet called *Common Sense*. It was speedily republished throughout the continent, becoming an instant sensation. Its influence was felt everywhere, appealing to all levels of society—from the man at the plow and in the street, to the soldier in the camp and on the line, to the statesman at his desk or before the Congress.[7] Amid all of this, as 1776 progressed, the British massively increased their troops and financial support, dedicating themselves entirely to prosecuting the war, and in so doing, at last pressed the United Colonies into declaring their independence.

Gen. William Howe would lead this reinvigorated British effort, at the head of massive invasion force that would depart Halifax and aim to take New York City. Washington's army was already on its way to fortify New York. But the full power and wrath of Great Britain was about to be unleashed upon Washington the gentleman farmer and his meager rabble army.

The War for Boston was over. The War for New York was set to begin.

ABBREVIATIONS

ADM	Admiralty Records, now part of the UK National Archives
BL	British Library
BPL	Boston Public Library
CHS	Connecticut Historical Society
Clements	Clements Library, University of Michigan, Ann Arbor
Coll.	Collections
Comm.	Committee
Corr.	Correspondence
First Year	French, Allen. *The First Year of the American Revolution.* Boston: Houghton Mifflin, 1934.
Hist.	Historical
Huntington	Huntington Library, San Marino, CA
Igniting	Beck, Derek W. *Igniting the American Revolution: 1773–1775.* Naperville, IL: Sourcebooks, 2015.
JCC	Ford, Worthington Chauncey, ed. *Journals of the Continental Congress.* Vol. 1–4. Washington, DC: Government Printing Office, 1904.
JEPCM	Massachusetts Provincial Congress. *The Journals of Each Provincial Congress of Massachusetts in 1774 and 1775.* Boston: Dutton and Wentworth, Printers to the State, 1838.

LGFO	Great Britain War Office. *A List of the General and Field Officers...of the Officers in the several Regiments of Horse, Dragoons, and Foot...Artillery...Engineers...Marines...* London: War Office, 1778.
LOC	Library of Congress
Mass.	Massachusetts
MHS	Massachusetts Historical Society
MS	Manuscript
MSS	Manuscripts
NDAR	Clark, William Bell, William James Morgan, and Michael J. Crawford, eds. *Naval Documents of the American Revolution*. 11 vols. Washington, DC: Naval History Division, Dept. of the Navy, 1964.
NEHGS	New England Historic Genealogical Society
NEHGR	New England Historic Genealogical Society. *New England Historical and Genealogical Register*. Boston: Samuel G. Drake, various volumes, as cited.
PBF	*Papers of Benjamin Franklin*
PGW	*Papers of George Washington*
PHE	Cobbett, William, John Wright, and Thomas Curson Hansard, eds. *The Parliamentary History of England from the Earliest Period to the Year 1803*. Vols. 16–18. London: T. C. Hansard, 1813.
PJA	*Papers of John Adams*
PRO	Public Records Office, now part of the UK National Archives
Proc.	Proceedings
Pubs.	Publications
NYPL	New York Public Library
NYHS	New-York Historical Society
Soc.	Society
UKNA	United Kingdom's National Archives
USNA	United States National Archives
WO	War Office, now part of the UK National Archives

APPENDIX I

CHRONOLOGY OF KEY EVENTS

May 21, 1775	Skirmish of Grape Island
May 27–28, 1775	Battle of Chelsea Creek (and the sinking of *Diana*)
June 17, 1775	Battle of Bunker Hill (Breed's Hill)
July 2, 1775	Gen. George Washington arrives in Cambridge
Sept 18–Nov 3, 1775	Siege of Fort St. Johns
Nov 13, 1775	Taking of Montreal
Dec 31, 1775	Battle of Quebec (City)
Mar 4–5, 1776	Washington fortifies Dorchester Heights
Mar 17, 1776	Evacuation Day; Siege of Boston ends

APPENDIX 2

BATTLE OF BUNKER HILL: TIMELINE

HMS *Lively*'s journal, among other sources, reports her opening fire at about dawn, 4:00 a.m. (Sunrise was at 4:06 a.m., per the U.S. Navy's Sun and Moon Data Calculator. Civil twilight began at 3:32 a.m., and sometime between then and sunrise, *Lively* beat to quarters.) Other ships soon joined in the barrage, as did Copp's Hill Battery (appendix 4).

The General Orders, June 17 (Howe's *Orderly Book*, 1–2) ordered the assault force "to parade at Half after 11 o'clock" (11:30 a.m.). As this parade was presumably on Boston Common (note the orders then tell them to march to their embarkation spots), the earliest this first wave of men could have arrived at Long Wharf (about three quarters of a mile from the center of the wharf to the eastern edge of the Common) and get aboard their boats would have been about an hour, putting us at 12:30 p.m. (Cf. HMS *Preston*'s journal in appendix 3, which gives the troops were ferried at about 1:00 p.m.)

The longboats then had to travel about 1.1 miles from Long Wharf to the edge of Moulton Point in Charlestown (at a modest 2 knots, given the tide coming in, this would take about 30 minutes), unload their men, and then return the approximately 0.6 miles (about 15 minutes) to North Battery. This took just over an hour or so (until 1:30 p.m.). Embarkation of the second wave of the assault force at North Battery, plus the field artillery (which understandably lagged behind the other boats), was at least another half hour (until 2:00 p.m.).

Howe, in his letter to Harvey, June 22 and 24, agrees with our timeline thus far and states that he and Pigot landed about two o'clock, "being the time of Tide most favorable for the descent". In his letter to Lord Howe, June 22, Howe added that it was necessary to delay until then because the "land was very flat". In other words, at low tide, the extended beach was a marshy mudflat. I have relied on *Bickerstaff's Boston Almanack of 1775*, which reports the day's high tides as 3:09 a.m. and 3:34 p.m., from which we deduce a low tide of 9:22 a.m. Thus, if Howe's time is to be believed, he landed about an hour and a half before high tide (at 2:00 p.m.). (French, *First Year*, 222n35, reports high tide as 2:51 p.m., citing Nathaniel Low's *Almanac of 1775*, which I have not seen.)

HMS *Somerset*'s journal gives a timeline, which, since she was nearby but not engaged in the battle, is more reliable than those of the other warships. The other ships' logs also generally agree, though *Cerberus*'s journal is mostly unreliable, as she was nowhere near the battle. (All of the ships' journals are listed in appendix 3.) *Somerset*'s journal agrees with the 2:00 p.m. landing of the troops. It notes too that the field artillery began to play about 3:00 p.m.

Howe's decision to call over his reserve from Boston required a few minutes for him to first size up the battlefield, have an aide row back over to Boston (15 minutes), embark the new troops (at North Battery), and have them cross the river (another 15 minutes) to disembark near the eastern edge of Charlestown. This took at least an hour and a half, if not more (3:30 p.m.).

If we give Howe a few minutes more to prepare his troop formation and give orders to his officers, as well as to order the burning of Charlestown, the timeline approaches say 3:45 p.m. as the start of the British march for the first assault. Meanwhile, assuming multiple couriers relayed the message to burn Charlestown, one to each warship and to Copp's Hill Battery, let us allot another 15 minutes (4:00 p.m.). This includes time to begin the bombardment, as the hot shot was already prepared. (*Glasgow*'s log also says about 4:00 p.m.) But it would have taken some time for the flames to spread and the conflagration to become general.

Also, this would have been about the same time as the attack began on the beach, or while the slow-moving main British force was still underway toward the redoubt and rail fence, per sources cited in the main text. Given time to finish the first result (including two attempts at the rail fence, say 20 minutes), then a retreat and reorganization (say another 20 minutes), this brings us to about 4:40 p.m. for the start of the march for the second, final assault. The battle was over shortly after five o'clock and *Somerset*'s journal reports at "1/2 past 5 the firing slackened". General Clinton landed at Charlestown about 5:00 p.m., as he was not there in time to fight, but he was still in time to do some service against the American retreat. He landed ahead of the reinforcement, which took considerable time to cross in part because the tenders had to first come from Charlestown to fetch them.

Determining the colonial timeline of events is murky at best. It can be guessed with logical assumptions based on the relative information to what was happening with the British. The colonists paraded in Cambridge about 6:00 p.m. on June 16, prayed, and then after dark, about 9:00 p.m., they marched (Chester and Samuel Webb to Joseph Webb, June 19, and Chester to Fish, July 22). They arrived at Breed's Hill about 10:30 p.m. (a guess) and argued about the fortification for about a half hour (Judge Prescott's account).

Gridley marked out the edges of the redoubt, and construction began about midnight, probably a little before. (Chester to Fish, July 22, and Prescott to John Adams, Aug 25, both say about midnight, but other primary sources say 11:00 p.m.).

Peter Brown to his mother, June 28, says "And about half after 5 in the Morn, we not having above half the Fort done, they began to fire." We know Peter Brown was wrong on the time, as the British began firing at 4:00 a.m., but we can glean from this that the redoubt was half finished after just four hours (midnight to dawn). Thus, the redoubt may have been completed in just four hours more, about 8:00 a.m., though the pace probably quickened once the Americans could actually see what they were doing and once they were literally under the guns to finish. Also, Prescott did not consider a breastwork until dawn revealed his untenable position, but as the redoubt was still underway, he probably waited until it was almost finished, say 7:00 a.m.

The undertaking of the breastwork was nearly as great as that of the redoubt, and so we might expect another eight hours or so on the breastwork, the construction probably continuing right up until the battle, if indeed it was ever finished. The arrival of the early detachment of 200 of Stark's men under Lieutenant Colonel Wyman certainly helped, as did the recall of the 60 men under Captain Nutting who had acted as sentries in Charlestown all night. It was probably with these fresh men that Prescott was able to start the breastwork before the redoubt was quite finished.

The cannon's timeline is a mystery, but let us try. Peter Brown to his mother, June 28, implies the cannon came up in late morning. William Tudor to Stephen Collins, June 23, in Dawson (June 1868), 2:3:376–78, indicates that two arrived (under Captain Gridley) by 8:00 a.m. The Ebenezer Bancroft statement in Spalding's *Bi-Centennial of Old Dunstable*, 58ff., gives that it was not until Putnam carried away the entrenching tools that the Americans began to dig out embrasures for the two cannon, which makes no sense. Instead, the lack of tools was probably due to the breastwork being well underway, and with Stark's 200 men having just arrived, there were not enough tools to keep everyone employed. It was only after the British embarkation became clear that Prescott could send Gridley's two cannon out of the redoubt with Captain Knowlton's soldiers, at which point Captain Callender's two guns came up.

Regarding the breastwork construction at Bunker Hill, see appendix 6, where I make the case that it probably began at noon.

The alarm in Cambridge could not have been raised until the troops were seen gathering for embarkation (the troops were to parade and march at 11:30 a.m.), and that message had to be passed to Cambridge by foot, for no horses were available. Chester to Fish, July 22, says he got the message after dinner (lunch), and in Chester and Samuel Webb to Joseph Webb, June 19, he specifies 1:00 p.m. It was also about this time that the rail fence was begun, and it was probably not finished until about the start of the battle. Stark received his marching orders at 2:00 p.m. from Medford (Stark to New Hampshire, June 19). Warren crossed at about the same time, perhaps before Stark, having heard the alarm in Cambridge before departing.

In the Prescott Family manuscript in Dawson, 2:3:437–38, and again in Judge Prescott's account, there is a note that Prescott sent two separate messengers to General Ward seeking reinforcements, the first courier being unnamed, the latter being Major Brooks. Both accounts claim that Brooks was sent at about 9:00 a.m., and so after a four-mile walk, he arrived in Cambridge about 10:00 a.m. Both sources also claim this resulted in Colonel Stark and Colonel Reed being sent to Charlestown, arriving just before the action. But Stark to New Hampshire, June 19, states he received his orders at 2:00 p.m., so he must have been sent in response to the general alarm of about 1:00 p.m., not to Brooks, who arrived at headquarters some four hours before Stark's orders. It seems unlikely that Brooks was responsible for either Stark's or Reed's orders to Charlestown. Was Brooks then responsible for the earlier order for Stark to send a 200-man detachment to Charlestown under Lieutenant Colonel Wyman? Perhaps so, since we have no sure evidence either way. However, it seems to me that if Brooks did not arrive in Cambridge until 10:00 a.m., Wyman's detachment could not have been in Charlestown until 11:00 a.m. at best, which seems too late in the morning.

Stark's letter suggests he was ordered to send these men in response to the "shipping" (the cannonade), which tends to suggest an early morning order. While Ward was cautious, it seems unlikely he waited until 11:00 a.m. to send Wyman's detachment, a delay that could have had disastrous results. We cannot know for certain, but I suspect that it was either Putnam's earlier meeting with Ward, or otherwise Prescott's first unknown messenger, that resulted in Wyman's detachment being sent. It was probably the former, as Putnam's request would have carried some weight. Governor Brooks's statement (in Swett, notes section, 3) tells us nothing about what Brooks really did that day. It is worth adding that, per these Prescott sources, the council in the redoubt that led to Brooks being sent to Ward was at 9:00 a.m., after it was "evident" the British were going to land and attack. How "evident" was this landing at so early an hour, really? The troops were not ordered to parade until 11:30 a.m., per the day's general orders. Tenders might have been then collecting at North Battery, but perhaps only a few, as the ships were still repositioning. One wonders if this claim is tainted by memory, since the Prescott statements were written years after the battle.

The following given times are often logical guesses, but the order of the events relative to one another is probably close to fact. (Cf. the timeline in Letter from Boston to a Gentlemen in Scotland, June 25, in Force, *American Archives*, 4:2:1093–94. While it generally agrees with the timeline presented here, the greatest discrepancies are in its estimation of the numbers engaged and the casualties.)

Notional Timeline for June 17, 1775

~12:00 a.m.	Colonists begin entrenching Breed's Hill
3:09 a.m.	High tide
3:32 a.m.	Begin civil twilight*
4:00 a.m.	HMS *Lively* begins cannonade; other warships follow
4:06 a.m.	Sunrise*
6:30 a.m.	Gage's war council meets[†]
7:00–10:00 a.m.	Warships reposition
7:00 a.m.	200 of Colonel Stark's regiment arrive under Lieutenant Colonel Wyman; colonial breastwork construction begins (continues up to battle); Prescott's 1st reinforcement request sent to Cambridge[‡]
8:00 a.m.	Breed's Hill redoubt completed; Captain Gridley's cannon arrive[‡]
9:00 a.m.	Prescott's 2nd reinforcement request (Major Brooks) sent to Cambridge[‡]
9:22 a.m.	Low tide
All morning	British preparations for embarkation
~10:30 a.m.	Colonial cannon setup in redoubt after embrasures built[‡]
11:45 a.m.	British troops begin to arrive at embarkation points (only those at North Battery visible to redoubt); alarm sent to Cambridge[§]
12:00 p.m.	Captain Knowlton, cannon sent out of redoubt; rail fence construction[§]
12:00 p.m.	Entrenchment begins on Bunker Hill proper**
12:30–1:00 p.m.	British First Landing: 1st Wave[§] 10 light infantry compys., 10 grenadier compys., 5th and 38th batt. depart Long Wharf and arrive at Moulton Pt.
1:00 p.m.	Alarm sounds in Cambridge; General Ward sends reinforcements
1:30–2:00 p.m.	British First Landing: 2nd Wave[§] 43rd and 52nd batt., Artillery, Pigot, Howe depart North Battery and arrive at Moulton Pt.
2:00 p.m.	Dr. Warren arrives on the field[§]

2:30 p.m.	Colonel Stark's regiment arrives, begins construction on cobble fence[§]
2:30 p.m.	Howe sends for British Reserve to embark[§]
3:15–3:30 p.m.	British Second Landing: Reserve[§]
	47th batt., 1st Marines batt., 4 light infantry compys., 4 grenadier compys. depart North Battery and arrive east of Charlestown
3:34 p.m.	High tide
3:45 p.m.	British commence march for first assault[§]
4:00 p.m.	Charlestown begins burning; beach attack begins[§]
4:40 p.m.	British commence march for second assault[§]
5:00 p.m.	General Clinton arrives[§]
5:15 p.m.	British Third Landing: Reinforcement[‡]
	63rd batt., 2nd Marines batt. arrive east of Charlestown (departed North Battery)
5:30 p.m.	Americans in full retreat; scattered fighting only
7:23 p.m.	Sunset*

* U.S. Navy's Sun and Moon Data calculator.

[†] An unsupported guess.

[‡] A reasoned guess, as given above.

[§] Deduced from evidence, as given above.

** See appendix 6.

APPENDIX 3

BATTLE OF BUNKER HILL: ROLE OF THE ROYAL NAVY

Naval Assets Present during the Battle of Bunker Hill

Rate	Name	Captain	Guns	Men
3	*Boyne*	Capt. Broderick Hartwell	68	520
	Somerset	Capt. Edward Le Cras	68	520
4	*Preston*	Capt. Jonathan Robinson	50	300
		VAdm. Samuel Graves (flagship)		
6	*Cerberus*	Capt. James Chads	28	200
6	*Glasgow*	Capt. Tyringham Howe	20	130
6	*Lively*	Capt. Thomas Bishop	20	130
Sloop	*Falcon*	Cmndr. John Linzee	16	125
Sloop	*Spitfire*	(a Cmndr. ?) (James Dickinson?)	6	40
Arm'd Trans	*Symmetry*	Lieutenant Boormasters	18	38+
5? Floating Batteries		Lt. Col. Thomas James, Royal Artillery	1	15 ea.?

NDAR, 1:700–704, gives journals (logs) for the larger vessels, which are also in UKNA. (*Somerset's* log is transcribed slightly incorrectly: ADM 51/906, UKNA.) Admiral Graves also notes many in his *Conduct*, the pertinent part in *NDAR*, 1:704. *Boyne's* journal is in neither, but in ADM 51/129, UKNA. The count of these vessels nearly agrees with the letter of Peter Brown to his mother, June 28, which states there were eight "ships of the line". (The three unrated vessels were not actually ships of the line.) Most of these vessels are not depicted on contemporary maps of the battle or, if so, not accurately depicted.

Position of the Vessels during the Engagement of Bunker Hill

Boyne and *Cerberus*: According to their journals, they were both moored in the south end of Boston Harbor, *Boyne* at King's Roads, *Cerberus* at Nantasket Roads. Neither of their journals mentions any action except lending their boats for the troop landing.*

Falcon: Comparing the noted journals, she was anchored somewhere in the harbor, probably near Long Wharf (since she borrowed 11 men from *Somerset*), then moved up to the mouth of the Charles. There she contributed to the bombardment and lent boats for the troop landings.

Glasgow: According to her journal, she was in Boston Harbor, probably on the north end near the mouth of the Charles River, where she struggled to move upriver to bear on Charlestown Neck (but the journal makes no mention of firing prior to her arriving near the neck). In contrast, *Preston*'s journal says that *Glasgow* did fire first, and *Preston* was moored just south of *Glasgow* and can therefore be believed. Perhaps *Glasgow* only fired for a short time, since the men were soon employed in heaving the ship on her anchor against the ebb tide of the Charles. (This was probably done by kedging: sending a boat ahead to drop an anchor while holding position with a second, then pulling up on the lead anchor, and then repeating.) To be in such a position to rake the neck, *Glasgow* must have been upriver beyond Breed's Hill and the town itself, near Barton's Point off Boston. She also had with her a yawl—a small two-masted sailing vessel—which she armed and sent over toward the troop embarkation point at North Battery.

Lively: Per her journal, was moored off Charlestown. As confirmed by many contemporary sources, at dawn, she began firing on the redoubt, but at 8:00 a.m., she unmoored and moved down the Charles toward the mouth, near a place called "Winesimet Ferry". (*Somerset*'s journal claims *Lively* was forced to warp [kedge] downriver.) This ferry connected Winnisimmit (northeast of Charlestown Peninsula) to Boston. Its dock was likely at "Ferry Way" (often labeled on period maps) near Copp's Hill. Page's 1778 Bunker Hill map seems to agree: it shows both positions of the *Lively*, with her new position between the east side of Copp's Hill Battery and the buildings of Charlestown center.†

Preston and *Somerset*: Graves later stated (in his *Conduct* for June 17) that Howe came aboard *Somerset* and talked with Graves, hoping to "have had that Ship warped in to cover the Landing, but there was not sufficient depth of Water: The

---

*On *Cerberus*: Barker's diary (June 1), in *British in Boston*, 53. Graves to Captain Wallace of the HMS *Rose* in Rhode Island, June 29, in *NDAR*, 1:776–77, says *Cerberus* sailed on the morning of June 27 for Britain.

†*Lively* had warped upriver circa June 2, per Graves's *Conduct*, June 2, and Graves to Philip Stephens, June 16, in *Conduct*.

larger Ships therefore could give no other assistance, than that was done." This seems to have been the service of both *Somerset* and *Preston*, the two largest ships in the vicinity, though both employed their boats in the troop transfer. Neither cannonaded. Both report being moored somewhere in Boston Harbor. Only *Somerset* reports donating men (to *Symmetry*), implying she was moored farther up harbor to do so, probably still near Hancock Wharf (a.k.a. Clarke's Wharf).* *Preston* then was probably farther south, close to Long Wharf, with easy access to shore since she was the flagship. This explains why Graves and Howe met aboard *Somerset* (for a better view of Breed's Hill) and not *Preston* (the flagship).

Though we have no journals for the *Symmetry* and *Spitfire*, their positions can be gleaned for the other sources.

Symmetry: *Somerset*'s journal claims *Symmetry* was "the transport next up the Harbor," so up harbor from *Somerset* at Hancock Wharf, probably somewhere at the mouth of the Charles. *Somerset*'s journal reports that 30 of her men were transferred to *Symmetry*. (In Graves's *Conduct*, he reports it was 2 officers and 36 seamen.) *Glasgow*'s log notes *Symmetry* was near her own final (upriver) position. Later in the day, *Glasgow* resupplied *Symmetry* with ammunition. *Symmetry* seems to have been closer to the neck and milldam than *Glasgow*.†

Spitfire: Per *Glasgow*'s journal, *Spitfire* was also near *Symmetry*. Graves's *Conduct* states, "*Preston* manned the *Spitfire*...and provided her with Ammunition". *Conduct* notes: "The *Lively*, *Falcon*, and *Spitfire* abreast of and below Charles Town..." Piecing these all together, *Spitfire* was probably southeast of *Glasgow*'s final position, west of Copp's Hill, closer to Charlestown Ferry, or near where *Lively* was moored before she moved downriver. Having received ammunition from *Preston*, *Spitfire* may have been closer to the harbor at the start of the day, later to move to

---

*There are various claims that *Somerset* was between Boston and Charlestown (for example, Frothingham, *History of the Siege*, 131, 139), a wrong assumption based on her position when Revere crossed on April 18. *Somerset*'s journals are sometimes specific on her position, as on Apr 18, which gives "Moored between Charles Town and Boston", though they often generic: "Moored in Boston Harbour" (even when she was still on the Charles). However, her journal reports she warped to a position off Charlestown on April 14, where she remained for a time. Barker's diary, May 13, in *British in Boston*, 46–47, gives she was still there to watch General Putnam's daring march into Charlestown. Graves's *Conduct*, May 9, notes that the 20-gun *Glasgow* was ordered to relieve the 16-gun sloop *Nautilus* on the Charles River, perhaps done in anticipation of moving *Somerset* off. (*Glasgow*'s journal reports she moved on May 10.) Finally, Graves's *Conduct*, May 29, gives an order for *Somerset* to move down harbor, and *Somerset*'s journal seems to record this movement on May 31. Graves to Philip Stephens, June 16, in Graves's *Conduct*, explains more, giving that, out of fear for his ship, particularly in low tide, he moved *Somerset* to just off Hancock's Wharf (Clarke's Wharf). To reconcile *Glasgow*'s position from May 10 to her warping up the Charles on June 17, as given above, she must have been well off the mouth of the river, perhaps near Noddle's Island, or perhaps she moved off Charlestown at some point, say when *Lively* came up. (See previous note.)

†Frothingham, *History of the Siege*, 139, has several errors, but see 131n3: "Boston letter, June 25, 1775", which appears accurate. Williams's journal, June 17, in *Discord*, 17, also confirms the positions of *Symmetry* and *Glasgow*, etc.

Charlestown Ferry. However, she could just as likely have received her ammunition by barges and may have kept her original position, never moving that day.

One strange observation: *Glasgow* and *Lively*, both ships of similar size and design, seem to have crossed paths on the Charles. It would have been simpler if *Lively* had moved upriver to cover Charlestown Neck while *Glasgow* took up position off North Battery, closer to the mouth of the Charles where she could cover the landing of the troops.

It should be noted that none of the ships take credit for burning Charlestown in their journals, though the warships were clearly involved. Graves states in *Conduct* that he "immediately sent to the Ships to fire red hot Balls (which had been prepared with that in View), and also to Copse Hill Battery to desire they would throw Carcasses, into the Town". The only ships in a position to burn the town were *Glasgow*, *Spitfire*, *Lively*, and *Falcon*. The small sloop *Spitfire* had only a few small guns, so she probably did not have the equipment to fire hot shot. *Glasgow's* journal claims she "saw" Charlestown on fire, which infers she did not fire on the town herself, though she was probably in the best position to do so. *Falcon's* journal gives that she fired "on the Rebells till 4 P M at which Time Charles Town took fire", as if she was too busy barraging the redoubt to fire on the town. Finally, *Lively* gives only that "Charles Town was set on fire", and though she does not take the credit, this is the only journal that leans toward that interpretation. In short, we cannot be sure which ships fired hot shot onto the town, but as Graves says "ships" in plural, it must have been at least *Glasgow* and *Lively*, being the larger candidates. In all likelihood, *Falcon* also helped, while *Spitfire* could not. In addition, Copp's Hill Battery also fired. Between these four attacks, as well as the marines that landed by rowboat to burn the waterfront, the town slowly went up in flames.*

Floating Batteries (Gunboats) at Bunker Hill

There are a number of references to floating batteries, also called gondolas, scows, *radeaux* (rafts), or gunboats. Letter of a British Officer, July 5, describes them as "covered boats, musket-proof, carrying a heavy piece of cannon, [which] might have been rowed close in". Lieutenant Barker's diary, June 19, in *British in Boston*, 61, refers to them as "large flat boats, sides raised and musquet proof". Captain Laurie [to Lord Dartmouth], June 23, calls them "flatt bottom'd boats which contains each a twelve pounder". Artillery Lt. Col. Thomas James describes them having "a heavy 12-pr. in each prow".† Coggins, *Ships*

---

*Marines: French, *First Year*, 742–43.

†Lt. Col. Thomas James to Francis Downman, June 23, in F. A. Whinyates's *Services of Lieut. Colonel Francis Downman, R. A.* (Woolwich: Royal Artillery Institution, 1898), 23–24. WO 10/145, UNKA, lists James as a captain.

and Seamen, 54, describes the boats as typically 37 feet long, beam of 12 feet, and probably rigged with a dipping lugsail. Coggins adds that the cannon had a "rail-type slide, elevated at rear to control recoil." Page's 1778 map depicts two gunboats, each with a dipping lugsail on a single mast. Thus, the gondolas were both equipped with oars and rigged to sail. Teams of five to nine men were required for the 12-pounder, plus the requisite seamen, giving a crew of about fifteen, all seamen per Graves below, except perhaps the officers.*

There is contradictory evidence on how many gunboats were of service this day. Graves's *Conduct*, June 17, notes: "two Scows with a 12 pounder in each [prow] end, manned from the Ships of War under the direction of [Lt.] Colonel [Thomas] James, went as near to the Mill house as possible; at first to prevent fresh Forces coming over during the Fight, and afterwards the routed from getting off: But the ebbing Tide would not admit either the Scows or small Vessels [*Glasgow* and *Symmetry*] to approach within the Distance desired." Howe to Lord Howe, June 22, states there were "five floating boat batteries" (Cf. Williams's journal, in *Discord*, 17, unsupported). Barker's diary, June 19, and Lieutenant Colonel James's statement, as cited, note three gunboats days later.

The gunboats probably all began the day near Charlestown Ferry. General Clinton reportedly placed them under the command of Lieutenant Colonel James of the Royal Artillery, who then sent perhaps just two of them up to the milldam near Charlestown Neck, keeping the others back as a reserve. In the afternoon, just before the battle, General Howe sent a messenger to recall them all, hoping to move the gunboats up the Mystic River and behind the colonial left flank. However, timing prevented that, because the gunboats had to fight the flooding Charles to move east and then the ebbing Mystic to round Moulton Point. Thus, the position between Charlestown and Boston as depicted on Page's 1778 maps is probably as far as they got before the battle was over.†

---

*Per William Tudor to John Adams, Sept 30, in *PJA*, American batteries built in late 1775 had crews of 30, though they mounted more guns: a 9-pounder and two 6s, plus swivels. Seamen: there were too few artillerymen in Boston.

† Page's 1778 map is the best map depicting the gunboats. That Clinton gave the order: Clinton MSS loose sheet "I was not a Volunteer…" in front of Box 280; but see French, *First Year*, 230n65, which cites a reference "145–2D" that seems to be the same French later calls by its first line "opinions on his arrival", a letter I could not find, likely in the unorganized portions of the Clinton MSS. *First Year*, 230, 233, gives Howe's plan to recall the batteries. Also see ibid., 241–43 and n31. The claim that the batteries did indeed make it to the Mystic in time to give aid is unsupported by primary sources. For example, Barker's diary, June 19, in *British in Boston*, 61–62, laments that only then, two days later, did three gondolas position on the Mystic.

APPENDIX 4

BATTLE OF BUNKER HILL: ON COPP'S HILL BATTERY

HMS *Lively*'s journal (appendix 3) states, "at 4 AM… Began to fire upon them [Americans] as did the Battery of Copps Hill" (followed soon after by *Spitfire* and *Falcon*). *Lively* was just off Copp's and thus credible. Lord Rawdon to Earl Huntingdon, June 20, states that after it was found that the ships "could not elevate their guns sufficiently to bear upon" the redoubt, four 24-pounders were sent to Copp's. Letter from Boston to a Gentleman in Scotland, June 25, in Force, *American Archives*, 4:2:1093–94, gives it was actually three brass 24s, plus some howitzers. Williams's journal, June 17, in *Discord*, 17, also says three 24s, plus a mortar, "drawn to the North end Battery on Corpse—hill, where there were already 6. 24 po[u]ndrs in Barbette. they began firing on the Enemy under Capt le Moine & Lieut Trotter."* Contemporary maps support that some 24s were already in place—for example, that of "an Officer on the Spot", which lists eight 24s there total. But Gage to Lord Dartmouth, June 25, [No. 33] in Carter, *Corr. of General Gage*, 1:405–06, gives that "within a few hours, a battery of six guns played upon their works", making no mention of additional pieces sent.

Admiral Graves's *Conduct*, Apr 22, describes ordering the original construction of the battery for the express purpose of protecting his ships from elevated positions such as Breed's Hill. It was then dubbed the Admiral's Battery, manned by seamen and marines, and supplied with four 24-pounders (two each from *Preston* and *Boyne*). Per Graves's *Conduct*, June 17, a few days after the *Diana* incident (circa May 31), Gage realized the value of the battery, and the "Corps of Artillery was therefore ordered to take possession and mount some of their own Cannon therein, those belonging to the men of war to be

---

LGFO, 202–03, notes these are Capt. John Lemoine and Lt. John Trotter.

carried aboard again". Afterward, "insensibly it lost its original nickname" and was thereafter called the New or Copp's Hill Battery.

We can safely assume that five or six 24s were in place at dawn, June 17. However, once the British realized that the Americans had no artillery yet, the cease-fire was probably given so that the additional cannon, mortars, and howitzers could be brought up. By around 9:00 a.m., the additional 24s were emplaced. Also about that time, Burgoyne and Clinton arrived and took command. Thus, after an hours-long respite, the battery almost literally redoubled its cannonade. This also explains some contemporary reports that only mention Copp's active at 9:00 a.m.

As Lieutenant Williams's journal adds, "these guns were well pointed & struck the redoubt every time, but they [Yankees] still continued their work." This deadly accuracy is confirmed by the eyewitness account in *Rivington's Gazette*, Aug 3, 1775, in Frothingham, *History of the Siege*, 397–98, which states that the American redoubt was nearly empty by the end "because the fire from Cop's hill poured in so thick that there was no living in it."

APPENDIX 5

BATTLE OF BUNKER HILL: ON THE COLONIAL CANNON

Frothingham, *History of the Siege*, 118, names the three key artillery captains that served that day: Samuel Gridley (49 men), John Callender (47 men), and Samuel R. Trevett (37 men). They were all of Col. Richard Gridley's regiment (ibid., 404), and he had only recommended these and other officers the day before the battle (Force, *American Archives*, 4:2:1354). Whether their commissions were yet signed is unknown. While Colonel Gridley was both a skilled artillery officer and engineer (artillerymen sometimes pulled double duty), many of his men had no training whatsoever (Force, 4:2:1477–78). (Samuel Gridley was the colonel's nephew, though Colonel Gridley also had a son by the same name, not in the Army.* Colonel Gridley had another son, Scarborough, introduced below.)

From combining evidence given below, the first two artillery companies to arrive that morning were that of Captains Gridley and Callender, with two guns each. Gridley dragged his into the redoubt.

Per the eyewitness William Tudor to Stephen Collins, June 23, in Dawson (June 1868), 2:3:376–78, at 8:00 a.m. the redoubt was nearly finished, "but the Embrasures were not cut, nor the Platform for the Cannon prepar'd. there were no Cannon there, only [Gridley's] two field Peices, 4 Pounders." Tudor, an unarmed spectator, then departed, but Capt. Ebenezer Bancroft's first-person story, though transcribed fifty years later by a Mr. Hill in Spalding's *Bi-Centennial of Old Dunstable*, 58ff., proves reliable and echoes Tudor. Bancroft gives that there were no entrenching tools by which to cut the embrasures because they were all in use. So Colonel Prescott asked Bancroft and his men to see what they could do. After attempting to dig by hand through the packed dirt, the artillerymen

---

*See J. L. Bell's blog *Boston 1775*, "A Digital Library from London" at http://boston1775 .blogspot.com/2008/11/digital-library-from-london.html [published Nov 16, 2008].

impatiently fired the cannon through the half-dug embrasures to force them open, absurdly wasting precious gunpowder and shot, proving their lack of discipline.

Swett, *History*, 24, states that when Maj. John Brooks was sent to General Ward to seek reinforcements, "he was directed to take one of the artillery horses, but the order was vehemently opposed by Capt. Gridley", confirming this was Gridley's company in the redoubt. Letter of a British Officer, Boston, July 5, states that in the early afternoon, from the corner of the redoubt, "they fired seven or eight shot into the North end of the Town; one shot went through an old house, another through a fence, and the rest stuck in the face of Cobb's [Copp's] hill." Burgoyne to Lord Stanley, June 25, states that Copp's was "out of danger; for, except for two cannon balls that went a hundred yards over our heads, we were not in any part of the direction of the enemy's shot." Peter Brown to his mother, June 28, adds that Gridley "fired but a few times, and then swang his Hat round three Times to the Enemy, then ceased Fire".

Prescott to John Adams, Aug 25, states, "I ordered the train, with two field-pieces, to go and oppose them [the British landing off his left flank], and the Connecticut forces [of 200 men under Captain Knowlton] to support them; but the train marched a different course... I suppose to Bunker's Hill." The train was likely just the horses and limbers (not a powder train, as the Yankees had little), positioned behind the redoubt, which joined Callender's artillery company waiting out back. (Nothing more is said of the opened embrasures—were the maybe two holes in each corner of the redoubt simply left open for the British assault?)

Swett, 29, gives that the two artillery companies repositioned to the "space between the breastwork and rail fence", and Frothingham, *History of the Siege*, 136, agrees. This seems to be near the three flèches behind the slough or swampy area. Little is written of these flèches, which appear on De Berniere's map. But from Livingston's *Israel Putnam*, 229, supported by Ezra Runnels (below), Putnam reportedly helped lead some construction near the redoubt's adjacent breastwork, and so was possibly responsible for the flèches too. They were either earthen or rail fence. (q.v. French, *First Year*, 227–28, 741ff.) There they fired for a short time.

Ezra Runnels of Gridley's company (Swett, *History*, notes section, 16) states: "Went on to the Hill with the company, and 2 small pieces... Capt. Gridley, having received some cartridges which were too large for our pieces, said that nothing could be done with them, and left his post, and our company was scattered. General Putnam came to one of the pieces, near which I stood, and furiously inquired where our officers were? On being told our cartridges were too big, and that the pieces could not be loaded, he swore, and said they could be loaded, taking a cartridge, he broke it open, and loaded the pieces with a ladle, which was discharged; and assisted us in loading two or three times in that manner." (Meanwhile, Callender's company was apparently still fully manned and continued to fire.)*

---

*A June 23 statement of a Mass. Provincial Congress committee, in Force, *American Archives*, 4:2:1438, confirms the oversized cartridges reported by Runnels.

The 2 companies (or 4 colonial guns total) then cannonaded for a time, but the Royal Navy quickly honed in on them.* One of Gridley's pieces was apparently disabled about this time (either its carriage shattered or the gun itself hit), and both were soon abandoned. This left only Callender's two pieces, which he began drawing off in great haste. According to his court-martial proceedings of June 23 (Force, *American Archives*, 4:2:1438), Putnam confronted him and "ordered the officer to stop and go back; he replied, he had no cartridges; the General dismounted and examined his boxes, and found a considerable number of cartridges, upon which he ordered him back; he refused, until the General threatened him with immediate death, upon which he returned up the hill again, but soon deserted his post and left the cannon..."

Per the court-martial, Callender lied, saying "he had no cartridges". Some secondary sources claimed Callender meant he had no proper-*sized* cartridges (for example, *Columbian Centinel*, July 22, 1818, p. 1), but such claims are likely influenced by Callender's exemplary service later in the war. Otherwise, Callender would have corrected himself once confronted by Putnam. In truth, Callender was retreating, probably getting no farther than the southern base of Bunker Hill.

Another story (Swett, *History*, notes section, 7), related by one of Putnam's sons (probably Daniel), says upon confronting Callender's men, Putnam "offered to lead them on himself, entreated, threatened, and broke his sword over them [the guns?] knocking down a non-commissioned officer [with a flying shard?]."†

In the end, Callender's men dragged the pieces back to the lines, but whether they fired them again is unknown. Soon after, theirs, like those of Captain Gridley, were entirely abandoned.

About this time, Col. Richard Gridley returned to the field, having spent the night resting due to his age. However, late claims that he manned the abandoned guns are totally unsupported.‡ Rather, he served in the redoubt where he was shot in the thigh during the battle (Swett, *History*, 44, 49).

The next evidence is from a late 1818 statement of Benjamin Pierce (Dawson, 2:3:414–15), who served in Capt. John Ford's infantry company of Chelmsford, Massachusetts.§ At Putnam's request, Ford convinced his resistant men to drag two of the cannon down to protrude from the rail fence, spaced "about half the distance from the redoubt on Breed's-hill to Mystic-river". From Chester and Samuel Webb to Joseph Webb, June 19, Putnam then fired

---

*Breed's Hill somewhat protected the American guns from Copp's Hill Battery.

†Benjamin Pierce's late 1818 statement in Dawson, 2:3:414–15 adds: "I think I saw [Putnam]... looking for some part of his sword", something non-witness John Barker, ibid., 433–35, thought ridiculous.

‡For example, Daniel Huntoon's rare *History of the Town of Canton, Norfolk County, Massachusetts* (Cambridge, MA: J. Wilson and Son, 1893), 369–71.

§Pierce was later a New Hampshire governor and father of future U.S. President Franklin Pierce.

the cannon for a time as a demonstration and, given the limited ammunition, likely only fired round shot (despite unsupported claims in Swett, *History*, 34, and French, *First Year*, 240).

Meanwhile, Maj. Scarborough Gridley was supposed to lead additional artillery companies across Charlestown Neck, but balked at the heavy fire from the armed transport *Symmetry* and the floating batteries there. Frothingham (*History of the Siege*, 146) gives that Major Gridley, "halted, and resolved to cover the retreat, which he thought to be inevitable. Col. Frye, fresh from the battle, urged him forward; but Gridley, appalled by the horrors of the scene, ordered his men to fire at the Glasgow [probably *Symmetry*]... He also ordered Colonel Mansfield to support him with his regiment, who, violating his orders, obeyed. Captain Trevett, however, disobeyed his superior, led his [artillery] company, with two field-pieces, to Bunker Hill, where he lost one of them, but drew the other to the rail fence." Swett (*History*, notes section, 20) specifies it was the gun carriage, not the gun itself, that was lost, along with one of his men. Trevett's statement (Dawson, 2:3:415) tells us little.

British Marine Lieutenant Waller (to a friend, June 21) confirms that three guns served at the rail fence, but being at the opposite side of the battle, is mistaken they did "much mischief" (to Jacob Waller, June 22).

As the battle became a colonial retreat, Swett (*History*, 47), perhaps drawing from an unpublished statement of Trevett (cf. Swett, 36), states Trevett was largely deserted by his men. Nevertheless, he convinced his remaining officers and some 30 infantrymen to haul off one of the guns. As they did, the British swarmed to within 30 yards and fired upon them. One Yankee dropped dead and another was wounded, but the rest managed to escape with that cannon, the only one saved from the battle, which Putnam ordered to Cambridge. British statements (below) give that only 5 pieces were recovered, confirming one was removed. It was probably dragged off, rather than literally carried off, and was likely the one still on Bunker Hill with a broken carriage. As it was perhaps a naval 4-pounder (if not larger, see below), it weighed about 1,200 pounds (Coggins, *Ships and Seamen*, 152), explaining the many men needed to remove it.

Frothingham (*History of the Siege*, 184) notes that Capt. Thomas Wait Foster's artillery company also made it as far as Bunker Hill, but was late to the fight, and so obliged to retreat.

After the British took the field, Marine Lt. John Clarke's *Narrative* gives that they found 5 cannon and 5 iron swivel guns, taken from the *Diana* schooner. Howe (to Gage, June 21) agrees. Multiple sources (for example, William Tudor's letter as cited) also confirm the guns were of *Diana*, but she mounted just four 4-pounders and twelve half-pounder swivel guns (Beck, *Igniting*, appendix 5), which does not account for the at least 10 guns sent to the field (including at least 2 with Scarborough). In fact, the Americans had at least a dozen cannon besides those of *Diana* (*JEPCM*, 516; cf. Frothingham, *History of the Siege*, 102n2).

Regarding horses, that Major Brooks sought one from Gridley confirms Gridley and likely Callender had some (maybe three per gun: Spring, *With Zeal*, 159), and so must have had limbers too. But since Trevett's company dragged their pieces across Charlestown Neck and afterward dragged a piece off, they must have abandoned any horses they had before first crossing the neck.

After the battle, Captains Gridley and Callender were the first courts-martial (Force, *American Archives*, 4:2:1438). Gridley's was postponed for a time (and stretched into October), but Callender's took just two weeks. One of General Washington's first acts as commander in chief, given in his General Orders, July 7 (in *PGW*), was to make an example of Callender, ordering him "cashiered, and dismissed from all further service in the Continental Army as an officer." Nevertheless, Callender continued as a volunteer and served so valiantly at the 1776 Battle of Long Island that, after being captured by the British and later released, Washington had his sentence stricken from the record.

Maj. Scarborough Gridley was demoted to second major (*JEPCM*, 373) as he awaited his court-martial, which dismissed him from the Massachusetts service for breach of orders (Force, 4:3:855). But per Washington's General Orders, Sept 24 (in *PGW*), "on account of his inexperience and youth, and the great confusion which attended that day's transaction in general, they do not consider him incapable of a Continental Commission, should the General Officers recommend him to his Excellency." Disobedience of a direct order is a serious charge, and his punishment is unfair in comparison to Callender's. But as his father Col. Richard Gridley, commander of the Artillery, had announced back on July 3 his plans to retire (Force, 4:2:1477–78), one must wonder if Scarborough's softer sentence was due in part to reverence for his father, whose favor and service the court hoped to retain. Whether Scarborough could find no general to endorse him, or never sought it, he apparently never served in the Continentals.

Finally came the sentencing of Capt. Samuel Gridley, nephew to the colonel. Though he was charged with "backwardness in the execution of his duty, and for negligence in the care and discipline of his camp", he was acquitted, the court giving the unanimous opinion that no part of the charge was supported (Force, 4:3:1049; General Orders, Oct 11, in *PGW*). Strange, considering what we know of his conduct. Meanwhile, Lt. Richard Woodward of Gridley's company was court-martialed and unanimously convicted of cowardice and "mutiny, and of a malicious, vexatious, and groundless accusation of Captain Gridley, at a late General Court-Martial." Woodward was sentenced to be "cashiered, and rendered incapable of serving in the Continental Army" (General Orders, Oct 13, in *PGW*). Yet we know nothing of Woodward's story. Perhaps he was a scapegoat.

Unfortunately, in the confusion immediately after the battle, Captain Trevett was also arrested for dereliction of duty, despite his gallant service. Once the mistake became clear, Trevett was instantly released, but not before his company dissolved away in disgust. The Massachusetts Provincial Congress then offered Trevett some kind of new commission, but whatever it was, it appears he declined it, though undoubtedly some of his men enlisted (*JEPCM*, 581).

There were other courts-martial against artillery officers in late 1775, unrelated to Bunker Hill. These serve as proof that Colonel Gridley's selection of officers was less than ideal, and it is exactly for this reason that he seems to have retired on Nov 17, 1775. His replacement was the very able Col. Henry Knox, a man whose experience came mostly from reading the books in his Boston bookstore (Force, 4:3:1921).

APPENDIX 6

BATTLE OF BUNKER HILL: ON THE BREASTWORK AT BUNKER HILL

Daniel Putnam to the Bunker Hill Assoc., Aug 1825, in *Coll. of CHS* (1860), 1:246, suggests construction of a breastwork on Bunker Hill began as the British were embarking in Boston (around noon). The work was likely slow until General Putnam had brought up to Bunker Hill the extra entrenching tools gathered in the back of the Breed's Hill redoubt. According to Heath's *Memoirs*, 13, that happened shortly before the action (4:00 p.m.). Heath was not on the field but appears accurate, because the tools were in use at the Breed's Hill breastwork until then. De Berniere's reliable contemporary map shows a rather complete line on Bunker Hill, supporting that the work was begun around noontime. But if the real reinforcements did not come onto the battlefield until after the 1:00 p.m. alarm in Cambridge (appendix 2), who was available to build this breastwork?

Putnam's regiment was defending Cambridge, per the diary (June 17) of Putnam's second-in-command, Experience Storrs, so it was not them. However, one unsupported claim gives that a detachment of Putnam's regiment did indeed come up that morning, under an Ensign Sprague (Dawson, 2:3:429, the statement of Isaac Bassett).

Otherwise, the only apparent supply of men was those on Breed's Hill, such as the 200 of Stark's regiment under Lieutenant Colonel Wyman that had lately arrived. However, Wyman's detachment seems to have come earlier that morning and was assigned to the breastwork on Breed's Hill.

Alternatively, some of Colonel Gerrish's men could have helped build it. We know Gerrish's regiment eventually did take up position on Bunker Hill (and mostly refused to join the battle). While most of his regiment came in after the Cambridge alarm, per statements in Dawson, 2:3:402ff., the statements also note that part of Gerrish's regiment was already on Bunker Hill.

In the end, we cannot know who built it.

APPENDIX 7

BATTLE OF BUNKER HILL: ON THE BRITISH LANDING AT CHARLESTOWN

We have no direct evidence of the number or size of the boats employed to land the British at Charlestown, but we can make some logical guesses. Each warship or sloop had a complement of various boats, depending on the vessel's size. The rated ships of the line typically carried three boats or more: typically a longboat of about 21–23 feet, a pinnace of about 28–30 feet, and a yawl of about 22–24 feet. Cutter boats were just coming into use, about 25–28 feet long, and many fourth-rate vessels (e.g. *Preston*) carried them in addition to the other types. Third-rate vessels (e.g. *Somerset*) typically carried all four varieties plus one additional boat. *Somerset* is known to have had a small sloop *Britannia*, likely in place of her fifth boat. Sloops-of-war (e.g. *Falcon*) usually carried only a longboat of 16–19 feet and a pinnace of 24–26 feet. Despite these various standards for the ships, boats were sometimes substituted with smaller launches or barges. Whatever its species, boats were often generically referred to simply as longboats, and each was typically manned with between 6–12 rowers, plus a coxswain (often a midshipman).*

Given the warships present (appendix 3), we have: third-rates *Boyne* and *Somerset* (5 boats each); fourth-rate *Preston* (4 boats); sixth-rates *Cerberus*, *Glasgow*, and *Lively* (3 boats each); sloops *Falcon* and *Spitfire* (2 boats each); and transport *Symmetry* (let us guess 2 boats). Though *Boyne* was at King's Roads, about 5 miles southeast from Long Wharf, and *Cerberus* was at Nantasket Roads, about a mile beyond *Boyne*, both ships' journals imply they employed their boats. So we have 29 boats available for the British landing.

Howe to Lord Howe, June 22, notes they had for the landing many

---

*W. E. May, *Boats of the Men-of-War*, 32–33, 40, 56–57 passim. Also see Williams's journal cited at the end of this appendix.

"species of boats (not one of our old accustomed flat boats amongst them)". Others besides Howe complained of not having "flat boats" or flat-bottomed longboats, a style of landing craft that could be rowed close to shore even at low tide when the harbor beaches about Boston were extended marshlands. (Landfill has long since removed this trait of Boston proper, but it can still be observed along the northern shores of Massachusetts.) In A Letter of Intelligence (Fortescue's *Corr. of George III*, 3:215–18), the unknown author complains of "*no proper boats* for Landing Troops" (italics per the original) and recommends "Every Transport Coming out, to bring a flat boat of Rather a Lesser Construction than those used Last war, as they wou'd be Stronger, & bear the motion of the Ship better." Gage himself acknowledged the want of such boats, requesting from England "flatbottomed Boats, used last War in landing Troops, big enough to hold sixty Men including the Rowers" (Gage to Dartmouth, June 12, in Carter, *Corr. of General Gage*, 1:404–05). (Cf. Philip Stephens of the Admiralty to Vice Admiral Graves, Aug 3, in *NDAR*, 1:1347–51, citing plans to order 20 flat-bottomed boats with a capacity of 40 soldiers and 16 rowers each, this after the trial run noted in Williams's journal for July 29, quoted below.) From Gage's request, we may draw at least one conclusion of the boats used on June 17: they carried fewer than 60 men each.

We come next to the contemporary letter of Peter Brown to his mother, June 28, which states, "there was a matter of 40 barges full of Regulars coming over to us: it is supposed there were about 3000 of them". As there were only about 29 physical boats available, not 40, Brown must have meant 40 *boatloads* (or trips) conducted by the 29 physical boats. The total of all British forces, including reinforcements and reserves, was about 3,000 troops (see appendix 9). But 40 boatloads to transport 3,000 men equates to 75 men per boatload, not counting the rowers—an impossibly large number given our upper limit of 60-man boats per Gage. In fact, Brown's reliable letter only makes sense if he meant 40 boatloads were used for the first landing (in two waves*). So, let us assume Brown did not have time to count those boatloads of reserves and reinforcements that came later while he was fighting (a good assumption based on other content of the letter).

Thus, the entire first landing (in two waves or trips) included about 1,799 men (soldiers, officers and artillerymen), plus 10 artillery pieces. With 40 boatloads, this equates to an average 45 men transported per boat and still affords room for the rowers and coxswain. If we assume a modest 6 rowers per boat (perhaps soldiers also rowed) plus 1 coxswain, the 40 boatloads carried an average of 52 men each.

To check our logic, note from appendix 9 that the first wave alone was

---

*40 boatloads with 29 physical boats requires that some went back to Boston to fetch more troops, and so the whole first landing must be considered to be in two waves, not just as the first wave.

1,174 soldiers and officers. At 45 troops (plus rowers) per boat, this first wave required 26 physical boats, which is in line with the number of physical boats we estimated available. And with our average 45 troops per boat, the second wave (of 619 soldiers, officers, and artillery crews) required about 14 boatloads more, plus a few extra boats for the artillery pieces, and one for Howe and his staff. This gives us very close to 40 boatloads for the entire first landing (first and second waves), as seemingly reported by Peter Brown.

Our two approaches thus count 26–29 boats in use. Any error could be from Graves's perhaps keeping a few boats for naval use, or our guess on the boats of *Symmetry*. It is worth noting that other boats were kept in Boston too, such as those of Charlestown Ferry, and might also have been used.*

---

*Cf. Williams's journal, July 29, in *Discord*, 27: "this morning a trial was made of some flat bottomed boats. they held 45 men besides 16 Rowers. all full acoutred. they drew with the above number of men in 17 i[n]ches." These were flat-bottomed boats, not of the style used for the landing this day.

APPENDIX 8

BATTLE OF BUNKER HILL:
ON THE BRITISH CANNON

Lt. Col. Samuel Cleaveland, local commander of the Royal Artillery, wrote in a June 24 letter (French, *First Year*, 232n72, original in WO 55/1537, UKNA) that he intended to send to Charlestown "a Detachm[en]t of Artillery 4 light 12 Pdrs, four 5 ½ Inch How[itze]rs and 4 light 6 Pdrs." Apparently, Howe overruled him. Howe to Harvey, June 22 and 24, notes the British instead brought "Six Field pieces, two Light 12 pounders & two Howitzers". Comparing the two letters, we can assume the howitzers were both 5½ inches and the fieldpieces were all 6-pounders. Tradition gives that the fieldpieces were "brass" (the usual misnomer for bronze pieces), which is likely true because references called them light guns (the alternative was heavy iron guns). The 12s and howitzers were also probably brass. Note that in addition to being light, the 12s had shorter barrels than standard guns, thus reducing their weight but also their accuracy. In A Letter of Intelligence (Fortesque, *Corr. of George III*, 3:215–18), the author laments, "we are in Great want of Medium Twelve Pr Guns", which, though heavier, were also more accurate. Per Howe to Lord Howe, June 22, the second wave (of the first landing) of troops was "followed by some Field Artillery" (and by implication, this artillery*men* came then too).

As for positioning once at Charlestown, each version of Page's map depicts the six brass 6-pounders and two howitzers on Moulton Hill, ahead of where the British right wing formed.* These would lead the British assault.

Per Page's original hand-drawn map, the heavier 12-pounders were apparently kept the entire battle in the British rear on Moulton Hill, where they could elevate sufficiently to bombard the colonial works. Page's has them

---

*De Berniere's map only depicts 6. Page's original hand-drawn draft only has 7, corrected to 8 in later versions.

depicted in tandem: the first between the two British lines, the other behind the rear line. Curiously, later engraved maps of Page omit these guns. (Only after the battle did the 12s finally get moved, under General Clinton, to protect Charlestown Neck.)

Howe's letter to Lord Howe, June 22, states, "We began the attack by a sharp cannonade from our [six] field pieces and two Howitzers, the lines advancing slowly, and frequently halting to give time for the artillery to fire."

As the first assault progressed, much is said of the troops having to slow to pass dozens of fences, but strangely, I found nothing of the cannon trying to pass the same. Somewhere along the way too, it was discovered that the 6-pounders had mostly 12-pound shot in their side boxes, which was too large in diameter to fit into the 6s. (Per Beck, *Igniting*, appendix 6, the difference between the two shot was less than an inch in diameter—a subtle difference, perhaps the cause of the mistake.) Certainly, the British had some 6-pound shot. Otherwise, the problem would have been discovered from the outset, and no such "sharp cannonade" could have set the battle in motion.

The primary theory behind the wrong-sized balls is advanced by *Letter of a British Officer*, July 5 (q.v. Ketchum, *Decisive Day*, 196–98; French, *First Year*, 749). The story goes that Lieutenant Colonel Cleaveland, though not on the battlefield, was derelict of duty because he was swooning over a woman in Boston, one of the daughters of South Latin Schoolmaster John Lovell. Because of this love interest, Cleaveland had made her brother Benjamin a clerk of the artillery stores, but Benjamin was influenced by yet another brother, James, a devout Whig, and thus intentionally sent over the wrong balls.

A second theory in French, *First Year*, (234n6, 741ff.) notes that at times, ill-trained infantry augmented the artillerymen, and these, if employed on this day, may have inadvertently brought up the wrong shot. (French also claims a company of grenadiers, he supposes the 35th, guarded the fieldpieces, though I have found no such proof.)

I have a different theory. If we return to the original order by Lieutenant Colonel Cleaveland, he intended to send two more 12-pounders and two fewer 6-pounders than were sent. Perhaps the clerk of the artillery stores then supplied the cannon as Cleaveland ordered them, not as Howe modified the order. If so, no wrongdoing was at work, and it was simply a communication failure that led to the wrong shot supplied.

Whatever the reason, the 6s grew silent (though the howitzers probably remained active), and Howe learned why. But per Letter of a British Officer, July 5, the gunners reported having grapeshot, so "Howe ordered them forward [and left] to fire grape."* As the artillerymen began to drag their pieces by

---

*Ketchum, *Decisive Day*, 153, unsupported, gives that Howe also ordered a resupply of proper cannon shot. This was a relatively fast-moving battle: it was useless for Howe to seek this resupply, so he did not do so.

hand—a slow process—Howe moved forward against the rail fence, only to be repulsed after two attempts (appendix 11). Meanwhile, the guns' progress was slowed by various fences, given they were advancing in a new direction that was not yet cleared. Only after Howe fell back did the field guns reach their final reposition. (Cf. Frothingham, *History of the Siege*, 143.)

Given that De Berniere's contemporary map depicts other final positions for troop units, it seemingly also shows that of the field guns, labeled "second Position of the cannon in advancing with the Grenadiers, but Stopt by the Marsh". Ahead of this swamp is where they halted, rather than getting mired in it, just south of the 3 American flèches (left of the British right wing).*

From there, they could fire along the entire colonial lines, including the breastwork and flèches (though not into the rear of the redoubt as some stories claim). And since they were still outside the accurate range of American musketry, and since the rather useless colonial cannon were by then mostly silent, this position was relatively safe. Soon the British field guns began firing their grapeshot, softening up the colonial lines, and according to Judge Prescott's account in *Proc. of MHS* (1876), 14:72, they were quite effective. Ultimately, the artillery ceased firing as the final British assault swarmed in that direction and took the field.

---

*French, *First Year*, 241, claims the cannon actually got mired in this marsh, but this is unsupported.

APPENDIX 9

BATTLE OF BUNKER HILL: BRITISH TROOPS ENGAGED

To estimate the number of British engaged in the battle, we start with the General Orders, June 17 (Howe's *Orderly Book*, 1–2):

> … The 10 Eldest Companys of Grenadiers and the 10 Eldest Companys of Light Infantry (Exclusive of those of the Regts lately landed) the 5th and 38th Regiments to parade at Half after 11 o'clock, with their Arms, Ammunition, Blanketts and the provisions Ordered to be Cooked this Morning, They will March by Files to the long wharf. The 43d and 52d Regiments with the remaining Companys of Light Infantry and Grenadiers to parade at the same time with the same directions and March to the North Battery. The 47th Regiment and 1st Battallion of Marines will also March as above directed to the North Battery after the rest are Embarked, and be ready to Embark there when Ordered.
>
> The rest of the Troops will be kept in readiness to March at a Moments Warning.
>
> 1 Subaltern, 1 Serjt 1 Corpl 1 Drummer and 20 private to be left by each Corps for the Security of their respective Encampments…

The best sources on the disposition of British troops are the three letters of Howe, dated within days after the battle, which I refer to explicitly where necessary: Howe to Lord Howe, June 22; Howe to Harvey, June 22 and 24; Howe to Gage, June 21 (see bibliography).

Before we begin our estimate, let us briefly discuss the makeup of a regiment. As detailed in Beck, *Igniting*, appendix 4, a regiment consists of 8 companies of infantry, which can generically be called battalion companies, plus 2 flank companies, one being the grenadiers, the other being the light infantry. It was too late in the publication process when I learned, thanks to the careful research of Mr. Don Hagist, that my estimates in *Igniting*, appendix 4, were a bit low (by approximately 6 percent), and that some of my guesses could have been checked against actual muster rolls in the UK National Archives, of which I was previously unaware. My estimates here are based on this new-found knowledge and the information Mr. Hagist generously shared with me. A company at full strength would therefore have had 42 men (38 privates, minus 2 ghost or "warrant men" kept on the books for financial purposes, plus 2 sergeants, 3 corporals, 1 drummer), plus generally 3 officers. The flank companies, the flower of the Army, comprised the very best men and were often detached from their regiments for special service. Per Gage's General Orders, June 4 and 6 (in Mackenzie Orderly Book 98 and 100, WO 36/1, UKNA), the grenadiers and light infantry were now formally detached and serving as two independent regiment-like corps, with Lt. Col. James Abercrombie and Lt. Col. George Clerk as their respective commanders.

As a foundation for my estimates, I consulted Murdock's *Bunker Hill*. However, we seek to derive a better guess of the effective strength of the British companies, drawing upon Murdock's estimates but tailoring them to equal the totals given in Howe to Lord Howe (presented below, of which Murdock was unaware). Thus, the average effectives of each infantry unit were:

Light infantry companies effectives (Army)	30 men avg.
Grenadier companies effectives (Army)	32 men avg.
Battalion companies effectives (Army) (except 5th Reg.)	27 men avg.

The above is effective strength: total strength less the ill, the wounded (from the Expedition to Concord), and those left to watch the camps (per the day's general orders given above). Note the flank companies suffered great losses in the Expedition to Concord, yet were augmented back to the above strength at the expense of the battalion companies.*

The Marine battalions (interchangeable with "regiments"), modeled after those of the Army, also had 2 flank and 8 battalion companies. This was the first battle the marines fought as 2 separate battalions. Howe notes the marines were close to full strength, which, from *Igniting*, appendix 4, was near 53 men per company. But this was their total, not their effective force. Our infantry estimates above account for the ill and wounded, as they are deduced (below) from actual forces in the field.

However, we do not have the same total force estimates for the marines, and so cannot calculate their effective company size. Therefore, let us make a crude estimate by applying the average effectives for the Army to the Marines. That is, note the Army's averages fit for duty were 30 of 42 light

---

*Cf. "Letter of a British Officer, July 5," which claims, "grenadiers and light infantry, forty men each", obviously referring to the theoretical company size.

infantry (71 percent), 32 of 42 grenadiers (76 percent), and 27 of 42 battalion men (64 percent), and then apply these averages to their counterparts in the Marine battalions which had a full strength of 53 men. This gives an effective size of:

Light infantry companies (Marines)	38 men avg.
Grenadier companies (Marines)	40 men avg.
Battalion companies (Marines)	34 men avg.

The other men we must consider, and who are so often ignored, are the officers. As noted in *Igniting*, appendix 4, there were 3 officers per company. While one subaltern per regiment was required to be left at the camp, per the general orders, I do not explicitly calculate for these few men because I am probably already underestimating the officers. (My calculations are approximated, and no doubt others came as volunteers, just as they did on April 19.) To our estimate of the officers, we must also add the two generals, plus Howe's entourage of various military aides, more than a dozen in all. (At least a dozen were wounded or killed, per Gage's Official Casualty List, June 17.) We will treat the artillery officers separately below. Nowhere in these estimates do I account for the noncombatants, such as the many officers' servants apparently on the field.* In this manner, we may derive a crude guess of the numbers of officers, ignoring the slight difference in the ratio of Marine officers to marines versus Army officers to soldiers.

Let us begin the analysis of the British troops engaged. Howe to Lord Howe notes the first wave of boats (from Long Wharf per the general orders) brought to the battle 1,100 "rank and file" (thus not accounting for the officers). Howe to Harvey specifically gives that this first wave included ten companies of light infantry (he says about 300 men), ten of grenadiers ("something more" than 300), the 5th ("230 Rank & File...the strongest in the Field except Marines"), and the 38th.

The ten flank companies, the eldest companies per the general orders, though not explicitly listed in any letter, can be derived from Ens. De Berniere's eyewitness map. Because the ten light infantry companies marched up the Mystic beach during the battle, De Berniere's map gives them explicitly, in the following order: the light infantry of the 23rd (Welch Fusiliers), 4th (King's Own), 10th, 52nd, 43rd, 65th, 59th, 47th, 35th, 38th, and finally, the 5th. Note eleven companies are listed here: the 35th did not cross with the other ten on this first landing, but came over with the reserve in the second landing (discussed below). With our estimated 30 men per light company, their column was about 330 men total. As given in appendix 11, this column may have been four men wide, and so about 82 men long.

---

*Several eyewitness letters (e.g. Captain Harris, undated, and Lieutenant Clarke's *Narrative*) refer to officers' servants, which were apparently drawn from the ranks.

Thus, the first wave (of the first landing), which embarked at Long Wharf and landed at Moulton Point, can be estimated as:

10 light infantry companies, given as 300 men (to Harvey), thus 30 men each (avg.)	300
10 grenadier companies, given as "something more" than 300 (to Harvey), thus guessed at 320, or 32 men each (avg.)	320
5th Regiment, 8 battalion companies, given as 230 men (to Harvey) the strongest battalion "except Marines", thus 28.75 men each (avg.)	230
38th Regiment, 8 battalion companies, guessed 27 men each (avg.)	216
Total Rank and File: Assault Force (first wave) (est.)	1,066
Total per Howe (to Lord Howe): Assault Force (first wave)	**1,100**

Our estimates (based on to Harvey) agree closely with the total number Howe gives (to Lord Howe), and Howe may have indeed rounded. Note it is from these estimates that we have deduced our estimates of effective company sizes given above.

For the officers in this first wave, we may estimate the following:

Lieutenant Colonels or Colonels	
1 for each regiment	
1 for the ten light infantry (Lt. Col. George Clerk)	
1 for the ten grenadiers (Lt. Col. James Abercrombie)	4
Majors	
1 for every colonel or lieutenant colonel	4
Captains	
1 for each company (20 flank and 16 battalion)	
less 1 per senior field grade officer (who also held companies)	28
Lieutenants (or Captain-Lieutenants)	
1 for each battalion company	
2 for each flank company	56
Ensigns	
1 for each battalion company	16
Total Officers: Assault Force (first wave) (est.)	**108**

A second wave, necessary only due to the lack of sufficient boats, was "the 43rd and 52nd Battalions; making about 450 addition to the former" (to Lord Howe). We may again assume this was just the rank and file. (Note that in Howe to Harvey, he inadvertently refers to the 43rd here as the 4th.) While the general orders state this second wave, embarking at North Battery, was to include "the remaining Companys of Light Infantry and Grenadiers", the hypothesis is that they were given oral orders to remain in Boston until called for. Howe does not include them in his explicit description of this second wave. (This varies from Murdock's *Bunker Hill* numbers. See below, in the discussion of the 35th flank companies.)

Thus, the second wave (of the first landing), which embarked at North Battery and landed at Moulton Point, can be estimated as:

43rd Regiment, 8 battalion companies, guessed 27 men each (avg.)	216
52nd Regiment, 8 battalion companies, guessed 27 men each (avg.)	216
Total Rank and File: Assault Force (second wave) (est.)	432
Total per Howe (to Lord Howe): Assault Force (second wave)	**450**

Again, our estimate agrees closely with the number Howe gives us. For the officers in this second wave, we may estimate the following:

Major General Howe, Brigadier General Pigot, a dozen military aides	14
Lieutenant Colonels or Colonels	
1 for each regiment	2
Majors	
1 for every colonel or lieutenant colonel	2
Captains	
1 for each company (16 battalion)	
less 1 per senior field grade officer (not generals or staff)	12
Lieutenants	
1 for each battalion company	16
Ensigns	
1 for each battalion company	16
Total Officers: Assault Force (second wave) (est.)	**62**

Between these two waves, which together comprised the first landing and were intended as the full assault force, there were about 1,500 soldiers (1,550 by Howe's estimate), plus officers.

Howe to Lord Howe adds that the 450 of the second wave were "followed by some Field Artillery" (presumably from North Battery, though unspecified*), as well as General Pigot and Howe himself, implying these boats comprised the rear of the second wave of the landing. French (*First Year*, 232n72) estimates the artillerymen at about 100. This is a believable number, since Howe to Harvey gives the British had "Six Field pieces, two Light 12 pounders & two Howitzers", or 10 artillery pieces total, and a gun crew of about 10 men each seems appropriate, particularly given there was no baggage train to support the artillery. These 100 men were more than half of the 178 total artillerymen available (perhaps underestimated), as noted in *Igniting*, appendix 4. We should also consider their officers, which were probably at least 2 to every piece (20 officers) plus an artillery commander for every 2 pieces (5 more), or 25 officers total. (This is in juxtaposition to the Americans, who seem to have employed as many as 25 men per cannon, 2 cannon per company, 4 officers commanding. See the statistics in Frothingham, *History of the Siege*, 404, under Gridley.) Some of the artillerymen may have been augmentees from the Army, but we need not count them differently.

Thus, for the artillery (part of the second wave of the first landing), which likely embarked at North Battery and landed at Moulton Point, we can estimate:

10 pieces, 10 men per piece (avg.)	100
Artillery officers	25
Total Artillerymen (second wave) (est.)	**125**

After the above forces all arrived, Howe opted to delay his assault while he ordered up his reserve from Boston. Per all three Howe letters, the reserve was comprised of the remaining light infantry and grenadiers, the 47th battalion companies, and the entire 1st Marines. The contemporary maps of De Berniere and Page both show these as having landed closer to Charlestown, along the British left. Howe's letters do not directly estimate the numbers for this reserve, but instead report his final total (to Harvey; to Lord Howe) as 2,200 rank and file. We may *guess* that, given Howe's estimate of 1,550 in the first and second waves, this reserve gave an additional 650 men (or an additional 702 total using our estimates, but see below).[†]

Before we continue, we must address one anomaly that troubles the calculations. The general orders for the day clearly state that, while the 10 eldest flank

---

*Note that in the excerpt above, the general orders do state "The Pioneers of the Army… to the South Battery… [under] Lieutt Colo Cleveland." However, while Cleaveland was indeed in charge of the Royal Artillery, he did not accompany the artillery to the battle, thus him being at South Battery does not indicate the artillery was also sent there. Moreover, why haul the pieces to South Battery, only to row them past North Battery to Charlestown? (Unless they were stored near South Battery.) The pioneers were not employed during the battle.

†Cf. Murdock, *Bunker Hill*, 17.

companies were to embark at Long Wharf, the remaining flank companies were to embark at North Battery along with the 43rd and 52nd battalions and thus should have been on the second wave. Murdock (*Bunker Hill*, 16) assumes the 35th flank companies were indeed sent over with the second wave, and gives an argument as to why they alone made their appointed embarkation. However, Murdock bases his conclusion on De Berniere's map, where the 35th is explicitly listed on the British right with the other ten light companies that marched up the Mystic beach.

In contrast, French (*First Year*, 741) notes that Howe's letters are consistent in reporting that only ten light companies crossed in the first two waves. Moreover, the 35th was among those lately arrived (June 12–13, see *Igniting*, appendix 3) and thus exempt from embarking on the second wave per the general orders ("exclusive of those of the Regts lately landed"). Thus, French asserts that no flank companies embarked on the second wave, that the second wave was simply the two battalions of the 43rd and 52nd, as explicitly stated by Howe to Harvey (which says nothing of flankers). Instead, French argues that all eight remaining flank companies (two each from the 1st and 2nd Marines, the 63rd and the 35th) were probably given "oral orders, not recorded" to remain at North Battery, and thus did not cross until the reserve was called over, which landed on what would be the British left.

I agree with French's theory, and Howe's letters do seem to support it, but that means the 35th was either ferried separately from North Battery to join the British right or landed on the British left and then they alone marched eastward to join the British right (where they are depicted on De Berniere's map).* Thus, of the reserve, the 35th flank companies joined the British right, while the rest (the flank companies of the 63rd, 1st and 2nd Marines; the battalions of the 47th and 1st Marines) remained in their landing zone, becoming the British left.

The reserve (the second landing, or third wave), which embarked at North Battery and landed on the eastern edge of Charlestown proper, can be estimated as:

47th Regiment, 8 battalion companies, guessed 27 men each (avg.)	216
1st Marines (entire force), including	
8 battalion companies (given as more than 230 of the 5th Regiment, per Howe to Harvey), using 34 men each (avg.) (as deduced above)	272
1st Marine Light Infantry (as deduced above)	38
1st Marine Grenadiers (as deduced above)	40
2nd Marine Light Infantry (as deduced above)	38
2nd Marine Grenadiers (as deduced above)	40

---

*While Howe's letters have occasional mistakes, he was not mistaken in reporting 10 light infantry companies in the first landing, for his reported 300 light infantry only makes sense if there were 10 companies, not 11.

35th Light Infantry (based on first wave lights avg.)	30
35th Grenadiers (based on first wave grenadiers avg.)	32
63rd Light Infantry (based on first wave lights avg.)	30
63rd Grenadiers (based on first wave grenadiers avg.)	32
Total Rank and File: Reserve (est.)	768
Total from Howe (to Harvey): Reserve (not given, inferred at)	**650**

Why is my estimate so much more than Howe's inferred number? On the reserve, Howe does not give an estimate of their number. Instead, he gives only the final number of about 2,200, which he reports in to Harvey and to Lord Howe. By using the rounded numbers given by Howe for the first and second waves, equating to 1,550, we are led to believe this third wave must then be 650. However, because Howe's rounding error has sufficiently accumulated with the three waves, we might instead compare the sum of my estimates (2,266 rank and file) to Howe's 2,200, which compares nicely, within 3 percent of his figure. These numbers do not count the artillerymen.

As to the officers of the reserve, we may estimate them as:

Lieutenant Colonels or Colonels	
1 for the 47th Regiment	
0 for the 1st Marines (see majors below)	
0 for the flank companies	1
Majors	
1 for every colonel or lieutenant colonel	
2 for the 1st Marines (Pitcairn and Tupper*)	3
Captains	
1 for each company (8 flank and 16 battalion)	
less 1 per senior field grade officer (except Marines)	22
Lieutenants	
2 for each flank company	
1 for each battalion company	32
Ensigns	
1 for each battalion company	16
Total Officers: Reserve (est.)	**74**

---

*Maj. John Tupper of the 2nd Marines was ordered over with his flank companies, ahead of his main battalion, per Major Pitcairn's orders (Tupper to John Montague, Lord Sandwich, June 21, in *NDAR*, 1:731).

In total, there were roughly 244 officers to lead about 2,266 men. In addition, there were about 100 artillerymen and perhaps 25 artillery officers. The grand total of British combatants was then about 2,635.

To compare, the British eyewitness Francis, Lord Rawdon (in his letter to his uncle, June 20) states "in all about 2400" troops, probably not counting the officers, in close agreement with my estimate above. Yankee references tend to exaggerate. One such report, Peter Brown to his mother, June 28, claims "it is supposed there were about 3000 of them". It is not clear whether Brown is describing the total who engaged in the battle (as given above) or the total who eventually came to the field (including a reinforcement, given below). If it is the former, it is a gross exaggeration (the likely scenario), but if it is the latter, it is rather close to the truth.

When the battle was nearly ended, the reinforcement arrived: the 63rd battalion companies and 2nd Marines (cited explicitly in Howe to Gage), which apparently landed about where the reserve had in the third wave. Howe seems to have ordered these up, perhaps after his first repulse. Per Howe to Gage, "they could not get to the field in time to have their share of the success". Unfortunately, Howe gives us no estimate of the size of this force, so we will use our above deduced averages for like units.*

The reinforcement (the third landing or fourth wave), which embarked at North Battery and landed on the eastern edge of Charlestown, can be estimated as:

63rd Regiment, 8 battalion companies, guessed 27 men each (avg.)	216
2nd Marines, the 8 battalion companies only, using 34 men each (avg.)	
(as deduced above)	272
Total Rank and File: Reinforcement (est.)	**488**

The officers of the reinforcement may be estimated as:

Major General Clinton (crossing separately)	1
Lieutenant Colonels or Colonels	
1 for the 63rd Regiment	1
Majors	
1 for the 63rd Regiment	
0 for the 2nd Marines (Tupper was in third wave)	1

---

*See notes in French, *First Year*, 241n28, which supersedes Murdock's claim in *Bunker Hill*, 122. Lieutenant Clarke's *Narrative*, in Drake, *Bunker Hill*, 44, gives a completely unbelievable claim of the size of this reinforcement.

Captains

    1 for each company (16 battalion)

    less 1 per senior field grade officer (except Marines)   14

Lieutenants

    1 for each battalion company   16

Ensigns

    1 for each battalion company   16

Total Officers: Reinforcement (est.)   **49**

Thus, the total forces at Charlestown by the end of the battle were about 3,180, including all officers and artillerymen.

To summarize, based on my estimates above (not counting noncombatants):

	Enlisted	Officers	Total
Assault Force (first wave of first landing)	1,066	108	1,174
Assault Force (second wave of first landing)	432	62	494
(Artillery with second wave)	(100)	(25)	(125)
Reserve (third wave, or second landing)	768	74	842
Total Ground Force (not artillery; est.)	2,266	244	2,510
Total Attack Force (incl. artillery; est.)	**2,366**	**269**	**2,635**
Did not fight:			
Reinforcement (fourth wave, or third landing)	488	49	537
Total Deployed Force (est.)	**2,854**	**318**	**3,172**

APPENDIX 10

BATTLE OF BUNKER HILL:
COLONIAL TROOPS ENGAGED

The number of Americans engaged at Bunker Hill is nearly impossible to deduce. The best attempt is in Richard Frothingham's *History of the Siege*, 401–04, summarized below. His estimates come from research in the Massachusetts Archives, but his assumptions are unknown. We might guess his numbers do not include those ordered to Charlestown but who refused to cross the neck, a valid supposition considering he does not list known derelict colonels like Scammans and Mansfield. Likewise, while Frothingham's list breaks down each regiment by company, for Colonel Gridley's artillery regiment, he gives only the three companies known to have come to the fight (those of Callender, Samuel Gridley, and Trevett). An alternate estimate, in Murdock's *Bunker Hill*, 74–79, uses the known casualty rate for a few regiments and assumes the same rate for regiments that only reported their losses to deduce their full strength. His numbers are far more general than Frothingham's but broadly agree. (I have corrected Murdock's minor math error, and I use his higher number for the Massachusetts men, as he seems unconvinced of the lower number.) The following is a summary of both estimates.*

Province	Regiment (Col. unless noted)	Frothingham	Murdock
Massachusetts	Jonathan Brewer	397	
	Ebenezer Bridge	460	
	Ephraim Doolittle	unk	
	James Frye	488	
	Thomas Gardner	unk	

---

*Swett (*History*, 5) adds what county each Massachusetts regiment came from.

	Samuel Gerrish	unk	
	Richard Gridley (Artillery)	133	
	Moses Little	456	
	John Nixon	unk	
	William Prescott	432	
	Jonathan Ward	unk	
	Benjamin Woodbridge	363	
		>2,729	2,400
New Hampshire	James Reed	486	377
	John Stark	unk	477
		>486	854
Connecticut	Brig. Gen. Israel Putnam	unk	
	Joseph Spencer	unk	
		unk	350
Total		**>3,215**	**3,604**

Using different methodologies, both historians derived similar estimates. In round numbers, there were about 3,500 Americans on Charlestown Peninsula, though some never actually fought.

Of those that served in the redoubt, Prescott (to John Adams, Aug 25) notes his party was about 1,000 strong, consisting of 300 of his own men, some portion of the regiments of Colonel Bridge and Colonel Frye, and 200 of Putnam's Connecticut men under Captain Knowlton.* Ketchum (*Decisive Day*, 245–46) guesses maybe 350 were of Frye's regiment and 210 were of Bridge's. Some of these 1,000 where later sent outside the redoubt to build the breastwork and may have there remained, though some deserted. Knowlton's 200 men were also sent outside and began construction of the rail fence.[†]

Others left the redoubt to entrench on Bunker Hill and there remained or deserted. Still more were sent outside under Lieutenant Colonel Robinson and

---

*Frye was ill with the gout, so Lt. Col. James Brickett was in charge, per French, *First Year*, 217n18. Late claims that Knowlton had but 120 men are unbelievable. Samuel Gray to Mr. Dyer, July 12, in Frothingham, *History of the Siege*, 393–95, says 400 men! Prescott was in charge and wrote his letter days later, so he is the best source.

[†]Before dawn, 60 men were sent to Charlestown as sentries under Captain Nutting, per Amos Farnsworth's diary, June 16, but they returned to the redoubt in the early morning.

Major Woods to "flank the enemy", presumably to snipe from Charlestown. Peter Brown (to his mother, June 28) indicates that only 700 were left in the redoubt at the start of the British landings, a rather high estimate. Prescott reports that before the final British assault he had only about 150 men left. Some historians venture that Prescott was augmented by late arrivals to the field, but no evidence supports this.

Most reinforcements that came to the field manned the long rail fence, the breastwork, or the three flèches that separated the two. Captain Knowlton's detachment probably positioned along the rail fence nearest the redoubt, perhaps at the flèches. Somewhere in the center of the rail fence were Colonel Reed's men. On the colonial far left, near the palisade down to the Mystic beach, were Colonel Stark's men. Some 200 of Stark's men had come earlier in the day (per Stark to New Hampshire, June 19), being the first reinforcements on the field and arriving well before the British landings, but it is not clear whether they helped with the redoubt's breastwork, which would have only just then begun construction, or elsewhere. But too many of the reinforcements stayed back on safe Bunker Hill where they gave no service, refusing to fight, or as Peter Brown explained: "500 Reinforcement that could not get so nigh to us as to do any good".

Per Chester to Fish, July 22, many would desert before the conclusion of the battle. Perhaps Swett (*History*, 50) was most accurate when he wrote, "The number of the Americans during the battle was fluctuating, but may be fairly estimated at 3500 who joined in the battle, and 500 more who covered the retreat", the latter being a polite reference to those who cowered on Bunker Hill. George Washington (to George Fairfax, July 25, in *PGW*) claimed, "nor had we...above one thousand five hundred men engaged on that day." This is an impossibly low number. We can only guess, but the actual number engaged at any one time was probably closer to 2,000.

Appendix II

Battle of Bunker Hill: On the British Assaults

There has long been debate about the number of assaults (cf. Murdock, *Bunker Hill*, 70–72; French, *First Year*, 743–46; Howe's letters, and so on). My conclusion is that the issue is really related to the definition of "assault" and is mostly semantics. I use "assault" as a concerted military action against a target, or as per the U.S. Department of Defense Joint Publication (JP) 3–18, "To make a short, violent, but well-ordered attack against a local objective, such as a gun emplacement, a fort, or a machine gun nest." "Attacks" or "offensives" are loose terms that simply mean attempted, usually destructive actions against a target. A "charge", "push", "phase", or "movement" is then a single drive or series of maneuvers toward an enemy objective, and one or more charges may comprise an assault. Where an assault ends and a new one begins is not always clear, but if the assaulting force merely recoils before continuing an attack, they are committing a second charge or maneuver; whereas if the assaulting force entirely retreats, only to regroup and try new tactics, this is clearly a new assault.

I propose there was one beach assault, and two assaults on the plain.

Initial British Troop Dispositions and the First Assaults

Once the first British landed, Howe (in two letters: to Gage, June 21; to Lord Howe, June 22) states that he formed the men in three lines on a "rising spot": the slopes of Moulton Hill. The grenadiers on the left and light infantry on the right comprised the front line, on which the maps of De Berniere and Page agree, though they disagree slightly on other troop positions. Then Howe called for his reserve. As he waited, Howe sought to protect his flanks by placing four light infantry companies forward in a small dell north of Moulton Hill, possibly the site of the clay pit (depicted on both maps). He also placed the 38th on the left, near a stone wall (Page's maps only).

The reserve (the 47th and 1st Marines) landed on Charlestown's eastern edge, well west of the first British force. Both maps show that the 38th and 43rd of the initial force then moved to join this new left wing. I have seen no reliable evidence to suggest the 38th and 43rd were sent to the left prior to the reserve's arrival, though Murdock (*Bunker Hill*, 21) suggests it, as does French (*First Year*, 231), both claiming this was done because the British were harassed by Charlestown snipers even while positioned on distant Moulton Hill, which should have been out of range. Per Charles Stuart to Lord Bute, July 24, (secondhand—Stuart arrived the day after the battle), "The men [reserve] were drawn up two deep on the beach in one line", a claim supported by both maps. This entire left wing was commanded by Brig. Gen. Robert Pigot.

Howe's remaining wing had just two lines: the grenadiers in the front, supported by the 5th and 52nd. The light infantry also started in the front line on Moulton Hill, but as the first assault commenced, they peeled off and moved in column up the Mystic beach. Given Charles Stuart's description of the British left, Howe's two lines were likely also each two ranks deep (apparently common: see French, *First Year*, 235), or four men deep in total. Clinton to William Phillips (Clinton MSS, 12:22), supposedly written sometime before Dec 5, 1775, seems to be a generic letter of little value, but when overlaid with a mask, reveals a secret military message. In it, Clinton gives that the British disposition "was one long stragling line two deep", suggesting the 5th and 52nd were spaced so far apart that the grenadiers ahead appeared almost between them (hence one straggling line).

I define the beach offensive of the light infantry column as the first charge of the first assault, coordinated with the grander maneuvers on the plain, which were dependent on the actions at the beach. Ketchum (*Decisive Day*, 154) claims this column marched four abreast, without reference, though this is plausible given the narrow beach. After their assault failed, they fell back to Moulton Hill.

Howe's right wing then converted their feint against the rail fence to an outright assault (the first on the plain). When they took heavy fire and fell back beyond musket range to regroup and then charge again, this was the same assault, as there was no retreat. (Had this second charge been a new assault, it would have suggested Howe was stupidly inflexible—not the case given the final assault, below.) Only with this second charge did the left wing attack for the first time that day, though it was but a feint against the redoubt. Howe's right was repulsed and fell back, and then Pigot called retreat on the left.

Final British Troop Dispositions and the Final Assault

The British regrouped in their approximate original positions, with the broken light infantry joining the grenadiers in the front of the British right wing.

Howe apparently had learned his lesson, and so the second, final assault on the plain employed column formation. But De Berniere's and Page's maps are not precise for troop movements, and Howe's own letters lead us to believe he changed nothing. Instead, Prescott to John Adams, Aug 25, tells us "they began to march to the attack in three columns."* Reliable Jeremy Belknap, founder of MHS, wrote June 17, in *Proc. of MHS* (1876), 14:92, "they made a feint as if they would attack the same part ag[ai]n, & when they got almost up, the rear made a sudden wheel toward the right of ye entrechmt & entered". And from the eyewitness account in *Rivington's Gazette*, Aug 3, 1775, in Frothingham, *History of the Siege*, 397–98: "They advanced in open order, the men often twelve feet apart in the front, but very close after one another, in extraordinary deep or long files. As fast as the front man was shot down, the next stepped forward into his place..." Finally, Judge Prescott's account, in *Proc. of MHS* (1876), 14:71, states that Howe "wisely gave orders for the troops to disencumber themselves of their knapsacks, advance in column, and enter the redoubt".

This brings context to Waller's letter to a friend, June 21, which describes his 1st Marines as they converged with other columns at the redoubt: "we were jumbled together. I say Jumbled, as the March over the Rails &c. had shifted the 47th Regt. (that was on our Right on leaving the low Ground) in such a manner as to divide the 2 Companies on the right of our Battalion from the other 6 on the Left, but as they were nearly in Column of Files we were not far asunder".

Since there were four regiments (1st Marines, 38th, 43rd, 47th) plus a detachment of six flank companies on the British left, there were probably four spacious columns total, with the detachment of flank companies as one or two long files somewhere in between. Each column then comprised multiple companies. And within each column, each single file of men was apparently spaced twelve feet apart, while the gaps between these spacious columns was greater still, to delineate one another.

What of the wheel maneuver mentioned by Belknap? There is almost no reference to it, though the generally unreliable 1818 statements of participant Henry Dearborn (Dawson, 2:3:402–07) note it. Other references hint at it too. Period military manuals give little detail on the maneuver, but some reference, without explanation, wheeling by platoons. Platoons were loosely defined in 1775, and was perhaps half a company.

It seems Pigot and the left wing began in columns, while Howe on the right began as before: two lines. This was a ruse, and as Howe's right wing approached the rail fence, his second line (the rear [5th and 52nd] per Belknap) broke off and "wheeled" toward the breastwork.

They might have wheeled by platoons, so that within each of their companies of the line, they effectively split in half, pivoting on their respective platoon's left flank. Given the battalion companies were about 27 men, this meant,

---

*Prescott thought one column was led by Clinton, but Clinton was not yet there, as noted in the main text. Prescott only describes the final assault, the only real attack against his redoubt.

that for each company, the platoons were about 14 men each, in 2 lines, with 7 men in the front line and 7 men in the rear line. If they wheeled by pivoting as platoons on their left flanks, the net result would have been a column of companies, about 7 men (or ranks) wide, each of the companies in this column about 4 men deep.

Alternatively, perhaps the lines of two deep merely faced left, becoming a column just two ranks wide. This was quicker, but it also meant a narrow and thus less threatening formation to assault the wide American redoubt breast-work and flèches.

However the 5th and 52nd became columns, the line of grenadiers and light infantry remained ahead as lines. Whether they charged together effec-tively as one long column or split into two directions and became almost side-by-side in their charge, they soon swarmed up Breed's Hill toward points along the redoubt's breastwork.

Meanwhile, Howe's front line (the flank companies) continued forward in line formation as a feint against the rail fence to keep it in check from a distance. But then the grenadiers next wheeled or faced left and charged in column against the breastwork as well. Though Page's map is imprecise for troop movements, it depicts this. Lord Rawdon to Earl Huntingdon, June 20, and Captain Harris, undated letter, in Lushington, *Life and Services*, 41–42, both authored by 5th Grenadier officers, support this.

Thus, the tattered light infantry alone kept the rail-fence defenders in check, and the maps suggest they remained in line formation there to give covering fire while the swarm of many British columns broke through the breastwork and redoubt, thus forcing the American retreat.

General Clinton's late arrival with reinforcements is a final action of this final assault.

Appendix 12

Battle of Bunker Hill: On the Contemporary Maps

French's *First Year*, appendices 21 and 23, examines the Bunker Hill maps of Page and De Berniere, the two critical contemporary maps from which we draw many conclusions (see bibliography).* Prior to *First Year*, many historians considered Page's map the best, noting that it is topographically accurate, based on a survey by British engineer John Montresor. But French argues that De Berniere's map is the one to rely on.

French explains that since Page was injured in the battle and soon after sent home to England, he never walked the grounds to gather the details. Moreover, Page did not produce his final engraved map until he was back in London (though he had a hand-drawn original based on his limited time on the field).

In contrast, De Berniere was able to freely examine the field after the battle and throughout the siege, and so included details not found on the other map, such as the three flèches, the brick kiln, the swampy ground, the cobble fence on the Mystic beach, and so on, all of which Page either forgot or was unaware. Page's map also wrongly shows a bend in the redoubt's breastwork, though his is the only one to include the many fences, being based on the survey.

Both maps are also inaccurate in regards to naval ship positions (Page is closest), specific unit positions (since they disagree with contemporary letters of those who fought, though the overall British lines are correct, and De Berniere

---

*There are several similar maps by Page; I refer here to the 1778 engraved version. Besides his and that of De Berniere, there are many later maps. However, they are generally quite flawed, being influenced by Dearborn's 1818 reworking of the De Berniere map. See Dawson, 2:3:406–07 for more.

is closest*), and both maps depict dashed lines inferring troop movements, but are inaccurate in these as well. At best, both maps seem to show only the first and last positions of each of the units, not their states in between (with the exception of the light infantry). For this reason, I conclude in appendix 8 that the cannon are also depicted in their first and last positions only. In summary, neither map can be heavily relied upon for determining warship or specific troop positions or movements.[†]

French rightly concludes: "The student should use the two contemporary maps, and adjust their discrepancies as best he can." Each map is useful, each has its merits and drawbacks, and I have noted this whenever applicable.

---

*Strangely, De Berniere also depicts some large unknown battalion marked "D. M.", perhaps meaning "Detached Marines" and referring to the flank companies of the 1st and 2nd Marines.

[†]N.b. Page's maps of 1778 and newer have a flap, on top of it showing the initial positions of all and the light infantry attack on the beach, but beneath the flap showing the final positions of all. His hand-drawn 1775 maps are essentially the 1778 map without the flap, depicting just the final actions.

APPENDIX 13

BATTLE OF QUEBEC: COLONIAL TROOPS ENGAGED

Per Arnold's letter to Washington, Nov 20, 1775, Arnold had about 550 effectives, and by comparing Arnold's two letters to Montgomery dated Nov 8 and Colvil Place, Nov 14 (15?), we learn that about 50 of these were Indians (all three letters in Roberts, *March to Quebec*, 82ff.). Meanwhile, Montgomery to Schuyler, Nov 24, 1775 (in Force, *American Archives*, 4:3:1695) gives that Montgomery brought by sail from Montreal "two or three hundred", a figure confirmed by Arnold to Washington, Dec 5, 1775, in Roberts, 101–02. This figure may not include Lamb's artillerymen and cannot include Livingston's Canadians, which were themselves perhaps 200 at this point, per Arnold to Wooster, Jan 2, 1776, in Roberts 103–06.* Livingston's Canadians seem to have marched from Montreal to Quebec, rather than sailed, and thus did not arrive until mid-December, by which time Quebec was already besieged (Montgomery to Schuyler, Nov 19, 1775, in Force, 4:3:1682–84; curious they did not employ captured vessels from Carleton's escape, as Montgomery's men had). Arnold to Wooster, Jan 2, 1776, adds that the Americans recruited perhaps an additional 200 Canadians, mostly locals from the Quebec suburbs, who seem to have been mostly augmentees, not permanently attached. If we sum these estimates: 550 from Arnold, 300 or so from Montgomery, 200 under Livingston, we arrive at 1,050 in the American force, plus a handful unaccounted for with Lamb's artillery company, or in round numbers, 1,100, not counting the 200 Canadian locals. This was the besieging force before Quebec City.

Of these, some had grown sick due to cold weather and inadequate clothing,

---

*Livingston seems to have had as many as 300 in late Sept or early Nov 1775, during the Siege of Fort St. Johns.

as well as an outbreak of smallpox that was beginning to take hold and would grow to a severe epidemic by January. By Dec 16, Montgomery (to Wooster, Dec 16, 1775, in Force, 4:4:288–89) reported, "We have not much above 800 men fit for duty exclusive of a few ragamuffin Canadians." I assume the ragamuffins were the local augmentees. We cannot know how many of each regiment contributed to the sick, but assuming 1,100 to start, less 800 effectives, gives 300 sick (about 25 percent). Given no other details, we will apply this deduction across all regiments.

Additionally, we know from Henry's journal (Jan 1) that some of the 200 local Canadians joined Arnold's assault, and probably the other assaults too. It seems justifiable to not factor sick against these 200, since, as they were local, they would have dissolved to the countryside if unable to fight. Let us arbitrarily assume these 200 were divvied up with 50 to Arnold, 50 to Montgomery (probably too high), and 100 to the frontal assault, perhaps put directly under Major Brown's command, since he had no men otherwise.

Thus, for Arnold's original 550, let us assume Captain Lamb's artillerymen, who joined Arnold, were about 25 (cf. appendix 5), giving Arnold a conceivable 575. With our 25 percent reduction for sick, Arnold's task force was about 430 (including artillerymen) plus 50 Canadians, or 480 total. Of Montgomery's original 300 (besides artillerymen), our 25 percent reduction gives him 225 plus 50 Canadians (probably less), or 275 total. Of Livingston's available 200 Canadians, his effectives were about 150, plus 100 local Canadians, or 250 total, which were apparently divvied up between Livingston and Major Brown since they conducted two separate feints against the Upper Town's walls. (Cf. American George Morrison's journal [Dec 30], in Roberts, 535, which does not count the Canadian locals but generally agrees. The otherwise reliable Thomas Ainslie's journal [Dec 31], in Würtele, *Blockade of Quebec*, 28, gives impossibly high numbers.)

This total assault force was then about 805 men plus 200 Canadian locals, in agreement with Montgomery's estimate of 800, giving a combined force of 1,005. I have not counted Captain Wool's artillery company, which fired mortars from St. Roch during the battle. Carleton to Howe, Jan 12, 1776, in Force, 4:4:656, counts only the "Two real attacks" (Arnold and Montgomery), and his upper estimate generally agrees.

What of the losses in battle? Per Henry's journal (Jan 1), some Canadians and Indians of Arnold's assault force fled over the frozen St. Lawrence, but they were likely few and later returned. Per Arnold to Wooster, Jan 2, 1776, American Major Meigs, though a prisoner, was sent out to the American lines for the officers' baggage, at which time he reported General Carleton's estimate of 100 Americans killed and wounded, though Meigs doubted the casualties exceeded 60 and guessed about 300 more were taken prisoner (cf. the cryptic Arnold to Washington, Jan 14). Henry Dearborn, also taken prisoner, reports in his journal (Dec 31) that "The number of Sergts Corporls & Privates Taken, but not wounded, are about 300" and lists some additional

30 plus officers also, or 330 total. As this estimate seems more specific, I use 330. British militiaman Ainslie's journal (Dec 31), in Würtele, 31, claims a high total of 426 captured, including 350 men, 32 officers, and 44 wounded officers and soldiers. Arnold to Wooster, Jan 2, 1776, suggests that by then Arnold was reduced further, probably accounting for some that marched away at year's end once their enlistments expired. (100 more marched off later, per Arnold to Washington, Jan 14, 1776, enclosure, in Force, 4:4:674–75 or Roberts, 113–15.)

American Siege Force mid-Dec 1775:

American siege force (incl. sick)	1,100
Canadian locals (augmentees)	200
Total Forces Available (incl. sick)	**1,300**

Battle of Quebec City:

Brigadier General Montgomery's attack:	225
plus, of the 200 local Canadians, say	<50
Colonel Arnold's attack (incl. Lamb's artillery)	430
plus, of the 200 local Canadians, say	50
Colonel Livingston's and Major Brown's feints (Canadian Regt.)	150
plus, of the 200 local Canadians, say	>100
(Not counting sick or those in St. Roch, e. g. Wool's artillery)	(295)
Colonial Assault Force (effectives, incl. local Canadians):	**1,005**

Prisoners, not wounded	–330
Killed or wounded held as prisoners by British	–60
Immediate departures upon enlistment expirations, guess	–50
Total American Losses	**–440**

Departures upon expiration of enlistments c. Jan 14, 1776	–100
American Siege Force by late Jan 1776 (incl. sick)	**760**

APPENDIX 14

BATTLE OF QUEBEC: BRITISH TROOPS ENGAGED

The British figures below are from Maclean's Nov 16 list in *NDAR*, 2:1038–39 (see also French, *First Year*, 607n37). They approximately agree with Ainslie's journal (Nov 22, 30), in Würtele, *Blockade of Quebec*, 18. Caldwell [to Murray], June 15, 1776, also generally agrees, but gives some specifics. Of the 200 Highlanders (186 men plus 14 officers), Caldwell gives about 100 were the initial, local recruits, and about 100 were recently recruited by a Captain Campbell and Malcolm Fraser from Newfoundland. Major Caldwell also states, "We were about 330, officers included", which probably meant the British militia, including augmentees. Caldwell agrees with the 60 fusiliers listed, men of the 7th Royal Fusiliers. (Of the other regiment that had been in Canada, it seems the entirety of the 26th Regiment was taken with St. Johns and Carleton's narrow escape from Montreal.) Arnold's own estimate of the British force was 1,900, with a thorough breakdown given in his letter to Montgomery, Nov 20, in Roberts, *March to Quebec*, 90–92.

Following Carleton's Nov 22 ultimatum for Quebec's citizens to serve the militia or flee, Ainslie's journal (Nov 30), in Würtele, 18, reports a new estimate of 1,800 total men. His numbers are approximate, and I ignore where his numbers appear lower than Maclean's Nov 16 list. I also ignore his greater numbers for the fusiliers and seamen, because it seems unlikely there were any more to be had after impressment. The numbers I do accept are listed below as augmentees, taking Ainslie's final number and subtracting for those already accounted for from Maclean's Nov 16 list. Ainslie also reports a total of 5,000 souls inside the walls of Quebec.

	Officers	Men
Royal Artillery	1	5
Royal Highlander Emigrants Regiment (new regiment)	14	186
HMS *Lizard* Marines	2	35
HMS *Lizard* Seamen (effectives)	19	114
HM Sloop *Hunter* Seamen (effectives)	8	60
Armed Sloop *Magdalen* Seamen (effectives)	4	16
Armed Sloop *Charlotte* Seamen (effectives)	4	46
Impressed Masters, Carpenters, Seamen, etc.		
of Merchant Ships		74
Artificers & Carpenters		80
British Militia (including officers)	?	200
Canadian Militia (including officers)	?	300
7th Royal Fusiliers (prev. aboard *Fell & Providence*)	3	60
Snow *Fell* & Schooner *Providence* Seamen	8	72
Total Force as of Nov 16, 1775 **1,311 total:**	**63**	**1,248**

		Men
Augmentees:		
Royal Artillery		16
Royal Highlander Emigrants Regiment		30
Artificers		40
British Militia		130
Canadian Militia		243
Total Force as of Nov 30, 1775 **1,770 total:**	**63**	**1,707**

APPENDIX 15

BRITISH EMBARKATION FOR DORCHESTER HEIGHTS

Timeline for the Embarkation on March 5, 1776

Some secondary sources claim the British plan was to wait until the evening to attack Dorchester Heights. There is no support for this, and it directly contradicts Howe to Lord Dartmouth, Mar 21, 1776, which gives he wanted to attack immediately that morning, a point echoed in the morning orders (also in the *Orderly Book*, 225).

Robertson's diary (Mar 5), 74, gives that the transports got underway at 11:30 a.m., about high tide, exactly when best to land at Dorchester Peninsula given the expansive mudflats there at low tide. (High tide was 11:25 a.m., per *Bickerstaff's New-England Almanack for 1776*. Rev. William Gordon to Samuel Wilson, Apr 6, 1776, in Commager and Morris, *Spirit of 'Seventy-Six*, 177–79, agrees the tide was an issue.) Again, the plan was to attack immediately. However, contrary winds and a brewing storm delayed the transports reaching the eastern side of Dorchester (near Castle William) to beyond high tide, so the plan shifted to delay the landing until the next high tide that night, thereby ensuring a safe British landing. The general orders were issued in three parts on March 5 (morning orders, general orders, and evening orders, all in Howe's *Orderly Book*, 225), and it was probably not until 1:00 p.m. (Robertson 74) when the second general orders were issued in response to the changing weather, and only these then called for an embarkation that night.

However, as given in the main text, the storm continued to strengthen, again delaying the attack until the next morning, March 6. By then, with the Yankees further entrenched, Howe aborted the mission and opted to quit the town.*

---

*Kemble's diary (Mar 5–6), in *Coll. of the NYHS* (1883), 1:71, generally supports the other evidence here, but adds confusion to the timeline. Cf. French, *First Year*, 770.

British Troops Embarked

The morning orders (as cited) list the regiments to be employed: the 40th, 44th, 49th, 52nd, and 55th were to be embark before noon, while the 23rd and 38th were ordered to be ready by 7:00 p.m., along with the corps of light infantry and grenadiers. Robertson's diary (Mar 5), 74, repeats these. Hunter of the 52nd Lights, in his journal, 14–15, says the light infantry were under arms from 6:00 p.m. to 1:00 a.m. that night. Some field artillery may have also been included in the first embarkation, despite no mention of such in the general orders, if only to serve as a diversion for the American artillery.

We can crudely estimate the numbers employed by using 30 men per company, 8 companies per regiment for the 5 regiments above, the flank companies having been formally detached (appendix 9). Note that while these regiments were mostly of the Second and Third embarkations, perhaps recruited to full strength of at least 42 men per company, this number would have dwindled by now due to winter and sickness. Thus, for the British embarkation:

40th Regiment, 8 batt. compys., guessed 30 men each (avg.)	240
44th Regiment, ditto	240
49th Regiment, ditto	240
52nd Regiment, ditto	240
55th Regiment, ditto	240
Total Rank and File: Forenoon Embarkation (est.)	**1,200**

Brig. Gen. Valentine Jones, plus half a dozen aides	7
Lieutenant Colonels or Colonels	
1 for each regiment	5
Majors	
1 for every colonel or lieutenant colonel	5
Captains	
1 for each company (40 battalion)	
less 1 per senior field grade officer (not general or staff)	30
Lieutenants	
1 for each battalion company	40
Ensigns	
1 for each battalion company	40
Total Officers: Prenoon Embarkation (est.)	**127**

A total of 1,327 officers and men, not counting any artillery, was quite a small force with which to the attack the Americans. If we include those meant to embark at 7:00 p.m., and for the possible flank companies note there were a maximum of 20 regiments and 2 battalions of marines in Boston to supply flanking companies (Beck, *Igniting*, appendix 3), we can estimate:*

23rd Regiment, 8 batt. compys, guessed 30 men each (avg.)	240
38th Regiment, ditto	240
(2?) Corps of Grenadiers, ~22 compys, guessed 30 men each (avg.)	660
(2?) Corps of Light Infantry, ditto	660
Total Rank and File: Evening Embarkation (est., probably too high)	**1,800**

Lieutenant Colonels or Colonels	
1 for each regiment or corps	4
Majors	
1 for every colonel or lieutenant colonel	4
Captains	
1 for each company (44 flank and 16 battalion)	
less 1 per senior field grade officer	52
Lieutenants	
1 for each battalion company	
2 for each flank company	104
Ensigns	
1 for each battalion company	16
Total Officers: Evening Embarkation (est.)	**180**

The total force planned for the aborted battle was thus 3,307, including officers and men but not artillery, or 3,000 rank and file. To compare, Howe to Clinton, Mar 21, 1776, in Clinton MSS, gives 2,200 rank and file were employed, and Colonel Stuart to Lord Bute, Apr 28, 1776, estimates a 2,500 total force. The difference is due to uncertainties in flank companies comprising the detached corps, true numbers of effectives versus sick, etc., and most of this error is likely in our calculation for the planned evening embarkation. About 2,500 is likely the more accurate number.

---

*The 22 or so light companies were now apparently separated into two corps; the same for the grenadiers. This implied from the day's general orders, as cited. On May 14, 1776, they were again reorganized, per Howe's *Orderly Book*, 272–73.

Appendix 16

Vessels Employed in the Evacuation of Boston

The vessels employed in the British Evacuation of Boston on March 17, 1776, included at least the transports *Francis, Adventure, Richmond* (a hospital ship), and Crean Brush's *Elizabeth* (see Shuldham to Stephens, Mar 17, 1776, in *NDAR*, 4:381–82; French, *First Year*, 666–67, 672–73). Transports rarely appeared on the Navy lists as they were often under the command of the Army, being supply ships for such. (See as evidence Graves's *Conduct* and Gage to Graves, Sept 4, 1775, in *NDAR*, 2:7–8) The five (probably Army) transports that embarked the first troops for the aborted Battle of Dorchester Heights were probably used, though nothing is reported of them after March 5. They were *Goodintent, Sea Venture, Venus, Spy*, and *Success* (Morning Orders, Mar 5, 1776, in Howe's *Orderly Book*, 225). *First Year*, 665, also mentions brigantine *Unity*.

Regarding the other vessels mentioned throughout this volume, *Symmetry* had been sent to Georgia and *Falcon* had been sent to North Carolina ahead of Clinton (Graves to Philip Stephens, Jan 26, 1776, in *NDAR*, 3:992–95). *Preston* sailed for England with Graves aboard. *Glasgow* was now in the Rhode Island area. *Somerset* left shortly after the Battle of Bunker Hill, presumably first to Halifax for repairs (she is on the September List in *NDAR*, 2:742), then onward to England (she is not on the January 1776 List in *NDAR*, 3:1008). *Canceaux*, the ship that bombarded Falmouth, was sent to England (ibid.). *Halifax* seems to have been fighting against whaleboaters along the New England coastline (*NDAR*, vol. 3 passim), but ultimately sailed for Halifax, arriving on March 29, 1776, just ahead of the fleet (her journal in *NDAR*, 4:590–91). *Spitfire* was damaged in the attack at Falmouth and was to be repaired, but is not mentioned as sailing to Halifax (Mowat to Graves, Oct 19, 1775, in *NDAR*, 2:513–16). (Note that *Spitfire* was rarely listed in the Navy reports because she apparently belonged to the Army, per Gage to Graves, Sept 4, 1775, in *NDAR*, 2:7–8.)

The January 1776 List in *NDAR*, 3:1008, also gives three ships then being fitted out, which should have been finished by March. They were *Tryal* Advanced Boat, *Dispatch* Schooner, and *Diligent* Schooner. HMS *Chatham*'s journal (Mar 21–22, 27, 1776), as well as that of the *Centurion* (Mar 27, 1776), in *NDAR*, 4:447, 537–39, mentions *Renown*, *Fowey*, *Lively*, *Nautilus*, *Savage*, *Diligent*, *Dispatch*, *Tryal*, *Kingfisher*, and *Niger* in the Evacuation. Shuldham to Stephens, Mar 23, 1776, in *NDAR*, 4:472, adds that the "Victualling Sloop" *Princess Augusta* arrived just before they flotilla set off for Halifax.

In all, the flotilla that departed for Halifax was "HM Ships [*Chatham*] *Centurion Lively Savage Tryal* Schooner with Sixty Six Sail of Transports & other Vessels" (*Chatham*'s journal for Mar 27, 1776, as cited). The flotilla also included *Kingfisher* and *Dispatch* (Shuldham to Philip Stephens, Mar 23, 1776, as cited, see note 2 there). If these 66 sails all had three masts (unlikely), then the transports and other vessels were at least 22 ships, plus the 7 warships explicitly named. Thus, it is fair to say the flotilla that departed for Halifax was at least 29 vessels, likely more. Finally, Shuldham to Stephens, Mar 23, 1776, reports that *Renown* with other small cruisers was to guard Boston Harbor to prevent vessels still sailing across the Atlantic from falling into the hands of the rebels.

Appendix 17

Particulars of the Death
of Joseph Warren

An unauthenticated story claims Dr. Warren may have been injured in the arm during the Battle of Bunker Hill, June 17, 1775, perhaps by a bayonet during the melee that ensued inside the American redoubt on Breed's Hill.[*] Finally, when the Americans retreated, Warren was among the last to leave the redoubt. He rallied the Yankees for one more volley when he was shot in the face by some British pursuer, the bullet passing through his left cheek and out the back of the skull at its base.[†] Based upon evidence presented below, despite many claims afterward that he gave dying speeches, he died instantly on the field of battle.[‡] Warren's killer was then "instantly cut to pieces" by the

---

[*]General Sumner's late statement, unsupported, in *NEHGR* (1858), 12:119. That Warren said, "I am a dead man, fight on" (ibid., 122) is impossible: read on.

[†]Previous sources debated *where* in the head Warren was shot, but the evidence below gives the truth. John Trumbull's *The Battle of Bunker's Hill, June 17, 1775* painting (1786; featured on the cover of *Igniting*) depicts the good doctor with just a hint of red dripping from behind the top of his head; his face is intact and his friends surround him, holding back the oncoming British bayonets.

[‡]There is a romantic (but false) story that first appeared in Daniel Putnam's 1818 statement, in Dawson, 2:3:412, that British Maj. John Small, while at Bunker Hill, was saved from being shot thanks to the urging of his longtime friend General Putnam, who was of course fighting with the Americans. Later, when General Howe saw Warren shot but not yet dead, he had Small rush forward and save Warren from being bayonetted. This is depicted in John Trumbull's painting *The Battle of Bunker's Hill, June 17, 1775*. Per the story, Warren then looked up at Small, smiled, and expired a moment later. Frothingham, *Life and Times*, 517n3, gives the rest of the story. Small later said of Trumbull's painting, "He [Trumbull] has paid me the compliment of trying to save the life of Warren; but the fact is, that life had fled before I saw his remains." Strangely, our otherwise reliable Lieutenant Clarke's *Narrative*, in Drake, 50, tells of Warren being bayoneted while still alive—impossible as he was shot through they head.

Americans.* Given the oncoming swarm of British, there Warren's body was left.

As given in the main text, the British first buried Warren with another body following the Battle of Bunker Hill. Following the British Evacuation, on April 4, 1776, Warren's brothers John and Eben, along with Paul Revere, found and identified the body, identifiable in part due to dental work Revere had done. Warren was then taken to Boston and buried in a formal ceremony on April 8.

Over time, the placement of the body was forgotten, though in 1825 it was rediscovered. Warren's nephew, Dr. John Collins Warren, identified the remains "by the eye tooth, and the mark of the fatal bullet... They were placed in a box of hard wood, and removed to the Warren Tomb, in St. Paul's Church, Boston."† Then on August 3, 1855, John Collins had the remains of Joseph and three other Warren ancestors disinterred and placed into urns, though he died before he could see them reburied. His son, Dr. Jonathan Mason Warren (grandnephew to Joseph), was for a time touring in Europe, which in part explains why a year more passed before the remains were finally reburied. At last, on August 8, 1856, John Mason had photographs taken of Joseph's skull, and then had the four family remains placed in the Warren family plot in Forest Hills Cemetery in Boston, where they remain to this day.‡

The original daguerreotype photos and their copies seem to be lost.§ However, third-generation photos exist in the Center for the History of Medicine, part of the Countway Library of Medicine under the auspices of

---

*Repeated and cited below.

†*Life and Times*, 524. Hidden by the ellipsis: "behind the left ear." (Another inaccurate account.)

‡*Life and Times*, 525; Arnold, *Warren*, 245. Yearlong delay: Sam Forman's research, citing an Interment Log, Forest Hills Cemetery Archive, Roxbury, MA. Forman also provided me a copy of the pertinent 1855–1856 entries of John Collins Warren's journal (late entries by Jonathan Mason Warren) vol. 96, John Collins Warren MSS, MHS.

§Where the original daguerreotypes reside is unknown. The photos in the Center for the History of Medicine are on photographic paper with the stamp of Dr. Lester L. Luntz on the back of each. Luntz was a dentist and forensic scientist who took these photos from a "photo composition" he claims were the originals (really a copy themselves), which he found in the Old South Meeting House "sub-basement". He published his third-generation photos in his *Handbook for Dental Identification* (Philadelphia: J. B. Lippincott Co. , 1973). J. L. Bell's *Boston 1775* blog has a related article: "Finding Dr. Joseph Warren's Head," http://boston1775.blogspot.com/2009/02/finding-dr-joseph-warrens-head.html (published Feb 4, 2009). In it, Bell cites Robert Shackleton's *The Book of Boston* (Philadelphia: The Penn Publishing Company, 1920), 118, which states: "A few relics of Revolutionary days are shown in this building [Old South], and there are photographs, to suit the taste of such as care for such a thing, of the skull of General Warren, showing the fatal bullet-hole: an exhibition which perhaps might have been spared." In reply to Bell's blog article, a respondent calling himself an employee of Old South said, "it appears Old South had more of a collage

the Harvard Medical School.* The authenticity of these photos is evidenced by the metal wire placed by Revere, barely visible between the eyetooth and the first premolar in the frontal view. From these copies, the particulars of Warren's death become apparent. (Note the various rumors that the skull was kept for display instead of buried with the remains have been sufficiently discredited.†)

The photos reveal a bullet hole just between the nostril and eye of Warren's left cheek. There is a much larger exit wound at the base of the back of the skull, just right of center when looking at it from behind, which Dr. John Mason Warren described as "crumbling at the margin."‡ Due to the low muzzle velocity of most weapons of that era, as evidenced by their extremely limited range, one can deduce that in order for a ball to pass entirely through the skull, the fatal shot was fired from close range.§

By careful examination and measurement of the photos, the entry hole appears to be approximately 0.50 inches in diameter, much smaller than the 0.75-inch caliber balls fired from the common Brown Bess musket as carried by British soldiers. The most likely conclusion is that the fatal shot was fired from a pistol. Pistols were primarily carried by British officers and came in a variety of sizes. But one old source, citing an unknown British account, claims Warren's shooter was "an officer's servant", who was afterward "instantly cut to pieces". This is

---

of images of Joseph Warren's skull, not the original prints. The images are apparently no longer in our collection." The "collage" is what Luntz reportedly photographed. My private correspondence with Old South led to the same conclusion: they no longer have this collage, and so it, like the originals, is now lost. There is a chance the photos were reversed (left-right inversion) when first copied from the original daguerreotypes.

*The photographs (there are three, plus a wide picture of the original collage) are part of the Harvard Medical School Faculty and Staff Portrait Collection, ca. 1774–2001, Series 00137, and are listed as: Image No. 00137. 718 [Profile of Joseph Warren's skull, showing the bullet hole]; Image No. 00137. 719 [The back of Joseph Warren's skull, showing the bullet hole]; Image No. 00137. 720 [The front of Joseph Warren's skull]; Image No. 00137. 721 [Multiple views of Joseph Warren's skull, showing the bullet hole]. Note their captions are misleading as to where Warren was in fact shot. Photocopies of two of these are also in the Warren MSS, II, MHS.

†From private correspondence (Mar to Apr 2009) with Ms. Emily Curran of the Old South Meeting House, she reports there was once a skull purported to be that of a soldier of Bunker Hill. Some concluded it was that of Warren, and it was on display in the 1970s, but it was then realized it was not a very honorable way to treat the soldier's remains, and the skull was de-accessioned in 1977. Nothing supports that it was Warren's.

‡Arnold, *Warren*, 245 (quote in note).

§Smoothbore muskets had an effective maximum range of only about 150 yards. Smoothbore pistols had a bit less, though neither was accurate at those ranges. Nonuniform, handmade balls, imprecision in the manufacture of the gun, etc., make determining actual muzzle velocities difficult. Thanks to reenactor Paul O'Shaughnessy (Apr 2009) and small-arms expert Sean Rich (June 2011) for their private discussions on this matter.

1856 PHOTOS OF JOSEPH WARREN'S SKULL (REVEALING A SHOT THAT ENTERED FROM THE FRONT AND EXITED THE BACK OF SKULL). COURTESY OF THE FAMILY OF LESTER L. LUNTZ, D. D. S. , TAKEN OF LOST DUPLICATES BY HIM FOR HIS *HANDBOOK FOR DENTAL IDENTIFICATION* (PHILADELPHIA: J. B. LIPPINCOTT CO., 1973). THE LUNTZ COPIES ARE NOW IN HARVARD'S COUNTWAY LIBRARY OF MEDICINE, BOSTON. ORIGINAL DAGUERREOTYPES PROBABLY TAKEN ON MAY 6, 1856.

plausible, as there were many servants on the battlefield, for which we have a few accounts, though we know little about their role. As it seems unlikely any civilian servant would have been so armed, since any combatant not in uniform would have been treated as a spy if captured, it must have been a soldier servant (a batman) or an aide. Whoever the shooter was, he did not use a standard Brown Bess musket but rather a pistol, and he was likely wearing a red coat.*

---

*Quotes from Frothingham, *Life and Times*, 519–20, citing an unknown British account of July 5, 1775 (thus not likely biased; this is not the "Letter of a British Officer, July 5, 1775"). This is the only one of the many eyewitness accounts of Warren's death that suggests a pistol was used, and so is likely to be true. On the bullet hole measurements: private correspondence with Sam Forman (Apr 2011). "cut to pieces": true, the Americans were running out of ammunition at the end of the battle, but only those in the redoubt, not those who had been along the breastwork and the rail fence.

These photos sufficiently disprove the claim that a 0.75-caliber musket ball archived at the New England Historic Genealogical Society was the ball that killed Warren (supposedly removed from his body a day later). Clearly, the 0.50-caliber ball that killed Warren passed through his skull, and thus may still be buried on the hill. (If the photos did not exist to prove otherwise, the idea that such a ball was dug out of Warren's brain seemed dubious. That the society's relic has still attached to it a piece of its paper cartridge makes it especially so.)*

With these long-lost photos, we now have visual proof to answer the particulars of the fatal shot. Dr. Joseph Warren was shot in the face, probably looking at his assailant, and given the exit wound, he undoubtedly died instantly, giving no speeches.

*Thanks to Timothy Salls of NEHGS for allowing me to examine this artifact. NEHGS has related letters, mostly of the donor William Montegue, attesting to its authenticity and describing how it came into his possession. There was a brief public argument on the ball's authenticity as well (copies in NEHGS), with the first blow by Samuel Swett, author of *The History of the Bunker Hill*, who, in the *Boston Daily Advertiser* newspaper of June 12, 1857, gave an (unconvincing) argument that the ball could not be genuine. In the same paper, on June 16, Montegue argued back, stating the ball's provenance and giving a sworn affidavit. The flat spot on NEHGS's ball is likely where the ball's sprue was cut off after casting, rather than indicative of, say, an impact into a skull.

NOTES

These notes employ short-form citations, which are explained in detail at the start of the bibliography on page 446.

CHAPTER 1: MOUNTING TENSIONS

1. From a Lady of Philadelphia to Captain S—, a British Officer in Boston, [n.d.], in Commager and Morris, *The Spirit of 'Seventy-Six*, 94–96.

2. *JCC*, 2:12. See note 125 on Franklin's departure and arrival.

3. Isaacson, *Benjamin Franklin*, 280–83, 293–94 passim.

4. Curiously, the American troops at Roxbury under General Thomas did very little to protect against a British incursion from Boston Neck, though one British officer noted the Yankee "sentrys were abt 200 yards from ours & were numerous." From Williams's journal, June 15, *Discord*, 6.

5. *JEPCM*, May 19, 243.

6. Adams, *Works of John Adams*, 3:277.

7. *JEPCM*, May 25, 258, also 253.

8. The National Park Service, at http://www.nps.gov/revwar/about_the_revolution/african_americans.html (accessed Nov 6 2008), reports as many as 5 percent of the men at Bunker Hill were African American. They were integrated and received the same pay as white men. Cf. George Washington to John Hancock, July 10–11 (with associated enclosures), in *PGW*. Lockhart, *Whites of Their Eyes*, 104–05, reports that at least 21 black men fought on April 19, while as least 88 fought at Bunker Hill, citing George Quintal Jr., *Patriots of Color: "A Peculiar Beauty and Merit": African Americans and Native Americans at Battle Road & Bunker Hill* (Boston: National Park Service, 2004), 21–36.

9. French, *First Year*, 405–06; Alden, *General Gage in America*, 258–59; Lockhart, *Whites of Their Eyes*, 105–06. Ibid., 320, indicates that at least 15 Indians fought at Bunker Hill, citing Quintal above.

10. Sparks, *Writings of Washington*, 3:491–92. The statement is undated.

11. Various references, such as Intelligence, Apr 25, in Gage MSS.

12. Barker, May 1, *British in Boston*, 39–40.

13. Intelligence, Apr 30, Gage MSS. There are three intelligence documents of this date, two of which

explicitly suggest an attack from the south. However, Intelligence, Apr 25, also in Gage MSS, states there were no plans for an attack.

14. Intelligence, May 12, Gage MSS.

15. Barker, May 2 passim, *British in Boston*, 40ff.

16. Intelligence, May 13, Gage MSS.

17. Barker, May 13, *British in Boston*, 46–47.

18. Amos Farnsworth's diary, May 11, appended, *Proc. of MHS* (1899), 2:12:79.

19. Daniel Putnam to Bunker Hill Assoc., Aug 1825, *Coll. of CHS* (1860), 1:236.

20. Silas Deane to his wife, July 20, George L. Clark, *A History of Connecticut: Its People and Institutions*, 2nd ed. (New York: G. P. Putnam's Sons, 1914), 286.

21. John Thomas to Artemas Ward, May 18, John Thomas MSS, MHS.

22. Barker, May 18, *British in Boston*, 48.

23. Barker, June 1, *British in Boston*, 53.

24. Barker, Apr 26, May 17–18, 30, *British in Boston*, 39, 47–48, 53.

25. *Igniting*, appendix 3. There is little doubt that with 460 veteran marines and 645 new arrivals, they were reallocated to form two equally sized battalions. Tupper was acting commander because Major Short was dying of the flux.

26. *Igniting*, appendix 4. This total includes the 17th Light Dragoons, and the 35th, 49th, and 63rd.

27. Lieutenant Williams's journal, June 12, *Discord*, 4–6. He was newly assigned to the 23rd Welch Fusiliers in Boston.

28. Barker, May 8, *British in Boston*, 44.

29. Compare the Reports of the Provisions of the British Army, May 12, 19, and 24 (this last one out of sequence and filed at the end of volume 136), all in Gage MSS.

30. Note in the Mackenzie MSS Orderly Book, [n.d., late May], 92, in WO 36/1, UKNA.

31. Samuel Stebbens to Colonel Linkhorn [Lincoln] in Hingham, May 26, in John Thomas MSS, MHS. It speaks of the hay belonging to a "Mr. Loveill", who French supposes is John Lovell the Tory (French, *First Year*, 188n29).

32. Barker, May 20–21, *British in Boston*, 48–49, gives a critical account. Which sloop this was is unknown.

33. *Bickerstaff's Boston Almanack for 1775* gives high tide at 5:15 a.m. and 5:39 p.m.; thus low tide was at 11:27 a.m.

34. Warren admits he was there in Warren to Samuel Adams, May 26, Frothingham, *Life and Times*, 495–96. He also admits that the article in Hall's paper (*Essex Gazette*), referred to in note 35, was his anonymous submission. See Bancroft, *History of the United States*, 4:193.

35. *Essex Gazette* (a.k.a. *New England Chronicle*), May 18–25, 3, mostly republished Frothingham, *Life and Times*, 492–93. Warren the author: see previous note.

36. Barker, May 21, *British in Boston*, 48–49.

37. General sources for this section: ibid.; *Essex Gazette*, May 18–25, as cited. Cf. *Providence Gazette*, May 27, *NDAR*, 1:549.

38. *JEPCM*, May 22, 249.

39. Number of Loyalists/Whigs: Robert M. Calhoon, "Loyalism and Neutrality" in *A Companion to the American Revolution*, Jack P. Greene and J. R. Pole, eds. (Malden, MA: Blackwell Publishing Ltd., 2004), 235. Meanwhile, Lt. Edward Gould, injured at North Bridge and captured by the Americans, was restored his liberty courtesy of a prisoner exchange (see Beck, *Igniting*, passim). Barker, May 22, *British in Boston*, 49; Lord Barrington to Gage, Mar 24, Gage MSS.

40. Mass. Provincial Congress to the Continental Congress, May 17, *JEPCM*, 229–31.

41. *JEPCM*, May 16, 229. In private correspondence, Dr. Forman, biographer of Warren, notes that Dr. Warren may have wanted to get Dr. Church out of the way for a while. Even though Warren did not yet suspect Church as a spy, Church had not proven himself terribly useful.

42. First quote: Warren to Samuel Adams, May 17 (appended to a letter to the same, dated May 12), Frothingham, *Life and Times*, 485. Second quote: between the same, May 26, ibid., 495–96.

43. Intelligence, May 24, Gage MSS.

44. Ibid.: French, *Informers*, 147ff., especially 155–57.

45. *Otter's* and *Cerberus's* journals (both May 24), *NDAR*, 1:518; Graves to Lord Dunmore, May 20, ibid., 1:372 and in Graves, *Conduct*, May 20. Ship specifications: Naval List, Sept 29, *NDAR*, 2:742–43 and Beck, *Igniting*, appendix 5. How many shots in the salute is unknown, but saluting was standard practice (May's "Gun Salutes," cited below). Also, Barker, May 15, *British in Boston*, 50.

46. French, *First Year*, 195–96ff.; Spring, *With Zeal*, 247ff.

47. Samuel Kirk to General Howe, Feb 10, and the response, Feb 21, both transcribed in the Godwin Pamphlets: G. Pamph. 475 (3) 138–41, Bodleian Library, Univ. of Oxford, UK. The whereabouts of the originals are unknown.

48. Clinton MSS, loose sheet "I was not a Volunteer..." in front of Box 280.

49. French, *First Year*, 198–99. One episode of his sensitivities given in detail in Murdock, *Bunker Hill*, 121ff.

50. Burgoyne's *Orderly Book*, xiv ff.; French, *First Year*, 199–200ff. The nickname "Gentleman Johnny" was something given him by historians in the early 1900s and is not contemporary.

51. Burgoyne in the House of Commons, Apr 19, 1774, *PHE*, 17:1271. For his cavalry experience, the 17th Light Dragoons would be put under his direct command, per Gage's General Orders, June 12, in the Mackenzie MSS Orderly Book, 104, WO 36/1, UKNA.

52. *London Evening Post* (England), Thursday, Apr 20, 1775, p. 4.

53. An overestimate. In Beck, *Igniting*, appendix 4, I estimated 4,036 officers and men, including losses from April 19 and those new arrivals before May 25. As for 10,000 colonists, as we have just seen in Church's report to Gage, Church claimed it was closer to 12,000.

54. Frothingham, *Siege*, 114n1, citing Boston newspapers circa early to mid-June 1775, though I have found none. The closest example I found was *New York Journal* (a.k.a. *The General Advertiser*), June 15, 3 (main paper, not the supplement), which gives the same idea but without the verbatim quotes. When Burgoyne returned to Boston as a prisoner in 1777, he suffered the taunts of an old woman who, "perched on a shed above the crowd, cried out at the top of a shrill voice: 'Make way, make way—the General's coming! Give him elbow room!'" (*Siege*, 114n1). See Moore, *Diary of the American Revolution*, 1:526–27, for another reference, apparently common.

55. Cmdr. W. E. May, "Gun Salutes", *The Mariner's Mirror*, 45, no. 4 (London: Cambridge Univ. Press, November 1959), 325–28.

56. Williams's journal, June 11, *Discord*, 3–4.

57. *Cerberus's* journal, May 25, *NDAR*, 1:523. On the flag: see note 67.

58. Gage to Graves, May 25, *NDAR*, 1:523. The owner's name, "Mr. Williams", is given in the account in the *New York Journal*, June 8, published in Force, *American Archives*, 4:2:719–20, and *NDAR*, 1:544–45; the quote from Graves, *Conduct*, May 27. Williams's full name is in his petition to the Mass. Congress for his losses, dated June 12, Force, 4:2:971, and his petition suggests he was a Whig. The statement of losses from Noddle's, Force, 4:4:365–66, suggests what Williams was compensated. Note the hay and stock was bought, providing support that the hay on Grape Island had also been.

59. Barker, May 25, *British in Boston*, 50.

60. *JEPCM* (Apr 24, 26, and May 3, 14, 23, 24) 522, 523, 533–34, 545, 554, 557, respectively. Church's Intelligence, May 24, states he intended to leave the next day (May 25), the same day Gage learned of the news, thus making Church (via his go-between) a plausible suspect as the informant.

61. Gage to Graves, May 25, *NDAR*, 1:523. This was, perhaps, by word of mouth: I have not seen any *written* intelligence that tipped Gage off to the planned raid.

62. Graves, *Conduct* (throughout May 25 entry). The details of this Act are provided in Beck, *Igniting*, 89.

63. Graves to Stephens, May 25, Graves, *Conduct* and *NDAR*, 1:523.

64. Graves to Stephens, June 7, Graves, *Conduct* and *NDAR*, 1:622–23.

65. Graves to Gage, May 25, *NDAR*, 1:523–24. This letter implies no guard was as yet on the island, though as evidenced in the following main body text, the marines were there in time for the skirmish. It is uncertain whether they came from the warships or from Gage's marines in Boston, but given that the early reinforcement of marines disembarked from the warships and that Gage did little to support the battle, the initial marines camped on the island seem to have belonged to Graves.

66. *New York Journal*, June 8, 1775, Force, *American Archives*, 4:2:719–20.

67. *Preston's* journal, [May 27?], *NDAR*, 1:546. I have not examined the original journal, but the transcription may be inaccurate, because the salute occurred on May 26, as evidenced in Barker, May 26, *British in Boston*, 50; *Somerset's* journal, May 26, in ADM 51/906, UKNA; and *Glasgow's* journal, May 26, in ADM 51/398, UKNA. On the flags and their placement: Perrin, *British Flags*, 96–97. Wilson, *Flags at Sea*, 21, gives the basic idea, but the figure does not depict the flags as they were in 1775, for by 1702, the plain white flag had been replaced with St. George's Cross (Perrin, 99). Additional details on the flags thanks to private correspondence with Peter Ansoff, former president of the North American Vexillological Association (NAVA), in Mar and Apr 2010.

68. Farnsworth's diary, May 26, *Proc. of MHS* (1899), 2:12:80. A strong tradition in secondary sources maintains that a portion of the party included men from the New Hampshire camp in Medford, led by their own Col. John Stark. However, there is no known original source material to support Stark's presence. Caleb Stark, *Memoir...of Gen. John Stark*, 29, suggests Stark had reconnoitered the islands, but nothing more.

69. U.S. Navy's Sun and Moon Calculator. On May 27, sunrise was 4:13 a.m.; civil twilight was 3:39 a.m.

70. What was once Noddle's Island is now roughly all of East Boston north of the present airport. (The airport was a later landfill extension from the old island.) Hog Island stood immediately east of Noddle's Island and is now roughly that section of East Boston's Orient Heights.

71. Some dated topography notes are in Mellen Chamberlain, *A Documentary History of Chelsea*, 2 vols. (Boston: Printed for the Mass. Hist. Soc., 1908), 2:442–43, and Robert D. McKay's unreliable *Battle of Chelsea Creek* (Chelsea, MA: Reprinted from *Chelsea Evening Record*, 1928). Knee-high inlets: *New York Journal*, June 8, Force, *American Archives*, 4:2:719–20.

72. Farnsworth's diary, May 27, *Proc. of MHS* (1899), 2:12:80–81. Owners' names given in the *New York Journal*, June 8, Force, *American Archives*, 4:2:719–20.

73. *Preston's* journal, May 27, *NDAR*, 1:546; Farnsworth's diary, May 27. According to *Bickerstaff's Boston Almanack for 1775*, the high tides were 9:59 a.m. and 10:22 p.m.; thus low tide was at 4:10 p.m. Their raid is observed at about two o'clock, per *Preston's* journal, hence they crossed at about 1:00 p.m.

74. Williams to Mass. Congress, June 12, Force, *American Archives*, 4:2:971.

75. *New York Journal*, June 8, Force, *American Archives*, 4:2:719–20; Farnsworth's diary, May 27. Time: *Preston's* journal, May 27, *NDAR*, 1:546. On 30 colonists: Report to Mass. Comm. of Safety, May 27, ibid., 1:545–46. (*New York Journal* states 20 to 30.)

76. *New York Journal*, June 8, 1775, Force, *American Archives*, 4:2:719–20.

77. *Preston*'s journal, May 27, *NDAR*, 1:546; Beck, *Igniting*, appendix 5. Report to Mass. Comm. of Safety, May 27, *NDAR*, 1:545–46, states *Diana* was usually stationed at Winnisimmet Ferry. Thomas the admiral's nephew: French, *First Year*, 191. Graves to Stephens, June 7, Graves, *Conduct*, and *NDAR*, 1:622–23, implies *Diana* was not given her instructions by signal flag. This same source claims *Diana* did not enter the river inlet until between three and four o'clock, in contradiction to both *Preston*'s journal (which says the orders were given at 2:00 p.m.) and the logical time it should have rounded the island and reached the inlet river if it were to cut off the rebel retreat. It must have reached the inlet by 3:00 p.m. at the latest.

78. Farnsworth's diary, May 27, *Proc. of MHS* (1899), 2:12:80–81; Beck, *Igniting*, appendix 5.

79. Report to Mass. Comm. of Safety, May 27, *NDAR*, 1:545–46; *New York Journal*, June 8, Force, *American Archives*, 4:2:719–20. The latter claims 2 killed and 2 wounded (1 mortally), but as this was about the total British casualties of the day, it seems unlikely they were all killed or wounded at the onset.

80. Farnsworth's diary, May 27, *Proc. of MHS* (1899), 2:12:80–81.

81. Journals for *Preston, Cerberus, Glasgow, Somerset*, all for May 27, *NDAR*, 1:546–47. By comparing those of *Preston* and *Somerset*, it becomes clear that *Britannia* is a tender of *Somerset* and the sloop referenced by the American accounts. One hundred marines: Barker, May 28, *British in Boston*, 51; Report to Mass. Comm. of Safety, May 27, *NDAR*, 1:545–46. The precise timeline is murky.

82. *Preston*'s journal, May 27, *NDAR*, 1:546.

83. *New York Journal*, June 8, 1775, Force, *American Archives*, 4:2:719–20; Report to Mass. Comm. of Safety, May 27, *NDAR*, 1:545–46.

84. *Cerberus*'s journal, May 27, *NDAR*, 1:546.

85. Graves to Stephens, June 7, *NDAR*, 1:622–23.

86. *Preston*'s journal, May 27, *NDAR*, 1:546. The "Letter Received in New York from the Provincial Camp", June 1, Force, *American Archives*, 4:2:874–75, gives a dubious 8 to 10 barges.

87. Farnsworth's diary, May 27, *Proc. of MHS* (1899), 2:12:80–81, which claims this was at sunset. U.S. Navy's Sun and Moon Calculator gives sunset at 7:10 p.m., with end of civil twilight at 7:43 p.m. Also, *New York Journal*, June 8, Force, *American Archives*, 4:2:719–20.

88. His uniform, if he had one, would have been like that described by Chester to Joseph Fish, July 22, Frothingham, *Siege*, 389–91.

89. *New York Journal*, June 8, Force, *American Archives*, 4:2:719–20. This latter source claims Putnam arrived about 9:00 p.m., and if he indeed arrived when *Diana* beached, this claim generally agrees with *Preston*'s journal, May 27, *NDAR*, 1:546. Foster is named as the artillery captain by Caleb Haskell's diary, May 27, Roberts, *March to Quebec*, 460–61. His company size is unknown, but three others (appendix 5) range from 37 to 49. He was selected to enlist a company, *JEPCM* (April 17), 515. Indication of Warren's presence is largely traditional (though highly probable, given his definite presence during the fighting of April 19 at Grape Island and at Bunker Hill), Frothingham, *Life and Times*, 497.

90. *New York Journal*, June 8, Force, *American Archives*, 4:2:719–20. It claims this encounter occurred at 9:00 p.m., but this is hard to believe considering the moonless night and end of civil twilight at 7:43 p.m. This encounter was probably more like 8:00 p.m. (per U.S. Navy's Sun and Moon Calculator).

91. *New York Journal*, June 8, Force, *American Archives*, 4:2:719–20.

92. "Letter Received in New York from the Provincial Camp", June 1, Force, *American Archives*, 4:2:874–75.

93. *New York Journal*, June 8, Force, *American Archives*, 4:2:719–20, claims more marines came *with* the 12s, which is not only plausible but likely, since they all came from Boston. Graves to Philip Stephens, June 7, *NDAR*, 1:622–23, suggests the 12s were on the scene before the vessel ran aground. Barker, May

28, *British in Boston*, 51, states that 100 marines were sent that night, but claims the 12s came in the next morning, in contradiction to other sources. Barker's account has other inaccuracies, suggesting he learned of the battle perhaps thirdhand. In contrast, the journal for *Preston* on May 28, *NDAR*, 1:554, gives that 200 marines were sent as reinforcements. Report to Mass. Comm. of Safety, May 27, *NDAR*, 1:545–46, also mentions the 12s.

94. Graves to Stephens, June 7, *NDAR*, 1:622–23.

95. *Bickerstaff's Boston Almanack for 1775* has high tide at 10:22 p.m. Per U.S. Navy's Sun and Moon Calculator, the moon was a 3 percent waning crescent and had set at 5:25 p.m., ahead of sunset. It would not rise again until 4:05 a.m. on May 28, after the beginning of civil twilight of 3:39 a.m., just before sunrise of 4:12 a.m. Graves to Stephens, June 7, *NDAR*, 1:622–23, claims *Diana* ran aground between 11:00 p.m. and midnight, helping to construct an accurate timeline. *New York Journal*, June 8, Force, *American Archives*, 4:2:719–20, gives a confused timeline for the later part of the battle. Stevens's diary, May 27–28, *Essex Inst. Hist. Coll.* (1912), 48:45–46, gives a little more detail.

96. *Preston's* journal, May 27, *NDAR*, 1:546; the quote: Report to Mass. Comm. of Safety, May 27, ibid., 1:545–46; the time: Graves to Stephens, June 7, ibid., 1:622–23; the distance: Barker's diary, May 28, *British in Boston*, 51; the location: Caleb Haskell's diary, May 27, Roberts, *The March to Quebec*, 460–61.

97. *Preston's* journal, May 27, *NDAR*, 1:546. *Bickerstaff's Boston Almanack for 1775* gives high tide at 10:22 p.m. on May 27 and the next at 10:45 a.m. on May 28; thus low tide was 4:31 a.m. on May 28. Since *Diana* was on mud at the low tide, she must have fallen over sometime before low tide; thus 3:00 a.m. seems close. Graves to Stephens, June 7, *NDAR*, 1:622–23, gives "about 3" as well.

98. *Preston's* journal, May 27, *NDAR*, 1:546.

99. Gage to Lord Dartmouth, June 12, [Separate], Carter, 1:404–05.

100. *New York Journal*, June 8, Force, *American Archives*, 4:2:719–20.

101. Ibid. On size of 12-pounder balls, Beck, *Igniting*, appendix 6. Sunrise: see note 95.

102. Timothy Newell's diary, May 27, *Coll. of MHS* (1852), 4:1:262; James Stevens's diary, May 28, *Essex Inst. Hist. Coll.* (1912), 48:46. Barker, in his May 28, entry in *British in Boston*, 51, was under the impression that the British destroyed their own ship. On the tide: see note 97.

103. Stevens's diary, May 28, *Essex Inst. Hist. Coll.* (1912), 48:45–46; "Letter Received in New York from the Provincial Camp", June 1, Force, *American Archives*, 4:2:874–75.

104. Barker, May 28, *British in Boston*, 51.

105. General source supplementing this section: French, *First Year*, 190–93, and especially the notes in appendix 17, 736–37.

106. Report to Mass. Comm. of Safety, May 27, *NDAR*, 1:545–46.

107. Farnsworth's diary, May 27, *Proc. of MHS* (1899), 2:12:80–81.

108. Graves to Stephens, June 7, *NDAR*, 1:622–23, suggests the 2 killed and 2 wounded were not inclusive of the seamen aboard the schooner and boats, and so must have been marines. Gage to Lord Dartmouth, June 12 [Separate], Carter, *Corr. of General Gage*, 1:404–05, and Barker, May 28, *British in Boston*, 51, generally support this number. There is no reason to suspect Gage exaggerated here, as his casualties listed for all other skirmishes appear to be accurate. Therefore, the exaggeration most likely lies with the Americans.

109. It was called the Apthorp House until it became part of Harvard's Adams House and is now known as the Master's Residence.

110. Putnam to Bunker Hill Assoc., Aug 1825, *Coll. of CHS* (1860), 1:235–36.

111. Silas Deane to his wife, July 20, George L. Clark, *A History of Connecticut: Its People and Institutions*, 2nd ed. (New York: G. P. Putnam's Sons, 1914), 286.

112. Putnam to Bunker Hill Assoc., Aug 1825, *Coll. of CHS* (1860), 1:235–36.

113. Warren to Arthur Lee, May 16, Frothingham, *Life and Times*, 488–90.

114. Warren to Samuel Adams, May 26, Frothingham, *Life and Times*, 495–96. Italics as in the original.

115. Stevens's diary, May 28, *Essex Inst. Hist. Coll.* (1912), 48:45–46.

116. Barker, May 29, *British in Boston*, 51–52.

117. Williams to Mass. Congress, June 12, Force, *American Archives*, 4:2:971. Fate of the livestock (500 sheep, 340 lambs, 30–40 horned cattle): Phillips Payson to Henry Williams, Feb 16, 1786; Statement of Moses Gill [n.d.]; Statement of Thomas Cheever [n.d.]; Noddle's Island Papers, Ms. S-678, MHS.

118. Barker, May 30, *British in Boston*, 52–53. See appendix 3.

119. The warehouse was burned June 10. Williams to Mass. Congress, June 12, Force, *American Archives*, 4:2:971, gives his petition. The statement of losses from Noddle's Island, Force, 4:4:365–66, suggests Williams was partially compensated.

120. Graves to Stephens, June 7, *NDAR*, 1:622–23. The same requests compensation for the private property the crew lost. The reply (*NDAR*, 1:1347–1351, Aug 3) accepted the sentence but denied compensation.

121. Barker, May 29, *British in Boston*, 51–52.

122. See appendix 4.

123. Graves to Stephens, May 15 and June 16 (the quote), both in Graves, *Conduct. Somerset* was ordered to move off the Charles River on May 29 and did so May 31. *Lively* came up circa June 2. *Glasgow* may have been there during the transition. See appendix 3.

124. French, *First Year*, 79–80ff. Greene's whereabouts are confusing: ibid., n20.

125. Franklin to Lee, Mar 19 (*PBF*, 21:534), is the last letter he wrote from London, passing off his responsibilities as a colonial agent. He writes another, aboard ship, to William Franklin, Mar 22 (*PBF*, 21:540), so he sailed circa Mar 20–21 on board the *Pennsylvania* packet, with a Captain Osborn commanding. He arrived the evening of May 5, per his letter to David Hartley, May 6, *PBF*, 22:31.

126. Rantoul, Cruise of the *Quero*, in *Essex Inst. Hist. Coll.* (1900) 36:3–7, 11.

127. Joseph Warren to the Inhabitants of Great Britain, Apr 26, as given in Force, *American Archives*, 4:2:487–88; first appeared in England published in the *London Chronicle* (England), May 27–30, 1775, p. 9.

128. Hutchinson, *Diary and Letters*, May 29, 1:455.

129. Rantoul, Cruise of the *Quero*, *Essex Inst. Hist. Coll.* (1900), 36:6.

130. Frothingham, *Life and Times*, 497, which notes this is the first time Warren's name was appended to an official document published in England.

131. Fred Junkin Hinkhouse, *The Preliminaries of the American Revolution as Seen in the English Press: 1763–1775* (New York: Octagon Books, orig. 1926, 1969), 188, citing the London Packet, June 7, 1775; also in the *Morning Chronicle and London Advertiser*, June 7, 1775. The page's note says to see an opposing paragraph in the *Morning Chronicle*, July 19, 1775.

132. Fischer, *Paul Revere's Ride*, 275, citing Lord George Germain to John Irwin, May 30, in Add. Ms. 42266 (f. 79), BL. (Fischer's typographical error here corrected.) According to the BL, it is not the original, but a printed *précis* with manuscript annotations.

133. Walpole to Sir Horace Mann, June 5, Mason, *Walpole*, 250–51. His quote references a line from the "Ballad of Chevy Chase", which gave the story of the Battle of Otterburn in 1388, at which another Lord Percy lost to the Scots.

134. Walpole to Rev. William Mason, June 12, Mason, *Walpole*, 251.

135. Hutchinson, *Diary and Letters*, May 31, 1:461. The officers were Lt. Col. William Dalrymple and Lt. Col. James Grant.

136. Lord Dartmouth to Gage, June 1, Carter, *Corr. of General Gage*, 2:198–99.

137. Hutchinson, *Diary and Letters*, June 10, 1:466.

138. Rantoul, Cruise of the *Quero*, in *Essex Inst. Hist. Coll.* (1900), 36:13–14, citing the "London Press", June 12. I have been unable to find the original.

139. Lord Dartmouth to Gage, July 1, 2:199–202.

140. Lord Mayor and Aldermen of London to King George III, June 14, Commager and Morris, *The Spirit of 'Seventy-Six*, 241–42.

141. George III to Lord Sandwich, July 1, Commager and Morris, *The Spirit of 'Seventy-Six*, 97.

142. Beck, *Igniting*, appendix 3.

143. Fischer, *Paul Revere's Ride*, 276, citing Lord Suffolk to Lord Germain, June 15, and the reply, also of June 15, Add. Ms. 42266 (ff. 98–100 and 101, respectively), BL. BL reports the letters are not the originals, but are printed *précis* with manuscript annotations.

144. Lord Dartmouth to Gage, Apr 10, 1773, Carter, *Corr. of General Gage*, 2:157–58; Lord Dartmouth to Gen. Frederick Haldimand, Apr 15, Gage MSS. This second letter, though dated April 15, was not received until about the end of May. (The actual copy in Gage MSS bears no mark on when it was received. However, the letter Dartmouth to Gage, [Private], Apr 7, and Dartmouth's Circular, Apr 15, were received June 3 and May 25, respectively. They are Carter, 2:189–90.) Also see French: *First Year*, 207–08 (and notes).

145. Intelligence, May 24, Gage MSS; Beck, *Igniting*, appendix 4. On Church's authorship: see note 44.

146. New York's upheaval: French, *First Year*, 140.

147. Beck, *Igniting*, appendix 4; ibid., appendix 3. The 7,800 number does not account for the losses of the coming battle.

148. *Falcon's* journal, May 11, *NDAR*, 1:311–12.

149. Nathanial Freeman to the Mass. Provincial Congress, May 29, *NDAR*, 1:558–59.

150. There are unsupported modern sources that claim the midshipman is Richard Lucas, but I cannot confirm.

151. Quote: *Massachusetts Spy* newspaper, May 24, 3. *Success* may be a name later ascribed to the American boat, appearing only in late sources such as *Lineage Book, Society of the Daughters of the American Revolution* (Washington, DC: 1904), 18:29, and Duane Hamilton Hurd, *History of Bristol County, Massachusetts with Biographical Sketches of Many of Its Pioneers and Prominent Men* (Philadelphia, PA: J. W. Lewis & Co, 1883), 269. Captain Egery is mentioned by name in the Nathanial Freeman letter cited in note 149.

152. The details are scant: *Massachusetts Spy*, May 24, 3; Graves to Stephens, May 15 and May 19 and June 16, all three in Graves, *Conduct*; *Falcon's* journal, May 11, 12, "17" [really 18], *NDAR*, 1:311–12, 322, 350–51, originals in ADM 51/336, UKNA; Ezra Stiles's diary, May 23, 1:560. Also, Beck, *Igniting*, appendix 5, for *Falcon*.

153. Graves to Stephens, May 15 and June 16.

154. Graves to Stephens, June 16. *Nautilus*: Graves's Sept 1775 list, *NDAR*, 2:742–43.

155. Barker, June 4–5, *British in Boston*, 54–55; Gage's General Orders, June 4, the Mackenzie MSS *Orderly Book* 98, in WO 36/1, UKNA.

156. Chester to Fish, July 22, 389–91.

157. Livingston, *Israel Putnam*, 207.

158. Per Coburn, *Battle of April 19*, 156–57, only 5 of these Yankee prisoners were taken during the Battle of the Nineteenth of April.

159. *New England Chronicle* (a.k.a. *Essex Gazette*), June 8, 3, mostly republished in Frothingham, *Siege*, 111–13. Also see the recount of the event in Force, *American Archives*, 4:2:920–21, dated June 6.

160. Beck, *Igniting*, appendix 4; ibid., appendix 3. This is the number available for the next engagement. A census taken on June 24, given on a list dated Oct 9, 1775, the Gage MSS, gives 6,247 Bostonians.

161. Graves, *Conduct*, May 25; Gage to Graves, May 24, 1:518–19. Gage desires it for more than just firewood, stating, "to bring fuel, Lumber &c". This is consistent with his troubles building barracks.

162. Machias Committee to Mass. Congress, June 14, Force, *American Archives*, 4:2:988–90, calls her the King's tender, but Graves, in *Conduct*, probably would have called her such had she been one. Though she does not appear on any of Graves's ship lists, she was probably purchased like *Diana*, perhaps in the wake of the *Diana* affair. If purchased, she was likely bought and lost between the issuance of lists (the Jan and Sept lists, *NDAR*, 1:47 and 2:742–43). The earliest reference I have found to her is in Graves, *Conduct*, Apr 7.

163. Graves to Midshipman James Moore, May 26, Graves, *Conduct*, appendix, and *NDAR*, 1:537–38. The letter states five ships, but the other sources cited herein give only two sailed besides *Margaretta*.

164. Machias Committee to Mass. Congress, June 14, Force, *American Archives*, 4:2:988–90.

165. Godfrey's statement, June 11, *NDAR*, 1:655–66.

166. Machias Committee to Mass. Congress, June 14, Force, *American Archives*, 4:2:988–90. The mob did capture one Stephen Jones, perhaps Ichabod's son.

167. Ibid.; Godfrey's statement, June 11, *NDAR*, 1:655–66. U.S. Navy's Sun and Moon Calculator lists sunset at 7:15 p.m., end civil twilight at 7:52 p.m., and a waxing gibbous, 94 percent visible.

168. Machias Committee to Mass. Congress, June 14, Force, *American Archives*, 4:2:988–90.

169. Unlike ibid., Godfrey's statement, June 11, *NDAR*, 1:655–56, states that she anchored near the sloop and was not lashed to it. Godfrey, being impressed, had no reason to talk up the British side of the story. Instead, he gives that they lashed to it the next morning.

170. French, *First Year*, 360–61, citing an unfound account.

171. Machias Committee to Mass. Congress, June 14, Force, *American Archives*, 4:2:988–90.

172. Ibid.

173. Joseph Wheaton's statement, undated, Coggins, *Ships and Seamen*, 15–16, uncited.

174. If only we knew what flag it was!

175. Godfrey's statement, June 11, *NDAR*, 1:655–66.

176. Graves, *Conduct*, May 25. Note the date: *before* the battle. Of course, *Conduct* was written almost two years after the battle, so this was likely a mistake. Graves gives little detail overall.

177. Beck, *Igniting*, appendix 4 and appendix 3.

178. Howe to [Lieutenant] General [Edward] Harvey, June 12, *Proc. of the Bunker Hill Monument Assoc.* (1907), 109ff.

179. Graves, *Conduct*, Apr 20.

180. Beck, *Igniting*, appendix 3.

181. Burgoyne to Lord Stanley, June 25, Force, *American Archives*, 4:2:1094–95, and de Fonblanque, 155–58.

182. Howe to Harvey, June 22 and 24.

183. From Howe's proposed plan, very near what was adopted. It is in Howe to Lord Richard Howe, June 12, *Proc. of the Bunker Hill Monument Assoc.* (1907), 112ff. Cf. Howe to Harvey, June 12, ibid., 109ff. One of several Clinton MSS variants of Clinton's MS Narrative, p. 3 of vol. 1 of that in Box 279, titled "Extract from *Narrative*", gives that a council was held on the subject on June 15 (and agrees with the plan given here). It must have been a second council, as the first was around June 12, given the Intelligence, June 15, Gage MSS, which reports the rebels knew of the British plan (more in later main text).

184. Date established in various letters, e.g., Burgoyne to Lord Stanley, June 25, and Howe to Harvey, June 22 and 24. Clinton has one letter that was mistaken: see French, *First Year*, 209n35.

185. Gage to Lord Dartmouth, June 12, 1:404–05; Haldimand to Gage, New York, June 27, Gage MSS.

186. Proclamation by Gage, June 12, Force, *American Archives*, 4:2:968–70, with minor corrections made based on an original at LOC, http://hdl.loc.gov/loc.rbc/rbpe.03801700 (accessed Sept 3, 2010). Italics changed from original.

187. *JEPCM*, June 13, 330ff.; ibid., June 16, 343–47, gives the drafted response to be considered further on June 20, but it was never again taken up. Cf. Williams's journal, June 14, *Discord*, 6.

188. Putnam to Bunker Hill Assoc., Aug 1825, *Coll. of CHS* (1860), 1:233. There are no quotes in the original, so these words are not purported to be verbatim of what was said.

189. Ibid., 1:242–44. Daniel claims his father, Israel, told him of the conversation afterward, so while Daniel was in Cambridge as Israel's aide, he apparently was not an eyewitness.

190. *JEPCM*, June 13, 565. See next note.

191. Intelligence, June 15, Gage MSS. The deacon's surname (no first given) is difficult to read: Stoser? Williams's journal, July 13, *Discord*, 25, notes a church sexton arrested for making smoke signals, perhaps this deacon. More on how the Americans might have first learned of the planned attack in French, *First Year*, 209n37. A claim in Swett, *History*, 58, that Warren canoed into Boston days before the battle is entirely unlikely and unsupported.

192. *JEPCM*, June 14, 333.

193. Frothingham, *Life and Times*, 503–04.

194. Presumably, they were awaiting Whitcomb's response.

195. Repeated often in May and June, e.g. in *JCC*, 2:57.

196. Elbridge Gerry to the Mass. Delegates in Congress, June 4, James Trecothick Austin, *The Life of Elbridge Gerry*, 2 vols. (Boston: Wells and Lilly, 1828), 1:77–79.

197. John Adams, *John Adams Autobiography*, cited in note 200.

198. Washington in uniform: John Adams to Abigail Adams, May 29, *PJA*.

199. I have not found this in primary sources, but it is often repeated without citation in secondary ones, such as Joseph J. Ellis, *Founding Brothers: The Revolutionary Generation* (New York: Vintage Books, 2002), 124.

200. John Adams, *John Adams Autobiography, Part 1*, "John Adams," through 1776, sheet 20–21 of 53, *PJA*. The original introduction in full (obscured by my careful use of the ellipsis) implies Washington at the beginning, which is contrary to what Adams then says of Hancock's response. As both quotes are from the same document, I imagine Adams mistakenly recorded the order of his introduction when he penned it in his autobiography. The date of this episode is uncertain.

201. *JCC*, June 15, 2:91. There is sometimes confusion over Washington's rank because in 1798, after his retirement from the presidency, President John Adams, faced with deteriorating relations with France, commissioned Washington as lieutenant general (the highest rank at the time) in the young U.S. Army. However, during the Revolutionary War, Washington was only referred to as "General and Commander in chief", as on his official commission by the Continental Congress (in LOC). Washington to Hancock, Jan 22, 1777, and Washington to a Continental Congress Camp Committee, Jan 29, 1778 that Washington appealed to Congress for lieutenant generals, implying his rank was higher. His calls went unheeded. The lieutenant general rank never existed in the Continental Army.

202. *JCC*, June 16, 2:92.

203. *JCC*, June 17, 2:97.

204. Washington to Martha Washington, June 18, *PGW*.

205. John Adams to Abigail Adams, June 11–17, *PJA*.

Chapter 2: Seizing the Offensive

1. Intelligence, June 15, Gage MSS.

2. *JEPCM*, June 15, 569.

3. Putnam to Bunker Hill Assoc., Aug 1825, *Coll. of CHS* (1860), 1:237–39. Though I use 1825 information carefully, anecdotes such as this are probably based in fact. One can imagine that such a scene would have been etched vividly into the 15-year-old's mind.

4. I believe there were 1,000 total after Knowlton's men were added, per Prescott to Adams, Aug 25, 395–96. Cf. French, *First Year*, 215, which implies there were 1,000, later joined by 200 of Knowlton's men.

5. *JEPCM*, June 15, 334.

6. The prayer's details are unknown. Its closing lines, as reported by a "Diary of Dorothy Dudley," are bogus: see Mary Beth Norton, "Getting to the Source", *Journal of Women's History* 10 (Autumn 98), 141.

7. Ill with the gout, Frye would send his subordinate, Lt. Col. James Brickett, in his stead: Swett, *History*, 18.

8. Capt. John Chester and Samuel Webb to Joseph Webb, June 19, Frothingham, *Siege*, 415–16, describes "one day's provisions, blankets, &c."

9. Frothingham, *Siege*, 121–22, describes both Prescott and the prayer. French, *First Year*, 219, describes Prescott wearing "home-spun clothes with his sword buckled on, and wearing over them a banyan, or light loose coat. The broad brim of his hat shaded his eyes." (Cf. Swett, *History*, 19: "calico frock".) Judge Prescott's account of the Battle of Bunker Hill, *Proc. of MHS* (1876), 14:68–78, mentions the banyan. Prescott is pictured, bald, at the unnumbered beginning of Caleb Stark, *Memoir...of Gen. John Stark.*

10. Swett, *History*, 19.

11. French, *First Year*, 215, was apparently the first to suggest Knowlton's men did not join the others until this point, suggesting they actually met near Inman's Farm, a likely possibility. According to Daniel Putnam to the Bunker Hill Association, Aug 1825, *Coll. of CHS* (1860), 1:236, Israel Putnam's men were mostly stationed at Phipps's Farm, well east of Cambridge, and Putnam was staying with a few companies at nearby Inman Farm. (Daniel was Putnam's son and present in Cambridge.) This seems to be where Knowlton's detachment met them. Various letters of 1818 in Dawson, 2:3, claim Knowlton had only 120 men (Cf. Gray to Mr. Dyer, July 12, Frothingham, *Siege*, 393–95). I go with Prescott to John Adams, Aug 25, written days after the battle. Since Prescott was commander of the detachment, I deem him the best source, and he indicates 200 men. Chester to Fish, July 22, mentions wagons, plural. They must have been horse-drawn. On Foster: Lockhart, *Whites of Their Eyes*, 189.

12. Samuel Bixby's diary, June 16, *Proc. of MHS* (1876), 14:286–87.

13. The waning gibbous was 87 percent full, according to the U.S. Navy's Sun and Moon Calculator.

14. Farnsworth's diary, June 16, *Proc. of MHS* (1899), 2:12:78ff.

15. Frothingham, *Siege*, 123, supplies in part the original source on 393–95: a letter of Samuel Gray to John Dyer in London, July 12. This source claims there were "two generals" and the engineer (Colonel Gridley). One general was Putnam, but Prescott, also present, was no general. Dyer was probably mistaken. It is unlikely that Gen. John Thomas or Gen. William Heath were present, since they were both stationed in Roxbury, nor General Ward, who was back at headquarters and probably suffering with his calculus, as he would be the next day. French, *First Year*, 215n14, agrees. If a second general was indeed present, the only possibilities are Gen. Joseph Spencer of Connecticut or would-be Gen. Joseph Warren, but I do not subscribe to their being there.

16. The colors are captured in various contemporary paintings, including John Trumbull's *The Battle of Bunker's Hill, June 17, 1775* (1786). They are the same as those described by Connecticut's Captain

Chester to Fish, July 22, 389–91. In Putnam to Bunker Hill Assoc., Aug 1825, *Coll. of CHS* (1860), 1:236, young Putnam states that he found his father after the battle and "he wore the same clothes he had on when I left him". Daniel did not call it a uniform. I suspect the general had some kind of uniform, given that the company under him also had uniforms. Perhaps Putnam simply chose not to wear it at the battle, just as Chester's company covered theirs.

17. *JEPCM*, June 15, 569.

18. Quantity of houses: a statement of the Mass. Provincial Congress on June 28, signed by James Warren, says 500 (in Dawson 2:3:380–81). Clarke's *Narrative* gives the impossibly low "about three hundred houses, a church, some public buildings." Captain Laurie [to Lord Dartmouth], June 23, gives "about 600 houses besides Store houses". Dr. James Thacher, *Journal*, 28, says "three hundred dwelling houses, some of them elegant, and about two hundred buildings of other descriptions".

19. On the heights, Swett, *History*, 16, and French, *First Year*, 213–15.

20. No source gives Gridley's preference, but I suspect that, as a master engineer, he was for Bunker Hill's higher ground. However, one could argue that as an artilleryman, he was for the closer ground (Breed's) where his small pieces could harry the British. Putnam was the most impetuous of the three and so is traditionally assumed to have been the one for taking Breed's Hill. But Lockhart, *Whites of Their Eyes*, 194–95, suggests Prescott might have been the advocate for that hill, given that Putnam would show no effort to dictate the order of battle throughout the day and would instead defer to Prescott.

21. Prescott's account states only "all's well", though that could be paraphrasing. Ship timekeeping: Danton, *Theory and Practice*, 282–83. French, *First Year*, 216, says Prescott went into Charlestown itself to listen for alarms, only there to hear the "all's well". He would have heard the bells at least, even from Breed's Hill.

22. *Watertown's Military History*, 127. Some (e.g., *Memorial History of Boston*, 3:108) suggest that Warren spent his last night in the Hastings House.

23. Frothingham, *Life and Times*, 506.

24. General sources for this section (each giving slightly varied accounts): Brown, *Stories about General Warren*, 63; Swett, *History*, 25 (quotes); Frothingham, *Life and Times*, 509–10, all secondary sources.

25. Various letters refer to the ditch, such as Waller to his brother, June 22, Nicholas, *Historical Record*, 1:87–89; Lord Rawdon to his uncle, June 20 (in Commager and Morris, *Spirit of 'Seventy-Six*, 130–31); and Wilkinson, "A Rapid Sketch," in Coffin, *History of the Battle*, 8–13 (p. 9).

26. Margin note of one of several Clinton MSS variants of Clinton's MS *Narrative*, 1:2 of Box 279, titled "Extract from *Narrative*". It is similar to other Clinton material. That Clinton's report was in writing (now unfortunately lost): Clinton to P [William Phillips], June 13 (with postscript on June 16), Clinton MSS. This June 16 postscript is clear: Clinton proposed in writing to Howe and Gage an assault on the Americans "at daybrake…Saturday" (June 17).

27. Clinton MSS loose sheet "I was not a Volunteer…" in front of Box 280. In that document, SW is Sir William [Howe] (not yet a knight in June 1775).

28. Clinton to P [William Phillips], June 13 (with postscript on June 16), Clinton MSS.

29. Howe to General Harvey, June 22 and 24, 3:220–24. The sentries may have remembered Putnam's previous march through Charlestown. As that affair turned out to be nothing, they thought the same of this one.

30. Coggins, *Ships and Seamen*, 177, or Danton, *Theory and Practice*, 282–83.

31. On sleeping between the guns, private correspondence with the USS *Constitution* Museum, Dec 2008.

32. On June 17, 1775, sunrise was 4:06 a.m., per U.S. Navy's Sun and Moon Calculator.

33. Estimate based on the original Mass. Committee of Safety Report, Force, *American Archives*, 4:2:1373–

76, which says about "eight rods square", thus 132 feet on each side. However, Peter Brown to his mother, June 28, (in Ezra Stiles's diary, 1:595–96), calls it "*ten Rod long and eight wide*, with a Breast Work of about *8 more*" (Brown's italics), believable if we compare the layout to the De Berniere map, which shows one part of it not quite square. Brown also mentions at 5:00 a.m. "we not having above half the Fort done". The only part of Brown's claim that is not believable when compared to De Berniere's map is that of an 8-rod breastwork. The oft cited, overly complicated rendition "Plan of the Redoubt and Intrenchment on the Heights of Charlestown, (commonly called Bunker Hill)…", June 17 (first published in Britain's *Gentleman's Magazine*; republished Frothingham, *Siege*, 198, "as a curious memorial") is completely inaccurate, published in Britain to help spin the story on why the British lost so many men. There seems to be no consensus among historians on the definite shape of the redoubt, but that shown on De Berniere's map seems most likely. Frothingham, *Siege*, 198, provides more information.

34. Mollo, *Uniforms*, color plate 31.

35. On the details of the ship, Beck, *Igniting*, appendix 5; on her logs for the day, appendix 3.

36. Appendix 4.

37. "Letter from Boston to a Gentlemen in Scotland", June 25, Force, *American Archives*, 4:2:1093–94, claims "The firing from the *Lively* was almost immediately put a stop to by the Admiral." There is no mention of this in Graves, *Conduct*. Moreover, none of the ships' logs record a cease-fire, and thus seem to have fired all morning.

38. We might assume they followed standard protocol in raising the red flag, as evidenced by other references given throughout this volume. Signal code instructions from 1653 require the solid red flag be raised to the fore-topmast head and two guns fired (Perrin, *British Flags*, 160–62). On what mast the red flag was flown in 1775 is unknown.

39. Appendix 3.

40. Outer quotes: "Reminiscence of General Warren", *NEHGR* (1858), 12:230, which describes the coat as light. Trumbull, *The Battle of Bunker's Hill, June 17, 1775 (1786)*, at Yale Univ. Art Gallery, depicts the coat as sky blue. Middle quote: "Letter of a British Officer", July 5, *Detail and Conduct of the American War*, 13–15: "in his best clothes; everybody remembered his fine, silk-fringed waistcoat". The late letter of Samuel Lawrence in Dawson, 2:3:422, adds, "He had a blue coat, and white waistcoat, and, I think, a cocked hat." Swett, *History*, 25, states Warren "with his fusil and sword, repaired to the post of danger." He certainly had a musket and sword of some sort.

41. Frothingham, *Life and Times*, 513; Swett, *History*, 25; "Reminiscence of General Warren", *NEHGR* (1858), 12:230.

42. The exact timeline is unclear. Whether Gerry attempted to dissuade Warren from leaving the evening before or just before, he departed in the morning. In either case, it would have still been dark if Warren was indeed to make it to Cambridge by daylight per Swett, *History*, 25. Dr. Sam Forman, author of *Dr. Joseph Warren*, alerted me to other stories of Warren's whereabouts that morning, but none seem credible or supported, and Forman agrees.

43. Putnam to Bunker Hill Assoc., Aug 1825, *Coll. of CHS* (1860), 1:247ff. Putnam had spent part of the night at the Inman Farm, and he probably rode to headquarters upon hearing the cannonade.

44. French, *Siege of Boston*, 264, claims Ward never left his house, as does Frothingham, *Life and Times*, 513. However, Martyn, *Life of Artemas Ward*, 126, states that Ward did leave for a time, but much has been reported of him being essentially (if not entirely) bedridden this day due to severe calculus (ibid., 127). Ibid., 129, reports he in fact left for a second errand related to his command. Putnam to Bunker Hill Assoc., Aug 1825, *Coll. of CHS* (1860), 1:247ff, tells of Daniel Putnam's visit to

headquarters, but Ward was off on an errand. A similar note is in "Reminiscence of General Warren", *NEHGR* (1858), 12:230.

45. A "fast-moving battle": while preparations took all day, the battle itself was fast: See appendix 2.

46. Since the Declaration of Independence was not yet conceived, nor was independence yet part of the public consciousness, it is arguable to call Ward an "American" commander in chief. Furthermore, he had no official authority over the armies of the other New England colonies. However, he was appointed such by the Mass. Provincial Congress, as noted in *JEPCM*, May 19, 243, though their authority to do so is debatable.

47. French, *First Year*, 59–61, gives a great discussion on localism.

48. There is much discussion of the Interim Army enlistment in French, *First Year*, 47–87.

49. In this period before the Army was adopted, it is interesting to wonder what might have happened if the British were to have retreated to, say, Rhode Island. Would Ward have remained responsible, despite the fight no longer being in Massachusetts, or would the entire organization have changed, perhaps passing authority to Gen. Nathanael Greene?

50. French, *First Year*, 86.

51. There is much debate over who had command. Putnam did not seem to interfere or direct command with Prescott's men in the redoubt. Furthermore, as shown, Putnam was willing to relinquish command to Warren. However, the fact that Putnam felt he had a command to relinquish suggests he was in command. Prescott would do the same when Warren arrived in the redoubt, so one could surmise that Prescott also had a command to give. The difference is that with Prescott, there seems to be no indication that his authority extended beyond his earthen redoubt. Putnam's jurisdiction seems more the question. Regardless of any understood commands, the rebel army was far from organized. In the 1818 Dearborn-Putnam public controversy, mostly in Dawson, 2:3:402ff., Dearborn supporters chastise Putnam for not leading Gerrish's men forward. Since Gerrish was of Massachusetts, regardless of Connecticut's placing itself under the command of Ward, Putnam ultimately had no authority over Gerrish.

52. Martyn, *Life of Artemas Ward*, 125–27. Frothingham, *Siege*, 128–29, describes Ward's motivations.

53. Stark to New Hampshire, June 19, Force: *American Archives*, 4:2:1029. Note that the 200 were a *portion* of Stark's regiment, which he gladly sent under Lt. Col. Isaac Wyman (Frothingham, *Siege*, 186). Stark stayed with his remaining force at Medford until he received new orders. See appendix 2 for more. The messenger is unknown, but it might have been Ward himself (note 44).

54. On the meeting held at the Province House, see Frothingham, *Siege*, 127 and notes; also in Adan's statement cited in note 56. Cf. Frothingham, *Siege*, 258–61, and French, *First Year*, 221–23.

55. The British Army in America was considered to have lesser status than the Army at home. A man could be in reality a colonel, elevated to brigadier general for the purposes of his tour in America, but his rank would revert back to colonel upon his return to the mother country. Thus, Percy and Pigot were colonels holding a position in America that elevated them to brigadier general. This is described more in Clarke's *Narrative*, Drake, *Bunker Hill*, 42–59. Details about Pigot remain almost as obscure as those of Valentine Jones, a lieutenant colonel serving as third brigadier. Jones apparently played no significant role at any point during the American Revolution but was probably at the council. He was intended to take command of the attack on Dorchester Heights, but that scheme was not to be. Valentine Jones to a friend, June 19, *Proc. of MHS* (1876), 14:91, mentions nothing of his role this day. Pigot a "little Man": Howe to Harvey, June 22 and 24, 3:220–24. More on both men in Beck, *Igniting*, appendix 3.

56. Frothingham, *Siege*, 127n, gives that Timothy Ruggles was present and supported what was Clinton's plan, although it claims Ruggles proposed the plan, unaware of proof in the Clinton MSS. Frothingham's

source "Ms. Letter" is difficult to trace, but it is probably Statement of John R. Adan, Dec 21, 1841 (secondhand of some British Mr. Erving at Boston in 1775), Richard Frothingham MSS II, 2:3, MHS. That Ruggles is a captain (not a general as some sources claim) and in charge of the 1st Company of Associators, each about 45 men strong, is in the returns for these 5 Associator companies, appearing in the Gage MSS under July 5, 1775. The 2nd Company was under Abijah Williard, the 3rd under Adino Paddock, the 4th under James Putnam[?], the 5th under Richard S/Jeltonotall[?]. Related: see the Loyalists' Pledge, May 3, signed by 220 Bostonians, Gage MSS.

57. Nothing supports Graves's presence, and Graves instead tells of Howe visiting him on *Somerset*. The fact that the Royal Navy was not employed in a strategic way for the battle seems to confirm he was not there.

58. Clinton states that Lieutenant Jourdain and Lieutenant Page are present in Clinton's unaddressed account "our opposite Neighbours…" in Clinton MSS, 10:5, quoted in French, *First Year*, 221. An Aug 2 war council, the minutes of which are in Clinton MSS, lists the following attendees, which gives us insights to the June 17 meeting: "Gage, Graves, Clinton, Burgoyne, Percy, Chief Justice Oliver, Attorney General, Mr. Secretary Flucker, Mr. Hutton [Henry Hulton?], Mr. Burch, Mr. Paxton, Mr. Hallowell." Howe was commanding in Charlestown then.

59. Howe to Harvey, June 22 and 24, 3:220–24.

60. Quote: ibid., emphasis as in original. Evidenced in other sources as well, for example, Lord Rawdon to Earl Huntingdon, June 20: "[the redoubt] if perfected, [would] have probably destroyed the greatest part of Boston." Clarke's *Narrative* gives that in Howe's speech, before the first assault, warned that the town would be destroyed if they did not achieve victory.

61. "Letter of a British Officer", July 5, *Detail and Conduct of the American War*, 13–15.

62. See next note.

63. On Clinton's proposal, Clinton MSS loose sheet "I was not a Volunteer…" in front of Box 280. On the redan versus a redoubt, Clinton MSS, 10:5, "our opposite Neighbours…" Other variations of these claims exist in the unorganized boxes of the Clinton MSS, such as Box 282, which has two variants of "Private Notes". One begins, "I Sir Henry Clinton advised that the Enemy might be attack'd"; the other begins almost verbatim, but with margin notes. Both are very close to a third variation, which I have not been able to find, quoted in French, *First Year*, 221. French cites this as "Clinton MSS., 136, Private Notes to the History". This source is lost within the unorganized portions of the Clinton MSS. A tradition holds that Gage also objected to Clinton's plan for fear of landing troops between two forces, apparently referring to those on Breed's Hill and those in Cambridge (French, *First Year*, 222).

64. Gage says this in "To Lord Barrington", June 26, [Private], Carter, *Corr. of General Gage*, 2:686–87, claiming it to be a common expression, but he does not seem to be the first to say it that day. Phrase as quoted: "Letter of a British Officer", July 5, 13–15.

65. Gage to Clinton, June 17, Clinton MSS.

66. French, *First Year*, 223n38, cites a letter in the Dartmouth MSS, June 19, where Percy states: "For my Part I happened to be upon Duty in the Lines that Day, so that I was in no way concerned in the Engagement, being only entertained by a pretty smart Cannonade which we kept up upon Roxburgh to amuse them on that Side." French's earlier work, *Siege*, 412, claims Percy did not play a bigger role this day due to his being ill, but gives no references, and French does not repeat this detail in *First Year*.

67. Graves, *Conduct*, June 17.

68. General Orders, June 17 and 18, Howe's *Orderly Book*, 1–3.

69. Of course, Howe could have burned Charlestown to the ground before landing on its docks.

70. Graves, *Conduct*, June 17. The discussion of the tenders is implied. Howe discusses his desire to land at high tide in his letter to Harvey, June 22 and 24. *Bickerstaff's Boston Almanack for 1775* gives high tide at 3:34 p.m. (See appendix 2 and note that the British did not wait until full high tide to begin landing.) See French, *First Year*, 222–23, on criticisms of these delays. Fleming, *Now We Are*, 345–50, makes a strong counterargument that the delays were *not* due to idleness on the part of the British, but that it took considerable time to amass an amphibious invasion, relating it to the efforts of WWII's D-Day invasion. Lockhart, *Whites of Their Eyes*, 233ff., echoes Fleming. However, unlike Bunker Hill, D-Day involved a strongly entrenched position at the landing site, plus the need to bring over heavy equipment and supplies for a massive army that might be pinned down for days. For Bunker Hill, the beaches were clear for a landing, provisions could have been ferried over later in the day, and few lines of supply were needed for the operation to commence. Faster action on the part of the British would have cost them fewer casualties and probably guaranteed them a swift victory. Moreover, while men fight better with dry feet, rapid initiative would have saved British lives.

71. Appendix 2.

72. Appendix 4.

73. Drought: postscript of Samuel Webster to the New Hampshire Committee of Safety, June 21, in Force, *American Archives*, 4:2:1056; Experience Storrs's diary, June 10: "Extreemly Dry & Dusty"; Letter to Jeremiah Powell, June 21, *Proc. of MHS* (1870), 11:226–27: "they were almost suffocated with dust".

74. Appendix 3.

75. Putnam to Bunker Hill Assoc., Aug 1825, *Coll. of CHS* (1860), 1:247ff.

76. Appendix 5.

77. Prescott to John Adams, Aug 25, Frothingham, *Siege*, 395–96. Ketchum, *Decisive Day*, 117–18, claims the breastwork was 165 feet. But if we assume the redoubt was in fact 132 feet ("eight rods square") as cited, and if we trust De Berniere's map, the breastwork was substantially longer than the redoubt face. Thus, the greater number is to be believed. Also see Peter Thacher's *Narrative*, in Dawson, 2:3:381–84, which describes constructing the redoubt's breastwork.

78. Farnsworth's diary, June 17, *Proc. of MHS* (1899), 2:12:78ff.

79. Peter Brown to his mother, June 28, Ezra Stiles's diary, 1:595–96.

80. I use Judge Prescott's account. A slightly different version, perhaps the original, is in the Prescott Family Manuscript in Dawson, 2:3:437–38. Neither gives it as a quotation.

81. Capt. Ebenezer Bancroft's statement in Spalding, *Bi-Centennial of Old Dunstable*, 58ff., gives that Bancroft, who fought in the redoubt and was blinded in one eye by the shock wave of a cannon ball that grazed him, thought the ball was fired by *Somerset*. Legend has ascribed this shot as being from *Somerset* too. However, *Somerset* was not in a position to fire on the redoubt (appendix 3). The best guess is that the victim was Asa Pollard, but for differing viewpoints, see J. L. Bell's "Besmeared with His Blood and Brains" on his blog *Boston 1775*, at http://boston1775.blogspot.com/2008/12/besmeared-with -his-blood-and-brains.html, Dec 9, 2008; which continues with six subsequent posts. A Lieutenant Spaulding would suffer a similar fate later in the battle (Swett, *History*, 29). Aaron Barr is supposed as the second victim of the day (Fleming, *Now We Are*, 161).

82. The events, the death of the man (probably Asa Pollard), etc., Frothingham, *Siege,* 126n1, where Prescott insists on the burial against the wishes of a horrified chaplain, though Bell, *Boston 1775*, (cited in note 81) gives evidence that such a funeral did not happen. (Cf. French, *Siege of Boston*, 290.) The quotes by Prescott are from Major Butterfield, who apparently had heard it from Prescott himself. They were published in several newspapers including the *Newburyport Herald*, June 7, 1825, and the *Salem*

Gazette three days later. Clarke's *Narrative* supposes a great number of colonists were buried that day before the British took the field. He writes: "The next day, also, we found a piece of ground, about twenty yards long and twelve wide, which appeared to have been freshly digged...a number of dead bodies were discovered...must have been killed by the shot and bombs from the shipping". That is a rather large burial plot to undertake during the preparations, and it is odd that no colonial evidence notes it. Could Clarke have stumbled upon one of the plots the British themselves dug later and not known it? Given the accuracy of Copp's Hill Battery (appendix 4), one wonders if Prescott walked the parapet only during the brief respite from there.

83. Prescott's account *Proc. of MHS* (1876), 14:76–77, and Sabine, *American Loyalists* (1847), 706. Variations exist in secondary sources, for example, French, *First Year*, 219, and Frothingham, *Siege*, 126. Lockhart, *Whites of Their Eyes*, 227, doubts Gage could have seen Prescott, given the primitive optics of the day. However, Prescott was only about a half-mile distant, and for someone who knew him, it should have been possible to identify him by his gait or posture at least, and perhaps by his blue frock. So it seems plausible, even with a modest spyglass (and Gage would have had a decent spyglass). There would have been little smoke over the battlefield at this point, as the Americans were not yet firing artillery.

84. Runnel's statement in Swett, *History*, Notes, 16.

85. Appendix 5. At least one protruded from the corner, but where they were is unclear.

86. Despite Ketchum, *Decisive Day*, 119, and other secondary sources, Prescott had no uniform.

87. Fatigued, no doubt, having worked all night. But were they also thirsty? Many sources (Swett, *History*, 23; Frothingham, *Siege*, 127–28; Ketchum, *Decisive Day*, 127, 168) give a story of rum and water being brought in, but Martyn, *Life of Artemas Ward*, 130n13, suggests (and I agree) they had plenty of water from Charlestown, and what they really wanted was rum, beer, or (hard) cider. Frothingham, *Battle of Bunker Hill*, 33, says barrels of beer arrived, while French, *First Year*, 219, cites Peter Brown: there was "no drink but rum". In all likelihood, they were not thirsty for water, as many sources claim. The best evidence that the Americans had water and simply wanted alcohol is in the Letter to Jeremiah Powell, June 21, 11:226–27: "they were almost suffocated with dust & choak'd for want of liquor".

88. French, *First Year*, 217. Some stories give that even Colonel Bridge and Lieutenant Colonel Brickett (in charge of Frye's regiment, who was ill) abandoned the work, taking shelter from the heat in a nearby house. Copp's Hill Battery: appendix 4.

89. Frothingham, *Siege*, 128n1, citing "Governor Brooks's Statement", which appears mostly in Swett, *History*, Notes, 3, but says nothing of the horse. Frothingham, *Siege*, 121, suggests he obtained a copy of an original from Swett, and perhaps it references the horse. It is unpublished, if so. Swett worked for Brooks for a time, and so is a reliable secondary source on this matter. Number of horses: Spring, *With Zeal*, 195.

90. "Letter of a British Officer", July 5, 13–15.

91. Burgoyne to Lord Stanley, June 25, Force, *American Archives*, 4:2:1094–95.

92. Brown to his mother, June 28, Ezra Stiles's diary, 1:595–96.

93. Beck, *Igniting*, appendix 5.

94. Appendix 7. It is likely *Falcon* delivered her perhaps two boats before coming up from the harbor.

95. HMS *Cerberus*'s journal (details in appendix 3) is unclear on whether she also donated tenders; she was at Nantasket Roads. HMS *Boyne* was nearer to Boston at King's Roads. They both guarded the harbor's entrance, 5 to 7 miles southeast. See appendix 3, appendix 7.

96. Appendix 9.

97. Appendix 9, appendix 7.

98. Swett, *History*, 37, says 125 pounds, a figure often repeated, but this is excessive. The General Orders, June 17 and 18, Howe's *Orderly Book*, 1–3, clearly state that camp gear was not brought until June 18. Thus, contrary to legend, the rank and file did go into this battle with full gear as if on campaign. Even so, Spring, *With Zeal*, 40, gives that the full gear weighed more like 60 pounds. Rolled blanket: carried by a leather strap. Knapsacks: buff, black or fur.

99. Clinton MSS loose sheet "I was not a Volunteer…" in front of Box 280, repeated in French, *First Year*, 261. For the uniform descriptions, I draw on Mollo, *Uniforms*; Smith and Kiley, *Uniforms*, 126ff.; *First Year*, 108; and Fischer, *Paul Revere's Ride*, 118–123.

100. The blue flag is noted in the day's general orders, in Howe's *Orderly Book*, 1–2, signifying "To Advance". The orders do not specify where this flag was to be flown, but likely on the flagship *Preston*, though which mast is uncertain. This blue flag was not a standard signal but one arranged for that day; thus we can only guess. Also in the day's orders: a red flag was the signal "To Land" and a yellow flag "To lay on Oars". The yellow flag was probably not used this day. See also, appendix 7.

101. On platforms and height: Frothingham, *Siege*, 125.

102. I have found no clear source on how the alarm was sent to Cambridge. Chester to Fish, July 22, 415–16, claims he first heard the alarm from Captain Putnam, likely Capt. Israel Putnam Jr. (Frothingham, *Siege*, 404, lists him under General Putnam's officers.) It was not Daniel Putnam (Putnam to Bunker Hill Assoc., Aug 1825, *Coll. of CHS* [1860] 1:247ff), who was mostly at Inman Farm all day. Trevett's statement, in Dawson, 2:3:415, claims that after he left Cambridge about 1:00 p.m., he saw General Putnam ride by, and since Trevett came to the field just before the battle, this may be a clue that General Putnam initiated the alarm.

103. Prescott to John Adams, Aug 25, Frothingham, *Siege*, 395–96; appendix 5.

104. Chester to Fish, July 22, ibid., 415–16.

105. Osgood and Joseph Ward: Martyn, *Life of Artemas Ward*, 90. Joseph is listed as Ward's "second cousin once removed". Knox: Frothingham, *Siege,* 146. Knox seems to have been Ward's eyes that day. Warren: see note 109.

106. Heath's *Memoirs*, 14. Also, Swett, *History*, 29. On abatis use: French, *First Year*, 246.

107. John Trumbull's *Autobiography* excerpt, quoted in F. S. Drake, *Town of Roxbury*, 274.

108. "Reminiscence of General Warren", *NEHGR* (1858), 12:230.

109. Ibid.; Frothingham, *Life and Times*, 513. How there were injured soldiers so early that day is unknown. There is a story in the notebook of Jeremy Belknap (founder of MHS), *Proc. of MHS* (1876), 14:92–93, which claims Warren was urged to not go to the battle by several men, who volunteered to execute Warren's orders in his stead. Warren finally agreed, saying he was going to Roxbury instead, only to go to Charlestown anyway. The source itself is from a statement to Belknap in Aug 24, 1787, some 12 years after the battle, while Warren was still at the height of his fame. While the story may be true, the late date and Warren's reported deception, which does not seem in character, lead me to discount it.

110. Red flag noted in the day's general orders (cited in note 98).

111. Appendix 9.

112. Appendix 11.

113. Wood and stone: Chester to Fish, July 22, Frothingham, *Siege*, 389–91; 600 feet back: Wilkinson, "A Rapid Sketch", Coffin, *History of the Battle*, 8–15 (see p. 9), claims the rail fence was about 300 yards (900 feet) long, though he warns that his figures are taken from a memorandum some 41 years after the event. My calculations using modern mapping tools suggest 300–350 yards long. Cf. French, *First*

Year, 219–220, which indicates 200 yards, without support. The cannibalized fence may have been of the same design as the one fortified or perhaps made only of wood.

114. Runnels's statement in Swett, *History*, Notes, 16; more in appendix 5.

115. French, *First Year*, 227–28. Connecting the flèches to Putnam: appendix 5. They might have been of rail fence rather than dug, but De Berniere's trustworthy map shows them in the same style as other earthworks.

116. The assumption is that Putnam did not waste precious powder and so fired a real shot at the British. All of this comes from Runnels's statement in Swett, *History*, Notes, 16. See appendix 5.

117. Livingston, *Israel Putnam*, 410.

118. Appendix 5.

119. Appendix 2. Given my theory that the redoubt's breastwork was still under construction, some of the entrenching tools must have still been in use.

120. Heath, *Memoirs*, 13. However, while this story is often taken as truth, Heath was not at Bunker Hill this day, but among the Roxbury lines. Thus, he is a secondary source and fails to give the original. In the end, most of the tools would fall into British hands anyway.

121. Mollo, *Uniforms*, 160 and color plate 21. The coat is blue, not black as it may appear. See also, appendix 9.

122. Appendix 8.

123. French, *First Year*, 220, says the neck was 30 feet wide; ibid., 213, says the milldam was 100 yards off.

124. Dearborn's controversial open letter of Mar 1818 (reprinted in Dawson, 2:3:402–06) is only considered accurate for his description of crossing the neck, since he was among Stark's regiment as it crossed. From his letter, we know there were two regiments ahead of Stark's crossing. Most statements in the Dearborn-Putnam controversy in 1818 (in Dawson, 2:3:402ff.) state they saw Gerrish on Bunker Hill upon their arrival, thus requiring Gerrish's men to have crossed before Stark's. Swett, *History*, 25, claims Reed was sent at the same time as Stark, and since Reed's men were posted near Charlestown Neck, while Stark's were in Medford, it is logical to conclude the other was Reed's. More on Reed in Frothingham, *Siege*, 186–88. Cf. French, *First Year*, 225, which states Reed followed Stark. But clearly, two regiments were ahead of Stark, and those of Reed and Gerrish seem the best candidates. Note that this was Stark's main force, not the 200 sent earlier. Where those earlier 200 served is unknown.

125. French, *First Year*, 226; Beck, *Igniting*, appendix 5; appendix 3.

126. Chester and Samuel Webb to Joseph Webb, June 19, 415–16, describes the cannon shot used as they crossed the neck.

127. Brown to his mother, June 28, Ezra Stiles's diary, 1:595–96.

128. Prescott's account *Proc. of MHS* (1876), 14:72, says on the retreat, "many killed by the fire of the British…not a few, in passing the neck".

129. Frothingham, *Battle of Bunker Hill*, 35.

130. Dearborn's controversial letter of Mar 1818 (in Dawson, 2:3:402–06, see notes). Despite Stark's proximity to the battle (Medford), he came this late because his men still had to prepare ammunition cartridges. What did they do all night?

131. French, *First Year*, 229.

132. Frothingham, *Life and Times*, 513. More on the hospital and the fate of the house in Swett, *History*, 49–50, and "Reminiscence of General Warren", *NEHGR* (1858), 12:230.

133. Wilkinson, "A Rapid Sketch", in Coffin, *History of the Battle*, 8–13 (see 9–10), describes the palisade. Few sources give other details on this often-ignored part of the battlefield. Note that he says the beach was "firm and flat". If so, where did the rock come from to build their barricade? He acknowledges he wrote this "almost forty years since".

134. Quote: Letter to Jeremiah Powell, June 21, *Proc. of MHS* (1870), 11:226–27, which is contemporary but not eyewitness. Swearing: Livingston, *Israel Putnam*, 410. Broken sword: appendix 5.

135. On the event, and Gerrish's weight: Swett, *History*, 37. However, this event could not have taken place after the first British assault, given the preponderance of claims that Gerrish had arrived even before Stark's men (who arrived in time to repulse the beach attack). Thus, Gerrish's arrival must have been before the first assault (see note 124). Frothingham, *Siege*, 402, does not give numbers for Gerrish's regiment, but Frothingham, *Battle of Bunker Hill*, 13, citing a June 9 return, lists Gerrish with 421 men. How many Febiger took is unknown, but it seems to have been a small percentage. Scant details exist in Frothingham, *Siege*, 147, and French, *First Year*, 244, and both sources disagree on the portion (the former claiming a mere company under Capt. Thomas Mighill, the latter claiming "most of the Gerrish's regiment"). On his fate: Force, *American Archives*, 4:3:251 (court-martial) and 252 (cashiered). He was court-martialed not only for his cowardice at Bunker Hill, but for a similar performance weeks later at a skirmish at Sewall's Point; Frothingham, *Siege*, 178–79.

136. Frothingham, *Siege*, 151, puts Reed at the rail fence and lists others who were there.

137. "Letter of a British Officer", Boston, July 5, 13–15.

138. Howe to Harvey, June 22 and 24, 3:220–24.

139. The positions of each light infantry company are on De Berniere's map. The 38th is depicted at the stone wall on Page's map.

140. Not depicted on the maps, but evidenced by Waller to a friend, June 21, at MHS. Howe's letters of the day also make it clear that the 43rd ended up on the left. Why the 43rd is not depicted this way on the maps is due to the maps' inherent flaws regarding troop positions. See appendix 12.

141. Frothingham, *Siege*, 133, notes.

142. Ibid., 131–32.

143. Wilkinson, "A Rapid Sketch", in Coffin, *History of the Battle*, 8–13: the author apparently was at the fight on the beach. The stake was said to be 8 or 10 rods distant. French, *First Year*, 226c27 and n54, gives French's theory that Knowlton's men doubled up the rail fence while Stark's stuffed it with hay. I agree. With 40–50 men posted here, it is logical, based on 3 lines and a beach of only a dozen feet wide at high tide.

144. Howe's 23rd: Beck, *Igniting*, appendix 3. Lieutenant Colonel Smith did the same with his 10th in the Expedition to Concord.

145. Putnam to Bunker Hill Assoc., Aug 1825, *Coll. of CHS* (1860) 1:247ff.; Williams's journal, June 17, *Discord*, 18.

146. Appendix 10. Gridley: appendix 5.

147. Frothingham, *Life and Times*, 515; Frothingham, *Siege*, 133, notes.

148. Frothingham, *Life and Times*, 515, appears to prefer Heath's telling (in Heath, *Memoirs*, 13–14), calling the other circumstantial. However, the other, by Judge Prescott, son of Colonel Prescott, seems no more circumstantial to the present author, given that Heath was not at the Battle of Bunker Hill any more than was Prescott's son. Both accounts effectively describe the same kind of transaction, even if the words differ, though admittedly, Heath's was written sooner after the battle than Prescott's. I prefer the telling of Prescott's son (in Judge Prescott's account, *Proc. of MHS* [1876], 14:77). Many statements in the 1818 Dearborn-Putnam controversy in Dawson, 2:3:402ff., offer similar accounts as well.

149. Appendix 9.

CHAPTER 3: BLOWS MUST DECIDE

1. George III to Lord North, Nov 18, 1774, Donne, *Corr. of George III with Lord North*, 1:214–15. Cf. British Lieutenant Williams's journal, June 15, *Discord*, 6–9, on his thoughts about the Yankees' desire of independence.

2. Burgoyne to Lord Stanley, June 25, Force, *American Archives*, 4:2:1094–95, gives a thorough description of the scene and notes "the hills round the country covered with spectators".

3. Cf. French, *First Year*, 219n24. The unreliable Caleb Stark, *Memoir...of Gen. John Stark*, 31, gives that Gage saw the battle from the cupola.

4. Appendix 9. The 35th flank companies join the British right. Whether they marched or were ferried there is unknown.

5. Tupper just acting: Beck, *Igniting*, appendix 3 (2nd Marine Battalion).

6. Careful math of units in appendix 9 will show the wings were approximately divided in half.

7. From private correspondence with Mr. Peter Ansoff (July 2010), former president of the North American Vexillological Association: the Americans probably had no flags at Bunker Hill, despite the occasional postwar claim of a "Bunker Hill Flag": a solid blue flag with a white canton featuring St. George's red cross, with a pine tree in the first quarter. (See Lossing, *Pictorial Field-Book*, 1:541n4). Instead, it seems based on unsupported tradition. Lieutenant Clarke's *Narrative*, in Drake, *Bunker Hill*, 55, states "nor did I see any colors to their regiments on the day of action." Cf. Trumbull, *The Battle of Bunker's Hill, June 17, 1775*, which features the red flag with a white canton featuring only a pine tree and no cross. Also see Frothingham, *Siege*, 192n1. It is uncertain when Graves and staff crossed. Time: appendix 2.

8. Waller to a friend, June 21, at MHS.

9. Graves, *Conduct*, June 17, the pertinent excerpt also *NDAR*, 1:704.

10. *Spitfire* was probably too small to have the equipment for hot shot.

11. Graves, *Conduct*, June 17. On the messengers sent by boat, Burgoyne to Lord Stanley, June 25, 4:2:1094–95. Further support in an unaddressed, undated Clinton narrative, beginning "our opposite Neighbours…", in Clinton MSS, 10:5.

12. Appendix 3. Tides: appendix 2.

13. Appendix 9. On the formation, appendix 11.

14. Lord Rawdon to Earl of Huntington, June 20, Commager and Morris, *Spirit of 'Seventy-Six*, 130–31; appendix 2.

15. Clarke's *Narrative*, in Drake, *Bunker Hill*, 42–59; also in Frothingham, *Siege*, 137. But Clarke was a marine on the British left, so how could he have heard this?

16. Ron Aylor, *British Regimental Drums & Colours*, http://www.fifedrum.org/crfd/drums.htm, Mar 23, 2003; which depicts most of the standards present.

17. Gage's Official Casualty Report, lists drummers and fifers wounded. Though often ignored, they were in battle.

18. Formation: appendix 11; their numbers: appendix 9.

19. Howe to Harvey, June 22 and 24, 3:200–24; Howe to Lord Howe, June 22, Murdock, *Bunker Hill*, 147–49, the latter more explicit. Fences: Burgoyne to Lord Stanley, June 25, 4:2:1094–95. Quote: Waller to a friend, June 21, MHS.

20. Waller to a friend, June 21, MHS.

21. Quotes: Pierce's statement in Dawson, 2:3:414–15. See appendix 5.

22. 330 men: appendix 9. Clerk commanded the 43rd. Butler came from the 65th, but per Gage's general orders (June 6, the Mackenzie MSS *Orderly Book*, 100, in WO 36/1, UKNA) was placed in charge of

the standing Corps of Light Infantry. Howe to Harvey, June 22 and 24, 3:200–24, calls him *Clark*. See Beck, *Igniting*, appendix 3.

23. Wilkinson, "A Rapid Sketch", Coffin, *History of the Battle*, 8–13. Wilkinson appears to have fought on the beach. Cf. French, *First Year*, 230 n64.

24. There is much evidence that some thought of Warren as commander. For instance, the letter of June 25, 1775, Force, *American Archives*, 4:2:1093–94, or Frothingham, *Life and Times*, 516n3, which give several first and second sources, though one of them, of Leland, I have not found. Cf. Needham Maynard's statement in the Warren MSS, published in Josiah H. Temple, *History of Framingham, Massachusetts: Early Known as Danforth's Farm, 1640–1880* (Framingham, MA: Published by the Town of Framingham, 1887), 288ff. Maynard fought at the battle and was in Colonel Brewer's regiment. While his statement speaks of events known to be false, and thus is not to be trusted, it is probably reliable in its claim that Maynard and others considered Warren a commander. (I highly doubt the story that Colonel Brewer sought orders from Dr. Warren or assigned Warren an aide, unsupported by all other evidence.) The connection between Needham Maynard and the unfound statement of "Hon. Horace Maynard" cited in *Life and Times*, 516n3, is unknown. Several of the British thought Warren was the commander too, e.g., Clarke's *Narrative*, in Drake, *Bunker Hill*, 50; and Williams's journal, June 17, *Discord*, 19. That Putnam and Prescott both offered their command to Warren shows they both felt they had a command to relinquish.

25. On Putnam back and forth: statements in Dawson, 2:3:426–29. The various encouragements (not all by Putnam), vary per source and likely are not verbatim. First quote: ibid., 429; other two: French, *First Year*, 230. "Yankee Doodle": Swett, *History*, 32, and Notes, 25nK.

26. Prescott's account, *Proc. of MHS* (1876), 14:70.

27. Appendix 8. Williams's journal, June 17, *Discord*, 17–18, gives the artillery officer in charge on the field as Capt. John Lemoine, though he says the same for Copp's Hill Battery (appendix 4).

28. The original reference on a shot blasting through the British line comes from Swett, *History*, 34, but see appendix 5.

29. The carcasses may have been fired from cannon, but this seems unlikely. The goal was to lob these into nearby Charlestown, not blast through the buildings. Thus, mortars or maybe howitzers were used. It is unknown how many of these were at Copp's Hill Battery, but they did have some. See appendix 4. Carcasses could have 3 or 5 holes, but 3 seems more common in this era.

30. A great description of revolutionary-era artillery in Robert Selig's "Artillery" essay at AmericanRevolution.org.

31. Burgoyne to Lord Stanley, June 25, Force, *American Archives*, 4:2:1094–95.

32. Hunter's journal, 10.

33. Details of the burning of Charlestown from Graves, *Conduct*, June 17, *NDAR*, 1:704; also *First Year*, 231, 742–43; Burgoyne to Lord Stanley, June 25, 4:2:1094–95. In some sources, the relative time of this event is ambiguous. Howe to Harvey, June 22 and 24, 3:200–24, suggests during the first assault ("at this critical time"); Thacher's *Narrative*, in Dawson, 2:3:381–84, gives during the first movement toward the rail fence; Farnsworth's diary, June 17, *Proc. of MHS* (1899), 2:12:78ff., states it was before the British began their march. (These last two sources give the American claim that the British burned the town to blind the battlefield with smoke. Not true. On actual wind direction: Murdock, *Bunker Hill*, 89n.) Clarke's *Narrative*, in Drake, *Bunker Hill*, 43, agrees the town was bombarded before the march. Perhaps all are right: it took time for the flames to spread.

34. Besides the tradition, Prescott's account *Proc. of MHS* (1876), 14:70. I have not found the traditional part in any contemporary source, but in French, *Siege of Boston*, 269–70, and Everett, *Life of Joseph Warren*, 171 (1902 ed., p. 161 of 1856 ed.).

35. Reuben Kemp's statement in Dawson, 2:3:428–29. Broken sword: appendix 5.

36. French in *First Year*, 237n17, assumes the light infantry never fired, because he has not seen a source that said so. The problem is that almost no sources cover the beach offensive, it being hidden from many of those who left us letters of the day. While French may be right, I find it hard to believe that they would retreat without firing at least one scattered volley.

37. This was Captain Blakeney, per Murdock, *Bunker Hill*, 143, probably William Blakeney of the 23rd, per *LGFO* (1778), xiv.

38. French, *First Year*, 237–38; Wilkinson, "A Rapid Sketch", in Coffin, *History of the Battle*, 8–13 (see 12). The latter lists those killed on the beach and states the British were repulsed three times. Wilkinson was among the cobble-fence defenders.

39. Mass. Comm. of Safety Report, July 7, Force, *American Archives*, 4:2:1373–76, says "they came within ten or twelve rods, and then began a furious discharge of small-arms." Also, Hide's account in Dawson, 2:3:378–79.

40. The exact number is unclear; we can only guess based on the final numbers in Gage's Official Casualty Report.

41. Appendix 9.

42. Thacher's narrative, in Dawson, 2:3:381–84. Why they did not go back to their boats: French, *First Year*, 238.

43. That the light infantry joined the grenadiers is supported by De Berniere's map. See appendix 11. However, when exactly they rejoined is uncertain.

44. Mass. Comm. of Safety Report, July 7, Force, *American Archives*, 4:2:1373–76, says "reserved their fire until…within five or six rods".

45. Everett, *Life of Joseph Warren*, 171 (1902 ed., p. 161 of 1856 ed.). I have found no primary source for it.

46. As with the other casualties, we cannot be sure exactly when he was shot. That he dies of an apparent flesh wound: Howe to Harvey, June 22 and 24, 3:200–24. See Beck, *Igniting*, appendix 3, for the 22nd Regiment.

47. On firing too high: French, *First Year*, 235n11.

48. A dozen aides were killed or wounded by the end of the battle, listed in Gage's Official Casualty Report. Unverified stories of how these aides were wounded: Ketchum, *Decisive Day*, 168–69; Swett, *History*, 39.

49. Burgoyne to Lord Rochfort, [1775], de Fonblanque, *Political and Military*, 191–98: "all the wounds of the officers were not received from the enemy." Cf. Murdock, *Bunker Hill*, 27n, which gives a letter, apparently unpublished, of Charles Stuart of the 35th. (It is *not* in the Stuart compilation *A Prime Minister and His Son*, edited by Wortley.) It states: "…caused the Corps naturally to crowd upon one another and made a confusion in which we suffer'd as much from our own fire as the enemy's."

50. Dearborn's controversial statement of 1818 (Dawson, 2:3:405) is probably accurate on this nuance, though his quotes in his statement probably are not.

51. Howe to Harvey, June 22 and 24, 3:200–24.

52. French, *First Year*, 747, gives that it was the ankle. The primary source for this is unknown. Fortunately, he lived and created one of the two most important contemporary battle maps. Ketchum, *Decisive Day*, 168, says he lost his leg, without reference.

53. On his being badly wounded, Burgoyne to Lord Stanley, June 25, 4:2:1094–95. Gage's Official Casualty Report calls him wounded. That he died: French, *First Year*, 221n32. The same note discusses the spelling variations on his name. In Gage's report, he is listed as "Jorden". Various claims, such as Ketchum, *Decisive Day*, 169, claim he was shot through the head, without reference. If so, how could he have been wounded and not instantly dead?

54. General note: we cannot be sure on which charge these aides were shot, but Howe's statement of having "a moment he never felt before" and the context of his letter to Harvey, June 22 and 24, suggests it was in the first real attack (the second charge) at the rail fence. For any particular in this section not explicitly cited, see Howe to Harvey, June 22 and 24, 3:200–24.

55. Ibid.

56. Swett, *History*, 37.

57. We cannot know the dead per assault. It is estimated from the final tally in Gage's Official Casualty Report.

58. "Letter of a British Officer", July 5, 13–15, states clearly that Pigot called for a retreat but does not tell when. It must have been after the first real attack (second charge) at the rail fence (see appendix 11), as Pigot's actions during the first charge did not amount to much. Noted later in the text, Clinton saw disorder on the British left following this retreat, prompting him to go to Charlestown. In contrast, Waller to his brother, June 22, 1:87–89, boasts they "did not retreat an inch."

59. There is not the level of detail in the accounts necessary to verify the warships began a cannonade after each assault. However, cannon were fired after the first assault at the rail fence, whether the two 12-pounders or those of the Navy, because Captain Trevett, who was to arrive shortly with two more colonial guns, would lose one to a ball (later in text). I presume the Navy was part of this barrage, that they did not sit idly after the battle began.

60. Burgoyne to Lord Stanley, June 25, 4:2:1094–95. Also, Murdock, *Bunker Hill*, chap. 5. Clinton's quote: Clinton MSS loose sheet "I was not a Volunteer..." in front of Box 280.

61. Isaac Smith to his son, July 1, *Proc. of MHS* (1878), 16:291, also in part in French, *First Year*, 340. Lovell was arrested after an incriminating letter was found on Warren: read on in main text.

62. Boardman, *Edes*, 15–16; Peter Edes's diary, June 19, ibid., 93ff.

63. A nice discussion is in French, *First Year*, chap. 4.

64. Prescott's account, *Proc. of MHS* (1876), 14:71 (source of quote, emphasis as in the original). Iron and nails: British Dr. Grant's letter Dawson, 2:3:361.

65. Chester to Fish, July 22, 389–91, "that one subaltern, one sergeant, and thirty privates, were draughted out over night to intrench". As a Connecticut company was typically 100 men (Frothingham, *Battle of Bunker Hill*, 3), this leaves about 70 marching on the day of the battle. Chester's company was from Wethersfield, Connecticut.

66. Chester to Fish, July 22, 389–91.

67. Ibid.

68. Ibid.

69. Frothingham, *Siege*, 146–47, gives others, such as portions of the regiments of Ward, Patterson, and Gardner. When they positioned is unknown.

70. Ibid., 146; French, *Siege of Boston*, 275. Cf. Swett, *History*, 30, for a kinder version. Scammans's court-martial is announced in Force, *American Archives*, 4:2:1661, and his acquittal on 1665. Lockhart, *Whites of Their Eyes*, 318–19, gives that he petitioned to raise a regiment for the Continental Army, but apparently nothing came of it.

71. Frothingham, *Siege*, 404, only reports the three artillery companies that served in the battle, averaging 44 men each. Colonel Gridley's total regiment size on June 9 was 370 men per Frothingham, *Battle of Bunker Hill*, 13. Dividing the total of 370 by 44 gives 8 companies, and with 2 in the field, 6 remained. (I have found no complete company list prior to the battle and thus must deduce it.) Each company had 2 guns it seems, thus 16 total guns in the regiment. Of these, 4 are accounted for with Captains Gridley and Callender. Major Gridley had at least 6 more, since Trevett and Foster attempted to bring 2 each

onto the field, and Gridley must have had something left with him near Cobble Hill. Some guns might have been at Roxbury and Cambridge too. See next note.

72. Gridley and Mansfield: Frothingham, *Siege*, 146; French, *Siege of Boston*, 275–76. Cf. Swett, *History*, 36, for a kinder version with more on Frye, given on authority of an apparently unpublished statement by Trevett. One version of the story tells that Major Gridley asked or "ordered" Mansfield to give his support, and that Mansfield, though a colonel and thus higher ranking, considered the young, inexperienced, untrained, lower-ranking Major Gridley, who had just received his commission the day before, "high military authority" and so obeyed his request.

73. Both Gridleys: appendix 5. Mansfield's court-martial in Force, *American Archives*, 4:3:250, 251, his sentence on 769–70.

74. Appendix 5. Number in his company: Frothingham, *Siege*, 404.

75. Brown to his mother, June 28, Stiles's diary, 1:595–96; appendix 10.

76. Blacks and Indians: see chapter 1, notes 8 and 9. On 3,500 New Englanders: appendix 10.

77. Prescott's account, *Proc. of MHS* (1876), 14:72, 77.

78. On 150 men left: Prescott to John Adams, Aug 25, Frothingham, *Siege*, 395–96. Quote: Prescott's account, *Proc. of MHS* (1876), 14:71. Per *Rivington's Gazette*, No. 120, Aug 3, 1775, the redoubt was nearly empty "because the fire from Cop's hill poured in so thick that there was no living in it." (See appendix 4.)

79. The stripping of the equipment and coats seems to be largely traditional, only appearing in later stories: Prescott's account, *Proc. of MHS* (1876), 14:71; Swett, *History*, 42; and Murdock, *Bunker Hill*, 29.

80. This is their final place depicted on all of Page's maps. See appendix 3.

81. New formation: appendix 11.

82. All of the secondary sources mention the brick kiln, depicted on De Berniere's map. I would be breaking a tradition by failing to mention it.

83. Many statements indicate that the British artillery was only now effective, and from this I deduce their deadliness. That they fired toward the breastwork and flèches is implied in Prescott's account, *Proc. of MHS* (1876), 14:72. See appendix 8. The diameter of the grape for the 6-pounder guns should have been about 1.6 inches. As for the 5½-inch howitzers, each grape ball should have been about 2.4 inches. (See Beck, *Igniting*, appendix 6.)

84. Number of British deduced from the final casualties in Gage's Official Casualty Report.

85. Prescott's account, *Proc. of MHS* (1876), 14:72.

86. French, *Siege of Boston*, 278, agrees that Prescott knew they were doomed.

87. While I have saved this quote until now mostly for dramatic value, it was possibly used throughout the day. Certainly, the final assault on the redoubt, when the men were running out of ammunition, would be a time to use it (again, if need be). We have no primary source for it that I have seen; it is apparently traditional. The closest example is an 1818 statement by Isaac Bassett, which says they were ordered to hold their fire until "they should see the *color* of their eyes" (his emphasis; in Dawson, 2:3:429). It is plausible the line was repeated throughout the day, along all of the lines. Who said it has been hotly debated, some giving it to Prescott, some to Putnam. They could have both said it, as neither appears to be the originator, despite their legends. Thus, even Warren might have said it. Two fascinating discussions are on J. L. Bell's blog *Boston 1775*, suggesting its earlier origins as German. The first is "Who Said, 'Don't Fire Till You See the Whites of Their Eyes'?" at http://boston1775.blogspot .com/2007/06/who-said-dont-fire-till-you-see-whites.html, June 21, 2007; accessed Nov 6, 2008; the second, on its true origins, suggested as a Prussian phrase or older, is "Who Coined the Phrase 'Till You

See the Whites of Their Eyes'?" at http://boston1775.blogspot.com/2007/06/who-coined-phrase-till
-you-see-whites.html, June 22, 2007.

88. While the maps of Page and De Berniere are unreliable for troop movements, Page's maps suggest the grenadiers turned to the breastwork on the final assault (appendix 12); this supported by notes 97 and 99. Howe would have been foolish to employ the grenadiers on the rail fence again, for they were some of his best soldiers.

89. Prescott's account: "within twenty yards". See *Proc of MHS* (1876), 14:72.

90. "Eyewitness Account of the Battle" in *Rivington's Gazette*, No. 120, Aug 3, Frothingham, *Siege*, 397–98.

91. The staggering is supported by the Pitcairn references given below (note 92), as well as Waller to a friend, June 21, at MHS, and Prescott's account, *Proc. of MHS* (1876), 14:72.

92. It seems purely traditional that Major Pitcairn fell into the arms of his son. Not only did Pitcairn possibly receive multiple shots, but as muskets were then very inaccurate, it is difficult to imagine any individual knowing he hit Pitcairn when the redoubt defenders were firing in scattered volleys, while blinded by dust and gunpowder smoke. The undated letter of Burgoyne to Lord Palmerston in de Fonblanque, *Political and Military*, 154, written shortly after the battle, tells the story of Pitcairn being carried back to the boats by his son and mentions the kiss. Major Tupper to Lord Sandwich, June 21, *NDAR*, 1:731, gives that he was wounded "a few Minutes before the Attack was made on the Redoubt and he died about two or three hours after". Waller to a friend, June 21, MHS, also claims Pitcairn was mortally wounded outside the redoubt after they were checked by colonial fire. Frothingham, *Siege*, 195, states, "Dr. John Eliot wrote in his [1775] almanac the following account of his fall: 'This amiable and gallant officer was slain entering the intrenchments. He had been wounded twice; then putting himself at the head of his forces, he faced danger, calling out, 'Now for the glory of the marines!' He received four balls in his body." Except for this unreliable Dr. Eliot source, no contemporary evidence claims Pitcairn died on the rampart wall or in the entrenchments, though the claim appears in unreliable late statements. Another take is the contemporary Henry Hulton, June 20, 1775 in Hulton, *Letters of a Loyalist Lady*, 97–100, which claims that Pitcairn was shot outside Charlestown. However, as Hulton was a spectator in Boston, he is unreliable. Hulton is also the source of the perhaps dubious "lost my father" story. Trumbull, *The Battle of Bunker's Hill, June 17, 1775* (1786), follows the tradition that a single black man—be it "Salem Poor", "Peter Salem", "Salem Prince", or whomever—killed Pitcairn, a tradition that has remained for some time, despite the likelihood Pitcairn was shot multiple times. Belknap's notebook, *Proc. of MHS* (1876), 14:93, includes a statement of 1787 that "A negro man belonging to Groton, took aim at Major Pitcairne, as he was rallying the dispersed British Troops, & shot him thro' the head, he was brought over to Boston & died as he was landing on the ferry ways." This seems to be the earliest reference to the claim of a black man killing Pitcairn. A thorough discussion on the legend surrounding Pitcairn's death is at Bell, *Boston 1775*, beginning with the article "Major Pitcairne was killed close by me" at http://boston1775.blogspot.com/2009/02/major-pitcairne -was-killed-close-by-me.html, Feb 8, 2009; and continues for nine subsequent posts. An anecdote of Pitcairn on his deathbed (difficult to confirm, secondhand, and unreliable due to its date) is in the statement of John R. Adan, Dec 21, 1841 (secondhand of some British Mr. Erving at Boston in 1775), Frothingham MSS II, 2:3, MHS. Pitcairn was buried in King's Chapel in Boston, and later his body was identified and sent to Britain, but the rumor persists that the wrong body was intentionally sent. For more on this, see Samuel Drake, *Old Landmarks of Boston* (Boston: 1873), 217.

93. Waller to a friend, June 21, MHS. Waller was adjutant of the 1st Marines.

94. Prescott's account, *Proc. of MHS*, 14:72.

95. On Prescott's orders to his men: Abel Parker's 1818 statement in Dawson, 2:3:421.

96. Daniel Putnam's 1818 statement in Dawson, 2:3:412. It seems to be legend. Howe does not reference in it in his own letters. Perhaps it was a grazing shot not worthy of noting.

97. The anecdote from Clarke's *Narrative*, specifically Drake, *Bunker Hill*, 48–49. That it mentions the grenadiers of the 23rd (Welch Fusiliers) tells us that Clarke, a marine on the British far left, did not see this incident firsthand. However, because it is a contemporary report, it is believable, though this one man's having shot 20 officers is not. This is added support that the grenadiers turned left toward the entrenchments.

98. Jacob B. Moore, "Memoir of Abel Parker", *Coll. of New Hampshire Hist. Soc.*, vol. 3 (Concord, NH: 1832), 258–66.

99. Rawdon to Huntingdon, June 20, 130–31; Captain Harris, [n.d.], letter, in Lushington, *Life and Services*, 41–42. Both letters affirm their authors as of the 5th Grenadiers, but their exact position is unknown. This is still more proof that the grenadiers turned left toward the entrenchments.

100. Rawdon to Huntingdon, Aug 3. A berm is a flat space between the ditch and the rampart wall.

101. Per Hunter's journal (see next note). Also in Rawdon to Huntingdon, June 20, 130–31. Rawdon admits the cap was not regulation and he wore it for convenience. As a grenadier, he should have been wearing a bearskin.

102. Ensign Hunter did seek out a surgeon after the victory, though it did not matter. Williams is on Gage's Official Casualty Report as killed. The story comes from the very rare journal of Gen. Sir Martin Hunter, 10ff., quoted more extensively in French, *First Year*, 248.

103. Waller to a friend, June 21, MHS.

104. Ibid.

105. Swett, *History*, 44.

106. Waller to a friend, June 21, MHS, seems to suggests his side was in the redoubt first: "am almost certain that Campbells Light Company, and part of the 47th & 43rd Regts. were the first Troops that mounted the Parapet". Waller says his friend Archy Campbell fell; the only Campbell listed dead on Gage's Official Casualty Report is of the 2nd Marines. So, Campbell's company is of the 2nd Marines and had remained on the British left, not with the light infantry on the rail fence. Captain Laurie [to Lord Dartmouth], June 23, says his 43rd took the redoubt by storm. Undoubtedly they did, coming up the center, but Laurie was with the Corps of Light Infantry and thus busy over at the rail fence. So, although his statement implies his 43rd may have been the first in the redoubt, we must dismiss it as secondhand information.

107. Waller to a friend, June 21, MHS.

108. Stones as bullets: Frothingham, *Siege*, 150, which adds that the "stones, revealed their weakness, and filled the enemy with hope." His source is unclear.

109. Prescott's account, *Proc. of MHS*, 14:72.

110. Ibid. If Prescott did indeed remove his banyan earlier in the heat, he once again had it on.

111. Appendix 17.

112. Account of the battle in *Rivington's Gazette*, No. 120, Aug 3, Frothingham, *Siege*, 397–98.

113. Prescott's account, in *Proc of MHS* (1876), 14:68–78.

114. Burgoyne to Rochfort [1775], 142–54. On Parker: see note 98.

115. Appendix 17.

116. Rawdon to Huntingdon, June 20, 130–31; Burgoyne to Rochfort, [1775], 142–54.

117. Swett, *History*, 47, 53.

118. Appendix 5.

119. All quotes are from Frothingham, *Siege*, 152, citing unknown statements of Elihu Wyman, Anderson Minor, and Colonel Wade. According to Rawdon to Huntingdon, June 20, "General Putnam, who commanded them (and is a very brave fellow), was shot through the thigh, but got off." I have been unable to verify this claim with other sources.

120. Clarke's *Narrative*, in Drake, *Bunker Hill*, 56, gives the story of a sergeant in the 63rd Grenadiers. The 35th Light Infantry Company was led by their senior private, in Dawson, 2:3:368–69.

121. Clinton MSS loose sheet "I was not a Volunteer…" in front of Box 280; Clinton MSS, 10:5, "our opposite Neighbours…"

122. The reinforcement is discussed in appendix 9. Quote: Howe to Gage, June 21, 1:196–98. One wonders if the longboat Clinton crossed with included any of the reinforcement, perhaps the first to cross. Otherwise, who in Clinton's longboat was shot? Rowers? Aides?

123. Several were counted as wounded as of the date of Gage's Official Casualty Report, but see Frothingham, *Siege*, 196n1, citing the *London Chronicle* of Jan 11, 1776, which states only Lieutenant Page survived his wounds.

124. Clinton MSS loose sheet "I was not a Volunteer…" in front of Box 280.

125. Ibid., and Clinton MSS, 10:5, "our opposite Neighbours…"

126. The list of these 31 men, and their fates, are in *New-England Chronicle/Essex Gazette* (one newspaper), Sept 7–14, 1775, p. 3, republished in *NEHGR* (1888), 42:168–69. Williams's journal, June 17, *Discord*, 19, notes that the British saw the Americans "drive off several carts during the action & even before it", perhaps the carts that had brought the entrenching tools.

127. Hide's statement in Dawson, 2:3:379, says, "We sustained our principal loss in passing the causeway." Prescott's account, *Proc. of MHS* (1876), 14:72, gives a similar sentiment.

128. Appendix 5.

129. On Pigot: loose narrative in Clinton MSS, 10:5, "our opposite Neighbours…" On snipers and Rawdon: Clinton to Huntingdon, June 23. The original is not in the Clinton MSS at Clements Library or in the Hastings Collection (which includes the Huntingdon papers) at Huntington Library. It is, however, copied in the "Memoranda" large vellum book (of two books) in Box 286 of the Clinton MSS, 6. The important part is also in a transcription on a loose sheet in the same box. Perhaps historian Harold Murdock had the original (see French, *First Year*, 252n57), but whatever his copy, his was dated June 23 and matches the words in the undated copy in the Clinton MSS.

130. Rawdon to Huntingdon, June 20, Commager and Morris, *Spirit of 'Seventy-Six*, 130–31.

131. See next note.

132. The story is relayed across two letters, beginning in Clinton MSS, 10:5, "our opposite Neighbours…", which ends abruptly but continues in Clinton to [Benjamin] Carpenter, [after June 17, 1775], MSS 10:7. Both are further quoted in French, *First Year*, 252–54.

133. Clarke's *Narrative*, in Drake, *Bunker Hill*, 44. Cf. Kemble's diary, June 17, *Coll. of the NYHS* (1883), 1:44, which says Dutton was killed by a random shot. Time: appendix 2.

134. By nightfall, the troops on guard at the neck are the grenadiers. Howe's General Orders, June 18 (the next morning), in his *Orderly Book*, 3, give that the light infantry are to replace the grenadiers at the advance entrenchment later that evening.

135. Clinton MSS loose sheet "I was not a Volunteer…" in front of Box 280; repeated in French, *First Year*, 254. This was probably one of the 12s from Moulton Hill, not one of the gunboats.

136. Dearborn's 1818 statement in Dawson, 2:3:405. A similar statement is on 418.

137. Prescott's account *Proc. of MHS* (1876), 14:73.

138. Storrs's diary, June 17.

139. Putnam to the Bunker Hill Assoc., Aug 1825, *Coll. of CHS* (1860), 1:241.

140. Howe to Harvey, June 22 and 24, 3:200–24.

141. Burgoyne to Rochfort, [1775], 148.

142. Letter between unknown correspondents, surely written by either Burgoyne or Clinton, probably the former, June 25. It is in the *Manuscripts of His Grace the Duke of Rutland, K.G., Preserved at Belvoir Castle* (London: Historical Manuscripts Commission, printed by Eyre and Spottiswoode, 1894), Report 14, Appendix, Part I, 3:2–3.

143. "Letter of July 12, 1775," in Force, *American Archives*, 4:2:1650–51.

144. Stark to New Hampshire Congress, June 19, 4:2:1029.

145. Both quotes from Lockhart, *Whites of Their Eyes*, 319; also see Frothingham, *Siege*, 209–210.

146. Gage's Official Casualty Report, in Force, *American Archives*, 4:2:1098–99. Note the totals at the end of the list disagree slightly with the actual sum of the numbers given, probably due to those first reported wounded that later died. Cf. French, *First Year*, 256n1, but note French's error in the wounded, which was just 808, or 41 percent not counting artillerymen: Appendix 9.

147. This exact quote comes from Clinton MSS loose sheet "I was not a Volunteer…" in front of Box 280, but the sentiment is repeated elsewhere too, such as in Clinton to Carpenter, circa June 17, 1775, Clinton MSS, 10:7. Various others repeat what appears to have been a common phrase.

148. Gray to Dyer, July 12, 393–95.

149. Murdock, *Bunker Hill*, 75–76.

150. Washington's numbers are reported in his letter to George Fairfax, July 25, *PGW*. Cf. Frothingham, *Siege*, 192–93, which gives both Ward's official estimates and those of Frothingham's original research.

151. Appendix 5.

152. Howe to Harvey, June 22 and 24, 3:220–24.

153. The official letter to the home government is Gage to Lord Dartmouth, June 25, [No. 33], (received July 25) with the Official Casualty Report, in Force, *American Archives*, 4:2:1097–99. It appears also in Carter, *Corr. of General Gage*, 1:405–06, but without the Casualty Report. The other is Gage to Lord Dartmouth, June 25 [Private], Carter 1:406–07. There is a third, of the same date, [No. 34], ibid., 1:407–08, but less relevant.

154. Gage to Lord Barrington, June 26, Carter, *Corr. of General Gage*, 2:686–87.

155. Clinton MSS loose sheet "I was not a Volunteer…" in front of Box 280, in which Clinton claims he had written this quoted detail to Adjutant-General Harvey.

156. Abstract of a letter from…Burgoyne, June 25, 3:224–27.

157. Captain Laurie [to Lord Dartmouth], June 23. Laurie adds, this "cannot be attempted with a less number than 20,000 Men."

158. "Letter of the Provincial Congress", June 20, *JEPCM*, 366. It continued for 24 hours.

159. The ruins of Charlestown are shown in an untitled sketch archived as Charlestown, Breed's Hill, and Bunker Hill in the Clinton MSS Map collection, Map 45, Clements Library call number 4-G-4.

160. Hunter's journal, 12, also in French, *First Year*, 255. Hunter's words are confusing, so I simplified with an ellipsis. It begins in full: "The cries of the wounded of the enemy, Charlestown on fire". He meant the British wounded.

CHAPTER 4: PASSING OF BATONS

1. Henry Hulton, June 20, Hulton, *Letters of a Loyalist Lady*, 99. Most of the source's letters are from his sister, Anne Hulton, but this is from Henry, despite many claims to the contrary.

2. Lister, *Concord Fight*, 43, 33–35.

3. Ketchum, *Decisive Day*, 186.

4. On the camp women as nurses, French, *First Year*, 262, citing some of Gage's orders.

5. Rhoda Truax, *The Doctors Warren of Boston: First Family of Surgery* (Boston: Houghton Mifflin Company, 1968), 42, unreferenced. She claims that circa 1770 the almshouse had just 8 beds. It may have had more in 1775.

6. Dr. Grant to a friend in Westminster, June 23, Dawson, 2:3:361, original cited as in the Upcott Collection at NYHS. His first name per returns in the Gage MSS and Carter, *Corr. of General Gage*, 2:687–89.

7. Waller to his brother, June 22, Nicholas, *Historical Record*, 1:87–89.

8. Henry Hulton, June 20, 99.

9. "Letter of a British Officer", July 5, 13–15.

10. Rawdon to Huntingdon, Aug 3.

11. Clinton MSS, 10:5 "our opposite Neighbours..."

12. Burgoyne to Rochfort, [1775], 191–98.

13. The fates of the 31 men in *New-England Chronicle/Essex Gazette*, Sept 7–14, 3, also in *NEHGR* (1888), 42:168–69.

14. Swett, *History*, 50.

15. Clarke's *Narrative*, Drake, *Bunker Hill*, 51.

16. Howe's *Orderly Book*, 2–4.

17. *Proc. of MHS* (1867), 9:348–50. Warren biographer Sam Forman believes MHS's sword is a fraud, not this sword.

18. "Letter of a British Officer", July 5, 13–15.

19. "Letter of July 12, 1775", Force, *American Archives*, 4:2:1650–51. Frothingham, *Life and Times*, 520, says there were 6 letters, citing an unknown British letter of July 5, 1775. Lovell: letter in Forman, *Dr. Joseph Warren*, 305.

20. General Sumner's account in *NEHGR* (1858), 12:113ff., gives that he was found stripped after the British Evacuation. Clarke's *Narrative*, in Drake, *Bunker Hill*, 50, notes that he saw Warren stripped "soon after" his death. However, French in *First Year*, 263n19, doubts these statements, saying the stories of Warren being stripped are unauthenticated. Laurie [to Dartmouth], June 23, reports nothing of it.

21. Sumner's account in *NEHGR* (1858), 12:119.

22. Laurie [to Dartmouth], June 23.

23. See next note.

24. Warren, *John Warren*, 44–46 (source of quotes, which comes from Warren's diary, June 17, published also in J. C. Warren, *Genealogy of Warren*, 87). Cf. Frothingham, *Life and Times*, 518–19. I have seen some secondary sources claiming that Ebenezer Warren was also with John, seeking out their brother, though no primary sources support this.

25. Various letters in Mercy Scollay MSS; appendix 17.

26. Abigail Adams to John Adams, July 5, *PJA*.

27. *JEPCM*, 356–57. There may be a very distant relation between James and Joseph Warren, but they were

not directly family. Heath's promotion in the stead of Warren: ibid., 367. Heath's later promotions with the Continentals are as difficult to follow as his earlier promotions. See Warren to Heath, June 16, 506–07; *JCC*, 2:103; French, *First Year*, 753–54; and for his earlier promotions, see Beck, *Igniting*, chapter 9, note 55.

28. *JEPCM*, 361, seems to suggest Church was back from Philadelphia on June 19, as he was selected for several committees. French, *Informers*, 172 affirms he was back in time to meet Washington upon his arrival. While he was gone, Benjamin White signed as Chairman of the Committee of Safety on June 18, *JEPCM*, 571.

29. Page's 1778 map *Boston, its Environs and Harbour* depicts various American entrenchments. Cf. French, *First Year*, 265–66. Also, Flick, "Ticonderoga Expedition" essay. Quote from Belknap's journal, Oct 20, *Proc. of MHS* (1860), 4:78ff. Lucy Flucker Knox was the daughter of General Gage's secretary Thomas Flucker.

30. One of several Clinton MSS variants of Clinton's MS Narrative, 1:3, in Box 279, titled "Extract from *Narrative*".

31. Both quotes from Clinton MSS loose sheet "I was not a Volunteer…" in front of Box 280. The underlining as in the original. Clinton's prophecy is very near what happened, though not quite from that hill. (Further commentary: French, *First Year*, 260n11.)

32. Delay given in Howe to Lord Howe, June 22, 147–49: expected to be "to-morrow [Friday] or on Saturday". Laurie [to Dartmouth], June 23, mentions the plan "this night" (June 23, a Friday) to take Dorchester Heights. That they were in their boats: French, *First Year*, 260n10; Williams's journal, June 23, *Discord*, 20–21.

33. Clinton MSS loose sheet "I was not a Volunteer…" in front of Box 280.

34. Ibid.

35. French, *First Year*, 261. The fort can be seen in detail in Frothingham, *Siege*, facing 331, (depicted upside down; the neck is to the bottom of the page). It and the entire network of British and American forts are on the map *Plan of Boston…with its Environs* (Pelham, 1777). The best map is Montresor's *Survey of the Peninsula of Charles Town shewing the three posts…* (Dec 10), the only apparent copy being at Clements Library (Map 4-I-20). Also see a profile *View of Charlestown from Copse Hill Battery* at MHS, reproduced in Barker, *British in Boston*, facing 64.

36. Visible on several contemporary maps, including Pelham's 1777 *A Plan of Boston…with its Environs* and Page's 1778 *Boston, its Environs and Harbour*. For the neck in particular, see Montresor, *Plan of the Neck and Fortifications*, delivered to Gage June 30. Also, French, *First Year*, 322.

37. A full list of promotions is in Clarke's *Narrative*, in Drake, *Bunker Hill*, 58–59, but his list seems incorrect for the marines (see Beck, *Igniting*, appendix 3, for the 2nd Marines). Tupper took command the evening of the battle. Maj. James Short was technically in charge of the marines for a few days after the battle, until he died of the flux. Adair was promoted to captain on July 24 and Pitcairn made captain on July 27, per *LGFO*, 210. They perhaps received these promotions from England and were in the interim promoted to captain-lieutenants, as suggested by Clarke.

38. Gage to Dartmouth, June 25 and July 24, 1:407–08 and 408–09, provide the first and final arrivals of the Second Embarkation, the latter stating they "landed on the 18th and 19th Inst" (see Beck, *Igniting*, appendix 3).

39. French, *First Year*, 308, suggests none but Washington had a uniform. However, perhaps at least General Lee also had a uniform, because he was flamboyant and pompous and would not have wanted to have been outdone by his rival Washington. (As previously noted, Putnam probably had a uniform too, but he was not in the entourage.)

40. See the essays of Batchelder and Anderson, cited below in notes 49 and 50. Cf. Frothingham, *Siege*, 214. While still en route to Massachusetts and just learning of the battle, Washington supposedly replied, "Then the liberties of the country are safe": Frothingham, *Siege*, 157–58n2.

41. Church and Gill: *JEPCM*, June 26, 398, 400.

42. Heath's *Memoirs* makes no mention of attending the arrival of Washington. But on p. 16–17, his entry for the day mentions another British bombardment that morning against Roxbury, a frequent event after the battle. It was probably that skirmish that, keeping Heath and Thomas on their toes, prevented their attending. Putnam may have been there, though we have no source. The selection of Putnam and Ward as major generals is in the General Orders, July 4, *PGW*.

43. General Orders, July 4, *PGW*. The orders refer also to Schuyler, who was stationed outside New York City. The orders do not give ranks for Mifflin or Reed, but they can be gleaned from Edmund Pendleton to Washington, July 12 (Mifflin) and Washington to Lt. Col. Joseph Reed, Oct 30 (Reed), both in *PGW*.

44. On the relative ranks of the generals, see French, *First Year*, 287n26. On the uniform, see note 39.

45. I suppose the commission came on July 8, as it is announced in the General Orders, July 9, *PGW*.

46. "Tradition" is the key word here. See the quotes in Martyn, *Life of Artemas Ward*, 152n17.

47. Ford, *Writings of George Washington*, 3:1–3 notes. More on the houses in Windsor, *Memorial History of Boston*, 3:106–07, 112, or the National Park Service website: http://www.nps.gov/long/.

48. See the essays of Batchelder and Anderson, notes 49 and 50. Also, Martyn, *Life of Artemas Ward*, 152–53n19.

49. Batchelder's essay "Washington Elm Tradition", reprinted in his *Bits of Cambridge History*, 262–63.

50. Anderson, "The Hinge of the Revolution", in the *Massachusetts Historical Review* (1999).

51. General Orders, July 3, *PGW*.

52. Heath's *Memoirs*, 17, does not record Washington inspecting the Roxbury lines until July 5.

53. McCullough, *1776*, 42. Lee was a slave at Mount Vernon and seems to have joined Washington on all of his travels.

54. Provincial Congress to Washington, July 3, *PGW*.

55. Washington to the Provincial Congress, July 4, *PGW*.

56. *JCC* (June 17, 19), 2:97, 99. A convenient list of the generals and staff is in the Gage MSS, filed under July 24, 1775, the English Series.

57. General Orders, July 4, *PGW*.

58. General Orders, July 7, *PGW*. Note Washington had earlier ordered several courts-martial to commence, as listed in the General Orders, July 5 and 6, but none of these were for officers, and none were yet sentenced. Callender was the first of either the officers or men to receive a sentence under Washington.

59. His fate: appendix 5.

60. Washington to Lund Washington, Aug 20, *PGW*.

61. Benjamin Thompson, Nov 4, *Report on the Manuscripts of Stopford-Sackville*, 2:13–18. Thompson is further introduced in the main text later.

62. Steuben to Baron de Gaudy [1787], Friedrich Kapp, *The Life of Frederick William von Steuben* (New York: Mason Brothers, 1859), 698–700.

63. Rev. William Emerson's statement, circa July 4, Sparks, *Writings of Washington*, 3:491–92.i.

64. French, *First Year*, 303, but seen throughout the general orders.

65. General Orders, July 15, *PGW*.

66. Thacher's journal, 32–33.

67. Abigail Adams to John Adams, July 17, *PJA*.

68. French, *First Year*, 283–84, 499 (the last being the source of the quote, from Belknap); Benjamin Rush's assessment from his *Autobiography*, excerpt in Commager and Morris, *Spirit of Seventy-Six*, 276–77; Abigail Adams to John Adams, Dec 10, Adams, *Familiar Letters*, 128ff., and *PJA*. See Bell, "The Real Story of 'Boiling Water'", *Boston 1775*, at http://boston1775.blogspot.com/2013/09/the-real-story-of -boiling-water.html, Sept 27, 2013.

69. The Lee-Burgoyne correspondence is in Force, *American Archives*, 4:2:925–28, 1610–12, 1638–39, with two letters by countrymen remarking on these continuing to 1642. Also in de Fonblanque, *Political and Military*, 160ff. The meetinghouse recommended is Enoch Brown's on Boston Neck. Ketchum, *Decisive Day*, 260ff., mistakenly associates a June 23 skirmish here with the Battle of Bunker Hill.

70. French, *First Year*, 272–73.

71. Anderson, "The Hinge of the Revolution", *Massachusetts Historical Review* (1999), citing Douglas Southall Freeman, *George Washington: A Biography* (New York: C. Scribner's Sons, 1951), 3:484, 509.

72. General Orders, July 26, *PGW*. The riflemen now arriving from the South were especially eager to show off their guns' accuracy, perhaps the source of the problem.

73. French, *First Year*, 272–73; General Orders, July 23, *PGW*.

74. French, *First Year*, 308. Request for hunting shirts: Washington to Continental Congress, July 10–11. The officers' insignias are in the General Orders, July 14. Those for junior officers and noncommissioned officers are in the General Orders, July 23. All are in *PGW*.

75. Letter of July 21, Force, *American Archives*, 4:2:1687.

76. Washington to Lee, July 10, *PGW*.

77. Ibid.

78. Washington to Samuel Washington, July 20, *PGW*.

79. Beck, *Igniting*, appendix 4; appendix 3. A census taken on June 24, given on a list dated Oct 9, Gage MSS, gives 6,247 Bostonians. Some passes were still granted; thus this number would dwindle to 5,389 by Oct 2, per the same record.

80. Washington to John Hancock, July 10–11 (with associated enclosures), *PGW*.

81. The observer's quote is from Benjamin Thompson, introduced in main text later; his full letter of Nov 4, 1775, is in *Report on the Manuscripts of Stopford-Sackville*, 2:13–18.

82. Abigail Adams to John Adams, Sept 10, Adams, *Familiar Letters*, 95–96. (q.v. ibid., 93–94, 102, 105–06ff.)

83. *JCC*, June 22, 2:103; *JCC*, July 19, 2:191; French, *First Year*, 303–306; Lockhart, *Whites of Their Eyes*, 336–38.

84. July 5 petition of Spencer's officers (and following) to the Connecticut Assembly, in Force, *American Archives*, 4:2:1585–1586; Gov. Jonathan Trumbull to Washington, July 13 (Note: there are two such letters!), and the reply (source of the quote), dated July 18, both in *PGW*; French, *First Year*, 303–306.

85. Roger Sherman to David Wooster, June 23, and an excerpt of the reply in note 3 (the quote) of Burnett, *Letters of the Members*, 1:142.

86. General Orders, July 22, *PGW*.

87. General Orders, Aug 14, *PGW*.

88. Anderson, "The Hinge of the Revolution", *Massachusetts Historical Review* (1999).

89. Washington to Lee, Aug 29, *PGW*.

90. Washington to Col. William Woodford, Nov 10, *PGW*.

91. Washington would several times in 1775 petition the Continental Congress for uniform enlistments

across the Thirteen Colonies that had terms for the duration of the war, but his requests were not heeded. The next enlistments would be for the next calendar year alone.

92. Washington to Lee, Aug 29, *PGW*; Sullivan to New Hampshire Comm. of Safety, July 29 [dated wrong, really Aug 29], Force, *American Archives*, 4:2:1755. Early Boston Neck skirmishes in Williams's journal, in *Discord*, 20ff.

93. Jabez Fitch's diary, Aug 15, *Proc. of MHS* (1895), 2:9:45.

94. John Trumbull, *Autobiography*, in Drake, *Town of Roxbury*, 274. I find no formal orders from Washington on this, so it must have been issued by General Thomas or more junior officers.

95. Washington to Lee, Aug 29, *PGW*.

96. A temporary position of surgeon general was not created until 1777: Henry C. Corbin, *Legislative History of the General Staff of the Army of the United States (its Organization, Duties, Pay, and Allowances), from 1775 to 1901* (Washington, DC: U.S. Gov't Printing Office, 1901), 361. Also, *JCC*, 2:209–11.

97. French, *First Year*, 323–24, citing the Annual Register for 1775, *Chronicle*, section 157 (1st ed.) or 170 (2nd ed.).

98. Compare the Reports of the Provisions of the British Army from June 12 and Sept 28, Gage MSS.

99. John Andrews to William Barrell, June 1, *Proc. of MHS* (1866), 8:406–08.

100. Hunter's journal, 13.

101. Newell's journal, Aug 1, *Coll. of MHS* (1852), 4:1:265; italics as in original.

102. "Letter of July 23, 1775", Clarke's *Narrative*, in Drake, *Bunker Hill*, 56.

103. Williams's journal, July 20, *Discord*, 25.

104. Quote: in French, *First Year*, 352.

105. Washington to New York Provincial Congress, Aug 8, *PGW*.

106. Newell's journal, July 23, Aug 15, *Coll. of MHS* (1852), 4:1:264–65.

107. French, *First Year*, 353–56; Tupper to Gates, Aug 3, 4:3:19–20. Gage knew of a plan to destroy this lighthouse per "[Intelligence] Memorandum", May 30, Gage MSS.

108. French, *First Year*, 353, citing Graves's *Conduct*. In my own research, I did not study this portion of the lengthy *Conduct*.

109. French, *First Year*, chapter 23, explains Graves's difficulties in detail, and chapter 24 tells about the start of an American Navy.

110. Letter between unknown correspondents in de Fonblanque, *Political and Military*, 194–99, which French claims is Burgoyne to Lord Germain, Aug 20, his *First Year*, 357n23.

111. Burgoyne to Gage, Aug 13, Gage MSS; Clinton to Gage, Aug 15, Clinton MSS, a more legible transcription in Gage MSS under Aug 26.

112. Gage's report probably reached London by July 26. Quote: Lord North to the King, July 26, No. 1682, Fortescue, *Corr. of George III*, 3:234.

113. Walpole to Sir Horace Mann, Aug 3, Mason, *Walpole*, 252. For other English responses to the battle, see Force, *American Archives*, 4:2:1099–1102.

114. King to Lord North, July 26, Fortescue, *Corr. of George III*, 3:235.

115. Ibid.

116. King to Lord North, July 28, 3:236–37.

117. Ibid.

118. Permanent grade of major general as of May 25, 1772, per *LGFO* (1778), iii.

119. Arnold aboard *Enterprise*: Nelson, *Arnold's Navy*, 54. Allen at Ticonderoga: Allen to Mass. Congress, May 12, Hall, *Ethan Allen*, 79–80.

120. *JCC*, 2:73–74; French, *First Year*, 154–57.

121. *JEPCM*, 717–19; Sparks, *Benedict Arnold*, 24–25; French, *First Year*, 157–59.

122. Arnold, *Life of Benedict Arnold*, 47.

123. Text of the Quebec Act in Force, *American Archives*, 4:1:216–20, which has the Parliamentary debates on it, beginning at ibid., 169.

124. Congress's quote from *JCC*, 1:88. Quebec Act far advanced: French, *First Year*, 399. *First Year*, 145, adds: "Why the English could not also see that an equal liberality toward their own colonists would be wise can be explained only by the human weakness which allows us to grant as a privilege what we will not yield as a right. What the Canadians did not ask was given them; but what the Americans demanded was denied. It is true that in law the cases are not the same, for politically the Canadians were kept in leading-strings. But in the larger view the difference was slight, and in the long run the granting of colonial rights was inevitable."

125. French, *First Year*, 68, 431. June 1 prohibition: *JCC*, 2:75.

126. *JCC*, 2:109–10.

127. French, *First Year*, 378–79.

128. French, *First Year*, 378–79; Shelton, *General Montgomery*, 17–36; Schuyler to Congress, Sept 19, Force, *American Archives*, 4:3:738.

129. Schuyler to Washington, July 18, *PGW*. On Wooster: French, *First Year*, 384, 426.

130. Schuyler to Congress, Oct 5, Force, *American Archives*, 4:3:952; French, *First Year*, 390–91.

131. Schuyler to Benjamin Franklin, Aug 23, Force, *American Archives*, 4:3:242–43; Shelton, *General Montgomery*, 85; Nelson, *Arnold's Navy*, 91. Before now, the Lake Champlain navy was by authority of the Provinces of Connecticut and Massachusetts.

132. On the Indian negotiations: Schuyler to Washington, Dec 15, *PGW*.

133. Intelligence: Major Brown to Montgomery, Aug 23, Force, *American Archives*, 4:3:468; Shelton, *General Montgomery*, 87.

134. See next note. The informant was probably Moses Hazen of Massachusetts who had settled at St. Johns sometime following the last war: French, *First Year*, 759.

135. Schuyler to Hancock, Sept 8, 4:3:669–70; Schuyler to Washington, Sept 20, *PGW*; Shelton, *General Montgomery*, 87–92.

136. Shelton, *General Montgomery*, 92–95. Last quote: Schuyler to Congress, Sept 19, 4:3:738–40.

137. "Letter from an Officer at Isle-aux-Noix", Sept 17, Force, *American Archives*, 4:3:726.

138. Schuyler to Congress, Sept 19, 4:3:738–40; Schuyler to Washington, Dec (reporting from Albany) and July 17, 1776 (the first letter not from Albany), *PGW*; French, *First Year*, 415–21.

139. Shelton, *General Montgomery*, 98–99; Montgomery to Schuyler, Oct 20, Force, *American Archives*, 4:3:1130–33, and cf. inventory, ibid., 1133–34.

140. Carleton to Gage, July 27, Gage MSS.

141. Montgomery to Schuyler, Sept 19, 4:3:797–98; Shelton, *General Montgomery*, 99.

142. Shelton, *General Montgomery*, 99–101; French, *First Year*, 428.

143. Benjamin Trumbull's journal, Sept 21, *Coll. of CHS* (1899)7:137ff.

144. Curiously, there is no statement whatsoever on Brown's failure or alibi, and none of the letters deriding Allen's affair mention Brown. That Brown was to help at all comes from only Allen himself. See next note.

145. Allen's *Narrative*, 14–23; Hall, *Ethan Allen*, 107, 162; French, *First Year*, 422–24. "English-Americans": Samuel Mott to Governor Trumbull, Oct 6, Force, *American Archives*, 4:3:972–74, calls them New Englanders.

146. Quote: French, *First Year*, 424. On blame: Montgomery to Schuyler, Sept 28, 4:3:952; Schuyler to Congress, Oct 5, 951; Washington to Schuyler, Oct 26, *PGW*.

147. Adjournment was Aug 2 to Sept 4, returning Sept 5: *JCC*, 2:239.

148. Stocking's journal, Sept 18, Roberts, *March to Quebec*, 197ff. French, *First Year*, 431–34 (see n40) claims just 10 companies, citing a secondary source which probably in turn cites Sparks, *Benedict Arnold*, 26–27. The General Orders, Sept 5, *PGW*, do not specify the number of musket companies, only the riflemen. Febiger is in Henry's journal, Oct 17, Roberts, *March to Quebec*, 299ff.

149. John Adams to Abigail Adams, June 11–17, *PJA*.

150. Smith and Kiley, *Uniforms*, 59, 82–83. The British primarily used muskets throughout the war, because it was easier to supply one common bullet to the soldiers.

151. See next note.

152. The whole of the story comes from Jesse Lukens to John Shaw Jr., Sept 13, Lossing, *American Hist. Record*, 1:546–50. General Orders, Sept 11 and 13 (the court-martial results), *PGW*.

153. General Orders, Sept 5, *PGW*; William Allen's account *Coll. of the Maine Hist. Soc.*, 1:500.

154. Benjamin Thompson, Nov 4, *Report on the Manuscripts of Stopford-Sackville*, 2:13–18.

155. Instructions to Col. Benedict Arnold, Sept 14, and Address to the Inhabitants of Canada, *PGW*.

156. Gage to Carleton, Sept 29, Gage MSS.

157. Abner Stocking's journal in Roberts, *March to Quebec*, 197ff.; Senter's journal, ibid., 197ff.; Thayer's journal, ibid., 247ff.; Meigs's journal, ibid., 173ff. The number of batteaux is perplexing: Senter for Sept 25 claims just 100 batteaux, and Thayer for Sept 22 claims 100 men dropped off to row them up to Fort Western, seemingly confirming Senter's number. Senter claims each boat could take about 5 people and continues by stating about 600 would march the course. (Senter does agree with the 1,100 total force, in his Sept 19 entry, so his numbers given here make sense.) Meigs, however, says on Sept 20 that it was 200 batteaux, the number French accepts in *First Year*, 432. (Meigs is the source for the batteaux being built in just 2 weeks.) That the journals and Arnold's letters (see following main text) refer to things like oxen being ushered along prove that some did march from the start. Haskell's journal says that he was one who traded on and off, going one day by batteau, the next by foot. Some whole companies would do as Haskell did, exchanging duty daily.

158. French, *Informers*, 178–83. The remainder of this section as cited in note 163.

159. Church's cipher letter: note 161 below.

160. He "kept" the woman, etc.: Washington to Hancock, Oct 5, *PGW*; also Force, *American Archives*, 4:3:956–58. "Girl of Pleasure": Stiles's diary, Oct 2, 1:618–20. Stiles dined with one of the principal actors (Maxwell) and they discussed the details.

161. Church's cipher letter to Major Cane in Boston [c. July 1775] (see bibliography for the translations). More on Cane below, note 165.

162. Stiles's diary, Oct 2, 1:618–19; Oct 23, 1:628 calls Wenwood "her former Enamorato" (inamorato or lover). Bell, "New Study of Dr. Benjamin Church", *Boston 1775*, at http://boston1775.blogspot .com/2013/10/new-study-of-dr-benjamin-church.html, Oct 23, 2013; theorizes she was Mary Butler Wenwood of Marblehead, estranged wife of Godfrey.

163. Washington to Hancock, Oct 5, *PGW* (which hints at the date of Church's arrest, stating "About a Week ago"); French, *Informers*, 183–201; Stiles's diary, Oct 2, 23, 1:618–620, 626–28. Extra minutiae from Bakeless, *Turncoats, Traitors*, 11ff.

164. Ibid., 17.

165. His pleas are in Church to Washington, Oct 3, *PGW*, and in his "From my Prison in Cambridge,"

Nov 1, Force, *American Archives*, 4:3:1479–86. Who Cane was is uncertain. A Lt. Col. Maurice Cane appears on the List of Army Officers, Jan 1, with additions to 1779, WO 64/15, UKNA, (which gives all officers in the Army, not just those in America), but Maurice Cane belonged to the 6th Regiment of Foot, not on station in Boston.

166. Council of War for Oct 3–4, *PGW*. Articles of War: *JCC*, 2:111ff.

167. The dissolution of the Provincial Government is in the *JEPCM*, 501.

168. French, *Informers*, 190–95, citing, among others, Church to James Warren, "October 23", Mass. Archives Coll., 138:321–322. A copy of this letter is in the Miscellaneous Collections of the Clements Library, but seems dated October 3. These two letters are indeed one and the same, for while I have not seen the original at the Mass. Archives, I have a transcription of it, and it matches. (This letter also includes Church's resignation.) On "utterly expel" and "any of the privileges": Mass. House Resolves in Force, *American Archives*, 4:3:1497–98. On if released by the military, to be apprehended: Mass. House Resolves in Force, 4:3:1518. The paragraph-by-paragraph explanation is in Church's From my Prison in Cambridge, Nov 1, Force, 4:3:1479–86.

169. French, *Informers*, 194–96; Adams's quote: John Adams to Charles Lee, Oct 13, *PJA*. N.b. as given in *PJA*: this letter was previously thought to be intended for James Warren but has since been proven as intended for Lee.

170. Paul Revere to Jeremy Belknap [circa 1798], original at MHS, *Proc. of MHS* (1878), 16:371–76.

171. His story and the case against him are in French, *Informers*, chapter 4; his invisible ink letter, ibid., 139–42; his departure to Newport, ibid., 144–45. He remained in Boston until the Evacuation, before sailing to England via Halifax. He fought for the British in South Carolina and New York.

172. French, *Informers*, 198–99; James Warren to John Adams, June 5, 1776, *PJA*.

173. The resolve is in SC1/Series 45X, Mass. Archives Coll., 168:142. Also, French, *Informers*, 199–201.

174. Much of this section from Alden, *General Gage*, 283–86. The same vessel would soon after sail to Rhode Island and then return with Benjamin Thompson.

175. Dartmouth to Gage, Aug 2, 2:202–04.

176. Dartmouth to Howe, Aug 2, and the attached Howe's Commission, Aug 2, as well as Gage to Carleton, Sept 29, all in Gage MSS.

177. Stephens to Graves, Sept 21, 2:724–26; two letters of the Lords Commissioners of the British Admiralty, both dated Sept 29, one to Graves, one to Shuldham, both in *NDAR*, 2:740–43. *Chatham*'s departure in *NDAR*, 2:785. Graves learned of his fate Dec 30: *NDAR*, 3:300, citing Graves's *Conduct*.

178. Gage to Barrington, [Private], Sept 28, Gage MSS. (Note: there are two letters of this date, only one "private".)

179. There are three addresses in total to Gage, one of which is unsigned and appears as if in draft. They are filed under September and October in the Gage MSS. Of the two signed, one has 76 signers, the other 97 signers. Frothingham, *Siege*, 248–49, cites portions of Gage's reply, the original of which I have not found.

180. Gage to Graves, Sept 30, Gage MSS.

181. Gage to Thomas Oliver, Oct 3, Gage MSS.

182. Gage to Dartmouth, Oct 15, 1:421–23.

183. Phillips to Clinton, Jan 1776, Clinton MSS. That Phillips is an artilleryman, Alden, *General Gage*, 283–84.

184. Alden, *General Gage*, 284, 15.

185. Ibid.

186. The letter referenced is Gage to Clinton, Jan 3, 1776, Clinton MSS; also Alden, *General Gage*, 285–

86. On the lasting relationship, perhaps not all good due to a suspected mistress: Alden, 287–89. Regardless, the myth of Mrs. Gage's being a secret rebel spy (see Beck, *Igniting*, 113) seems further debunked by this.

187. Clinton MSS loose sheet "I was not a Volunteer…" in front of Box 280.

188. Howe to Harvey, June 22 and 24, 3:220–224. Italics as in the original.

CHAPTER 5: STRUGGLES OF AUTUMN

1. Montgomery to Schuyler, and "Proceedings of a Council of War", both Oct 13, Force, *American Archives*, 4:3:1097–98; Shelton, *General Montgomery*, 107–08.

2. Schuyler to Congress, Oct 18, 4:3:1093–1095 (source of quotes); Schuyler to Congress, Oct 21, ibid., 4:3:1130–32; Congress's order to Wooster: *JCC*, 3:282–83. Though many letters prior to October refer to Wooster as a brigadier general, it is clear he did not consider himself such, given Schuyler to Congress, Oct 18, and especially given the letter by Deputy Muster Master General Gunning Bedford to the Continental Congress, Aug 30, Force, 4:3:460. The exact date Wooster accepted his commission as a brigadier general was Oct 19: in Schuyler to Wooster, Oct 19, Schuyler asked very directly on this matter, and in the reply, Wooster to Schuyler, Oct 19 (both in Force, 4:3:1107–08), Wooster stated he would accept whatever rank Congress had bestowed on him, but as for his men, which were under Connecticut law, they would continue to be a provincial regiment.

3. Schuyler to Montgomery, Oct 20, 4:3:1132–33; Shelton, *General Montgomery*, 108, 211n33. More on the schooners below, note 17.

4. Montgomery to Schuyler, Oct 20, and Schuyler to Congress, Oct 21, 4:3:1130–33; the articles of capitulation and inventory list, ibid., 1133–34. The 7th Regiment's standard is now at the Museum of the U.S. Military Academy at West Point. It is also depicted at Ron Aylor, *British Regimental Drums & Colours*, http://www.fifedrum.org/crfd/drums.htm, Mar 23, 2003. Additional minutia from Shelton, *General Montgomery*, 109–10.

5. Washington to Schuyler, Nov 5, *PGW*.

6. Montgomery to Major Stopford, Oct 20, Force, *American Archives*, 4:3:1134.

7. Carleton to Lord Dartmouth, Oct 25, Cruikshank, *History of the Organization*, 2:111–13.

8. Schuyler to Congress, Oct 21, 4:3:1130–32; Shelton, *General Montgomery*, 111 (source of the 4th New York's numbers), gives no relevant citation.

9. "An Account of the State of Quebec, etc., at the End of November, 1775", Force, *American Archives*, 4:3:1723–1725 (see ibid., 1725, for Maclean with 80 men, though Caldwell [to Murray], June 15, 1776, suggests 100). Cf. French, *First Year*, 606–07n35, for other resources. Also, see note 93 below.

10. Montgomery to Schuyler, Nov 3, 4:3:1392–93; "Extract from a Letter Dated La Prairie, Nov 3", ibid., 4:3:1343; Ritzma's journal, Oct 31; Shelton, *General Montgomery*, 112–13 (which claims the flotilla was 40 boats, not 34).

11. Ritzma's journal, Oct 29, Nov 1; Montgomery to Preston, Nov 1, 2:114; Shelton, *General Montgomery*, 113–14. "Royals" defined in W. H. Smyth's *The Sailor's Word Book*, 583.

12. Shelton, *General Montgomery*, 114.

13. Montgomery to Preston, Nov 1, 4:3:1393–94.

14. Montgomery to Schuyler, Nov 3; Preston to Montgomery, Nov 1; Montgomery to Preston, Nov 1; Preston's proposed articles of capitulation, 4:3:1392–95. Trumbull's journal, Nov 2, gives more on the back and forth of the articles of capitulation.

15. "State of the Troops..." in Cruikshank, *History of the Organization*, 2:115.

16. "Schuyler's Return of discharged sick Men", Oct 12, Force, *American Archives*, 4:3:1097.

17. Trumbull's journal, Nov 2, 3, lists the spoils, also two Nov 3 reports in Force, *American Archives*, 4:3:1395. Both schooners would serve in Benedict Arnold's navy and fight at the 1776 Battle of Valcour Island (Nelson, *Arnold's Navy*, 113, 168).

18. Washington to Schuyler, Oct 26, *PGW*.

19. Montgomery to Schuyler, Nov 13, 4:3:1602–03.

20. This entire section is an amalgamation of several journals. See note 28.

21. Senter's journal, Oct 16.

22. Arnold to Enos, Oct 24, Roberts, *March to Quebec*, 75–76.

23. Arnold to Washington, Nov 8, Roberts, *March to Quebec*, 84–85, and *PGW*.

24. Enos's court martial is announced in the General Orders, Nov 30, his acquittal in General Orders, Dec 4. He resigned in this letter: Enos to Washington, Jan 18, 1776. All in *PGW*. Cf. French, *First Year*, 438 and n46 (source of the last quote).

25. On 7 batteaux: French, *First Year*, 439, giving no citation.

26. The exact number is hard to determine. Arnold to Montgomery, Nov 8, gives that about two-thirds of the original detachment (of 1,100 men) made it to Point Levi, "most of them in good health and spirits", and in the same letter adds that he now had some 40 Indian recruits. But in his letter to Montgomery, Colvil Place, Nov 14 [15?], he states "his party of five hundred men". If we assume about 500, plus the 40 Indians, this gets us close to the third number Arnold gives, to Washington, Nov 20: "about five hundred and fifty effective men", though this letter also notes about 100 additional sick, thus 650 total (or 500 effectives plus 50 Indians). Later letters suggest he had just 550 before Quebec, so perhaps these 100 sick remained behind at Point Levi or later in St. Roch. All of these letters are in Roberts, *March to Quebec*, 82ff.

27. More on *Hunter* and *Lizard* in Beck, *Igniting*, appendix 5.

28. This entire section is an amalgamation of the several journals written on the expedition, namely, in order of precedence I give them: Senter's, Stocking's, Henry's, Thayer's, Haskell's. Arnold's was also consulted, but gives little additional detail. Supplemental information comes from Arnold's letters in Roberts, *March to Quebec*, 67ff. and William Allen's account *Coll. of the Maine Hist. Soc.* 1:499ff. Cf. French, *First Year*, 431–42.

29. Kemble's diary, Oct 11, *Coll. of the NYHS* (1883), 1:60.

30. The sloops: *Unity* and *Polly*, as given in chapter 1. In Jan 1776, Machias would burn 3 more ships: Colonel Stuart to Lord Bute, Apr 28, 1776, Wortley, *A Prime Minister and His Son*, 76–80.

31. Graves [Orders] to Mowat, Oct 6, 2:324–26; French, *First Year*, 539–40.

32. List of British Ships, Sept 29, *NDAR*, 2:742–43.

33. Mowat to Graves, Oct 19, 2:513–16; Graves's Narrative and Gage to Graves, Sept 4, both in *NDAR*, 2:7–8 (original from Graves, *Conduct*, Sept 4); Graves [Orders] to Mowat, Oct 6, 2:324–26; French, *First Year*, 539–40.

34. "Extract from a letter from Bristol, Oct 8", in the *New York Gazette*, Oct 23, republished in Commager and Morris, *Spirit of 'Seventy-Six*, 170–71. Wallace's squadron can be gleaned from the lists in *NDAR*, such as 1:47 and 3:1008.

35. *Canceaux*'s journal, Oct 6, *NDAR*, 2:326, says *Symmetry* and *Spitfire* were this day embarking troops, while *Canceaux* herself was still moored in Boston Harbor. *NDAR* fails to give the journal entry for the ship's actual departure, but does give the Oct 9 entry, ibid., 2:374, reporting her 3 leagues (17 nautical miles) northwest by north of Cape Cod, or at sea about straight east from the entrance to Boston

Harbor. Thus, without obtaining the actual ship's journals for the day from UKNA, we can surmise she probably departed Oct 7, otherwise the 8th. See next note.

36. *Canceaux*'s journal, Oct 9, *NDAR*, 2:374, states that the ship spotted and chased a schooner. Perhaps this is the same one *Halifax* reported as captured on Oct 11 (see note 44; this journal entry not published in *NDAR*). Some schooner was added to the fleet at least, as 2 statements of inhabitants of Falmouth, both ibid., 2:487–89, reference 5 ships arriving there under Mowat (though the first also mentions a bomb sloop).

37. Mowat to the People of Falmouth, Oct 16 [17?], Force, *American Archives*, 4:3:1171. Despite the date of that letter, *Canceaux*'s journal (Oct 17, *NDAR*, 2:489) gives she arrived on Oct 17, and only then was the letter delivered. Other evidence cited hereafter confirms this timeline.

38. Graves [Orders] to Mowat, Oct 6, 2:324–26.

39. Pearson Jones Deposition, Oct 16 [18?], Force, *American Archives*, 4:3:1152; Sons of Liberty demanding no submission: Letter of Rev. Jacob Bailey, [Oct 17], in *NDAR*, 2:487–88. See also French, *First Year*, 765–66.

40. Quote: Mowat to Graves, Oct 19, *NDAR*, 2:513–16; Mowat to the People of Falmouth, Oct 16 [17?], 4:3:1171.

41. All quotes from the "Report by the Selectmen of Falmouth" in Force, *American Archives*, 4:3:1172–73. No injuries: French, *First Year*, 542.

42. "Report by the Selectmen of Falmouth", Force, *American Archives*, 4:3:1172–73.

43. Washington to Hancock, Oct 24, *PGW*.

44. Mowat to Graves, Oct 19, 2:513–16. Mowat apparently seized 2 schooners and 2 sloops along his cruise, though the 2 sloops were apparently destroyed in gales off Cape Ann while en route back to Boston. The 2 schooners both made it to Boston; one was salvaged from Falmouth, and the other seized by *Halifax* on Oct 11. All this per *Canceaux*'s journal, Oct 19, *NDAR*, 2:516 (see the notes, which refer to other journal entries not published).

45. The Olive Branch Petition (also known as the Second Petition to the King) is in *JCC*, 2:158–62, also in Force, *American Archives*, 4:2:1870–72. This petition was first proposed in May, but it was not until June 3 that a committee was formed to draft it (*JCC*, 2:79–80), and the draft was not debated until July 5 (*JCC*, 2:127). See the impressions on it in Adams, *John Adams Autobiography, Part 1*, "John Adams," through 1776, sheet 19 of 53, page 3–4, *PJA*. The First Petition to the King is in Beck, *Igniting*, 59ff.

46. Suffolk: Bancroft, *History of the United States*, 4:269–70. Delivery of the petition in following main text.

47. Proclamation, Aug 23, Force, *American Archives*, 4:3:240–41. The version I quote, slightly different, from USNA, is online at http://www.archives.gov/exhibits/charters/charters_of_freedom_1.html.

48. Penn arrived in London on Aug 14, per notes in *JCC*, 2:162. Richard Penn and Arthur Lee to John Hancock, Sept 2 (source of the quotes), states they sent the copy of the Olive Branch Petition to Dartmouth on Aug 21. (*JCC*, 2:162, notes, claims Dartmouth did not receive it—perhaps did not read it—until Aug 26.) The same Penn and Lee letter gives that they hand-delivered the original on Sept 1. Penn and Lee's letter was read before Congress on Nov 9, per *JCC*, 3:343, just 4 days before the proclamation was received. (See next note.) Their letter only appears in excerpt in *JCC*, but appears in full in *Minutes of the Provincial Congress...of New Jersey* [1775–1776] (Trenton, NJ: Naar, Day & Naar, 1879), 286. Congress also swore an oath of secrecy on Nov 9, *JCC*, 3:342–43, perhaps given the reply of Penn and Lee. In Britain on Nov 7, the Olive Branch Petition was read in the House of Lords (*PHE*, 18:895ff.), and they afterward determined to examine Penn (ibid., 900ff.), which occurred on Nov 10 (ibid., 910ff.).

49. The copy of the proclamation was sent to Washington by unknown means. He forwarded it as an

enclosure to Hancock, Nov 2, *PGW*, and his letter states he only received the copy on "Monday last", Oct 30. On Nov 13, it was read before Congress (four days after receiving the Penn and Lee letter from London, see last note) and a committee was formed to draft a reply, per *JCC*, Nov 13, 3:352–53.

50. *JCC*, Dec 6, 3:409–12.

51. Force, *American Archives*, 4:6:1, 18.

52. The speech is in *PHE*, 18:695–97, also in Force, *American Archives*, 4:6:1–3, dated Oct 26. This speech is one of the earliest references to explicitly call the various Parliamentary Acts of 1774 the "coercive acts", previously referred to in Parliament as the "coercive measures".

53. King's departure, and so on: Force, *American Archives*, 4:6:3. Quotes: next note.

54. Shelburne's quote: *PHE*, 18:723; Grafton: ibid., 710; Fox: ibid., 769–70 (to which Lord North replied he held the pity and contempt of Fox in equal indifference); Johnstone: ibid., 752. Both of these quotes are from Oct 26 (or into the morning hours of Oct 27).

55. Dr. Price [unaddressed, circa 1776], Commager and Morris, *Spirit of 'Seventy-Six*, 251–52. General discontent in Britain: various letters, ibid., 243–46.

56. Both quotes: Clinton to [Sir John] Vaughan [and possibly Edward Harvey and Benjamin Carpenter], undated [1775], Clinton MSS, 12:48.

57. Colonel Stuart to Lord Bute, Apr 28, 1776, Wortley, *A Prime Minister and His Son*, 76–80. Stuart thought the British should have kept that spot as an outpost.

58. Washington to Reed, Nov 27, 1775; Dec 25, 1775; Jan 23, 1776; and Feb 10, 1776, all four in *PGW*; Colonel Stuart to Lord Bute, Apr 28, 1776, Wortley, *A Prime Minister and His Son*, 76–80. The first citation says a fort at Lechmere was begun sometime before Nov 27, yet Stuart's letter claims the Lechmere fort appeared overnight on Dec 17, contradictory to Washington's letter of Dec 25, which claims the fort was still not done. Howe to Lord Dartmouth, Mar 21, 1776, Dawson's *Battles*, 1:94–96, claims it was completed by the end of January. This is the same geographical point where the British had landed to begin their Expedition to Concord.

59. Nathanael Greene to Gov. Nicholas Cooke, Aug 9, Rhode Island Hist. Soc. Coll. (1867), 6:117–18.

60. Congressional committee conference proceedings in Force, *American Archives*, 4:3:1155–61.

61. Washington to Reed, Nov 8, *PGW*.

62. French, *First Year*, 505–11.

63. General Orders, Nov 16, *PGW*.

64. General Orders, Nov 12, *PGW*.

65. General Orders, Nov 17, *PGW*.

66. Washington to Hancock, Nov 19, *PGW*, gives 966 men.

67. French, *First Year*, 516–19, expands considerably on the nuances of the pay issues.

68. Washington to Hancock, Sept 21, *PGW*.

69. Washington to Hancock, Nov 19, *PGW*.

70. General Orders, Nov 23, *PGW*.

71. General Orders, Nov 20 and 23, *PGW*.

72. Their address is in Force, *American Archives*, 4:3:1666–67.

73. Washington to Hancock, Nov 28, *PGW*, reports 2,540 since last report (see note 66 above), for a total of 2,540 + 966 = 3,506.

74. Washington to Reed, Nov 28, *PGW*.

75. Washington to Reed, Jan 14, 1776, *PGW*.

76. French, *First Year*, 521–22.

77. Marines: *JCC* (Nov 10), 3:348. Gridley's official departure and Knox's selection in *JCC*, Nov 17, 3:358–59. Also, French, *First Year*, 521, especially n40. (See also appendix 5.)

78. Instructions to Knox, Nov 16, *PGW*. Knox's findings in New York were of limited value, per Knox to Washington, Nov 27, *PGW*, though much of the ammunition would come from there.

79. Daniel Morgan's autobiography (incomplete and just a few pages), in Dawson (1871), 2:9:379–80.

80. On the British taking the boats away: Ainslie's journal, Nov 3, Würtele, *Blockade of Quebec*, 16; On Arnold's obtaining boats: Arnold to Montgomery, Nov 8 (20 canoes) and Nov 14 (40 canoes), Roberts, *March to Quebec*, 82ff.

81. Montgomery to Schuyler, Nov 3, 4:3:1392–93; Brown to Montgomery, Nov 8, 4:3:1401.

82. The ships are all named between the two lists in Force, *American Archives*, 4:3:1693. *Maria* is one of the armed escorts.

83. Trumbull's journal, Nov 13; Ritzma's journal, Nov 19–28; Montgomery to Schuyler, Nov 13, 4:3:1602–03; Smith, *Our Struggle*, 1:485–87. (Trumbull's journal, as cited, claims they entered the city on the thirteenth evening.) Terms of surrender: Force, *American Archives*, 4:3:1597–98. There is quite a bit of confusion on the name of the ship Carleton boarded, but while Ritzma's journal, Nov 28, calls it *Gaspé*, many other records call it *Gaspé*. The Admiralty Records *NDAR*, 2:742–43, report only of one *Gaspee*, under command of a William Hunter. Graves to Hunter, Sept 4, *NDAR*, 2:11–12, makes it explicit that Hunter's *Gaspee* is indeed the ship at Quebec. Meanwhile, Carleton to Lord Dartmouth, Nov 20, Cruikshank, *History of the Organization*, 2:133–34, gives in its transcription *Gaspé*. The report of provisions taken from this ship after Carleton's escape, in Force, 4:3:1693, calls it *Gaspee*. We can safely conclude then that *Gaspee* and *Gaspé* are indeed the same ship, with different spellings. Which is the official—that is, which was painted on its stern—is unclear, but it was probably *Gaspee*, since this is how it appears in the Admiralty Records *NDAR*, 2:742–43.

84. Ainslie's journal, Nov 12, Würtele, *Blockade of Quebec*, 16; Arnold to Montgomery, Nov 14, 87–88; Caldwell [to Murray], June 15, 1776.

85. Arnold to Washington, Nov 20, 93–94, and *PGW*.

86. Arnold's letters in Roberts, *March to Quebec*, 85–90, are mostly all dated Nov 14, suggesting the first three, dated from Point Levi, were written late on Nov 14, while the first of his troops were crossing starting at 9:00 p.m. The rest are all dated from outside Quebec for the same day of Nov 14. Most of the journals agree the crossing was on the night of Nov 13. (See French, *First Year*, 605n30.) Major Brown seems to have been in charge at Sorel first (when Maclean was sent scurrying); then Easton was sent (he repulsed Carleton). When the transition happened is unclear. Arnold's letter is generically addressed to the commanding officer at Sorel, which was probably Colonel Easton by Nov 14.

87. Sixty-five percent waning gibbous per U.S. Navy's Sun and Moon Calculator; sunset was 4:14 p.m.; moonrise was 9:42 p.m., based on Quebec City.

88. *Hunter* and *Lizard*; *Providence* and *Fell* may have also been near.

89. Henry's journal, Nov 13.

90. Arnold to Montgomery, Point Levi, Nov 14, and another between the same, dated Colvil Place, Nov 14, Roberts, *March to Quebec*, 85–88; Ainslie's journal, Nov 9, 13, Würtele, *Blockade of Quebec*, 16.

91. Henry's journal, Nov 13–14.

92. Arnold to Montgomery, Colvil Place, Nov 14, Roberts, *March to Quebec*, 87–88 (see the postscript). Details of the capture are unknown, but see Hugh T. Harrington, "The Strange Odyssey of George Merchant, Rifleman", *Journal of the American Revolution* at http://allthingsliberty.com/2013/01/the-strange-odyssey-of-george-merchant-rifleman/, Jan 21, 2013.

93. Ainslie's journal, Nov 14, Würtele, *Blockade of Quebec*, 16; also appendix 14.

94. I have seen no definite number of cannon to report. However, Caldwell [to Murray], June 15, 1776, reports the city eventually mounted an astounding 140 pieces, though they "had not originally above 30 carriages made from the King's ships". What this means is unclear, and when exactly 140 were available for use is also unclear. Some of these, as is hinted in this passage, were off-loaded from the *Hunter* and *Lizard*, as they were useless on the ships, which were either beached or stuck in the frozen St. Lawrence all winter. See Beck, *Igniting*, appendix 5, for hints on the cannon changes for *Hunter* and *Lizard*.

95. Maclean to Barrington, Nov 20, Cruikshank, *History of the Organization*, 2:132–33.

96. The second two letters are in Roberts, *March to Quebec*, 88–90. We must infer the results of the third, as we have no fourth letter complaining of Arnold's man being fired upon. Smith, *Our Struggle*, 2:27–28, has no better information.

97. Montgomery to Schuyler, Nov 24, 4:3:1694–95, claims he had but 800 effectives as he prepared to depart for Quebec. (Some remained as a garrison at Montreal.) If we are to believe the 2,000 number (see note 8), this gives more than half lost. Some who left were sick, taking this logical opportunity to depart. Cf. French, *First Year*, 596 and n5.

98. Schuyler to Congress, Nov 27, 4:3:1681–82.

99. Easton to Carleton, Nov 15, Smith, *Our Struggle*, 1:487.

100. *NDAR*, 2:742–43, gives details for the *Gaspee*.

101. Smith, *Our Struggle*, 1:485–91, which claims the canoe was a small whaleboat; French, *First Year*, 598–99; Schuyler to Washington, Nov 28, 4:3:1692–93 and *PGW*; Shelton, *General Montgomery*, 119–20; number of prisoners taken: Force, 4:3:1694. Caldwell [to Murray], June 15, 1776, reports that it was a birch canoe. *Tourte* was a New France variation of the Classical (pre-Modern) French *tourtre*, generically meaning "pigeon", but used in reference to the passenger pigeon (now extinct), known in Modern French as *tourte voyageuse* or *pigeon migrateur*.

102. Ainslie's journal, Nov 19, Würtele, *Blockade of Quebec*, 17.

103. Shelton, *General Montgomery*, 120.

104. Maclean to Barrington, Nov 20, 2:132–33.

105. Arnold to Montgomery, Nov 20, 90–92; Ainslie's journal, Nov 19, Würtele, *Blockade of Quebec*, 17.

106. Montgomery to Schuyler, Nov 24, 4:3:1695.

107. Both quotes from the same letter (different order): Montgomery to Schuyler, Nov 13, 4:3:1602–03.

108. Shelton, *General Montgomery*, 38–39 passim.

109. Schuyler to Congress, Nov 18, 4:3:1595–96.

110. Schuyler to Washington, Nov 22, *PGW*.

111. Hancock to Montgomery, Nov 30 (the quote) and to Schuyler, Nov 30, Burnett, *Letters of the Members*, 1:263–64.

112. Washington to Schuyler, Dec 24; see also Washington to Schuyler, Dec 5, *PGW*. While Schuyler probably intended to forward to Montgomery a copy of the letter of Dec 24, or at least the sentiments therein, it likely would not have made it in time for the Attack on Quebec.

113. French, *First Year*, 600. Which citation in n14 applies to this quote is unclear, and I have not stumbled upon it in my own research.

114. Ritzma's journal, Nov 28; Montgomery to Schuyler, Dec 5, 4:4:188–190.

115. Montgomery to Schuyler, Nov 19, 4:3:1682–84.

116. Appendix 13. Montgomery to Schuyler, Nov 24, 4:3:1695; Ritzma's journal, Nov 28. Ritzma calls it the *Mary*, but the two lists of provisions taken when the ship was captured (Force, 4:3:1693) call her *Maria*.

117. Henry's journal, Dec 2.

118. Henry's journal, Dec 1.

119. Thayer's journal, Dec 2.

120. Morison's journal, [Dec 2?], Roberts, *March to Quebec*, 534.

121. Montgomery to Schuyler, Dec 5, 4:4:188–90.

122. Appendix 13.

123. Appendix 14.

124. Caldwell [to Murray], June 15, 1776.

125. "Under pain" from the proclamation itself, in Cruikshank, *History of the Organization*, 2:134–35.

126. Caldwell [to Murray], June 15, 1776. Also see Ainslie's journal, Nov 22, Würtele, *Blockade of Quebec*, 17.

127. Appendix 14.

128. Montgomery to Schuyler, Dec 5, 4:4:188–90.

Chapter 6: Desperate Measures

1. Various evidence supports this: Howe's *Orderly Book*, 131; Archibald Robertson's diary, Dec 10, 70; Barker, *British in Boston*, Jan 23, 1775, 22–23, and Dec 14, 1774, 11, etc. Cf. Newell's journal, Nov 16, 24, *Coll. of MHS* (1852), 4:1:270, also in Commager and Morris, *Spirit of 'Seventy-Six*, 149. Newell was in Boston, but the people he describes as turned out of their homes must be those sent off to Point Shirley days later, as described later in main text.

2. Letter sent to England by an officer at Boston, Aug 18, Commager and Morris *Spirit of 'Seventy-Six*, 166–68.

3. Newell's journal, Oct 27, Nov 16, *Coll. of MHS* (1852), 4:1:269–70, but on the Nov 16 entry, see note 1 above.

4. Newell's journal, Nov 19, *Coll. of MHS* (1852), 4:1:270. The Report of Provisions of the British Army, Sept 28, Gage MSS, lists about 79 days' worth of salt pork, 97 days' worth of flour.

5. Washington to Hancock, Nov 28, *PGW*; Newell's journal, Nov 24, *Coll. of MHS* (1852), 4:1:270. Point Shirley is the southern extremity of modern Winthrop, Mass. The date of this expulsion was Nov 24. *Halifax* may have been the vessel; else another load of poor was later expelled by *Halifax*: Graves, *Conduct*, Dec 14, this excerpt *NDAR*, 3:97. See also Report of Provisions of the British Army, Sept 28, cited in note 4 above.

6. Letter sent to England by an officer at Boston, Aug 18, Commager and Morris *Spirit of 'Seventy-Six*, 166–68.

7. Newell's journal, Oct 30, *Coll. of MHS* (1852), 4:1:269.

8. Unsupported tradition claims General Howe spent much time gambling and currying favor with a supposed Bostonian mistress, Mrs. Elizabeth Loring, wife of a Joshua Loring Jr. (to whom Howe supposedly gave several lucrative posts in exchange for his acquiescence). However, there is nothing to support that Mrs. Loring was more than a friend. A single 1778 political poem suggests more, but political slander is hardly proof. Later historians expanded on this, stating Howe lost his military prowess because of the mesmerizing Mrs. Loring—an absurd claim.

9. French, *First Year*, 537.

10. Graves to Stephens, Dec 15, 3:112; Howe's *Orderly Book*, 304, states that he arrived in England on Dec 27.

11. *New London Gazette* (Connecticut), Dec 8, 1775, p. 3. He would not return to Boston until 1777, as a prisoner of the Continental Army.

12. Percy: Howe's *Orderly Book*, 102–03. Smith: ibid., 135; q.v. Beck, *Igniting*, appendix 3.

13. Dartmouth to Gage, Aug 2, 2:204–06. Compare to Beck, *Igniting*, appendix 4.

14. Washington to Reed, Nov 20, *PGW*.

15. Coggins, *Ships and Seamen*, 23–25. Congress had contemplated this new Navy ever since October 5.

16. Ibid. See Instructions to Captain Nicholson Broughton [of the Hannah], Sept 2, *PGW*.

17. Stephen Moylan and Col. John Glover to Washington, Oct 9; "Instructions to Captains Nicholson Broughton and John Selman", Oct 16; both in *PGW*. The citation in the next note gives that Captain Broughton of the Hannah moved to the schooner *Lynch*.

18. "List of the Armed Vessels and a State of Them", signed by Joseph Reed, Oct 29, Force, *American Archives*, 4:3:1251–52. These 6 schooners were (after the *Hannah*): the *Lynch*, *Franklin*, *Lee*, *Warren*, *Washington*, and *Harrison*.

19. French, *First Year*, 497; Washington to Hancock, Nov 11, *PGW*.

20. Washington to Hancock, Dec 4, *PGW*.

21. Coggins, *Ships and Seamen*, 25, also in French, *First Year*, 497, citing William Watson to Moylan, Dec 4, Washington MSS, 21:2682, LOC.

22. See note 18.

23. Washington, not far away from Gloucester, learned of it on Nov 29, per Washington to Hancock, Nov 30. It is in *PGW*, but the enclosures are not; instead, see it plus the list of stores in Force, *American Archives*, 4:3:1721ff.

24. French, *First Year*, 498; complete list of her stores in Force, *American Archives*, 4:3:1721–23.

25. *JCC*, 3:443, spelling his first name Ezek.

26. See note 58.

27. General Orders, Dec 3, *PGW*.

28. Simeon Lyman's journal, Nov 29–Dec 10, Commager and Morris, *Spirit of 'Seventy-Six*, 158–59.

29. Greene to Ward, Dec 10, 4:4:231–32.

30. Trumbull to Washington, Dec 7, *PGW*.

31. Greene to Ward, Dec 10, 4:4:231–32; Washington to Hancock, Dec 4, *PGW*.

32. He fears their coming: Washington to Hancock, Nov 28; the militia come in fast: ibid., Dec 11; Washington is pleased with their service: Washington to Reed, Dec 25. All in *PGW*.

33. French, *First Year*, 465.

34. See the 1777 map *Plan of Quebec and Environs* by Des Barres. On the cannon: Caldwell [to Murray], June 15, 1776.

35. Shelton, *General Montgomery*, 130–31; the letter in Cruikshank, *History of the Organization*, 2:138, which states that a second copy, from which this is taken, was shot with an arrow over the city wall some days later.

36. Carleton to Howe, Jan 12, 1776, 4:4:656; Shelton, *General Montgomery*, 131; Montgomery's letter to the people of Quebec, Dec 6, is in Cruikshank, *History of the Organization*, 2:136–37.

37. Caldwell [to Murray], June 15, 1776.

38. Ainslie's journal, Dec 7, Würtele, *Blockade of Quebec*, 21.

39. Ibid.

40. Caldwell [to Murray], June 15, 1776; Smith, *Our Struggle*, 2:104–05; Shelton, *General Montgomery*, 134–35. The battery's guns are probably those referred to in Montgomery to Wooster, Dec 16, 4:4:288–89, the only reference to the howitzer.

41. Montgomery to Schuyler, Dec 18, 4:4:309–10.

42. Montgomery to Wooster, Dec 16, 4:4:288–89.

43. Or were these the ones Arnold had left at Point Levi?

44. "sensible and concise": Morrison's journal, [Dec 25? 26?], Roberts, 535, which gives the full description of the event. Remaining quotes: Stocking's journal [Dec 31?], Roberts, 562.

45. Montgomery to Schuyler, Dec 26, 4:4:464–65.

46. Schuyler to Congress, Dec 26, 4:4:463–64. How prophetic! Read on.

47. Washington to Schuyler, Dec 18, *PGW*.

48. Montgomery to Wooster, Dec 16, 4:4:288–89. Smallpox: Caldwell [to Murray], June 15, 1776. See also, appendix 13.

49. Meigs's journal, Dec 21, Roberts, *March to Quebec*, 187.

50. Caldwell [to Murray], June 15, 1776 (the quote); Shelton, *General Montgomery*, 138–39.

51. French, *First Year*, 613, note 56.

52. Ainslie's journal, Dec 23, Würtele, *Blockage of Quebec*, 26. Shoveling out the ditches: Senter's journal, Dec 27, and Caldwell [to Murray], June 15, 1776.

53. The disposition is scattered throughout the many journals, but in particular, Senter's journal, Dec 31, supported by Thayer's journal, Dec 30. See also Appendix 13. Wool: see Chapter 7, note 1.

54. Shelton, *General Montgomery*, 141, citing Montgomery to Robert R. Livingston, Dec 17, Robert R. Livingston Papers, NYPL.

55. Senter's journal, Dec 31, is the only one to claim hail.

56. Senter's journal, Dec 31. Maybe they also continued to wear hemlock sprigs.

57. Washington to Reed, Jan 4, 1776, *PGW*.

58. Washington to Hancock, Dec 4, reports 1,300 since last week, last week's being to Reed, Nov 28, which reports 3,500 (hence 4,800 total). A week later they were 5,253: Washington to Hancock, Dec 11. Then 5,917: Washington to Reed, Dec 15. Then 7,140: Washington to Hancock, Dec 18. On Christmas, they were 8,500: Washington to Hancock, Dec 25. At the end of the year, they were 9,650: Washington to Hancock, Dec 31. All in *PGW*.

59. French suggests, in *First Year*, 267, that America could have won the war herself, without the help of France, if only she had fully devoted herself.

60. Beck, *Igniting*, appendix 4.

61. Washington to Reed, Feb 10, 1776, *PGW*.

62. See letter between unknown correspondents in de Fonblanque, *Political and Military*, 194–99, which French claims is Burgoyne to Germain, Aug 20, 1775, per French, *First Year*, 357n23.

63. Burgoyne to Gage, Aug 13, Gage MSS; Clinton to Gage, Aug 15, Clinton MSS, and a more legible transcription in Gage MSS under Aug 26.

64. Perrin, *British Flags*, 96–97; Wilson, *Flags at Sea*, 21.

65. Their arrival and numbers: Beck, *Igniting*, appendix 4; Washington to Reed, Jan 4, 1776, *PGW*.

66. Shuldham's selection to fleet admiral in America (Sept 29, 1775): *NDAR*, 2:740–42; Graves's recall, Sept 29: *NDAR*, 2:740; Graves's response (the quote) in his *Conduct*, Dec 30, the pertinent part *NDAR*, 3:300; change of command, Jan 15, 1776: *NDAR*, 3:794. For the last, see ibid., n2, which gives Shuldham's promotion as Dec 7, but that he would not hear of it until May 16, 1776, Halifax. *Chatham* had departed about Oct 27 (*NDAR*, 2:785), so Shuldham did not yet know of his promotion. Graves was still performing administrative functions in Boston as of Jan 27 (see *Conduct* or *NDAR*, 3:1006). Graves, aboard *Preston*, lingered for fair weather from Jan 27 to Feb 1: his *Conduct*, Feb 1; also *NDAR*, 3:1078–79, which has a letter to Stephens giving the same information (also see *NDAR*, 3:1096). Feb 1 was the same day the British in Boston learned of the Battle of Quebec: Kemble's diary, Feb 1, 1776, *Coll. of the NYHS* (1883), 1:66–67.

67. *JCC,* 3:444–45. (Resolution was on Dec 22, 1775.)

68. Hancock to Washington, Dec 22. Washington acknowledges it to Hancock, Jan 4, 1776, while he notes in his letter to Hancock, Dec 31, 1775, that he had not received a letter from Hancock for some days. Thus, Washington received the letter of Dec 22 later on Dec 31, or between Jan 1 and 4, 1776. All are in *PGW.*

Chapter 7: Battle amid the Blizzard

1. Ainslie's journal, Dec 31, calls them two Royals (brass 5½-inch mortars, firing 24-pound shells), three Cohorns or Coehorns (brass 4½-inch mortars, firing 12-pound shells), and two brass 3-pounders. (Caldwell [to Murray], June 15, 1776, claims seven pieces, all Royals, plus notes the capture of Lamb's piece.) Mortars: Smyth, *The Sailor's Word Book.*

2. Ainslie's journal, Dec 25, Würtele, *Blockade of Quebec,* 27.

3. For the curious, see French, *First Year,* 606n31, on the dubious story, which French himself doubts, that the St. John's Gate, at the front westward wall of the Upper Town, was left open. Smith, *Our Struggle,* 2:25–27, believes the story, but I do not.

4. Caldwell is on special assignment to the American Service per *List of Army Officers,* 1 Jan 1775, with additions to 1779, WO 64/15, UKNA. I found nothing to support the claim in French, *First Year,* 411, that he was a half-pay retired officer. In fact, Caldwell received a promotion to lieutenant colonel in June 1776, per WO 64/15, UKNA.

5. Ainslie's journal, Dec 31, says two; Thayer's journal, Dec 30, says three.

6. Shelton, *General Montgomery,* 143, citing Col. Donald Campbell to Robert R. Livingston, Mar 28, 1776, the R. R. Livingston Papers, NYPL.

7. Shelton, *General Montgomery,* 143.

8. Thayer's journal, Dec 30; Dearborn's journal, Dec 31.

9. Arnold to Wooster, Jan 2, 1776, Roberts, *March to Quebec,* 103–06 (and Force, *American Archives,* 4:4:670–71).

10. Henry's journal, Jan 1, 1776.

11. Almost every reference fails to say which leg. But Arnold reveals it is his left leg in his letter [probably to Hannah Arnold], Jan 6, 1776, Roberts, *March to Quebec,* 108–09 (also in Force, *American Archives,* 4:4:589–60). Senter's journal, Dec 31, gives explicit detail on Arnold's wound and describes how the ball must have shattered before hitting him.

12. Stocking's journal, [Dec 31?], Roberts, *March to Quebec,* 564, says two 12-pounders; Thayer's journal, Dec 30, also claims two pieces.

13. Henry's journal, Jan 1, 1776, claims 30 defenders, as does Meigs's, Dec 31, but Thayer's, Dec 30, claims 60.

14. If grape was fired at Lamb from a 12-pounder, each of the 9 balls was about 2 inches in diameter (see Beck, *Igniting,* appendix 6). Claims that it was grape or canister: Henry's journal, Jan 1, 1776.

15. I have found no number to use here, but as Carleton by now realized the feints were just that, and as Montgomery's approach was lightly guarded, we must conclude that the main city defenders were now all surging to this location.

16. Henry's journal, Jan 1, 1776, 378–79.

17. Shelton, *General Montgomery,* 148–49.

18. The letter attributed to Coffin is in the Royal Historical Manuscripts Commission's Eleventh Report, Part 5, Appendix, *The Manuscripts of the Earl of Dartmouth* (London: Royal Stationery Office, 1887), 406. The argument that the letter is Coffin's comes from French, *First Year,* appendix 46. Additional

detail from Caldwell [to Murray], June 15, 1776 (source of the quote). Caldwell claims just four cannon and a 4-pounder.

19. Grape for a 3-pounder gun was about 1.3 inches in diameter (Beck, *Igniting*, appendix 6).

20. Shelton, *General Montgomery*, 153.

21. French, *First Year*, 615.

22. Henry's journal, [Jan 1, 1776?], 387, describes how he was given permission to help identify the body, and describes how he found the bodies.

23. None of the men who witnessed Montgomery's fall wrote journals. The results are all slightly circumstantial. Where Montgomery was shot comes from Meigs's journal, Dec 31. Henry's journal, Jan 1, 1776, gives the most vivid account, as he was afforded the opportunity to walk the grounds within days after being taken prisoner.

24. Caldwell [to Murray], June 15, 1776.

25. Ainslie's journal, Dec 31, Würtele, *Blockade of Quebec*, 31.

26. Coffin's letter as cited above (note 18); Caldwell [to Murray], June 15, 1776.

27. Caldwell [to Murray], June 15, 1776, and Ainslie's journal, Dec 31, mostly agree and are relied on here.

28. Dearborn's story comes from his journal, Dec 31. The case of his interaction with a British or Canadian soldier parallels one in Caldwell [to Murray], June 15, 1776, though Caldwell claims his opponent was someone in Morgan's company (see note 32).

29. Henry's journal, Jan 1, 1776, Roberts, *March to Quebec*, 379 (the quote); Ainslie's journal, Dec 31.

30. Caldwell [to Murray], June 15, 1776.

31. The confusion is adequately represented in the journals, and it is impossible to accurately discover who was where at exactly when. Anderson issued from a gate in the barricade, per Stocking's journal, [Dec 31?], Roberts, *March to Quebec*, 565, and Caldwell [to Murray], June 15, 1776, states he arrived at "the second barrier which our people got shut just as I arrived", presumably referring to the troops as they pulled Anderson's body back inside. These are the two primary sources of this section, augmented by French, *First Year*, 618–620.

32. Caldwell [to Murray], June 15, 1776.

33. Some of the sources say as early as 8:00 a.m. (such as Ainslie's journal); some say as late as 10:00 a.m. (such as Meigs's journal, in Roberts, *March to Quebec*, 191), others suggest 9:00 a.m. (Henry's journal, in Roberts, 381). (All of these journal entries are for Dec 31.)

34. Graham, *Life of General Morgan*, 103, citing a dubious reference: "Dr. Hill".

35. Senter's journal, Dec 31.

36. See note 1.

37. Arnold to Wooster, Dec 31, Roberts, *March to Quebec*, 102–03 (and Force, *American Archives*, 4:4:481–82).

38. Henry's journal, [Jan 1? or 2?, 1776], 387–88, states "The disgust caused among us, as to Campbell, was so great as to create the unchristian wish that he might be hanged. In that desultory period though he was tried, he was acquitted". I have found no evidence that Campbell was actually tried for anything, and he simply seems to disappear from all reference a few days after the battle.

39. Caldwell [to Murray], June 15, 1776.

40. Carleton to Howe, Jan 12, 1776, 4:4:656. Ainslie's journal, Dec 31, 31, agrees.

41. Caldwell [to Murray], June 15, 1776; appendix 13.

42. See the lists in Roberts, *March to Quebec*, 27–40.

43. Appendix 13.

44. Henry's journal, Jan 1, 1776, 380, 381, and Jan 3 or 4, 1776, 389.

45. Arnold to Washington, Jan 14, 1776, enclosure, Roberts, *March to Quebec*, 113–15; also in *PGW* (version quoted) but missing the enclosure.

46. Shelton, *General Montgomery*, 158.

47. Schuyler to Washington, Jan 13, 1776, *PGW*.

48. Washington to Schuyler, Jan 18, 1776, *PGW*.

49. Lee to Washington, Jan 24, 1776, *PGW*.

50. Ainslie's journal, Jan 2, 4, 1776, 33.

51. Henry's journal, Jan 4, 1776, 389.

52. Meigs's journal, Dec 31, 192.

53. Shelton, *General Montgomery*, 179–81.

54. Congress promoted Montgomery on Dec 9, *JCC*, 3:418; promoted Arnold on Jan 10, 1776, *JCC*, 4:47. These promotions never seem to have been explicitly announced to the selectee. Instead, they simply started receiving letters addressing them at the new rank.

55. In the 1778 Boston oration memorializing the "Boston Massacre", as the war continued to drag on and with no end in sight, Jonathan Williams Austin exhorted his audience, "Let not the ashes of Warren, Montgomery, and the illustrious roll of heroes, who died for freedom, reproach our inactivity and want of spirit, in not *compleating* this grand superstructure [Revolution]; the pillars of which have been cemented with the richest blood of America." In *Orations Delivered*, 114, and Shelton, *General Montgomery*, 168.

56. Washington to Wooster, Jan 27, 1776, *PGW*.

57. Washington to Reed, Jan 31, 1776, *PGW*.

58. Shelton, *General Montgomery*, 162–63.

59. Washington to Hancock, Feb 9, 1776, *PGW*.

60. Hancock to Washington, Sept 24, 1776, Force, *American Archives*, 5:2:488–90. (The *PGW* copy is missing the pertinent enclosure.)

61. Caldwell [to Murray], June 15, 1776.

62. Arnold [probably to Hannah Arnold], Jan 6, 1776, Roberts, *March to Quebec*, 108–09 (and Force, *American Archives*, 4:4:589–60).

CHAPTER 8: A NEW YEAR BEGINS

1. *NDAR*, 3:794.

2. Dunmore's proclamation, Force, *American Archives*, 4:3:1385.

3. Col. William Woodford to the Virginia Convention, Dec 10, 1775, Force, *American Archives*, 4:4:228; Journal of a midshipman on board HMS *Otter*, in Commager and Morris, *Spirit of 'Seventy-Six*, 113–14; French, *First Year*, 575–582.

4. Col. Robert Howe to the Virginia Convention, Jan 2, 1776, Force, *American Archives*, 4:4:538; French, *First Year*, 642–43.

5. There were also troubles in the Carolinas, which I only briefly allude to in the text.

6. Washington to Richard Henry Lee, Dec 26, 1775, *PGW*.

7. See next note.

8. Washington to Reed, Jan 4, 1776, *PGW*. The primary flag on Prospect Hill is the subject of much controversy. For this and reference to the striped flag, see Ansoff,"The Flag on Prospect Hill", in Raven, *Journal of Vexillology*, 13 (2006), 77–100. The date of the actual flag raising is uncertain, but it was clearly before Jan 4 (Washington's letter) and after Dec 31, as just-arrived Shuldham must have

brought the speech. Washington to Reed states they raised the flag on "the day which gave being to the New Army". The Army was officially formed Jan 1, per Washington's General Orders, Jan 1, 1776, which state: "This day giving commencement to the new-army... Every Regiment now upon the new establishment... This being the day of the Commencement of the new-establishment". Thus, despite the controversy on the date (see French, *First Year*, 630n18; various sources in Ansoff's essay), the event was likely Jan 1. The British Union Flag of 1606 was St. George's red cross overtop the white St. Andrew's cross on a dark blue field.

9.   *Mercury's* journal, Jan 20, 1776, *NDAR*, 3:900, also *NDAR*, 3:649–50. Three transports: Graves to Stephens, Jan 26, 1776, 3:992–95. They were: *Glasgow Packet*, *Three Sisters*, and *Kitty*.

10.   Instructions to Major General Charles Lee, Jan 8, 1776, *PGW*.

11.   French, *First Year*, 622–23, 685–86.

12.   MacDonald, *Select Charters*, 391ff. (the actual bill).

13.   Hunter's journal, 13–14 (the quotes); Letter of Jan 9, 1776, Force, *American Archives*, 4:4:612–13; Washington to Hancock, Jan 11, 1776, *PGW*; Frothingham, *Siege*, 287–88; Kemble's diary, Jan 8, 1776, *Coll. of the NYHS* (1883), 1:65. Moon: U.S. Navy's Sun and Moon Calculator gives it was a 92 percent waning gibbous moon.

14.   Council of War, Jan 16, 1776; effectives given in Council of War, Feb 16, 1776. Both in *PGW*.

15.   Enclosure of Knox to Washington, Dec 17, 1775, which gives just thirty-nine cannon including six 12s. The other four 12s were obtained at the last minute, and Knox to Washington, Jan 5, 1776, describes them. Both are in *PGW*. Some of the pieces selected were originally from Crown Point (cf. Enclosure of Arnold to Mass. Comm. of Safety, May 19, Force, *American Archives*, 4:2:645–46). However, Knox's diary, Dec 5–9, 1775, *NEHGR* (1876), 30:323, gives no mention of his going to Crown Point, so they must have been brought down before his arrival. Artillery rounds from New York: evidence in Flick, "Ticonderoga Expedition" essay, for example, Knox to Colonel McDougal [of New York], Dec 17.

16.   Knox to Washington, Dec 17, 1775, *PGW*; Knox's diary, Dec 5–9, 1775, *NEHGR* (1876), 30:323. By land: the narrow and overly shallow waterway connecting the two lakes would have been frozen by this time. Knox's diary references a bridge. Cattle were used, probably to get the guns over the bridge at least: receipt, ibid., 326.

17.   Knox's diary, Dec 9, 1775, *NEHGR* (1876), 30:323. Scow sinks: Knox to his brother William, Dec 14, Flick, "Ticonderoga Expedition" essay.

18.   Knox's diary, [Dec 25?], 26–31, 1775, *NEHGR* (1876), 30:323–24. Horses: see next note.

19.   Knox to Lucy Flucker Knox, Dec 17, 1775, Flick, "Ticonderoga Expedition" essay. Knox to Washington, Fort George, Dec 17, *PGW*, claims Knox "provided [for?] eighty yoke of Oxen to drag them [the sleighs] as far as Springfield". Fort George was at the south end of Lake George, about 50 miles north of Albany. Yet Knox wrote of this plan too soon, as Knox's diary, Dec 27–31, 1775, *NEHGR* (1876), 30:324, gives that the negotiation with George Palmer only then took place in Albany. His diary also reports that the artillery was not transported from Fort George to Albany until after this negotiation (due to a heavy snow, not just a lack of transportation), and thus was indeed brought by the horse-drawn sleighs. (Sadly, a few pertinent pages of his diary are lost.) Thus, contrary to tradition, it seems Knox had few oxen on his journey. Still, his diary (Jan 11, 1776, ibid., 325) suggests Knox remained eager to hire oxen whenever he could, as he hired "two teams of oxen" on Jan 11 alone. Knox's Dec 10 Instructions for their [Artillery] Transportation, in Flick, suggests Knox always expected to use horses, only to discover Palmer's supply of oxen (so when the oxen negotiations broke down, Knox simply

returned to his original plan for horses). Palmer was apparently hopeful to profit on the expedition with more than just oxen: he secured a contract with Knox to build carriages or sleighs for the artillery, but once it was determined there were enough existing sleighs to be hired, Palmer refused to cancel the contract (George Palmer to Knox, Dec 25, Flick). It is unclear which sleighs were actually employed.

20. Knox's diary, Jan 1–4, 1776, *NEHGR* (1876), 30:324.

21. Knox's diary, Jan 5–8, 1776, 30:324–25; "thaw": Knox to Washington, Jan 5, 1776, *PGW*.

22. Knox's diary, Jan 9–10, 1776, 30:325. On the horses and oxen: see note 19.

23. General source for this section: Knox's diary, in *NEHGR* (1876), 30:321–26; also, Flick, "Ticonderoga Expedition" essay. On the date of Knox's arrival, not recorded in his diary, instead: Flick, and French, *First Year*, 656. Quote: Knox to Washington, Dec 17, 1775, *PGW*.

24. Washington to Reed, Jan 23 and Feb 10, *PGW*.

25. All quotes: Washington to Reed, Feb 26 [to Mar 9], 1776, *PGW*.

26. Council of War, Feb 16, 1776, *PGW*.

27. Building of batteries, and British aware of the coming attack: Colonel Stuart to Lord Bute, Apr 28, 1776. Mission to Dorchester: Howe to Dartmouth, Mar 21, 1776, Dawson, *Battles*, 1:94–96. (The date Howe gives is Feb 13, *before* Washington's war council.)

28. French, *First Year*, 654.

29. It is strange there are no war council records in *PGW* after Feb 16, leading up to the fortification of Dorchester Heights.

30. See Pelham's 1777 *Boston and its Environs* map, but note its orientation to north as marked. Additional details from Page's 1775 *Boston, its Environs* map, though it is less accurate in its topography and mislabels Foster's Hill. The hill it calls Dorchester Hill is Foster's Hill. It does, however, depict the town of Dorchester. Additional details from *Record of the Streets...of Boston*, 157, 310, 425, 467.

31. Rev. William Gordon to Samuel Wilson, Apr 6, 1776, Commager and Morris, *Spirit of 'Seventy-Six*, 177–79.

32. French, *First Year*, 656: the idea was proposed by Col. Rufus Putnam, who had been instrumental in the fortification of the Roxbury lines. Also see McCullough's *1776: The Illustrated Edition*, 90.

33. Washington to Ward, Mar 3, 1776, *PGW*.

34. Lt. Samuel Webb's journal [of the Continental Army], Mar 1, 1776, Commager and Morris, *Spirit of 'Seventy-Six*, 176–77.

35. Cutting a trench: Webb's journal, Mar 1, 1776, Commager and Morris, *Spirit of 'Seventy-Six*.

36. Washington to Hancock, Mar 7–9, 1776, *PGW*. On the signals: John Sullivan to John Adams, Mar 15–19, 1776, *Proc. of MHS* (1876), 14:283–85.

37. Washington to Hancock, Mar 7–9, 1776, *PGW*.

38. Howe to Dartmouth, Mar 21, 1776. Cf. Stuart to Bute, Apr 28, 1776, which claims one shot killed 8 men of the 22nd.

39. Washington to Hancock, Mar 7–9, 1776, *PGW*. Thomas claims these are the only 2 killed in the whole affair, in Thomas to Mrs. [Hannah] Thomas, Mar 9, 1776, Coffin, *Life of Major General Thomas*, 20–21.

40. Washington to Hancock, Mar 7–9, 1776, *PGW*.

41. Stuart to Bute, Apr 28, 1776.

42. Gordon to Wilson, Apr 6, 1776, gives: "It was hazy below so that our people could not be seen, tho' it was a bright moon light night above on the hills." U.S. Navy's Sun and Moon Calculator gives the moon was 100 percent full at 4:33 a.m. on Mar 5, 1776 for Boston. Sunset on Mar 4 was at 5:39 p.m., end of civil twilight was at 6:07 p.m.

43. Washington to Ward, Mar 3, 1776, *PGW*, recommended these points, and it is reasonable to believe this plan was the one followed. Gordon to Wilson, Apr 6, 1776, mostly agrees.

44. Thomas to Mrs. [Hannah] Thomas, Mar 9, 1776, Coffin, *Life of Major General Thomas*, 20–21; Gordon to Wilson, Apr 6, 1776, which claims 300 wagons.

45. Washington to Ward, Mar 3, 1776, *PGW*.

46. Robertson's diary, Mar 4, 1776, 73. The lieutenant colonel is identified as Campbell of the 22nd, ibid., 74.

47. The quote is Allen French, from *First Year*, 659. That Howe did not receive the information is supported by his response the following day.

48. Gordon to Wilson, Apr 6, 1776.

49. Dawn was 6:12 a.m., per the U.S. Navy's Sun and Moon Calculator. Civil twilight began at 5:44 a.m.. On the relief: French, *First Year*, 660, unreferenced. Six thousand provincials at dawn: see next note.

50. Howe to Dartmouth, Mar 21, 1776, claims three forts. He wrote the letter more than two weeks later. Was he counting the third fort built on Foster's Hill days later? No other reference supports three forts on the first day. The "majick" quote and the opening of embrasures is from Stuart to Bute, Apr 28, 1776. Stuart counted 6,000 provincials at dawn, feasible if the original 3,000 did not accept relief by the 3,000 that came early morning.

51. John Sullivan to John Adams, Mar 15–19, 1776, *Proc. of MHS* (1876), 14:283–85.

52. See the journals of HMS *Centurion* and *Chatham NDAR*, 4:192, 4:211–12. Neither reports opening fire.

53. Gordon to Wilson, Apr 6, 1776.

54. Howe to Dartmouth, Mar 21, 1776.

55. Gordon to Wilson, Apr 6, 1776.

56. Ibid.; appendix 15. Some contemporary American letters believed it was Lord Percy who was to lead the attack (such as Sullivan to Adams, Mar 15–19, 1776, 14:283–85), but this is unsupported by British sources. More on this: French, *First Year*, 770.

57. Appendix 9.

58. Beck, *Igniting*, appendix 4.

59. Lechmere's Point: Sullivan to Adams, Mar 15–19, 1776, 14:283–85. The claim is that Lord Percy saw them. Defending Boston: Howe to Clinton, Mar 21, 1776, Clinton MSS.

60. Robertson's diary, Mar 5, 1776, 74–75.

61. Gordon to Wilson, Apr 6, 1776.

62. Thomas to Mrs. [Hannah] Thomas, Mar 9, 1776, Coffin, *Life of Major General Thomas*, 20–21. Were these 2,000 among the 6,000 Colonel Stuart counted earlier? See note 50.

63. Timeline: Appendix 15. The transports were: *Goodintent*, *Sea Venture*, *Venus*, *Spy*, and *Success*, listed in the Morning Orders, Mar 5, 1776, Howe's *Orderly Book*, 225.

64. Gordon to Wilson, Apr 6, 1776.

65. Washington to Hancock, Mar 7–9, 1776, *PGW*.

66. Appendix 15.

67. Stuart to Bute, Apr 28, 1776; appendix 15.

68. Hunter's journal, 14–15.

69. Stuart to Bute, Apr 28, 1776.

70. Hunter's journal, 14–15.

71. Gordon to Wilson, Apr 6, 1776.

72. Timothy Newell's journal, Mar 5, 1776, *Coll. of MHS* (1852), 4:1:272.

73. Gordon to Wilson, Apr 6, 1776.

74. Hunter's journal, 14–15.

75. Washington to Hancock, Mar 7–9, 1776, *PGW*.

76. Stuart to Bute, Apr 28, 1776.

77. Howe to Dartmouth, Mar 21, 1776.

78. Stuart to Bute, Apr 28, 1776.

79. Howe to Dartmouth, Mar 21, 1776.

80. Ibid.

81. On the ships: Shuldham to Stephens, Mar 17, 1776, 4:381–82. The five transports used for the intended landing of troops against Dorchester Heights may have also been employed, though nothing more is said of them. On the vessels employed: appendix 16.

82. Quote: "the want of which…", Howe to Dartmouth, Mar 21, 1776, Washington to Reed, Mar 19, 1776, *PGW*; Quote: "Notorious Rebel Hancock", Shuldham to Stephens, Mar 17, 1776, 4:381–82. Howe's letter mentions the wool, and Robertson's diary, Mar 6, 1776, 75, claims he made the suggestion, via his boss, Capt. John Montresor.

83. French, *First Year*, 666–67, 672–73.

84. Barker, Mar 10, 1776, *British in Boston*, 71.

85. Gordon to Wilson, Apr 6, 1776.

86. Stuart to Bute, Apr 28, 1776.

87. Ibid.; Robertson's diary, Mar 9, 1776, 76.

88. Washington to Hancock, Mar 7–9, 1776, *PGW*.

89. Barker, Mar 5–17, 1776, *British in Boston*, 70–72; Robertson's diary, Mar 6–17, 1776, 75–80. Also Washington to Hancock, Mar 7–9, 1776, and Mar 13, *PGW*.

90. Washington to Hancock, Mar 7–9, 1776, *PGW*.

91. Morning Orders, Mar 11, 1776, Howe's *Orderly Book*, 231.

92. Shuldham to Stephens, Mar 17, 1776, 4:381–82. King's Roads is now President Roads, and is north of Long Island (Massachusetts).

93. Stuart to Bute, Apr 28, 1776.

94. Quote: French, *First Year*, 665.

95. Hunter's journal, 14–15 (the quote); Howe to Dartmouth, Mar 21, 1776. Despite the former source's claim, Adair was promoted to captain on July 24, 1775, per *LGFO*, 210.

96. Robertson's diary, Mar 17, 1776, 79–80.

97. Howe to Dartmouth, Mar 21, 1776.

98. Beck, *Igniting*, appendix 4; French, *First Year*, 672 (the source of the other statistics; I disregard his troop numbers); ibid., 675.

99. Vessels employed in the evacuation: appendix 16. It is unclear which ship Howe and his staff were on prior to their coming aboard *Chatham*, but compare *Chatham*'s logs to those of *Fowey*, *NDAR*, 4:382–84.

100. See multiple journal entries for *Fowey*, *Centurion*, and *Chatham*, *NDAR*, 4:382–84, 447.

101. Coffin, *Life of Major General Thomas*, 24, claims General Thomas was there, though he was immediately ordered to Canada with a promotion, given in *JCC* (Mar 6, 1776), 4:186.

102. McCullough, *1776*, 105, claims Ward marched in first at the head of 500 men, without reference. (His only reference does not provide support.) McCullough was probably citing French, *First Year*, 671, also unreferenced, but *First Year* does not quantify the men as 500. I have never uncovered proof that Ward was the first to enter, only Putnam, at the head of 1,000, per Washington to Hancock, Mar 19, 1776,

PGW. Cf. Timothy Newell's journal, Mar 17, 1776, *Coll. of MHS* (1852), 4:1:275–76, which claims 2,000 entered under Putnam, and that they entered the next day. Newell tells that Ward interacted with the Boston selectmen at the Roxbury lines, but does not claim Ward entered the town. Perhaps it is tradition? After all, how fitting would it be to have had the Massachusetts general enter Boston first!

103. French, *First Year*, 671, citing various sources.

104. All quotes: Washington to Reed, Mar 19, 1776, *PGW*.

105. Sullivan to Adams, Mar 15–19, 1776, 14:283–85.

106. Samuel Cooper to Benjamin Franklin, [Mar 17, 1776], *NDAR*, 4:380, and *PBF*.

107. Washington to Reed, Mar 19, 1776, *PGW*. The full military inventory, including that which was useless, is *NDAR*, 4:445–46.

108. Washington to Hancock, Mar 19, 1776, *PGW*. More anecdotes on Boston fortifications in John Warren's diary, Mar 17, 1776, J. C. Warren's *Genealogy of Warren*, 95–96.

109. Robertson's diary, Mar 18–20, 1776, 80–81 (see plate 25 for a sketch of the Castle's destruction, appearing after 242). Howe to Dartmouth, Mar 21, 1776, mentions it without particulars, but *Chatham*'s journal, Mar 20, 1776, *NDAR*, 4:447, gives more detail. Also, Washington to Hancock, Mar 24, 1776, *PGW*.

110. Both quotes: Washington to Reed, Mar 19, 1776, *PGW*.

111. Appendix 16.

112. Washington to Hancock, Mar 27, 1776, *PGW*.

113. Beck, *Igniting*, appendix 3. But there were other troops in the backcountry, so the modern U.S. was not devoid of troops (see Gage to Barrington, July 21, Enclosure, 2:689–91). Additionally, the Port of Boston had been closed for just under two years, but with the Evacuation of Boston, was now reopened.

114. Timothy Newell's journal, Mar 17, 1776, *Coll. of MHS* (1852), 4:1:275–76.

EPILOGUE

1. Frothingham, *Life and Times*, 522, gives the date.

2. *NEHGR* (1858), 12:113ff.; quote: ibid., 119, by William Sumner, an interested party but not an eyewitness. I thank J. L. Bell for leading me to this source.

3. J. C. Warren, *Genealogy*, 47. Whether the eyetooth was the false tooth, or whether the false tooth was secured to it by the wire is unclear.

4. Frothingham, *Life and Times*, 523. Washington, also a Freemason, left for New York on April 4 (before the funeral), per General Orders, Apr 3 and 4, 1776, *PGW*.

5. Frothingham, *Life and Times*, 523ff.; various letters in Mercy Scollay MSS; appendix 17.

6. Benjamin Franklin to William Franklin [Journal of Negotiations in London], Mar 22, 1775, *PBF* (21:540). Cf. the Intelligence, May 12, 1775, Gage MSS, which reports, in response to the Concord Expedition: "Doctr Franklin has sent an Express to the [Mass.] Provincial Congress Approving of their Conduct... Assuring them...that now is the time to Declare for Independance". The source of the intelligence is unknown, and if Franklin really said this, no other evidence exists to confirm it. It seems false.

7. Commager and Morris, *Spirit of 'Seventy-Six*, 272.

BIBLIOGRAPHY

On endnotes in this volume: Any letter, diary entry, or other source given without a year should be assumed to be of the year 1775, unless context clues suggest otherwise.

On sources: Letters are cited in the format of author to recipient, place, date, in source. I only include place when it provides clarity. Likewise, personal diaries and journals are cited in the format author's journal, date of entry, in source. However, if the letter or journal is one I cite frequently, I generally do not give its source in the endnotes, but instead list those key letters or journals explicitly here in the bibliography, and only here include its full citation. But even in these cases, I sometimes also specify the source in the endnotes when it provides clarity, particularly in lengthy letters and journal entries.

On style: For all quotes of original written documents, which are the majority of those in this volume, I have retained all spelling and grammar errors and have mostly left the abbreviations and punctuation as in the original, except where necessary for clarity. However, I have at times slightly modified quotes first uttered as spoken words that were later recorded in letters, correcting punctuation and misspellings only in these instances and only for clarity. In doing so, I have on very rare instances found it necessary to correct the tenses and pronoun choices of some of the words used. In these rare cases, or in any other departure from the original, I have described my changes in the related endnotes.

Lastly, I employ the "logical quotation" style. That is, I have carefully transcribed all written quotations such that any punctuation included within the quotation was there in the original. (So, "quotation," indicates the comma was in the original, while "quotation", indicates there was no comma in the original, usually because I ended my quote mid-sentence of the original.) While I generally follow the Chicago Manual of Style (CMOS), this quotation style is from the Council of Science Editors (CSE) Scientific Style and Format. The only exception to logical quotations is in adding punctuation (per CMOS) to article names in full citations, as listed in this bibliography.

Archives

Citations to the Evans Collection refer to the massive microform collection available at most research libraries and also online in the Archive of Americana database by Readex.

Adams Papers. Digital Edition. Massachusetts Historical Society, Boston. http://www.masshist.org /publications/apde2/ Formerly titled *Founding Families: Digital Editions of the Papers of the Winthrops and the Adamses*.

Clinton, Henry. Papers. University of Michigan William L. Clements Library, Ann Arbor, MI.

Franklin, Benjamin. Papers. Yale University, New Haven, CT. http://www.franklinpapers.org.

Gage, Thomas. Papers. University of Michigan William L. Clements Library, Ann Arbor, MI.

Scollay, Mercy. Papers. Cambridge Historical Society, Cambridge, MA.

Sparks, Jared. Papers. Harvard University Archives, Cambridge, MA.

Thomas, John. Papers. Massachusetts Historical Society, Boston.

Warren, Joseph. Papers. Massachusetts Historical Society, Boston.

Washington, George. Papers. University of Virginia, Charlottesville, VA. http://rotunda.upress .virginia.edu/founders/GEWN.html. Note: As of this writing, one can gain free access via the Mount Vernon website. Many of the originals in the George Washington MSS at LOC are at http://lcweb2.loc.gov/ammem/gwhtml/gwhome.html.

Primary Sources
Almanacs (and Calculators)

George, Daniel, ed. *George's Cambridge Almanack, or, The Essex Calendar for the Year of Our Lord 1776*. Salem, MA: E. Russell, 1775. Evans Microfilm, 14062. Reprinted with Joseph Warren Memorial. Salem, MA: E. Russell, 1775. Evans Microfilm, 14063. No other years seem to exist for this almanac.

Gleason, Ezra, ed. *Bickerstaff's New England Almanack for the Year of Our Lord 1776*. Newburyport, MA: Mycall and Tinges, 1775. Evans Microfilm, 14066.

Thomas, Isaiah, ed. *Thomas's Boston Almanack for the Year of Our Lord 1775*. Boston: Isaiah Thomas, 1774. Evans Microfilm, 42711. No other years seem to exist for this almanac.

U.S. Navy's Sun and Moon Calculator website. http://aa.usno.navy.mil/data/docs/RS_OneDay.php Note: All times given throughout this volume are in Eastern Standard Time.

West, Benjamin, ed. *Bickerstaff's Boston Almanack for 1775*. Boston: Mills & Hicks, 1774. Evans Microfilm, 13763.

Books and Articles (of Primary Source Material and Letters)

Adams, John. *Familiar Letters of John Adams and His Wife Abigail Adams, During the Revolution*. Edited by Charles Francis Adams. New York: Hurd and Houghton, 1876.

———. *The Works of John Adams, Second President of the United States*. 10 vols. Edited by Charles Francis Adams. Boston: Little, Brown and Co., 1850–56.

Burnett, Edmund C., ed. *Letters of the Members of the Continental Congress.* Vol. 1, *Aug 29, 1774–July 4, 1776.* Washington, DC: Carnegie Institution, 1921.

Carter, Clarence Edwin, ed. *The Correspondence of General Thomas Gage with the Secretaries of State and with the War Office and the Treasury 1763–1775.* New Haven: Yale University Press, 1931–33.

Clark, William Bell, William James Morgan, and Michael J. Crawford, eds. *Naval Documents of the American Revolution.* 11 vols. Washington, DC: Naval History Division, Dept. of the Navy, 1964.

Clarke, Lt. John. *An Impartial and Authentic Narrative*: See Letters, Bunker Hill.

Cobbett, William, John Wright, and Thomas Curson Hansard, eds. *The Parliamentary History of England from the Earliest Period to the Year 1803.* Vols. 16–18. London: T. C. Hansard, 1813.

Commager, Henry Steele and Richard B. Morris, eds. *The Spirit of 'Seventy-Six.* Edison, NJ: Castle Books, 2002. First published 1958 by Harper Collins.

Dawson, Henry B., ed. *The Historical Magazine.* Morrisania, NY: Dawson, various dates. Note: all generic citations to Dawson refer here.

Donne, William Bodham, ed. *The Correspondence of King George the Third with Lord North from 1768 to 1783.* 2 vols. London: John Murray, 1867.

Force, Peter. *American Archives.* 4th ser., 6 vols. Washington, DC: M. St. Clair Clarke and Peter Force, 1837–1846.

Ford, Worthington Chauncey, ed. *British Officers Serving in the American Revolution, 1774–1783.* Brooklyn, NY: Historical Printing Club, 1897.

———. *Journals of the Continental Congress.* Vols. 1–4. Washington, DC: Government Printing Office, 1904.

———. *The Writings of George Washington.* Vol. 3, *1775–1776.* New York: G. P. Putnam's Sons, 1889.

Fortescue, John William, ed. *The Correspondence of King George the Third from 1760 to December 1783.* Vol. 3, *July 1773–Dec 1777.* London: Macmillan and Co., 1927–28.

Great Britain War Office. *A List of the General and Field Officers…of the Officers in the several Regiments of Horse, Dragoons, and Foot…Artillery…Engineers…Marines…* London: War Office, 1778. Later editions titled *A List of the Officers of the Army and of the Corps of Royal Marines.*

Hulton, Anne. *Letters of a Loyalist Lady.* Edited by Harold Murdock and "C. M. T." Cambridge, MA: Harvard University Press, 1927.

Kennedy, John Pendleton, ed. *Journals of the House of Burgesses of Virginia.* Vol. 13, *1773–1779.* Richmond, VA: 1905.

Mason, Alfred Bishop, ed. *Horace Walpole's England as His Letters Picture It.* Boston: Houghton Mifflin Company, 1930.

Massachusetts Provincial Congress. *The Journals of Each Provincial Congress of Massachusetts in 1774 and 1775.* Boston: Dutton and Wentworth, Printers to the State, 1838.

Prescott, Judge. "Account of the Battle of Bunker Hill": See Letters, Bunker Hill.

Roberts, Kenneth, ed. *March to Quebec: Journals of the Members of Arnold's Expedition.* New York: Doubleday, Doran & Company, Inc., 1938.

Scull, Gideon Delaplaine, ed. *The Montresor Journals.* In *Collections of the New York Historical Society for the year 1881.* Publications Fund Series. Vol. 14. New York: NY Historical Society, 1882.

Sparks, Jared. *Life and Treason of Benedict Arnold*: See Secondary Sources.

————. *The Writings of George Washington*. Vol. 3. Boston: American Stationers' Company, 1837.

Wortley, E. Stuart, ed. *A Prime Minister and His Son*. New York: E. P. Dutton and Company, 1925.

Würtele, Fred C, ed. *Blockade of Quebec in 1775–1776 by the American Revolutionists*. Quebec: Daily Telegraph Job Printing House, 1905. Contains the Thomas Ainslie journal.

Collections and Proceedings of Societies and Archives
A partial list, various volumes of each as cited throughout the endnotes:

Bunker Hill Monument Association. *Proceedings of the Bunker Hill Monument Association at the Annual Meeting*. Boston: Published by the Association, June 17, 1907.

Connecticut Historical Society. *Collections of the Connecticut Historical Society*. Vol. 1. Hartford, CT: Printed for the Society, 1860.

Historical Manuscripts Commission (Britain). *Report on the Manuscripts of the Late Reginald Rawdon Hastings, Esq., of the Manor House, Ashby de la Zouche*. 4 vols. London: Historical Manuscripts Commission, 1928–1947.

————. *Report on the Manuscripts of Mrs. Stopford-Sackville*, 2 vols. London: Historical Manuscripts Commission, 1904.

Maine Historical Society. *Collections of the Maine Historical Society*. Vol. 1. Edited by William Willis. Portland, ME: Bailey & Noyes, 1831. Reprinted 1865.

Massachusetts Historical Society. *Collections of the Massachusetts Historical Society*. Boston: Mass. Hist. Soc., various volumes, as cited.

————. *Proceedings of the Massachusetts Historical Society*. Boston: Mass. Hist. Soc., various volumes, as cited.

New England Historic Genealogical Society. *New England Historical and Genealogical Register*. Boston: Samuel G. Drake, various volumes, as cited.

Peabody Essex Museum (formerly the Essex Institute). *Essex Institute Historical Collections*. Salem, MA: Essex Institute, various volumes, as cited.

Journals, Diaries, and Autobiographies (Personal)
Ships' journals (logs) are not listed here, but are as cited throughout the endnotes.

Adams, John: See Archives, Adams Papers.

Ainslie, Thomas. "Journal of the Most Remarkable Occurrences in the Province of Quebec from the Appearance of the Rebels in September 1775 until Their Retreat on the Sixth of May 1776," in Würtele, *Blockade of Quebec*, 9ff.: See Primary Sources, Books.

Allen, Ethan. *Narrative of Ethan Allen*. Bedford, MA: Applewood Books, 1989. First published in 1779.

Arnold, Benedict. In Roberts, *March to Quebec*, 45ff.: See Primary Sources, Books.

Barker, John. *The British in Boston—The Diary of Lt. John Barker*. Edited by Elizabeth Ellery Dana. Cambridge, MA: Harvard University Press, 1924. First published in part in *Atlantic Monthly*, 1877.

Dearborn, Henry. In Roberts, *March to Quebec*, 129ff.: See Primary Sources, Books.

Edes, Peter. In Boardman, *Peter Edes*: See Secondary Sources.

Farnsworth, Amos. In *Proceedings of the Massachusetts Historical Society.* 2nd ser., vol. 12, *1896–1899*, 78–102. Boston, Massachusetts Historical Society, 1899.

Fitch, Jabez. "Diary of Captain Jabez Fitch." In *Proceedings of the Massachusetts Historical Society*, 2nd ser., vol. 9, *1894–1895*, 41ff. Boston, Massachusetts Historical Society, 1895.

Franklin, Benjamin: See Archives, Franklin Papers.

Haskell, Caleb. In Roberts, *March to Quebec*, 459ff.: See Primary Sources, Books. Also published separately as *Caleb Haskell's Diary, May 5, 1775–May 30, 1776*. Edited by Lorthrup Withington. Newburyport, MA: William H. Huse and Company, 1881.

Heath, William. *Memoirs of Major-General William Heath By Himself.* Edited by William Abbatt. New York: William Abbatt, 1901.

Henry, John Joseph. In Roberts, *March to Quebec*, 299ff.: See Primary Sources, Books. Also published separately as *Account of Arnold's Campaign against Quebec and of the Hardships and Sufferings of That Band of Heroes Who Traversed the Wilderness of Maine from Cambridge to the St. Lawrence in the Autumn of 1775*. Albany, NY: Joel Munsell, 1877.

Hunter, Martin. *The Journal of Gen. Sir Martin Hunter.* Edinburgh: The Edinburgh Press, 1894. Note: The book is very rare. A copy is at the Huntington Library, CA.

Hutchinson, Thomas. *The Diary and Letters of His Excellency Thomas Hutchinson.* Vol. 1. Compiled by Peter Orlando Hutchinson. Boston: Houghton, Mifflin, and Co., 1884.

Graves, Samuel. *The Conduct of Vice Admiral Samuel Graves, Considered during the Period That He Held the Command of His Majesty's Naval Force, in North America, 1774–1776.* [Edited by George Gefferina?]. Circa Dec 11, 1776, to Dec 1, 1777. Original in British Library, Ad. 14.038 and 14.039; a transcription in MHS with selections in *NDAR*. Note: Editor appears to be George Gefferina, Graves's flag secretary while in Boston (see *NDAR*, 2:1025), for in the introduction it is twice signed G. G., and many letters throughout, especially in the appendices, are signed "G. Gefferina, by order of the Admiral". Though Gefferina was the editor, much of this work was probably dictated by Graves himself.

Kemble, Stephen. "Kemble's Journals, 1773–1789." *Collections of the New-York Historical Society for the year 1883*. Vol. 16, 1–247. Publications Fund Series. New York: NY Historical Society, 1884.

Knox, Henry. "Diary to and from Fort Ticonderoga," in *New England Historical and Genealogical Register. Vol. 30* (1876):321–26.

Lister, Jeremy. *Concord Fight: Being so much of the Narrative of Ensign Jeremy Lister of the 10th Regiment of Foot as pertains to his services on the 19th of April, 1775, and to his experiences in Boston during the early months of the Siege*. Edited by Harold Murdock. Cambridge, MA: Harvard University Press, 1931. Written in 1782.

Meigs, Return Jonathan. In Roberts, *March to Quebec* 173ff.: See Primary Sources, Books.

Montresor, John. "1761 Journal to Quebec," in Roberts, *March to Quebec*, 5ff.: See Primary Sources, Books.

———. All other journals in Scull, *The Montresor Journals*: See Primary Sources, Books.

Morison, George. In Roberts, *March to Quebec*, 505ff.: See Primary Sources, Books.

Mott, Edward. "Journal of Capt. Edward Mott." In *Collections of the Connecticut Historical Society*. Vol. 1, 163–174. Hartford, CT: Printed for the Society, 1860.

Newell, Timothy. "A Journal Kept During the Time that Boston was Shut Up in 1775–6," in

Collections of the Massachusetts Historical Society. 4th ser., vol. 1, 261–276. Boston: Massachusetts Historical Society, 1852.

Ritzma, Rudolphus. "Journal of Col. Rudolphus Ritzma" in Magazine of American History with Notes and Queries. Vol. 1, 98–107. Edited by Martha J. Lamb. New York: A. S. Barnes & Company: 1877.

Robertson, Archibald. His Diaries and Sketches in America. New York: New York Public Library & Arno Press Inc., 1971 reprint edition. First published New York Public Library, 1930.

Senter, Dr. Isaac. In Roberts, March to Quebec, 197ff.: See Primary Sources, Books. Also in Magazine of History with Notes and Queries, Extra, no. 42 (1915):11–60, edited by William Abbatt; Tarrytown, NY: 1915 and published as The Journal of Isaac Senter, Physician and Surgeon to the Troops Detached from the American Army Encamped at Cambridge, Mass. on a Secret Expedition against Quebec. Philadelphia: Historical Society of Pennsylvania, 1846.

Stevens, James. "The Revolutionary Journal of James Stevens of Andover Massachusetts." Essex Institute Historical Collections. Vol. 48, 41ff. Salem, MA: Printed for the Institute, 1912.

Stiles, Rev. Ezra. Literary Diary of Ezra Stiles, D.D., LL.D. Vol 1. Edited by Franklin Bowditch Dexter. New York: Charles Scribner's Sons, 1901.

Stocking, Abner. "Interesting Journal of Abner Stocking of Chatham, Connecticut." In Roberts, March to Quebec, 545ff.: See Primary Sources, Books. Also in Magazine of History with Notes and Queries Extra 75, ed. William Abbatt (Tarrytown, NY: 1921).

Storrs, Experience. In New England Quarterly 28 (Mar 1955):72–93.

Thacher, Dr. James. A Military Journal during the American Revolutionary War from 1775 to 1783. 2nd ed. Boston: Cottons & Barnard, 1827.

Thayer, Simeon. In Roberts, 247ff.: See Primary Sources, Books. Also in Rhode Island Historical Society Collections. Vol. 6, 1ff. Edited by Edwin Martin Stone. Providence, RI: Knowles, Anthony & Co, 1867.

Trumbull, Benjamin. A Concise Journal or Minutes of the Principal Movements Towards St. John's of the Siege and Surrender of the Forts there in 1775. In Collections of Connecticut Historical Society. Vol. 7, 137ff. Hartford, CT: Printed for the Society, 1899.

Warren, Dr. John. In J. C. Warren, Genealogy of Warren, 85ff.: See Secondary Sources.

Washington, George: See Archives, Washington Papers.

Williams, Lt. Richard. Discord and Civil Wars; being a portion of the Journal kept by Lieutenant Williams of His Majesty's Twenty-Third Regiment while stationed in British North America during the time of the Revolution. Buffalo[?], NY: Easy Hill Press for the Salisbury Club of Buffalo, 1954.

Letters (and Reports)

These are only the *key letters* frequently drawn upon in the endnotes, for which I have used shorthand notation, properly citing them here only (referencing sources listed in this bibliography). The endnotes throughout this volume cite many other letters not listed here.

Bunker Hill

Regarding the source material for the Battle of Bunker Hill, there are essentially three sets of data. The first consists of the contemporary documents. The second is statements related to a newspaper-based public controversy in 1818 between Henry Dearborn (who spoke ill against the memory of the deceased Israel Putnam) and supporters of Putnam. Many of these 1818 statements were firsthand, but because they were collected forty-three years after the fact, not to mention biased, they must be used cautiously. Finally, there are statements collected by the Bunker Hill Memorial Association for the fiftieth anniversary of the battle in 1825. These are considered so unreliable that I have generally avoided them entirely. Of the other two sets of sources, I rely primarily on the contemporary material. However, since there are many gaps in the story based on contemporary evidence alone, the 1818 material—most of which appears in Dawson, *The Historical Magazine* (June 1868) 2:3:402ff.—must be considered. In the event of a contradiction, I rely on the contemporary, though if I have doubts, I describe my reasons in the endnotes.

Brown, Peter. Peter Brown to his mother, June 28, 1775. In Ezra Stiles's *Diary*, 1:595–96.

Burgoyne, Maj. Gen. John. Maj. Gen. John Burgoyne to Lord George Germain, Aug 20, 1775. In de Fonblanque, *Political and Military Episodes*, 191–98.

———. Maj. Gen. John Burgoyne to Lord Rochfort, [circa 1775], in de Fonblanque, *Political and Military Episodes*, 142–54.

———. Maj. Gen. John Burgoyne to Lord Stanley, June 25, 1775, Force, *American Archives*, 4:2:1094–95, and de Fonblanque, *Political and Military Episodes*, 155–58.

Chester, John. Capt. John Chester to Rev. Joseph Fish, July 22, 1775, Frothingham, *Siege*, 389–91.

———. Capt. John Chester and Samuel Webb to Joseph Webb, June 19, 1775, Frothingham, *Siege*, 415–16 (of the 3rd edition or later only).

Clarke, Lt. John. *An Impartial and Authentic Narrative of the Battle Fought on the 17th of June, 1775, &c.* In Drake, *Bunker Hill*, 42–59.

Gage, General Thomas. Official Casualty Report on Bunker Hill, June 17, 1775, enclosed with his letter to Lord Dartmouth, June 25, 1775 (received July 25, 1775), Force, *American Archives*, 4:2:1097–99 (dated wrong in that source). Note: A copy of the letter appears in Carter, *Corr. of General Gage*, 1:405–06, but the Casualty Report enclosure is not included with it.

Harris, Capt. George. Capt. George Harris (to his cousin?), undated letter. In Lushington, *Life and Services*, 41–42, and Drake, *Bunker Hill*, 37–38.

Howe, Maj. Gen. William. Maj. Gen. William Howe to Lt. Gen. Thomas Gage, June 21, 1775, in Belcher, *First American*, 1:196–98, original in Gage MSS.

———. Maj. Gen. William Howe to Lord [Adm. Richard] Howe, June 22, 1775, in *Report on the Manuscripts of Mrs. Stopford-Sackville*, 2:4, reprinted in full except the last paragraph in Murdock, *Bunker Hill*, 147–49.

———. Maj. Gen. William Howe to the Adjutant-General [Lt. Gen. Edward Harvey], June 22 and 24, 1775, in Fortescue, *Corr. of George III*, 3:220–24.

Laurie, Capt. Walter Sloane. Capt. Walter Sloane Laurie [presumably to Lord Dartmouth],

June 23, 1775, in William Legge, 2nd Lord Dartmouth MSS, D(W)1778/II/1330, Staffordshire Record Office, Stafford, UK (never published).

Letter of a British Officer, Boston, July 5, 1775. It appears in full in *Detail and Conduct of the American War*, 13–15. It also appears in excerpt in two sources. The fuller excerpt is in Dawson, *The Historical Magazine* (June 1868) 2:3:367; the lesser is in Commager and Morris, *Spirit of 'Seventy-Six*, 135–36.

A Letter of Intelligence, in Fortescue, *Corr. of George III*, 3:215–18.

Letter to Jeremiah Powell, June 21, 1775, *Proc. of MHS* (1870), 11:226–27. The letter is missing the final page(s), and so the sender is unknown, but is possibly the recipient's brother-in-law, John Bromfield.

Massachusetts Committee of Safety Report on the Battle of Bunker Hill, July 7, 1775, Force, *American Archives*, 4:2:1373–76, and Frothingham, *Siege*, 381–85. Discussed in detail in Murdock, *Bunker Hill*, 83–96.

Putnam, Daniel. Daniel Putnam to the President and Directors of the Bunker Hill Monument Association, Aug 1825, *Coll. of CHS* (1860), 1:227ff.

Prescott, Judge. "Account of the Battle of Bunker Hill," *Proc. of MHS* (1876), 14:68–78, not to be confused with the two following sources.

Prescott [Family] Manuscript in Dawson, *The Historical Magazine* 2, vol. 3 (June 1868): 437–38.

Prescott, Col. William. Col. William Prescott to John Adams, Aug 25, 1775, Frothingham, *Siege*, 395–96.

Rawdon, Lord. Francis, Lord Rawdon, to his uncle, Francis, tenth Earl of Huntingdon, June 20, 1775. Original at Huntington Library Hastings Collection, published in *Report on the Manuscripts of the Late Reginald Rawdon Hastings, Esq., of the Manor House, Ashby de la Zouche*, 3:154–55. (London: Historical Manuscripts Commission, 1928–1947). Also in Commager and Morris, *Spirit of 'Seventy-Six*, 130–31.

———. Francis, Lord Rawdon to his uncle, Francis, tenth Earl of Huntingdon, Aug 3, 1775. Original at Huntington Library Hastings Collection, in *Report...Ashby de la Zouche* (as cited in letter above), 3:156–59.

Stark, Col. John. Col. John Stark to the New Hampshire Congress, Medford, June 19, 1775, Force, *American Archives*, 4:2:1029.

Tupper, Maj. John. Maj. John Tupper to John Montague, Lord Sandwich, June 21, 1775, *NDAR*, 1:731.

Waller, Lt. John. Lt. John Waller to a friend, June 21, 1775, at MHS.

———. Lt. John Waller to his brother [Jacob Waller], June 22, 1775, in Nicolas, *Historical Record*, 1:87–89, and Drake, *Bunker Hill*, 28–30.

Other

Caldwell, Maj. Henry. Maj. Henry Caldwell [to Gen. James Murray], June 15, 1776, in *The Invasion of Canada in 1775*, Quebec: *Morning Chronicle* Office: 1887 [reprint].

Church, Benjamin, Jr. Benjamin Church Jr. to Major Cane in Boston [circa July 1775], [in cipher], in the George Washington MSS, LOC, 1741–1799: Series 4, General Correspondence, 1697–1799; digitized into LOCs *American Memory* online database as images 754–55.

———. Benjamin Church Jr., cipher letter translated by Col. Elisha Porter, in Force, *American Archives*, 4:3:958–960.

———. Benjamin Church Jr., cipher letter translated by Rev. Samuel West, in Force, *American Archives*, 4:3:1480–83.

———. Benjamin Church Jr. to General Washington, Oct 3, 1775, in *PGW*.

———. Benjamin Church Jr., "From my Prison in Cambridge, November 1, 1775," Force, *American Archives*, 4:3:1479–86.

Gordon, Rev. William. Rev. William Gordon to Samuel Wilson, Apr 6, 1776, in Commager and Morris, *Spirit of 'Seventy-Six*, 177–79.

Howe, Maj. Gen. William. Maj. Gen. William Howe to Lord Dartmouth, Mar 21, 1776, in Dawson, *Battles*, 1:94–96.

Stuart, Col. Charles. Col. Charles Stuart to Lord Bute, Apr 28, 1776, in Wortley, *A Prime Minister and His Son*, 76–80.

Maps and Sketches
Boston

Montresor, Capt. John. *[Plan of the Neck and fortifications]* "Delivd. to H.E. Gl. Gage, June 30th. 1775." 1775.

Page, Thomas Hyde, and John Montresor. *Boston, its Environs and Harbour, with the Rebels Works Raised against that Town in 1775*. William Faden, 1778.

Pelham, Henry. *A plan of Boston in New England with its Environs*. 1777.

Price, William. *A new plan of ye great town of Boston in New England in America, with the many additional buildings, & new streets, to the year 1769*. 1769.

Bunker Hill/Charlestown

"an Officer on the Spot". *A Plan of the Battle, on Bunkers Hill*, including a published letter from John Burgoyne to Lord Stanley, June 25, 1775, London: printed for R. Sayer & J. Bennett, 1775. Held at MHS, reprinted in MHS's *The Battle of Bunker Hill* picture book.

De Berniere, Henry. *Sketch of the Action on the Heights of Charlestown, June 17th 1775, between his MAJESTY'S Troops, under the command of Major Gen.l Howe, and a large body of AMERICAN REBELS*. (1775). Engraved version, which claims it was taken from an original sketch now in the hands of "J. Cist, Esq.", held in the Emmet Collection, NYPL. It is reprinted in a variety of sources, including French, *First Year*, between 226–27, and Ketchum, *Decisive Day*, 170–71.

Jefferys, Thomas and William Faden. *A sketch of the action between the British forces and the American provincials, on the heights of the peninsula of Charlestown, the 17th of June 1775*. 1775. Held at BPL, reprinted in MHS's *The Battle of Bunker Hill* picture book.

Page, Thomas Hyde. *A plan of action at Bunkers Hill, on the 17th of June 1775. Between His Majesty's Troops, Under the Command of Major General Howe, and the Rebel Forces*. It appears in at least four forms with slightly different titles:

    ———. 1775 Original, hand-drawn draft, held at LOC. Probably made the evening of the battle, because Page was on the field as General Howe's aide-de-camp.

———. 1775 Second draft, hand-drawn, greater detail, held at LOC.

———. 1778 Engraved form with much greater detail, published in London and held at BPL.

———. 1793 Engraved form almost identical to 1778, engraved for inclusion in a history book of the Revolution, held at BPL.

Pelham, Henry. *Map of Bunker Hill, 1775.* 1775. Held at Clements Library, Univ. of Michigan.

Quebec

Des Barres, Joseph F. W. *A Plan of Quebec and Environs, with its defenses and the occasional entrenched camps of the French commanded by Marquis de Montcalme.* 1777.

Faden, William. *Plan of the city and environs of Quebec...1775 to...1776.* At the Norman B. Leventhal Map Center at the Boston Public Library.

Newspapers
A partial list:

Columbian Centinel (of Boston)
London Chronicle
London Evening Post
Massachusetts Spy
New England Chronicle (*Essex Gazette*)
New London Gazette (of Connecticut)
New York Journal (*General Advertiser*)
New-York Gazette
Rivington's *New York Gazetteer*

Orderly Books

Arnold, Benedict. Regimental Memorandum Book, in *Bulletin of the Fort Ticonderoga Museum* No. 1, Vol. 14 (Summer 1981): 71–80.

Burgoyne, Gen. John. *Orderly Book.* Edited by Edmund Bailey O'Callaghan. Albany, NY: J. Munsell, 1860.

Howe, Gen. William. *General Sir William Howe's Orderly Book at Charlestown, Boston and Halifax, June 17, 1775 to 1776 26 May.* Edited by Benjamin Franklin Stevens. London: Benjamin Franklin Stevens, 1890.

Washington, Gen. George. General Orders: See Archives, Washington Papers.

SECONDARY SOURCES

Adams, Charles Francis. "The Battle of Bunker Hill from a Strategic Point of View" (1895). *Proceedings of the American Antiquarian Society.* New Series, 10:387–98. Worcester, MA: American Antiquarian Society, 1896.

Alden, John Richard. *General Gage in America.* Baton Rouge, LA: Louisiana State Univ. Press, 1948.

Anderson, Fred W. "The Hinge of the Revolution: George Washington Confronts a People's Army, July 3, 1775". *Massachusetts Historical Review* 1 (1999).

Ansoff, Peter. "The Flag on Prospect Hill." *Raven: A Journal of Vexillology* 13 (2006): 77–100.

———. "The Sign Their Banners Bore: The Pine-Tree Flag in the American Revolution". Paper presented at NAVA 38, Indianapolis, Indiana, 2004 (unpublished).

Arnold, Howard Payson. *The Memoir of Jonathan Mason Warren, M.D.* Boston: 1886.

Arnold, Isaac Newton. *The Life of Benedict Arnold: His Patriotism and His Treason.* Chicago: Jansen, McClurg & Co., 1880.

Bakeless, John Edwin. *Turncoats, Traitors, and Heroes.* New York: Da Capo Press, 1998. First published Lippincott, 1960.

Bancroft, George. *History of the United States from the Discovery of the Continent.* 6 vol. (New York: D. Appleton and Co., 1895–96 [Author's Last Revision]).

Batchelder, Samuel Francis. "The Washington Elm Tradition: 'Under this Tree Washington First Took Command of the American Army'. Is it True?" *Proceedings of the Cambridge Historical Society* (1925), reprinted in Batchelder, Samuel Francis, *Bits of Cambridge History*, 234ff. Cambridge, MA: Harvard University Press, 1930.

Beck, Derek W. *Igniting the American Revolution: 1773–1775.* Naperville, IL: Sourcebooks, 2015.

Belcher, Henry. *The First American Civil War: The First Period 1775–1778.* 2 vols. London: MacMillan and Co. Ltd, 1911.

Boardman, Samuel Lane, ed. *Peter Edes: Pioneer Printer in Maine: A Biography.* Bangor, ME: Printed for the De Burians, 1901. Includes his diary.

Boston Street Laying-Out Department. *A Record of the Streets, Alleys, Places, Etc., in the City of Boston.* Boston: City of Boston's Printing Office, 1910.

Bradford, Alden. *A Particular Account of the Battle of Bunker, or Breed's Hill, on the 17th of June, 1775.* Boston: Cummings, Hilliard, & Company, 1825.

Brown, Rebecca Warren. *Stories about General Warren in Relation to the Fifth of March Massacre and the Battle of Bunker Hill* "by a Lady of Boston". Boston: James Loring, 1835.

Coburn, Frank Warren. *The Battle of April 19, 1775, in Lexington, Concord, Lincoln, Arlington, Cambridge, Somerville, and Charlestown, Massachusetts.* 2nd ed. Boston: Wright & Potter Printing Co., 1922.

Coffin, Charles. *History of the Battle of Breed's Hill.* Portland, ME: D. C. Colesworthy, 1835.

———. *The Life and Services of Major General John Thomas.* New York: Egbert, Hovey & King, 1844.

Coggins, Jack. *Ships and Seamen of the American Revolution.* Harrisburg, PA: Stackpole Books, 1969.

Cruikshank, Ernest, ed. *A History of the Organization, Development, and Services of the Military and Naval Forces of Canada.* 3 vol. Ottawa: Canadian Government, 1919–20.

Danton, Graham. *The Theory and Practice of Seamanship.* 11th ed. New York: Routledge, 1996.

Dawson, Henry B. *Battles of the United States.* 2 vols. New York: Johnson, Fry, and Company, 1858. Note: default Dawson reference.

———. *The Historical Magazine*: see Primary Sources, Books.

The Detail and Conduct of the American War, under Generals Gage, Howe, Burgoyne, and Vice Admiral Lord Howe. 3rd ed. London: Richardson and Urquhart: 1780.

Drake, Francis S. *The Town of Roxbury: Its Memorable Persons and Places, Its History and Antiquities...* Boston: Municipal Printing Office, 1908.

Drake, Samuel Adams. *Bunker Hill: The Story Told in Letters from the Battle Field by British Officers Engaged.* Boston: Nichols and Hall, 1875.

Everett, Alexander. *Life of Joseph Warren.* Edited by Jared Sparks. New York: Harper and Bros.,

1856. Republished in Wilson, James Grant and John Fiske, eds. *Appleton's Cyclopaedia of American Biography*, 10:91. New York: D. Appleton and Co., 1888. (10:101 of the 1902 ed.). The pages cited in the present text correspond to Sparks's compilation.

Fischer, David Hackett. *Paul Revere's Ride*. New York: Oxford University Press, 1994.

Fleming, Thomas J. *Now We Are Enemies: The Story of Bunker Hill*. New York: St. Martin's Press, 1960. Note: My limited use of this source is with caution, as it is entirely unreferenced.

Flick, Alexander C. "General Henry Knox's Ticonderoga Expedition". New York State Historical Association, *Quarterly Journal* 9 (Apr 1928): 119–35.

de Fonblanque, Edward Barrington. *Political and Military Episodes… Life and Correspondence of the Right Hon. John Burgoyne: General, Statesman, Dramatist*. London: Macmillan and Co., 1876.

Forman, Samuel A. *Dr. Joseph Warren: The Boston Tea Party, Bunker Hill, and the Birth of American Liberty*. Gretna, LA: Pelican Publishing Co., 2011.

French, Allen. *The First Year of the American Revolution*. Boston: Houghton Mifflin, 1934.

———. *General Gage's Informers*. Ann Arbor: Univ. of Michigan Press, 1932.

———. *The Siege of Boston*. New York: The Macmillan Company, 1911.

Frothingham, Richard. *The Centennial: Battle of Bunker Hill…* Boston: Little, Brown, & Co., 1875.

———. *History of the Siege of Boston*. 3rd ed. Boston: Little, Brown, & Co., 1872.

———. *Life and Times of Joseph Warren*. Boston: Little, Brown, & Co., 1865.

Graham, James. *The Life of General Daniel Morgan*. New York: Derby & Jackson, 1856.

Hall, Henry. *Ethan Allen: The Robin Hood of Vermont*. New York: D. Appleton and Company, 1892.

Isaacson, Walter. *Benjamin Franklin: An American Life*. New York: Simon & Schuster, 2003.

Ketchum, Richard M. *Decisive Day: The Battle for Bunker Hill*. 2nd ed. New York: Doubleday, 1974.

Livingston, William Farrand. *Israel Putnam: Pioneer, Ranger, and Major-General, 1718–1790*. New York: G. P. Putnam's Sons, 1901.

Lockhart, Paul. *The Whites of their Eyes*. New York: Harper Collins, 2011.

Lossing, Benson. *American Historical Record and Repertory of Notes and Queries*. 3 vols. Philadelphia: Chase & Town, 1872–74.

———. *The Pictorial Field-Book of the Revolution*. 2 vols. New York: Harper & Bros., 1851–52.

Lushington, S. R. *Life and Services of General Lord Harris, G.C.B.* London: John W. Parker, 1845.

MacDonald, William. *Select Charters and Other Documents Illustrative of American History, 1606–1775*. New York: Macmillan Co., 1899.

Martyn, Charles. *The Life of Artemas Ward*. New York: Artemas Ward, 1921.

May, W. E. *The Boats of Men-of-War*. Annapolis, MD: Naval Maritime Museum, 1974. Reprinted with additions by Simon Stephens. Annapolis, MD: Naval Institute Press, 1999.

McCullough, David. *1776*. New York: Simon & Schuster, 2005.

———. *1776: The Illustrated Edition*. New York: Simon & Schuster, 2007.

Mollo, John. *Uniforms of the American Revolution in color*. Illustrated by Malcolm McGregor. New York: Macmillan Publishing Co., Inc., 1975.

Moore, Frank. *Diary of the American Revolution from Newspapers and Original Documents*. 2 vols. New York: Charles Scribner, 1860.

Murdock, Harold. *Bunker Hill: Notes and Queries on a Famous Battle*. Boston: Houghton Mifflin Company, 1927.

Nelson, James L. *Benedict Arnold's Navy: The Ragtag Fleet that Lost the Battle of Lake Champlain but Won the American Revolution.* Camden, ME: McGraw-Hill Professional, 2006.

Nicolas, Paul Harris. *Historical Record of the Royal Marine Forces.* 2 vols. London: Thomas and William Boone, 1845.

Orations Delivered at the Request of the Inhabitants of the Town of Boston to Commemorate the Evening of the Fifth of March, 1770... Boston: Peter Edes, 1785. Note: This rare volume is in the Evans microfiche, No. 18997, available at most research libraries.

Perrin, William G. *British Flags, Their Early History, and Their Development at Sea.* London: Cambridge University Press, 1922.

Sabine, Lorenzo. *American Loyalists...* Boston: Charles C. Little and James Brown, 1847.

Selig, Robert A. "Artillery." AmericanRevolution.org. Accessed Nov 7, 2008. http://www.american revolution.org/artillery.html.

Shelton, Hal T. *General Richard Montgomery and the American Revolution.* New York: New York University Press, 1994.

Smith, Digby and Kevin K. Kiley. *An Illustrated Encyclopedia of Uniforms from 1775–1783: The American Revolutionary War.* London: Lorenz Books, 2008.

Smith, Justin Harvey. *Our Struggle for the Fourteenth Colony.* 2 vols. New York: G. P. Putnam's Sons, 1907.

Smyth, Adm. W. H. *The Sailor's Word Book: An Alphabetical Digest of Nautical Terms.* London: Blackie and Son, 1867.

Spalding, Edward Henry, ed. *Bi-Centennial of Old Dunstable: Address by Hon. S. T. Worcester, October 27, 1873.* Nashua, NH: E. H. Spalding, 1878.

Sparks, Jared. *Life and Treason of Benedict Arnold.* Boston: Hilliard, Gray, and Co., 1835.

———. *The Writings of George Washington*: See Primary Sources, Books.

Stark, Caleb. *Memoir and Official Correspondence of Gen. John Stark...* Concord, Mass.: G. Parker Lyon, 1860.

Spring, Matthew H. *With Zeal and with Bayonets Only: The British Army on Campaign in North America, 1775–1783.* Norman, OK: University of Oklahoma Press, 2008.

Swett, Samuel. *The History of the Bunker Hill Battle, With a Plan.* 2nd ed. Boston: Munroe and Francis, 1826. Originally published in 1818.

Tzu, Sun. *The Art of War.* Translated by Thomas Cleary. Boston: Shambhala Publications, 1988.

Walker, Jeffrey B. *The Devil Undone: The Life and Poetry of Benjamin Church, 1734–1778.* New York: Arno Press; 1982. Originally presented as the author's doctoral thesis at Pennsylvania State University, 1977.

Warren, Edward. *The Life of John Warren, M.D.* Boston: Noyes, Holmes, and Company, 1874.

———. *The Life of John Collins Warren, M.D.* 2 vols. Boston: Ticknor and Fields, 1860.

Warren, John Collins. *A Genealogy of Warren with Some Historical Sketches.* Boston: Printed by John Wilson and Son, 1854.

Watertown's Military History. Boston: David Clapp & Son, Printers, 1907.

Wilson, Timothy. *Flags at Sea.* Rev. ed. Annapolis, MD: Naval Institute Press, 1999. First published by H. M. Stationery Office, London, in 1986.

Windsor, Justin, ed. *The Memorial History of Boston...1630–1880.* 4 vols. Boston: James R. Osgood and Company, 1881–82.

INDEX

ABOUT THE AUTHOR

Derek W. Beck has always had a passion for military history, which inspired him to start his career in the U.S. Air Force. He has served as an officer on active duty in science roles and in space operations. In 2005, he earned a master of science degree at the Massachusetts Institute of Technology (MIT), where he also fell in love with Boston's revolutionary past. To more fully pursue writing, he later transitioned to the Air Force Reserves, though he still remains quite active, presently holding the rank of major. Derek's first book, *Igniting the American Revolution: 1773–1775*, was published in October 2015 by Sourcebooks. When not working on future history books, Derek is a frequent contributor to the online *Journal of the American Revolution*. You can follow or connect with him through his website at www.derekbeck.com.

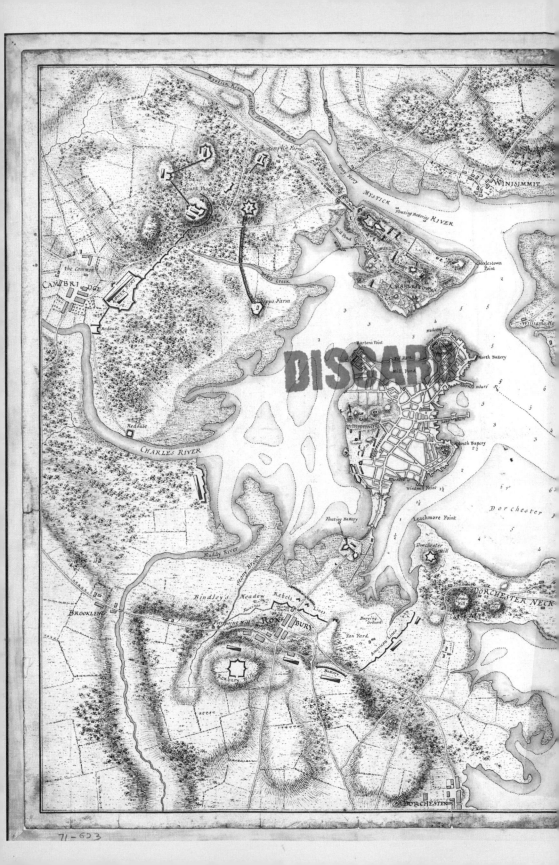